Mass Communication in India

FOURTH COMPLETELY REVISED & UPDATED EDITION

Mass Communication in India

FOURTH COMPLETELY REVISED & UPDATED EDITION

Keval J. Kumar

JAICO PUBLISHING HOUSE
Ahmedabad Bangalore Bhopal Bhubaneswar Chennai
Delhi Hyderabad Kolkata Lucknow Mumbai

Published by Jaico Publishing House
A-2 Jash Chambers, 7-A Sir Phirozshah Mehta Road
Fort, Mumbai - 400 001
jaicopub@jaicobooks.com
www.jaicobooks.com

© Keval J. Kumar

MASS COMMUNICATION IN INDIA
ISBN 81-7224-373-1

First Jaico Impression: 1994
Thirty-ninth Jaico Impression (Fourth Edition Revised & Enlarged): 2010
Fifty-sixth Jaico Impression: 2017

No part of this book may be reproduced or utilized in
any form or by any means, electronic or
mechanical including photocopying, recording or by any
information storage and retrieval system,
without permission in writing from the publishers.

Printed by
SRG Traders Pvt. Ltd.
B-41, Sector 67,
Noida 201301, U.P.

For Eve, Sneha and Ranjit

CONTENTS

Preface   xvii

SECTION I

Introduction to Communication Theory   1-48
  Communication as a Social Science
  The Need for Communication
  Communication and Language
  Communication and Information
  The Right to Communicate
  Defining Communication
  Types of Communication
  The Three Stages of Interpersonal Communication
  Group Communication
  Mass Communication
  Mass-Line Communication
  Interactive Communication
  Western Models of Communication
  Indian Communication Theories
  Barriers to Communication
  Information Technology and Society: A Brief History
  Mass Communication and Culture
  'Mass Culture', 'Popular Culture' and 'Folk Culture'

  For Further Reading
  Web Resources
  Review Questions
  Suggested Projects

SECTION II

The Mass Media : History, Practices, Values   49-447
  Functions of the Mass Media
  Theories of the Press/Media

Journalism   *61-165*
    What is Journalism?
    Tabloid and Yellow Journalism
    What is News?
    Journalism as Public Relations
    Journalism for Development: 'Alternative' or
        'Public' Journalism
    The Role of the Press
    The 'Power' of the Press
    A Short History of Indian Journalism
    News and News Values
    The Making of a Newspaper
    Print Media: The Magazine Sector
    The 'Business' of News: New Trends
    Freedom of the Press: The Right to Publish and
        the Right to Privacy
    Press Codes and Ethics
    Press Council's Guide to Journalistic Ethics
    Censorship and Control in the Press
    Media Laws
    Press Ownership and Monopolies
    Some Media Organisations: PCI, ABC, RNI and INS
    International News Agencies
    Challenging the Transnationals' Dominance
    News Agencies in India
    The Struggle for NWICO
    The MacBride Report

    For Further Reading
    Web Resources
    Review Questions
    Suggested Projects

Cinema   *166-250*
    The Beginnings
    The Pioneers: The Lumiere Brothers

The 'Talkies'
The Studio System
Satyajit Ray
The Golden Age: Sohrab Modi, Raj Kapoor and
   Guru Dutt
The Angry Young Man and the Return of the
   Action Genre
The 'New Wave'
The 'Middle' Cinema
Regional Language Cinema: Tamil, Telugu, Marathi,
   Bengali, Malayalam, Kannada, Oriya, Punjabi,
   Gujarati, Assamese, Manipuri, Bhojpuri
Documentary and Short Films
The Indian Documentary
The Indian Newsreel
The Films Division
Independent Documentary Producers
Film Studies in Indian Universities
'Impact' of Cinema on Society
Ethics of Cinema
Film Censorship
Censorship Guidelines

For Further Reading
Web Resources
Review Questions
Suggested Projects

Radio   *251-293*
   Development of Radio as a Mass Medium
   Indian Broadcasting: The Early Years
   The War Years
   Underground 'Congress' Radio
   All India Radio at Independence
   All India Radio in the Late 1990s and Early
      Years of 2000

All India Radio Services: National, Regional,
  Local and External
Radio Formats and Genres
Programme Composition of AIR
Broadcasting Policy
Broadcasting Code
FM Broadcasts (1997-2000)
FM Radio – Auctioning the Airwaves
Projected Growth of the Radio Industry
New Developments: Community and Campus Radio
Digital Audio Broadcasting
Satellite Radio
Visual Radio
Ethics of Broadcasting
Listenership Surveys

For Further Reading
Web Resources
Review Questions
Suggested Projects

Television 294-360
Early Experiments in Television
The Story of Indian Television
Enter: Film Directors and Film Stars
Advertising Revenues
Distribution of Television Content
Television Genres: Television News
Advertising in the News
TV Documentaries or Features/Factual Television
Talk Shows
Children's Programmes
'Talent Hunt' Shows
Reality TV
Religious Programmes
Soap Operas

Video and Cable Television (1980s and 1990s)
Video, Cinema and Television (1980s)
Cable TV
Satellite TV
Ownership, Control and Regulation of Television
The Broadcasting Bill
Television for National Development
Television and Higher Education
Television and Corporate Social Responsibility
The Cable Television Networks (Regulation) Act, 1995
Guidelines for Advertising on All India Radio and
 Television

For Further Reading
Web Resources
Review Questions
Suggested Projects

The Recorded Music Industry   *361-370*
Music Industry after Independence
The 'Remix' Phenomenon
Music Genres
'Indi-pop' Challenges Film Music
Music on Radio and Television

For Further Reading
Web Resources
Suggested Projects

Book Publishing   *371-383*
The Beginnings
Publishing after Independence
Paperbacks and Textbooks
The Multinational Presence
New Trends in the New Millennium

For Further Reading
Web Resources
Review Questions

Folk and Traditional Media   *384-400*
Advantages of the Folk Media
Electronic Media and Folk Media
Folk Theatre Forms: Tamasha, Powada, Keertana, Yakshagana, Dashavatar, Nautanki, Bhavai, Therukoothu, Jatra, Ram Lila, Rasa Lila, Puppetry
Street Theatre

For Further Reading
Web Resources
Review Questions
Suggested Projects

Advertising and Public Relations   *401-447*
History and Development of Advertising
Modern Advertising
History of Indian Advertising
Advertising in the Early 20th Century
The Inter-War Years
Post-Independence Advertising
Evolution of the Public Relations Industry
The Need for Public Relations
The Business of Advertising and Public Relations
Types of Advertising
Outdoor or Out-of-Home (OOH) Advertising
Online Advertising
Mobile Advertising
The Nature and Role of Advertising and Public Relations
Advertising/Account Planning
Media Buying and Selling

Testing Advertising Effectiveness
Public Relations in Industry
Media Relations
Going Beyond Media Relations
Advertising and Corporate Social Responsibility
Ethics in Advertising and Public Relations
ASCI Code
PRSI's Code of Ethics
PRCAI's Code of Ethics

For Further Reading
Web Resources
Review Questions
Suggested Projects

SECTION III

Psychology and Sociology of Media Audiences   448-480
Communication and the Social Sciences
Media Audiences
The Audience as 'Market'
Psychology of Audiences
The 'Mass' Audience
The Public and Public Opinion
Public Opinion Surveys
Mass Media and Politics
Persuasion and Propaganda
Audience Measurement: The 'Ratings' Game
Audience Surveys
Readership Surveys

For Further Reading
Web Resources
Review Questions
Suggested projects

SECTION IV

Mass Communication and Society: Uses, Effects, Representations 481-516
The Meaning of 'Effects'
Theories of Media Effects and Media Uses
Effects of Media on Education
The Mass Media and the Indian Family
Children and the Media
Representations of Women in the Mass Media
Women in the Media Professions
Need for Audience Studies
Media and Consumerism
Violence in the Media and Violence in Society

For Further Reading
Web Resources
Review Questions
Suggested Projects

SECTION V

Mass Media, Culture and Development 517-556
The Cultural Context of Development
Development Communication
'Modernization' Models of Development Communication
Dependency/Structuralist Models
'Alternative' Approaches to Development
Revival of 'Modernization' Models
ICT, the Internet and Mobile Telephony for Development
The Need for National and International Regulations
Media, Development and Social Change: The Indian Experience
Broadcasting as Public Service

Mahatma Gandhi: The Communicator
Role of TV in Promoting Literacy and Social Change
SITE (Satellite Instructional Television Experiment)
Kheda Communications Project
Radio Rural Forums
Media and Family Planning
Traditional Media and Development
The Press and Development
Voluntary Agencies

For Further Reading
Web Resources
Review Questions
Suggested Projects

SECTION VI

Information Technology, Telecommunications and the Internet 557-594
From Stand-Alone Technologies to 'Convergence'
History of Information Technology in India
New Computer Policy (1984)
The Private Phone STD/ISD Booth Phenomenon
National Telecommunications Policy (1994)
Regulating Telecommunications
Information Technologies: Developments in India
The Information Revolution
The 'Information Superhighway'
The Internet in India
The Internet, Civil Society and Social Movements
Family and Social Networks
'Globalisation'
E-Commerce, E-Banking and E-Governance
National Task Force on Information Technology
Mobile Telephony
Serving the Urban and Rural Poor

Social and Cultural Implications
The Gaming Industry
Online Gambling Industry
InforWars, Hate Speech

For Further Reading
Web Resources
Review Questions

SECTION VII

Mass Media, Intellectual Property Rights   **595-609**
and the Public Domain
IPR: An Historical Perspective
India's Copyright Act
The Meaning of 'Copyright'
Adaptations and Derivative Works
Indian Broadcasting
Rights of Broadcasters
Cable and Satellite Broadcasting
Doctrine of Fair Use
Home-Taping, Rentals, Piracy
Conclusions

For Further Reading
Web Resources
Review Questions
Suggested Projects

Preface

The first decade of the new millennium has been perhaps the most tumultuous period for mass communication in India. The proliferation of television channels, FM radio stations, newspaper editions, special-interest magazines, multiplexes, websites, blogs and social networks on the Internet, and above all of telecom service providers and mobile telephony has been unprecedented. To keep pace with this growth there has been the mushrooming of media training institutes in New Delhi, Noida, Mumbai, Pune and Chennai. However, research in media and communication studies has not been given the attention it deserves in academe or in the media industries. Market research often does not go beyond counting heads and the segmentation of 'target audiences' in terms of demographics and psychographics. Social science institutes/departments continue to overlook the need for research in media studies.

This fourth revised and updated edition of Mass Communication in India builds on the earlier three but updates and expands every chapter and section so as to provoke critical reflections on recent developments and trends in both the traditional and 'new' media. For the media researcher, the publications listed 'For Further Reading' that follows each chapter has been made more comprehensive, with a list of relevant Journals and 'Web Resources'.

Certain worrying trends are threatening the future of the mass media as public resources and public services. Cross-media ownership, for one, has given rise to cross-promotion in different media properties and even to oligopolies. The growing strength of giant media conglomerates (ADAG-Reliance Adlabs, Tata's, BCCL/Times of India, Zee, Star, Sony, NDTV, Living Media/ India Today, Jagran Prakashan, Dainik Bhaskar, Eenadu, TV-18, UTV, Sun TV, Sahara, etc) threatens pluralism in our democracy.

An equally disturbing trend is the media ownership by political parties and their open espousal of political affiliations. Tabloidization and the 'Page 3' approach to the news media transform every issue into 'infotainment'. Practices like 'Medianet' and 'private treaties' with commercial firms pose a danger too. Advertisers, PR lobbies and media managers often cross the 'lakshman-rekha' that should separate advertising from 'editorial' and 'programmes'. Regulations are considered anathema despite the phenomenal success of TRAI in furthering mobile telephony. The credibility of the news and that of the other media suffers as a result. Further, media convergence has enhanced the number of revenue streams for 'content'. These are some of the key trends that are taken up for discussion in this latest edition.

A whole new chapter on 'Mass Media and Intellectual Property Rights' has been added because IPR impacts upon all the media and their financial growth in terms of a variety of 'revenue streams' across a whole range of content-delivery platforms. It's not 'piracy' that is a major concern as much as the 'public domain' ('the commons') from the perspective of media users. It is from this 'media-as-public domain' perspective that the history, practices and values of mass communication in India have been analysed here.

KEVAL J. KUMAR
Director,
Resource Centre for Media Education and Research
4 'Chintamani'
Kale Path, Bhandarkar Road
Pune-411004.
Email: kevalj.kumar@gmail.com

SECTION I

INTRODUCTION TO COMMUNICATION THEORY

'Communication' (together with its twin 'information') is perhaps one of the most loosely defined terms in contemporary media and cultural studies. Perhaps it is because the term encompasses a multitude of experiences, actions and events, as well as a whole variety of happenings and meanings, and technologies. Thus, a conference or a meeting or even a *mela* or procession is a 'communication event', newspapers, radio, video and television are 'communication media', phones, computers, satellites and the internet are 'communication technologies', and journalists, advertisers, public relations personnel, and even camera crew and news-readers are 'communication professionals'.

The contemporary period has come to be labelled variously the 'Information Age', the 'Communication Age', and most recently, the Cyber or Networking Age. The uses and understanding of Communication have come a long way from its original association first with 'means of transport' and later with 'transmission'. The English word 'communication' is derived from the Latin noun 'communis' and the Latin verb 'communicare' which means 'to make common'. Terms closely related to communication and with similar etymological origins include community, communion, commonality, communalism and communism. The closest Indian language equivalent to the original concept of communication is 'sadharanikaran'.

Communication, in its simplest sense, then is a human relationship, involving two or more persons who come together to share, to dialogue and to commune, or just to be together, say, at a festival or a time of mourning. Communication is thus not so much an act or even a process but rather social and cultural 'togetherness'. Communion with oneself, with God, with nature, with the world of spirits, with one's ancestors are also forms of communication.

Communication as a Social Science

The study of Communication in its multitudinous forms, whether in its human or technological dimensions, has now taken on the characteristics of an interdisciplinary and multi-disciplinary social science. To begin with, Communication Science or Communication Studies was based in university departments of Sociology, Psychology and Political Science, and it borrowed heavily from these social science disciplines. In its turn, Communication Studies brought about a re-orientation in the social and behavioural disciplines through a greater involvement with popular cultures, and with men and women as communicators at home and in the workaday world. Studies of propaganda by political scientists resulted in greater interest in the 'power' of communication strategies among governments and the business communities. Government departments of defense provided generous funding for propaganda research, and business and industry promoted media research so as to better exploit communication for advertising and marketing their products and services. Thus government departments, private companies and the media themselves were the prime supporters of university courses and research in the mass media.

Communication Studies has been largely influenced by such needs and such research, as well as by the rapid growth of the press, and later by the cinema, radio, television, and the new digital media. The discipline of Communication owes its origins to the political concerns of the United States in the 1930s, a time when Nazi propaganda was rife; the US government established an Institute of Propaganda Research to develop techniques to counter such propaganda and to influence public opinion. In

Britain and France, the discipline had its roots in literary and linguistic studies, while in Germany the origins are traceable to the neo-Marxist scholars of the Institute of Social Research (the Frankfurt School).

In India, the discipline of Communication came into its own with the post-Independence Government's need for propagating national integration, socio-economic development and family planning throughout the vast country. The Indian Institute of Mass Communication was established in 1965 by the Ministry of Information and Broadcasting to provide training and also to conduct research to assist in this effort. University departments of Communication/Journalism joined in this effort as well. In the new millennium, however, several private media institutes have wrested the initiative from public universities by offering a variety of professional training programmes in film and television production, journalism, media management, advertising and public relations.

The Need for Communication

Communication is a fact in the world of human beings, animals, and plants, and is an ever-continuing process going on all the time. It is as necessary to human, animal and vegetable existence as life itself. Halt communication and the life processes wither and die. The need for communication is as basic as the hunger for food and drink, perhaps even more so. In the beginning after all was 'Aum' or the 'Word', the first sound ever made or heard. In Indian tradition the 'Word' is the Shabda Brahman, the divine word.

According to one definition, 'Communication is the name we give to the countless ways that humans have of keeping in touch – not just words and music, pictures and print, nods and becks, postures and plumages; to every move that catches someone's eye and every sound that resonates upon another's ear.'[1] But this

---

1   Ashley Montagu and Floyd Matson: *The Human Connection*, New York: McGraw-Hill, 1979.

observation is true also for animals, birds and bees, and other land, sea and air creatures. The singing and chirping of birds, the croaking of frogs, and the many visual and olfactory signals among bird and beast are forms of communication too; some simple, others very highly sophisticated. The dance of the honeybee, for instance, is an advanced means of communication for it conveys to other bees the precise direction and distance of the place where nectar will be found.

A human being's need for communication is as strong and as basic as the need to eat, sleep and love. It is both an individual and a social need. It is 'both a natural individual demand and a requirement of social existence to use communication resources in order to engage in the sharing of experiences, through symbol-mediated interaction'.[2] The severest punishment for a child is to be isolated, to be left alone, not to be spoken to. North Indian children mete out this punishment when they say 'kuttie' to their playmates, holding out their thumb as an accompanying gesture.

Grown-ups too and especially the aged need company, need to communicate. Society punishes criminals by locking them up in solitary cells, thus starving them of the basic need, and indeed the fundamental right to communicate. Communication involves active interaction with our environments – physical, biological and social. Deprived of this interaction we would not be aware of whether we are safe or in danger, whether hated or loved, or satisfied or hungry. However, most of us take this interaction and this relationship for granted, unless we experience some deprivation of it. When that happens we adapt ourselves to the environment so that we don't lose touch, in both the literal and figurative senses. For, to lose touch is to suffer isolation.

The basic human need for communication can perhaps be traced to the process of mankind's evolution from lower species. Animals, for instance, have to be in sensory communication with their physical and biological surroundings to find food, protect themselves and to reproduce their species. A loss of sensation –

---

2 Luis Beltran: 'Farewell to Aristotle', in *Communication* 5, pp. 5-41.

the inability to hear a predator, for instance – can mean loss of life. Similarly, to be lost from primitive social communication – from the pack, from the herd or the tribe – is to be condemned to death.[3]

What happens to a person who is 'excommunicated' – literally, cut off from communication – by his group or his society? Malcolm X, the Black Muslim leader, described the experience of being expelled from his group as 'a state of emotional shock'. Elaborating, he said that this state was like that of someone 'who for twelve years had an inseparable, beautiful marriage partner and then suddenly one morning at breakfast the marriage partner had thrust across the table some divorce papers. I felt as though something in nature had failed, like the sun or the stars. It was that incredible a phenomenon to me – something too stupendous to conceive.'

Others who have been isolated for a period of time from human company are known to have experienced nightmarish hallucinations. Indeed, social isolation can also be hazardous to the heart as much as to the mind. It is estimated that single men without close friends run two or three times the risk of developing heart disease as their more sociable counterparts.

However, lack of communication can be as disorienting an experience as too much of it. Indeed, the apparent effects of sensory deprivation and sensory overload are frequently similar: anxiety, apathy, impaired judgement, strange visions, and something akin to schizophrenia. The 'information explosion' brought about by the Internet and other technologies is an instance of this sensory overload.

Communication and Language

But sensory communication alone was not enough for man to survive. Hence the evolution of symbolic communication called language – from non-verbal gestures, grunts and grimaces to the

---

[3] David Clark and William Blankenburg: *You and Media: Mass Communication and Society*, New York: Canfield Press, 1973.

verbal, and then to the written and printed word. Language is inseparable from culture which is its very source of sustenance; language embodies and expresses a community's culture. The 'arts' have grown out of this same fundamental desire and need to express oneself and to reach out to others. Cro-Magnon men and women adorned their caves with paintings of animals and hunters; the modern artist shows a preference for the abstract and 'pop', for the electronic and computer arts, for 'virtual reality'. But the human need to communicate has remained the same; only the forms and languages have changed.

The death of a language leads to the extinction its culture and its forms of communication; as many as 400 languages are close to extinction while over three thousand are on the endangered list. The world today has as many as 6800 languages (and many more dialects) according to Ethnologue, a database maintained by the Summer Institute of Linguistics, Dallas. The Asia and Pacific region accounts for the largest number of languages (3200), with Papua New Guinea alone speaking over 800); Africa accounts for 2400, while the Americas for about a thousand and the whole of Europe for just 200. Mandarin Chinese has the highest number of speakers: over a sixth of the world's population of six billion.[4]

Communication and Information

Communication and information are not similar concepts or experiences. Communication is not the mere sending or receiving of information in whatever form. Rather, it is a whole situation and an experience; a human relationship, in sum. Information, on the other hand, is made up of bits of messages, verbal and non-verbal, and is essentially unilinear. Significant information can bring about a communication relationship, but not when the exchange of information is on an unequal or commercial basis. Then information turns into a 'commodity', an

---

4 Cf. Special report on 'Endangered Languages' in *The Economist,* January 1, 2005. pp. 62 ff.

item to be bought and sold in the market place. A commodity, by definition, has a price attached to it. Authentic communication is not helped but rather distorted by such 'commodotized' information. Business communication thus, is a contradiction in terms; when communication becomes a business it turns into a commodity with an exchange value.

An Argentinian scholar, Ricardo C. Noseda, distinguishes between communication and information thus: Communication is not an act but a process by which an individuality enters into mental co-operation with another individuality until they come to constitute a common conscience. Information, instead, is just a unilateral translation of a message from an Emitter to a Receiver.[5]

The Right to Communicate

The right to information has been declared a fundamental right by a United Nations Charter (and such a right is recognised in India's Right to Information (RTI) Act, 2005), but what human beings need much more fundamentally is in fact the right to communicate. It is such a right that gives men and women their dignity and their freedom, as well as the ability to participate in the social, religious, economic and political life of a nation.

The right to communicate is now seen as a fundamental human right, much more comprehensive than existing freedoms of speech, the press, etc. It is the basic right of an individual and it extends, in some degree at least, to groups, nations and the international community, and to have important legal, economic and technological implications. It is closely related to the democratisation of communication within and between countries, and to concepts of 'access', 'participation' and the 'two-way' flow.[6]

---

5 Quoted in Luis Beltran, op cit.
6 Fisher and Harms: *The Right to Communicate*, 1983.

Defining Communication

Interaction, interchange, transaction, dialogue, sharing, communion and commonness are ideas that crop up in any attempt to define the term 'communication'. According to Denis McQuail, communication is a process which increases commonality – but also requires elements of commonality for it to occur at all.[7] A common language, for instance, does bring people together but language alone does not suffice for communication to take place. There are other factors too at play such as a shared culture and a common interest which bring about a sense of commonality and more significantly, a sense of community.

The Sanskrit term *sadharanikaran* comes closest to the sense of 'common' or 'commonness' usually associated with communication. Sadharanikaran is a social process which can be achieved only among *sahridayas*, people with a capacity to receive messages. This is an innate ability acquired through culture, adaptation or learning.[8] The focus here is not on the sender but the receiver of the message. Moreover, communication according to this Sanskrit concept is a relationship based on common and mutual understanding and feeling, for *sahridaya* literally means 'of one and the same heart'. The derivation of this ancient Indian concept of communication from the aesthetic theory of 'rasa' will be examined in a later section.

Communication thus presupposes a shared symbolic environment and a social relationship among those who participate. What it leads to is social interaction, and in combination with a set of other factors, contributes to a sense of community. Since the world of man, bird and beast too possesses and communicates such a social relationship, the need arises to speak of 'human communication' rather than 'communication' alone in

---

7 Denis McQuail: *Towards a Sociology of Communication*, London: Collier-Macmillan, 1975.

8 I.P. Tewari: 'Sadharanikaran: Indian Communication Theory', in *Indian and Foreign Review*, June 1980. See also I.P. Tewari: 'Towards an Indian Communication Theory', in *Communicator*, New Delhi, pp.

our study, though many communication researchers do not like the distinction.

Denis McQuail sees 'human communication' in linear terms as the sending of meaningful messages from one person to another. These messages could be oral or written, visual or olfactory. He also takes such things as laws, customs, practices, ways of dressing, gestures, buildings, gardens, military parades, and flags to be communication.[9] In contemporary urban culture, shopping malls, department stores, multiplexes, fairs and exhibitions may also be considered as forms of 'communication' since they bring people together to shop, share and experience a new ambience.

Ashley Montagu and Floyd Matson go a step further. In their view 'human communication', as the saying goes, is a clash of symbols, and it covers a multitude of signs. But it is more than media and message, information and persuasion; it also meets a deeper need and serves a higher purpose. Whether clear or garbled, tumultuous or silent, deliberate or fatally inadvertent, communication is the ground of meeting and the foundation of the community. It is, in short, the essential human connection.[10]

W.S. Cardon, a leading exponent of kinesics, the science of body language, develops the argument still further. He stresses that interaction within a culture is governed not so much by language, but by 'body synthesizers' set in motion almost immediately after birth and thereafter conditioned by culture. Communication, therefore, is not a matter of 'isolated entities sending discrete messages back and forth, but a process of mutual participation in a common structure of rhythmic patterns by all members of a culture'. For sociologists like Thompson, however, communication is a 'form of action' which takes places in a social context and is related to questions of economic, political, coercive and symbolic power in society.[11] The uses of

---

9 Denis McQuail: op cit.
10 Montagu and Matson: op cit.
11 John B. Thompson: *The Media and Modernity: A Social Theory of the Media*, Stanford, California: Stanford University Press, 1995. pp. 12-13

the mass media and the new digital media, in terms of this perspective, 'involve the creation of new forms of action and interaction in the social world, new kinds of social relationship and new ways of relating to others and to oneself... In a fundamental way, the use of communication media transforms the spatial and temporal organization of social life, creating new forms of action and interaction, and new modes of exercising power, which are no longer linked to the sharing of a common locale.'[12]

Types of Communication

Communication has been classified into several types: in terms of the verbal and non-verbal; the technological and non-technological; the mediated and non-mediated, the participatory and the non-participatory, and so on. Most of these typologies, however, are primarily for pedagogic or instructional purposes; in actual practice, there is much overlapping and mixing of the various types. The typologies must be seen as attempts at coming to grips with the apparently simple but really complex phenomenon of communication.

One common typology relates to the size of a social group or the number of people involved in the experience of communication. Such a typology ranges from the intrapersonal and interpersonal and transpersonal, to the group and the mass. Another typology relates to the extent of interactivity between the participants in the context of different technologies. So we can speak of face-to-face non-mediated communication', 'mediated communication' and 'computer-mediated communication', for instance.

Intrapersonal Communication

Intrapersonal Communication is individual reflection, contemplation and meditation. Transcendental meditation, for instance, is an example of such communication. Conversing with

---
12 Ibid. p. 4.

the divine, with spirits and ancestors, may be termed 'transpersonal' communication. This is a vital experience in the religious and monastic life, and in ashrams and places of prayer.

Interpersonal/Face-to-face Communication

Interpersonal Communication is direct face-to-face communication between two persons. It is, in other words, a dialogue or a conversation without the intervention of another person or a machine like the telephone or a two-way radio or television set-up. It is personal, direct, and intimate, allowing for maximum interaction and exchange in word and gesture. Indeed, it is the highest, the most perfect form of communication that two persons can attain. It is more persuasive and influential than any other type of communication such as group communication or mass communication, for it involves the interplay of words and gestures, the warmth of human closeness and in fact all the five senses. All interpersonal exchange is, therefore a communion and a sharing at the most intimate and open level. It is total communication for it takes within its compass words, body movements, physical characteristics, body odours, and even clothes. This is not to deny that interpersonal exchanges can be used by confidence tricksters and conmen to throw wool over people's eyes. A man may smile and smile and yet be a villain for all we know. That perhaps explains why we cherish our privacy so much and are constantly on our guard in face-to-face encounters, much more so than in group or mass gatherings. Only the ones who have our trust, and have proved themselves are allowed to cross the barriers of an intimate relationship. Most are kept at a distance.

In the area of business communication that distance is ritualized. For instance, interpersonal exchanges between a medical representative and a doctor or that between a manager and a clerk, are generally carried out on a professional level. As the saying goes they usually 'talk shop', but on occasions, even business chatter can lead to close and abiding friendships. That potential lies in the nature of interpersonal communication; hence the frequent barriers we raise lest people invade our space, our 'territory'. Interpersonal communication involves the sharing of a common space and time. Co-presence in a shared locale is imperative for this type of communication. So is a shared timeframe; we need to be together in time and space.

Konrad Lorenz and Desmond Morris have reported how animals and birds often turn aggressive when their territories are invaded by outsiders. This is because of the 'territorial imperative' – the obsession with protecting one's space.[13] The elephant has his herd, the lion his pride, the wolf his pack, and the birds and bees their nests and hives. Any encroachment from other groups is resented, and fought off, sometimes violently. Human beings react in an equally savage manner when their spatial privacy is encroached upon. In European cultures, it is considered bad manners and bad communication to get too close (literally and figuratively) and too intimate unless you have been permitted to enter the sanctum sanctorum of another. Among Indians and Arabs, however, physical closeness in Interpersonal Communication does not generally imply intimacy, nor does constant gazing into each other's eyes. This is a part of Western and South Asian cultures. According to Buddhism, the four social emotions that should guide interpersonal communication are: *metta* (loving kindness), *karuna* (compassion), *murdita* (sympathetic joy) and *upekkha* (equanimity).[14]

Focused and Unfocused Interactions

Interpersonal communication is conducted on the basis of focused and unfocused interactions. In his study of *Behaviour in Public Places*, Erving Goffman[15] argues that most interpersonal communication is of an unfocused nature. It takes place whenever we observe or listen to persons with whom we are not

---

13 Cf. Desmond Morris: *The Naked Ape.*
14 Wimal Dissanayake: 'Asian Theories of Communication', in *Media Development*, 1983 (2), p.9.
15 Erving Goffman: *Behaviour in Public Places.*

conversing, for instance in buses, trains, lifts or in public places like stations, bus stops, or on the street. It's the kind of activity we indulge in when we are 'people watching' without their being aware we are doing so. And what do we come to know about them? Our inferences may not all be valid or meaningful, but the fact remains that we do make inferences all the time about people. The young man who passes us by in a street dressed in pyjama and kurta evokes different associations from one clad in jeans and a jazzy shirt, depending of course on our own background, and the location of the street. The girl in a simple cotton sari, with her hair tied in a 'plait' say in a city like Bombay, conveys different impressions from the girl in a dress and with her hair bobbed. Additional sources of information about these persons are height, weight, and build. For instance, a well-built tall man is regarded as handsome, a stout fat woman as ugly, a thin wiry figure as athletic. Body movements such as gestures, the manner of standing, sitting or walking too convey certain meanings to us. Very broad gestures and loud talk, for example, are considered uncouth in polite society, but not necessarily so among working class groups. Thus it is that we draw conclusions on a person's qualities, cultural and religious background, socio-economic status, political ideology and other preferences without ever speaking to him or to her.

Focused interactions

Focused interactions, on the other hand, result from an actual encounter between two persons. The persons involved are fully aware that they are communicating with each other. Sitting or standing face-to-face either close or distant, they know fully well that they are exchanging both verbal and non-verbal messages, though they may not realize how these messages are being interpreted. Also, they are generally not conscious of the meanings they are conveying through 'body language'. An unfocused interaction usually is set off by eye contact. The meeting of eyes indicates that both parties are willing to have an interpersonal exchange. The turning away of eyes, on the other hand, cuts off the attempts to come together and start a conversation. It shows lack of interest. Similarly, reduction in eye involvement during a conversation is a non-verbal signal which indicates that it is time to bring the conversation to a close. Indeed, there is no more effective way of ending a face-to-face interaction than refusing to continue eye contact.

The Three Stages of Interpersonal Communication

The Phatic Stage: The initial exploratory stage of communication determines the course conversation will take. This first stage is known as the phatic period (from the Greek "phases", an utterance). It begins with a "Hi!" or a "Hello! How are you?", "Good Morning" or even a simple 'namaste' or 'vanakkam' or 'Jairam'. The accompanying gestures are the meeting of the eyes, a smile, perhaps a handshake, and moving in closer to a talking distance. In a formal encounter, the distance is greater (though not among all cultures) than an informal friendly meeting. The conversation then may veer to talk about the weather or queries like "How's life?", "How are things with you?" "What have you have been doing with yourself?", "What's the news?", "How are the folks at home?"

The Phatic stage is, therefore, a warming-up time during which ritualized greetings are exchanged. In themselves, the words and gestures exchanged during this period do not mean much. Indeed, the questions asked are not meant to be taken literally. They are only a formalised manner of showing interest and attention. They are a way of saying "I am glad to have met you. Let's have a chat". The answers we give to the queries made are equally formalised. "I'm fine, thank you", for example is a stock reply even if you're not doing too well. No deception is involved at all: what we are doing through words is merely sending signals that we would like to have a conversation. So at this stage we don't literally mean what we say, but we mean well. It's the meaning after all, and not the words that really matter. The words are only symbols or ways of getting across. The meaning is more often than not behind the words rather than in them. More accurately, meaning lies in a situation and a context, seen not so much in isolation but in a social and cultural environment. This is as true of verbal as of non-verbal communication. For instance, the North Indian's gesture of touching an elder's feet connotes respect and reverence among people of that culture, but is considered a demeaning gesture in some cultures of the south and the north-east. The phatic stage then is patterned according to social and cultural norms and rituals.

The Personal Stage: The second stage, called the personal stage, introduces a more personal element into the conversation. During this period we generally lower our social guard a little and are prepared to take some risk in exposing ourselves and our feelings. Having moved on to this personal stage, we are likely to be willing to talk about personal matters such as one's profession, the family, health problems and the like. If, on the other hand, we were hesitant to enter this stage, we would have broken off the conversation at the phatic stage itself or continued talking in a formal manner. Professional discussions rarely go beyond the personal stage. Most business communication, therefore, takes place at this level, for it does involve personal interests and we are ready to go along to promote them.

The Intimate Stage: This stage is reserved for friends and relatives, the degree of intimacy depending upon the closeness of the relationship. To some we open our hearts out completely; to others, though good friends, we are reluctant to tell all. Nevertheless, it's a stage when social barriers fall and we are at ease; interpersonal communication achieves its highest form in this mode, and words seem inadequate. Says Robert Shuter, "In this period, communicators reveal their innermost thoughts and feelings – their fears and joys, weaknesses and strengths. Marked by intimate revelations, this stage is reserved for individuals who have established a deep union, one based on love, respect and understanding".[16]

Group Communication

Group communication shares all these qualities, though in a much less measure. The larger the group the less personal and intimate is the possibility of exchange. In fact, as the group grows in size communication tends to become more and more of a monologue, for participation becomes problematic. The degree of directness and intimacy, therefore, depends upon the size of the group, the place where it meets, as also the relationship of the members of the group to one another, and to the group leader. Group communication is thus a more complex process than interpersonal communication. The level of mutual participation and understanding among the members suffers as a result. In Interpersonal Communication too understanding and participation may not be complete, especially if the non-verbal cues and the socio-cultural contexts are not paid attention to. However, the possibility of checking up and correcting misunderstanding is much quicker and easier in much interpersonal communication.

Feedback is the key word here. While in interpersonal communication, feedback is instantaneous, it is not so in group communication, especially in large groups. What is more, it allows for instant response to feedback received. In Group Communication, on the other hand, feedback is more difficult to measure, and to respond to. It takes time before meanings are clarified and responses assessed. That explains why the art of effective public speaking (an example of one-way top-down communication) is more necessary at the group level than at the interpersonal level. Feedback is a term from cybernetics, the study of messages, particularly of effective message control. When feedback is employed for this kind of social engineering, as in consumer advertising, it is no more communication but

---

16 Quoted in Lee O. Thayer: *Administrative Communication*, Illinois: Richard D. Unwin, 1961.

propaganda and manipulation.

Face-to-face communication, nevertheless, is more persuasive and influential, particularly in an unequal communication situation. It involves the interplay of words and gestures and above all, the warmth of human closeness. No wonder, advertising people still depend on door-to-door salesmen and salesgirls even where the mass media such as radio, television and the press are widespread. Sincerity and enthusiasm are far easier to convey, and to react to in a face-to-face situation. In Group Communication, particularly where the group is large, deception and pretence cannot be detected immediately. That must be the reason why 'acting' is associated with Group Communication. The theatre, religious services, dance performances, carnivals, the Kumbh Mela, Rama Lila, Rasa Lila and other folk events, are examples of Group Communication. Village markets, bazaars and melas too are instances of informal Group Communication. Then there are 'gossip groups', 'tea-shop groups' and other informal traditional groups that come together either regularly or occasionally for sharing information. These are 'micro-groups' that communicate among and within themselves in terms of their status and the nature of their relationships.

Mass Communication

Group Communication has now been extended by the tools of mass communication: books, the press, the cinema, radio, television, video and the Internet. Mass Communication is generally identified with these modern mass media, but it must be noted that these media are processes and must not be mistaken for the phenomenon of communication itself. Exaggerated claims have been made for the 'power' of the mass media. Daniel Lerner termed them 'mobility multipliers' and Wilbur Schramm considered them to be 'magic multipliers'. Indeed, both the terms 'mass communication' and 'mass media' are inappropriate in the context of developing societies. None of the 'mass media' reach the masses of people in these societies, though increasing numbers are acquiring access to them with every passing decade. Yet, where access to, and distribution of, the mass media in India is concerned, only the comparatively well-off in urban and rural areas are at an advantage. They are elite media in another sense too: the stories they tell and the information they disseminate are more relevant to elite interests: the poor, marginalized groups and minority groups are barely visible.[17]

Newspapers, transistors, films and television are still beyond the economic reach of at least 20% of our population that lives below the poverty line. Traditional community media like the keertana and yakshagana, and the whole treasure-house of folk song, folk dance and folk theatre are the real organs of mass media in India. They are far less expensive organs, are easy of access, are frequently participatory in nature and communicate much more effectively than the electronic media and at a direct and personal level. Their reach too is far and wide in the country. However, the modern mass media are produced and distributed like other consumer and industrial products – on a mass scale. Mass communication then is 'communication at a distance' with technology mediating production, transmission and reception. To Thompson this is a form of 'mediated quasi-interactive communication'. In all types of mass communication, he observes, the context of production is generally separate from the context of reception... the flow of messages is a *structured* flow in which the capacity of recipients to intervene or contribute to the process of production is strictly circumscribed.'[18] Phone-in programmes and SMS voting in television contests and game shows have made little difference to this fundamental separation of producers and receivers.

---

17 For further analysis of this issue, see my article on 'Poverty, Advertising and the News Media in India', *Media Development* (Toronto), January 2008.
18 John B. Thompson: *The Media and Modernity: A Social Theory of the Media*, Stanford University Press, 1995.

'Mass-line' Communication

Mao Zedong, who led the Chinese Cultural Revolution, used a type of communication to talk to the masses. He termed it 'mass-line' communication. Mahatma Gandhi too employed a similar type of communication, the essence of which was personal example, respect for the peasant's knowledge, and non-manipulative information. Kusum J Singh's comparison of the two leaders' use of the mass-line type of communication brings out the relevance of this type of grass-root level communication even today for mobilizing the masses in developmental efforts.[19]

Interactive Communication

Communication via the 'new' media such as video, cable, videotex, teletext, video-on-demand, tele-shopping, computers, the Internet and mobile telephony is usually termed 'interactive communication'. Telecommunication-based services such as telephones, pagers, cellular or mobile phones, electronic mail are also considered to be 'interactive'. They are point-to-point communication systems, and can approximate to the inter-personal (as in the basic telephone and the various 'value-added' services), the group (as in teleconferences and videoconferences) or the mass (as in the Internet's World Wide Web where companies or people with their own web-sites can reach millions of individuals across the globe at their own convenience. A major characteristic of interactive communication is 'asynchronicity', that is the sending and receiving of messages is at one's convenience, rather than at the same time, as in radio, television. Audio, video and digital recording facilitates listening and watching at a time later than the time of transmission; voice mail, electronic mail and SMS/MMS messages, can be sent and accessed at times convenient to communicators.

Western Models of Communication

Western theories and models of communication have their

---

19 Kusum Singh: *Gandhi and Mao as Mass Communicators*, Ann Arbor, 1978.

origin in Aristotle's Rhetoric. According to Aristotle, rhetoric is made up of three elements: the speaker, the speech, and the listener. The aim of rhetoric is the search for all possible means of persuasion.

Perhaps the most widely quoted definition of mass communication in terms of Aristotelian rhetoric is that of Harold D. Lasswell, the American political scientist. He stated that 'a convenient way to describe an act of communication is to answer the following questions:
Who
Says What
In Which Channel
To Whom
With What Effect?

WHO	SAYS WHAT	IN WHICH CHANNEL	TO WHOM	WITH WHAT EFFECT?
COMMU-NICATOR	MESSAGE	MEDIUM	RECEIVER	EFFECT

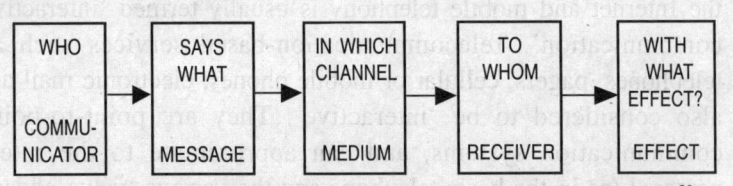

Fig. 1: The Lasswell Model of the Communication Process[20]

Lasswell saw communication as performing three functions: surveillance of the environment, correlation of components of society, and cultural transmission between generations. Such a mechanistic and 'effects' approach to communication was to influence communication theory for decades to come. Essential to this understanding were the notions of transmission and transfer of information for intended effects.

A definition on similar lines was given by Berelson and Steiner: 'The transmission of information, ideas, emotions, skills, etc., by use of symbols-words, pictures, figures, graphs, etc. It is the act or process of transmission that is usually called communication'.

---

20 Denis McQuail and Sven Windahl: *Communication Models for the Study of Mass Communication*, London: Longman, 1993.

The primary goal of communication, according to Western communication theory, was influence through persuasion. Osgood's definition is an illustration. In the most general sense, he explains, we communicate whenever one system, source, influences another, the destination, by manipulation of alternative signals which can be transferred over the channel connecting them.

The Shannon and Weaver Model

The effects-oriented models or approaches to mass communication derive from Shannon and Weaver's Mathematical model of communication. They conceived of communication as a system composed of five essential parts plus 'noise': (1) an information source, (2) a transmitter, (3) a channel, (4) the receiver, and (5) the destination. As engineers during World War II at the Bell Telephone Laboratories in the United States, their primary concern was finding out the most efficient means of using the channels of communication (the telephone cable and the radio wave) for the transfer of information. They, however, claimed that the mathematical model they worked out as a result of their research at Bell, was widely applicable to human communication as well.

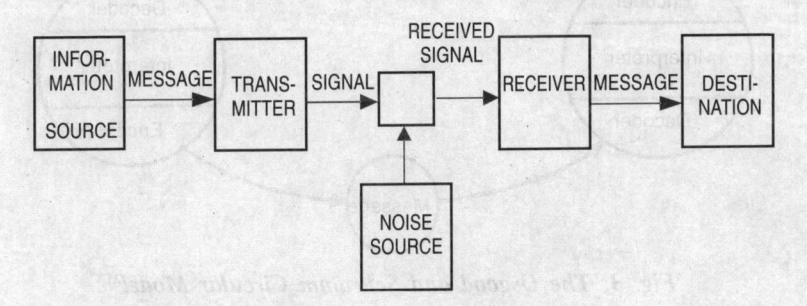

Fig. 2: The Shannon and Weaver 'Mathematical' Model of Communication[21]

---

21 Ibid.

Wilbur Schramm, whose theories have influenced much Indian planning on the role of communication in development, adapted Shannon and Weaver's model to human communication, but stressed the encoding-decoding aspects as crucial. He defined communication as 'the sharing of information, ideas or attitudes'. He endorsed the Aristotelian principle that communication always requires at least three elements – source, message and destination. The encoding and decoding of the message were the most important components to him. As he explained: Substitute 'microphone' for encoder, and 'earphone' for decoder and you are talking about electronic communication. Consider that the 'source' and 'encoder' are one person, 'decoder' and 'destination' are another, and the signal is language, and you are talking about human communication.[22] In a communication model he developed with Charles Osgood, Schramm suggested that communication was circular in nature, where both the sender and the receiver were involved in encoding and decoding, and were equal partners in the exchange.

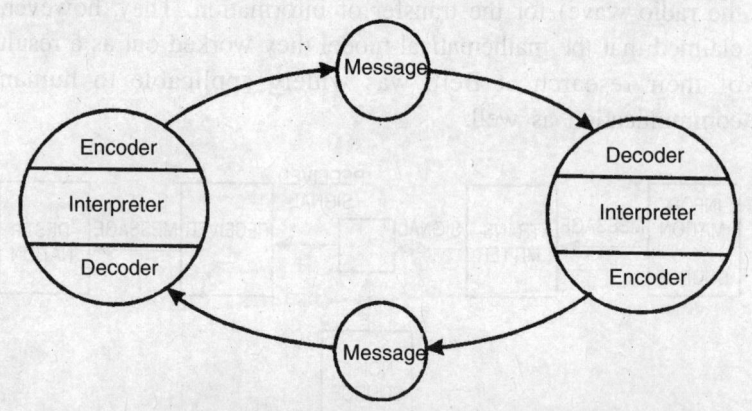

Fig. 3: The Osgood and Schramm Circular Model[23]

Berlo, on the other hand, saw communication as a 'process' and

---

22 Wilbur Schramm: *Mass Media and National Development*, Stanford University Press, 1964.
23 McQuail and Windahl, op. cit.

the events and relationships of this process as dynamic, ongoing, ever-changing, continuous. He argued that you cannot talk about the beginning or the end of communication or say that a particular idea came from one specific source, that communication occurs in only one way and so on. He termed this the 'bucket' theory of communication wherein ideas were dumped from the source into a bucket – such as a film, a lecture, a book, a television program or what have you – and shipped the bucket over to the receiver and dumped the contents into his head.

In sum, Western communication theories and the models (especially of development communication) built on them have been largely unilinear, wrongly postulating a mechanical notion of communication as the transmission of information from active sources to passive receivers. Further, these individual-based models wrongly assume that communication is an act, a static phenomenon privileging the source, not a dynamic process involving all elements in a social relationship.

In recent years, however, the focus in Western communication theory has shifted – from mechanistic 'effects' models of communication acts to those concerned with communication relationships and the communication 'experience'. Semiotic models look at communication as 'social interaction through messages'. The focus of attention in these models is language (both verbal and non-verbal) as a sign-system; how 'meaning' is generated and understood is central to this approach. The crucial questions the semiotic approaches address themselves to are: What is a Sign? What is the Meaning of Signs? What is the relationship between signs, users and external reality? The user is seen as active, as a creator of meaning, as one who makes his or her own meaning. Meaning is thus not so much in the words, gestures or symbols (the 'text') but in the cultural interpretation of the participants (the 'readers') in the communication experience. The semiotic approaches to communication are based on the work of C.S. Pierce, who established the American tradition of semiotics; C.K. Ogden and I.A. Richards of Britain; and the Swiss linguist, Ferdinand de Saussure.

Communication as 'Ritual': The Ritual Model of Mass Communication

James Carey, the American anthropologist, has been foremost in promoting a 'ritual' model communication. Horace Newcomb, Robert Alley and others also promote this perspective. They base their approach on Victor Turner's extensive anthropological studies of the role of ritual in societies. 'All members of the public – not just message senders – are considered to be actors contributing in some way to the pattern of meaning of a nation or region'.[24] They object to a 'transportation' model which defines communication as the 'transmission of messages for purposes of social control. Public communication such as television is more closely analogous to the moment of ritual in which myths, values and meanings of life are recalled and re-enacted. Communication is thus a process of creation, representation and celebration of shared beliefs'.[25]

Communication as 'Dialogue'

Communication as a dialogic and 'participatory' relationship is at the heart of the South American perspective. The key elements of the perspective are 'liberation', 'participation' and 'conscientization' derived from liberation theology and the writings of the late Paulo Freire, the Brazilian educationist. This perspective of communication challenges the traditional Aristotelian model of communication as 'transmission' and 'transportation'. Much of South American research in communication is based on this model.

---

24 Robert A. White: 'The significance of recent developments in the field of mass communication', paper presented at the 1985 meeting of the Foundation for Mass Communication Research in the Netherlands, March 1985. See James A Carey: Communication as Culture.
25 ibid.

Communication as a Power-Relationship

In some situations, Communication is an exercise in power-relations, the power of one individual over another, of an individual over a group, and of mass media owners and producers/professionals over audiences. This perspective of Communication focuses on the inequality among people involved in a communication experience: the inequality in class, caste, economic and social power. This perspective has its basis in Marxism which sees 'conflict' and class differences rather than consensus as the function of communication. Communication is a relationship of power in the family, the classroom, the workplace, and the mass media situation.

Indian Communication Theories

In recent years communication scholars in India and Sri Lanka have made attempts to develop theories of communication based on Indian classical texts and on popular Indian culture.

According to Tewari, the Indian theory of communication forms a part of Indian poetics; and can be traced to a period between second century B.C. and first century A.D. in the works of Bharata. It hinges on the concept of *sadharanikaran* which is quite close in meaning to the Latin term communis, commonness, from which the word 'communication' is derived.[26]

The most important assumption in the process of *sadharanikaran* is that it can be achieved only among *sahridayas*, i.e., only those who have a capacity to accept a message. This is an innate ability acquired through culture, adaptation and learning. Thus communication is an activity among sahridayas. It is to be noted that, says Tewari, the concept of *sahridaya* is not co-terminus with predisposition or in favour or against. It only denotes the quality of mind or receptivity on the part of the audience. It does not speak of the quality – positive or negative – of attitude on the part of the audience. It

---

26 I.P. Tewari: 'Indian Theory of Communication', Communicator, New Delhi, March 1992, pp.35-38.

may, however, qualify the depth or level of sensory experience that shapes the human personality.[27]

The human psyche in terms of this theory is composed of permanent moods, called *sthai bhava*. These moods are capable of arousing a corresponding state of feeling, *rasa*. There are nine permanent moods and they give rise to nine *rasas* or forms of aesthetic pleasure. For instance, the permanent mood *bhayanaka* arouses the *bhayanak* (furious) *rasa,* the *hrsha* (joy) triggers the *hasya* (laughter) *rasa*, the *dina* the *karuna* (compassion) *rasa* and so on. The entire range of human emotions is encompassed in this categorisation. The state of arousal of the nine permanent moods is termed *rasa utpathi*.

The *sthai bhavas* are accompanied also by many fleeting or secondary moods that are common to several dominant moods and serve the purpose of completely manifesting the permanent mood, such as *nirveda* (despondency) or *glani* (fatigue), and may help to manifest the permanent moods, like the erotic helps the pathetic. These are called *sancharis* or *vyabhichari bhavas*. In addition, there are *vibhavas* and *anubhavas,* the emotions that unite a man and woman in love. It is at the climax of this relationship that *sadharanikaran* is attained.

The concept of *sadharanikaran*, one of the fundamental concepts in Indian aesthetics, also has religious implications. As in the Vedanta, objects of experience are held to be not the ultimate reality but only manifestations of that reality; so words and the expressed meaning are regarded as the mere external experience of art, and the emotional mood which a work communicates is thus the essence of reality – the highest communication endeavour indeed.[28]

There is a certain elitism present in the concept, however. Rasa is the art of the ordinary, but it can be understood only by the *sahridaya* and the only proof of its existence is the aswada,

---

27 Tewari, op cit.
28 ibid.

the taste, which only a *sahridaya* has. He or she alone is capable of *sadharanikaran*.

Yadava points out that the term was first used in the tenth century by Bhattanayaka in a commentary on the Natya Shastra to explain the sutras related to *rasa*. Bhattanayaka stressed that the essence of communication lay in achieving commonness and oneness.[29]

Yadava draws out two implications or resonances of the term, *sahridaya*, literally of one heart. He believes that the term is synonymous with 'identification' and 'simplification' – the identification of communicator with the receiver through the process of simplification. Mahatma Gandhi, for instance achieved this identification with the masses through 'simplification' of his message, the common religious symbols he employed, and above all, the utter simplicity of his life.

At the community level, Yadava notes, the saints, sufis and brahmins of old propagated religious and cultural values through simplification and illustration. He sees this practice as continuing today in the conversation and traditional media of rural folk throughout the Indian sub-continent. This dimension of *sadharanikaran*, seems to have become the common heritage of the Indian people.[30]

Yet, the process of *sadharanikaran* is fundamentally 'asymmetrical', and the sharing or oneness it connotes is among sahridayas alone, unequal perhaps but one in heart. The goal of *sadharanikaran*, therefore, is not persuasion so much as the very enjoyment of the process of sharing. At the same time, the source is perceived as having a higher status, and the receiver of the message, a lower status. As Yadava puts it, the relationship is hierarchical, of 'domination' and 'subordination'. The source is held in high esteem by the receiver of information, a relationship idealized and romanticised in the guru-chela tradition.[31]

29 J.S. Yadava: 'Trends in Communication Research', Paper presented at the National Seminar on Communication Research: Trends and Priorities, New Delhi: Indian Institute of Mass Communication research, 1984.
30 Ibid.
31 Ibid.

Yadava hypothesizes that the asymmetrical aspects of *sadharanikaran* helped in the blossoming of Indian civilization in earlier times through efficient communication and division of labour, but in centuries resulted in highly rigid and hierarchical closed social structures.[32]

Wimal Dissanayake draws on the Vedas, the Upanishads and non-philosophical traditions (such as Bhartrhar's *Vakyapadiya*, a fifth century text on grammar or Bharat Muni's *Natyashastra*) to build an Indian model of communication. The primary focus of interest in his model is how the receiver makes sense of the stimuli he receives so as to deepen his self-awareness. In Indian tradition, he argues, 'communication is an inward search for meaning – a process leading to self-awareness, then to freedom, and finally to truth'. Thus it transcends language and meaning and is interpretation or reception-orientated, not expression-orientated like the Western models. The intrapersonal dimension is of greater importance than the interpersonal in the Indian approach, for individualism and manipulation have no place in it.

Neville Jayaweera, also a Sri Lankan with a deep interest in Indian philosophy, observes that the Vedantic philosophy of 'advaita' (absolute monism) has profound implications for contemporary understanding of communication.[33]

Dissanayake also propounds a Buddhist theory of communication derived from the concept of dependent co-origination, *pattica-samupadda/pratitya-samutpada*. This concept lies at the heart of the Buddha's teaching. It is related to the three principles that sum up worldly existence: *anitya* or impermanence, *dukkha* or suffering and *anatma* or no-self. It is a highly connotative concept which implies that every phenomenon, including communication, is in a state of impermanence and flux.[34]

---

32 Ibid.
33 Gunaratne, 1991.
34 Wimal Dissanayake: 'Asian Theories of Communication', in *Media Development*, 1983 (2), p.9.

A Philosophical View

T.B. Saral looks at communication theory from a Hindu philosophical perspective.[35] The Hindu's concept of the universe is based on the 'Virat Purush' (cosmic man) view. A natural extension of this concept is that it espouses the systems approach, the authority of Universal law, the law of Dharma. Dharma is the basic principle of the whole universe and is existing eternally. This natural law of Dharma regulates human existence and governs relations of individual beings; communication too is governed by the same law.

Saral believes that most western studies of communication are confined to the study of what may be termed 'surface structure' features, such as verbal language, body language, nonverbal gestures, facial expressions, etc. But it is often the 'deep structure' features that make a critical difference to our understanding of communication. This 'deep structure' is shaped by the cultural and metaphysical assumptions about the definition of truth and reality, the place of an individual in the universe, and one's relationship with other living and non-living elements of the environment, the concepts of time and space, and so on.

Western models and theories of communication are thus reflective of the biases of western thought and culture. The distinctive marks of this philosophy are categorisation, classification, linear sequencing and rational logic. Indian philosophy, on the other hand, is characterised by complexity and pluralism; it is holistic and intuitive, and believes that reality is one. In Indian rhetoric, opposites are co-ordinates, contradictions are illusory, and the world is a dramatic portrayal of God playing hide-and-seek with himself, trying to reassemble all the divergent parts back into their original unity.[36]

---

[35] T.B. Saral: 'Hindu Philosophy of Communication', *Communication 6*, pp.47-58. For another Indian analysis of Western transmission models, see Achal Mehra: 'Western Communication Theory: An Asian Critique', Paper presented at the IAMCR Conference, Lake bled, Yugoslavia, August 26-31, 1990.

[36] T. Oliver: *Communication in Ancient India and China*, Syracuse: Syracuse University Press, 1971.

An Islamic 'Communitarian' View

Hamid Mowlana and Majid Teharanian, two Iranian-American media scholars have developed an Islamic or 'Communitarian' model of communication.[37] The 'umma' or the community is at the centre of communication in Islam, as against the individual who is the primary focus of attention in Western models. The primary purpose and experience of communication, according to this view, is to build relationships in a community rather than persuasion or propaganda.[38]

Barriers to Communication

'Barriers' are any obstacles or difficulties that come in the way of communication. They may be physical, mechanical, psychological, cultural or linguistic in nature. In business communication, for instance, the major obstacles arise because of the set-up of an organisation – the organisational barriers. The size of an organisation, the physical distance between employees of an organisation, the specialisation of jobs and activities, and the power and status relationships, are the main organisational barriers. Besides, there are the barriers, raised by interpersonal relationships between individual and groups, the prejudices of both individuals and groups, and the channels they use to communicate.

In the 'jargon' of communication, all barriers whatever their nature are clubbed under a common label – 'noise'. A term from modern physics, it denotes not only atmospheric or channel disturbance, but all barriers that distort communications in any manner.

Is there such a thing then as 'perfect' communication free of all barriers? This is hardly ever true, except perhaps at higher spiritual or mystic levels where communication is transformed

---

37 See also Sohaib Jamal-Al-Barzinji: *Working Principles for an Islamic Model in Mass Media Communication,* International Institute of Islamic Thought, 1993.
38 Cf. special issues of *Asian journal of Religion and Communication* on 'Religious Perspectives of Communication, 2006. Includes research papers on Hindu/Indian, Islamic, Buddhist, Confucianist and Christian perspectives.

into a 'communion'. For us, mere mortals, the wrestling with imperfect communications must continue.

Physical Barriers

Four main kinds of distractions act as 'physical barriers' to the communication process. These are –

(1) The Competing Stimulus in the form of another conversation going on within hearing distance, or loud music or traffic noise in the background. The cawing of crows or a plane passing overhead can, for example, drown out messages altogether.
(2) Environmental Stress: A high temperature and humidity, poor ventilation, vibrations felt, a strong glare – all can contribute to distortions in the sending and receiving of messages.
(3) Subjective Stress: Sleeplessness, ill health, the effects of drugs and mood variations give rise to forms of subjective stress that often lead to great difficulties in listening and interpretation.
(4) Ignorance of the Medium: The various media for communication in business are: oral, written, audio, visual and audiovisual. The use of a medium with which the communicators are not familiar would turn the medium itself into a barrier. For instance, the use of visual media like maps and charts to instruct workers who have not been taught to read maps and charts would alienate the workers immediately; they would 'switch off' for lack of knowledge of the medium.

Psychological Barriers

Each of us has a certain 'frame of reference', a kind of window through which we look out at the world, at people, and events and situations. A frame of reference is a system of standards and values, usually implicit, underlying and to some extent controlling an action, or the expression of any belief, attitude or idea. No two individuals possess exactly similar frames of reference, even if they should be identical twins. To a large extent our frames of reference are influenced by our experiences, particularly our childhood experiences, and the cultural environment we have grown up in. Heredity too has a great influence.

However, learning and deeper experiences modify these 'mental sets' as we grow and mature, and develop diverse frames of reference to meet different needs – our own and that of the group we identify ourselves with. This is the 'reference group', whose attitudes towards religion, politics, education and so on we adopt as our own – without being fully aware that we are doing so.

Self-Image

Tied up with the term 'frame of reference' is the term 'self-image' or 'self-concept' – i.e., the way an individual looks at himself, or the picture he has of himself. It is this 'self-image' that makes us always defend our point of view, to interpret messages in the way we wish to interpret them, and to see 'reality' according to our own pre-conceived notions. That is why few people see things alike: Freud, Jung and Adler interpreted the same dream in three different ways; Indian historians differ on who was responsible for 'the partition', and people understand 'love', 'beauty', 'honour' and 'freedom' according to what suits their 'self-image'. The American poet Wallace Stevens wrote that there were 13 ways of looking at a blackbird. He was mistaken, for there were as many ways as there were cultural contexts.

Thus, we tend to listen attentively to, and interpret favourably those messages which give a boost to our self-image, and reject or misinterpret messages which threaten that same image. The consequence is: Communication selectivity. It is not only with regard to the sending and receiving of messages that we are selective, but also in the extent we remember them. For instance, we retain only that information that is pleasant to us or reinforces our ego, and very conveniently forget details that are unpleasant or humiliating.

Resistance to Change

"The risk of being changed is one of the most frightening prospects many of us can face" (Carl Rogers). No wonder, we resist change in any form with all our might, except where we are convinced it is to our benefit. So new ideas that do not support our own views are resisted outright. In fact, most of the time we do not actually hear views which conflict with our own. But we hear with rapt attention any communication that reinforces our beliefs, and our self image.

The effective communicator, therefore, does not wait till resistance builds up against an intended change or innovation, but takes the people into confidence even at the planning stage. Instead of springing a surprise on them, he listens to their point of view with respect, involves them in the change; talks to them about the benefits the change will bring; assures them their job security will not be affected; and explains the reasons why the change is necessary.

Defensiveness and Fear

Closely related to the barrier raised by our 'resistance to change' is the barrier of defensiveness. One of man's most compelling needs is to justify himself. Even when we are convinced we are wrong, few of us admit it, as it means a loss of face. More often than not, therefore, we tend to 'rationalize' (explain away) the mistakes we make, the attitudes and opinions we hold so dear.

'Fear is an affect of great potency in determining what the individual will perceive, think and do' (Izard and Tomkins). Indeed, together with the allied emotions of nervousness, anxiety and tension, fear is the most constricting of all the affects, resulting often in 'tunnel vision' (near-blindness to a great part of the communication). It also gives rise to slow and narrow thinking which selects and distorts communications.

During an interview, a candidate's fear, tension and anxiety tells on his performance: he fumbles for words, misinterprets questions and in general gives a poor show of himself. During a written examination, nervous candidates misread the instructions, misunderstand the questions asked. Some psychologists, however, are of the view that a little anxiety is good, for it brings into use brain-cells otherwise inactive, and heightens attention, improves performance, releases certain hormones, and facilitates learning by a greater spread of nerve messages in the brain. In other words, fear and anxiety can be turned into a source of energy and confidence.

Linguistic and Cultural Barriers

A language is the expression of the thoughts and experiences of a people in terms of their cultural environment. When the same language is made use of in a different culture, it takes on another colour, another meaning. When, for instance, English is employed in India, it comes under the influence not only of the accent of the local language, but also of the meanings and connotations of words, phrases, and idioms of that language, and of the culture that has given rise to it.

Each language shapes the reasoning of its speakers. Thus English enforces 'either/or' thinking and reasoning, which Chinese does not. Indeed, 'no human is free to describe nature with strict objectivity; he is a prisoner of his language' and even the same language has to cross not only cultural and generation gaps, but political and social gaps as well.

What is more, 'in our own familiar environment we switch our type of language fairly frequently, probably quite unconsciously; we modify it according to whom we are talking to, where we are, and according to what we talk about; there is a different language for discussing profit margins and for talking about the merits of the domestic help....... we are aware of the situational differences'.

This is equally true of non-verbal language: a nod of the head does not mean assent in all cultures; the 'thumbs up' gesture has different associations for urban and rural groups in India; the touching of an elder's feet is a mark of respect in North India, but a mark of humiliation in other cultures.

Language and Meaning

Language facilitates understanding, but there are times when it can be a barrier to communication. In the first place, a language (whether verbal or non-verbal) is ambiguous by nature. The words of language, for instance, are mere symbols, and by themselves rarely represent only one meaning. Further, these symbols are understood differently by participants in communication. And words (or symbols) possess objective and subjective meanings. While objective (or denotative or dictionary) meanings point to objects, people and events, subjective (or connotative) meanings point to emotional and evaluational responses. The favourable and unfavourable associations of a word depend upon the cultural context in which it is used. Take the words 'fascist', 'capitalist' or 'communist', for example: they carry different associations in communist and non-communist states.

Meanings, therefore, exist not in words themselves but in the minds of people who use them. Even simple words like 'love', 'freedom', 'happiness' and 'tragedy' carry numerous associations depending upon the political and cultural situations people find themselves a part of.

Mechanical Barriers

Mechanical barriers are those raised by the channels employed for interpersonal, group or mass communication. Channels become barriers when the message is interfered with by some disturbance, which (1) increased the difficulty in reception or (2) prevented some elements of the message reaching its destination or both. The absence of communication facilities too would be a mechanical barrier. Technically, such barriers are clubbed together under one general term 'channel noise'.

This type of barrier includes any disturbance which interferes with the fidelity of the physical transmission of the message. A telephone that is in poor working order, making demands on the yelling ability of Sender and Receiver, is a mechanical barrier in interpersonal communication. So also is 'cross-talk' often heard over an 'intercom' link in an office, or during long-distance calls. Thus, hearing is the physical act of receiving sound waves, a natural process. Listening, however, is a skill that has to be learned and developed, requiring hard work and practice.

In Group Communication, a rundown or 'whistling microphone' and the wrong placement of loudspeakers are disturbances which are mechanical in nature. (The communicator who stands too close or too far from the mike is another matter). In mass communication, mechanical barriers would include such disturbances as static on the radio, smeared ink in a newspaper, a rolling screen on television, a barely readable point-size, or a film projector or video that does not function perfectly.

Information Technology and Society: A Brief History

The beginnings of modern mass communication, where the use of technology defines the nature of communication, are perhaps traceable to the invention of printing and paper in China, Korea and other parts of Asia, more than four centuries before Guttenberg in Europe. It was around 1440 in Mainz, Germany, that Johannes Guttenberg introduced his machine for printing from movable type. Instead of having to make copies laboriously by hand, numerous copies could be turned out of a machine that was worked by hand. Books like the Bible became easily available to all those who were literate. Indeed, the invention of printing made possible the spread of education in schools and universities. No more was learning the monopoly of a few monks with access to hand-copied manuscripts in remote monasteries.

With the growing sophistication in the techniques of printing (the steam press and later the rotary press), communication with the literate masses by writers and leaders became a simple matter. Religious revolutions like the Protestant Reformation, political revolutions like the French and the American and freedom struggles like those in Asia and Africa could involve the masses in the uprisings because of speedy and efficient communication.

The First Wave

The invention of printing (which Marshall McLuhan, the Canadian media sociologist, considered an 'extension of the eye') led to 'the tendency to see reality in discrete units, to find causal relations and linear serial order, and to find orderly structure in nature'. It allowed individuals to withdraw, to contemplate and meditate outside of communal activities. Printing, therefore, encouraged 'privatization, the lonely scholar, and the development of private points of view'. Indeed, 'the very linear and rectilinear layout of words on the printed page transformed the nature of spelling, grammar and prose style'. An oral face-to-face 'tribal' culture gave way with the help of the new technology of printing to a 'detribalized' visual, linear and symmetrical culture. The logical, the orderly, and the linear now come to prominence in man's ways of seeing and communicating. So did McLuhan speculate on the deterministic nature of technology. To McLuhan, all the media (not just the communication media) were 'the extensions of man'.[39]

By the early 19th century, power press printing helped introduce the daily newspaper – the greatest challenge to the printed book. The arrangement of news and later of pictures as well on the pages of a newspaper was not linear, but in the form of a mosaic. There was no specific order in which the news and

---

39 Marshall McLuhan: *Understanding Media: The Extensions of Man*, Penguin, 1969.

pictures were arranged, and no specific order in which they had to be read or looked at. Thus, the linear and the symmetrical communication culture gave way under the onslaught of the mosaic and montage modes of communication. Technology had once again revolutionised our way of seeing – and of sending and receiving communication.

The Second Wave

The 19th century also saw the inventions of the telegraph, the telephone and photography. Then along came Thomas Edison with his phonograph and his movie camera and projector which made it possible to store sound and moving pictures. DeForest's invention of the triode vacuum tube in 1907, opened up the new worlds of radio and television. All these technological innovations led to another revolution in communication. This dramatic development has been called 'the second wave' of modern communication, 'the first wave' being ushered in by print technology.

Just as print extended the eye, radio proved to be an extension of the ear. McLuhan argued that 'printing upset the balance between oral and written speech; photography upset the balance of ear and eye.' With radio, oral speech and the sense of hearing regained their importance. Together with the phonograph (or gramophone), a new aural culture was beginning to take shape, when the movies and later television launched an audio-visual revolution in communication. In McLuhan's words, "If the movie was the mechanization of movement and gesture, TV was the electronification of the same."

Satellite communication via television and cable has now transformed the world into a 'global village'. Man has been 'retribalized', returned to the state of the tribe, to his 'sensorial wholeness' (the balanced use of all his senses). "The speed of information in the global village", wrote McLuhan, "means that every human action or event involves everybody in the village in the consequences of every event." Wishful thinking! While this might have been true of the small close-knit primitive tribe, it does not apply to the scattered millions of the universe who are caught up in the little worlds of their own castes, religions, ethnicities, communities and nationalities.

The Third Wave

The third wave of modern communication between man and machine was set in motion almost at the same time as the first, but climaxed only in the 20th century. Computers, and the concept of information storage, retrieval and transmission have brought about mind-boggling changes in the processing of information and communication. It is now possible for computer programmers to instruct machines to develop and work other machines ('artificial intelligence'). This has resulted in automation – and the dawn of the fourth wave.

The Fourth Wave

First it was 'Teletext', then 'Videotex' bringing us the latest headlines on the TV screen; but from the early nineties, the rapid diffusion of multi-media, paging and cellular telephony, and above all, the Internet, especially in developed societies, has given rise to the 'Age of Information', an age in which information has been turned into the primary commodity of commerce and trade.

Further, Cable TV technology combined with satellite and digital technologies, has led to a profusion of broadcasting channels worldwide. (Direct-to-Home or DTH broadcasting already brings more than five hundred channels to the small screen). The choice in communication has become virtually unlimited for the urban affluent. The 'information explosion' is however largely restricted to the young, educated and better off classes in developed societies; the business and academic elite in developing societies.

In India, multinational companies and several public and private sector organisations have already gone in for the use of computers on a massive scale. The armed forces, the police departments, the courts, the airlines, railways, meteorological departments and the telecommunications division, find the computer indispensable. The INSAT series of domestic satellites, and our membership in INTELSAT, INMARSAT and other consortia, are helping us considerably in improving communications on a nationwide and international scale.

McLuhan's is a media-centric account of the development of Western civilization, largely influenced by his compatriot, Harold Innis.[40] Other futurists like Alvin Toffler (author of *Future Shock*, *The Third Wave*, and *Powershift*), Daniel Bell (*The Post-Industrial Society*), John Naisbitt (*Megatrends*), have advocated a similar view. Like Jacob Bronowski, such writers see the 'ascent of man'[41] only in terms of the history and experience of Western civilization. The domination of the social sciences by such one-sided linear accounts has made other more ancient traditions 'invisible'. The colonisation of history, knowledge and information continues unchallenged.

Mass Communication and Culture

Modes of communication and culture are not as far apart, nor as distinct from each other, as is often argued. Both communication and culture develop together, one supporting the other. Indeed, communication is an expression of a community's culture, and culture in its turn embodies a community's communication and information needs and practices. Communication and Culture are thus inextricably tied to each other; we cannot understand one without understanding the other; nor can we speak of one without referring to the other. Most Indian languages do not have separate words for each; 'sanskruti' for instance takes both within its compass; so does 'sadharanikaran'. Communication, language, culture, society and civilization, and

---

40 Harold Innis: *Empire and Communications*, Oxford University Press, 1950; *The Bias of Communication*, University of Toronto Press, 1951.
41 Cf. the BBC series entitled 'Ascent of Man' (1989) presented by Jacob Bronowski.

their Indian equivalents, may have meanings of their own, but they are intimately linked to each other, and have evolved together, though the pace of evolution might differ from community to community. Moreover, changes and developments in one influence the others.

Has mass communication led to changes in the people's various cultures? Has the cinema, for instance – which is in every sense the most popular and the most widespread form of mass entertainment in our country – made any dent in our centuries-old cultural values and behaviour? Or, has television (which in the Indian context is nothing more than an extension of cinema) in any way affected the culture of our city folk in any significant manner?

The reach of mass communication through the electronic media is mostly limited to the urban areas and to the better-off sections of rural parts of the country. It would, therefore, be ridiculous to suggest that the modern mass media have in any tangible way influenced Indian culture which itself is an extremely composite phenomenon, and impossible to define precisely. Indeed, the word 'culture' too is so comprehensive that it encompasses every facet of our lives from the most superficial to the most profound and intimate.

Mass Communication does influence (and even reflect) social values and practices, but this influence is always in combination with a whole lot of other socio-cultural and economic and political factors. By themselves, the media have little power to influence, change or develop.

For instance, Hindi films may start new fashions for men and women in the areas of clothes, hairstyles, manner of speech (the use of 'yaar' for example, or the sprinkling of conversation with English expressions), manner of greeting, or ways of socializing or of making love or even on our life-style and outward behaviour. We may even go to the extreme of acting out what we see or hear in the mass media, say a violent gesture or a protest, but it takes much more than film or TV to transform our social and cultural values.

'Mass Culture', 'Popular Culture' and 'Folk Culture'

The understanding of 'mass culture' depends on our point of view and on what 'culture' means to us. Thus the term 'mass culture' can be used pejoratively or positively. The 'mass' is the rabble, the uncouth, illiterate and uncultured lot; the 'mass' is also vast, homogeneous, scattered, anonymous. But from a positive perspective, the mass is volatile, dynamic, revolutionary; what Carl Sandburg in his poem, 'The People, Yes', termed the 'teeming, seething mass'.

The concept of 'mass culture' (popularised by neo-Marxist social theorists of the Frankfurt School)[42] refers to a whole range of popular activities and artefacts – to entertainments, spectacles, music, books, comics, films – but it has become identified with the typical content of the mass media, and especially with the fictional, dramatic and entertainment material which they provide.[43]

So, 'mass culture' according to this definition has little reference to the culture of the masses, that is the vast general population of a nation. It primarily refers to the 'content' of radio, TV, cinema and the press. What then is the relationship between this 'mass culture' of the media and the people's own culture/s?

The reach of the mass media is so limited in India that one wonders what relevance Denis McQuail's description of mass culture has to our society. 'Mass' culture in our country is still by and large the one that prevails in our villages where over 70% of our people live, and where Indian culture is barely touched by the mass media, except perhaps in South India. Folk media continue to provide the main source of entertainment, and also of

---

42 Social theorists associated with the Frankfurt School (the Institute of Social Research founded in 1923 in Frankfurt, in 1933 moved to New York) include Theodor Adorno, Max Horkheimer, Herbert Marcuse. They were primarily neo-Marxists who regarded the mass media of that time as 'cultural industries' that commoditized culture that indoctrinates and manipulates and promotes a 'false consciousness ...which is immune against its falseness' (See Marcuse's *One-Dimensional Man*) (1972).

43 Denis McQuail: *Towards a Sociology of Mass Communication*, 1969, p. 22.

instruction and education in religious, social, economic and political matters. While there are a great variety of folk forms in every region, and numerous languages and dialects in which they are presented, the themes have their source in the two epics, the Ramayana and the Mahabharata. The Muslims who make up the second largest religious community in the country have preserved their own traditional folk forms like the *ghazal*, the *Quwali* and the *mushaira*. The tribals too continue to entertain themselves with age-old folk songs and folk dances. The mass media have, however, entered into the lives of the upper and middle classes in cities and towns. The cinema is the most popular entertainment, as is evident from the production of nearly a thousand films a year, and the screening of them in over 12,500 theatres. This popularity is also seen in the number of film-oriented programmes on Vividh Bharati and Doordarshan, as well as on the many cable and satellite television channels.

The Indian cinema has the qualities of a mass culture product, but it is doubtful if it has given rise to a 'mass culture' among the general population.

As understood by Western sociology, Mass Culture has three main features:
(1) Immense popularity among all classes, but particularly among the working class in industrial societies,
(2) Mass production and mass distribution,
(3) Unlike elite or 'high' culture its aesthetic and literary standards are low, and commercialised, as its mass produced programmes aim at the mass market.[44]

Examples of such mass culture products are the films for the big and the small screens (what is sometimes derisively termed 'the commercial cinema'), soap operas like *Hum Log*, *Buniyaad*, *Shanti*, *Kyunki Saas Bhi Kabhi Bahu Thi*, and *Kahani Ghar Ghar Ki*; the 'mythologicals' such as the *Mahabharat*, *Ramayana*, *Shri*

---

44 ibid.

Krishna and *Hanuman*, situation comedies ('sitcoms'), film-based programmes, reality shows, game shows and the like.

The culture propagated by the mass media is not necessarily the popular culture of the masses. More often than not, as in the Hindi cinema, it is a 'synthetic' North-Indian or Bombay culture, paying lip service occasionally to the values of popular culture. This is not to suggest that there are no links whatsoever to the popular cultures; these links, however, tenuous, make for 'connections' with the myths of the community and the nation. But 'mass culture' is itself a non-entity; like mass communication it largely exists in the minds of the elite fearful of the 'vulgar mob', the common people.

The mainstream Hindi and regional language cinema, the glossy film magazines, the Amar Chitra Katha comics and the garish type of calendar art, greeting cards, and cinema and advertising posters and billboards, offer examples of mass culture in our cities. But are they mere 'kitsch'? 'Kitsch' is an expressive German word often used to describe the art forms of the new culture of the mass media. It may well be defined 'as artistic rubbish'. The German verb from which 'kitsch' is derived means 'to make cheap', to 'vulgarise'. A well-known commentator on the Indian cultural scene, Ka Naa Subramaniam, dismisses the division between elite and 'pop' ('high' and 'mass') culture as meaningless in the Indian context, since the influence of the mass media have not yet advanced much, and the spirit of the community continues to prevail. He argues that 'to talk of pop and elitist art in India is to confuse the issues in an already confused milieu. Neither 'pop' nor elitist art exists in India as of today. We have not yet lost the old purpose of art nor discovered new ones.'[45]

'Mass culture' then is a complex cultural phenomenon which is a creation of the mass media. It is, therefore, more precise to term it 'mass media culture', to distinguish it from the majority culture or folk culture or even popular culture. Mass media

---

45 Ka Naa Subramaniam: 'Pop Goes Our Culture', *The Times of India*, 1980.

culture is an entirely urban phenomenon, resulting from rapid industrialization, and alienation from the majority culture.

Dwight MacDonald sums up the characteristics of this culture which is manufactured collectively by production-line specialists, to tested formulas, packaging and marketing, in these words:

"The lords of Kitsch (or mass culture) sell culture to the masses. It is a debased, trivial culture that voids both the deep realities (sex, death, failure, tragedy) and also the simple, spontaneous pleasures... The masses, debauched by several generations of this sort of things, in turn come to demand trivial and comfortable cultural products which came first... the mass demand or its satisfaction (and further stimulation) is a question as academic as it is unanswerable".[46]

This is evidently an elitist and patronizing view of what culture is and what the masses are susceptible to. A more balanced approach to the popular forms of various cultures, would make for a more realistic evaluation of the relationship between the mass media and popular culture. Do television audiences, for instance, watch a soap opera or a sitcom as a 'mass' or rather as members of a cultural community, in terms of what James Lull calls 'interpretative communities'? Theorists of 'mass culture' (like those of the Frankfurt school) assumed that audiences were passive absorbers of media messages; ethnographic and qualitative research since the mid-1980s suggests otherwise, that audiences often negotiate, resist and even poach the texts that they read; far from being 'dupes', audiences 'appropriate' the messages in terms of their own experiences and cultures and interests.[47] [48]

---

46 Quoted in Mahadev L Apte: *Mass Culture, Language and Arts in India*, p.12.
47 For a fuller discussion of this approach to media audiences, see especially John B. Thompson: The Media and Modernity: A Social Theory of the Media, Stanford University Press, 1995. See also the work of David Morley, Janice Radway, Ien Ang, and Purnima Mankekar. Later sections of the book examine the contribution of these researchers to media studies.
48 For a perceptive analysis of cultural 'resistance' in the Indian context, see Michael Amaladoss: 'Resistance and Adoption in India's Cultural History, in Michael Traber: Globalisation, Mass Media and Indian Cultural Values, New Delhi: ISPCK. pp. 41-57.

FOR FURTHER READING

1. Mahadev L. Apte: *Mass Culture, Language and Arts in India*, Bombay: Popular Prakashan, 1978.
2. Subrata Banerjee (Ed.): *Culture and Communication*, New Delhi: Patriot Publishers, 1986.
3. David Clark and William Blankenburg: *You and Media: Mass Communication and Society*, Canfield Press, 1973.
4. David Crowley and David Mitchell (Eds.): *Communication Theory Today*, Cambridge: Polity Press, 1994.
5. John Downing, Denis McQuail, Philip Schlesinger and Ellen Wartella (Eds.): *The Sage Handbook of Media Studies*, New Delhi: Sage Publications, 2004.
6. John Fiske: *Introduction to Communication Studies*, London: Methuen, 1982.
7. Stephen W. Littlejohn: *Theories of Human Communication*, Thomson/Wadsworth. (Indian Reprint), 7th Ed. 2002.
8. Denis McQuail: *Towards a Sociology of Mass Communication*, London: Collier-Macmillan, 1969/ 1975.
9. Denis McQuail: *McQuail's Mass Communication Theory*, London/New Delhi: Sage, 2007.
10. Ashley Montagu and Floyd Matson: *The Human Connection*, McGraw-Hill, 1979.
11. P.N. Malhan: *Communication Yesterday, Today and Tomorrow*, New Delhi: Publications Division.
12. Everett K. Rogers: *Communication Technology: The New Media in Society*, New York: Free Press, 1986.
13. Michael Traber (Ed.): *Globalisation, Mass Media and Indian Cultural Values*, New Delhi: ISPCK, 2003.
14. John B. Thompson: *The Media and Modernity: A Social Theory of the Media*, Stanford University Press, 1995.

WEB RESOURCES

1. www.comminit.com (Communication Initiative's site for media and communication research)
2. www.thehoot.org (India's foremost website for an analysis and critique of the mass media in South Asia, edited by Sevanti Ninan)
3. www.righttoinformation.gov.in (Official site of the Commission for Right to Information)
4. www.righttocommunicate.org
5. www.mediastudies.org

6. www.mib.gov.in (Official site of the Ministry of Information and Broadcasting, Government of India)
7. www.oneworld.org (An invaluable resource for alternative approaches to news, media and communication).

REVIEW QUESTIONS

1. What are the problems involved in defining 'communication' and 'mass communication'?
2. What is 'mass communication'? What are its major characteristics?
3. What is 'Interactive Communication'? How does it differ from Mass Communication?
4. What is 'Mass' culture? Write a critical account of the concept.
5. What has been McLuhan's contribution to our understanding of how technology influences communication?
6. How important is the role Mass Communication plays in our society? Illustrate your answer with reference to the uses of the mass media in India.
7. What are the problems encountered in communicating on a mass scale?
8. How did developments in communication technology contribute to the growth of the nation-state and to democracy?

SUGGESTED PROJECTS

1. Look up a dictionary to discover the many meanings of 'communication'. Note the different contexts in which they are used.
2. Write down what you understand by 'culture'. What are the 'connotations' of the word? Find out the Indian language equivalents of the word? Do the Indian language equivalents have the same connotations?
3. Make a list of words that have more than two or three different meanings depending upon the context. Are the meanings precise? (To start with, take simple words like 'short', 'tall', 'big').
4. Draw up a list of 10 emotionally powerful words. Write out the 'associations' or 'connotations' they have for you. Compare them with the 'associations' noted down by your class-mates or friends.
5. Play the game 'Whispering Gallery' with a group of 10-15 fellow-students (the more, the merrier!). The game begins with a group leader whispering a message to the first member of the group, who then whispers it to the second, who whispers it to the next... and so on, till the message reaches the last of the group. The Leader then checks to see how much the

message has been distorted! Write down what the game tells you about the communication process. Discuss the reasons for the distortion.
6. Select a country of your choice. Search the internet for information and hard data on mass media in that country. Make a Powerpoint presentation of your findings.

SECTION II

THE MASS MEDIA: HISTORY, PRACTICES AND VALUES

In essence, the mass media are the tools or technologies that facilitate dissemination of information and entertainment to a vast number of receivers. They are the tools of large-scale manufacture and distribution of information and related messages. These tools 'mediate' the messages; they are not the messages themselves. However, Marshall McLuhan, the media prophet, liked to proclaim that 'the medium is the message', though the title of one his books suggests rather that 'the medium is the massage'[1]. So while the media are technologies; they are also messages and massages. They can also be looked at as industries, as cultural or entertainment industries. For Manuel Castells, author of the trilogy on *The Information Age*, and a number of other scholarly works on 'the network society', it's the 'network' that is the message.[2]

While cinema, radio, television, cable, and the press can easily be recognised as 'mass media', it requires some stretching of the established meaning of the term to include recent technologies (sometimes termed the 'new media') such as pagers, iPods, cellular phones, satellites, computers, electronic mail and the Internet as 'mass media'. More correctly, these new media may be termed 'interactive communication media' for they are not so much production and transmission technologies dissemi-nating messages far and wide to many receivers, as interactive technologies which involve feedback, exchange and participation.

---

1 Marshall McLuhan and Quentin Fiore: *The Medium is the Massage: An Inventory of Effects*, Toronto: Penguin, 1967.
2 Manuel Castells: *The Information Age: Economy, Society and Culture*, Vols. 1-3, Beverly Hills, CA: Sage, 2000.

'A mass medium' says Wilbur Schramm,[3] 'is essentially a working group organised round some device for circulating the same message, at about the same time, to large numbers of people'. Such a definition excludes the folk media, group media, and interpersonal communication such as word-of-mouth publicity, or education and preaching, where communication is not 'mediated' by a 'device'. Further, the pejorative term 'mass' (a way of looking down at people as 'masses') suggests that the modern media are 'experienced' not by individuals and groups in terms of their own cultures but as part of the 'mass' and as 'mass culture'. (See Section I for a detailed analyses). The term 'mass' also suggests that people's interaction with the media is homogeneous, inactive and unquestioning. In Communication Studies today, however, the term 'mass media' has come to be a useful collective phrase, though it slurs over the distinctions among the various media.

As generally interpreted the 'mass' media are the press, cinema, radio and television. But books, magazines, pamphlets and direct mail literature and posters also need to be included in the label. They are so termed because their reach extends to vast heterogeneous masses of the population living in a wide and extensive area of a country. The means they employ to communicate messages to the masses are technological – printing machines, records, cameras, fax machines, cable, modems, computers and satellites. Their communications are thus interposed and 'mediated'; they are not as direct or face-to-face as in interpersonal exchanges.

The organs of the mass media are thus technological means of transmitting messages to large numbers of people. But they are much more than that. As they require a very expensive infrastructure, (particularly the cinema, radio, television, video, cable, computers, and satellites) they have to be run by institutions like the Government or well financed private commercial firms. Further, they require a group of people ('media professionals') to organise and administer, to produce,

---

3   Wilbur Schramm: *Mass Communication*, Illinois:University of Illinois Press, 1960.

distribute, transmit and constantly maintain in working order the whole set up of, say, a studio, a transmitting centre, or a publishing house.

Yet another feature of the mass media is that they are founded on the idea of mass production and mass distribution – the marks of an industrial society. Copies of newspapers and magazines, for instance, are printed in thousands (some national and regional dailies in India have a circulation of over a million copies) and are reprinted and distributed in several cities across the country. But to enjoy a mass audience, the media have to cater to a taste that is not very 'cultured' or sophisticated. What the mass media therefore reflect and propagate is a popular culture. The culture made popular by mainstream films and film music in Hindi, Tamil, Telugu and a host of Indian languages is a case in point. With the rapid expansion of television, video, the internet and mobile telephony in cities and towns, popular culture is likely to take on new forms; the 'myths' of our culture will find expression in ever new ways.

But access to the mass media in India is still restricted because of poverty, low literacy levels, and little familiarity with Hindi and English, the major languages used in the various media; moreover, reach is limited to populations living in metros and large cities and the better-off sections in rural India. The folk media, in contrast, have a wider audience; they are media close to the hearts and minds of the people and suited to a poor country, and help facilitate identification and participation. It is no wonder then that the mass media incorporate various popular elements of the folk media. And that folk media, in their turn, incorporate elements (such as music and dance) of the mass media.

Functions of the Mass Media

Modern mass media serve functions very similar to those

---

4 For instance Cf. Harold Lasswell: 'The Structure and Function of Communication in Society' in L. Bryson (Ed.): *The Communication of Ideas*, New York: Harper, 1948; and Denis McQuail: *Mass Communication Theory: An Introduction*, London: Sage, 1994.

fulfilled by traditional media in some ancient societies, and in some developing countries today. Western media theorists[4] generally identify three major functions; surveillance of the environment, interpretation of the information and prescription for conduct, and the transmission of heritage. The developmental and liberation or empowerment functions, or even the ritualistic or celebratory functions of the media rarely find mention in Euro-American media theory. South American media theorists have contributed to our understanding of media for 'liberation' while African and Asian scholars have explored the relevance of media to 'national development'.

Information

Surveillance of the environment relates to information or 'news' about happenings in society. The mass media carry out this function by keeping us posted about the latest news in our own region and around the world. In rural societies, however, the word-of-mouth method is still the most credible means of spreading news.

But the mass media cannot or should not stop at watching the horizon for us, through news bulletins or advertisements or documentaries. They need, and often do help us 'to correlate our response to the challenges and opportunities which appear on the horizon and to reach consensus on social actions'.[5] In rural India, the panchayat meetings help the village elders to decide on the challenges and the opportunities. The mass media help us to keep the culture and heritage of our society alive, and to transmit it to others. This is what the media should ideally do, but often don't. Folk media serve a similar purpose in developing countries.

Entertainment

A fourth function is the vital function of entertainment. Entertainment has been a legitimate function of the traditional folk media, but the mass media provide it with a vengeance.

---

5   W.L. Rivers, W. Schramm and C.G. Christians: *Responsibility in Mass Communications*, New York: Harper, 1980. p.15.

They help to pass the time, and to relax with family and friends.

Anthropologists of culture and communication discern a symbolic function of the media: the media provide a 'shared symbolic environment'. Victor Turner, for instance, believed that the media provide a 'liminal' ritualistic experience. George Gerbner[6] saw television as the central symbol of American culture today. Horace Newcomb[7] and other 'culturalists' (such as James Carey[8] and Robert White[9]) perceive the media as providing a ritualistic and 'liminal' experience. Besides, the mass media lead us to re-work and re-define our 'self-identities' and our 'collective identities'.[10]

Advertising

An equally vital function is that of the mass media helping to sell goods and services through sponsorships and commercials. The commercial function has indeed been served well, perhaps too well, especially in the United States, where the networks would have to close down if the support from commercials were to dry up. At the same time, it would be suicidal to let this function dominate the mass media at the expense of the other four functions. India too promotes the commercial function, and has allowed its representatives to take over the programming of radio and television. This is equally true of the press and its dependence on advertising.

---

6   George Gerbner: 'Born A.T. (After Television): What Difference Does it Make?', Talk at Conference on Early Childhood Education, Tel Aviv, June 1981. Much of Gerbner's theorising on 'violence' and 'cultural indicators' is based on this premise.2 For instance Cf. Harold Lasswell: 'The Structure and Function of Communication in Society' in L. Bryson (Ed.): *The Communication of Ideas*, New York: Harper, 1948; and Denis McQuail: Mass Communication Theory: An Introduction, London: Sage, 1994.
7   Horace Newcomb: 'Television as Popular Culture: Towards a Critically Based Curriculum' in M. Ploghoft and J. Anderson: *Education for the Television Age*, Illinois: Charles C. Thomas, 1981.
8   James Carey: Communication as Culture, Boston: Unwin Hyman, 1988.
9   Robert A. White: 'Audience Interpretations of Television', *Communication Research Trends*, 1994, Vol. 14, No.3.
10 For a more detailed discussion, see John B. Thompson: *The Media and Modernity: A Social Theory of the Media,* Stanford: Stanford University Press, 1995.

Development

In the developing countries of Asia, Africa and Latin America, the mass media, which include traditional media, have a different function to perform. In a word, development communication i.e., communication that focuses on the information needs of the poor and the oppressed, and their socio-economic and cultural interests.

Uses of the media

While these may be the five functions of the mass media, it does not necessarily follow that audiences go to them for the same reasons. In his book *The Play Theory of Mass Communication*, William Stephenson argues that fun is both the greatest impact and the greatest public service of the mass media. Audiences use them as a form of play, or *lila*.

So, for a good number of the audience, the mass media may be marvellous time-fillers, like listening to the radio while cooking or while driving, or reading a book during a long train journey. Further, some people use the media to fulfill psychological and social needs. They perhaps get vicarious enjoyment out of sex and violence in the media, and use the media to get topics for conversation at work, or to solve their own problems. Still others might seek information, merely to be well-informed, or perhaps to learn how higher-status people dress and live. Or, they might watch advertisements on TV not so much to know more about a product as to assure themselves that they have bought the best product! These are the variety of 'uses and gratifications' of the media.

So whatever functions the media pundits say the mass media have, the people will continue to use them in the way they (the people, not the pundits) like. It is in this sense that audiences are 'active' rather than 'passive' users of the mass media. It is the members of the audience, after all, who have to actively interpret and make sense of the media in terms of their own needs, interests and experiences. Therein lies the real power of audiences.

Theories of the Press/Media

Western theories of the mass media (particularly of the news media) were first propounded by Fred Siebert, Theodore Peterson and Wilbur Schramm in their book *Four Theories of the Press*.[11] These theories have now come to be termed 'normative' in the sense that they 'mainly express ideas of how the media ought to, or can be expected to, operate under a prevailing set of conditions and values.'[12] So, strictly speaking they are hypotheses rather than theories. These 'theories' were first enunciated in the United States during the height of the 'cold-war' against communism and the Soviet Union. They were thus part of American propaganda and only loosely based on actual practices in the media. They idealised the American practices which are touted as being democratic and socially responsible, and derided 'Soviet' and 'Communist' practices as being 'dictatorial' and 'authoritarian'. They did not take into account the 'public service' models of print and electronic media widely accepted in Western Europe, and in many countries of Asia and Africa.[13] [14]

The 'original' four theories of the press/media are: authoritarian theory, libertarian theory, social responsibility theory, and Soviet media theory. Each of them suits particular political and economic circumstances, and focuses not so much on the relationship between the press and readers as on the relationships between the press and Government. The major concern is with ownership and control rather than with different perspectives of Journalism or the people's right to information. Siebert, Peterson and Schramm limit their analysis to 'four'

---

11 F. Siebert, T. Peterson and W. Schramm: Four Theories of the Press, Urbana, IL.: University of Illinois Press, 1956.
12 Denis McQuail: Mass Communication Theory: An Introduction, London: Sage.
13 For incisive critiques of the Four Theories of the Press, see J. Herbert Altschull's 'Agents of Power: The Role of the News Media in Human Affairs' (London/New York: Longman, 1984) and John C. Merrill's 'The Imperative of Freedom: A Philosophy of Journalistic Autonomy' (New York, 1974).

See also Shelton Gunaratne: *The Dao of the Press: A Humanocentric Theory*, London: Hampton, 2005, for a critique of the 'Four Theories' from a Buddhist perspective.

theories; three more need to be added to the original four to take account of circumstances in the developing countries of Asia, Africa and Latin America. The last three could be termed 'Developmental or Alternative Theories' of the media.

Authoritarian Theory

According to this theory the mass media, though not under the direct control of the State and the ruling classes, must do their bidding. The press and other media are expected to respect authority, to be always subordinate to established power and authority, and therefore should avoid offending the majority or dominant moral, political and economic values. Journalists lack independence and freedom; their reports have to be submitted for advance censorship. This censorship is justified on the ground that the State must always take precedence over an individual's right to freedom of expression. Such censorship is more rigidly enforced in times of war and during 'internal' and 'external' emergencies. It needs to be noted that both dictatorial and democratic regimes resort to such authoritarian control of the media. The strictness with which the Official Secrets Act is enforced in Britain and in India is a case in point.

Libertarian or Free Press Theory

The basis of this 'free press' theory goes back to 17th century England when the printing press made it possible to print several copies of a book or pamphlet at a comparatively low price. In contrast with the authoritarian theory, libertarianism is founded on the fundamental right of an individual to freedom of expression. Western liberal democracies swear by this belief. The First Amendment in the American constitution is an embodiment of this theory; it flows from the individual's right to life, liberty and the pursuit of happiness. The individual, not the State or society, is supreme, and popular will (vox populi) is granted precedence over the power of the State. The argument is that 'truth' can be arrived at only through the free expression of diverse points of view, no matter how erroneous. The great apologists of this theory were John Milton, the epic poet (in his *Aeropagitica*) and John Stuart Mill (in his essay, *On Liberty*). A free press is seen as essential to a free society and the dignity of the individual. Moreover, the freedom to publish is often linked to the right to property and the free market system.

In practice, however, the theory provides the prerogative of free speech only to the rich and the powerful elites of a society. The marginalized groups do not have access to, and indeed, cannot afford the means or the tools of free expression. What happens on the ground is that media merchants and media monopolies (e.g. the big newspaper chains, the television companies) exploit that freedom to expand their empires. Market forces rather than public good mould the kind of information to be purveyed. The theory thus protects media owners rather than the rights of editors and journalists, or of the public. What the theory offers, in sum, is 'power without social responsibility'.

Social Responsibility Theory

This theory can be said to have been derived from the Hutchins Report (entitled 'A Free and Responsible Press: A General Report on Mass Communication: Newspapers, Radio, Motion Magazines and Books'). The Hutchins Commission on Freedom of the Press (1947) was established and financed by Henry Luce of Time Magazine at a time in the history of American Journalism when press barons like Luce sensed that government regulations on 'yellow journalism' were round the corner. Moreover, the years following the Second World War witnessed the rise of the Democratic Party in the United States, the restraints on business under the New Deal, and the strengthening of the trade union movement. The American press (which was known to be largely pro-Republican) feared that the federal Government would issue legislation to regulate the 'freedom of the press', despite the First Amendment.

Robert Hutchins, the Chairman of the Commission, was the Chancellor of the Chicago University at the time, and he was assisted by twelve others who were experts in different fields.

The Report appeared in two volumes: the first on newspapers, the second on the other media.

The Commission found that the free market approach to press freedom had not met the informational and social needs of the less well-off classes; in fact, it had increased the power of a single class. There was little expression of diverse views; the emergence of radio, film and television also suggested that some public control and some means of accountability had become necessary. Thus, the theory had its roots in the view that the media had certain obligations to society – to serve its needs, rather than that of the free market. Hence the need for high professional standards; of truth, accuracy, objectivity and balance. Self-regulation and also state regulations were imperative. Public interest was a greater value than unregulated freedom of expression. Thus news offensive to religious and ethnic minorities, or news likely to lead to social violence needed to be underplayed. The Hutchins Report led to the establishment of Press Councils, the drawing up of codes of ethics, anti-monopoly legislation, and to press subsidies to small newspapers. State and public intervention in the exercise of free expression was therefore considered legitimate under certain circumstances.

Soviet Media Theory

This theory is derived from Lenin's application of Marx and Engels' dictum in *The German Ideology* that, 'the ideas of the ruling class are in every epoch the ruling ideas'. The media are thus a means of 'mental production' of the ideology, in other words. Hence the need for their control by the working class, that is, through the Communist Party, so that the interests of the working class rather than those of the ruling or elite class are projected. In a Socialist society, therefore, the media should be used as tools to 'socialize' the people; the primary functions of the media are to educate, inform, motivate and mobilize citizens, and to support 'progressive' movements everywhere. What is expected is 'objective' (or 'scientific') presentation of society.

Censorship and restriction on the media are legitimate for the media are accountable to the State, to the public and to the Party. The public is encouraged to provide feedback, as it is only in this way that the media will be able to serve the public interest.

Development Communication Theory

The 'four theories of the press' are not fully applicable to the experience of the non-aligned countries of Asia, Africa, and South America. While in most Asian and African countries, the media (especially the broadcast media) are owned and run by the State, in Latin American countries, commercial ownership of all the mass media is the norm. A common factor in the experience of the majority of the non-aligned countries is the dependence on industrialized countries for both hardware and software. Another common factor is the commitment of these nations to social and economic development on their own terms; they would like to employ the mass media as tools for 'development', for 'nation-building'. The larger national interest and the public good are of paramount importance to them. So certain freedoms need to be curbed in the interest of say national integration, and economic and social development. Hence the stress on 'development communication' and 'development journalism'. According to development theorists, journalists have the responsibility to support national governments in their efforts at eradicating literacy, promoting family planning, promoting national integration, and increasing production and employment. The weakness in the theory is that 'development' is often equated with government propaganda.

Democratization Theory

Latin American critics (notably Paulo Freire, Reyes Matta, Luis Beltran, Diaz Bordenave and Valerio Fuenzalida) of commercialized ('commodotized') media have come out strongly against the top-down, one way and non-participative character of contemporary mass media. Like the development theorists, they lay stress on the positive uses of the media, on the need for 'access' and the 'right to communicate'. They insist on the need for local and community participation in media and news production. The people must speak for themselves, they argue, not through professional journalists and producers.

What is vehemently opposed also is commercial, political or bureaucratic control of the media, which exist to serve audiences, not the interests of government or commercial enterprises. The 'demassification' of the media, according to this theory, is as vital as 'democratization'. The ultimate purpose is to put the media in the hands of communities (as in people's radio or community media) for their own 'liberation' through a process of 'conscientization'. Thus is created, in Reyes Matta's words, a 'critical national audience'.[15]

---

15 F. Reyes Matta: 'A Model for Democratic Communication', Development Dialogue, Vol. 2, pp.79-97.

JOURNALISM

Journalism as a craft, a profession and even as a cultural industry and a business is over three centuries old. It was made possible by the coming together of a number of technologies as well as of several social, political and economic developments. The main technologies that facilitated the development of large-scale printing and distribution of print material were the printing press, the telegraph and the railways. The industrial revolution and the growth of capitalism, democracy and the public sphere provided the impetus and the support for rapid developments in the press. Technological determinists like Harold Innis[1] and Marshall McLuhan[2], two Canadian media sociologists, credited the printing press with the evolution of democracy and the nation state overlooking the vital role of capitalism and socio-political movements in Europe and its colonies worldwide. Going beyond technological determinism, Benedict Anderson later spelt out the role of print media, vernacular languages and capitalism in the emergence of nationalism and nation-states ('imagined communities') in Europe, Latin America and Asia without however establishing a clear 'causal link' between print capitalism and national consciousness.[3]

As a craft Journalism involves specialisation in one area (editorial, design, photojournalism, printing, or marketing); for the reporters and the sub-editors for instance, it entails writing to a deadline, following routines in a conveyor-belt like workplace, while respecting the division of labour in the newsroom and the whole production process. In earlier times, a knowledge of

---

1. Cf. Harold A. Innis: *The Bias of Communication*, Toronto: University of Toronto Press, 1964; and *Empire and Communications,* Toronto: University of Toronto Press, 1972..
2. Cf. Marshall McLuhan: *The Gutenberg Galaxy: The Making of Typographic Man* (Toronto: University of Toronto Press, 1962, and *Understanding Media: The Extensions of Man*, New York: McGraw-Hill, 1964.
3. See Benedict Anderson: *Imagined Communities: Reflections on the Origin and Spread of Nationalism*, London: Verso, 1991. See also John B. Thompson: *The Media and Modernity*, Stanford University Press, 1995, pp. 62-63, for an evaluation of Anderson's argument.

typewriting and shorthand were the main skills required of journalists; today, computing and internet skills as well as DTP (Desk Top Publishing) and multimedia and multi-tasking skills are in demand for all areas of Journalism. QuarkExpress is perhaps the most widespread software programme which print journalists are required to be proficient in. Also, the divisions among the different specialisations have become blurred. That's true also of electronic, Internet (or Online) and Mobile Journalism. Radio and television journalists need to familiarize themselves with the special demands of audiovisual media (Writing news for radio and television, Stand-Up reporting, Anchoring, Camera work, Editing etc.) and Online journalists need to hone their skills in writing for the digital media. Mobile Journalists are essentially headline writers who encapsulate the news in fewer than 160 characters for SMS transmission to mobile phones.

So, as a profession Journalism is markedly different from other established professions like law, medicine, engineering, management or teaching. While the established professions require some specialised educational qualifications and training to be recruited to them, Journalism does not make any such requirement essential. There is no bar to anyone entering the profession, no matter what one's educational background or professional experience. From the very beginning, Journalism (like the other media professions: Advertising, Public Relations, Event Management, Radio, Film and Television Production, Animation and Gaming, Theatre, and Publishing) has been, and still remains, an 'open' profession.

Further, journalism has no distinct body of knowledge that defines the profession and marks its relationship with its clients (readers, advertisers, advertising agencies, public relations officials and others) and other professions. It may be argued that journalism is 'a way of knowing different from that produced in social science' or that it has its own specific approach to reality. However, there is no consensus in the journalistic community on this. Nor is there a universally accepted Code of Conduct or Code of Ethics, and where it does exist, it is loosely enforced.

Opinions vary on whether journalism is a 'calling', a public service, an entertainment, a cultural industry motivated by profit, or a tool for propaganda, public relations and advertising. Journalism can be a combination of all these, or each of these separately. Opinions are not so varied about the other professions.

As a cultural industry and business, Journalism involves publishing on a regular basis for profit, with news considered as the primary product. Hence the need to attract advertisers and readers through marketing strategies that focus on circulation and readership. But this need to attract advertisers often leads to the de-politicisation and localization of news where 'soft stories' take precedence over 'hard stories' and where news is transformed into 'infotainment' and editorials into 'advertorials'. The primary goal therefore of newspaper publishers begins to be the purchase, first of advertisers and then of readers. This results in turning newspapers into 'products' and reading citizens into 'consumers'. When this takes place the 'public sphere' shrinks and Journalism ceases to be the 'Fourth Estate'.

What is Journalism?

Who then is a 'Journalist'? And what is 'Journalism'? The words 'journalist', 'journal' and 'journalism' are derived from the French 'journal', which in its turn comes from the Latin word 'diurnalis' or 'daily'. The Acta Diurna, a handwritten bulletin put up daily in the Forum, the main public square in ancient Rome, was perhaps the world's first newspaper. In later periods of history, pamphlets, tracts, reviews, periodicals, gazettes, newsbooks, corantos, news sheets and letters came to be termed 'newspapers'. Those who wrote for them were first called 'news writers' or 'essayists' (even 'mercurists') and later 'journalists'. The Mughal rulers in India employed 'vaquia-navis' and 'confia-navis' as public and secret news-writers to record once a week in a 'vaquia' (a sort of gazette or mercury) the events of importance in the empire. These news letters were read to the king every evening by the women of the court. The British colonial rulers used a system of 'informers' for their intelligence networks.

Journalism has come a long way since then. Today, a journalist is anyone who contributes in some way to the gathering, selection, and processing of news and current affairs for the press, radio, film, television, cable, the Internet, blogs, the mobile, the PDA and the iPod; and Journalism is the profession to which they belong. Thus, editors, correspondents, assistant editors, reporters, sub-editors, proof-readers, cartoonists, photographers ('photo-journalists') and online journalists and news-oriented bloggers are journalists; so are, camera crew, audio and video editors, news readers, producers, directors and managing editors. 'Stringers' are part-time journalists, while 'free-lance' journalists are those who are occasional contributors to newspapers. Here is how the Working Journalists' Act (1955) defines a 'working journalist':

"Working Journalist" means a person whose principal avocation is that of a journalist and (who is employed as such, either whole-time or part -time in, or in relation to, one or more newspaper establishment), and includes an editor, a leader writer, news-editor, sub-editor, feature-writer, copy-tester, reporter, correspondent, cartoonist, news-photographer and proof-reader, *but does not include* any such person who:

a) is employed mainly in a managerial or administrative capacity or
b) being employed in a supervisory capacity, performs, either by the nature of duties attached to his office or by reasons of the power vested in him, and function mainly of a managerial nature.

Tabloid and Yellow Journalism

Journalists work for the 'broadsheet' (or 'quality' or 'serious') press and the 'tabloid' (or 'popular' or 'sensational') press. The terms 'broadsheet' and 'tabloid' (or 'compact') usually describe the two main formats of newspapers, but the labels also connote two kinds of news stories selected, and more importantly, the presentation, treatment and style as well. However, this distinction is now blurred, especially when the serious or quality papers (such as *The Times of India*, the *Indian Express* and *The Asian Age*) choose to highlight the private lives of public figures and the tabloids (such as *Midday*, the *Afternoon Dispatch and Courier*, and *Today*) to publish serious investigative stories of corruption in high places. A third format is termed the 'Berliner' which is popular with European (*Le Monde*, *The Guardian*, and *La Stampa*) and some North American (*The Journal and Courier*) daily newspapers. HT Media's business daily *Mint*, published in partnership with the *Wall Street Journal*, uses the Berliner format. The 'Berliner' is a little narrower and shorter than the broadsheet and slightly taller and wider than the tabloid. Like the broadsheet, it connotes quality and serious journalism.

'Tabloid Journalism' is frequently termed 'yellow journalism' primarily because of its tendency to sensationalize and trivialise events, issues and people. The staple of the 'tabloids' is the private lives of famous people, crime, accidents, disasters, public corruption, sex, etc. (E.g. *Midday*, *Mumbai Mirror*, *Pune Mirror*). Tabloid journalists are believed to indulge in 'Chequebook Journalism' which implies that the subjects of the news stories are bribed to sell their 'true confessions'. Such journalists are also believed to indulge in 'keyhole journalism' or 'sting journalism' in their attempts to probe the private sexual infidelities and peccadilloes of well-known people and public officials. Then there is 'Page 3' Journalism which focuses on the social lives of celebrities and film stars and sports heroes. These journalistic practices raise several ethical questions about the invasion of the privacy of individuals and the public's right to information. In most democracies, reasonable restrictions are imposed on these intrusions on privacy, especially if they are not in any way related to the 'public interest'.

'Tabloid television' follows the pattern of selection, treatment and style of the tabloid press. In the pre-satellite television era (the 1980s) the video newsmagazines 'Newstrack' and

'Eyewitness' were in the tabloid tradition. In recent years, India TV, Janmat (now Live India) and the crime-based programmes on several television news channels verge on the sensational and the tabloid.

What is 'News'?

The nature of Journalism and one's approach to what Journalism is, therefore, depends on one's perspective of news and news values. 'News is the account of an event, not something intrinsic in the event itself'. Hence 'news' is the written, audio or visual construction of an event or happening or person. There is nothing in the event itself that makes it news; the event is not the news. Rather, the 'news' is the write-up or the audio or visual presentation of the event. Further, such a presentation or 'representation' or 'construction' of an event has to be in a particular format and is selected according to a certain professional value-system to make it 'news'. It needs to be emphasised that 'news is the end-product of a complex process which begins with a systematic sorting and selecting of events according to a socially constructed set of categories'. So, it is not the event which is reported that determines the form, content, meaning or 'truth' of the news, but rather the 'news' that determines what it is that the event means. The meaning results from the cultural discourse that 'news' employs. As one social linguist puts it: 'News is a social institution and a cultural discourse which exists and has meaning only in relation to other institutions and discourses operating at the same time'.[4]

Like language, news is a map, not the terrain which the map represents. A map uses codes, conventions, signs and symbols which have to be 'read' or actively interpreted. So does news; news as it were 'maps' the world. News selects, processes, produces and shapes an event or happening, but it is we as readers who select what is of interest to us and make our own sense of the news.

Mainstream journalism treats news as a commodity to be

---

4   Roger Fowler: The Language of the News, London:

bought and sold in the market place of information. In order to keep costs of news-gathering down, newspapers and other media subscribe to news agencies for news stories and visuals; their primary sources of revenue are advertising and circulation. The media are run, like any other business or industrial enterprise, in the tradition of mainstream journalism. The focus is on the 'exceptional' and the 'elitist', and the preferred format is the 'inverted pyramid' news report; other formats include features, editorials and columns/opinion pieces.

Journalism as Public Relations

Where news is used primarily for the publicity of an organisation or a product or a particular perspective on issues national and international, the kind of journalism that results may be termed 'public relations'. The chief objective is not the reaping of profits but in advancing causes and perspectives, or in fighting a 'cold war'. Political party newspapers and television channels fall in this category. Thus the *Organiser* and *Panchajanya* are the mouthpieces of the BJP and *People's Democracy*, of the Marxist party; the Malayalam television channels of the Marxists, the Congress and the Catholic Church in Kerala are nothing more than PR wings of the respective organizations, and Sun TV, Kalaignar TV and Jaya TV speak for their political masters, the DMK and AIDMK.

At the international level, most overseas broadcasts like that of the Voice of America, Radio Moscow, the BBC World Service, Deutsche Welle, France's TV5, Australia's ABC Asia Pacific, China's CCTV, and AIR's and Doordarshan's external services are examples of the use of broadcasting for public relations. Governments and corporate groups the world over spend millions of dollars to do public relations under the cover of journalism. They present views and perspectives as 'facts' in the form of news stories. Newspapers in India, especially the local and business sections, are packed with reports and features that have their source in 'press releases' and 'backgrounders' issued by social, political and business groups who wish to publicise their activities.

In recent years, newspapers and magazines have begun publishing glossy sections which are interestingly termed 'response features' or 'space marketing' supplements. Such supplements are no more than a marketing ploy to woo advertisers and to involve the corporate world in the newspaper business. Take the *Times of India*'s 'Ascent' or *The Indian Express*'s 'Express Careers' supplements for instance. The main contributors are from the corporate world; so are those who contribute to 'space marketing' supplements. Several journalists too write for such supplements; however, they do not equate this with journalism, but rather with public relations and publicity. Such is the case also for 'sponsored features' (*India Today* terms them 'impact features') and 'response supplements'; *Frontline*; the Hindu's newsmagazine, carries such features on individual states and cities under the broad title 'Focus' but does not tell the reader that they are 'sponsored'. That they are 'sponsored' is evident from their totally positive publicity-oriented approach, with hardly any analysis or critique. The most blatant of these practices in public relations but disguised as Journalism is the *Times of India*'s initiative (for its daily city supplements) called 'Medianet'. It is a business arm of the newspaper which sells editorial space to publicity-seekers for a price. The price is determined according to a published 'rate card'. The reports and photographs in these city supplements are presented as the work of staff journalists; nowhere are readers told that these are 'sponsored' or that they are indeed advertisements and have been directly paid for. Other daily newspapers such as the *Hindustan Times* and *Dainik Bhaskar* too have gone the 'Medianet' way though in not so unabashed a manner as the *Times of India*.

A second initiative of the Times of India/BCCL is termed 'Times Private Treaties' (TPT) wherein the newspaper group trades a stake in companies in return for providing advertising and branding. So far the group has taken such stakes in over 112 companies (including Pantaloon, Apollo Hotels and Paramount Airways) and has invested over Rs. 1500 crore in the venture.[5]

---

5 Gurbir Singh: 'Times in PR Mode' in Business World, 25 February 2008, p. 32.

A third BCCL initiative has been the joint venture that it has entered into with the Public Relations agency, Adfactors. The joint venture (on a 33:67 basis) has been named Tatva Public Relations.[6] These initiatives in the news media raise serious concerns about the independence and the credibility of editorial practices in the publications and television news channels of the Times of India Group.

Journalism for Development: 'Alternative' or 'Public' Journalism

Shelton Gunaratne describes development journalism as an integral part of a new journalism that involves 'analytical interpretation, subtle investigation, constructive criticism and sincere association with the grassroots (rather than with the elite)'[7]. Development or 'alternative' journalists reject the 'mainstream' Western-style approach to news and news values. They argue that 'mainstream' journalism is subservient to government and private business interests. They also argue that Western-style journalism aims at upholding, supporting and justifying confidence in the status quo. Development (or developmental) journalism rejects the 'famous five' of traditional journalism: balance, consensus, impartiality, objectivity and value-neutrality. It also rejects the traditional news values as the criteria for news selection: timeliness, immediacy, proximity, oddity, conflict, mystery, suspense, curiosity and novelty. This 'man-bites-dog' approach to journalism, according to development journalists, promotes sensationalism, elitism and conservatism, and thus indirectly suppresses the voice of the silent and oppressed majority. Development journalism is thus deliberately pro-Third World, pro-development/liberation, and pro-marginalised and poor

---

6 Ibid.
7 Shelton Gunaratne: 'Media Subservience and Developmental Journalism', *Communications and Development Review*, Vol. 2, No. 2, pp.3-7, Quoted in Shelton Gunaratne and Mohd. Safar Hasim: 'Social Responsibility Theory Revisited: A Comparative Study of Public Journalism and Developmental Journalism', *Javnost/ The Public*, Vol. 3, No. 3, pp. 97-107.

groups. The main sources of information for Development Journalism are the poor, the rural, the weak, the marginalised, the voiceless,[8] not the powerful, the elite or the rich. The language of alternative journalism differs from 'the laconic, sterile staccatto of the wire-service ticker and ventures boldly into innovative forms of creative prose.'[9] Further, such an approach rejects the format of the 'inverted pyramid' structure for news reporting; opting instead for the analytical essay or feature-type of writing, with context and the background of issues always spelt out at length. For the development journalist it is not the 'sound bite' or the 'scoop' or the information 'leaks' that make for news as much as social issues and developments in their global and national contexts. Rather than present news as a series of isolated events with little or no explanation, the development journalist is concerned with explaining 'why?' and asking 'so what?' Development Journalism is thus not propaganda and certainly not government propaganda, as mainstream Anglo-American journalists tend to believe it is. Rather, it could be 'a partner of government in discovering what sort of development the people want and need, and what sort of policies the authorities might pursue'.[10] Beyond this relationship, development journalism is equally an independent investigator of what type of development is taking place; and it is an honest and free critic in pointing out what may be going wrong and what dangers may be building up as a result.[11] Development or alternative journalism is practised by Inter Press Service (IPS), the Rome-based international news agency, and other news services such as Depthnews, Gemini and South-North News; www.indymedia.org, www.infochangeindia.org, www.indiainfo.com, and www.oneworld.org offer excellent examples of alternative

---

8   Kunda Dixit: *Dateline Earth: Journalism as if the Planet Mattered*, InterPress Service/Asia Pacific, p.154.
9   ibid.
10 Pran Chopra: 'Why Development Journalism?' in M.V. Desai and Sevanti Ninan (Eds.): *Beyond Those Headlines: Insiders on the Indian Press*, New Delhi: The Media Foundation/Allied Publishers, 1996, pp.112-121.
11 ibid.

Online Journalism. In the United States, such an open advocacy of human rights and the public interest is termed 'Public Journalism'. Mainstream journalists are disdainful of such an approach to what is termed 'Professional' Journalism. The biggest challenge to Professional Journalism today comes from news blogs on the Internet; most newspapers, newsmagazines and television news channels run their own news blogs in response to the challenge (e.g. blog.expressindia.com, blogs.reuters.com/India). However, the popularity and credibility of the personal news blog continue to engage web surfers and journalists alike.

The Role of the Press

Prior to Independence, the press in India had a clear-cut role to play in the nation's struggle against British rule. It had put up a brave fight in its heroic effort to expose the brutality of the regime, particularly in its suppression of the freedom movement. Many editors of the Indian language press defied censorship regulations to keep the nation informed (and agitated) about the progress of the movement[12], and especially of the plight of national leaders like Gandhi and Nehru.

With the goal of Independence being achieved at long last, the Indian press seemed to have lost its moorings. It was in a quandary. Should it play the role of an adversary to the government in power - the role it had played with remarkable success - or, should it transform itself into an ally, and support the government in its efforts at national development. That quandary of the press has yet to be resolved. Girilal Jain, the late editor of *The Times of India,* believed that one is an 'Indian first, and a journalist next.' (Interestingly, Dan Rather, the renowned CBS anchor, echoed a similar sentiment after 9/11, though he came to regret it later).

According to the First Press Commission, the press should help secure and protect a social order in which justice (social,

---

[12] Cf. Robin Jeffrey: *India's Newspaper Revolution*, and Sevanti Ninan: *Headlines from the Heartland: Reinventing the Hindi Public Sphere*; P. Sainath: *Everybody Loves a Good Drought.*

economic and political) would prevail. But the role of the press in India need not be that of an adversary or of an ally of the government. The press should be a watch-dog and act as a catalytic agent to hasten the process of social and economic change. The perspective of an adversary role for the press derives from the assumption that the press is the voice of the public, is above corruption, and that the government, though deriving power from the people, might misuse it. It must be noted that the press is part of the political process, craves for power, is made up of people with personal ambitions and aversions, preferences and prejudices. As perhaps the largest advertiser, the government supports and strengthens the press. Both the government and the press represent the 'power elites', and therefore reflect their interests. Most professional journalists in India belong to the higher castes. According to Robin Jeffrey's survey of Indian journalists, this is perhaps why the interests of the poor and the dalits are rarely on the agenda of public discussion.[13]

Jeffrey's conclusion is confirmed in a survey conducted in June 2006 of 315 senior journalists working for 37 English and Hindi dailies and television news channels. The survey found that 'India's national media lacks social diversity and does not reflect the country's social profile... Hindu upper-caste men dominate the media. They are about 8% of the population but among the key decision makers of the national media; their share is as high as 71%. Twice-born Hindus ('dwijas' comprising Brahmins, Rajputs, Vaishyas and Khatris) account for about 16% of the population but are 86% among key decision-makers. Brahmins (including Bhumihars and Tyagis) alone constitute 49% of key media personnel; if non-dwija forward castes like Marathas, Patels, Jats and Reddys are also added to this list, the total share of the upper-castes would be 88%. Dalits and adivasis are conspicuous by their absence among the decision makers: not even one of the sample of 315 journalists belonged to the SCs

---

13 For a comprehensive survey and analysis of Indian journalists in terms of caste-representation, see Robin Jeffrey, op. cit.

or STs. The proportion of the OBCs is abysmally low: only 4% compared to their population of around 43% in the country.'[14] Muslims comprise 13.4% of the population but have a share of only 4% in top media posts. However, the share of Christians who make up only 2.3% of the population is 4%. And women make up 17% of key decision makers in the media.[15]

The press is so obsessed with national and regional politics, cricket, crime and Bollywood that even silly rumours about people associated with these subjects hit the front page. What the press urgently needs is creative, investigative and development reporting chiefly on non-political themes like unemployment, malnutrition, exploitation of the poor, miscarriage of justice, police atrocities, development schemes and the like. The exposure of the genocide in Gujarat and the subsequent plight of the displaced in communal ghettos, which would have never come to light but for an alert press, is just one example of the heights the Indian press can sometimes scale. Recent examples include the Bofors pay-offs, the Harshad Mehta securities scam, the 'hawala' payments to top politicians, the Telgi Stamp Paper scam, the animal husbandry scandal in Bihar, the fake police 'encounters' in Gujarat and elsewhere, the shooting down of protesters in Nandigram and Singur, the Noida murders, the Gurjjar (or Gujjar) protestors in Rajasthan...But follow-up investigations of these public scandals are lacking, and are rarely pursued to the end. The news media whips up interest in a scam or a murder to a crescendo, then forgets about it when another more sensational scam is unearthed. Such 'crisis' reporting sells newspapers but does little to bring the guilty to book or to educate the public about the contexts of corruption and crime. But there have been several exceptions to this: the courageous exposes of lies and corruption in high places by www.tehelka.com, the *Tehelka* news magazine, the *Indian Express*, *Frontline* and a clutch of other newspapers, news

---

14 Yogendra Yadav, Anil Chamaria and Jitendra Kumar: National Media Devoid of Social Diversity: Survey, UNI Report in *Maharashstra Herald*, Pune, 6 June 2006. p. A7.
15 Ibid.

magazines and news channels.

Credibility is indeed the very life-blood of the news media, no matter which government is in power. The period of the Emergency showed how the credibility of the press could suffer. There are other reasons why credibility suffers, the chief being the unduly heavy dependence on official press handouts by business, the police and government. When, for example, there is a strike or riot, the Police Department's handout is printed and telecast without comment. On-the-spot investigative reports are few and far between. 'Trials by the media' of crimes and corruption have become commonplace on television news channels. While miscarriage of justice has to be certainly brought to light by the media, journalists have no business trying to replace the police and the courts.

Further, journalists are inclined to accept many favours from government such as subsidised housing and medical facilities, and it is therefore not surprising that they rush to the same government when they have differences with editors, and with management, or when they demand higher salaries and better working conditions. "An awesome responsibility", remarks the veteran editor, S. Nihal Singh, "rests on the shoulders of journalists because in the final analysis they are the custodians of the freedom of the press. If they prefer careerism to standing up for their rights, they are letting down their profession." However, the press is much too important in a democracy to be entrusted entirely to journalists; an ever vigilant public, the courts and the Press Council are needed to keep a watchful eye on it.

The 'Power' of the Press

The 'power' of the press to bring about social and political change or economic development is extremely limited. In capitalist societies, the press is primarily like any other business or industry: it exists to raise advertising revenue and circulation with the aim of making profits. 'Public service' and 'public interest' are not the main concerns. This is not to suggest that the press does not make attempts to exercise its 'power' in favour of one political or economic ideology over another, or of one group or class or caste over another. These attempts, it must be acknowledged, are sometimes successful and at other times disastrous failures. At most times, however, the attempts are not paid much heed to, unless it affects some group's interests in a radical manner. In the ultimate analysis, the 'power' of the press depends on its credibility among readers, as well as on how the news reported is understood and interpreted. Different groups 'read' the same news item in varied ways depending on their own social backgrounds. How news is read is not entirely in the hands of journalists. Indeed, the press often succeeds only in reinforcing widely held beliefs and the status quo rather than bringing about change and development.

Does the press 'set the agenda' for us and for society? There is no doubt that the press (62,483 registered publications strong in 2006)[16] keeps us informed about selected events, issues and people. But the public too has a role in 'setting the agenda' of the press. The public has interests, beliefs and expectations that are catered to by the press. While the press tells us what to think about, and also what to think, it has little power to change our ideas, beliefs and attitudes even when it attempts to do so. Only when there is a general consensus on an issue among all the elements of the press and the other media, and this consensus fits in with a community's needs, is there is some likelihood of a change being effected. Even in this case, several other factors would have to come into play before any real change can be felt.

The public attitude to the 'internal emergency' imposed by the Indira Gandhi regime is a case in point. One could argue, however, that it was not so much the press that brought about the downfall of that regime as the people's hostility to the crackdown on their fundamental rights. The press, after all, was easily silenced during the emergency. In the post-emergency period, the press only reflected the public's seething anger against the regime.

By and large, then, the press rarely initiates change,

---

16 RNI's Annual Report – 2006. See www.rni.nic.in for the latest data.

innovation and development. Because of its dependence on commercial interests and the dominant groups, it is of necessity conservative and status-quoist. The widespread support that the anti-Mandal riots and the 'liberalisation' policies of the Government have received from the 'national' and the 'regional' press is a reflection of that dependence. How is it that murders and other crimes perpetrated in upper middle class areas of Noida (where several TV news channels, incidentally, have their studios) and Gurgaon get saturation coverage in the news media, while those in poor rural areas (e.g. Khairlanji) are given short shrift?

It appears then that the news values of Indian journalists are no different from the news values of their counterparts in the Anglo-Saxon world. These are timeliness, immediacy, proximity, oddity, conflict, mystery, suspense, curiosity, and novelty. The new development/alternative journalists, however, challenge these elite- and immediacy-oriented values, and the 'man-bites-dog' approach to news. They believe that the voice of the silent, suffering majority should be heard through the press and other media. Not politics, business, finance, sports should be the staple of news but rather what is of value in terms of equality, human rights, social justice and peace. As N. Ram, the editor-in-chief of *The Hindu*, argued in his welcome at Joseph Stiglitz's lecture in 2007: The key question that needs asking is, do our news media contribute, in substantial measure, to empowering ordinary people – or are they interested in empowering and enriching themselves? We believe that promoting these values and these functions of serious, quality journalism necessarily involves a commitment to promoting informed public discussion of issues that matter.[17]

A Short History of Indian Journalism

"The over-200-year history of the Indian press, from the time of Hicky to the present day, is the history of a struggle for

---

17 N. Ram, in his welcome address at the Joseph Stiglitz lecture, Chennai, on January 4, 2007. Report in the *Hindu*, January 6, 2007, p. 14.

freedom, which has not yet ended. There have been alternating periods of freedom and of restrictions on freedom amounting to repression. The pioneering works on the Indian press, like that of Margarita Barns, were stories of arbitrariness and despotism, of reforms and relaxation. The story of the Indian press is a story of steady expansion but also one of press laws."[18]

The first newspaper meant for publication was 'announced' in 1776 by William Bolts. He asked those interested to come to his residence to read the news. This 'newspaper' had the twin function of informing the British community of news from 'home', and of ventilating grievances against the colonial administration.

Hicky's Gazette

But it was not until James Augustus Hicky dared to start his *Bengal Gazette* (also called *Hicky's Gazette*) in 1780 that the age of Journalism dawned in the country. England had already had a taste of the Spectator papers of Addison and Steele, and of lesser known periodicals as well, and learnt about the power of the periodical essayists, to laugh to scorn the manners and mores of society, and of those in high places.

Political and social corruption was rife among the British sent to rule the country when Hicky, a printer by profession, launched his Gazette 'in order to purchase freedom for my mind and soul'. He described the *Bengal Gazette* (later called *Hicky's Gazette*) as a 'weekly political and commercial paper open to all parties but influenced by none'. His venom was aimed at individuals like Mrs. Warren Hastings and their private affairs. He published announcements of marriages and engagements, and of 'likely' engagements.[19] The *Gazette* was, in essence, no better than a scandal sheet. Barely a year later, Sir Warren Hastings denied all postal facilities to Hicky who hit back with these ringing words:

'Mr. Hicky considers the Liberty of the Press to be essential to the very existence of an Englishman and a free Government.

---

18 Chalapathi Rau: '200 Years of the Indian Press', in *Vidura*, February 1980.
19 Margarita Barns: *The Indian Press*.

The subject should have full liberty to declare his principles and opinions, and every act which tends to coerce that liberty is tyrannical and injurious to the community'.

In June the following year (1781), Hicky was arrested and thrust into jail, from where he continued writing for the *Gazette*. He was stopped from 'bringing out his weekly only when the types used for printing were seized'.[20]

Five newspapers made their appearance in Bengal in six years' time – all started by Englishmen. Some of these newspapers received government patronage. The *Madras Courier* and the *Bombay Herald* (which later merged with the *Bombay Courier*) were then launched in the two cities. They were subservient to the government, and therefore flourished. The total circulation of all these weeklies was not more than 2,000; yet, the government issued Press Regulations (1799) making the publication of the name of the printer, editor and proprietor obligatory. The regulations also ordered these to declare themselves to the Secretary of the Government; and to submit all material for prior examination to the same authority. Pre-censorship was to dog the Indian journalist for many years to come.

Indian language Press

The pioneers of Indian language journalism were the Serampore Missionaries (led by William Carey)[21] with *Samachar Darpan* and other Bengali periodicals, and Raja Ram Mohan Roy with his Persian newspaper *Miratool Akbar*. The object of Rammohan Roy, the social reformer, in starting the paper was 'to lay before the public such articles of intelligence as may increase their experience, and tend to their social improvement', and to 'indicate to the rulers a knowledge of the real situation of their subjects, and make the subjects acquainted with the established laws and customs of their rules'. Roy ceased publishing his

---

20 ibid.
21 See the film documentary 'Candle in the Dark' (The Story of William Carey), Bombay: Galilean International Films and TV Services, 2005.

paper later in protest against the Government's Press Regulations.

The *Bombay Samachar*, a Gujarati newspaper, appeared in 1822. It was almost a decade before daily vernacular papers like *Mombai Vartaman* (1830), the *Jan-e-Jamshed* (1831), and the *Bombay Darpan* (1850), began publication. In the South, a Tamil and a Telugu newspaper was established with the aid of a government grant, and in the North West Provinces, a Hindi and an Urdu periodical started off under the government's patronage. The Bengali press with as many as nine newspapers in 1839 had a circulation of around 200 copies each, even as the British press with 26 newspapers (six of them dailies) grew in strength and power, under the liberal rule of Lord Metcalfe, and later of Lord Auckland.

Censorship and the 'Mutiny'

The year of what the British historians term 'the Sepoy Mutiny' (and some Indian historians the 'first war of independence'), however, brought back the press restrictions in the form of the Gagging Act, 1857. Lord Canning argued for them, stating that 'there are times in the existence of every state in which something of the liberties and rights, which it jealously cherishes and scrupulously guards in ordinary seasons, must be sacrificed for the public welfare. Such is the State of India at this moment. Such a time has come upon us. The liberty of the press is no exception.'

The Mutiny brought the rule of the East India Company to a close, with the Crown taking over the 'colony', with the promise of religious toleration, and press freedom. How the English press and the international news agencies such as Reuters covered the 'Mutiny' is a scandal exposed by the Australian researchers, Chandrika Kaul and Peter Putnis, in their historical accounts of the London-based 'steamship press' – actively promoted by British colonial and business interests.[22]

---

22 See Chandrika Kaul: Peter Putnis: 'The British Transoceanic Steamship Press in Nineteenth Century India and Australia': An Overview', Journal of Australian Studies, March 1, 2007.

The main topics of discussion in the English and vernacular press before and after the Mutiny were sati, caste, widow remarriage, polygamy, crimes, and opposition to the teaching of English in schools and colleges. Bombay's Gujarati press, in particular, excelled in the defence of the Indian way of life. In 1876 the Vernacular Press Act was promulgated.

During the next two decades *The Times of India*, the *Pioneer*, the *Madras Mail*, and the *Amrit Bazar Patrika* came into existence – all except the last edited by Englishmen, and serving the interests of English educated readers. The English press played down the inaugural meeting of the Indian National Congress on December 28, 1885 in Bombay, but it was reported at length by the vernacular papers such as *Kesari* (founded by Lokmanya Tilak). The *Amrit Bazar Patrika* and *Kesari* soon gained a reputation for opposing government attempts to suppress nationalist aspirations. The *Amrit Bazar Patrika*, for instance, denounced the deposition of the Maharaja of Kashmir, and *Kesari* was foremost in attacking the Age of Consent Bill of 1891, which sought to prohibit the consummation of marriage before a bride completed the age of 12. The *Kesari*'s stand was endorsed by the *Amrit Bazar Patrika* and *Bangabasi* of Calcutta on the ground that the government had no right to interfere with traditional Hindu customs. Tilak charged the government with disrespect for the liberty and privacy of the Indian people, and with negligence in providing relief during the countrywide famine in 1896-97, which resulted in the death of over a million people.

Such savage anti-government sentiments could not be allowed free play and so Lord Elgin added sections to the Indian Penal Code to enable the government to deal with promotion of 'disaffection' against the Crown, or of enmity and hatred between different classes. Also prohibited was 'the circulation of any reports with intent to cause mutiny among British troops, intent to cause such fear or alarm among the public as to cause any person to commit an offence against the State, or intent to incite any class or community to commit offences against any other class or community'. The penalties for offences ranged from life imprisonment to short imprisonment or fines.[23]

The man who became the most noteworthy victim of these new laws was none other than Bal Gangadhar Tilak, editor of *Kesari* and its English companion, *Mahratha*. He was arrested, convicted and jailed for six years, but *Kesari* continued to build up its reputation and influence as a national daily, as India woke to the 20th century. Other champions of press freedom who were prosecuted at about the same time were Aurobindo Ghose of *Bande Mataram*, B.B. Upadhayaya of *Sandhy*a, and B.N. Dutt of *Jugantar*.

The Indian Press Act

In 1910, the Indian Press Act clamped further controls on newspapers in the wake of the partition of Bengal and violent attacks by terrorists in Ahmedabad, Ambala and elsewhere. The Act required owners of printing presses to deposit securities of Rs. 500 to Rs. 2,000, which were forfeited if 'objectionable matters' were printed. The threats of seizure of the printing press, and confiscation of copies sent by post were also included in the Act. The vernacular press suffered rigorous suppression during this period (1910-1914). The government banned 50 works in English and 272 in the vernacular, which included 114 in Marathi, 52 in Urdu and 51 in Bengali.[24]

World War I introduced still more severe press laws, but there was no let-up in nationalist agitations. Annie Besant's New India became the mouthpiece of Home Rule advocates, ably supported by the *Bombay Chronicle* (edited by Benjamin Horniman), *Maratha* (edited by N.C. Kelkar) and other publications. The government reacted swiftly by exiling Annie Besant, deporting Horniman and imposing new securities on offending publications. The Rowlatt Act of 1919 infuriated Indian opinion, which now came under the leadership of Mahatma Gandhi. His Non-Cooperative Movement took the press by storm. Gandhi was to remain front-page news for years to come. His arrests and

---

23 Sharad Karkhanis: *Indian Politics and the Press*, New Delhi: Vikas, 1980.
24 ibid.

imprisonments were covered with relish by the English and the vernacular press, whose readership now rose dramatically. The Swaraj Party led by C.R. Das, Vallabhbhai Patel and Motilal Nehru, launched its own publications – the *Banglar Katha* in Calcutta, the *Swadesh Mitram* in the South, and *Hindustan Times, Pratap* and *Basumati* in the North.

The Indian Press Ordinance (1930), like the Press Act of 1910, and five other Ordinances gave added power to the government in dealing with acts of terrorism, and inflammatory literature. The Swadeshi Movement, covered prominently by the press, as in The Hindu (Madras) led to the imprisonment of leaders like Gandhi and Nehru, and of editors like S.A. Brelvi of Bombay Chronicle and Ganesh Shankar Vidyarthi of *Pratap*. The Indian Press (Emergency Powers) Act of 1931 raised deposit securities and fines, and gave Magistrates the power to issue summary actions. Several other Acts were made law during the thirties, forcing the closure of many presses and publications.

Meanwhile, the *Free Press of India*, which began as a news agency, started *The Indian Express* and *Dhenamani* in Madras, the *Free Press Journal* in Bombay, and Gujarati and Marathi journals. The news agency collapsed after it forfeited Rs. 20,000 security under the Indian Press (Emergency Powers) Act, but its publications continued under different owners, and the Free Press editors started a new agency called the United Press of India (U.P.I.)

Then came the Quit India Movement, and World War II, and the press in India, including the English language press and that in the Indian Native States played a commendable role in reporting the struggle for freedom fairly. It opposed communal riots and the partition of the country, and when partition did take place in the glorious year of independence, lamented it. Indeed, it could be said that the press played no small part in India's victory to freedom. Free India's Constitution upheld the citizens' right to freedom of speech and expression, which included the freedom of the press. While the obnoxious Press Acts were repealed or amended, the Official Secrets Act and Sections of the Indian Code dealing with disaffection, communal hatred and incitement of armed forces to disloyalty, were retained.

The Nehru Government passed in October 1951 the Press (Objectionable Matters) Act which was reminiscent of earlier press laws enacted by the colonial rulers. The 'objectionable matters' were quite comprehensive. So fierce was the opposition to it that in 1956, it was allowed to lapse, and the first Press Commission was formed.

The national and regional press covered the campaigns of the first national elections of 1951-1952 with professional skill. So were the other events of the Nehru era, like the formation of the linguistic States, the second and third general elections, the Chinese attack, and the take-over of Goa. Unlike her father, Indira Gandhi had never been at ease with the press. 'How much freedom can the press have in a country like India fighting poverty, backwardness, ignorance, disease and superstitions?' asked she in the first year of her regime. The national dailies grew strident in their attacks on her government, especially on the question of nationalisation of banks, privy purses, the Congress split, but joined forces with her during the Bangla Desh war of liberation. The attacks reached their climax in the period prior to the emergency, with open accusations of rampant corruption, and demands for her resignation, followed the Allahabad High Court's verdict of her being guilty of corrupt election practices.

Press Censorship under the Emergency

During the British regime, Indian newspapers were not allowed to publish any material considered 'seditious'. Yet few printing presses were confiscated, and fewer journalists arrested. Complete censorship was imposed only on rare occasions as when Gandhiji's arrest led to countrywide disturbances and the detention of over 60,000 persons.

Though some papers like the Bengali weekly *Jugantar*, or the daily *Sandhya* (also Bengali) were banned in the thirties, they were published secretly. Restrictions were imposed on the press during the Quit India Movement of 1942. Yet major papers could publish the arrest of national leaders and reports of demonstrations and protests. Moreover, pre-censorship was never enforced and that explains why articles critical of the British Government were carried freely.

In 1975, however, an internal emergency was clamped on the nation, and pre-censorship imposed in a draconian manner. The government suppressed transmission of news by imposing censorship on newspapers, journals, radio, TV, telex, telegrams, news agencies and on foreign correspondents. Even teleprinter services were subjected to pre-censorship. The censorship was total and unparalleled. News agencies had to get all their material censored in Delhi prior to transmission. Further, newspapers had to submit already censored news for re-censorship in their respective headquarters. What is more, even advertisements, cartoons, and comic-strips were subjected to pre-censorship. Foreign papers and journals were confiscated if they carried criticism of the emergency; some issues of *Time* and *Newsweek* were banned outright.

The underground press was, however, very active. More than 34 printing presses were seized and over 7,000 people arrested in connection with the publication and circulation of underground literature. Small publications such as A.D. Gorwala's *Opinion*, A.B. Shah's *Quest* (now *New Quest*), were forced to close down. Underground literature flourished in Gujarat, Tamilnadu, Bihar and Maharashtra. Letters from Jayaprakash Narayan and George Fernandes were published regularly and distributed discreetly around the country. From Bihar alone more than 2,000 titles were circulated.

The RSS distributed underground literature in the form of news-sheets which contained only news and quotations. They were published in English and the major Indian languages. Indians abroad published anti-emergency literature e.g., *Swarajya* (England), *Satyavani*, *Indian Opinion* (USA).

Among the few overground publications that opposed the emergency despite stringent censorship regulations were: *Sadhana* (Gujarati), *Himmat* (edited by Rajmohan Gandhi), *Freedom First* (owned by M.R. Masani), *The Statesman*, *The Indian Express*, *Daily Morosoli* (Tamil), *Tughlak* (Tamil) and

Radical Humanist. Most other major national dailies like *The Times of India*, *The Free Press*, the *Hindustan Standard*, and the *National Herald* "crawled when they were only asked to bend".[25]

The post-Emergency period too was witness to attempts by the Congress Party to control the press. In 1984, Bihar's Chief Minister, Dr Jagannath Mishra, mooted the *Bihar Press Bill*, but protests by journalists forced him to withdraw it. Three years later, an Anti-Defamation Bill (1987), initiated by Prime Minister Rajiv Gandhi, also met the same fate. More recently, veteran Congressman V.N. Gadgil introduced the Right to Reply Bill (1994), but this too had to be withdrawn.

News and News Values in Mainstream Journalism

Pick up half a dozen newspapers of different publishing houses on a single day, and scan through the news items on the front pages of the newspapers. What strikes you at once is that most of the same items ('news stories') appear in each paper, often with similar headlines and in similar positions on the front page. Stories appearing on the top half of the front page ('above the fold') are considered to be more important than those appearing 'below the fold'. Prominence and significance of stories is suggested by type-size of headlines, placement, and column centimetres of space; sometimes news items are 'boxed' to suggest their greater significance. The 'anchor' story (the final article at the bottom of the front page) generally focuses on a human interest story; this is to provide a semblance of balance in the selection of front page stories. The 'solus' position on the extreme right hand corner of the front page is generally given over to a display advertisement.

Clearly, there is a 'hierarchy' in the selection of news. Political stories receive more prominent coverage than say stories of heroism; disaster and crime stories get greater attention than social or civic problems. The focus, it becomes clear, is on 'events' rather than issues and processes; on eminent and elite

---

25 Cf. Dass Report (1977) ; also known as the 'White Paper on Misuse of Mass Media During the Internal Emergency', August 1977.

people rather than the poor and the marginalised;[26] on the exotic and the novel rather than the ordinary, the everyday and the usual. Evidently, certain 'values' are at work in the way some happenings, some people, some nations and some cities, are considered news-worthy and others are not. Numerous happenings are not reported; a strict selection process sifts out what is not *newsworthy*, and what is. From whose perspective and in terms of which value-system is this selection being made?

Table 1: Top Ten 'Mainstream' Newspapers and Magazines (In terms of Readership)

Daily Newspapers	Magazines
1. Dainik Jagran (Hindi)	1. India Today (Hindi)
2. Dainik Bhaskar (Hindi)	2. Saras Salil (Hindi)
3. Daily Thanthi (Tamil)	3. India Today (English)
4. Amar Ujala (Hindi)	4. Kungumum (Tamil)
5. Hindustan (Hindi)	5. Kumudum (Tamil)
6. Malayala Manorama (Malayalam)	6. Sarita (Hindi)
7. Lokmat (Marathi)	7. Grihashobha (Hindi)
8. Eenadu (Telugu)	8. Swati SVP
9. Mathrubhumi (Malayalam)	9. Vanitha (Malayalam)
10. The Times of India (English)	10. Malayala Manorama Weekly

(Sources: IRS-Round 1 – 2006; FICCI Report-2006)

It appears that journalists in all newspapers think alike and work according to the same set of values. It is true that they use the same sources (the news agencies) for the majority of their news stories, but even where newspapers have their own special correspondents, say as in New Delhi or the state capitals, one finds that exactly the same stories come to be selected for reporting. It appears that reporters hunt in packs; they have a similar sense of what makes for news. An earthquake takes place in Latur, and the world's press is there the next day in hordes;

---

26 See the special issue on 'Communication Poverty' in *Media Development* (Toronto), 2008/1. Cf. Keval J. Kumar: 'Poverty, Advertising in the Indian News Media', and I. Arul Ram: 'Indian Media Devote Little Space to Poverty' in the same issue.

Anna Hazare of Ralegaon Siddhi threatens a fast unto death, and Maharashtra's reporters queue up outside his temple-residence. The Prime Minister comes to town, even on a personal visit, and the press is busy sniffing around.

This approach to journalism is sometimes labelled 'Pack Journalism'. Further, how is it that journalists the world over swear by the 'inverted pyramid structure' when writing up the news? Such a structure came into existence with the telegraph; the electronic media and the internet have a potential for experimenting with other formats, but journalists cannot shed their old habits of thought and their old routines of working to deadlines. With round the clock news on news channels (such as CNN, BBC World, DD News, Star News, Zee News, NDTV, CNN-IBN and Times Now) and on the Internet, the traditional forms of journalism and traditional routines of journalists have taken a thorough beating.

The Making of a Newspaper

News Reporting

News reports are classified into two broad types: straight news reports, and investigative or interpretative reports. Straight news reports present what has happened in a straight-forward, factual, and clear manner. They draw no conclusions, nor offer any opinions. There is no attempt to probe deeper than the surface happenings, or to provide elaborate background information, or even to examine claims made. The main sources (generally attributed) are: Government officials, elite groups, news agencies, eminent people, businessmen, and others.

Both these types of news stories merely present the claims, without in any way trying to question or rebut, or ask why. Investigative reports, on the other hand, would make an effort to go behind the claims, and see how valid they are. They report happenings in depth, present fairly all sides of the picture in the context of the situation, and generally, put some meaning into the news so that the reader is better able to understand and analyse the event.

Disaster stories e.g. accidents, famines and floods get pride of place in the daily press, and these provide many 'human interest' stories. Developments in science, industry and agriculture are increasingly coming to be considered as interesting news, as also the exposure of corruption in high places, the exploitation of the lower classes and workers, and social injustice and inequalities resulting from the social, economic and political structures. Of course, all the news reported is not news of the highest interest to everybody. Politics interest some, sports others, crime still others. However, it is rare that newspapers touch on the information needs and interests of the poorer sections of society; they are largely 'invisible' and 'unheard' in the mass media.[27]

Investigative and Interpretative Reporting

Investigative and interpretative reporting is not necessarily getting 'scoops' and sensationalising them but rather 'situation reporting' in place of event or personality reporting. It is indeed a calm, restrained and detached manner of arriving at conclusions or at studied opinions from factual bits of evidence at hand. It may be reflective, even speculative, but always based on hardcore evidence.[28]

An investigative report begins with a hunch that there is something more than meets the eye. Ashwini Sarin of the *Indian Express* had heard of the wretched conditions in the Tihar Central Jail, but felt there was much more than mere hearsay in the reports. He wanted to do an investigative report on the jail and so got himself arrested on a flimsy charge. In mid-1979, the Indian Express carried four investigative reports by him on the inside story of Tihar Jail. Later, the same reporter disguised himself and 'bought' a girl to acquire firsthand knowledge of, and report on, the 'flesh trade' in an area not far from Delhi. News magazines like *India Today*, *Outlook*, *Tehelka* and *The Week* have exposed the Bhagalpur blindings, and other police

---

27 See the special issue of *Media Development*, Toronto, January 2008, for a series of articles on 'Poverty and the Mass Media'. Cf. Keval J. Kumar: 'Poverty, Advertising and the Indian Mass Media', pp. in the same issue.
28 M.V. Kamath: Professional Journalism, New Delhi: Vikas, 1980.

atrocities (often termed 'encounters') in many parts of the country. The carnage in Gujarat in 2002 following the Godhra train incident was well investigated by both print and electronic media. The tradition of 'investigative journalism' has strong roots in the Indian press. At the global level there has been an impressive growth since 1989 in the practice of investigative journalism 'fuelled by globalization, international aid, and the efforts of journalism groups'.[29]

Newspapers and news magazines are turning more and more toward investigative and interpretative reporting, as TV, radio and the Internet have a clear edge over them in giving up-to-the minute developments in news around the world. The morning's papers of course provide news in much greater detail, but it is all the same yesterday's news, which is undoubtedly stale news. However, TV and radio cannot match the press in in-depth reporting and critical analysis.

Investigative stories have to be done with the active support of the editor, else they may be 'killed' at the last minute. That is because such stories could tread on many toes, especially governmental and business toes. They often demand months of tedious work, and when finally published can have dramatic effects. An offshoot of investigative reporting is consumer reporting, which exposes business practices that exploit consumers. Indian newspapers have yet to take on big business in a big way. Occasional reports have focused on pharmaceutical and soft-drink companies, but without much real impact. The findings of consumer organizations and Consumer Redressal Courts are rarely given wide publicity, and 'complaints' columns in the press do not follow-up the complaints made. As M.V. Kamath points out, "the line dividing an in-depth (report) from a feature article or an investigative report is pretty thin indeed and one can often be confused for the other".[30]

In the ultimate analysis, the daily newspaper is the result of

---

29 'Global Investigative Journalism: Strategies for Support' – A Report to the Centre for International Media Assistance (CIMA), December 5, 2007, p. 4.
30 ibid.

a glorious team effort. The members of the team are often a restless lot getting on each other's nerves, but pulling together nevertheless. They know that come what may, it's better to hang together than to hang separately! For they share the 'values' of the profession. Indeed, even as they belong to one big team, (if they work for a large national daily) they are also members of smaller teams called 'departments'. For instance, reporters, sub-editors, news editors, assistant editors and editors belong to the editorial department. Compositors, makeup men and printers form the printing or mechanical department. But it isn't enough for the paper to be edited and printed; it needs to be advertised (more importantly, to collect and handle advertising), and sold, and regular accounts have to be maintained. The three departments responsible for these activities are the advertising, circulation, and accounting or accounts departments respectively. The five departments work in close co-ordination.

The editorial department is the creative organ of a newspaper. It is, therefore, manned by writers and re-writers. The writers are the editor and his assistants, as well as reporters and correspondents. The re-writers are called sub-editors (or copyreaders). In the jargon of the profession, the 'subs edit copy' before it is sent down to the compositor in the printing department. Desktop publishing (DTP) has eliminated the roles of the compositor and the layout artist, and has simplified the production process considerably.

The Sub-editor

The sub-editor's job is much less glamorous than a reporter's, but as important. While a reporter is an out-of-doors man with a 'beat' to cover, a sub-editor is a deskman. Again, while a reporter is well known to newspaper readers as his reports frequently carry a 'by-line', a sub-editor hardly ever sees his name in print. He is an obscure figure working back-stage to give a face-lift to the paper, but his worth is rarely acknowledged even by reporters to whose 'copy' he gives spit and polish, rendering it readable to the average newspaper reader. Indeed, a sub-editor is a 'super-reporter', for he sits in judgement on a reporter's news story, checking its accuracy, its language, and its intelligibility. It is often due to his alertness that a story is 'killed', and the editor is saved from being hauled up by the police and the courts, or from having to apologise to readers for carrying fake stories, and for errors in names, designations, dates and the like. The credibility of the paper rests in his hands. As one appreciative editor puts it: 'The sub-editor is the private detective, the motorcycle cop escort, nay even the army, navy and marine corps to the newspaper's most treasured possession – the confidence of the reader. He wears neither star nor chevron, and his bosom never bulges with gold medals, nor his pockets with coins; he is the lifeguard of the newspaper office'.

Headlines

The sub-editor has other creative duties as well. The most significant one is that of providing headlines and sub-headlines to news reports. The significance of this task can be realised from the fact that most readers glance through the headlines before they pick and choose items for detailed reading. Headlines, therefore, have the function of attracting the readers' attention, and of grading and organising the news. Besides, they make a newspaper page spring to life, lending it the character of a mosaic, with a form, symmetry and beauty all its own. Headlines capsule whole stories into a few words, which fit into the limited space of newspaper columns, and in typography that pleases the eye. Yet, headlines are not mere summaries. To be effective, they need to be packed with punch, to shoot fast and straight. This is achieved by the use of 'action' words like 'stab' (for murder), 'raid' (for search), 'hike' (for raise), 'flay' or 'rap' (for criticize), 'probe' (for investigate), and 'scam' (for fraud).

Headlines are usually written in the historical present tense and in a positive tone, as these lend an air of immediacy to the news. Besides, they must convey the spirit of their stories. Disaster stories need to bear headlines that convey the tragedy E.g. '51 die in gas line blast'. Amusing stories like the case of a minister who panicked on his first flight in a helicopter: 'Minister yells for life, guard runs for his!'

Headlines are of several types: the 'banner' which stretches across many columns: the 'boxed' headline which is framed in a small rectangle, the 'flush' headline which is multi-deck and printed flush left; the 'cross' line which is centred in column; the 'inverted pyramid' headline which as the name suggests is multi-deck, with the decks below centred with the upper: the hanging indent headline which is also multi-deck but with the lower decks indented from the left, the 'jumphead' which is the secondary head that carries the continued part of a news story in an inside page. There are numerous other types of headlines, some with fancy names like 'shoulder headline' and 'curiosity headline' but the ones that have been listed are those most frequently encountered by readers.[31]

Feature-Writing

While news reports present brief write-ups on events, issues and people, features present detailed analyses of the same, often in the form of discussions, narratives or critiques. Further, while news reports are written mostly in the inverted pyramid formal structure and style, features follow the structure of essays and discussions, and present a distinct point of view. News reports are written by staff reporters, stringers or correspondents but features are usually contributed by senior reporters, assistant editors, editors, but also by outside experts who may be academics, free-lancers, researchers and others.

A feature, then, is an essay-like piece written for publication in a newspaper or magazine. News reports dominate in a newspaper, but in magazines features take up most space. 'Cover stories' in magazines are usually written in the form of features, while in newspapers the main or lead story would be written in the form of a news report. Newspapers do not usually carry features on the front page, except perhaps in the 'anchor' position. Features also figure on the editorial page and on the

---

31 For a fascinating account of the variety of headlines in Indian newspapers, see Sunil Saxena's monograph on *Headline-Writing*, New Delhi, Sage Publications, 2006.

oped page, as well as in the Sunday/weekend magazine supplements.[32]

Interviews

Features may sometimes take the form of interviews, or use interviews as important sources of information. Features frequently quote several opinions which have been collected through interviews. The Sunday papers carry interviews with eminent people in art and literature. These interviews are sometimes presented in a 'question-and-answer' format, without any comments from the writer; at other times, the interviews are presented in the form of a news report or a feature where excerpts from the interview are highlighted, but the whole interview is not presented verbatim.

Interviews are a major source of information for a journalist. They may be conducted over the phone, in person, at press conferences or over the internet. Journalists are not expected to offer their own opinions in news reports; however, they are expected to give the views and opinions of people in power. Common people are asked their views when the issues concern them. But common people are rarely 'nominated' (named), whereas eminent people always are. The reasoning behind this is that people with power and position make news while common people do not. This is a major 'value' among mainstream journalists the world over.

Print Media: The Magazine Sector

The 1980s saw a boom in the publication of magazines in India, not only in English but in the major Indian languages as well. The magazine boom was perhaps set off by the launch of *India Today* in the mid-seventies, and the new-look *Illustrated Weekly of India* under the editorship of Khushwant Singh. (*India Today* was initially targeted at Indians settled abroad, but having failed miserably to make an impression, changed gears to target its product at the upper and middle class at home). Its inspiration

---

32 See Huned Contractor: *Feature Writing,* Bombay: Sangam Books, 2003.

right from its red-border cover page to its mode of gathering and editing and 'packaging' news has been TIME - International. So it came as no surprise when in 1992, *India Today* became the official agent of TIME magazine in India, collecting subscriptions and advertisements for it. It was only the national policy opposed to the entry of the foreign press that has kept TIME from publishing its Asian edition from New Delhi. (The Living Media Group which publishes *India Today* has, however, now launched the publication of *Cosmpolitan, Men's Health, Money Today* and *Harvard Business Review*).

Other magazines to be launched in quick succession in the early eighties included *Gentleman, Gentleman Fashion Quarterly* (GFQ), *Onlooker, New Delhi, Bombay, The Week, G* and a few others. Several new film magazines and computer magazines also took off around the same time. The new magazines introduced colour, gloss and a snazzy style of reporting which 'personalised' and 'dramatised' issues and events. Photographs, illustrations, charts and graphs enlivened each page, and the focus was on 'soft' features. High quality printing on imported glazed paper lent the magazines an expensive look. This pleased the advertising community immensely.

The boom continued into the 1990s despite the closure of long-established magazines like *The Illustrated Weekly of India, Sunday* and *Bombay*. The growth was spectacular in the case of special interest magazines, especially those dealing with business and finance, computers and electronics, fashion and lifestyles. Several special interest periodicals were launched in 1993: *Parenting, Young Mother, Auto India,* and *Car & Bike*. Other new magazines of the mid-1990s included *Studio System*, a bi-monthly on audio, video and recording, *Eating Out, Indian Thoroughbred* (on horse-rearing), *Golfingly Yours, Dost* (for homosexuals), and *TV Today*. The last, a publication from the Living Media stable, folded ten months after it hit the stands.

The magazine boom almost went bust by the close of the millennium, but by 2006 it was boom time again for magazines. In 2006 as many as 2600 magazine titles were registered with the

Registrar of Newspapers for India (RNI) and during the first six months of the following year, another 2100 were registered. At the Indian Magazine Congress in 2007, the Association of Indian Magazines (AIM) claimed that magazine advertising was growing faster than newspapers and television – at 24% per annum as against 18% for newspapers and television.[33] This was perhaps a consequence of the Government's policy of opening up the print media to foreign investment. So while FDI in the news sector was restricted to a 26% stake, the non-news sector was permitted up to 100% FDI. In 2006-2007, the Information and Broadcasting Ministry approved licenses for over a hundred non-news international titles.

But Readership Surveys by NRS and IRS and circulation audits by ABC seemed to suggest that there was a decline in magazine reading. A possible explanation for this trend was the many supplements (and even little magazines) that became part of the daily and Sunday papers. Also, newspapers were gradually beginning to take on the look and the function of general interest magazines, offering supplements or pages on health, environment, beauty, films and information technology. Since daily newspapers have indeed been transformed into magazines the future of magazines is under serious threat. News magazines were an exception though. *India Today* (with editions in Hindi, Tamil, Malayalam and Gujarati) was challenged by *Outlook* and *The Week*, and later by *Hard News*, *Alive*, *Tehelka*, and *Covert*. The Association of Indian Magazines (AIM), however, at their Congress in 2006 argued that the problem perhaps lay with the research methodology and the newspaper-oriented focus of both ABC and NRS surveys.[34]

Magazine Genres

Nearly four out of every five Indian periodicals are in the Indian languages. Hindi alone has more than 3,000 periodicals, followed by English with over 2,670. Periodicals in Tamil,

---

33 See reports of the 2007 Congress on AIM's website www.aim.org.
34 See reports of the 2006 Congress on AIM's official website www.aim.org.in.

Malayalam, Gujarati, Bengali, Marathi, Urdu and Telugu too enjoy a fairly good circulation and readership. Out of a total of 6,343 periodicals published regularly (with a circulation of 91.3 million copies), 3,428 are weeklies, 955 fortnightlies, 1,471 monthlies, 219 quarterlies and 49 annuals.[35] The circulation of the weeklies is 50.5 million copies while that of the monthlies and fortnightlies is 21.1 million and 12.3 million respectively.[36] The total readership of magazines is 359 million, 68% of which is in Hindi.[37]

Broadly speaking, there are two types of magazines: general interest magazines and special-interest niche (SIN) magazines. General interest magazines are those that attempt to cater to a wide variety of reading interests such as *India Today*, *The Week*, *Frontline*, '*G*'; and several others. Though they are largely newsmagazines, such magazines carry features on the arts, culture, environment, films, reviews, business and economics, gossip, etc. General interest magazines with the focus on news and current affairs number over 4,500 and have the largest readership and advertising revenue.

Special interest niche magazines are those that cater to the interest of a specific profession or interest group. Thus business magazines like *Business India*, *Business World*, *Business Today* and *Outlook Business* are of special interest to the corporate world, to business and finance professionals. *Outlook Money*, *Money*, *Investment* and similar magazines cater to the interests of investors in the stock market.

Other genres in the special-interest category are film magazines (*Movie, Filmfare, Stardust, Cine Blitz*), women's magazines (*Femina, Savvy, Women's Era, Celebrity*), computer and technology magazines (*Computers Today, Computers & Communications, Telematics, Computer Express*), environment magazines *(Down to Earth, Sanctuary)*, children's magazines (*Tinkle, Champa, Balaram* and *Chandamama*), career and

---

35 RNI's Annual Report – 2005.
36 Ibid.
37 National Readership Survey (NRS) – 2006.

*Table 2: Top Ten General-Interest Magazines
(In terms of Share of Advertising revenue)*

Magazine	Publication Group
1. Outlook	The Outlook Group
2. India Today (National)	The India Today Group
3. The Week	Malayala Manorama Group
4. Chitralekha (Gujarati)	Chitralekha Group
5. Time	Time International
6. Chitralekha (Marathi)	Chitralekha Group
7. India Today (Delhi)	The India Today Group
8. India Today (Bombay)	The India Today Group
9. Newsweek	Newsweek International
10. Swati (Telugu)	Swati Publications

(Source: *A Ready Reckoner for Indian Magazine Industry - 2007*)[38]

competition magazines (*Career and Competition Times*), police and detective magazines (*Police Times, Dakshatha*), travel and leisure (*Outlook Traveller*) and many others targeted at readers interested in astrology, agriculture, literature, environment, interior decoration, architecture, sports, etc. Besides these genres there are trade magazines and technical magazines catering to each trade and each branch of medicine, engineering, management (*Indian Management*), mass communication, advertising and marketing (*Pitch, Impact, Brand Reporter, USP Age, 4P's, Broadcast & CableSat),* etc. One of the largest players in the computer and telecommunications segment is the Cyber Media Group with over 15 magazines (*Dataquest, PC Quest, Living Digital, Bio Spectrum, Voice and Data, Global Services* etc.) and a dozen websites. A prolific publisher in the lifestyle segment is Lana Publishing (now called Magna); in the 1980s it launched *Stardust, Savvy, Society, Island* and *Parade* in quick succession.

News and current affairs periodicals (around 4,500) account for 27% of the total periodical circulation. Next in popularity are literary and cultural periodicals (around 2,000), commanding a

---

[38] *A Ready Reckoner for the Indian Magazine Industry – 2007*, PITCH, May 2007.

circulation of around 25%. An example of this type of periodical is the Tamil magazine *Kumudam*, which has a circulation of nearly half a million copies. Surprisingly, religious or philosophical periodicals have a circulation of over 8% of the total distribution. Film magazines are growing in number and circulation. Often obscene 'stills' from films accompany serious reviews. Even the so-called respectable family magazines resort to this gimmick to step up sales. Political and film gossip makes up the staple fare of most general-interest and news magazines, which in terms of circulation are on the decline compared to specialised periodicals aiming at target-groups such as youth (e.g. *JAM*), children, women, film buffs, professionals, executives, business groups, computer users, sports lovers and others.

With the spurt in the number of dailies and periodicals has come 'investigative' reporting, though some of it invades privacy and verges on gossip. The film magazines are particularly guilty of this approach to journalism. However, exposes of corruption in high places have given the national dailies in particular a new crusading spirit. Further, competition has shaken the complacency of the so-called monopoly press which has begun sending out more reporters into the field for 'spot' and investigative reporting.

Advertisers like to target their products and services at specific rather than general audiences; they term this strategy 'niche marketing'. They like, for instance, to target housewives who they believe are the chief decision makers in Indian homes, especially with regard to consumer and consumer durable items. So, women's magazines are selected for peddling not only products of interest to women, but also products for the men folk in the family. Is this perhaps the explanation for the sexiest ads being found in women's magazines? Up-market premium products are generally advertised in expensive English magazines (e.g. *Femina, Savvy, GQ*) while the down-market products are advertised in low-priced and not-so-glossy magazines (e.g. *Women's Era*).

Table 3: Top Ten Women's Magazines
(In terms of Share of Advertising Revenue)

Magazines	Publication Groups
1. Cosmopolitan	India Today Group
2. Femina	Worldwide Media (BBC World/Times of India)
3. Vanitha (Malayalam)	Malayala Manorama Group
4. Sananda (Bengali)	ABP Group
5. Women's Era	Delhi Press Group
6. Grihshobha (Hindi)	Delhi Press Group
7. Kanyaka (Malayalam)	Mangalam Publications
8. Mangayar Malar (Tamil)	Kalki Group
9. Jagran Sakhi (Hindi)	Jagran Group
10. 4th D Woman	Fourth Dimension Media

(Source: *A Ready Reckoner for Indian Magazines – 2007*)

In advertising, the name of the game is 'segmentation' – the categorisation of potential consumers in terms of demographics, psychographics and lifestyles. The advertiser aims at giving potential consumers the maximum number of 'exposures' to a 'vehicle' which carries an ad: that is, the maximum number of OTS (opportunities to see). The greater the exposure to an advertisement the greater is the chance of the product being purchased: so goes the assumption. Quality, price, and usefulness and relevance are criteria which do not concern the advertiser very seriously when it comes to exploiting magazines for selling products, services and ideas.

International Magazines

Foreign special interest magazines have entered the Indian market ever since FDI in that sector was opened to outsiders. They have found several Indian partners to assist them in their ventures, notably Living Media, The Times of India/BCCL and Media Transasia. Up to 26% FDI is now allowed in newspapers and news magazines and 100% in the non-news sector. The Times of India has a joint venture with BBC publications to publish and distribute its various periodicals in the Indian market. Media Transasia publishes the international magazines *Maxim, Travel and Leisure, Better House and Garden,* and *Child,* besides its own publications: *Swagat, Discover India* and *Architecture and Design.* Bangalore-based IDG India, a wholly-owned business unit of IDG Media Pvt Ltd, publishes *PC World, Channel World* and several other computer magazines. Yet another well known international title to be published in Mumbai and Delhi is *Time Out,* by Paprika Media Pvt Ltd and Time Out International. *OK,* a celebrity magazine from the UK which publishes nine editions in nine different countries, now has its tenth edition in India published by VJ Media, a Vijay Mallya venture. (VJ Media is the publisher of *Cine Blitz* and *Hi! Blitz).* The international content in these magazines is usually re-edited to suit local tastes.

Table 4: Indian Editions of International Magazines

Title	Publisher
1. Hello!	BBC Worldwide & TOI Group
2. Better Homes and Garden	Meredith Corporation
3. Channel World	International Data Group (IDG)
4. Prevention	Rodale (US) & India Today

Readership and Popularity of Magazines

Readership and popularity are not necessarily identical. A large readership might be one of the indicators of popularity, though not the only indicator. While readership relates to an activity, popularity relates to a positive feeling, of liking and of enjoying what one reads. But who is a 'reader' in the first place? Is a 'reader' one who has merely 'seen' a magazine or can recognize its masthead, as market researchers assume when they conduct National Readership Surveys (NRS) and Indian Readership Surveys (IRS)? Then there are what might be termed 'primary readers' and 'secondary readers' or even 'tertiary readers'. Primary readers are those who read every piece in the magazine with attention and care, and are not distracted by other activities. Secondary readers are those who read magazines while they are watching television, listening to the radio or to the audio-recorder, looking after children, answering telephones or doorbells, etc. For a third group of readers, magazine reading is an incidental superficial activity carried out while changing nappies, laying the table, cooking for the family, washing clothes, etc.

A further complication arises because most magazine readers are selective in what they choose to read. And what they select to read may not sometimes be to their liking. Measuring popularity is as slippery an exercise as the attempt by marketing agencies to measure 'readership'. Such attempts can at best provide only 'guestimates' rather than accurate statistical data. But since such guessing exercises are presented in statistical terms and in convincing graphics, the impression propagated (by the media primarily) is that 'scientific' surveys have been conducted.

Table 5: *Projected Growth of Print Media in India*

Year	Circulation (in '000s)
2007	135,000
2008	153,000
2009	173,000
2010	195,000

(Source: *FICCI-PwC – 2006*)

The Business of News: New Trends

The print media continue to obtain the largest slice of the total annual advertising spend of around Rs. 17,500 crore. Their share amounts to 45-48% while that of the broadcast media is about 40%.[39] Daily newspapers garner as much as 95% of the print media's share of advertising revenue; magazines fetch a

---

39 AdEx-India – June 2008. Quoted in *Business Standard*, 9-10 August 2008, p. 4.

mere five per cent.[40] What's most striking is the share of the Times of India/BCCL group of media companies: it grabs no less than 20% of the country's total adspend.[41] It is this mighty clout that has transformed the group into India's most powerful media conglomerate. It is no wonder therefore that the Times of India publications rule the roost, charge exorbitant ad rates and hike them regularly. In mid-2008, for instance, their ad rates were raised by a hefty 40% at one go in order 'to offset higher input cost'; the international price of newsprint had gone up by 50% around the same time. The Indian Newspaper Society (INS) pleaded with the Directorate of Advertising and Visual Publicity (DAVP) to raise its ad rates (which are much lower than commercial rates) by at least 50%.[42] DAVP commercials make up about 15% of the total ad volumes of the Times of India, and 10-15% of the Hindu.[43] Data from INS' annual report for 2007-2008 reveals that DAVP contributed Rs. 113.97 crore to the total ad revenues of Rs. 11,262 crore, reported by 273 members.

While INS has 737 members, the reporting members are the larger, profitable publications that usually account for more than 80% of the industry's revenues. DAVP, various government entities, and tender ads together contributed Rs. 998 crore, or about eight per cent of ad revenues.[44]

Table 6: Top Advertisers in Print Media[45]

Category/Sector	Share (%)
1. Educational Institutions	17
2. Services	12
3. Banking/Finance/Investment	11
4. Social Advertisements	7
5. Properties/Real Estate	4
6. Automobile Sector	3
7. BSNL/Telecom Sector	3

40 Ibid.
41 Ibid.
42 K.K. Sruthijith: '*Government Rates on Print Ads Go Up*', MINT, 1 September 2008, p. 1, 3.
43 Ibid.
44 Ibid.
45 AdEx-India. Op. cit.

The unprecedented growth of the print and electronic news media in India over the last decade has given rise to new patterns of media ownership and to unexpected changes in the news values and news formats. In mid-2007 there were 62,483 newspapers registered with the Registrar of Newspapers for India (RNI); AC Nielsen/TAM-India reported that as many as 50 around the clock television news channels in English and 18 Indian languages. From 2003 to 2007 more than 30 newspapers and magazines were launched in quick succession and most established publications increased the number of their local editions. In no other country in the world has such a phenomenal expansion taken place. While most developed economies reported a decline in circulation and readership of news in the traditional media, the recent FICCI-Price Waterhouse Coopers survey (2007) as well as the World Association of Newspapers (WAN) survey (2007) suggests that print and electronic media in India has witnessed remarkable growth.

The Indian newspaper industry is estimated to be worth Rs. 96 billion today, but is expected to become a Rs. 170 billion business by 2010.[46] In 2006, the Government of India opened up the news media business to foreign investors. Up to 26% of foreign paid-up equity was allowed in news, with of course a whole lot of conditions. So, few international publishers have made large investments in the Indian news media. The Financial Times of London has teamed up with *Business Standard*, Henderson Media with the *Hindustan Times*, Ireland's Independent News and Media with Jagran Prakashan (publishers of *Dainik Jagran*), and the Wall Street Journal with *Mint*, a business daily of the Hindustan Times Group. *Midday* and *Asian Age* too have benefited from foreign investments.

---

46 FICCI-PcW – 2006.

Table 7: Foreign Partners of Indian Publications

Indian Publication	Foreign Investor / Partner
1. Bennett, Coleman & Co. Ltd. (BCCL)	BBC Worldwide (UK)
2. Jagran Publications/Dainik Jagran	Independent News and Media (Ireland)
3. Dainik Group/Dainik Bhaskar	Warburg Pincus
4. HT Media Ltd./Hindustan Times	Henderson Ventures
5. Ushodaya Enterprises/Eenadu	Blackstone Group
6. Amar Ujala	D E Shaw
7. HT Media Ltd. (Printing)	Hubert Burda Media (Germany)
8. HT Media Ltd.	News Corporation
9. Mint (HT Media Ltd.)	Wall Street Journal (USA)
10. Business Standard (Anand Bazaar Patrika)	Financial Times (UK)

Most Indian media companies have found that going 'public' and being 'listed' in the stock market are much more efficient strategies of acquiring funds for growing their business than the FDI route. Several media companies are now 'listed': India Today, Midday, The Hindustan Times, NDTV, and Sun TV. BBC Worldwide has bought a 20% stake in Midday Multimedia, a listed media group; CNN has a joint venture with IBN/TV-18 bouquet of TV news/business channels. And Reuters has a joint venture with the Times of India in an English news channel, *News Now*. (This came to an abrupt end in early 2008).

Further, facsimile editions of foreign news publications have come to be permitted, provided that the companies concerned are incorporated and registered in India. Such editions would, however, not be allowed to carry any Indian advertisements. In order to protect the indigenous press, the Indian Government has issued guidelines on 'Syndication'. A striking trend in the English press is the widespread use of news reports, features and columns sourced in the international newspapers such as the *New York Times*, *The Washington Post*, *The Guardian*, *The (London) Times*, *The Los Angeles Times*, and news magazines such as *Time*, *Newsweek*, *The Economist*, and *Business Week*. The editorial and op-ed pages of English dailies are packed with such 'syndicated' pieces. The government guidelines permit the publication of 'syndicated' articles in Indian newspapers but these should not exceed 20% of the total printed area of the publication. What is more, the source has to be clearly specified (say as a byline) and the article concerned should already have been published in the foreign newspaper.

Several Indian newspapers and news magazines have had a make-over during the last few years. Rapid computerization of the newsroom, digitization of news and faster and more sophisticated web offset printing equipment, has brought a new look and new feel to the print media. The challenge from television has led the revamp. The highly-commercial oriented *Times of India* set the trend by going 'all-colour'. *The Hindustan Times*, and others quickly followed suit. Even the conservative and left-of-centre *The Hindu* and its newsmagazine, *Frontline*, went the same way. *The Business Standard*, the pink paper, flush with investments from *The Financial Times* (London) took on a new look too. Further, the Indian news media have a more youthful appearance than they did about a decade ago. 'From *Malayala Manorama* in Kerala to Jagran Prakashan in Uttar Pradesh, almost every major publishing company in India has seen younger managers, usually the sons, nephews or heirs of the publishers taking over. Many of them have been educated abroad and want to grow their businesses.'[47] This is equally true of the broadcasting, digital and mobile news media where young and well-educated professionals have begun to rule the roost.

Towards 'Localisation' of the News

Owing to the immense linguistic diversity among the Indian population, the news media in India have had perforce to be as local as possible. Except for some English newspapers and news magazines, the Indian press cannot claim to be 'national'.

---

47 Vanita Kohli-Khandekar: *The Indian Media Business*, New Delhi: Response Books, 2006. p. 25.

Indeed, there is no real national daily, despite the Hindu's claim of being 'India's national newspaper since 1878'. It is printed at only a dozen cities, compared say to the Indian Express which has over 18 editions from as many cities. But Dainik Jagran and Dainik Bhaskar, the nation's top Hindi dailies, are published from more than sixty cities in north India.

By 2005, most multi-media newspapers coming out of the state capitals in the Hindi-speaking states were releasing an edition every hour, starting from the evening, with pages finely tuned to cater to combined parts of different districts in some cases. In 2003, Hindustan was releasing 24 different editions a day from three centres to cover Bihar. By mid-2005 *Dainik Jagran* was putting the number of different editions from printing centres in Uttar Pradesh at 68. While the national and international news would remain the same in these editions, the front pages looked different because of the local stories chosen to go on them, and the inside pages changed to accommodate the changing focus on different circulation areas.[48] Local editions of newspapers did create a 'local-level public sphere'[49] but also led to a 'print-mediated fragmentation of community identity, all the more ironical because of its occurrence in an information society where Internet networking was making the coming together of different levels community possible'.[50]

The key concern about such a pervasive trend in large newspapers in English, Hindi, Kannada and other languages, relates to its disastrous consequences for regional identity and regional consciousness. Newspapers established editions not so much in terms of information needs of local populations as in the need to capture the local advertising business. Ninan's study though suggests that 'the segmentations of editions had its own logic, based on circulation and market feedback. It took into account contiguity of locations and methods of distribution. But in an editorial sense the overriding logic endorsed by marketing

---

48 Sevanti Ninan: *Headlines from the Heartland*, New Delhi: Sage Publications, 2007, p. 248.
49 Ibid. p. 257.
50 Ibid.

teams was one of catering to cultural aspirations and geographical affinities. Editions were devised accordingly, cutting across administrative divisions and parliamentary as well as legislative constituencies'.

As a result, a chief minister of a state had to read several local editions of the major newspapers each morning to keep track of his state. State and district officials, bureaucrats and police make similar complaints since they need to monitor areas under their control in terms of administrative and legislative divisions. Social workers have their own grouse: they do not know what is happening outside their block. They therefore find it difficult to mobilize people for a mass movement. As one social activist of Rajasthan told Ninan: The classification of editions is anti-people. A movement originating in Udaipur remains confined to Udaipur, you never get to hear of it in Ganganagar; it never will become a movement as a result. Earlier Rajasthan Patrika used to bring it all to the whole state, whatever was happening in any district. First you made people think of themselves as part of a state, then as part of a district, then division, you shrink his identity. Now I have become someone who only belongs to one town.[51] Ninan concludes: it was the fragmenting of regional identity thanks to a multiplicity of editions, so that news that might mobilize intervention across the state remained completely localized. It would big play in the local edition, four columns, maybe even a picture. But a wry activist described it as amounting to a peacock dancing in a forest. Nobody sees it.[52]

'Localisation' is also a strong trend in television news. Here it is local cable channels that are responsible for fragmenting audiences. But Indian language news channels in English, Hindi, Tamil, Marathi, Bengali, Kannada and Malayalam integrate speakers of these languages across the nation and where these channels are accessible overseas (and a good many of them are, especially in Asia), across the whole globe. Community radio,

---

51 Ibid. p. 255.
52 Ibid.

campus radio and FM radio have the potential to provide local news in different languages and dialects across the country.

News on the Internet

Even though almost all major newspapers and news magazines have their Internet versions, few Indians read news on the Internet unless of course they live or travel overseas. They have easy and cheap access to newspapers in their own languages across the country. Daily newspapers cost much less than a cup of tea. Access to the Internet is fairly widespread in the cities, though mainly via CyberCafes, schools, colleges and offices, though the cost of access at home is still unaffordable for most Indians. Home access to the net is limited to a small minority of the upper middle class in Tier 1 and Tier 2 cities. The situation in rural areas is far worse. Except for around five thousand e-choupals (Internet Kiosks), rural India is ill-served. The largest segment of around 42 million users are in the 18-35 age group; they comprise half of all users. But only 66% of these are 'active users', that is, those who use the net at least once a month. Most are 'ever' users', those who access the net once in a way.[53]

Indian websites that are at the forefront of online journalism are timesofindia.com, hindustantimes.com, Indianexpress.com and newindpress.com. The two Indian news agencies, Press Trust of India (PTI) and the United News of India (UNI) also have their own websites, though they appear to be reluctant to make all their news stories and features available free. According to Saxena[54] most of these news sites are still a prisoner of non-resident or NRI traffic which accounts for 50-75% of all traffic. The traffic was a great bonus in the initial years of the Internet in India, when very few Indians had access to the net, and the sites could tout these figures to show their popularity... today, however, the sites want the traffic to flow from within India. But this is not happening, at least not in the numbers that the

---

53 *The Marketing White Book*, 2007-2008.
54 Sunil Saxena: 'Online Journalism in India' in Nalini Rajan (Ed.): *Indian Journalism in the 21st Century*, New Delhi: Sage Publications, 2006. pp. 275-282.

advertisers want. The result is that media sites are still not a favoured property as far as Indian advertisers are concerned. Their reluctance to include New Media in their campaign plans means less revenue for media sites and continued dependence on parent companies.[55] Where content is concerned, Saxena observes that 'three quarters of content of any newspaper site is content generated for newspapers. The remaining quarter is content that has been sourced from news agencies. There is virtually no content that is generated by the media sites.[56]

But this situation is changing rapidly. Certain types of advertising are certainly moving over to the new media. Classified advertising for matrimonials and recruitments, for instance. Take www.simplymarry.com of the Times of India Group, or www.shaadi.com, and where job sites are concerned www.naukri.com and www.jobstreet.com. They attract millions of registered users from India and also from Indians across the world. Advertising revenues from travel and holiday/leisure/ hospitality industries is gradually shifting to the net, thus depriving traditional media of much advertising support.

News Alerts on Mobiles

A few telecom service providers have begun offering 'news alerts' as a value addition service (VAS) on mobile phones. These are in the form of SMS messages. School exam results, cricket scores, results of contests, emergency messages, scotching rumours by authorities are other kinds of 'news alerts' which are offered by mobile operators. Several newspapers, news channels and telecom operators offer 'news alerts' via email. BBC, CNN, IBN and NDTV were the first to offer these services free. Further, the majority of daily newspapers and news channels pose questions for audiences to respond to via email or SMS. Polls are conducted on a daily basis by the news media on questions and issues of the day. However, while the results of the polls are widely publicized and discussed by anchors and

---
55 Ibid.
56 Ibid.

experts, the total sample of respondents and their representative nature is rarely revealed. A number of Indian newspapers and individual journalists run their own news blogs but these have not made much of a mark.

Some Controversial Practices in the Indian Press

Some newspaper publishers, under the pretext of doing 'media education' have entered schools to market their products. Such is the attempt of *The Times of India*, one of the foremost national dailies, (with a circulation of over two million copies every day), to market their daily newspapers in the schools of New Delhi, Mumbai, Pune and Bangalore. The experiment is termed 'Newspapers in Education' (NIE), and is conducted during regular school hours, not by school teachers but by young men and women carefully recruited by the Response Department (read 'Advertising Department') of the publishing house. The newspaper is used to instruct children about history, geography, science and current affairs. Children are required to buy copies of the paper in school; copies of other papers are not available in school nor are they referred to in any way by the 'visiting' teachers. In the city of Pune, parents have protested against their children being asked to buy copies of the paper in schools but to little effect; rival city dailies have got into the act too. They have offered to publish supplements with drawings and articles by school children, each issue of the supplement devoted to different schools. Officials of the Paris-based World Association of Newspapers which propagates NIE all over the world have clarified to this researcher that NIE is meant to promote education in and through newspapers, and that it is certainly not a tool for marketing specific titles. This venture is no more than a marketing strategy to promote the daily newspaper among India's school children. It's a crying shame that school authorities have given free rein to marketers from the world of the media. Newspapers undoubtedly have a place in the classroom but 'newspaper/media education' should be left to school teachers rather than to those specially recruited and paid for by the Times of India![57] Other newspapers and news channels too have made similar attempts to 'invade' the classroom. As a quid pro quo, schools receive free publicity in the media.

Another Times of India innovation in marketing is 'Medianet', the practice of selling editorial space in newspapers (especially in the city supplements) to Public Relations agencies. Paid features occur routinely in the Lifestyle sections of the City supplements of The Times of India. There would be nothing wrong with such a marketing strategy if the reader was told that it is a paid or sponsored feature. All of them carry reporters' bylines. Such features are presented as news items and lifestyle articles, giving the reader the impression that they are part of editorial space.[58] Public relations officials have gladly accepted and supported this paid-for publicity. The fear of professional journalists is that other newspapers too would emulate this practice and such 'advertorials' would become the norm in the Indian press. An even greater concern is that 'soft' stories and 'lifestyle' features will dominate the 'newshole' in order to attract the biggest advertisers.[59] Yet another uniquely Times of India practice is the so-called 'invitation price' of one rupee charged for its tabloid Mumbai/Pune/Bangalore Mirror; the tabloid is foisted on all Times of India subscribers without as much as by-your-leave! The Press Council of India and the MRTPC have evidently not been doing their job.

Like the Times of India's practice of 'Medianet' in daily newspapers, *Frontline*, the newsmagazine of the Hindu Group, has popularized a section called 'Focus' wherein institutes, companies and even state governments receive publicity, even as

---

57 I raised this concern with the representatives of the World Association of Newspapers (WAN) at a UNESCO-sponsored conference on 'Media Education and Literacy' in Paris in June 2007. WAN promotes 'Newspaper in the Classroom' worldwide as part of courses in 'media literacy' where the primary focus is critical media analysis. The representatives were amazed to learn that the Times of India, a member of WAN, used NIE to market its own newspaper to children.

58 For a more detailed discussion, see G.S. Bhargava: *The Press in India: An Overview*, New Delhi: Publications Division, 2005.

59 For some other questionable practices of the Times of India Group, see discussion above under 'Journalism as Public Relations'.

they provide advertising support on alternate pages of the section. The column/section nowhere indicates that it is an 'advertorial' or a sponsored feature.

Freedom of the Press: The Right to Publish and the Right to Privacy

The Indian Constitution confers no special rights or privileges to the press as does the First Amendment of the United States Constitution. However, Article 19(i)(a) of the Constitution does guarantee freedom of expression for every citizen which includes:

(i) the right to lay what sentiments he pleases before the public, or the right to impart information and ideas;
(ii) the right to receive information and ideas from others through any lawful medium.

It is this Article that gives editors and journalists the right to publish news or any kind of information, and to comment on public affairs, and the public the right to receive information of which the United Nations Charter of Human Rights speaks so forcefully. These are fundamental human rights. The freedom of the press rests on the same fundamental rights, and implies the right to print, publish, comment and criticize without any interference from the State or any public authority. It includes the right not to publish or comment as well. However, the freedom of the press is not absolute, just as the freedom of expression is not. Public interest has to be safeguarded; so has private interest, and the right to privacy.

Public interest is safeguarded by Article 19(2) which lays down reasonable limitations to the freedom of expression in matters affecting:

(a) sovereignty and integrity of the State
(b) security of the State
(c) friendly relations with foreign countries
(d) public order
(e) decency or morality

(f) contempt of court
(g) defamation, and
(h) incitement to an offence.

The Right to Privacy

The right to privacy, a fundamental and legal right, is enshrined in Article 21 of the Constitution which says 'No person shall be deprived of his life or personal liberty, except according to procedure established by law'. The expression 'personal liberty', according to Justice P.N. Bhagwati (in the Menaka Gandhi case, 1978), 'is of the widest amplitude and it covers a variety of rights which go to constitute the personal liberty of man'. Personal liberty gives dignity to the individual, providing him the freedom to live his own life and to do his own thing. It is the necessary means to creativity, growth, autonomy, relaxation and mental health. That explains why the dignity of the individual is ensured in the preamble of our Constitution.

Besides the Constitution, the Law of Torts assures the right to privacy of the individual. This is a branch of law based on various decisions of judges on aspects of civil wrongs which are not provided for by statutory laws but which constitute the first principles of law relating to civil wrongs.

Further, privacy is protected by laws relating to defamation, under the Indian Penal Code. Defamation is making known through words spoken or written, or through signs or visible representations (e.g., a painting, a photograph, a cartoon, and illustration), an imputation which is intended to harm the reputation of a person. The exposure of the private love-lives of film stars in film periodicals can thus be challenged under the law. However, it must be pointed out that persons who are in public life cannot claim privacy to the same extent as ordinary citizens. Sometimes, a case can be made out for the view that, such exposures have been done 'in good faith', and in the public interest or for the 'public good'. Thus, exposures of political scandals by reporters are not always defamatory. But care has to be taken that the reports or photographs published are not obscene, do not offend morality or decency, and above all, do not affect 'public order'. Further, the reports need to be substantially correct. So it is not defamatory to comment on or criticize the conduct of a public figure in the discharge of his or her public duties.

There is, then a conflict between the right to publish and the right to privacy. Yet both are equally precious in a free society. While commercial exploitation of the private lives of public figures, and of lesser fry, can help step up sales of publications, a balance has to be struck between the two rights. Journalists, therefore, have to tread warily lest they be hauled up by the law for infringement of privacy. They have to act in 'good faith' and in 'the public interest'; they must not forget that they have no legal basis to keep their sources of information to themselves. Sources have to be disclosed when asked for, either by the police, or by the Courts of Law. In most cases, however, the law respects the confidentiality of the journalists' sources unless public interest and justice are involved.

In addition to the right to publish reports on events and individuals keeping in mind the public interest, a journalist is privileged to publish 'a substantially true report of either House of Parliament or the Legislative assembly'. This 'privilege' was withdrawn during the internal emergency, but was reinstated by the 44th Amendment Act, 1978.

Press Codes and Ethics

Codes of ethics for journalists began to be formulated since the early 1920s. Today, more than 60 countries around the world have drawn up and are enforcing such codes. Of course, they vary in form and scope from one country or region to another. In some countries, the codes have been voluntarily drawn up and are imposed by professional bodies of journalists; in others, they are imposed by the governments in power. Several states enforce such codes which speak of such high-minded principles as objectivity, impartiality, truthfulness, and freedom of information.

The MacBride Report states that all journalists have responsibilities to their own convictions, but equally important are their responsibilities to the public. The Report spells out journalists' responsibilities:
(1) Contractual responsibility in relation to their media and their internal organisation.
(2) A social responsibility entailing obligations towards public opinion and society as a whole.
(3) Responsibility or liability deriving from the obligation to comply with the law.
(4) Responsibility towards the international community, relating to respect for human values.

Media Ethics
Journalistic codes usually take into account the following concepts:
(a) Safeguarding freedom of information.
(b) Freedom of access to information sources.
(c) Objectivity, accuracy, truthfulness or the non-misrepresentation of facts.
(d) Responsibility to the public, and its rights and interests and in relation to national, racial and religious communities, the nation, the State and the maintenance of peace.
(e) The obligation to refrain from calumny, unfounded accusations, slander, violations of privacy.
(f) Integrity and independence.
(g) The right of reply and of correction.
(h) Respect of professional confidentiality.
(i) Consideration for the cultural, social or ethnic codes of individual countries.

However, "the scope of professional ethics is much wider than the texts of legal codes. For, in attempting to achieve a just balance between freedom and responsibility, the ethical aspects of this dichotomy depend not only on conscious decisions by a journalist, but also on practices in the media and the general social environment."⁶⁰

The MacBride Report says that the adoption of codes of ethics at national, and in some cases, at the regional level is desirable, provided that such codes are prepared and adopted by the profession itself, without government interference. It recommends that Codes of Ethics aim at the following objectives:
(a) to protect the consumer readers, listeners, viewers, or the public in general;
(b) to protect and inspire the working journalist, broadcaster or others directly concerned with the gathering, writing, processing and presenting of news and opinions;
(c) to guide editors and others who take full legal responsibility for what is published and broadcast;
(d) to define the responsibilities of proprietors, shareholders and governments who are in a position of absolute control over any particular form of mass media communications activity;
(e) to deal with issues of advertisers and others who buy into the services of the media.⁶¹

A Code of Ethics for Indian Journalists

Attempts to draw up a code of ethics for journalists in India have so far drawn a blank. Neither the Press Council nor the All India Editors' Conference has come up with a code acceptable to the whole profession.

In 1966, the Press Council did circulate a list of guidelines to over 10,000 newspapers and journals, for their observations, but the feedback was not promising enough. In January 1976, a committee of 17 editors presented a Code of Ethics and Editors Charter to parliament, but it was suspect, evolved as it was during the emergency regime. It gave a rather tall order in stating that the press must present a truthful, comprehensive and reliable account of the events in a context which gives them meaning,

---

60 MacBride Report: *Many Voices, One World*, 1980, p.242
61 MacBride Report: p.243.

project a representative picture of constituent groups in society, regard itself as a forum for comment and criticism and discharge its social responsibilities by clarifying the goals and values of society. The All-India Small and Medium Newspapers' Association had drawn up a Code of Ethics in 1975; however, it was not approved of by the general body. The Second Press Commission (1982) maintained that it would not be desirable to draw up a Code of Ethics for newspapers. It supported the Press Council's stand that a code should be built up case by case over a period of time.[62]

The consensus, however, appears to be that the press should be trusted to regulate itself, and where it invades privacy, or distorts facts, or fosters communalism or fanaticism, the Press Council has powers enough to pull up the offending papers and magazines. One of the penalties suggested is the withdrawal of government advertisements; the other is withdrawal of accreditation to journalists. However, the Press Council has been reluctant to impose any such penalties. (For a discussion of a code of ethics for broadcast journalism, see the Section on Television).

Press Council's Guide to Journalistic Ethics

The Press Council of India has been established to 'preserve the freedom of the press and to maintain and improve the standards of newspapers and news agencies'. The Council is enjoined to 'build up' a Code of Conduct for newspapers, news agencies and journalists in accordance with high professional standards. A compendium of broad principles evolved by the Press Council through its adjudications/principles was first published in 1983-84. In October 1992, the Council published 'an updated but succinct compilation of the principles of journalistic ethics sorted out from the adjudications of the Council and the guidelines issued by it in their wake'. (The Guide to Journalistic Ethics was further revised and updated in 1995 by

---

62 K.E. Eapen: *'Journalistic Ethics and Professional Training'*, paper presented at IAMCR Barcelona, 1988.

the present Chairman, Mr. Justice P.B. Sawant). Below are excerpts from the Guidelines:

1. *Accuracy and Fairness*: The fundamental objective of journalism, declares the Guide, is to serve the people with news, views, comments and information on matters of public interest, in a fair, accurate, unbiased, sober and decent manner. Publication of inaccurate, baseless, graceless, misleading or distorted material should be avoided. All sides of the core issue or subject should be reported.

1(a) Verification and checking of news before publication is necessary where its publication and the comments based thereon can create complications, such as:
(i) where it is likely to incite communal passions
(ii) where it is of a slanderous nature.

1(b) However, failure to observe strictly this rule as to pre-publication verification would not necessarily amount to a breach of journalistic ethics on the part of the editor
(i) where the impugned news item was merely a statement made by a responsible political leader of the ruling party at a press conference or a public statement of a recognised leader, or
(ii) where the impugned news item was based on the report of an accredited correspondent.
Provided in either case it was in respect to a matter of public concern.

1(c) Unjustified rumours and surmises should not be set forth as facts.

2. Journalists should judge no one unheard.

3. *Cautions against Defamatory Writings*: Newspapers should not publish anything which is per se defamatory or libellous against any individual or organisation unless after due care and checking they have sufficient reason to believe that it is true and its publication will be for public good.

4.(a) *Pre-publication Verification of Reports Necessary*: Whenever a newspaper receives a report or article containing defamatory or derogatory imputations or comments against a public figure, public servant or public organisation, touching his/her or its public conduct or character in so far as it appears in that conduct, the editor should, before publishing it, check with due care and attention, its factual accuracy – apart from other authentic sources, with the person or the organisation concerned to elicit his/her or its version, comments or reaction and publish the same. If the person or the organisation likely to be affected by that report/article refuses to give his/her counter-version or reaction, despite sincere efforts made by the editor, a footnote to that effect should be published along with the report or the article. If from the counter-version given by the person or organisation concerned, the editor's mind is left rocking with doubt in regard to the veracity of any part of the report/article, he should omit from publication that part and publish the rest with consequential amendment, provided the editor is satisfied that the remainder is substantially accurate and its publication will be for public benefit. If such doubt permeates the whole of the report/article, the prudent course for him is not to publish it at all.

4.(b) This salutary rule of journalistic ethics and fairness follow as a necessary corollary from two basic principles: the first is a fundamental canon of natural justice, that no one should be condemned unheard. The second is, that freedom of the press is not merely a right of the publishers and editors but also of the readers'/peoples' right to know all sides of an issue of public interest. The editor, therefore, cannot refuse to publish the reply or rejoinder merely on the ground that in his opinion the story published in the newspaper was true. That is an issue to be left to the judgement of the readers.

5. *Privacy*: Instruction or invasion on the privacy of individuals is not permissible unless outweighed by genuine overriding public interest, not being a prurient or morbid curiosity. (Explanation: Things concerning a person's home, family, religion, health, sexuality, personal life and private affairs are covered by the concept of privacy excepting where any of these impinge upon the public or public interest).

Victims of Sex Crimes – Caution against Publication of Names or Pictures.

6. While reporting crimes involving rape or molestation of women, of sexual assault on children, or raising doubts and questions touching the chastity, personal character and privacy of women, the names, photographs of the victims or other particulars leading to their identity should not be published. While such publication serves no legitimate public purpose, it may bring social opprobrium to the victims and social embarrassment to their relations, family, friends, community, religious order or the institution to which they belong.

7. Newspapers to eschew suggestive guilt by association. They should not name or identify the family or relatives or associates of a person convicted or accused of a crime, when they are totally innocent and a reference to them is not relevant to the matter reported.

8. *Corrections*: When any factual error or mistake is detected or confirmed, the newspaper should publish the correction promptly with due prominence and with apology or expression of regret in a case of serious lapse.

9. (a) *Right of Reply*: The newspaper should promptly publish at the instance of the person feeling aggrieved/or concerned by the impugned publication, a contradiction/reply/rejoinder sent to the editor in the form of a letter or note. The editor has the discretion either to publish it, in full or publish its abridged and edited version, particularly when it is inordinately long. But the remainder should be an effective reply to the allegations. However, the editor is not entitled to alter, omit or refuse to publish important portions of the reply/rejoinder which effectively deal with the material allegations in the news item. If the editor doubts the truth or factual accuracy of the contradiction/reply/rejoinder, even then, it is his/her duty to publish it, with liberty to add separately at the end, an editorial comment doubting its veracity, but only when this doubt is reasonably founded on unimpeachable documentary or other evidential material in his/her possession. The editor should not,

in a cavalier fashion, without the application of mind, append such note, as: 'we stand by our story'. It must be remembered that the liberty to append an editorial comment to a rejoinder or reply, is not absolute right. It is a concession which has to be availed of sparingly with due discretion and caution in appropriate cases.

9. (b) However, where the reply/contradiction or rejoinder is being published in compliance with the direction of the Press Council, it is permissible to append a brief editorial note to that effect.

10. *Letters to the Editor*: An editor who decides to open his columns for letters on a controversial subject, is not obliged to publish all the letters received in regard to that subject. He is entitled to select and publish only some of them either in entirety or the gist thereof. However, in exercising this discretion he must make an honest endeavour to ensure that what is published is not one-sided but represents a fair balance between the views for and against with respect to the principal issue in controversy. In the event of rejoinder upon rejoinder being sent by two parties on a controversial subject, the editor has the discretion to decide at which stage to close the continuing column.

11. *Conjecture, Comment and Fact*: Newspapers should not pass on or elevate conjecture, speculation or comment as a statement of fact. All these categories should be distinctly stated.

Paramount Interests of State, Society and Rights of Individuals not to be Jeopardised.

12. Newspapers should, as a matter of self-regulation, exercise due restraint and caution in presenting any news, comment or information which is likely to jeopardise, endanger or harm the paramount interests of the State and Society, or the rights of individuals, for the protection of which reasonable restrictions may be imposed by law on the right to freedom of speech and expression under Clause (2) of Article 19 of the Constitution of India.

13. *Newspapers may Expose Misuse of Diplomatic Immunity*:

The media should make every possible effort to build bridges of co-operation, friendly relations and in developing better understanding between India and foreign states. At the same time, it is the duty of a newspaper to expose if any diplomat is trying to misuse or take undue advantage of the diplomatic immunities.

14. *Covering Communal Disputes/Clashes*: News, views or comments relating to communal or religious disputes/clashes should be published after proper verification of facts and presented with due caution and restraint in a manner which is conducive to the reaction of an atmosphere congenial to communal harmony, amity and peace. Sensational, provocative and alarming headlines are to be avoided. Acts of communal violence or vandalism should be reported in a manner as may not undermine the people's confidence in the law and order machinery of the state. Giving community-wise figures of the victims of communal riot, or writing to inflame passions, aggravate the tensions, or accentuate the strained relations between the communities/religious groups concerned, or which has a potential to exacerbate the trouble, should be avoided.

Headings should not be Sensational/Provocative and must justify the matter printed under them.

15. In general, and particularly, in the context of communal disputes or clashes –
(a) Provocative and sensational headlines should be avoided.
(b) Headings must reflect and justify the matter printed under them.
(c) Headings containing allegations made in statements should either identify the body or the source making it or at least carry quotation marks.

16. *Plagiarism*: Using or passing off the writings or ideas of another as one's own, without crediting the source, is an offence against the ethics of journalism.

17. *Recording Interviews and Phone Conversations*: Journalists should not tape-record anyone's conversation without

that person's knowledge or consent, except where the recording is necessary to protect the journalist in a legal action, or for other compelling good reason.

18. (a) *Obscenity and Vulgarity to be Eschewed*: Newspapers/journalists should not publish anything which is obscene, vulgar or offensive to public good taste.
(b) Newspapers should not publish an advertisement containing material which is unlawful or illegal, or is contrary to good taste or to journalistic ethics or proprieties.
(c) Newspapers should not display advertisements which are vulgar or which, through picture of a woman in nude or lewd posture, provoke the lecherous attention of males as if she herself was a commercial commodity for sale.
(d) While publishing the tape-recorded statement of another, the editor should delete obscene or filthy epithets offensive to good public taste, with which the person stating might have punctuated the tenor or tone or his/her answers.

19. *Glorifying violence to be Eschewed*: Newspapers/journalists should avoid presenting acts of violence, armed robberies and terrorist activities in a manner that glorifies their acts or death in the eyes of the public.

20. *Glorification/Encouragement of Social Evils to be Eschewed*: Newspapers should not allow their columns to be misused for writings which have a tendency to encourage or glorify social evils like Sati Pratha.

21. (a) *Caution in Criticizing Judicial Acts*: Excepting where the court sits in camera or directs otherwise, it is open to a newspaper to report pending judicial proceedings, in a fair, accurate and reasonable manner. But it should not publish anything:
(i) which, in its direct and immediate effect, creates a substantial risk of obstructing, impeding or prejudicing seriously the due administration of justice;
or
(ii) is in the nature of a running commentary or debate, or records the paper's own findings, conjectures, reflections or

comments on issues, sub-judice, and which may amount to arrogation to the newspaper the functions of the court
or
(ii) regarding the personal character of the accused standing trial on a charge of committing a crime.

(b) Newspapers should not as a matter of caution, publish or comment on evidence collected as a result of investigative journalism, when, after the accused is arrested and charged, the court become seized of the case; nor should they reveal, comment upon or evaluate a confession allegedly made by the accused.

(c) While newspapers may, in the public interest, make reasonable criticism of a judicial act or the judgement of a court for public good; they should not cast scurrilous aspersions on, or impute improper motives or personal bias to the judge; nor should they scandalise the court or the judiciary as a whole, or make personal allegations of lack of ability or integrity against a judge.

(d) Newspapers should, as a matter of caution, avoid unfair and unwarranted criticism which, by inured, attributes to a judge extraneous consideration for performing an act in due course of his/her judicial functions, even if such criticism does not strictly amount to culpable Contempt of Court.

22. *Newspapers should avoid crass commercialism*: While newspapers are entitled to ensure, improve or strengthen their financial viability by all legitimate means, they should not engage themselves through the print media, in gross commercialism or unseemly, cut-throat competition with their rivals, for earning ever more profits for their proprietors, in a manner which is repugnant to high professional standards and good taste, and tends to downgrade the primary role of the free press as an essential institution of democracy to a secondary, subservient place.

23. *Photographs of Dead Bodies of Victims of Crimes/ Accidents*: Photo-journalism is an important part of the print media. While intrusion through photography into personal grief likely to hurt sentiments or arouse communal passions, should be

avoided, publication of photographs serving the larger public interest cannot be termed unethical or in bad taste.

In the Indian environment, publication of the photographs of the dead bodies of the victims of accidents or natural calamity may not be per use wrong unless objected to by near relations of the deceased.

24. (a) *Caste, Religion or Community Disclosures to be Generally Avoided*: In general, the identification of a person belonging to scheduled caste or depressed class, with reference to his caste or by use of the word 'Harijan' should be avoided, particularly when in the context it conveys a sense or attributes a conduct or practice derogatory to that caste.

(b) It is not desirable for a journalist to describe a person accused of an offence by mentioning his caste when the caste does not have anything to do with the offence or the crime and plays no part either in the identification of any accused or proceeding, if there be any.

(c) Except when it becomes relevant and material, it is not proper and desirable to mention the caste, religion or community of an assailant or victim in a news item. Mention of caste, creed, religion, or community usually serves no useful purpose, but may at times have the unfortunate effect of creating ill-feeling among communities and individuals.

25. *Editor's Responsibility for all matter published in the Newspaper*: The editor shall assume responsibility for all matter, including advertisements, published in the newspaper. If responsibility is disclaimed, this shall be explicitly stated before hand.

(b) Unconfirmed news shall be identified and treated as such.

26. *Confidence to be Respected*: If information is received from a confidential source, the confidence should be respected. The journalists cannot be compelled by the Press Council to disclose such source; but it shall not be regarded as a breach of journalistic ethics if the source is voluntarily disclosed in proceedings before the council by the journalist who considers it necessary to repel effectively a charge against him/her. This rule requiring a newspaper not to publish matters disclosed to it in

confidence, is not applicable where
(a) consent of the source is subsequently obtained.
(b) the editor clarified by way of an appropriate footnote that since the publication of certain matters were in the public interest, the information in question was being published although it had been made 'off the record'.

27. *Dummy Advertisements*: Publication of dummy advertisements that have neither been paid for, nor authorised by the advertisers, constitute breach of journalistic ethics.

Censorship in the Press

With the return of the emergency regime in 1978, the threats of freedom of the press grew more ominous than ever. In a case involving a newspaper, the Supreme Court ruled that "the freedom of the press rests on the assumption that the widest possible dissemination of information from diverse and antagonistic sources is essential to the welfare of the public". It also held that "it would certainly not be legitimate to subject the press to laws which would curtail circulation".

The newsprint advisory committee of the Central Government once considered proposals to deny newsprint to papers 'indulging in anti-national activities', as also to those 'found guilty by a court of law or censured by the Press Council for publishing material which is obscene or against good taste or which advocates violence, spreads ill-feeling between various communities or is likely to endanger the unity and integrity and defence of the country'. Such a move would kill whatever semblance of press freedom we have today, for as the Editors' Guild's response indicates, 'the powers sought by the government are omnibus in nature and the so-called defences are vaguely defined'. As though the monopolistic control in newsprint were not enough, the Government has licensed all import of printing machinery, and prohibited any direct subscription to a foreign news agency. It has to be channelled through the government. By mid-2008, however, the Government had 'liberalised' the import of newsprint, printing machinery and other infrastructure-related equipment. (India has to import fifty per cent of its annual newsprint consumption of 1.6 million tonne: in 2006 it imported 0.8 million tonne).[63]

Yet another lever of control exercised tactfully by the Government is the issue of advertisements by the Directorate of Advertising and Visual Publicity (DAVP) – a body that undertakes visual publicity campaigns on behalf of various ministries, departments and autonomous bodies. Besides, State Governments too have their own publicity departments. Medium and small newspapers are beholden to these bodies for very often their very sustenance depends on the largesse from them.

Volume 2 of the Annual Report of the Ministry of Information and Broadcasting provides an exhaustive list of the amount paid each year by the DAVP to the big, medium and small newspapers for buying space for advertising. The big papers earn the highest amounts. For instance, the Mumbai edition of the *Times of India* earns as much Rs. 14 million and the *Indian Express* around Rs. 4 million every year.[64]

Moreover, the threats of pre-censorship, of confiscation of printed copies and seizure of printing presses, and of the cutting off of electricity to newspaper establishments – all reminiscent of the dark days of the emergency – are not imaginary fears. The suppression of the *Asli Bharat* and some other publications that reported the Moradabad riots, and of the Assam press during the agitations in that State, are still fresh in freedom-lovers' minds. The Assam High Court's striking down of the Assam State's Special Powers Press Act, under which pre-censorship was clamped, demonstrates how the only protection press freedom in India can hope to get is from the Courts. Or, from a vigilant public, as the withdrawal of the Bihar Press Bill (1982) demonstrates. In early June 2008, another type of censorship reared its ugly head, this time in Gujarat where the Resident Editor of the *Times of India* was charged with 'sedition' (rather than 'defamation') by Ahmedabad's police commissioner whose

---

63 Report in *Business Standard*, 6-7 October 2007, p. 12. The country's 600-odd paper mills together have an installed capacity of eight million tonne.
64 Ministry of Information and Broadcasting: *Annual Report – 1996*.

alleged links with the underworld mafia had been exposed by the paper.

Far more worrying than the external threats of censorship are the internal threats from proprietors, senior journalists and news editors who would rather play safe than endanger their own interests, both professional and material. 'Self-censorship' in journalism, not so much out of concern for public welfare and interest, but rather out of a desire to curry favour with local politicians, advertisers and other lobbyists, has led to a decline in the credibility of the press. In Maharashtra, for instance, it is a regular practice for journalists to act as the public relations agents of sugar barons, builders and local politicians.

Media Laws

Besides the restrictions imposed on the press by the Constitution, there exist various other laws which further curtail press freedom and the right of the citizen to information, as well as the right to freedom of speech and expression. They are all in force in the interest of public order and the sovereignty and security of the State.

(1) The Indian Penal Code, 1860 which makes it an offence (a) to incite enmity between different classes of citizens, (b) to spread any rumours or reports likely to incite members of the Armed Forces to mutiny or failure of duty, (c) to cause alarm to any section of the public whereby there is an inducement to commit an offence against the State or against public peace, (d) to incite one class or community against another, (e) to utter words or to make visible representations with intent to wound religious feelings or beliefs of another person, or of any class of citizens.

(2) The Indian Telegraph Act, 1885 which empowers the State to intercept, detain, or not to transmit any message, in the interest of public safety, public order, the sovereignty and integrity, and security of the State. Press messages intended to be published in India by correspondents accredited to the Central Government or a State Government can be intercepted or detained only during a public emergency.

(3) Indian Post Office Act, 1898 which gives the State or its representative the right to intercept, detain or not to send any indecent or obscene publications or representations.
(4) The Police (Incitement to Disaffection) Act, 1922, which provides for a penalty for spreading disaffection among the police and for related offences.
(5) Official Secrets Act, 1923 which prohibits obtaining, collecting, recording or publishing of secret government documents or photographs or sketches or models. It is this Act which prevents Indian journalists from publishing inside information about the government.
(6) The Security and Public Safety Acts of the various States. These deal with penalties for inciting commission of 'subversive' acts.
(7) The Drugs and Magic Remedies (Objectionable Advertisement) Act, 1954, which, in the interests of public health, bans advertisements of magic cures of sexual ailments, and the like.
(8) Section 11 of the Customs Act, 1962 which gives Government the power to ban import and export of goods in the interests of security, public order, and decency and morality.
(9) The Criminal Procedure Code, 1973 which empowers the State to forfeit copies of a publication that offends Indian Penal Code provisions relating to public order or security of the State.
(10) The Young Persons (Harmful Publications) Act, 1956 disallows publication and circulation of any literature likely to encourage anti-social tendencies among children.
(11) Contempt of Courts Act, 1971 relates to the wilful disobedience of judicial orders and the like, and to any publication which interferes with or undermines the administration of justice. For example, a journalist is guilty of contempt of court if he or she publishes a report on a case held in camera (in the private chamber of the judge).
(12) The Copyright Act, 1957 (as amended up to August 1984) which protects the original works of writers, artists,

musicians, dramatists, film and video producers and other creative persons from being pirated.
(13) The Indecent Representation of Women (Prohibition) Act, 1986.
(14) The National Security Act, 1980.
(15) The Unlawful Activities (Prevention) Act, 1967.

Press Ownership and India's Media Conglomerates

The Indian press has been a private commercial enterprise from the days of its pioneers, Buckingham and Hickey. The trend towards individual ownership and later concentration of ownership was already discernible in pre-Independent India. Today, individuals own the largest number of newspapers with a circulation of more than a third of the total circulation. Joint stock companies, many of them industrial and commercial ventures, constitute another third of the share of circulation. It is to be noted that Government publications are few in comparison, and have a mere two per cent of the circulation. Most of these government publications would be by Government departments at the Centre or in the States. Finally, there is a small number of newspapers brought out by cooperatives, religious and political groups, or by journalists themselves.

Table 8: Ownership Pattern of Newspapers

Form of Ownership	Number of Newspapers	Percentage
Individuals	5,680	78.6
Joint Stock Companies	973	13.5
Firms/Partnership	169	2.3
Trusts	147	2.2
Societies and Associations	134	1.9
Government (Central/State)	64	0.9
Others	48	0.7
TOTAL	7,225	99.9

(*Source: Press in India – 2006). N.B. This data relates only to the 7225 publications that submitted their Annual Reports to RNI in 2006.*

Concentration of ownership or monopolies in the sphere of newspaper and magazine publishing takes the form of industrial houses bringing our multiple-audience publication such as morning and evening papers and dailies for the general reader, specialist dailies for businessmen and professionals, as well as women's magazines, children's periodicals, business weeklies, science journals, and even comics. The Times of India group (Bennett, Coleman & Co. Ltd.) is the largest publishing house bringing out regularly all these types of publications, but the group cannot be said to have a monopoly.

Table 9: Major Newspaper Publishing Groups

1. Bennett, Coleman and Co. Ltd.	8. Malayala Manorama Group
2. Jagran Prakashan	9. The Thanthi Trust
3. The Hindustan Times Group	10. Ushodaya Enterprises
4. Dainik Bhaskar Group	(Eenadu Group)
5. Anand Bazaar Patrika Group	11. Deccan Chronicle Group
6. Kasturi and Sons	12. Lok Prakashan
(The Hindu Group)	13. Sakaal Papers
7. Living Media India	14. Rajasthan Patrika.

The Indian Express group, its closest competitor, is owned by the Goenka industrial house, and publishes its daily from as many as 20 cities, and boasts the largest circulation. Goenka may be a 'press baron', but like Sahu Jain, he does not have a sole monopoly. The Times of India Group, the Anand Bazar Patrika group, and the Hindustan Times group (owned by the Birlas), Living Media (publishers of India Today and the owners of the Aaj Tak bouquet of TV channels) are the other contenders. In Kerala, the Malayalam Manorama group rules the roost.

Ownership of newspapers is thus concentrated in the hands of these few groups which as a result wield much power. The concentration of ownership is a major threat to a free press, for it considerably narrows the range of opinion and the field of debate. This range is further narrowed when cross-media ownership becomes the norm. Newspaper publishers like the

Times of India, India Today, Eenadu and Dainik Jagran have moved into television network ownership, and television networks (e.g. Zee Television, Sun TV), in their turn have turned their attention to newspaper publishing. This consolidation of media properties leads to greater commercialization of news, as also to the decline of the public sphere. It is true, as Vanita Kohli-Khandekar[65] argues, that there are no 'media conglomerates' in India to match the size of News Corporation, Time-Warner, Disney or Viacom; neither are there 'media monopolies' such as those of Silvio Berlusconi in Italy. Most media companies in India are in the Rs. 200-500 crore range. India's largest media house, Bennett, Coleman and Company Limited (BCCL) stands at a grand Rs. 1,808 crore. That is equal to just over $420 million. Rupert Murdoch's News Corporation, the world's fifth largest media company, is $22 billion or over Rs. 94,600 crore. So India's largest media company is a fraction of the size of the world's fifth largest. But News Corporation is a major player in India through the STAR network in Hindi, Vijay TV (in Tamil), FM radio channels, film and TV production and its web portals www.indya.com, www.indyarocks.com (a video-sharing site) and www.myspace.com (a social networking site). Major newspaper publishing groups have tried to emulate the News Corp example.

True again, that Indian media ownership is fragmented because of the large populations and the many languages that need to be catered to. So *Dainik Jagran* (with 32 editions in 11 States) dominates the Hindi belt, Sun TV and *Dinakaran* the south Indian belt, and Eenadu (the newspaper and TV network) dominates in Andhra Pradesh, but also parts of other States where part of its TV network in various languages (Bangla, Marathi, Urdu) is transmitted. But the growing trend towards cross-media consolidation is undeniable. Reliance Communications (RComm) is perhaps the foremost example of this.

---

65 Vanita Kohli-Khandekar: 'Do We Need Cross-Media Regulation?' in Asha Rani Mathur (Ed.): *The Indian Media: Illusion, Delusion and Reality*, New Delhi: Rupa & Co., pp.224-232.

THE MASS MEDIA - HISTORY, PRACTICES, VALUES

Table 10: India's Major Media Conglomerates

• ADAG-Reliance Communications (RComm)
• Bennett, Coleman & Co. Ltd. (BCCL)
• Jagran Prakashan
• Dainik Bhaskar Group
• Zee Network
• STAR-India
• NDTV (New Delhi Television)
• Sahara India
• Hindustan Times Media
• Living Media
• Eenadu/Yashodaya Group	• Sun Network
• UTV Software Communications
• Ananda Bazaar Patrika
• Malayala Manorama
• Sony Entertainment Television (SET)
• The Hindu Group (Kasturi & Sons)
• INX Media
• Pritish Nandy Communications
• Rajshri Productions
• BAG Films
• IBN (Global Broadcast News)
• Sakaal Group
• Network-18

Almost every major newspaper publisher in India owns at least one television and FM radio channel. So, the country's largest chain of newspapers, the Bennett Coleman/Times of India Group, has *Times Now*, a television news channel in partnership with Reuters, and also a lifestyle channel called simply *Zoom*. The Times of India Group has teamed up with the BBC to publish the latter's magazines. Living Media, the publisher of *India Today* (in English and four Indian languages) and a host of American/European magazines, such as Cosmopolitan, Vogue, Men's Health, owns a bouquet of news channels: *Headlines Today, Aaj Tak,* and *Aaj Tak Delhi*. TV18, a television production house, has teamed up with CNN to launch *CNBC-TV 18* and *Awaaz*, two business news channels, and IBN has joined with CNN to launch the *CNN-IBN* and *IBN-7* news channels. Other major players in the news media include the Star network and the Zee network which run news, business news and entertainment channels. Eenadu, Sun, Sahara and Asianet are the other Indian language networks that include news channels and sports channels in their bouquets. The public service Doordarshan network has a huge bouquet of over 20 channels, with DD News being their flagship news channel. BBC World and CNN-International too are major players in the Indian news media scene; other overseas players include Deutsche Welle-TV, ABC-Asia Pacific, CCTV and TV-Monde Asia.

The Business Press

Business magazines like *Business India*, *Business World*, *Business Today* and *Outlook Business* are of special interest to the corporate world, to business and finance professionals. Business/Financial Journalism has grown in esteem over the last decade, and is one of the highest paid professions in communications today. Every daily newspaper of repute has its 'pink' counterpart in the form of a sister publication or of a separate section/supplement. Thus the Times of India has *The Economic Times*, the Indian Express the *Financial Express*, the Hindu its *Business Line*, the Ananda Bazar Patrika its *Business Standard*, the Hindustan Times (in collaboration with the Wall Street Journal) its *Mint*, and the Deccan Chronicle its *Financial Chronicle*. Among the Indian language business dailies are *Nafa Nuksan* (Hindi) from the Jagran Group, *Vyapar* (Hindi and Gujarati) from the Janmabhoomi Group and *Vyapar Kesari* (Hindi) from the New Delhi-based News Services Online.

Table 11: Readership of Business Newspapers

The Economic Times	868,000
Hindu Business Line	173,000
Financial Express	93,000
Business Standard	75,000

(**Source:** *Indian Readership Survey – IRS: 2006, Round 1.*)

Table 12: Readership of Business Magazines

Business Today	716,000
Business India	526,000
Business World	335,000
Outlook Money	1,91,000
Capital Market	104,000
Dalal Street Investment Journal	182,000

(**Source:** *Indian Readership Survey –IRS: 2006-Round I*)

Some Media Organisations

The Press Council of India

The practice of instituting a Press Council to safeguard the interests of a free press was first initiated by Sweden. Presently, more than 40 countries have set up Press Councils. In India, the institution of a Press Council functioned from November 1966 to January 1, 1976, under the Indian Press Council Act 1965. But the emergency regime wound it up. The short-lived Janata regime reconstituted it in April 1979 under a new Press Council Act, 1978, as it felt that the liberty of the press needed to be upheld by the press itself.

The Press Council of India is a statutory body, and not a voluntary organisation as in the U.K. and other Commonwealth countries. It consists of 28 members, headed by a Chairman who is nominated by a committee made up of the Chairman of the Rajya Sabha, the Speaker of the Lok Sabha and an elected representative of the Council members. Of the 28 members, 13 are nominated in accordance with the procedure prescribed from among working journalists, of whom six are editors of newspapers and the other seven working journalists other than editors. Six members represent various interests like those of the owners of big, medium, and small newspapers, and of news agencies. Besides, there are five MPs nominated by the Speaker of the Lok Sabha, and two from the Rajya Sabha. Representation is also provided to specialists in law, education, literature, science and culture.

This representative body has the power to warn, admonish, and censure any editor or journalist who flouts the standards of journalistic ethics or public taste. It has the powers of a Civil Court and can, therefore, summon witnesses, inspect documents and receive evidence. Cases relating to the laws of libel, obscenity and contempt, as also the invasion of privacy can be taken up by it for adjudication. It handles about 500 complaints against newspapers and journalists every year.

The Indian Press Council has, besides, 'not only to help

newspapers and news agencies to maintain independence, but also to build up principles for maintenance of high standards of the journalistic profession with a stress on public taste, and fostering a due sense of rights and responsibilities of citizenship. It is for the Press Council to keep under review all developments likely to restrict the supply and dissemination of news of public interest, including the question of concentration of ownership of newspapers and news agencies, that may affect the freedom of the press.'[66]

In June 1980, the Council decided to recommend to the Central Government the need to amend the Press Council Act, 1978 so as to empower it to take penal action against defaulting newspapers 'which are indicted or censured', for infringement of journalistic ethics. The action suggested against newspapers was cessation of Central and State Government advertisements; and against journalists and editors, the withdrawal of accreditation facilities. The Second Press Commission recommended the arming of the Press Council with power to improve penalties but the Editors' Guild has not approved the move.

Audit Bureau of Circulation Ltd. (ABC)

The ABC is a private body whose members are 252 regional and national publishers, and 208 leading advertisers, news agencies, and advertising agencies. It surveys the circulation of publications in English, Hindi and 12 regional languages, in more than 50 major Indian towns.

ABC carries out circulation surveys on a regular basis and issues 'Certificates of Net Paid Circulation' every six months. It has a very high reputation for reliability and impartiality, and is therefore quoted with authority. Like the NRS, ABC too is urban-oriented. Ninety percent of publications are not members of the ABC; barely 20 of the English weeklies, and an equal number of the Hindi dailies are enrolled as members. Yet it is contended by advertisers, that ABC covers the entire 'Indian'

---

[66] Justice A.N. Grover, Former Chairman, Press Council of India, Vidura, February, 1980.

daily press. The fact is that a good number of members do not submit their circulation figures for verification. 'Not Received' (NR) is a familiar feature in the auditor's reports.

Registrar of Newspapers for India (RNI)
Established on July 1, 1956, the RNI functions as a Central Government body (under the Ministry of Information and Broadcasting) responsible for the compilation of a Register giving particulars like ownership and circulation of all newspapers published in India. Besides, it oversees the allocation of titles, newsprint, and certificates for the import of printing and allied machinery required by newspaper establishments. It also sees to the enforcement of the provisions of the Press and Registration of Books Act, and has the authority to inspect newspapers' records and documents. It carries out frequent checks to find out whether the newspapers registered with it are published regularly, and also whether the circulation figures claimed by newspapers are credible. It compiles the Annual Report, 'Press in India', which is a major source for hard data on the over-48,000 newspapers and magazines in the country.

Indian Newspaper Society (INS)
The INS, formerly the Indian and Eastern Newspapers Society (IENS), was established in 1939 to represent the interests of newspaper publishers and to promote the freedom of the press in the sub-continent. After independence, the INS negotiated the import of equipment and newsprint price and, in general safeguarded the business and the profession from interference from the government. It stood opposed to the entry of foreign newspapers and foreign investment. After liberalization of the economy though, this policy has been watered down. As a consequence, the INS has gone along with the Government's policy of allowing FDI up to 26% in newspapers and news magazines and 100% FDI in non-news publications.

In 2008 INS had only 670 members out of a total of over 45,000 publications. Around 50 mainstream publications controlled the body whose main occupation now has become the accreditation of advertising agencies and more significantly, the monitoring of payments due to newspaper publishers from advertising agencies. It issues notices to ad agencies for delaying payments and where dues are not cleared de-accreditation is threatened. More than 775 advertising agencies have been accredited by the INS. It is widely believed that the primary mission of INS today is to safeguard the business interests of its members rather than the promotion of the freedom of the press and ethical professionalism.

Other trade associations of the news media in India include: Indian Federation of Working Journalists (IFWJ), the Indian Journalists Union (IJU), the Indian Language Newspapers Association, the Hindi Samachar Patra Sammelan, the Association of Small Newspapers of India, the Editors Conference, the Editors Guild, the Working News Cameraman's Association, and the News Broadcasters Association (NBA).

International News Agencies

A news agency, according to a UNESCO definition, is "an undertaking whose principal objective, whatever its legal form, is to gather news and news material of which the sole purpose is to express or present facts, and to distribute this to a group of news enterprises, and in exceptional circumstances to private individuals, with a view to providing them with as complete and impartial a news service as possible against payment, and under conditions compatible with business laws and usage." In the new millennium, however, such a definition of a news agency sounds rather dated. Transnational agencies today are large corporations making their profits largely from the sale of financial and market data provided to clients around the world; the commercial clients far outnumber news enterprises. Further, the kind of 'facts' they present are highly selective, of primary interest to the world of business and commerce in the West, and thus are in no way 'complete' and 'impartial'. The services the agencies provide are not just text, but also relate to audio, video, photography and all kinds of data. The business of some national agencies too has grown and expanded through diversification.

The major transnational news agencies continue to be 'the big four': Reuters of Britain, AP (Associated Press) of the United States of America, AFP (Agence France Presse), and UPI (United Press International) of the United States, though the last has lost much of its international market since the late eighties, except in South America. Other large transnational news agencies include DPA (Deutsche Presse Agentur) of Germany, Itar-Tass of Russia, and MENA (Middle East News Agency) of Egypt. Reuters-TV and APTN (Associated Press Television News) are the television wings of the agencies; AFP too has entered the television news business. The Eurovision News Exchange (EVN), a 66-member consortium of public broadcasters, is yet another major player in television news serving EuroNews, the pan-European television channel, and also the English, French, German, Italian and Spanish broadcasters as well as broadcasting channels around the world. EVN's exchange with regional broadcasting consortia like Arabvision, Afrovision, Caribvision and Asiavision is largely one-way.[67]

The major financial and business news agencies are Reuters, Dow Jones, Bloomberg Information Service and Bridge Information Systems. In early 1998, Dow Jones sold its market units to Bridge Information Systems for $510 million. While Reuters distributes financial data to over 362,000 computer terminals, Dow Jones and Bridge Information Systems offers its data on equities, foreign exchange, derivatives and commodities to over 105,000 subscriber, and Bloomberg to over 75,000 terminals.[68] Reuters has a staff of over 17,500 in 94 countries; as many as 2400 of this number are editorial staff, journalists, photographers and camera crew posted in 196 countries and

---

67 See Daya Kishan Thuss: *International Communication*, London: Arnold, 2000. p. 160.
68 'Dow Jones sell market unit to Bridge Information Systems for $510 million', Report in *The Economic Times*, March 19, 1998, p.11.

serving 131 countries.[69] More than ninety per cent of its revenue is from its financial services business.[70] In 2007-2008, the Thomson Group (Canada) took over Reuters (it is now Thomson-Reuters plc) while NewsCorp bought up Dow Jones and its prestigious Wall Street Journal. The merger and acquisition (M and A) trend has yet to touch the Indian media business, despite the liberalization of the economy and the entry of big players like Reliance, Tata's, NewsCorp, Time Warner and Reuters into the news business.

Thomson Reuters in India

Thomson Reuters has set up shop in a big way in the cities of New Delhi and Bangalore, with a staff of over three thousand. It has taken a 26% stake in News Now, the television news joint venture with the Times of India and a 41% stake in Asia News International (ANI). Reuters has launched a web portal www.reuters.co.in and a WAP portal http://wap.reuters.co.in, on which news videos from News Now and ANI feature regularly. Besides, Reuters-India has, in collaboration with the Maharashtra government, established Reuters Market Light (RML) to provide timely information to farmers in rural areas of the State. Reuters' other ventures include 'Pluck' a blog syndication network. At the time of India's independence Reuters' most profitable market was this country; it has now returned with a vengeance to reclaim that territory. The post-millennium history of the news agency business is being quietly re-written by Reuters-India.

Challenging the Transnationals' Dominance

Regional 'news exchanges' were started in the 1980s to counter the dominance of the 'big four'. These included OPECNA – the news agency of the OPEC countries; the Non-Aligned News Agency Pool (NANAP); and Deterrin, the transnational news agency founded by both developed and developing countries, and operated by all participating countries.

---

69 See Reuters' official website http://about.reuters.com. Accessed on 8 April 2008.
70 Ibid.

Two news exchanges serve the South American region: the Accion de Sistemas Informativos Nacionales (ASIN) and the Agencia Latinamericana de Informacio (ALAI). The Pan African News Agency (PANA) serves the African Continent, CANA, the Carribean region, OANA, the Asia-Pacific region, and PACNEWS the Pacific region. An international news agency established recently, and of interest to Indian newspapers, is the IANS (India Abroad News Service) with its headquarters in New York. But none of these has made the slightest dent in the international news business.

The biggest challenge perhaps to western dominance of international news has come from the tiny Gulf kingdom of Qatar. Al-Jazeera, the independent Arabic television channel launched in 1996 in Qatar's capital Doha, with assistance from the Emir of Qatar, has covered the invasions of Afghanistan and Iraq as also the Israeli occupations of Palestinian territories and the invasion of Lebanon with a perspective that has drawn flak from the western media, terming it propagandistic and supportive of Al-Qaida, merely because it happens to broadcast audiotapes and videos from that group's leaders. But what really irritates the dominant news players is that it presents an alternative perspective of the news and exposes the ground realities of the invasions and the occupations. Several Arab nations have banned the channel's reporters; cable companies in the United States have banned it too, but its popularity among Arab communities around the world has grown manifold. By mid-2007 its viewership was estimated to have crossed 40 million. While it is available free in Arab countries, it is a pay channel in North America and Europe. Al-Jazeera launched its English channel in 2007; its website www.aljazeera.net (which was defaced in New York when it first launched), is available in Arabic and English versions (www.english.aljazeera.net). For Indian viewers, the prime time daily news bulletin of the channel is available on India TV, though dubbed in Hindi.[71] Al-Arabiya,

---

71 Cf. M. El-Nawawy and A. Iskander: *Al-Jazeera: The Story of the Network that is Rattling Governments and Redefining Modern Journalism*, Cambridge, MA: Westview, 2003.

the satellite TV channel of the Saudi royal family, has tried without much success to wean away Al-Jazeera viewers; Al-Arabiya, with its headquarters first in London and now in Dubai, has little credibility in the Arab world. Al-Jazeera and Al-Arabiya are news channels, not news agencies, but they compete with the transnationals in the sale and distribution of actuality footage about the Arab world.

One of the world's foremost 'alternative' news agencies is the Inter Press Service (IPS), with its headquarters in Rome. It has a bureau in New Delhi, besides other capitals of developing countries. IPS takes a deliberate 'third world' approach to social processes and issues. It decries 'spot reporting' and event and people-oriented news, and concentrates on analytical features. Its major interest is in placing issues in their context, to offer discussions on the 'why' of issues rather than the 'what', when', 'where' or 'who'.

There are now more than a hundred news agencies in the world. Around 90 countries have their own national news agencies while 40 countries do not have any agency at all. News agencies in 50 out of the 90 countries are directly under the control of the State, while the remaining 40 are owned and run jointly by newspapers and the media. Yet few of them are really autonomous, and totally free from political and commercial influences.

News Agencies in India

K.C. Roy, an Indian journalist during the early years of this century, set up the first Indian news agency called the Press News Bureau (PNB). S. Sadanand established a nationalistic news agency in the 1930s, known as the Free Press of India (FPI), but could not afford to keep it going for more than a couple of years. In 1933, the United Press of India (UPI), rose out of FPI's ashes, and proved to be a great success. Until independence, Reuters (a British news agency), and UPI were the main sources of news for Indian newspapers.

By 1949, the Indian and Eastern Newspaper Society had started its own agency – The Press Trust of India (PTI), which purchased Reuters, while UPI still struggled on, providing little or no competition. In 1958, UPI died a slow death, leaving PTI alone in the field, with a vast countrywide teleprinter network, and employing many journalists and stringers.

United News of India (UNI)

Before long, however, United News of India (UNI), a competitive news agency was set up by Dr B.C. Roy, and sponsored by eight national dailies. Within a decade, it could match the services of PTI in the collection and distribution of news. It now has correspondents in over 200 Indian towns and cities, and around a hundred bureaux across the nation. The various services it offers to its over a thousand subscribers in India (and 30 abroad), include UNIFIN, a finance and banking service, UNISTOCK, a service for stock exchanges, and UNISCAN, a news service fed directly into television sets. Besides, it has a national photo service and supplies computer-designed graphics in ready-to-use form on economic and other topics.

Press Trust of India (PTI)

PTI too has expanded its services considerably, and has foreign correspondents in New York, Moscow, Kathmandu, Colombo, London and other world capitals. It employs over a thousand journalists and technical staff manning around a hundred offices in the country. Its news services have been computerised, and among the many services it offers to its subscribers are: PTI-Stockscan, PTI-Stockscan Elect, PTI-MAG, Data India, and a screen-based news service called NEWSCAN. It has arrangements with Reuters, AFP and other agencies for news, with AP for international photographs, and with AP-Dow Jones for international economic and financial news. PTI has teamed up with AAP (Information Services of Australia), Nihon Keizai Shimbun of Japan, Antara news agency of Indonesia, and YONHAP of South Korea to form a joint venture company to gather and distribute business news on the industrialised economies of the Asia-Pacific. PTI is also part of a cooperative agreement among 12 news agencies of the Asia-Pacific region for the distribution of corporate and government press releases.[72] In March 1998, speculation was rife that Dow Jones would tie up with PTI to take on Reuters[73]. At present, the Dow Jones Services are provided by PTI because of government restrictions against direct distribution to Indian media houses. Dow Jones is reportedly helping PTI with technical assistance in its modernisation plans.[74] PTI also distributes the general news service of Reuters in India, but Reuters sells its screen-based business news independently to the press and to business.

With development loans made available by the Central Government, the two national news agencies have updated their technology of news reception and news distribution. Towards the end of 1978, UNI and PTI stepped into the age of satellite communication, discarding the outmoded radio-teletype system. They thus began to receive foreign agency and foreign correspondents' reports via satellite, and to disseminate agency copy using networked computers.

Another landmark in the modernisation of the news agencies has been the use of computers and satellite communications for prompt and in-depth analysis of the Lok Sabha and State Assembly elections since 1980. This was the first time that news agencies in any developing country had employed computers to report national elections.

While the UNI and PTI have made a great impact in the distribution of national and international news in India, they have yet to tap the interest of many foreign countries, especially of Asia, Africa and Latin America in Indian affairs. Despite the soaring costs of communications today, the effort to sell Indian news to the press, radio and TV networks around the world has yet to make a mark. A major vacuum in the Indian news business is the dire absence of Indian language news agencies. The total dependence of Indian language newspapers and television news

---

72 INDIA - 1998, New Delhi: Research and Reference Division/Publications Division.
73 'Dow Jones may tie up with PTI to take on Reuters', Report in *Business Standard*, May 25, 1998.
74 ibid.

channels on PTI and UNI and the international news agencies (Reuters, AP, AFP, DPA, ANI and IANS) which disseminate news in English distorts the process of selection and reporting of news in the various Indian languages. PTI-Bhasha and UNIVARTA, the Hindi units of PTI and UNI respectively, are exceptions to this.

Hindi News Agencies
PTI-Bhasha and UNIVARTA are the Hindi units of the two national news agencies. Until the 1980s, two Hindi news agencies: the Hindustan Samachar and the Samachar Bharati served the Hindi press. They were brought under one banner during the emergency for the ostensible purpose of starting a national news agency directly under government sponsorship. With the lifting of the emergency, however, SAMACHAR – the label under which the four agencies were merged – broke into its separate constituents again. For all practical purposes SAMACHAR functioned under government control. The Janata regime saw it as 'a deliberate design to make the news agencies serve as a tool of the ruling party', and so restored the status quo ante from April 14, 1978.

Hindustan Samachar, India's first multilingual news agency, was founded by S.S. Apte, as long back as 1948. It sought "to educate the masses to participate in national development and to strive for national integration through the promotion of all Indian languages". It achieved these aims through the distribution of news among local newspapers, first through Devanagari telegrams, and later through Devanagari teleprinters. By 1975, it had spread its network throughout the length and breadth of the country, catering to its subscribers in as many as ten Indian languages.

Samachar Bharati began its operations in 1967 supported by the governments of Bihar, Gujarat, Rajasthan and Karnataka which held almost fifty per cent of its shares. Jayaprakash Narayan was its first Chairman. Like Hindustan Samachar, though on a much more modest scale, it disseminates news in

Indian languages to the vernacular press. (Hindustan Samachar and Samachar Bharati were wound up in 1988).

Reports of the First and Second Press Commission

The First Press Commission was appointed on September 23, 1952 as a Commission of Inquiry for the purpose of 'making an inquiry into the state of the press in India, its past, present and future lines of development'. The Chairman of the Commission was Justice G.S. Rajadhyaksha; the other 10 members included Dr C.P. Ramaswami Aiyar, Dr Zakir Hussain, Dr V.K.R.V. Rao, P.H. Patwardhan, J. Natarajan, Chalapathi Rau. Its brief was to examine in particular the following vital areas of the Indian press:

1. The control, management and ownership and financial structure of newspapers, periodicals, news agencies and feature syndicates;
2. The working of monopolies and chains and their effect on the presentation of accurate news and fair views;
3. The effect of holding companies, the distribution of advertisements, and other external influences on healthy journalism;
4. The method of recruitment and training of journalists;
5. Newsprint supplies, and printing and composing machinery;
6. Machinery for ensuring high standards of journalism, liaison between Government and the press; the functioning of Press advisory committees and organisations of editors and working journalists;
7. Freedom of the press and repeal or amendment of laws not in consonance with it.[75]

Cooperation from the press and other agencies was minimal. The Commission had to send several reminders to journalists' associations, newspaper owners and editors in order to collect preliminary evidence. Out of 362 associations addressed for information, only 81 responded: only 26 out of 86 associations

---

75 MacBride Report, p. 2.

of working journalists; only one of the four associations of editors; and only eight out of 101 chambers of commerce, bothered to return the questionnaire. The response to the General Questionnaire sent out was no better: the response rate was less than five per cent: barely 318 out of 11,780 copies of the questionnaire mailed. Only 111 out of 7,335 editors of newspapers and periodicals, 41 out of 88 working journalists, ten out of 300 advertising agencies, and 77 out of 1,350 members of the public, returned the copies duly filled in. The Commission also conducted a sample survey of readers, and collected oral evidence *in camera* of over 400 witnesses in the metros.

The Commission's Report was submitted in 1954 in two parts: Part I contained the massive report and recommendations; Part II was a detailed study of the history and development of Journalism in India, researched and written up by J. Natarajan, the editor of The Tribune, and also a member of the Commission.

'It is the point of view of the public that dominates the Report and it is within this framework that the commission deals with the over-riding social aspect, the true nature of the freedom of press, the need for restraint and regulation, the healthy growth of the press, the place of small newpapers, the working of news agencies or the meaning of editorial freedom. Even the recommendations on collective bargaining and service conditions had to be viewed within the framework of public interest' (Rau, p.138).

The Report found that out of 330 dailies published at the time, five owners controlled 29 newspapers and 31.2 per cent of circulation, while a mere 15 owners controlled 54 newspapers and over fifty per cent of the circulation. The Commission warned against this tendency towards concentration of ownership, and towards monopolies. It provided a list of unfair and restrictive practices in the press, and in general the lack of financial soundness and the excessive dependence on advertising, in the industry.

The Commission's recommendations were aimed at the

development of a public service-oriented press. A major recommendation was the appointment of a Press Registrar to maintain accurate data on the press, and its working, and a Press Council to act as a watchdog on the press (through self-regulation), to help raise standards of journalism and to build up a Code of Ethics to guide journalists. It also strongly recommended the development of the Indian language press, especially the growth of small newspapers in the smaller towns. To assist in this development, it recommended to the Government the setting up of a State Trading Corporation for newsprint, a reasonable scale of tariff for news services, a price-page schedule, readjustment of advertisment allotments and rates, and elimination of unfair and restrictive practices, including crossword and other prize competitions.

Also recommended was the principle of collective bargaining and trade unionism, and the fixation of minimum wages for working journalists.

The Report argued against concentration of ownership and the rise of monopolistic trends, recommending 'diffusion of ownership and control among a large number of persons so that the chances of any dominant interests among the group of owners could be eliminated or cancelled mutually'. It further recommended that 'diffusion be brought about by the gradual distribution of shares to the employees, and to a small extent to the public, both in existing undertakings and in those to be started in future'.

The Press Registrar and the Press Council were given the responsibility of investigating into the existence of monopolies that went against public interest. The Report deprecated the pressures brought to bear on newspapers by advertisers, both corporate and Government. It condemned practices such as the publication of 'supplements' where 'a large amount of space is devoted to puffs', of reviews of the balance sheets and annual reports of only those companies that regularly advertised, of the influence of advertisers on news columns and editorials, and of the Government practice of withholding advertisements from

'Communist' and 'Communal' publications.

The Report upheld the authority and status of the Editor, and recommended that he be given administrative control over his staff, and that appointments of editorial staff be made with his consultation, as 'the future of the press depends on the independence of the editor'. It also recommended that the press eschew 'yellow journalism' and be independent, accurate and fair in the presentation of news. Besides, it recommended the streamlining of procedures of recruitment and training of journalists, and of some of the laws that related to the practice of journalism.

The Second Press Commission

The second Press Commission was set up in May 1978; the Report was submitted in 1982. Its brief was to 'enquire into the growth and status of the Indian Press since the last Press Commission reported and suggest how it should develop in future'. To begin with, Justice P.K. Goswami chaired the Commission, but he and his colleagues resigned when a new Government came to power at the Centre, in January 1980. The new Chairman was Justice K.K. Matthew and the members included Girilal Jain, Rajendra Mathur, Ranbir Singh, Amrita Pritam, P.V. Gadgil, Prof. H.K. Paranjape and others.

The terms of reference were revised, though many of the areas covered were very similar. They included the following areas:
1. The role of the Press in a developing and democratic society;
2. The adequacy of the present constitutional guarantees on the freedom of speech and expression;
3. Constitutional and legal safeguards to protect the citizen's right to privacy;
4. Safeguarding the independence of the Press against economic and political pressures, and against pressures from proprietors and management;
5. Responsibilities of the Press, especially with regard to

developmental policies;
6. The Press as an industry, a social institution and a forum for discussion of public affairs;
7. Ownership pattern, chain newspapers, management practices, financial structure, and the economics of the Press;
8. Advertising – Government and private, educational and commercial;
9. Government, Press Relations and role of official agencies;
10. Growth of small and medium newspapers and of the Indian language press; the periodical press and specialist journals;
11. News coverage and news values; news agencies and feature agencies; flow of news from and to India; the new international information order;
12. Training of journalists; research in journalism and mass communication; newspaper development.

The methods of collecting data were the same as those followed by the First Press Commission: the use of questionnaires (32 in all on various areas enumerated in the Terms of Reference), evidence from over 800 witnesses, recording of memoranda from 230 individuals and institutions, and 245 commissioned studies on various aspects of the Indian press. The Report critically analyses each of the above areas in 12 chapters, focusing on developments since 1952. Comparisons with developments in the press of other countries are frequently made. Based on this detailed analysis and criticism, the Commission drew up recommendations on each area of study.

Recommendations

The Commission saw the role of the press in a developing and democratic society as being 'neither that of an adversary nor an ally of the Government'. It declared: 'To be a mindless adversary or an unquestioning ally would be to abdicate judgement. A free press should be a constructive critic'. Hence the need for Development Journalism, for news values that are 'in the interest of social health and national development', and for Investigative Journalism which is oriented to social and economic issues.

A major concern of the Commission was 'objectionable communal writing'. It recommended that 'on the outbreak of a communal disturbance, newspapers should refrain from sensational presentation of the news and from giving community-wise figures of those killed and injured. However, when the situation gets stabilised, there should be no hesitation in investigating the causes of the rioting and its consequences, with identification of the communities concerned'. It recommended 'a stricter enforcement of the provisions in the Indian Penal Code with regard to communal incitement.' The Report thus argued for a 'positive role of the press – of bringing together the diverse elements in the nation's life by emphasising those aspects which tend towards unifying the communities', and 'strengthening of the moral fabric of society and discouraging the trend towards conspicuous and excessive consumption'. 'Public interest' should be the main criterion in Journalism, for 'the press has a social responsibility and accountability to the public'.

The Commission recommended that the Press Council should continue, but should be given powers to deny facilities of accreditation for a specific period if held guilty thrice, of violating journalistic ethics. However, 'it would not be desirable to draw up a Code of Ethics for newspapers; such a code could be built up case by case over a period of time.' A further recommendation was the amendment of Press Council Act to enable the Council to review the quality and adequacy of training facilities for journalists and for monitoring the performance of newspapers. A third recommendation was the inclusion of 'respect for privacy' in the Press Council Act of 1978, rather than any legislation incorporating a general right to privacy.

It further recommended that the editor take the responsibility for all matter published in his newspaper, including advertisements. The editor's authority should extend not only to the contents of advertisements but also to the proportion of space devoted to them. Complaints of violation of the codes of ethics governing advertising should be examined by the Press Council. The commission wanted journalists to resist external pressures and 'to be on guard against the temptation to enjoy favours, whether from Government authorities, employers, advertisers or others'.

A significant recommendation of the Report was the establishment of a Newspaper Development Commission, a body to promote the development of the press 'in directions which will facilitate the growth in particular of Indian-language newspapers of whatever circulation category, and of local interest and other publications of small and medium size in terms of circulation'. The Commission would promote research and development in the entire newspaper industry, liaise with various Government Departments concerned with the needs of the industry, and promote and coordinate training in journalism. It would be funded by an initial grant from the Government, a small cess on all newsprint consumption and a tax on advertising revenue of newspapers.

The New World Information and Communication Order (NWICO)

Proposals for a 'New World Information and Communication Order' (NWICO), during the late 1970s and early 1980s, stirred up a hornets' nest of controversy in the United Nations Educational Scientific and Cultural Organization (UNESCO). On the one side it was seen as a demand for a fair and balanced flow in international news. On the other, fears were expressed that it was an invitation to States to control the 'free' collection and distribution of news. At the centre of the turmoil were the transnational news agencies, such as Reuters, Associated Press (AP), Agence France Presse (AFP), and their television units. Criticizing them for lack of fairness and balance, the non-aligned nations established their own national and international agencies and news pools, which often were attacked, in turn, as government-controlled.

The demand for a more just and more equitable 'flow' of information and news across international borders had its roots in the struggle of the nations of Asia, Africa, Latin America and, later, Eastern Europe to break free of colonial chains. Already, early in the freedom movements, defiant efforts were made to counter the information disseminated by colonial governments through news agencies, the press and other media. The development of the vernacular press and 'alternative' forms of news distribution such as small magazines, pamphlets, letters (often handwritten), street plays and public meetings, played a vital role in spreading the message of independence. Several leading nationalist leaders were active journalists.

Once independence was won, the struggle became part of the effort to follow the path of non-alignment and self-reliant development. Indeed, information was valued, from the beginning, as a public resource and a 'social good' linked to development. The transnational agencies were, therefore, replaced by national agencies; not all of them under direct government control, though in most cases subsidized by the new governments. The transnationals did not go gracefully. Reuters, for instance, refused to let go of its profitable market in India until the Prime Minister himself forced it to withdraw. In some other countries like Nigeria, Ghana and the Caribbean, Reuters' managers were retained to help establish the national news agencies. Furthermore, journalists of some developing countries were sent to the West for training. Others were offered 'attachments' at the BBC and other Western broadcasting organizations. These efforts resulted in the entrenchment of Western and transnational news values in the press of the developing countries, helping to extend the dominance of the transnational news agencies long after the hold over managers and experts had been replaced by native journalists.

New Regional Alliances

Meanwhile, governments of the developing countries began to form new alliances, keeping clear of the 'power blocs'. The

Non-Aligned Movement (NAM) came into existence in 1961, with twenty-five member countries. Today, it has 102 members. In 1963, the independent nations of the African continent came together to form the Organization of African Unity (OAU), and two years later the Association of South-East Asian Nations (ASEAN) brought together Indonesia, the Philippines, Malaysia, Singapore and Thailand in a regional alliance. The Organization of American States (OAS) was formed in the Western Hemisphere. Of all these, the most significant was NAM, and its influence was increasingly felt in the United Nations. During the late 1960s and early 1970s, the non-aligned nations banded together to fight the international economic order which offered unfair and unequal trade advantages to the richer nations. They argued that 'free trade' was in reality a one-way trade, from North to South, and 'free-flow' of information likewise was regarded as a one-way flow of news and information, again from North to South.

They further argued that political freedom without economic and cultural freedom was meaningless; a de facto colonialism prevailed, their national and cultural identities were under threat of extinction. Their mass media were dominated by material from the West: films from Hollywood, TV serials from the networks, popular music from the multinational record companies, and news in all media from the transnational news agencies. Direct broadcasting was seen as the ultimate threat to their national and cultural identity. The flow was 'free' all right, but there was no equity or balance in it.

The NAM countries therefore sought to re-write the United Nations Charter, which had been adopted at a time when most of the developing world was under colonial rule. They felt that the Charter reflected colonial interests and values, which were repugnant to the free non-aligned countries.

The Role of UNESCO

Resentment about this obvious imbalance gave rise to speculation about its causes. Herbert Schiller contends that the

United States' advocacy of the 'free flow of information' was necessitated by imperialistic designs, corporate needs of business and trade, and the Cold War atmosphere. He argues that the historical coincidence of the 'imperial ascendancy' of the United States and its advocacy of the policy of 'free flow of information' is not fortuitous. He suggests that 'the genesis and extension' of the doctrine are roughly coterminous with the 'brief and hectic interval of US global hegemony'. It was also seen as needed to maintain the Cold War environment. As early as 1948, the United States and its allies had the major influence in drawing up the UN Declaration of Human Rights. Article 19 of the Declaration stated that 'everyone has the right to freedom of opinion and expression, and to seek, receive and impart information and ideas through any medium and regardless of frontiers'. News agencies thus had an unimpeded right to collect and distribute news and information 'regardless of national frontiers'. In reality, the right could only be exercised by the transnational news agencies, for they alone had the resources, the technology and the trained personnel to do so.

The interest of UNESCO in the communication field goes back to the early 1950s. It derives from UNESCO's 1945 Charter, which underscores the principles of the 'free flow of information' and 'the pursuit of objective truth'. UNESCO carried out its first study of 'news flows' in 1953, a comparative study of seven major dailies of the world, which included a survey of the structure and operations of news agencies. Three years later, a second study focused on the problems of transmitting press messages. Thus by the early 1960s, UNESCO had come to identify the major Western news agencies as 'one of the vital factors in the flow of information'.

UNESCO stepped up its communication activities with sponsorship of regional news agencies. A UNESCO-sponsored conference in Bangkok in 1961 led to the creation of the Organization of Asian News Agencies (OANA). In 1962, a similar conference in Santiago recommended the establishment of a news agency for Latin American countries. A conference in

Tunis in 1963 proposed the creation of a Union of African News Agencies. These activities attracted little attention or controversy in the West, at that time.

In 1970, however, the general conference of UNESCO issued a call to 'examine communication policies'. This drew severe criticism from the United States and its allies in Europe. The spectre of direct satellite broadcasting seemed, to some governments, to pose the ultimate threat to cultural independence. In 1972, a Soviet sponsored resolution, 'A Declaration of Guiding Principles for the Use of Satellite Broadcasting for the Free Flow of Information, the Extension of Education and the Development of Culture Exchanges', was adopted by UNESCO members, and a related General Assembly resolution to formulate principles governing direct satellite broadcasting also received overwhelming approval. Only the United States consistently opposed these resolutions.

NIEO and NWICO

Meanwhile, the non-aligned nations had drawn up a charter for a 'New International Economic Order' (NIEO), which was approved at a special session of the UN General Assembly in May 1974. NWICO was seen by them as integral to NIEO. The NAM Summit Conference, in Algiers in 1973, made it clear that the transformation of the international economic system required that non-aligned nations 'take concerted action in the field of mass communication in order to promote a greater interchange of ideas among themselves'. Thus it was at the Algiers meeting that the issue first surfaced as one of major international concern; however, the thrust of the resolution adopted at Algiers was toward achieving a freer flow of information among the non-aligned. Thus was born the idea of a non-aligned news pool, which was not conceived of as a rival or a supplanter of the big four news agencies. Only later was the pool felt to be a 'threat' by the transnationals. The non-aligned Group of 77 felt the Western agencies were using their vast resources to carry on a propaganda war against the just demands embodied in both

NIEO and NWICO. Western attitudes towards 'free trade', which the non-aligned labelled pure 'neo-colonialism', were exacerbated when the West persisted in regarding information as just another commodity, to be traded for profit without regard to its cultural implications.

The MacBride Report

The strengthening voice of the non-aligned nations in the United Nations led to the establishment of an International Commission for the Study of Communication Problems by UNESCO, in 1977, under the leadership of the Irish diplomat, Sean MacBride. Its mission was to do a thorough analysis of world communication problems, with special stress on the international implications of the modern media. The 'MacBride Report' was published under the title, *Many Voices, One World*, in 1980.

Although not an expression of UNESCO's official position, the Report served to define the issues underlying the debate. The commission members – prominent media personages from varying national and ideological backgrounds – produced a text, but not a consensus, and the Report's uneven style reflects its 'mosaic' character.

The 'new world' of the NWICO is the one that is brought into being by the newly gained independence of more than eighty nations since the end of the Second World War. Although other designations were already in use, such as 'New International Information and Communication Order' (NIICO), the 1978 UNESCO and UN General Assembly resolutions agreed that the goal they envisaged was a 'new, more just and more efficient world information and communication order'.

The Report gives a full airing to the many complaints of the non-aligned nations about the defects in the prevailing system of international news flow, such as the general neglect of news of the summit conferences and other activities of the non-aligned movement.[76] On the other hand, it does not neglect to present

---

76 Mulay, 1987.

legitimate Western fears, warning in several places, for example, that declarations defining the 'responsibilities' of journalists, calling for their licensing, or even saying that their rights and freedom should be given special consideration, all contain the danger of placing undue restrictions on their work. While seeing some problems in the kinds of news distributed by the transnational agencies, the Report also notes that they provide reliable news which cannot be obtained from other sources, and many of their deficiencies are offset by a 'growing capacity in developing countries to make appropriate critical selection of news coming from abroad'.[77] Much responsibility, both for failure to use diverse sources and for distorting acts of 'gatekeeping', lies with local editors; and many efforts to establish a truly 'two-way' flow of news are acknowledged to have been made in recent years.[78]

Neither the MacBride Report nor the general declaration embodying NWICO, drawn up by UNESCO in 1978, fully pleased anyone. But even the minimal unity manifested in these unsatisfactory compromises was a relief, in view of the heated debate which had preceded them.

Although, many disparities between developed and non-aligned countries still exist, and many basic issues in the debate have not been resolved, other authorities claim that it promoted some improvements in the coverage of non-aligned countries by Western media. Training and development have been slow in coming, but a few centres for training have been built and funding supplied. Technological changes have reduced the costs of news transmission greatly. High newsprint costs have hampered newspaper growth in many countries, but the spread of radio, television, the Internet and mobile telephony has more than compensated for a decline in newspapers. Interest in communication development has shifted its focus from mass media to telecommunication, which many have suddenly realized must be at the core of broad-spectrum development planning.

---

77 Ibid. p. 85.
78 Ibid. p. 146.

'Free Flow' versus 'Free and Balanced Flow'

Many observers in the non-aligned nations nevertheless see the fundamental problem in news flow as still unresolved. The debate, as they interpret it, is not simply between the proponents of 'free flow' and those arguing for a 'free and balanced flow' of information across borders. It is, rather, between radically diverse approaches to news and news flows, which have their roots in distinct social philosophies and cultures.

As the non-aligned countries perceive the situation, the patterns of news flows as they exist today are determined by a 'cartel' of transnational news agencies which embody the political economic and cultural interests of the Western bloc. The 'free flow' of information which they defined is, in fact, uni-directional and vertical, from North to South for the most part. News about the South that is transmitted around the world presents a distorted picture, for it is collected and processed with a Western audience and readership in mind. What is more reprehensible is that the nations of the South, which have different communication needs and interests, are fed similarly distorted images.

Furthermore, news about the South is gathered and processed by Western journalists few of whom possess an in-depth understanding of the cultural, social, and political ethos of developing countries. Foreign correspondents and Special Correspondents are based in the national capitals of the developed world and report with authority and expertise on a host of subjects. They are no more than 'parachute journalists'. (War correspondents in Iraq and Afghanistan who cozied up to the invading army commanders and sought their protection have come to be called 'embedded journalists'.) The result is that the 'images' of the developing countries thus disseminated are distorted and often superficial, with the emphasis on poverty, famines, floods, and other disasters and *coups d'etat* – generally presented as 'exceptional' events without a context. Thus, the philosophy of news espoused by the transnationals – news as exceptional events and exceptional people, as commodity for the market – is alien to the philosophy of non-aligned countries which see news as a developmental process, as fulfilling social, political, economic and cultural needs of their people.

FOR FURTHER READING

A. History of Indian Journalism
1. Margarita Barns: *The Indian Press*, London: George Allen & Unwin, 1940.
2. Moti Lal Bhargava: *Role of the Press in the Freedom Movement*, New Delhi: Reliance Publishing House, 1987.
3. Sharad Karkhanis: *Indian Politics and the Role of the Press*, New Delhi: Vikas, 1981.
4. Chandrika Kaul: *Reporting the Raj: The British Press and India (1880-1922)*, Manchester University Press, 2003.
5. Chandrika Kaul (Ed.): *Media and the British Empire*, Hampshire: Palgrave Macmillan, 2006
6. Milton Israel: *Communications and Power: Propaganda and the Press in the Indian Nationalist Struggle*, 1920-1947, Cambridge University Press, 1994.
7. Mohit Moitra: *A History of Indian Journalism*, Calcutta: National Book Agency Private Ltd., 1969.
8. J. Natarajan: *History of Indian Journalism*, New Delhi: Publications Division, 1955; Reprinted 1997.
9. S. Natarajan: *A History of the Press in India*, Bombay: Asia Publishing House, 1962.
10. Chalapathi Rau: *The Press*, New Delhi: National Book Trust.
11. Rangaswamy Parthasarthy: *Journalism in India*, New Delhi: Sterling, 1989, 2005.
12. G.N.S. Raghavan: *Indian Journalism: A New History*, New Delhi.
13. Mitchell Stephens: *A History of News*, New York: Oxford University Press, 2007, 3rd Ed.

B. Practices, Representations and Political Economy
14. Sonia Bathla: *Women, Democracy and the Press: Cultural and Political Representations in the Press,* New Delhi: Sage, 1999.
15. Robin Jeffrey: *India's Newspaper Revolution*, New Delhi: Oxford University Press, 1999.
16. Nalini Rajan (Ed.): *21st Century Journalism in India*, New Delhi:

Sage Publications, 2007.
17. Nalini Rajan (Ed.): *Practising Journalism: Values, Constraints, Implications*, New Delhi: Sage Publications, 2005.
18. M.V. Desai and Sevanti Ninan (Eds.): *Beyond The Headlines: Insiders on the Indian Press*, New Delhi: Allied Publishers/The Media Foundation, 1996.
19. Asha Rani Mathur (Ed.): *The Indian Media: Illusion, Delusion and Reality: Essays in Honour of Prem Bhatia*, New Delhi: Rupa & Co., 2006.
20. Sevanti Ninan: *Headlines from the Heartland: Reinventing the Hindi Public Sphere*, New Delhi: Sage Publications, 2007.

C. Media Laws and Media Ethics
21. Durga Das Basu: *Laws of the Press in India*, New Delhi: Prentice Hall, 2006.
22. Rajeev Dhavan: *Only the Good News: The Law of the Press in India*, New Delhi: Manohar Publications, 1987.
23. Government of India: *White Paper on Misuse of Mass Media (1977)*, New Delhi: Publications Division.
24. B. Radhakrishnamurthi: *Indian Press Laws*, Guntur: India Law House, 1980.

D. Professional Journalism
25. M.V. Kamath: *Professional Journalism*, New Delhi: Vikas, 1980.
26. Patanjali Sethi: *Professional Journalism*, Bombay: Orient Longman, 1974.
27. T.J.S. George: *Editing*, New Delhi: Indian Institute of Mass Communication, 1991.
28. Sunil Saxena: *Headline-Writing*, New Delhi: Sage Publications, 2006.
29. Sunil Saxena: *Breaking News: The Craft and Psychology of Online Journalism*, New Delhi: Tata McGraw-Hill Publishing Company, 2004.
30. Rangaswami Parthasarthy: *Basic Journalism*, New Delhi: Penguin, 2003.
31. B.G. Verghese (Ed.): *Breaking the Big Story – Great Moments in Indian Journalism*, New Delhi: Penguin, 2003.

E. International Communication
32. Stuart Allan: *News Culture*, Milton Keynes: Open University

Press, 2004, (Second Edition).
33. Suhas Chakravarthy: *Press and Media: The Global Dimension*, New Delhi: Kanishka, 1997.
34. Jaap van Ginneken: *Understanding Global News: A Critical Introduction*, London: Sage Publications, 1998.
35. Shelton A. Gunaratne: *The Dao of the Press: A Humanocentric Theory*, London: Hampton, 2005.
36. Keval J. Kumar and W. Biernatzki: 'International News Flows', *Communication Research Trends* (London), 1989.
37. Philip Lee (Ed.): *The Democratization of Communication*, Cardiff: University of Wales Press, 1995.
38. D.R. Mankekar: *Whose News? Whose Freedom?* New Delhi: Clarion, 1978.
39. Michael Traber and Kaarle Nordenstreng (Eds.): *Few Voices, Many Worlds: Towards a Media Reform Movement*, London: WACC, 1992.
40. Daya Kishan Thussu: *International Communication: Continuity and Change,* London: Arnold, 2000.
41. Ingrid Volkmer (Ed.): *News in Public Memory: An International Study of Media Memories Across Generations,* New York: Peter Lang, 2006. (See Keval J. Kumar's chapters on 'India' and 'Construction of Memory').
42. Madanmohan Rao (Ed.): *News Media and New Media: The Asia-Pacific Internet Handbook*, Singapore: Nanyang University/ Eastern University Press, 2003.

F. General
43. Prem Bhatia: *All My Yesterdays*, New Delhi: Vikas Publishing House, 1972.
44. G.S. Bhargava: *The Press in India: An Overview*, New Delhi, National Book Trust, 2005.
45. T.J.S. George: *Pothan Joseph's India: A Biography*, New Delhi: Sanchar Publishing House, 1992.
46. D.R. Mankekar: *Sheer Anecdotage,* Bombay: Somaiya, 1984.
47. J.P. Chaturvedi: *The Indian Press at the Crossroads*, New Delhi: Media Research Associates, 1992.
48. S.N. Bhattacharya: *Mahatma Gandhi – the Journalist*, Bombay: Asia Publishing House, 1965.
49. B.G. Verghese: *Ramnath Goenka.*, New Delhi.

G. Journals
1. *Communicator* (Indian Institute of Mass Communication, New Delhi).
2. *Vidura* (Press Institute of India, New Delhi).

WEB RESOURCES

I. News Search Engines
1. news.google.com
2. newsbot.msnbc.msn.com
3. search.news.yahoo.com
4. www.altavista.com/news
5. www.rocketnews.com
6. www.alltheweb.com

II. Websites for News and News Analysis
1. www.thehoot.org (For critical comments and analyses of Indian Journalism; started by B.G. Verghese but now edited by Sevanti Ninan).
2. www.newsdirectory.com (For access to the newspapers and magazines of the world, country by country and city by city).
3. www.indymedia.org
4. www.oneworld.org
5. english.aljazeera.net
6. www.ptinews.com (Press Trust of India)
7. www.uniindia.com (United News of India)
8. www.reuters.com
9. www.samachar.com (For access to the top English, Hindi, Tamil newspapers)
10. www.webduniya.com (For access to Indian language press)
11. www.ijuindia.com
12. www.presscouncil.nic.in
13. www.topix.net ((Online news service that gathers stories from thousands of sources)

REVIEW QUESTIONS

1. Distinguish between Journalism, Advertising and Public Relations.
2. Sketch the history of Indian Journalism from *Hicky's Gazette* to the time of Independence.
3. Log on to Pradyumna Maheshwari's news blog www.mediaah.com. Comment on news blogs as an 'alternative' form of Journalism.
4. Do Indian journalists need a Code of Ethics? Which are the principal areas which such a Code should give priority to?
5. What are 'news values'? Comment on the need for 'alternative' values in news selection?
6. Write critical notes on:
   (a) Magazine Genres
   (b) The 'Power' of the Press
   (c) News Agencies in India
   (d) The MacBride Report
   (e) The Journalist and the Right to Privacy
   (f) Restrictions on Press freedom in India
   (g) Online Versions of Daily Newspapers
   (h) News Blogs
   (i) The Times of India's 'MediaNet'

SUGGESTED PROJECTS

1. Conduct a comparative analysis of presentation and treatment of the main news story today in any two dailies of your city. Which presentation and treatment appealed to you most? Compare the layout, the kind of headlines and the typography employed to make the front page attractive. How have photographs and cartoons been positioned to give variety and balance to the front page?
2. Comment on the difference in approach and emphasis in the editorials of two rival papers on the same subject/news story. What is the point of view expressed in the two editorials? Is it subjective or based on facts? If it is subjective, which words/phrases/statements make this evident? If it is objective, what are the reasons/facts put forward?

3. Choose any one issue of a popular film or women's or youth or general interest magazine, and state the elements which have kept it popular. Is it only the content? Or also the layout and the mode of presentation? Name other magazines of the same genre.
4. Write a news report on an important meeting/function you have attended, using the 'inverted pyramid structure'.
5. Choose a news report which strikes you as not being well written, from this morning's paper. Edit it yourself and give it a striking headline.
6. Carry out a small readership survey among students in your class/college, to find out which is the mostly widely read daily/magazine. Draw up a suitable questionnaire and circulate copies of it or question each participant individually. Write out a report of the results for a local daily or the college magazine.
7. Do a feature-article on a topic of current interest. Use relevant websites and telephonic interviews to gather information about the topic. Make sure that it is not a 'copy and paste' job!
8. Visit a newspaper office. Talk to a reporter/sub-editor to find out about his/her work. Write a report on the visit.
9. Conduct a critical analysis of the amount of space devoted to news, advertising and public relations in a selected newspaper. When does a news item/or feature become a form of advertising and public relations?

CINEMA

The Beginnings

The years preceding the dawn of cinema in India were witness to the growth of musical dramas (*sangeet natak*), the Parsi theatre,[1] the drama companies of Madras, and the *jatra* in Bengal. Music, dance, song were an integral part of these performing traditions; this was the heritage of Sanskrit drama and later popular folk performing traditions such as the *ram lila*, the *ras lila*, the *nautanki* and the *thirukoothu*. In painting, the calendar art (sometimes termed 'bazaar art') of Raja Ravi Varma and others was well-known and stage sets incorporated some of the designs and colours of this new art form.[2]

So, when the first 'cinematographic exhibitions' of the Lumiére Brothers were held in Bombay on July 7, 1896, Indian dramatists, photographers, magicians, musicians and singers saw in them great potential for the re-telling of Indian myths and folklore. *The Times of India* advertised these early exhibitions as "the marvel of the country, the wonder of the world". The 'exhibitions' included 'living photographic pictures' in 'life-sized reproductions' of the arrival of a train, of workers leaving

---

1 For an historical account of the Parsi theatre cf. Somnath Gupt: *The Parsi Theatre: Its Origin and Development*, Calcutta: Seagull, 2005. (Translated and Edited by Kathryn Hansen).

2 For a more detailed account of the influences at work on early Indian cinema, see Ashish Rajadhyaksha's two papers: 'The Phalke Era: Conflict of Traditional Form and Modern Technology', in *Journal of Arts and Ideas*, Nos.14-15, July-December 1987; 'Neo-traditionalism: Film as Popular Art in India', in *Framework*, Nos. 32/33, pp.20-67; Anuradha Kapur: 'The Representation of Gods and Heroes: Parsi Mythological Dramas of the Early Twentieth Century', in *Journal of Arts and Ideas*, Nos. 23-24, January 1993, pp.85-107; Geeta Kapur: 'Ravi Varma: Representational Dilemmas of a 19th Century Indian Painter', in *Journal of Arts and Ideas*, Vols. 17-18, 1988, pp.59-80. For a recent evaluation of the influence of contemporary painting and graphic arts on commercial cinema, film posters and show-cards, see Kajri Jain: 'Figures of Locality and Tradition: Commercial Cinema and the Network of Visual Print Capitalism in Maharashtra' in Raminder Kaur and Ajay J Sinha (Eds.): *Bollyworld: Popular Indian Cinema through a Transnational Lens*, London/ New Delhi: Sage Publications, 2005, pp. 71-89.

a factory, of a sea-bath, and of ladies and soldiers on wheels. The exhibitions continued to draw crowds to four shows daily for over two months. Meanwhile, a British cinematographer held exhibitions of a similar kind in Calcutta, then the capital of British India. It is significant that the cinema had its beginnings in India almost at the same time as in other major film-producing countries. Indeed, barely six months after the first Lumiére Brothers' cinematograph projected moving pictures on to a screen in a Paris basement, and two years after Edison's invention of the Kinetoscope in New York.

Among the numerous crowds that watched the first screenings at Bombay's Watson Hotel with utmost fascination was a photographer named Harishchandra S. Bhatwadekar (alias Save Dada). He ordered for a moving picture camera from London, and when it arrived took it along to a wrestling match in Bombay's Hanging Gardens, and shot the match live (*Two Wrestlers*).[3] He soon acquired a projector and processing equipment. To him must go the credit of shooting one of the earliest Indian newsreels, *Return of Wrangler Paranjpe,* which recorded the triumphant welcome in December 1901 accorded to R.P. Paranjpe, an Indian student who had won honours in mathematics at Cambridge. Another Bhatwadekar short was *A Man and His Monkey*. Jag Mohan, the historian of the Indian documentary, credits Bhatwadekar with being 'the father of the Indian factual film'.[4] However, it is likely that the first Indian short films were *Coconut Fair* and *Our Indian Empire*, both made and exhibited in 1897 by unknown English camera persons.

Just as Indian photographers and studios proliferated soon after the introduction of the camera in 1840, so the arrival of the motion picture attracted a large number of business people,

---

3 This was perhaps the beginning of the 'action genre' in Indian cinema. For an historical account of this genre, see Valentina Vitali: *Hindi Action Cinema: Industries, Narratives, Bodies*, New Delhi: Oxford University Press, 2008.

4 Jag Mohan: Documentary Films and Indian Awakening, New Delhi: Publications Division, 1990.

artists and craftspeople into film production and exhibition.[5] Photographers in particular took to the new enterprise with enthusiasm. They turned out such items as *Poona Races, Train Arriving at Bombay Station, Tilak's Visit to Calcutta, Bathing Ghats at Benaras, Great Bengal Partition Movement,* and *Terrible Hyderabad Floods.* Some of them became professional showmen taking their equipment all over the country and holding exhibitions even in remote towns and villages. The first rural travelling cinemas had begun operating by the end of the twenties. On May 18, 1912, R.G. Torney filmed a Marathi stage play, *Pundalik,* while it was being acted out. The play was based on the legend of a famous Maharashtrian saint. Torney's screen version of *Pundalik* gave India its first filmed play (or 'photoplay') but the credit for making the first full length feature film must go to Dadasaheb Phalke's *Rajah Harishchandra,* released a full year later.

The Pioneers: The Lumiére Brothers

'The cinema is an invention without a future', declared Louis Lumiére who together with his brother, Auguste, pioneered what was to develop into an international cultural industry. The Lumiére brothers were the inventors of the 'cinematographe', a compact and portable machine that with a few adjustments could be used as a camera or projector or printing machine. As professional photographers themselves, cinema for them was no more than an extension of photography; hence they sought to capture events from a static position and therefore from a single point of view, in brief 'actualities' such as: the arrival of a train, a train leaving the station, workers leaving a factory, a sea bath, ladies and soldiers on wheels. Like still photographs, these 'living photographic pictures' were no more than attempts to reproduce reality. They narrated no story, but reproduced a place, time and atmosphere. These brief moving reproductions were therefore termed 'actualities'.

---

5 Geeta Kapur: 'Revelation and Doubt: Sant Tukaram and Devi' in Tejaswini Niranjana, P. Sudhir and Vivek Dhareshwar (Eds.): *Interrogating Modernity*: Culture and Colonialism in India, Calcutta: Seagull Books, 1993; Sumita S Chakravarty: *National Identity in Indian Popular Cinema (1947-1987)*, New Delhi: Oxford University Press, 1996, pp.33-34.

It was another pioneer, the French magician Georges Méliès, who was to revolutionise the cinema from being a 'photoplay' to a mass medium for the creation of fantasies and dreams. Several of his creations had the words 'nightmare' or 'dream' in their titles. He used elaborate sets and editing techniques to make science fiction films like *Voyage to the Moon* (1902).

So while the Lumiére brothers laid the foundation of realism in cinema, Méliès pointed the way to 'expressionism' and to the magic of cinema. The Lumiéres' realism introduced cinema to the 'mise en scene' while Méliès pioneered the technique of 'stop motion photography' to create magical special effects in his many 'trick films'. Elaborate stage sets and special effects were the hallmarks of his films. It is this historical tension between traditions of realism and traditions of expressionism that is at the heart of the aesthetics of cinema.

Realism and Soviet Cinema

The cinema of realism climaxed in the work of the early Russian film-makers, especially that of V.I. Pudovkin and Sergei Eisenstein. Eisenstein was not only a prolific film maker of the Revolution, but also a film theorist. His 'materialist' approach to the form of cinema is exemplified in his masterpieces, *Battleship Potemkin, Ivan the Terrible* and others. Both Pudovkin and Eisenstein theorised extensively about the concept and practice of 'montage'. Pudovkin (who directed *Mother*) identified five basic types of montage: contrast, parallelism, symbolism, simultaneity and liet-motif. He developed a theory of the interaction between shots variously called 'relational editing' or 'linkage'. Eisenstein, on the other hand, saw the relationship between shots as a collision rather than a linkage, and further refined the theory to deal with the relationships between elements of individual shots as well as the whole shots themselves. This he called the 'montage of attractions'[6]. Other early Soviet film-makers and theorists include Lev Kuleshov, Vertov (*Kino Eye*) and Dovzhenko (*Earth*): a major concern of

---

6   James Monaco: *How to Read a Film: The Art, Technology, Language, History and Theory of Film and Media*, Oxford: Oxford University Press, Rev. Ed. 1981, p. 185.

the film-makers of the early Soviet cinema was ideology and the socialist state. Their films had the appearance of a documentary style.

Evolution of Film Language

Thus, before becoming the means of expression familiar to us, cinema was a simple means of mechanical recording, preserving, and reproducing moving visual spectacles – whether of life, of the theatre, or even of small mises-en-scene, which were specially prepared and which, in the final analysis, remained theatrical. It was only when the cinema confronted the problems of narration, particularly in the years between 1910 and 1915 when films like *Quo Vadis?*, *Enoch Arden*, *The Battle of Gettysburg* and *Birth of a Nation* were made, did film language start inventing its own vocabulary to describe its techniques and procedures.

The pioneers of film language were Méliès, E.S. Porter and D.W. Griffith who 'cared little about the symbolic, philosophical or human message of their films', but who were ace story-tellers. Méliès it was, for instance, who invented 'double exposure', the device of 'multiple exposures' with a mask and a dark backdrop, the 'dissolve' and the 'fade in', and also the 'pan shot'.

Méliès was present at the Lumiére brothers' first exhibition of the cinematograph. In fact, he offered to buy up the machine. As a theatre owner and a magician he believed he could make his magic shows more lively with a projector. Accordingly, he bought a projector from an English photographer and used it for his magic shows. He turned the projector into a simple camera to record objects in motion. Once it so happened that the camera jammed, and so goes the legend – it was this accident that led to his discovery of 'quick' and 'slow' motion, of 'stop-motion', and also of the 'fade' and 'dissolve'.

Méliès' masterpieces were *Cindrella* and *A Trip to the Moon* – the first perhaps to combine paintings with studio-sets. (This technique was later perfected by the German expressionists). Méliès regarded film-making as an extension of his career as a magician. Most of his work was destroyed during World War II;

the few films that have survived reveal a film-maker who resorted to photographic tricks, to 'enchantments' and to actuality recording to create his movie magic. Edwin S. Porter, who made the first story film, *The Great Train Robbery*, was deeply influenced by Méliès.

The first occurrences of some other procedures of filmic language are attributed to the same pioneers as also to the Englishmen G.A. Smith and J. Williamson, and to the Russian, Sergei Eisenstein. The procedures are: the 'close-up', the 'pan shot', the 'tracking shot', 'parallel montage', and 'interlaced', or 'alternate montage'. Of these, the most significant and the most revolutionary was 'montage', derived initially from the masterpieces of D.W. Griffith. Indeed, it was montage that "gave birth to film as an art, setting it apart from mere animated photography; in short, creating a language" (Andre Malraux). Alfred Hitchcock and Jean-Luc Godard developed film language further with the introduction of new types of shots and camera and cutting techniques. The digitization of the film-making process has not radically changed the cinematic language but rather speeded up the process, reduced the costs involved and made it accessible to many more amateurs and to much larger audiences via television, VCD and DVD players, computers, the internet, game consoles and handheld devices like palm-tops, PDAs and mobile phones.

Pioneers of Indian Cinema: Dadasaheb Phalke

One of the pioneers of the silent feature film in India was Dhundiraj Govind Phalke (alias Dadasaheb Phalke), a Bombay printer, photographer, painter and magician. It is reported that he was converted to cinematography when he saw the film, *Life of Christ*, at a Christmas cinema show[7]. The idea of a similar full-

---

[7] Erik Barnouw and S. Krishnaswamy: Indian Film, New Delhi: Oxford University Press, 1980, p.11. However, as Kajri Jain (2005) points out, 'it is not clear whether this Life of Christ was the Pathe film from 1902 or Alice Guy's 1906 film for Gaumont' (Cf. Kajri Jain: 'Figures of Locality and Tradition: Commercial Cinema and the Network of Visual Print Capitalism in Maharashtra' in Raminder Kaur and Ajay J Sinha (Eds.): Bollyworld: Popular Indian Cinema through a Transnational Lens, London/New Delhi: Sage Publications, 2005. p.73n.

length feature on the life of Lord Krishna took hold of him, and he made it his life's ambition. But financial stringency and the blatant unwillingness of women, even prostitutes, to act in his films, were crucial issues he would have to contend with through his long career as a film-maker. He broke ground in 1913 with *Rajah Harischandra*. So successful did it prove with audiences in all parts of the country (though it was hardly noticed by the English-language press) that Phalke went on to make as many as 96 full length feature films and 26 short films. His most popular features were *Savitri, Lanka Dahan, Sinhasta Mela, Krishna Janma*, and *Bhasmasur Mohini*. The young man whom Phalke selected to play the women in his films was A. Salunke, a restaurant cook "with slender features and hands".[8] Phalke's last silent film was *Sethbhandan* (1932). His short films were on a variety of subjects including *How to Make a Film* and *Growth of a Pea Plant*.

Only a few scattered fragments of Phalke's silent films are extant. "The overall structure of each film is forever lost, but the fragments show a fine pictorial sense and remarkable technical resourcefulness. Like another magician who became a film pioneer, George Méliès, Phalke was a special effects genius. He explored a vast range of techniques, including animation. He experimented with colour, via tinting and toning."[9] His approach to film making was influenced by the tribal Bohada form of story-telling, a folk art tradition of the Nashik district (Maharshtra).

But the religious (or 'mythological') genre held little appeal for some of the other film-makers of the 'twenties and 'thirties. D.G. Ganguly of Calcutta specialised in satirical comedies like *England Returned* (1921) and *Barrister's Wife*, Chandulal Shah of Bombay in films dealing with social problems – *Gun Sundari* (English title: *Why Husbands Go Astray*), *Typist Girl* (1918), and Himansu Rai, sponsored by the Germans, made the brilliant

---

8   Barnouw and Krishnaswamy, op. cit. p.19.
9   ibid.

films, *The Light of Asia* (1925), *Shiraz* (1926), *A Throw of Dice* (1929), and *Karma* (1934) which immortalized the actress Devika Rani.

In South India, as in most other parts of the country (with the exception perhaps of Kerala), the mythological genre held sway. The foundation for a flourishing film industry in South India was laid by R. Nataraja Mudaliar, a businessman trained in cinematography in Poona. In 1917 he set up his own Indian Film Company and by 1923 had made six silent films – all based on mythological characters from the epics. The first was *Keechaka Vadha* (1917); the others included *Draupadi* (1919), *Lava Kusha* (1920), *Markandaya* (1922) and *Mayil Ravana* (1923). The films carried inter-titles in English and Indian languages.

During the Silent Era (1896-1930) over a thousand films of various genres were made in India; however, only ten of them survive, now restored and preserved in the National Film Archive of India (NFAI), Pune.[10] Regular film production though did not actually take off until 1919, when as many as eleven films were made.[11] By then, Indian-controlled exhibition networks were firmly in place.[12] Meanwhile, American and European films continued to grow in popularity, though a major source of worry for the Imperial Government was that they would 'corrupt' Indian minds. In 1917, the European Association warned the Government against a film called *The Serpentine Dance*, which 'was certainly calculated to bring the white men and women into low esteem in the Indian mind'.[13] A greater worry of course was the threat to British rule from nationalist film makers like J.B.H. Wadia who in many subtle and indirect ways promoted the struggle for independence and freedom.

---

10 Cf. *Cinema Vision India*, Vol. 1, No. 1
11 Valentina Vitali: *Hindi Action Cinema: Industries, Narrative, Bodies*, New Delhi: Oxford University Press, 2008. p. 4.
12 Ibid.
13 Quoted in Margaret MacMillan: *Women of the Raj*, London: Thames and Hudson, 1988, p. 53.

The Talkies

The films of the Silent Era did not 'talk' but they were never watched in 'silence'. Dialogue was presented through inter-titles which were often in English and two or three Indian languages. Almost every film had a background score which ran through the length of the film. The score was 'live', and helped to dramatise the narrative. Sometimes there was only piano accompaniment, but there were several films where a violin, a harmonium and other musical instruments could be added.

The 'Talkies Era' was set in motion by *The Melody of Love* (1929), the first 'talkie' to be screened in India. The first Indian talkie *Alam Ara* (1931) directed by Ardeshir Irani, was released two years later, with Master Vithal and Miss Zubeida as the lead actors. It was based on a play by Joseph David. Like most films of that era it was a straight adaptation of the play. A fourth of the film was silent. The premiere was a proud occasion at the Majestic theatre in Bombay, with the Governor as the chief guest. It included seven songs – so enchanted was the director with the novelty of sound! *Indra Sabha* which was released the following year had 70 songs.[14] (Though the novelty has long worn off, the enchantment remains to this day). No commercial film dared cutting out song-and-dance sequences altogether, except in rare cases such as J.B.H. Wadia's *Naujawan* (1937), B.R. Chopra's *Kannoon* and K.A. Abbas' *Munna* (1954).[15] Hindi films dominated right from the start: from 1931 to 1947, over 6,590 Hindi films were produced, while from 1947 to 1987, around 5,074 films were released.

The Studio System

With many new hands needed for the production of films, now gradually developing into a small industry, the "studio

---

14 Ashok D. Ranade argues that the songs in the early talkies were not all 'songs' but rather 'recitations' in the traditional Indian mode. Cf. Ashok D. Ranade: *The Hindi Film Song*, New Delhi : D K Publishers Distributors, 2006.
15 For a recent study of the 'songless film' in Bollywood, see Ian Garwood: 'The Songless Bollywood Film', *South Asian Popular Culture*, Vol. 4, No. 2, October 2006. pp. 169-183.

system" made its appearance in Bombay, Calcutta and Madras. In Bombay, V. Shantaram and three others set up the Prabhat Film Co., and went on to roll out films at regular intervals. Most of the films were directed by Shantaram himself. Among the outstanding films were: *Ayodhyacha Raja* (1932), *Sant Tukaram* (1936), *Amar Jyoti*(1936), *Duniya Na Mane* (the Marathi version was entitled *Kunku*), and *Adm*i. The Prabhat Film Co. later moved to Pune on the site where the Film and Television Institute of India (FTII) now stands.

Led by Himansu Rai, the Bombay Talkies (established in 1935) flourished as much as Prabhat, turning out three mythological films a year. The Imperial Film Co., another minor Bombay film venture, produced over seven features annually. Wadia Movietone, established by J.B.H. Wadia and his brother Homi, produced 130 films, with J.B.H. himself writing several of the screenplays. The credit for making the first railroad thriller shot on location (*Toofan Mail*, 1932) and the first film on Hindu-Muslim unity (*Jai Bharat*, 1936) must go to the Wadias, as well as the first stunt-film (*Hunterwali,*1935).[16]

In Calcutta, the foremost studio company was the New Theatre Co., which under the baton of B.N. Sircar and Dhiren Ganguli produced *Chandidas* (1932), *Devdas* (1936), and *Mukti* (1939). K.C. Barua's *Devdas*, was made in Hindi and Bengali, and introduced audiences to Bimal Roy, the cameraman who was to go on to make his own films, notably the classic *Do Bigha Zameen* (1953), and also to the immortal voice of Kundalal Saigal. Studios were opened in Madras, Salem and Coimbatore, but it was the Madras United Artists' Corporation under the leadership of K. Subrahmanyam, that turned to film-making in Tamil, Telugu and Malayalam. The southern studios, just as the Madras Studios do today, produced films also in Hindi.

---

16 For a fascinating account of the Wadia brothers and the stunt queen Nadia, see Rosie Thomas: 'Not Quite (Pearl) White: Fearless Nadia, Queen of the Stunts' in Raminder Kaur and Ajay Sinha: *Bollyworld: Popular Indian Cinema through a Transnational Lens,* New Delhi: Sage, 2005. See also Dorothee Wenner: *Fearless Nadia: The True Story of Bollywood's Original Stunt Queen*, Penguin Books, 2005.

Decline of the Studio System: Enter the 'Movie Stars'

During the forties, however, the big companies lost their hold on the studio system. Shantaram left Prabhat in 1941 to make films under his own banner. So did Mehboob Khan and others. This gave rise to the 'star system', the 'formula' film and the injection of 'black' money into the film world – three interrelated evils which have beset the commercial cinema ever since. Shantaram with the help of the writer K.A. Abbas, made *Journey of Dr. Kotnis*, a war-effort film, *Dharti Ke Lal*, and others. Sohrab Modi's films (notably *Pukar*) and Mehboob Khan's *Mother India, Aurath, Sister, Roti* were box-office draws. Gemini Studios' *Chandralekha* was the greatest Tamil draw in the south, and later in the entire country when the Hindi version was released. Still later, an English version was distributed overseas. It was a spectacular song and dance extravaganza. Its music appeared to anticipate the 'fusion' of the post-MTV Hindi film such as *Hum Aapke Hain Koun*. 'The songs are based on Carnatic, Hindusthani, Bharatnatyam, Latin American and Portuguee folk music, as well as the Struass Waltz, each distinct and standing on its own, with barely any background score attempting to interlink anything, just periods of silence'.[17] A significant event at the close of the forties was the starting of the Calcutta Film Society by Satyajit Ray.[18]

Satyajit Ray

It was not until 1954, however, that Ray could ring up the curtain on his long career as a film-director. He followed up his Apu Trilogy – *Pather Panchali* (1954), *Aparajito* (1957) and *Apur Sansar* (1959) – with such masterpieces as *Jalsaghar* (1958), *Devi* (1969), *Teen Kanya* (1961), *Charulata* (1964), *Nayak* (1966), *Gupy Gyne Bagha Byne* (1968), a fantasy musical, *Aranyer Din Ratri* (1970), *Seemabadha* (1971), *Sonar Kella* (1974), *Ashani Sanket* (1973), *Ghare Bhaire* (1985),

---

17 M. Bhaktavatsala: 'Music in the Movies', in *Screen*, Bombay, April 24, 1998, p. 36.
18 For an insightful account, see Chidananda Dasgupta: *Seeing is Believing: Selected Writings on Cinema*, New Delhi: Penguin/Viking.

Ganasatru (1989), and *Aguntak* (1991). *Shatranj Ke Khilari* (1977) was Ray's only Hindi feature and *Sadgati* his only short fiction film in Hindi made for television. Ray's documentaries include the moving *Rabindranath Tagore*, a one-hour documentary narrated by Ray himself, and *Sikkim* (1980).[19] "Ray's work traces the essential outline of the middle class in modern India. More importantly, it is an affirmation of faith in the human being," says Chidananda Das Gupta, a film maker in his own right and author of several books on Indian cinema.[20]

The Golden Age: Sohrab Modi, Raj Kapoor and Guru Dutt

During the fifties and sixties, Sohrab Modi and Mehboob Khan continued their film ventures. But with a difference – the films were all in colour. Modi's *Jhansi Ki Rani* (1953) was India's first colour feature; it flopped at the box-office. But they had now to compete with two other stalwarts in Indian cinema. The first was Raj Kapoor who began his career as a clapper-boy in Bombay Talkies; the second, Guru Dutt. Raj Kapoor acted in and directed his own films – *Awara, Barsaat, Shri 420, Sangam*, and *Mera Naam Joker*. In the seventies he directed the phenomenal success *Bobby*, and later the controversial *Satyam Shivam Sundaram*, and *Ram Teri Ganga Maili*. Raj Kapoor's films were runaway successes in the Soviet Union and the Arab world. An Indo-Soviet co-production, *Pardesi* (1957), starring Nargis and Balraj Sahni, told the tale of Afanasy, the first Soviet explorer to visit India in 1468. (In the English sub-titled and dubbed version, the title of the film is 'Journey Beyond the

---

19 For an analysis of Ray's documentaries, cf. Andrew Robinson: 'Ray's Documentaries' in Sanjit Narwekar (ed.): *Spectrum India -1994*, Third Bombay International Film Festival for Documentary, Short and Animation Films, February 1994, pp.86-90.

20 For a detailed analysis of Satyajit Ray's work, see Chidananda Dasgupta: *The Cinema of Satyajit Ray*, New Delhi: Vikas, 1980; Bidyut Sarkar: *The World of Satyajit Ray*, New Delhi: UBSPD, 1992; Ben Nyce: *A Study of his Films*, New York: Praeger, 1988; Sauranjan Ganguly: *Satyajit Ray: In Search of the Modern*, London: Scarecrow Press, 2000; Darius Cooper: *The Cinema of Satyajit Ray: Between Tradition and Modernity*, Cambridge University Press, 2000; Andrew Robinson: *Satyajit Ray: A Vision of Cinema*, I.B. Tauris, 2005.

Three Seas).[21]

Guru Dutt excelled in delineating the tragic mood in films like *Kagaz Ke Phool, Baazi, Pyaasa,* and *Sahib Bibi Aur Gulam.* Kamal Amrohi's studies of Uttar Pradesh's elite, *Mahal, Dawa* and *Pakeezah* belonged to the same period.

The two great money-spinners of the decade after independence were V. Shantaram's *Jhanak Jhanak Payal Baje* (1955) and Mehboob Khan's *Mother India* (1957). Shantaram's film had a record run of 104 weeks at a single cinema theatre in Bombay. It was basically a song-and-dance extravaganza in technicolour, featuring Sandhya and Gopikrishna. The colourful decor, costumes, locations and dances accompanied by lilting music gave the cue to Indian film-makers that a story could be dispensed with if such light entertainment were provided in full measure. *Mother India*, on the other hand, showed that a mother's suffering and sacrifice could touch the hearts of millions in India.

The sixties saw *Mughal-e-Azam* (1960) – a costume epic dependent on luxurious sets, dance and music sequences, and easy flowing Urdu dialogue for its success. It set the pace for films with a Moghul background. In 1961 *Ganga Jamna* introduced the figure of the wronged man turning into a dacoit as also the stock-characters of contemporary Hindi cinema – two brothers, one a law-keeper, the other a law-breaker. Raj Kapoor's *Sangam* (1964) started the trend of shooting on foreign locations, the necessity of a smooth camera technique and in terms of plot, made the friendship between two males (*Yaarana*) and their falling out over a woman as a result of circumstances, everlasting on the screen.

The Angry Young Man: Return of the Action Genre

The seventies began with *Bobby* (1973) proving how big a draw the portrayal of young love on the Indian screen could be. But perhaps the greatest spectacular of post-independence

---

21 The Hindi version of the film is not extant. The Russian version, subtitled and dubbed in English was screened at the NFAI in 2007.

cinema has been *Sholay* (1975), a 'curry western'.²² Shot in 70 mm and moving at a rapid-fire pace, it glorified the stocky and lovable dacoit chief, Amjad Khan. For the next decade or so excessive violence became the norm of the mainstream Hindi cinema and Amitabh Bachchan the 'angry young man' who set out to right the wrongs in Indian society. In film after film – *Zanjeer* (1973), *Deewar* (1975), *Amar, Akbar, Anthony* (1977), *Muqaddar-ka Sikandar* (1978), *Shaan* (1980), *Naseeb* (1981), – the actor represented the common man at the mercy of 'the system' but willing to stand up and fight back.²³ In the eighties the box office draw was disco – and music and dance sequences tied together with dollops of vendetta and romance. Feroz Khan's *Qurban*i remained the pace-setter for this genre. Ramesh Sippy, Manmohan Desai and Prakash Mishra were the foremost directors of these decades.

But during the nineties, the family drama genre, with the usual ingredients of romance, song, dance and endless arguments about what it means to be 'Indian', promised to be the main attraction, despite the phenomenal growth of television channels. Sooraj Barjatya's *Hum Apke Hain Koun* ('Forever Yours' in English, 'Anbaalayam' in Tamil) and Aditya Chopra's *Dilwale Dulhaniya Le Jayenge* were runaway successes at the box office, helped along by savvy marketing strategies, and the strict monitoring of cable operators' attempts to screen pirated versions; so were Yash Chopra's *Dil To Paagal Hai*, *Pardesh*, *Border* and *Rangeela*. Besides, David Dhawan's wafer-thin comedies-cum-romances (*Hero No. 1, Judwaa, Coolie No. 1* and *Gharwali Baharwali*) breathed new life into the ailing Bombay film industry.

The closing years of the 20th century and the first decade of the new millennium were marked by a revival of the mainstream Hindi, Tamil and Telugu cinema and the return of audiences to

---

22 Cf. Wimal Dissanayake and Malti Sahai: Sholay: A Cultural Reading, New Delhi: Wiley Eastern, 1992, for an interesting cultural analysis of the film. See also Gaston Roberge's analysis in his Mediation.
23 For an analysis of the literature on the 'angry young man', see Vitali, op. cit. Chapter 5.

the big screen. The new digital technologies, a booming Indian economy and the mushrooming of 'multiplex' theatres played no mean role in this revival. But first, a word about the 'New Wave' movement in Indian cinema.

The New Wave

What is termed the 'New Wave' in the history of Indian cinema is not the 'nouvelle vogue' of French cinema with which Bresson, Godard and other experimental filmmakers were associated in the fifties and sixties. In the Indian context, the term is rather loosely used to describe the deliberately realist (or 'neo-realist') and non-commercial style of film-making that sometimes experiments with form and content. Its roots are in IPTA (Indian People's Theatre Association) theatre, the realist novel, and European cinema (especially Russian, French and Italian). It eschews the escapist Hollywood and the Bombay film traditions, and is concerned more with real-life issues of Indian society than with just entertainment. Other terms used to talk about this cinema are 'alternative', 'parallel', and even 'another'[24] or 'the third cinema'.[25]

The establishment of the Film Finance Corporation (FFC) in 1960 raised the expectations of serious film makers though they were wary of the terms of the loans provided by it. The FFC began in a business-like manner giving loans only to established filmmakers. But from 1968 onwards, low-budget ventures by young filmmakers too began to be granted loans. Mrinal Sen's *Bhuvan Shome* (1969) set the trend for the 'New Wave' Indian film. *Bhuvan Shome* was filmed on location with a small cast, 'simple in structure though rich in resonance', breaking from the 'formula' film. It made a mark as a commercial success, and won the year's Best Feature Film, Best Actor, and Best Director awards; it won laurels abroad too. Like Satyajit Ray, Mrinal Sen continued to turn out films at regular intervals. His prolific work includes: *Baishey Shravan, Akash Kusum, Interview, Padatik,*

---

24 Cf. Gaston Roberge: *Another Cinema for AnotherSociety*, Calcutta: Seagull Publications, 1985.
25 Cf. The Third Cinema

Chorus, Ek Din Pratidin, Parashuram, Mrigaya, Ek Adhuri Kahani, Ek Din Achanak, and *Genesis.*

Basu Chatterji was a different type of 'new wave' film director. His debut was *Sara Akaash,* scripted and directed by him, with camera work by K.K. Mahajan. Chatterji whose forte was ridicule of the 'formula' film went on to make *Rajinigandha* (1974), *Chhoti Si Baat* (1975), *Chitchor* (1976), *Swami* (1977) and TV serials like *Rajan*i.

Table 13: Production of Feature Films (1973-2006)

Year	No. of Films
1973	447
1974	435
1975	475
1976	507
1977	557
1978	619
1979	714
1980	742
1981	737
1982	763
1983	741
1984	833
1985	913
1986	840
1987	806
1988	779
1989	780
1990	948
1991	910
1992	836
1993	812
1994	754
1995	795
1996	683
1999	764
2002	943
2003	877
2006	1091

In 1973, two FFC-aided films broke new ground. (The FFC is now the NFDC, the National Film Development Corporation). Avtar Kaul's *27 Down* was a paen to railway lore and mystique in the outward form of a love story. It won the year's Best Hindi feature award and later an award at the Locarno festival. Of a different genre was M.S. Sathyu's *Garam Hawa* (1973) which told the story of India's partition through the eyes of a Muslim family in Agra. FFC assisted in funding the making of more than a hundred films, many of which did not make it to the box-office. Notable among these have been Kumar Shahani's *Maya Darpan* and *Tarang*, and Mani Kaul's *Uski Roti, Ashad Ka Ek Din*, and *Duvidha* ('... they do not form a trilogy. They are about women yes, aspects of women, that's all'[26]), *Satah Se Utha Admi* (on Muktibodh, the Hindi poet), *Siddheshwar*, a tribute to the thumri singer, and *Naukar Ki Kameez*.

The Middle Cinema

Hindi cinema, dominated in the 1970s by the Sippys, Hrishikesh Mukherjee, B.R. Ishara and Vijay Anand, was jolted out of its wits when Shyam Benegal assisted by Blaze Enterprises, shot into prominence with *Ankur* (1974), and later with *Nishant* (1975), *Manthan, Bhumika* (1977), *Kondura* (1977) and *Junoon* (1979). Benegal turned his back on the standard *Kalyug* and *Aaradhana* (1981) genre, injecting a dose of caste-politics into his first three films. He was closely associated with the making of Govind Nihalani's *Aakrosh* (1980), a political film about the exploitation of illiterate Adivasis. *Ardh Satya* (1984), *Party* (an expose of the upper middle class), and his TV serial on the partition of India, *Tamas*, have been significant successes.

While the films of Mrinal Sen, Mani Kaul and Kumar Shahani did not fare very well at the box office, those of the 'middle cinema' reaped a good harvest. Saeed Mirza's *Albert Pinto Ko Gussa Kyon Aata Hai, Mohan Joshi Hazir Ho*, and *Salim Langde Pe Math Ro*, Rabindra Dharmaraj's *Chakra*, and Ketan Mehta's *Bhavni Bhavai* (in Gujarati and Hindi), *Mirch*

---

26 Mani Kaul: 'I am opposed to story-telling', in an interview with Sameer Shah in *The Sunday Observer*, July 11, 1982.

Masala, and later *Maya Memsahib*, and *Sardar*, started a trend in the making of socially conscious and political films which were entertaining as well. Both the New Wave and the Middle Cinema wilted under the impact of multi-channel television, 'commercial cinema', the commercialization of the National Film Development Corporation (NFDC), and above all the abysmal paucity of exhibition outlets. The gradual decline of the Film Society movement too played a significant role in the fading away of 'parallel cinema'.

The Second New Wave

As the century drew to a close, there was a revival of the New Wave spirit, with some assistance from the NFDC, Doordarshan, overseas TV companies such as Channel Four of Britain, and private financiers. Some termed this revival the 'Second New Wave',[27] even though most of the film makers involved in the revival were also part of the first New Wave. Mani Kaul (*Nazar, The Idiot, Siddeshwari*), Shyam Benegal (*The Making of the Mahatma, Mammo, Saatvan Ka Ghoda, Sardari Begum*), Saeed Mirza (*Naseem* (1996)), Adoor Gopalakrishnan (*Kathapurusham* (1995)), Girish Kasaravalli (*Mane* (1996), *Thai Saheb* (1998)), Govind Nihalani (*Hazaar Chourasi Ki Maa* (1998)), Kumar Shahani (*Chaar Adhyay* (1997)) and others in different regional languages of the country helped keep the spark of 'alternative' cinema alive. The establishment of the National Centre for Children and Young People (NCYP) provided an impetus to the making of films targeted at the Indian youth.

New Trends

The early years of the 21st century witnessed several dramatic developments in Indian cinema. Cinema was at last declared an 'industry' in May 1998 by the BJP Government (just a day prior to India's nuclear test on May 11) and no sooner did this happen than the gradual 'corporatisation' of the entertainment and media

---

27 Cf. Khalid Mohamed: 'The Second New Wave', in *The Times of India*, February 16, 1992.

industry took off. Banks, insurance companies and the Federation of Indian Chambers of Commerce and Industry (FICCI) were persuaded to support the industry. Active support from banks and financial institutions has resulted in the professionalization of the industry and also in the decline of its dependence on funding from the 'underworld' of Bombay and other shady sources of financing.

But perhaps the biggest impetus to the shake-up of the industry has been the rapid proliferation of 'multliplexes' (multi-screen theatres) and digital cinema theatres, first in the metros and later in the big cities such as Bangalore, Hyderabad, Ahmedabad and Pune. Multiplexes offered a different experience to cinema-goers, for in most cases they are part of a shopping and restaurant complex. Multiplexes receive direct tax benefits under the Income Tax Act (1961) and are integrated into shopping malls and comprise theatres of different sizes. This perhaps accounts for their rapid proliferation throughout urban India. Thus small-budget films could be released first in multiplexes and digital cinema theatres and later in single-screen theatres. Ticket rates are much higher in multiplexes than in single-screen theatres and therefore attract upper middle class families; they also exclude the poorer sections of the film-going audience. Multiplex cinemas have thus succeeded in enticing the upper middle classes back to film viewing in theatres.

Major Multiplex Chains	Major Home Video/DVD Companies
1. PVR Cinemas Ltd.	1. Moser-Baer
2. INOX Leisure Ltd.	2. Shemaroo
3. Pyramid Saimira	3. Eros International
4. Valuable Media	4. Excel Home Video
5. Mukta Adlabs	5. Time
6. Real Image	6. Bombino
7. Sathyam Cinemas	7. Ultra
8. Shringar Cinema	8. UTV
9. Fame India Ltd.	9. GV Films
10. Cinemax India Ltd.	
11. Fun Cinemas (E-Square)	

This has given rise to what has come to be known as 'multiplex films', that is small-budget, experimental films on subjects which are rarely touched on in mainstream cinema. Further, the films are personal, urban, and reflective; usually without any songs and the dominant language used is English or Hinglish. Young directors like Nagesh Kukunoor (*Hyderabad Blues, Bollywood Calling* and *Iqbal*), Sudhir Mishra (*Hazaaron Khwaishein Aisi*) and Anurag Kashyap (*Black Friday*) have been able to make a mark thanks to the multiplex phenomenon. Small low-budget films like *Being Cyrus*, *Mixed Doubles*, *Joggers Park*, *Split Wide Open*, *Everybody Says I'm Fine*, *White Noise*, *Jhankar Beats*, *Dharam*, *Bheja Fry*, and other feature films were released in such theatres. At the end of 2007, a decade after the first multiplex was established by Ajay Bijli in a refurbished theatre in New Delhi, there were over 500 screens in around a hundred multiplexes across urban India.

The potential of low-budget films at the box-office has led to the tackling of new and bold themes by young directors both in the mainstream and parallel traditions. Homosexuality, old age (*Being Cyrus*), HIV-Aids (*My Brother Nikhil*), live-in relationships (*Salaam-Namaste*), communication with the physically and mentally challenged (*Black, Iqbal*), religious fundamentalism (*Parzania*), nationalist history (*Mangal Pandey: The Rising*), patriotism (*Lagaan, Bose: The Forgotten Hero*), and rural development (*Swades*) have been some of the issues taken up for analysis in feature films and documentaries over the last decade. Yet another issue raised in film after film, especially after 9/11, and in reponse to the series of patriotic films of the 1990s where India's 'enemy' was represented as Muslim (e.g. *Roja, Sarfarosh, Mission Kashmir, Gadar, Border*), has been the case of the 'moderate' Muslim (e.g. *Chak De India*, Subhash Ghai's *Black and White*, Karan Johar's *My Name is Khan*, Pooja Bhatt's *Dhoka* and Shoab Mansoor's *Khuda Ke Liye*).[28]

---

28 Cf. Minakshi Sinha: 'Moderate Muslims in the Movies', *The Times of India*, 12 May 2008, p. 9. For a study of how Indian media students perceive Islam and Muslims in popular films, see my paper on 'Representations of Islam in the Indian Mass Media', presented at IAMCR Conference, Barcelona, 22-26 July 2002.

'Cross-Over Cinema': The Second New Wave

The term 'cross-over cinema' is rather loosely used to describe films in English and/or Hindi made by Indians of the diaspora: Gurinder Chaddha (*Bhaji on the Beach, Bend it Like Beckham, Bride and Prejudice*, and *Mistress of Spices*), Mira Nair (*Salaam Bombay, Monsoon Wedding, Kamasutra, The Namesake*) and Deepa Mehta (the 'elements trilogy': *Earth, Fire*, and *Water*) which have been successful at the box office both in India and overseas. Chaddha is British, while Nair is an American and Mehta a Canadian.

A second group of films that is sometimes labelled 'cross-over' include several films in English and/or Hindi made by Indian directors but set in London, New York, Sydney, Melbourne and Amsterdam (e.g: *Cheeni Kum, Kabhi Alvida Na Kehna, Heyy Babyy, Salaam Namaste*, and *Hum Tum*) which have proved to be successful in Indian and overseas markets. Other recent films that have been shot in foreign locations include: *Diwaana Hue Pagal* (Dubai), *Chocolate* (London), *Bachke Rehna Re Baba* (Mauritius), *Raniji London Waley* (London), and *Jo Boley So Nihal* (United States).

A third category of the cross-over film relates to mainstream Bollywood films such as *Kabhi Khushi Kabhi Gam, Hum Dil De Chuke Sanam, Chak De India* and *Om Shanthi Om;* these have been phenomenal successes in the overseas market. It is therefore not surprising that films targeted at the growing NRI market in North America, Britain, South Africa, West Asia and South-East Asia have been on the rise in 'Bollywood'. This trend was started in the 1990s by blockbusters like *Dilwale Dulhaniya Le Jayenge* and *Hum Aapke Hain Koun*.

The cross-over film is however not a new phenomenon in Indian cinema. Right from the early days of the silent and talkies eras, Indian films were invariably released overseas, especially in countries like South Africa, Fiji, Great Britain and the United States where large diasporic communities lived. A true crossover film, however, is one that succeeds in drawing non-diasporic audiences worldwide. This has been the case with Hindi films in the Arab world, Russia and East Europe, parts of Africa like Nigeria and Kenya, and of course the whole of South Asia and

South-east Asia. In recent years, Tamil films starring the superstar Rajnikant have proved popular in Japan and other parts of South-east Asia.

Production, Distribution and Marketing of 'Bollywood' Films

'Bollywood' is not the only Indian cinema; the term largely restricted to the production of around 250 Hindi films every year in Bombay/Mumbai. Hindi films are produced in Madras/ Chennai too, as they have been since the early days of Indian cinema. During some years though, a larger number of Telugu and Tamil films are produced in Hyderabad and Madras respectively than Hindi films in Bombay. But while Hindi films are marketed and distributed across six 'territories' of India and also in the overseas territory ('the seventh territory'), South Indian language films are widely distributed in the southern states. Tamil films in particular have found a potential market in South and West Asia as well as in South-East Asia (particularly in Japan and Korea) and South Africa.

The process of marketing a Hindi film begins with the public announcement of the 'muhoorat'; this is billed as a huge media event with publicity as the primary goal. Publicity/Public Relations managers are hired to flood the media with 'breaking news'. Most films now have one or more media partners/ sponsors, and other commercial 'sponsors'. Product placements ('in-film' advertisements) are negotiated with advertisers/ advertising agencies even as the script is being written. Sometimes, titles incorporate brand names as in *Cheeni Kum – A Sugar Free Romance* (where Sugar Free is a well-known sugar supplement brand) or *26th July at Barista* (where Barista is the coffee bar chain). A brand name in the title of film is believed to rake in ten to fifteen per cent of the production cost of a film.

'Merchandising' is yet another stream of revenue for film producers; this too is often negotiated with potential manufacturers and marketers. Songs to be incorporated in the film are then sold to music companies; the songs create a 'buzz' about the film and facilitate its marketing nationwide. Negotiations for the sale of video/DVD, television, satellite and internet rights to media companies are also held. Thus, more than a third of the production cost is financed even before the film goes on the shooting floor. On occasion, the proposed film is sold to different 'territories' much before the 'muhoorat'.

Table 14: Major Film Producers and Distributors

Major Producers-Distributors[29]	Major Distributors[30]
• Yash Raj Films • Percept Picture Company • UTV • Pritish Nandy Communications • Mukta Arts • Adlabs Films (ADAG)-Reliance, also in Exhibition (Reliance Big Entertainment) • Sony Pictures • K Sera Sera • Shringar Cinemas • BAG Films • Saregama • Studio-18	• Mukta Arts • Yash Raj Films • Cinevista • Varma Corp/K Sera Sera • E-City Entertainment • UTV Motion Pictures • PVR Pictures • Sahara One Motion Pictures • Shri Ashtivinayak Cinema Visions • Eros International (for 'Overseas' Territory) • India Film Company (Network-18)

Table 15: Revenue Streams for Indian Feature Films

1. Cinema Theatres
2. Television, Cable, Satellite, DTH, HITS, IPTV : Movie Channels, Film-based programmes, news, reviews – Video-on-Demand (VOD)
3. Film Music on AM and FM Radio Stations
4. Recorded Music Companies
5. Internet: Online movie portals, websites; downloads, online digital sales
6. Home Video: VCDs/DVDs, rentals
7. Mobile Telephony: Ring-tones, wall-papers, games
8. Merchandising
9. In-flight screenings
10. Events, festivals, wedding receptions, hotels, pubs, discos, restaurants, etc.
11. Brand names in film title, In-film advertising, in-theatre advertising.
12. Commercial Sponsors, Media Sponsors.

---

29 Cf. Vanita Kohli-Khandekar: *The Indian Media Business*, New Delhi: Response Books, 2007. Second Ed. p. 107.
30 Ibid.

Table 16: Film Distribution: 'Territories'

1. *Mumbai*: includes parts of Maharashtra, southern Gujarat and Karnataka.
2. *Delhi*: Uttar Pradesh, Uttaranchal and the National Capital Region
3. *East Panjab*: Panjab, Haryana, and Jammu and Kashmir
4. *East Circuit*: West Bengal, Bihar, Jharkand, Nepal, Orissa and Assam
5. *Rajasthan*: Rajasthan, Chhatisgarh, Madhya Pradesh and Northern Maharashtra
6. *South*: Nizam (parts of Andhra and Southern Maharashtra), Mysore (Bangalore and those parts of Karnataka which are not in Mumbai territory), Andhra (remaining parts of AP) and Tamilnadu (entire states of Tamilnadu and Kerala)
7. *Overseas/Multiple Territories*.

The 'Overseas' Territory

The 'overseas' territory has become more and more lucrative over the years, what with more than 22 million Indians of the diaspora, resident in over a hundred countries. In the United States, Indians of the diaspora (3.2 million) are called Indian Americans, in Great Britain (Indian population: 1.2 million), the resident Indians in Southall, Leicester, Bradford, Birmingham or Glasgow are called 'Asians' by the natives (and this encompasses Pakistanis, Bangladeshis, Sri Lankans, Tamils, the lot). But among the Indians themselves, Panjabis, Gujarathis, Goans, East Indians (and more recently Kashmiris) club together and maintain their separate identities and cultures zealously. Other countries which make up the Indian diaspora include Myanmar (2.5 million), Malaysia (1.6 million), South Africa and Kenya (around one million each), Canada (850,000), Mauritius (715,000), Trinidad and Tobago (500,600), Fiji (337,000), Singapore (300,000), Australia (190,000), New Zealand (55,000), Hong Kong (45,000). The Gulf nations do not offer citizenship, only worker status to around two million Indians (Saudi Arabia: 1.5 million; Kuwait: 295,000, Bahrain: 130,000, Qatar: 131,000, Oman: 312,000), Europe has a small community of Indians: France: 65,000, Germany: 35,000, and the

Netherlands 215,000), a few of them workers, not citizens.[31]

These various scattered groups of Indians comprise what Arjun Appadurai terms 'communities of sentiment',[32] for they do share a lot in common: Indian films are a way of keeping in touch with the religions, traditions and cultures of their forefathers and a powerful source of nostalgia. Indeed, for the diaspora the Bombay Hindi film is not mere entertainment but appears to relate to questions of identity of Indian communities living overseas, as well as to the nostalgia for a world they left behind in recent times (the new diaspora) or more than a century ago as plantation workers in far off lands (the old diaspora). Such films also speak of the traditional values of the Indian/Hindu joint family, often romanticising practices such as arranged marriages, respect for parents and religious rituals. This has given rise to a new genre which could be termed the 'NRI film'. The genre focuses attention on the cross-cultural dilemma of Indians living in the West, and in particular of their nostalgia for India. Perhaps unwittingly, the genre tends to foster a strong nationalist fervour and to endorse support for religious fundamentalism.[33]

The 1990s and the first decade of the new millennium witnessed the growing interest of international audiences in Indian cinema. Indeed, the biggest growth in Indian cinema has been in the overseas market. The international box office has begun listing Bollywood releases on its charts and foreign newspapers have started reviewing Indian films. Indian film makers have opened offices in London, New York and Tokyo while overseas distributors like Eros International and Ayangaran International have established offices in India, United States, Britain, UAE and Fiji. Around 130-140 Bollywood films make it

---

31 The data for NRIs and PIOs has been compiled from various sources. See *India Today*, May 20, 2002 for earlier data.
32 Arjun Appadurai: *Modernity at Large: Cultural Dimensions of Globalisation*, Minneapolis: University of Minnesota Press, 1996.
33 For further discussion of this theme, see my paper on 'New Trends in Indian Cinema', Siegen University Conference on Media and Universals, February 3-5, 2005. See also Patricia Uberoi: *Freedom and Destiny – Gender, Family and Popular Culture in India*, New Delhi: Oxford University Press, 2006.

to the overseas market every year, helping film makers to earn 15-20% of their income from overseas. For instance, Yash Raj Films earned Rs. 30 crore from the overseas territory out of its total earnings of Rs. 90 crore last year. Indian film exports earn about Rs. 10 billion per annum, with an estimated growth of two billion rupees every year.

Distribution and Exhibition of Indian Films Overseas

Indian films have been distributed and exhibited overseas, either formally or informally, right from the beginnings of cinema in the closing years of the 19th century. Cinema was perhaps the first entertainment industry to turn 'global' as it expanded rapidly around the world within months of the first 'actualities' screened in a basement in Paris. The Indian diaspora in Britain, Africa and North America were quick to take to the early mythologicals of Dadasaheb Phalke, the socials of Chandulal Shah and the oriental tales of Himansu Rai. The Rangachariar Committee established by the then British government in 1920 found ample evidence to suggest that Indian silent films were distributed in Asia, Africa and Europe. The diaspora at the time comprised mostly plantation labour and small business groups. The Indian diaspora today has increased manifold to about 22 million in over 110 countries, according to the Singhvi Report (2002) and comprises a diversity of professional groups, as well as a diversity of linguistic and religious groups. To both the first generation as well as the second or third generations of immigrants, films from India are not just a source of entertainment but rather a medium for keeping in touch and for feeding the nostalgia for a land they or their parents left behind.

Indian films are extremely popular in Nigeria and other countries of East Africa among the local populations who have little knowledge of Hindi (the films are shown without dubbing or sub-titles).[34] They are also popular among Arab viewers across

---

34 For an interesting analysis of Indian cinema in Nigeria, see Brian Larkin: 'Indian Films and Nigerian Lovers: Media and the Creation of Parallel Modernities', *Africa*, 67 (3), pp. 406-440.

the Middle East where of course the films carry Arabic subtitles.

Indian films, especially those in Hindi and made in Bombay have found their way to the diaspora of 22 million scattered in over a hundred countries. This is not a new phenomenon, for Indian films have been released overseas right from the days of Dadasaheb Phalke, the director of the first feature film, *Rajah Harishchandra* (1913). Some of the Phalke films were shown to Indian audiences in Burma, Singapore and East Africa.[35] In 1914, Phalke travelled to London with his first three films. The films were shown to a film industry group by the proprietor of the Bioscope.[36] But it is not clear if the films were actually distributed for the Indian community living in England.

The silent films of other directors too found their way to the diaspora. The films of Chandulal Shah, for instance, were comedies and satires which often carried English titles such as *Typist Girl, Why Husbands Go Astray, Educated Wife*. He produced as many as 130 feature films. Indian audiences at home and abroad were regaled by them, though 'Western audiences found them mild and hackneyed'.[37]

Himansu Rai, the founder of Bombay Talkies, was yet another film producer who released his films overseas, particularly in Europe. Rai's first film, *Light of Asia*, directed by the German film maker, Franz Osten, opened in Berlin, Vienna, Budapest, Venice, Genoa and Brussels, with personal appearance by Rai himself. It ran for four long months in London. The film, perhaps the first instance of an Indo-German co-production, proved a phenomenal box-office success. Rai got the finance necessary for his subsequent films (*Shiraz* (1926), *A Throw of Dice, Karma* (1930)) from Emelka Films and other European studios. Franz Osten of Emelka Films, Munich, later joined the staff of Rai's Bombay Talkies.

---

35 Eric Barnouw and S. Krishnaswamy: *Indian Film,* New Delhi: Oxford University Press, 1980, p.16
36 Ibid. p. 20.
37 Ibid. p. 36.

Shantaram's *Shakuntala* and *Dr Kotnis Ki Kahani* were released in London. They did not make a mark, but the films of Raj Kapoor were a phenomenal success, especially in the Soviet Union. Raj Kapoor and his fellow stars were taken in procession in the streets of Moscow and greeted everywhere. For decades, the songs in the Hindi films became as popular as the films themselves.

Regulating the Film Conglomerates

While Hollywood studios focus on production and international distribution ('vertical integration' of the production, distribution and exhibition sectors is prohibited by a 1948 anti-trust law laid down by the Supreme Court),[38] there are no such restrictions on Indian producers, distributors and exhibitors. Thus, several Indian film conglomerates such as Adlabs-Reliance BIG Entertainment, Yash Raj Films, PVR Pictures and Sahara One Motion Pictures are active in all three sectors. It is likely, therefore, that major Indian film companies will soon have their own chain of multiplexes around the country and distribute and exhibit their own productions in these very chains, thus effectively blocking the release of films from rival companies. At the end of 2007 there were a mere 13,000 cinema screens with 20% of them part of mobile cinemas meant primarily for small towns and cities in the interior of the country. Around a hundred e-cinemas got their digital content delivered via a satellite distribution network, and multiplexes were rapidly becoming part of the urban landscape.

So, while the 'content' of films is scrutinized by the CBFC there is hardly any regulation of monopolistic trends in the distribution and exhibition sectors. With the entry of the

---

38 See United States Supreme Court v. Paramount Pictures Inc. (1948). It is a landmark decision of the Supreme Court to rein in the Hollywood 'majors' as they monopolized theatre ownership at the time. It is also known as the Hollywood Anti-Trust Case of 1948, the Paramount Decree, the Paramount Decision or the Paramount Case. For a fuller discussion of the political economy of Hollywood cinema, see Janet Wasko: *How Hollywood Works,* London: Sage Publications, 2003, and Arthur de Vany: *Hollywood Economics*: *How Extreme Uncertainty Shapes the Film Industry*, London: Routledge, 2004.

Hollywood 'majors' in the Indian film market via co-production and joint ventures, such trends are likely to be aggravated. The film industry is in dire need of a FRAI (Film Regulatory Authority of India) so that there is a level playing field, as there is in telecommunications and other media-related businesses.

The 'corporatisation' of the film business (following the Central Government's declaration in 1998 that film entertainment is an 'industry') has led to the entry of major legitimate investors and fianciers into the production, distribution and exhibition sectors. (IDBI has financed 38 regional films under its film financing scheme, the Indian Overseas Bank financed the Rajnikant blockbuster, *Sivaji*, and Exim Bank is known to finance films that have a potential in overseas markets).[39] Some film labels such as Mukta Arts and Cinevista have already issued IPOs, entered the Bombay stock market and become 'listed' companies. The traditional modes of doing business are being challenged by the emergence of nationwide chains of 'multiplex' theatres and a new crop of young film makers and entrepreneurs. Where in earlier times a film would take years to be produced since the largely improvised script depended on the availability of 'stars' and of 'advances' from distributors, now a film has its beginnings in a 'bound script' and is shot at one go within a couple of months. Large companies like Yash Raj Films, UTV and Percept Communications sign deals with creative houses like Ram Gopal Varma's or with dozens of individual directors.[40] Ambani's Big Entertainment has negotiated deals worth over a billion dollars to finance Hollywood film directors including Steven Spielberg. And Hollywood studios have begun not just to release Bollywood films in India and overseas but also to finance or co-finance them. The rules of the game in terms of distribution and exhibition too stand changed. Age-old practices where the distributor was supreme are under threat; managers of multiplex

---

39 Cf. Shobha Kannan: Film Financing: Banks Sing Regional Tune, *Business Line*, 30 August 2007, p. 7.
40 For a detailed analaysis of the 'churn' in the business, see Vanita Kohli-Khandekar op. cit. p. 124 ff.

chains and digital theatres now call the shots. They can make or break even a potential blockbuster. Digital theatres (over 850 of them by mid-2008), digital modes of delivery and digital prints (VCDs and DVDs) have reduced the costs of distribution immensely. Indeed, the future of cinema is digital and above all in cyberspace where films have already begun to be distributed and exhibited worldwide without the need for cinema theatres or even digital prints. The Working Group of the 11th Five-Year Plan (2007-2012) on Information and Broadcasting Sector recommends that the Government 'should formulate a National Digital Policy for the film industry, encompassing all aspects of the industry i.e. production, distribution and exhibition.'[41] It also recommends that all Acts, Rules and Regulations that inhibit the development of the industry should be reviewed, and that import duties on capital goods required for the industry be reduced.[42] Further, it recommends that the Film and Television Institute of India (FTII) and the Satyajit Ray Film and Television Institute of India (SRFTII) be 'transformed into global film and television schools'.[43]

Table 17: Growth in the Cinema Business[44]

Year	Rs. Crore
2003	19
2004	23
2005	32
2006	55
2007	104.5
2008	157

---

41 Working Group Report of the 11th Five-Year Plan (2007-12) on Information and Broadcasting Sector, January 2007. Cf. http://planningcommission.gov.in.
42 Ibid.
43 Ibid.
44 Source: Pitch-Madison Survey – 2008.

Table 18: *National Box-Office Revenues (2001-2006)*[45]

Year	Revenue – US$	No. of Movie-goers	No. of Multiplexes
2001	593 million	2.8 billion	10
2002	658	3.2	19
2003	643	3.42	34
2004	707	3.59	54
2005	1.19 billion	3.77	68
2006	1.41 billion	3.95	101

'Regional Language' Cinema

At the national level, films in Hindi made in Mumbai and Chennai, continue to reign supreme. During the 1990s, however, some films made in the languages of the South, either re-made or dubbed in Hindi, have found a good market nationwide. Mani Ratnam's *Roja, Bombay, Dil Se, Yuva, Hey Ram!* and *Guru* are examples of such films. The omnibus term 'Regional Language' refers to Indian languages other than Hindi and English; strictly speaking though this is incorrect, since under the Indian constitution all 23 recognised languages are 'national'. For Hindi is as much a 'regional' language as say Tamil or Telugu or Bengali.

Several Hollywood films too began to be dubbed in Hindi, beginning with *Jurassic Park, Schindler's List, Pretty Woman* and *The Lion King*, though not all of them managed to succeed at the box-office. The various Hollywood companies such as Sony/Columbia, MGM, Twentieth Century Fox, Paramount/ Viacom and Disney have a significant presence in Mumbai and other large cities. A recent trend is the production of Indian films in English, such as *The Making of the Mahatma*, and *English August.* Yet another trend is the making of films on India-related themes by NRI film makers such as Mira Nair (*Salaam Bombay, Monsoon Wedding, Mississippi Masala, Kamasutra*) and Deepa

---

45 Source: *India Today*, 14 April 2008, p.70.

Mehta (the 'elements' trilogy: *Earth, Fire* and *Water*).

Tamil Cinema
Madras has been a centre for film production in Hindi and the South Indian languages, from the early years of Indian cinema. Several silent features based on the mythology and the puranas were produced, and proved to be very popular among the masses. The first silent film was *Keechakavatham* (The Extermination of Keechakan) (1916), a mythological, and the first talkie *Kalidas* (1931) contained no fewer than 50 songs. Tamil cinema was seen as an extension of the popular performing arts such as company drama, therukoothu, the circus and wrestling. The repertoire of the (drama) companies was limited to a few mythologicals, written as musicals. The stories were standardised as a series of songs[46]. In keeping with the tradition of company drama, the talkies carried a large number of songs and placed less emphasis on dialogue.[47] Right from the beginnings of Tamil cinema, the Brahmin elite despised cinema (just as it did company dramas and therukoothu (folk street theatre), regarding it as 'low culture', in contrast to Bharatnayam and Carnatic music which constituted 'high culture'.[48]

The first three phases of Tamil cinema, according to one analyst, were (i) the puranic, mythological and folklore period (1931-50), (ii) the melodramatic story period (1951-75), and (iii) the partly realistic anti-sentimental stories period (1951-75)[49].

The perspective is of course elitist; realism is seen as the ideal towards which cinema must aspire. The 'parallel' cinema, which was marked by social realism, had its influence on the Tamil cinema of the late seventies. The pioneers were K. Balachander, Bharathi Raja, Mahendran, Balu Mahendra, Dorai, Jayabharati, Bhagyaraj, Rudraiyya and H.A. Kaja. Mahendran's *Utharipookal* and Dorai's *Pasi* continued the realistic genre

---

46 S. Theodore Bhaskaran: 'Music for the Masses: Film Songs of Tamilnadu', in Economic and Political Weekly, March 1991.
47 S.S. Pandian: 'Tamil Cultural Elites and Cinema: Outline of an Argument', in Economic and Political Weekly, April 13, 1996, pp. 950-955.
48 S.S. Pandian: op cit. p.950.
49 ibid.

started by the late Bhim Singh's *Sila Narangalil Sila Manithangal* which challenged the myth of the ideal heroine. Bharathi Raja set the trend of locating films in villages, and Mahendra gave the villagers 'solidity, depth and relevance' in his *16 Vayadinile*. There was a radical move away from the dialogue-oriented film, as in J. Mahendran's *Mullum Malarum* and the co-operative venture of some young people under the leadership of Robert and Rajasekaran, *Oru Thalai Ragam*. The demise of film-star and Chief Minister M.G. Ramachandran[50] in 1988, and the ouster of Jayalalitha as Chief Minister has not affected film production though some studios have closed and attendance has fallen, owing to cable, the Sun, Vijay, Jaya and Raj TV channels, and Sun Movies, the round-the-clock film TV channel of the Sun TV group. Mani Ratnam, Illayarajah and A.R. Rehman have put Tamil cinema on the all-India map.[51,52] Mani Ratnam is prolific as he works not only in Tamil cinema but also in Hindi, Kannada and Telugu. Several of his Tamil films are dubbed in other Indian languages. Beginning with *Mouna Ragam* a romantic tale of an aged couple, he has gone on to tell stories of politics, terrorism, youth and business in box-office hits like *Iruvar*, *Thalapathi*, *Roja*, *Bombay*, *Yuva*, and *Guru*. But it is the films starring Rajnikant that draw the fans and the crowds in Tamilnadu to the larger-than-life representations of the superstar, his latest being *Sivaji, the Boss* (2007). The 'fan clubs' associated with Rajnikant and other film stars continue to thrive and to direct Tamil film and political culture.[53]

---

50 For a critical study of cinema and politics in Tamilnadu, cf. S.S. Pandian: *Image Trap: MGR in Film and Politics*, New Delhi: Sage Publications, 1992. See also S. Rajnayagam: *Cultural and Political Ramifications of Popular Screen Image in Tamilnadu: A Comparative Study of the Films of M G Ramachandran and Rajinikanth*, Unpub. Dissertation submitted to Madras University, January 2002.
51 For a recent analysis, cf. S. Theodore Bhaskaran: *The Eye of the Serpent: An Introduction to Tamil Cinema*, Madras: East West Books (Madras) Pvt. Ltd., 1996.
52 For an analysis of Tamil cinema from a religious perspective, cd. C.R.W. David: *Cinema as Medium of Communication in Tamilnadu*, Madras: Christian Literature Society, 1983.
53 See Sara Dickey's *Going to the Movies in Madurai*, for an ethnographic analysis of Tamilnadu's 'fan clubs'.

Telugu Cinema

In terms of the number of films produced no state has been as prolific as Andhra. Most of the Telugu films made are potboilers *a la* Hindi cinema, loaded with song and dance sequences. Mythologicals, folk love fantasies, social and crime thrillers dominate. The first Telugu talkie was H.M. Reddi's *Bhakta Prahlad* (1932); Reddi's *Grihalakkshmi* (1937) was a path-breaking film: it broke away from the tradition of using *grandhikam* in dialogue and employed a colloquial spoken style.'[54] From the 1930s onwards, Telugu films were made in Rajahmundy, Vizagapattnam, Madras and even Kolhapur. Some of the classics of early Telugu cinema are: G. Ramabrahman's *Mala Pillai Raita*, K.V. Reddi's *Bhakta Potana*, *Yogi Vemana*, Chittoor V. Nagaiah's *Thaiagaiah* and B.N. Reddi's *Malleswari*[55].

Shyam Benegal with *Anuragham*, Mrinal Sen with *Oka Cori Katha* did try to break into Telegu films but without much commercial success. B.S. Narayana has won national and international acclaim with his two features, *Oorummadi Bratukulu*, a naturalistic film about the struggle of the poor, and *Nammajjanam* which deals with the suicide of a young bride who is the victim of rape. Two other outstanding films are Ravindran's *Harijan* and Gautam Ghose's *Maa Bhoomi*, which focus on the plight of the have-nots in an exploitative situation.

Telegu cinema shot into the limelight in 1981 with K. Viswanath's *Sankarabaranam* which bagged the Golden Lotus for Mass Entertainer with Aesthetic Values. In 1989, his *Sevarna Kamalam* was selected for the Indian Panorama. Vishwanath went on to make several other films, such as *Sita Mahalakshmi*, *President Peramma*, *Saptapadi*, *Subalekha*, and *Sagar Sangamam*. Among the other directors worthy of mention are K.V. Reddi, L.V. Prasad, Dasari Narayana Rao, K. Raghavendra Rao and U. Vishveshwara Rao.[56]

---

54 Gudipoodi Srihari: 'Telugu Cinema' in T.M. Ramachandran, op. cit. p. 479.
55 For a filmography and discussion of B.N. Reddi's prolific output, cf. Randor Guy: B.N. Reddi, Pune: National Film Archive of India, 1986.
56 For a fuller discussion of Telugu cinema, cf. K.N.T. Sastry: Telugu Cinema, Secunderabad: Cinema, 1986.

What accounts for the big crop of films each year in Andhra is the State Government's support. It is perhaps the only State Government that ploughs back about 7% of the receipts from entertainment tax into the film industry. The Andhra Pradesh State Film Development Corporation supports films made in Telugu.[57]

Marathi Cinema

Indian cinema had its beginnings in the Bombay Province. The earliest feature films, *Pundalik* and *Rajah Harishchandra*, were unmistakably Maharashtrian in form and substance. The traditions of the Marathi stage were followed closely. The mythological genre was clearly dominant in the early Marathi cinema, but there were historical and social themes taken up as well. Indeed, the mythologicals invariably carried social messages, in the manner of popular folk traditions such as Ram leela, Krishna leela, and keertans. The first studios for making films in Marathi were established in Kolhapur, Nashik and Pune.

Baburao Painter made mythological films like *Sairandhri* and *Vatsala Haran*, historicals like *Sinhagad*, and a remarkable social realist film, *Savkari Pash*, which told the tale of a Marathi peasant family in the context of the exploitation of poor illiterate farmers by moneylenders[58].

But it was Prabhat Talkies' *Sant Tukaram* (directed by Damle-Fatehlala) that won plaudits at home and abroad; the film represented Indian cinema at the 1937 Venice Film Festival. This and other films produced by Prabhat Talkies have inspired Marathi cinema over the years. The first studios, however, were set up in Kolhapur – the Maharashtra Film Co. – by Baburao Painter who together with Anandrao, pioneered the silent film

---

[57] For a recent study of the action genre in Telugu cinema, see S.V. Srinivas: 'Hong Kong Action Film and the Career of the Telugu Mass Hero' in Meaghan Morris, Siu Leuing and Stephen Chan Ching-kiu (Eds.): *Hong Kong Connections: Transnational Imagination in Action Cinema*, Durham: Duke University Press, pp. 111-25.

[58] V.P. Sathe: 'Marathi Cinema' in T.M. Ramachandran (Ed.): *70 Years of Indian Cinema (1913-1983)*, Bombay: Cinema-India International, 1985, p. 423-439.

era in Western India. Sardar Balasaheb Yadav, the owner of Chhatrapati Cinetone, also in Kolhapur, made mythologicals like *Kurukshetra* (1933), with draperies and other paraphernalia provided by Baburao Painter after he had wound up his own studio.

Bhalachandra Gopal Pendharkar (better known as Bhalji Pendharkar) of Jaiprabha Studios, also in Kolhapur, made over 50 films, including nine silent films which he wrote, produced and directed himself. Pendharkar was a journalist, a stage actor, a translator, but above all a nationalist. The cinema for him was a weapon to serve his country, to add to her glory and to enhance the reputation of everything Indian. He made both mythological and historical films, as also films on social issues, to further these goals. In *Shyamsundar* (1932), for instance, Lord Krishna is a revolutionary out to destroy the evil Kaunsa. His oeuvre includes *Meethbhakar* (1949), *Saadhi Mansi* (1965) and *Taambdi Maati* (1969); Dada Khondke debuted as an actor in the last film.

The films of Master Vinayak who worked in collaboration with P.K. Atre, were brilliant social satires of the forties. The foremost director of the 1950s was Raja Paranjpe, who collaborated with the poet and screenplay writer, G.D. Madgulkar. The role of literary figures in the making of Marathi films climaxed in the work of P.L. Deshpande. In these hands cinema lost much of its visual character and was turned into a literary and verbose product. A significant film of the fifties was Anant Mane's *Sangtye Aika*, based on the life of a popular contemporary actress. The film ran for over 130 weeks in a Pune theatre. Mane's other box-office triumphs were *Aboli* (1953), *Manini* and *Dhatki Jaoo*.

The few films that were produced during the sixties and early seventies were formula films – either of the tamasha or the family drama genres. Dada Khondke made his debut as a director in 1971 with *Songadya*, and followed it up with a string of successes. His racy comedies laced with double entrendes, his khakhi shorts which barely held up, his Chaplinesque walk, catchy lyrics and folksy music, provided a heady mix at a time when violence and gang wars reigned supreme in the Hindi cinema.

The eighties and nineties saw some welcome trends in both the popular and parallel streams of Marathi cinema. The renaissance came about mainly because of the 'entertainment tax refund scheme' (ETRS) introduced by the State Government in 1975. Under this scheme, a filmmaker had only to make a second film to get a refund of upto 80 per cent of the entertainment tax collected by the State Government from his or her first film. Entertainment tax on all Marathi films has now been scrapped and a subsidy scheme introduced whereby an A Grade film receives a reimbursement of Rs. 20 lakhs, a B Grade film Rs. 10 lakhs and a Grade C film Rs. 5 lakhs. For a Dolby Digital enabled film an additional Rs. 10 lakhs is provided.

In the early Marathi cinema, men of letters were collaborators, but in recent years they have turned into filmmakers in their own right. Jabbar Patel, a paediatrician by profession, is easily the most eminent among them. Scripted by Vijay Tendulkar, his first venture *Saamna* (Confrontation) is about the changing scene of rural Maharashtra, dominated as it has been all these years by sugar barons and power-politics. The second, *Jait Re Jait*, deals with tribal life, and the third *Simhasan* (Throne), is a political satire on the goings-on in Maharashtra politics. His *Umbartha* (*Subah* in Hindi) based on the novel by Shanta Misal, has a feminist theme.

Films based on well-known Marathi stage successes have also proved popular. *Ghasiram Kotwal* and *Shantata Court Chalu Ahe* by Vijay Tendulkar, the latter directed by Satyadev Dube and shot by Govind Nihalani, are cases in point. Other outstanding films of the eighties include *Sarvasakshi* (Omnipresent) directed by Ramdas Phutane, *22nd June 1897*, directed by Chinoo and Jayoo Patwardhan, and Raj Dutt's *Devki Nandan Gopala*, a biographical film on the life of Gadge Maharaj, a modern saint.

Ramdas Phutane went on to make a film based on a Marathi drama, *Down with Festivals*, and Shriram Lagoo, a veteran stage actor and director, made his debut as a film director with *Zaakol* (Ominous Shadow). Vijaya Mehta, Arvind Deshpande and Amol Palekar, three big names of the Marathi stage, have also entered the world of cinema, Mehta as a director, Deshpande as an actor, and Palekar as both an actor and director. Mehta's film ventures include *Smriti Chitre* and *Rao Sahib*, while Palekar has directed *Bangarwadi* and *Daayra*.

In 1991, a record 29 films were made but the only real box-office hit was Vijay Kondke's *Maherchi Saadi* which set off a trend in family dramas. Despite being a remake of the 1983 Gujarati film *Mahiruni Chunnari*, it proved to be such a phenomenal success (it ran in Pune's Prabhat theatre for more than a year) that even films by Sachin (*Ayatya Gharat Gharoba*) and Mahesh Kothare (*Jivalaga*) could not hold the audiences.[59]

At the end of the nineties, Marathi cinema was gasping for survival, with only nine films produced in 1996, and 10 in 1997. The era of Dada Kondke came to an end with his passing away in early 1998. Shravani Deodhar's *Sarkarnama* (1997) focused on political corruption, while Nachiket and Jayoo Patwardhan's *Limited Manuski* (1996) used slapstick to satirise middle-class values. Other remarkable films of the time were Arun Khopkar's *Katha Don Ganpathivanchi* (1996), Sumitra Bhave and Sunil Sukhtankar's *Doghi* (1996), Ramesh Deo's *Senani* (1996), and *Piaj Lagnachi* (1997).

However, it appears that Marathi cinema will get a new lease of life with the State Government granting liberal subsidies to all film makers except for their maiden ventures, and making it obligatory for theatre owners in Maharashtra to screen Marathi films for at least four weeks a year. (In 2008, the State Government suspended the licenses of 35 theatres as they did not adhere to this ruling). In 2005, for instance, as many as 43 films received grants worth Rs. 8.5 crore. This financial assistance has

---

[59] Chandreshekhar Joshi: 'What Ails the Marathi Film Industry?', *The Times of India/Pune Plus*, October 16, 1992.

resulted in the production of around a hundred films every year, with some of them being sent to international film festivals at Cannes, Toronto and Rotterdam. Several Marathi films also figure regularly in the 'Panorama Section' of IFFI and the Pune International Film Festival (PIFF): Amol Palekar's *Anaahat* and *Thang* (Quest), Nishikant Kamat's *Dombivili Fast*, Chitra Palekar's *Bayo*, Kedar Sinde's *Jatra*, and Gajendra Ahire's *Divsendivas* and *Sarivar Sari*. Shwaas was nominated for the Oscar's in 2006. Beginning with *Sade Made Teen*, recent films that have done well at the box office include: *Kadachit* (Ashwini Bhave), *Valu* (Umesh Kulkarni), *Dombivli Fast, Tingya, Checkmate, Sakhi, De Dhakka, Amhi Satpute*. A prominent trend in contemporary Marathi cinema, is the making of films targeted at the VCD/DVD market for worldwide circulation. With Subhash Ghai's Mukta Arts, Amitabh Bachchan's A.B. Corporation and Subhash Chandra's Zee Telefilms entering the Marathi film market the growth of Marathi cinema in the years to come is assured.

Bengali Cinema

The Bengali cinema was dominated for over four decades (1950 -1995) by Satyajit Ray, Mrinal Sen, Tapan Sinha and Ritwik Ghatak. Ghatak died in 1976, and Satyajit Ray in 1993. Talented young film makers who joined the ranks of the 'parallel' cinema in later years included Purnendu Pattrea, Buddhadeb Dasgupta, Utpalendu Chakravorty, Nitish Mukherjee, Gautam Chakravorty, Gautam Bose and Aparna Sen.[60] But since all of them work at their art like lone wolves there's no 'movement' worth the name to provide them the support that comes from a cooperative effort. The result is that their films win laurels abroad, but can find few exhibitors at home. The Nandan Film Centre in Calcutta has now come to their rescue. The Centre has exhibition and documentation facilities, conducts seminars and workshops which draw film

---

60 For a study of Aparna Sen's work, see Shoma A. Chatterjee: *Parama and Other Outsiders: The Cinema of Aparna Sen*, Calcutta: Parumita Publications, 2002.

makers from all over the country. The Satyajit Ray Film and Television Institute, and the Film Studies programme at Jadavpur University have given further impetus to the Bengali film industry.

Buddhadeb Dasgupta launched his career as a director with *Dooratwa* (Distance) (1978), a close look at middle class mores in contemporary Calcutta through the story of a young lecturer's disillusion with leftist politics. *Neem Annapurna* (Bitter Morsel) followed a year later, and *Grihayuddha* (The Civil War) in 1982, the latter focusing on the inevitability of class conflict. *Andhi Galli* (Blind Alley) (1985), a film in Hindi, explored the erosion of Bengali youth's values against the backdrop of police 'encounters' of the 1970s for bumping off young leftists. He returned to Bengali with *Phera* (The Return) (1987).

Utpalendu Chakravorty made his debut with a documentary *Mukti Chai* and a feature on bonded labour *Moyna Tadanta* (Post Mortem), both of which have won national film awards. He went on to make *Chokh* (The Eye) (1982), *Debshishu* (Child God) (1985), *Phansi* (1989), the tragic tale of a professional hangman, *Chandanneer* (The Nest of Rhythm) (1989), a musical, and *Kanna* (1989), a documentary on a Bharat Natyam dancer.

Gautam Ghose made documentaries (*New Earth, Chains, Bondage, Hungry Autumn*) before he started directing feature films in Bengali, Hindi and Telugu. His first feature was a Telugu film *Maa Bhoomi* (Motherland) (1979), which focused attention on the Telangana peasant uprising in Andhra in the early forties. *Dhakal* (Occupation) (1981) told the story (in Bengali) of a gypsy woman's struggle to keep her land against the local landlord who is in collusion with the district officer. The Hindi feature *Paar* (The Crossing) (1984) told the dramatic tale of survival of a poverty-stricken couple, while the Bengali *Antarjali Yatra* (The Voyage Beyond) (1987) drew attention to the practice of sati.

Other Bengali filmmakers of note are: Aparna Sen (*36 Chowringhee Lane, Paroma, Sati, Picnic* and *Mr. and Mrs. Iyer*), Raja Mitra (*Ekit Jiban*), Sandip Ray (*Himghar*), Nitish Mukherjee (*Ekdin Surya, Nayan Shyama* and *Rabidar*),

Purnananda Pattrea (*Streer Patra, Chentra Tamsukha,* and *Malancha*)[61]. However, the most prolific of Bengali film makers in the last decade has been Rituparno Ghosh who has directed over 15 feature films (in Bengali, Hindi and English) and scripted over a dozen films. His award-winning Bengali films include: *Unishe April* (1994), *Bariwali* (1999), *Asukh* (1999), *Chokher Bali* (2003), *Dosar* (2006) and *Sunglass* (2008).

Malayalam Cinema

The seventies was the 'golden' period of Malayalam cinema. The pioneers of the 'parallel' cinema in Kerala were Adoor Gopalakrishnan, G. Aravindan, John Abraham and Shaji. Gopalakrishnan's oeuvre includes some finely crafted narratives made over the last three decades: *Swayamvaram, Kodiyettam* (1977), *Elipathyam* (Mousetrap) (1981), *Mukhamukham* (Face to Face) (1984), *Anantaram* (1987), *Mathilukal* (1989), *Vidheyan* (1993), *Kathapurusham* (1995), *Nizhalkkuthu* (2003) and *Naalu Pennungal, The Dance of Shiva* (2008).

The late G. Aravindan's films *Utharayanam* (1974), *Kanchana Sita, Thamp, Kummati, Esthappan, Sahaja, Oridath, Marattam, Chidambaram* (1985), and *Vasuthuhara* (1990) have won international renown for their asthetic and poetic qualities. Aravindan observed, 'Subtlety is my lifestyle, and I believe that it is more acceptable and suited to our way of life, culture and aesthetics. I cannot overlook the importance of social values. I enjoy making movies that are in communication with nature.'

Malayalam films have had the largest representation at the Indian Panorama of our international film festivals since the seventies. Film co-operatives (like Chitralekha), film societies (like Odessa), and loyal audiences have been the major reasons for the steady growth of Malayalam cinema. Besides, the State Government has set up a film complex in Trivandrum and provides subsidies to established filmmakers.

The other filmmakers who have made valuable contributions

---

61 For recent studies of Bengali cinema, cf. Prabhod Maitra: *Seven Decades of Bengali Cinema,* Calcutta: Nandan, West Bengal Film Centre, 1990; and Kironmay Raha: *Bengali Cinema,* Calcutta: Nandan, 1991.

in terms of form and content, include: Vasudevan Nair (*Nirmalayam Bandhanam*), P.A. Backer (*Kabani Nadi Chuvannappol*), Padmarajan (*Peuyazhiambalam* and *Kallan Pavithran*), V.R. Gopinath (*Greesham*), John Abraham (*Amma Ariyan* (Letter to Mother); *Cheriyachante Krogra Krithyangal* (The Wicked Deeds of Chediyachan), Sivan (*Yagam*), and K.R. Mohanam (*Ashwa Thama*) and Shaji (*Piravi*). K.G. George (*Journey's End*), Lenin Rajendran (*A Tale of the Past*), K. Ravindran's (*Ore Tahvool Pakshigal* and *Varikuzha*), are some of the other distinguished directors. The films that stood out in the early nineties were Shaji N. Karun's *Swaham*, Hariharan's *Parinayam* and Padmakumar's *Sammohanam*, and in the mid-nineties T.V. Chandran's *Ormakalundayirrikanam*, Hari Kumar's *Sukrutham*, and Lohitdas' *Bhootakannadi* (Magnifying Glass). Jeyraj, the maker of *Deshdanam*, won the Best Film Award for his *Kaliyattam* in 1998.[62] Chandran continues to produce films at regular intervals: *Susannah*, *Danny* and *Padam Onnu Oru Vilapam* have stormed the box office. So have the films of R. Sarath (*Sayahnam* and *Stithi*), Murali Nair (*Maranasimhasanam*, *Puttiyude Divasam* and *Arimpara*), Satish Menon (*Bhavam*), Rajiv Vijayaraghav (*Margam*) and Ashok Nath (*Sabhalam*).

Around 35 films are produced in Kerala every year but these have to compete for audiences with a spate of Tamil, Hindi and Telugu films (many of them dubbed in Malayalam). In 2007, for instance, as many as 80 Tamil films and 14 Telugu films were released in the State.

Kannada Cinema

Perhaps the earliest film in Kannada was *Bhakta Dhruva* (1934), but Kannada cinema really took off only after the mid-fifties under the leadership of Dr. Raaj Kumar. Its heyday was of course the 1970s when one daring film after another challenged the status quo and ushered in the Kannada 'new wave'. The State Government of Karnataka was perhaps the first to encourage the

---

[62] For a critical analysis of recent Malayalam films, cf. 'Focus on Malayalam Cinema, *Deep Focus*, Bangalore, Vol. VII, No. 1, 1997.

regional cinema by offering generous subsidies, and granting tax exemptions to films made in Kannada. In the space of two decades, Kannada cinema, largely under the influence of the 'Naavya' (modernist) movement in literature began to wrest national awards. *Samskara* (1970), *Vamsha Vriksha* (1971), *Kaadu* (1973), *Chomana Dudi* (1975) and *Hamse Geethe* won national and international acclaim. The ventures of Puttanna Siddhalingayya and Raaj Kumar which attempted to blend art with popular entertainment also proved successful.

The 'new wave' has receded in Karnataka as elsewhere in the country, with Karanth and Girish Karnad leaving the State, and the new film-makers taking to big-budget films. M.S. Sathyu of *Garam Hawa* and *Bara* (famine) fame, made two big-budget Kannada films – *Kanneshwara Rama* and *Chitegu Chinte* – and Girish Karnad *Ondanondu Kaladalli* and *Tabaliyu Neenade Magane* (jointly with Karanth). P. Lankesh's *Pallavi* too made a mark. But it has been Girish Kasaravalli who remains the foremost director now with a whole corpus of visually arresting 'humanist' films.[63] His contribution to Kannada cinema over the last three decades has been remarkable: *Ghattashradha* (The Ritual) (1977), *Aakramana* (The Siege) (1979), *Mooru Darigallu* (Three Pathways) (1980), *Tabarane Kathe* (Story of Tabare) (1987), *Mane* (House) (1988), Bannade Vesha (The Mask) (1990), Kraurya (The Tale of a Story-teller) (1995), *Thayi Sahiba* (Lady of the Manor) (1997), Dweepa (Island) (2002), *Hasina* (2005) and *Nayi Neralu* (In the Shadow of the Dog) (2006).[64] 'Central to Kasaravalli's oeuvre is the dynamic relationship between the humanism of the individual's story and the detached description of the outside world'.[65] In the popular film genre, commercial blockbusters continue to rule the roost.

---

63 For an insightful account of Kasaravalli's oeuvre, see N. Manu Chakravarthy (ed.): *Culturing Realism: Reflections on Girish Kasaravalli's Films*, Bangalore: Nudi Pustak, 2007.
64 For a critical history of Kannada cinema, cf. T.G. Vaidyanathan: 'Kannada Cinema' in T.M. Ramachandran, op cit., pp. 385-395.
65 Maithili Rao: 'Girish Kasaravalli: The Critical Insider' in N. Manu Chakravarthy: *Culuring Realism: Reflections on Girish Kasaravalli's Films*, Bangalore: Nudi Pustak, 2007, p. 85.

Since 2005, these have included the Shivraajkumar-starrer *Jogi* (2005), *Mungalu Male* (2006) and *Duniya* (2007).

Gujarati Cinema

The first Gujarati film was a short feature entitled *Mumbaini Sethani*, released on April 9, 1932, while the first full-length feature was *Narsinh Mehto*. Other early films included *Sati Savitri*, and *Ghar Jamai*. As in other parts of the country, Gujarati films had to compete with Hindi films made in Bombay and Madras, because of the samll number of theatres. So until the early seventies, only 130 Gujarati films had been made, the most remarkable being Kantilala Rathod's masterpiece *Kanku*. However, even *Kanku* could be released only in one theatre for just a week.

Then came the film 'boom' consequent upon the State government's generosity in granting subsidies and in exempting films produced in studios within the State, from entertainment tax. As many as 40 films were produced each year during the 1970s, but less than 30 during the 1980s, though the quality of films was rather indifferent. Popular Gujarati cinema has been largely based on mythology, folk tales and novels.

Some graduates of the Film and Television Institute, Pune, have set up a film co-operative called Sanchar. Sanchar's first venture, *Bhavni Bhavai (1980)*, made in 16 mm and shot on location and directed by Ketan Mehta, won a national film award and the acclaim of critics. So has *Mirch Masala* (1985). Mehta's Hindi films have met with greater success at the all-India box-office. They include *Holi* (1984), *Hero Hiralal* (1988), *Maya Memsahib* (1992), *Darling! Yeh Hai India (1995), Aar Ya Paar* (1997), *Mangal Pandey: The Rising* (2005) and *Rang Rasiya* (2007). He has also made seven documentaries, most notably the biographical film, *Sardar* (1993).

The spirit of *Kanku* and *Kashi No Dikro* returned to Gujarati cinema between 1980 and 1985 (the 'golden period' of Gujarati cinema), but for the next decade or so mythologicals and folk dramas continued to dominate. Gujarati cinema received a boost at the close of twentieth century with a string of blockbusters by

Govindbhai Patel, the foremost being *Unchi Medi Na Uncha Mol* (1996) and *Desh Re Joya Dada Pardesh* (1997). Like *Hum Aapke Hain Koun* and *Dilwale Dulhaniya Le Jayenge*, Patel's films are in the family drama genre, with the focus on the joint family system and the search for an Indian identity.[66]

Assamese and other North-Eastern Films

Cinema in Assam and the North-East has received much attention at national film festivals in recent years. The state film development corporations have provided the primary impetus for this gowth of interest in indigenous cinema. For instance, active support from the State-run Assam Film Finance and Development Corporation has played a vital role. It provides loans to talented filmmakers, and has plans of establishing a chain of 'Janata halls' for regular exhibition of films. Mobile cinemas are also being encouraged by exemption from entertainment taxes. The first Assamese film was Jyotiprasad Agarwala's *Joymati*, released in 1935. Agarwala later made *Indra Malati*, but received little recognition. He is believed to have been the first director to introduce playback singing in Indian cinema.

The following two decades saw a crop of films by Rohini Kumar Barua, Parvati Barua and Phani Sharma. In 1955 Piyali Phukan won a national award. In the sixties, the best known film-makers were Bhupen Hazarika, Padma Barua, Abdul Mazid, Attul Baroli and Manoranjan Sur. By the end of the eighties, however, film production had slumped. In 1986 only 11 films were made, and only eight in the following year. But this too is creditable since the whole state has only one government owned studio and minimal infrastructure. Most post-production work has to be completed in laboratories in Calcutta, Bombay or Madras. Exhibition theatres do not number more than 143 in the entire state.[67]

---

66 For further discussion of the history of Gujarati cinema, cf. Kantilala Rathod: 'Gujarati Cinema: A Critique', in T.M. Ramachandran, op cit., pp.349-353.
67 Sriprakash Menon in *The Indian Post*, Bombay, April 16, 1989.

Jahanu Barua and Bhabendranath Saikia have now put Assamese cinema on the international festival circuit. Saikia's major films include *Sandhya Rag, Anirban, Agnisaan, Kolahal* 1988) and *Kalsandhya,* and Barua's are: *Aparoopa* (1979), *Papori* (1985), *Halodhia Choraye Boodhan* (1987), *Bannai* (1989) *Hkhagoroloi Bohu Door* (1996) and *Firingoti. Halodhia Choraye Boodhan* won the Golden Lotus in 1988, and also the Grand Prix for Best Film and Best Actor at Locarno.

Barua and Saikia are filmmakers in the tradition of 'new wave' Indian cinema. They strive for an authentic portrayal of the village ethos, of the struggle of men and women against oppression and exploitation. Other filmmakers of note in Assam include Siba Thakur (*Asouta Prahor*), Padum Barua (*Ganga Chilaner Pakhi*), Jones Mohalia, Gautam Bora, Mirdul Gupta and Hemanta Das.[68] Recent Assamese films that have made a mark at home and abroad are: Santwana Bardoli's *Adajya* (The Flight), Manju Bora's *Laaz*, Sanjib Hazarika's *Matsyagandhya* (Outrage), Jwangdoa Bodosa's *Hagramayo Jinahan* (Rape in the Virgin Forest) and Sanjib Sabhapandit's *Juye Poora Xoon* (The Self-Triumphs).[69]

Manipuri Films

Around ten films have been produced so far in the Manipuri tongue, with the first film made in 1972. Perhaps the most acclaimed Manipuri film has been *Imagi Ningthem* (My Son, My Precious) (1981), directed by Aribam Syam Sharma. It won the Grand Prix at Nantes, France, in 1981. The film weaves a sensitive tale of a boy who, following his unmarried mother's death in childbirth, is brought up by his grandfather. The boy's father is traced by the local school teacher, and is found to be married; but his wife is only too happy to adopt the boy as her own. Sharma's *Ishanou* (1990) has been equally acclaimed. Among the other Manipuri films of note are: *Matamgi Manipur* (1972), *Ngak-ke-ko Ngangse* (1974), *Lamja Parusaram* (1975),

---

68 Pankaj Barua in *Cinema in India*, Bombay, January-March, 1989.
69 Cf. Lakshmi B. Ghosh: 'A Rare Peep into World of Assamese Cinema', *The Hindu*, 5 January 2006.

Khuttang Lamjet (1979), *Olangthagee Wangmadasoo* (1980), *Khonjel* (1981), *Wangma Wangma* (1982), M.A. Singh's *Sanakeithel* (1983) and Oken Amakchen's *Mayophy Gee Macha* (1994). 'The Manipuri Film is basically Meitei in content, theme and behaviour, though not mainly in form and style. The Meitei film is Imphal-based and middle-class in outlook and temper. And the middle-class mind is what constitutes the 'Manipuri mind'.[70][71]

A small number of films have also been made in the *other* languages of the north-east, such as Khasis *Manik Raiting* (Manik, the Miserable), and *Lawei Ha Ki Kti Jong Ngi*.

Oriya Cinema

Perhaps the first film to be made in Oriya was *Sitavivah* in 1934. As in the cinema of the other Indian languages, the early Oriya films were for the most part mythologicals. Time was when Oriya films matched the popularity of Bengali films. Notable films up to the fifties were: *Lalita*, *Mahalakshmi Puja*, *Dasyu Ratnakar* and *Parinam*. Mrinal Sen made *Matira Manisha* in Oriya, a film based upon Kalandi Charan Panigraha's Oriya novel of the pre-Independence period. One of the most popular films of the 1960s was Prabhat Mukherji's *Nua Bou*, replete with songs and the lead role played by the veteran Dhira Biswal.

Around 16 feature films are made each year in Orissa which has only one film laboratory, namely, the Prasad Kalinga Film Laboratories. A clutch of Oriya film makers of the last two decades, most of them alumni of the Film and Television Institute of India, have made a valuable contribution to Oriya cinema. One of the most distinguished is A.K. Bir, whose work includes *Aadi Mimansa*, *Lavanya Preeti*, *Aranyaka* and *Shasha Drushti* (The Last Vision). Nirad Mahapatra, an FTII alumni, has been relentless in his scrutiny of the Oriya family system in films like *Maya Miriga* (The Illusion) (1983). Other filmmakers like

---

[70] Lokendra Arambam: 'Imagi Ningthem: Social Content of Manipuri Films', in *Deep Focus*, Bangalore, Vol. 6, Nos. 2&3, 1996, pp.4-7.
[71] For a fuller discussion of Manipuri cinema, cf. Thounaojam Kishorchand Singh: 'Manipuri Cinema' in T. M. Ramachandran, op cit. pp. 415-421.

Sagir Ahmed focused on children who grow up without love and care in *Dhaare Aalua* (1983), and Prafulla Mohanty on child marriage in *Bhanga* (Broken Slate) (1987).

Manmohan Mahapatra has given us a whole range of sensitive yet incisive films on traditions and practices in urban and rural Orissa: *Sita Raati* (Winner's Night) (1982), *Neerabadha Jhada* (The Silent Storm) (1984), *Klanta Aparaha* (Tired Afternoon) (1986), *Majhi Pahacha* (The Middle Step) (1987), and *Trisandhya* (1988).[72] His recent oeuvre includes: *Kichi Smruti Kichi Anubhuti* (1989), *Andha Diganta* (1990), *Nishidhaa Swapna Veena* (1991), *Vinnay Samay* (1993), *Muhurta* (2002) and *Vijay Matiro Swarag* (2005).

Panjabi Cinema

Prior to partition, Panjabi films were made in Bombay and Lahore where modern studios hummed with activity. There were three studios in Lahore (Panjab Film Company, United Players and Kamla Movietone) established during the silent era. Himansu Rai's *Love of a Mughal Prince* was made in the Lahore studios, but the most successful was A.R. Kardar (who owned United Players) who made around nine silent films, with English titles such as *Golden Dagger, Brave Heart, Serpent, Shepherd, Mysterious Eagle* and *Wandering Dancer*.[73] The English titles invariably had alternative titles in Panjabi. *The Victim*, for example, was called *Bhukh nu Bhog*, *Wooing Nightingale* bore the Panjabi title *Bol Tu Bulbul*, *Jewelled Arrow* was *Poonam nu Chand*, in Panjabi, and *The Dancing Girl* had the creative title *Gutter nu Gulab*.[74] However, the 'talkies' in the early 1930s and later the partition brought an end to the Lahore ventures. The first Panjabi film, K.D. Mehra's *Sheila* (1935), inspired by Tolstoy's *Resurrection*, was premiered at the Corinthian Theatre in Calcutta; Mehra's *Heer Sayal*, based on Warris Shah's *Heer*

---

72 B.D. Garga: *So many Cinemas: The Motion Picture in India*, Bombay: Eminence Designs, 1996.
73 K.D. Mehra: 'Panjabi Cinema', in T.M. Ramachandran, op cit. p.452.
74 Nirupama Dutt: 'Partitioned Cinema', in *The Indian Express*, July 10, 1994, p. 9.

Ranjha, the immortal tale of young love, revived the studios of Lahore, though only until the partition.

Dalsukh Pancholi (*Soni Mehiwal, Gul Bakawli* and *Yamla Jat*), Roshan Lal Shorey (*Chaman*) (1948) and Roop Shorey (*Mangti, Dulla Bhatti, Koel and Tarzan Ki Beti*) contributed much to Panjabi cinema during the post-partition years. Bombay became the hub of Panjabi cinema after the partition, but Pakistan's ban on Indian films, the further division of the state of Panjab, and above all the competition from Hindi films dealt a deathly blow to Panjabi films. Devotional films (*Nanak Nam Jahaz Hai, Nanak Dhukia Sab Sansar, Dhanna Jat, Dukh Banjan Tera Nam, Man Jeeta Jag Jeet,* and *Sherni*) proved to be a big draw during the years of the Green Revolution, followed closely by years of fear and terrorism. Other films of the 1990s worthy of note are: Virendra's *Sarpanch* and *Lamberdarni*, Dharmakumar's *Daaj*, Peepat's *Chann Pardesi* (1980) and Vijay Tandon's *Kachehari* (1993). After 2000, Harbhajan Mann, the singer-turned-actor and Manmohan Singh, the choreographer-turned director, breathed new life into Panjabi cinema. The big hit in that year was *Shaheed Udham Singh*. *Jee Ayan Nu, Asa Nu Maan Watna Da* and *Des Hoyaa Pardes* were the major box-office successes from 2003 to 2005. In recent years the potential of the overseas market has led producers to venture into patriotic films such as *Dil Apna Panjabi* (2006), *Waris Shah* (2006), *Rustom-e-Hind* (2007) and *Mitti Wjan Mardi* (2007).

Bhojpuri Cinema

Bhojpuri cinema is a Rs. 500 crore business.[75] With over 200 million speakers in Bihar and Uttar Pradesh and also among the 20-million strong Indian diaspora in Fiji, Mauritius, Suriname, South Africa, and Trinidad and Tobago, Bhojpuri films are often more successful at the box-office than Hindi films. What is more, they are low-budget films with an occasional star like Amitabh Bachchan, Ravi Kishen or Manoj Tiwari playing the

---

75 Vanita Kohli-Khandekar: 'The Bhojpuri Plug', *Business Standard*, April 20, 2008, p. 8.

lead role. Perhaps the earliest Bhojpuri films were Nitin Bose's *Ganga Jamuna* (1961) and Kunden Kumar's *Ganga Maiya Tohe Piyari Chadhaibo* (1962). Since then they have been fitfully produced, though by 2000 around 30 films were being released in North Indian and overseas territories. In 2005, *Sasura Bada Paisawala* and *Daroga Babu I Love You* were runaway hits. The following year *Gangaa, Ab Ta Banja Hamaar* and *Dulha Milal Dildar* drew larger audiences than Bollywood films. *Deal in Crime* and *1971* were the major box-office hits of 2007. Bhojpuri films now feature regularly in film review columns in Sunday newspapers and film magazines. For the most part, Bhojpuri films are family melodramas set in foreign locales and tell familiar stories. So successful has this home-grown low-budget cinema turned out to be that production houses are keen on either re-making Bhojpuri versions or dubbing Bollywood films into this popular dialect of Hindi. These films are targeted not at the multiplex audiences in the metros but rather at small town and rural audiences for whom, as Ravi Kishen puts it, 'Bhojpuri cinema is like home-cooked food'.[76]

The Documentary Film: Evolution of the Genre

The documentary or non-fiction film is an elaborate method of recording the lives and activities of real people, but 'constructed' or 'recreated' nevertheless to tell an interesting story. A Committee set up by the Government of India in the sixties under the chairmanship of M.D. Bhat to define the term 'Documentary Film' for the guidance of bodies like the Film Advisory Boards and the Film State Awards Committee, stated that the following definition drafted by the World Union of Ducumentary in 1947 was most appropriate:

'By the documentary film is meant all methods of recording on celluloid any aspect of reality, interpreted either by factual shooting or by sincere or justifiable reconstruction, so as to appeal either to reason or emotion, for the purpose of stimulating

---

76 Quoted in Amarnath Tiwary: 'Move Over Bollywood, Here's Bhojpuri', 15 December 2005. http://news.bbc.co.uk/2/hi/south_asia/4512812.stm.

the desire for, and the widening of human knowledge and understanding, and of truthfully posing problems and their solutions in the spheres of economic, culture and human relations'.[77]

The documentary had its beginnings in 1922 when Robert Flaherty, an Englishman, took his camera to the Arctic regions to film the life of an Eskimo family. The result was *Nanook of the North*, a documentary film that pioneered the documentary tradition in cinema and later in television. But it was John Grierson who popularized the term and who turned the documentary into a popular artistic form. He shot his documentary entitled *Drifters* on location in the North Sea. It provided a glimpse of the fishermen of that region. Some of his other outstanding documentaries are *Weather Forecast, Song of Ceylon, Coal Face,* and *Night Mail.*

By the 1930s the documentary film was an established form and came to be patronised and supported by national governments, particularly during the war years. Film-makers and governments were soon convinced that the purpose of a documentary was social – "setting forth public and private crises and victories, to showing us where man has been, and what inevitably man would become unless proper action is taken". 'We have to think of communications', argued Grierson, 'of involving our people in building a future. But this belief in the future is not imported from the top, it is built from the bottom so that the common people themselves are in the forefront of the whole exercise of persuasion'.

Documentary Genres

The label 'Cinema verite' or Cinema of Reality sums up the type of film a documentary aims to be. John Grierson defined a film documentary as 'the creative interpretation of reality'. S. Sukhdev, the veteran documentary filmmaker, however, revised this definition to: 'the creative interpretation of *recreated*

---

[77] K.L. Khandpur: 'Compulsory Screening of Documentaries in India', in T.M. Ramachandran, op cit., p.510.

reality'.[78] Satyajit Ray wondered if Grierson's definition 'was not a little misleading' since even fictional films and even fantasies and fairly tales dealt with reality.[79] The documentary evolved as a reaction to shooting in a studio with a selected cast, generally chosen from among the urban elite. The pioneers of the documentary frowned upon the synthetic fabrication of the studio and insisted on the existence of real men and women, real things and real issues. They believed in story-material taken from life in the raw and in spontaneous gestures and unrehearsed speech. They wanted the cameras and the sound recording equipment to be taken from the studio to the field and the factory, to the road and the dockyard.

Several genres of the non-fiction evolved over the years: they ranged from the 'naturalist' and 'realist', to the 'experimental' and the 'abstract'. Somewhere in between were 'ethnographic' films, 'training' or educational/instructional films, and 'propaganda' films. The genres were defined in terms of the methods of filming (and editing) actual people and events. The video documentary is perhaps the most recent format, with its beginnings going back to the 1970s. CENDIT of New Delhi and SEWA of Ahmedabad were the foremost organisations that promoted the video documentary in India.[80] A Video Festival is now held every year in Trivandrum, and the Mumbai International Film Festival for Documentary, Short and Animation Films, has a Video Vista Section where over a hundred video documentaries are screened. The video format is inexpensive, flexible and easily accessible, and therefore is the ideal alternative to the big media. This format has now been overtaken by the digital (DVD) format which can be uploaded to television channels, Internet sites like www.youtube.com, // in.youtube.com, www.indyarocks.com and www.freedocumentaries.

---

78 Jag Mohan: *Sukhdev,* Pune: National Film Archive of India, p. 13.
79 Satyajit Ray: 'The Question of Reality', in Sanit Narwekar (ed.): *Spectrum India -1994,* Third Bombay International Film Festival for Documentary, Short and Animation Films, February 1994, pp.91-93.
80 Cf. Paromita Vohra: 'A Documentary is a Documentary is a...', in R.D. Burra (Ed.): *Video Vista - 96,* 4th Mumbai International Film Festival for Documentary, Short and Animation Films, 1996.

com as well as to mobile phones, iPods, vPods and PDAs.

The Indian Documentary: The Early Years

The Indian documentary was pioneered by three Europe-trained filmmakers. The first was P.V. Pathy, who had his training in Paris; the second D.G. Tendulkar, a student of Sergei Eisenstein in the Moscow Film School; and the third K.S. Hirlekar, who studied film making in Germany. These three led the development of the Indian documentary. They introduced editing, a vivid commentary style, effective music and sound effects. Between 1920 and 1940, more than 1500 short films were produced.

In 1947, Paul Zils together with Fali Billimoria established the Documentary Unit of India. A master editor and producer trained in Germany, Zils made a number of notable films: *Hindustan Hamara, Zalzala, The Ripening Seed, The Vanishing Tribe* and *Kurvandi Road*. Zils got together with Jag Mohan to edit the quarterly periodical, *Indian Documentary*.

In 1949 and 1950 as many as 32 black-and-white documentaries were made. The films were dubbed in five Indian languages – English, Hindi, Bengali, Tamil and Telugu. (Today, as many as 16 languages are in use in the Indian documentary). In June 1949, the first three documentary films were released: *Kashmir Carries On, India Independent*, and *Immersion of Gandhiji's Ashes*.

The first Indian documentary to win an international award in a foreign film festival was *Rajasthan Series I - Jaipur*. The first feature-length documentary made by the Films Division was released in 1955. This was *Mitrata ki Yatra*. Other films that won prizes in overseas film festivals were: *Symphony of Life* in 1955, *Wonder of Work* in 1957, and *The Challenge of Everest*, which won four awards. Thus, in the first two decades of the Indian documentary, over 250 documentaries were produced both by the Films Division and 'outside producers. Some of the award-winning 'outside producers' were:- S. Sukhdev, who made *India '67*; Clement P. Baptista, *Handicrafts of Rajasthan*, Shyam

Benegal, *Close to Nature*; N.S. Tappa, *Song of The Snows*; Satyajit Ray, *Rabindranath Tagore*, and Tapan Sinha, *Jagdish Chandra Bose*. Other filmmakers of note who made a valuable contribution to the development of the Indian documentary were: V.M. Vijayakar, K.T. John, Santi P. Choudhary (first generation); K.S. Chari, Pramod Pati, S.N.S. Sastry, T.A. Abraham and Neil Gokhale (second generation), and Loksen Lalvani (third generation).[81]

Commenting on the development of the Indian documentary film, P.V. Pathy said in 1957, "The rightful claim to credit for having fostered the adolescence of the documentary film goes to our government. Even the future of our documentary seems to be linked with Government sponsorship". In the mid-1990s, that future was uncertain as multi-channel television grabbed audience interest, and cinema exhibitors' resentment against obligatory screening of documentaries and newsreels rose to a crescendo.

The Indian Newsreel: Indian News Review

The short film in India has had a long history, going back to the first decade of the 20th century. Even before the first feature film was produced in 1912, film directors like Dadasaheb Phalke, made many short films both in the 'Silent' and the 'Talkies' Era. The common subjects for such short films (called 'topicals') were political meetings, funerals of national leaders, strikes, burning of foreign cloth, and visits by foreign dignitaries. 'The 'topicals' produced in India were confined to the installation functions and weddings of the Maharajahs... The Delhi Durbars of 1903 and 1911 were filmed. Dussehra celebrations, fairs and festivals, the day to day life of people in various parts of India, snippets from Parsi theatre plays and even industries came within the camera range of the early newsreel cameramen'.[82]

---

[81] ibid.
[82] Jag Mohan: *Documentary Films and Indian Awakening*, New Delhi: Publications Division, 1990, p. 3.

There were numerous such short films made by private companies like Bombay Talkies, Maharashtra Film Company, Kohinoor and many others. The "shorts" were screened along with the company's feature films. The Aurora Film Corportion pioneered a regular newsreel named 'Calcutta Film Gazette'.

During World War II, the Government set up the Film Advisory Board which later became the Information Films of India (IFI), for the production of propaganda films and newsreels. The newsreels were distributed under the banner of 'The Indian News Parade'. In 1946, these organisations ceased to exist, but two years later, when India became independent, the Indian News Review was started as a successor to the Indian News Parade. Thus there was no official organisation to film the historic transfer of power on August 15, 1947.

In the early years of the Indian News Reel, the emphasis was on projecting national leaders and events. However, with greater experience and the necessity of educating the masses, the emphasis shifted from personalities to issues such as family planning, insurance, savings, the Green Revolution, etc. The commentary which played such an important part in the early newsreels was now given little importance, and the tape recorder was taken to the fields and the factories as also to remote areas of the country where the common people's reactions were recorded on camera.

The Directorate of Field Publicity, which runs over 150 units in the rural and urban non-theatre areas, screens Films Division's newsreels regularly. The Films Division has arrangements for free exchange of newsreel material with 26 international organisations. The widespread expansion of television led to the winding up of the weekly newsreel from April 1, 1984, and the reduction in the number of documentaries, from 250 to a mere 52 per year.[83]

The Films Division

The Films Division was set up in Bombay at the end of 1948

---

[83] N.S. Thapa: 'Reality in 35mm', in *The Times of India*, August 14, 1993.

as a 'media unit' of the Ministry of Information and Broadcasting. It was closely modelled on the Information Films of India, the Indian News Parade and Kinematographic Services, the organisations established by the British to make propaganda films during World War II. Indeed, during the early years, the Films Division was identified with the the Information Films of India, and audiences looked upon its products as government propaganda. That perception has not changed over the past four decades.

The objectives of the Films Division were well chalked out: 'the production and distribution of newsreels and short films required by the Government of India for public information, education, motivation and for instructional and cultural purposes'. Besides, it aimed at mobilising the use of the dynamic medium of film to disseminate information to the broadcast spectrum of Indian and foreign audiences and to focus attention on important aspects of the country's life and to assist the growth and development of documentary films as a medium of education and communication.

During the first year the Films Division concentrated on producing news reels. The following year documentaries were taken up and 31 were released, one in colour. In the first two decades the Films Division made over 2,700 films, many of them documentaries on India's cultural heritage. Some notable examples were *Taj Mahal, Mahabalipuram, Jain Temple, Hill Temples of Gujarat* and *Cave Temples of India*. A series of films on Indian classical folk dances were also completed. The titles suggest the subjects filmed – *Bharat Natyam, Kathak,* and *Folk Dances of Assam*. Short biographies of national leaders like Gandhi, Nehru, Tagore and Tilak also proved popular. The Indian Documentary Producers' Association (IDPA) was established in the early fifties; its journal, Indian Documentary, though published only for a few years, offered a record of the documentary movement of the post-Independence years.

By the 1980s, the Films Division had been transformed into a more streamlined organisation making each year over 200 documentaries, training films for the armed forces, instructional films for farmers and factory workers, and 104 national and regional newsreels.[84] Asiad '82 challenged the Division to record for posterity the excitement of the Asian Games held in New Delhi. However, it continued to be used as an arm of the political party in power, especially during the Emergency years.

Until 1983 the Division was one of the largest film making agencies in the world, including the National Film Board of Canada and the documentary film studios of Moscow. It has full-fledged centres in Bombay, Madras and Calcutta. It used to release as many as 700 prints of one documentary and one newsreel every week. Several of its documentaries were screened on national and international TV channels.

Some States like Gujarat, Maharashtra, UP, Bihar, Andhra and West Bengal ran their own Film Units to make films of regional interest. Thus it was that about a hundred million people are exposed to the documentaries and newsreels week after week. Some departments like Family Welfare, National Savings, the Directorate of State Publicity, the LIC and the Tea-Board have mobile units but nearly all of them are in the border areas. A large number of mobile units would make for more frequent and regular exposure in far-flung villages. Further, a streamlined non-theatrical exhibition circuit needs to be built up to cover factories, educational institutions, hospitals, panchayats, etc. A greater variety of documentaries could thus reach special target groups.[85]

The Future of the Films Division

In 1989, the Films Division's collection of documentaries, short films, short fiction films, animation films and newreels, was 7,012 films[86]. Its main source of revenue has always been rentals from cinema theatres. The rate per film per week ranges

---

84 ibid.
85 For an insider's view of Films Division, cf. N.S. Thapa: 'The Documentary Film in India: Films Division at Work,' in T.M. Ramachandran, op cit., See also Jag Mohan: *Documentary Films and Indian Awakening*, New Delhi: Publications Division, 1990.
86 Jag Mohan: op cit.

from Rs. 2.50 to Rs. 400 depending on the status, size and collection of theatres. The exhibitors and the distributors share this expense. Under section 122 of the Cinematograph Act of 1952, the Films Division screens its films for upto 20 minutes compulsorily in each theatre. Theatre-owners complain that they lose over Rs.30 million annually on account of this show time. In 1988-89, the Films Division earned Rs. 77,826,000, a little more than half its expenditure (Rs. 139,028,074) during the same period.[87] It also earns about a million rupees a year from the sale of stock shots from its extensive film library. In 1996-97, the Films Division produced 22 news magazines, 52 documentaries and short feature films, and released 20,131 prints of 42 documentaries and 18 news magazines. The revenue earned during that year was Rs. 16,633,000.[88]

The Films Division can easily break even and become a profit-making body if it adopts a commercial approach to the sale and exhibition of its prints, and archival footage. It needs to charge for the prints it makes available to Doordarshan, the various Central and State Government bodies, and more importantly, sell prints abroad where there is a promising market for short films, particularly among television networks. At present only Indian embassies and Tourist Boards abroad are provided prints. The External Affairs Ministry has set up a cell for sales promotion of documentaries abroad. Already some of the documentary films have found a good market in West Asia, East Asia, and the West. The Films Division now organises an annual international festival for documentary, short and animation films called MIFF (Mumbai International Film Festival) where over 500 entries are received from around the world over every year.[89] It has tied up with the National Film Development Corporation (NFDC) which commissions short films for the Metro Channel, and also helps the Division to

---

87 Jag Mohan: op cit.
88 INDIA - 1998, New Delhi: Research and Reference Division/Publications Division.
89 See MIFF's official website http://miffindia.in for a list of short films (fiction and non-fiction) from India selected for screening at the festival each year since 1990.

market its documentaries, short films and animation films at international film festivals. Doordarshan too has begun to commission the Division to make documentaries for its national and regional networks. The Division has already adapted itself to the video/DVD and television formats.

Fifty years after its establishment, the Films Division continues to remain a 'unit' of the Ministry of Information and Broadcasting, and to do its bidding. An autonomous corporation status which has now been granted to All India Radio and Doordarshan would perhaps best ensure its future, and its distinct identity. With over a thousand employees, an annual budget of around Rs. 17 crores (Rs. 170 million), an infrastructure (for animation films in particular) in Bombay and Bangalore that is the envy of many media organisations, and a library with over 40 million feet of precious historical material,[90] the Films Division will need to become part of the new competitive multi-channel audiovisual environment if it is to survive as a vibrant and creative organization.

Films Division's 'Independent' Documentary Producers

Most of the films produced by the Films Division every year have been the work of its own employees. Only a handful of short films were given out to a panel of outside or 'independent' producers, through a tender system, a practice which put off young and ambitious filmmakers, particularly those graduating from the Film and Television Institute, Pune. Further, documentaries could be screened in theatres around the country only through the Films Divison circuit. Even after the film by the independent producer had been made, the threat of censorship at various levels remained, as happened in the case of several controversial films. In the words of Kumar Shahani, the director of the feature *Maya Darpan*, and of the Films Division-sponsored documentary *Fire in the Belly* (on the drought in Maharashtra) – 'Once a film is made, there are various stages of censorship, first the Films Division approves, then the Board of

---

90 N.S. Thapa: 'Reality in 35 mm', in The Times of India, August 14, 1993.

Censors has to clear it and finally the Film Advisory Board, which is the super Censor Board, has a big voice and even decides what shot should be there, and what should not be there, which amounts to aesthetic censorship'.[91]

B.D. Garga, who made documentary films for four decades, and was well-known for his films on Amrita Sher-Gil, Sarojini Naidu and Ananda Coomaraswamy, commented thus on how the Films Division functioned: 'Independent film producers of repute are also having a tough time in getting films. Film Division sometimes invites a film maker to make a film on a negotiated contract. It takes at least ten days to get an application processed via the Indian Documentary Producers Association (IDPA), Raw Film Steering Committee, the NFDC, and ORWO, but almost all of the films are given on the basis of the lowest tender and it's the money which determines whether you get a film or not. The tender system harms the cause of the documentary film movement. In their anxiety to get a film, some film makers underquote to such an extent that they cover only the raw stock and the laboratory charges. As a result the quality is bad and sometimes films remain unfinished'.[92]

The Working Committee on film policy has recommended the abolition of the system and advocated negotiations. Echoing Kumar Shahani's plaint he points out: 'The script has to be approved by the subject specialist – an official in the Ministry – who has very little idea of the media. He is very particular about his points. The freedom is curbed at the conception level, and also at the shooting stage where every film maker projects himself. The subject specialist has to approve narration, presentation, etc. With the various checks and guards which the ruling party employs, there is not a ghost of a chance for a film maker to bring in his vision. The only freedom he has is to bring in a certain amount of sophistication. The government policy is such that you can make slick films but you can't make thought-provoking ones'.[93]

---

91 Quoted in *The Economic Times*, November 16, 1980.
92 ibid.
93 Quoted in the Working Group's Report on National Film Policy, p. 45.

The ruling party's absolute control is evident in the subjects chosen at the start of each financial year, not by Films Division but in consultation with the Ministries of Defence and Agriculture, and with public sector undertakings. As though this were not enough, officers are appointed by these organs of Government to help in the production. It is no surprise, therefore, that the Division's films are simple narratives loaded with government propaganda. It is this credibility gap that makes the public suspect even the worthwhile offerings of the Films Division.

Despite these stringent regulations, the Films Division has been turning out a good number of award-winning films. On average 75 films are sent to international film festivals every year, and 40-45 bag prestigious awards. Sukhdev, Mushir Ahmed, N.S. Thapa, S.N.S. Sastry, Loksen Lalwani, B.D. Garga, Clem Baptista, Fali Bilimoria, Mani Kaul and a host of others have thus made a mark in the world of documentary cinema. But John Grierson, the father of the modern documentary, is reported to have warned that 'the Films Division is falling prey to some of the cheap film festivals of the Western affluent countries... of getting prizes for having caught the sickness of some of the frustrated countries in the West'.[94]

While the Films Division has gained world-wide recognition, it has woefully failed the country in the area of development communication. It is much too centralised a body to turn out films meaningful to the millions in the rural areas. A study carried out by the Indian Institute of Mass Communication, New Delhi, has revealed that only 10% of the films produced between 1975 and 1978 were primarily oriented to the rural classes, who make up 76% of the population. The study also found that the frequency of screening of films in villages was low. It concluded that the level of recall of films in villages among village folk was low because of the lack of socio-economic or cultural relevance of the films' backdrops to villagers' surroundings, complicated technique, an overload of statistics, difficult language and rapid

---

94 ibid.

speed of commentary.[95]

The Films Division has supported several feature-length documentaries. Some of these include Benegal's three hour film on Satyajit Ray, Jabbar Patel's film on *Indian Drama and Theatre*, Prakash Jha's *Parampara* (on the guru-shishya tradition in various styles of Indian dance), Girish Karnad's *Kanak Purandara* (on the Bhakti traditon in Karnataka), and Tapan Sinha's two one-hour featurettes: *Manas* and *The Story of Tiblu*, and Mani Kaul's feature film *Siddeshwari*.

Independent Documentary Movement

During the late seventies and early eighties several independent documentary producers like Mani Kaul (*The Nomad Puppeteer*, *Arrival*), Loksen Lalvani (*Burning Stone*, *They call Me Chamar*) and others made sensitive documentaries for the Films Division. By the mid-eighties, however, the clear trend among independent film-makers, was to go in for private sponsorships, or to seek support from the NFDC and other sources. The focus of attention of the young film-makers, in particular, was marginalized groups in Indian cities. Anand Patwardhan, for instance, focused attention on political opposition led by Jayaprakash Narayan to the Indira Gandhi regime (*Waves of Revolution*, *Prisoners of Conscience*) and the plight of Bombay's slum-dewellers (*Hamara Shaher*), and Pradeep Dixit documented the two-year-long strike of 250,000 textile workers of the same city (*Although the City Looks Quiet*). Patwardhan has gone on to document the movement against the Narmada Dam (*Narmada Story*), and the rise of Hindutva in his trilogy (*In Memory of Friends, In the Name of God*, and *Father, Son and Holy War*). He has also made *A Time to Rise*, a scathing expose of the exploitation of Sikh farm labour in Canada, with assistance from the National Film Board of Canada. Patwardhan has had to go to the courts in appeal against the censors for almost every documentary of his, including his recent *War and Peace*.

---

95 ibid.

Rajan Palit, a cameraman-director trained at the FTII, Pune turned the searchlight on the exploited weavers of Bhivandi, and went on to boldly record the struggle of the peasants of Baliapal to stop the government from converting their region into a missile site, in *Voices from Baliapal*. The film is co-directed by Vasudha Joshi. Bhopal has been the subject of a number of independently produced documentaries. Perhaps the most soul-searching was *Bhopal: Beyond Genocide* made by Tapan Bose, Suhasini Mulay and Salim Sheikh. A similar social concern is reflected in *Man Versus Man*, a sympathetic portrayal of Calcutta's rikshaw-pullers by Sashi Anand, and in *Famine '87* by Sanjiv Shah, and an Indian Story on the Bhagalpur blindings. The genocide in Gujarat too has been the subject of documentaries by Rakesh Kumar and others. So has the clash between the farmers and the West Bengal government over the acquisition of land for SEZ at Nandigram and Singur. The most telling of these documentaries has been Ladly Mukhopadhyay's *Whose Land Is It Anyway?*[96]

Women film-makers (such as the six young women of Delhi's Mediastorm) have turned attention on the Deorala sati tragedy of Roop Kumar, in *From the Burning Embers*. Suhasini Mulay has directed two documentaries, *Pani* and *Chithi*, Deepa Dhanraj questions the family planning campaign in *Something Like A War* and Chandita Mukerjee demythologises the working woman in *Totanama*.

The dramatic growth of television channels, particularly those dedicated to nature, the environment, geography, and history (E.g. Discovery, History, National Geographic, and Planet Earth) has provided a new fillip to the independent documentary movement in India. This has been spearheaded by the Independent Documentary Producers Association (IDPA). It actively promotes and supports the making of documentaries for the big and small screens, and frequently organizes festivals of documentary films.[97] Besides, video-sharing websites and social

---

96 For a detailed list of award-winning documentaries, see the annual IFFI and MIFF brochures.
97 IDPA's official website is www.idpaindia.org.

networking sites now afford new opportunities for documentary filmmakers to screen their work worldwide.

Film Studies in Indian Universities

It is only in recent times that the cinema has come to be looked upon as a serious art form worthy of academic study in Indian universities. While accepting an Honorary Doctorate from the Jadavpur University in 1980, Satyajit Ray made a strong plea for including the teaching of cinema as part of the educational curriculum. Only two universities, Jadavpur and Calcutta, have a Master's level programme in Film Studies. Most other universities have full-fledged departments of Communication/ Journalism where brief courses in film appreciation are taught as part of the discipline of Communication. Government institutes like the Film and Television Institute of India, Pune, the Madras Film Institute, and the Satyajit Ray Film and Television Institute, Calcutta, and private institutes like the Xavier Institute of Communications, Bombay, Chitrabani, Calcutta, and Whistling Woods, Bombay, offer diploma programmes in film appreciation and film production. With the mushrooming of media institutes around the country since 2005, the opportunities for the critical study of film have increased manifold. Scholarly research in film and cultural studies, however, is promoted in few such institutes.

The popular attitude to cinema as a means of mass entertainment has its origin in the type of films made up to the 'fifties in India. Satyajit Ray told the Working Group that 'the works of the early filmmakers suffered from a low level of conception, as right from the beginning cinema in India was aimed at the lowest common denominator and became primarily concerned with providing entertainment. Even when well-known writers became involved with cinema, they deliberately changed the quality of their writing. It is only in the last decade or so that intellectuals have begun associating actively with the making of films and thereby raised the status of cinema to an art form'.

The Government's attitude too has reinforced the popular view that cinema is a means of cheap entertainment. As the Working Group's Report notes: 'One of the major factors which has impeded the growth of cinema as an art form and as a medium of cultural expression is that despite a history of about 70 years of film-making, cinema in India continues to be treated almost as a sub-culture. This general attitude seems to permeate the total spectrum of the Government's policies towards cinema. The high taxation rates and the stringent rules for licensing of cinema houses gives the impression that cinema is an undesirable activity which needs to be kept at an adequate distance from the social life of the community. At the same time, it must be acknowledged that the Government has set up a Directorate of Film Festivals, a National Film Institute, a National Film Archive, the NFDC, and instituted National Film Awards to give a fillip to cinema. The film society movement indirectly supported by the Government has spread to many cities, making it possible for film lovers to be exposed to outstanding films of other countries.

To continue these efforts at promoting film as an art form, the Working Group recommended the establishment of the Chalachitra Akademi, on the lines of the Sahitya Akademi, the Sangeet Natak Akademi and the Lalit Kala Akademi. It also recommended the setting up of a Film Educational Advisory Service for inculcating a critical attitude towards cinema in schools and colleges as well as a Film Information and Documentation Centre, a National Film Museum, and a Children's Film Centre.

The cinema is the art of today, just as drama was in earlier ages. It is, as Pudovkin, the Russian theorist of film wrote in 1933: 'a synthesis of each and every element – the oral, the visual, the philosophical; it is our opportunity to translate the world in all its lines and shadows into a new art form that has succeeded and will supersede all the older arts, for it is the supreme medium in which we can express today and tomorrow'.

Impact of Cinema on Society

The three terms 'impact', 'cinema' and 'society' are extremely complex and much too comprehensive to take at surface-value. The term 'impact' is frequently used synonymously with 'effect' and 'influence' but its connotative meanings point to an effect or influence that is deep and long-lasting. These terms also suggest that the influence is one powerful force upon a passive inorganic receptor. A further complication arises when one realises that an 'impact' can be weak, moderate or strong, that it can relate to the psychological, social, economic, cultural, political and even physical. The reality is that it is well-nigh impossible to look at 'impact' of cinema or any other media in isolation from social life.

The term 'cinema' is equally complex today, with television, video, cable and satellite TV vying with each other to screen films on the small screen. Further, does the term refer to films shown on the big screen alone? Or, does 'cinema' refer to the whole industry of film production, distribution and exhibition, as well as the marketing of different genres of films whether for the big screen or the small screen? That is a huge field, and to analyse its 'impact' on 'society' is a daunting task for any researcher. Moreover, there are so many genres of cinema, each genre perhaps having an 'impact' of its own. 'Horror films', for instance, might have the impact of frightening viewers, and slapstick comedies of entertaining and relaxing them. Kung-fu and karate films might offer a 'cathartic' experience, leading to a purgation of the emotions of pity and fear.

The third term 'society' is an infinitely more complex phenomenon. The term takes within its compass all social institutions (such as the family, the school, the university, the state, the legislature, the class and caste-systems, religion, culture, political and economic institutions, etc.). How does one assess the 'impact' of 'cinema' on such an all-encompassing phenomenon? It therefore seems that the 'impact' of 'cinema' on 'society' is a very tricky subject for study. For several decades now, 'impact' or 'effects' studies have been conducted (though mostly in laboratory settings), but these have been narrow psychological studies on the 'effects' of violence and sex in specific films on specific groups such as school children, college and university youth. Most such studies have been carried out in the United States. In India, the Indian Institute of Mass

Communication, New Delhi, conducted a 'sociological' study on the 'Effects of Cinema'. The first research study on the influence of Hindi Cinema on Bombay Youth was conducted by Panna Shah in 1948.[98] More interesting perhaps would be to look at the politics and economics of cinema, of the relationship between cinema with the actual lives of the people, or how audiences use and incorporate cinema and the tales they tell into their daily lives.

Ethics of Cinema

While censorship is imposed by the authorities and the law, the matter of 'ethics' is imposed by individuals on their own professional practices. Thus, some communication professionals like advertisers and public relations practitioners have drawn up 'Codes of Ethics' for themselves but journalists, film producers, radio and television broadcasters in India have yet to agree on a common set of ethical practices in their respective media professions.

The need for ethics in cinema and the other mass media arises from the fear that children and sensitive adults might be harmfully influenced by certain portrayals and actions. Film makers must be concerned about the possible influence on individuals and groups of their artistic efforts. For instance, the stereotypical portrayal of women and minorities in Indian films could help to reinforce cultural stereotypes rather than stimulate new thinking about their roles in society. Few are the films that show women as intelligent, independent and hard working; fewer still are the films that show minority communities in a positive light. This is where 'ethics' comes in: a concern for the sensitivities of audiences and the nation's cultural pluralism. Unethical practices would include the insertion of 'adult sequences' in films meant for family viewing; the insertion (by cinema exhibitors) of pornographic sequences in films that have been already censored; the portrayal of excessive violence for minutes on end, when such portrayal is irrelevant and

---

[98] For recent research studies, see the section 'For Further Reading' at the end of this srction.

unnecessary; titillating bedroom and 'rain' sequences when they are not germane to the plot. There is a long tradition of Indian film makers of plagiarizing Hollywood films, sometimes shot by shot. These cloned versions are palmed off as original Indian language films. Adaptations of film themes and stories are considered creative, but cloned versions without acknowledgement of the original are undoubtedly plagiaristic and unethical. Further, it would be unethical to use scenes in film posters which do not exist in the film itself.

A recent WHO report entitled 'Bollywood – Victim or Ally? A Study of the Portrayal of Tobacco in Indian Cinema' raises serious questions about the ethics of glamourising smoking in feature films.[99] The study, conducted over a four year period from 2000 to 2004, used a mix of quantitative and qualitative research methods to examine the prevalence of incidents of tobacco smoking in 395 feature films released during one decade (1991 to 2002); on average a sample of 30-35 films from each year. Besides, focus groups and in-depth interviews were held: focus groups with a sample of male and female respondents aged 16-18, and 31 in-depth interviews with the film industry's leading film makers and exhibitors. The majority (80%) of the film makers stated that Hindi films do not glamourise smoking; the others said it was not done consciously. In the focus group discussions, most smokers openly admitted that films influenced their smoking habits as it was fashionable to do so.

The content anlaysis of Hindi and South Indian language films clearly indicated that tobacco smoking incidents occurred in 76% of the sample: cigarette smoking comprised 72% of all incidents. The occurrence of smoking among the 'good guys' increased from 22% in 1991 to 53% in 2002. In most incidents, smoking was portrayed as a 'normal' activity.

The study found that in the decade long sample of films, out of a total 2,463 incidents of smoking as many as 1,775 (72%)

---

99 *Bollywood: Victim or Ally? – A Study of the Portrayal of Tobacco in Indian Cinema,* Strategic Media Work for the Tobacco-free initiative of WHO Report 2003, Geneva: WHO, 2003. This Report is part of the Global Youth Tobacco Survey, supported by WHO and Centres for Disease Control and Prevention.

tobacco incidents related to cigarette smoking, 266 (10.8%) to cigar smoking, and only 135 (5.4%) to bidi-smoking. The total duration of tobacco-related incidents amounted to 13,334 seconds. There were two smoking incidents on average per hour of each film, and each incident was for a duration of five seconds on average.[100]

The table below provides a tally of the total number of smoking incidents in a sample of 395 films and the film stars associated with such incidents.

Table 19: On Branded/Unbranded Tobacco Usage by Leading Film Stars[101]

Actor	Total No. of Smoking Incidents	Percentage of Total Incidents
Shahrukh Khan	109	4.43
Rajnikanth	103	4.18
Ajay Devgan	55	2.23
Aamir Khan	44	1.79
Sanjay Dutt	31	1.26
Akshay Kumar	30	1.22
Manoj Bajpai	25	1.02

The overall conclusions of the WHO study are:
1. Tobacco consumption is today viewed as a 'normal activity' by Indian youth.
2. In both Hindi and South Indian films more and more 'good guys' are smoking.
3. There is a strong linkage between films and youth behaviour.
4. Smoking incidents in films are much higher than actual cigarette consumption among the Indian population.[102]

---
100 ibid.
101 Ibid.
102 Ibid.

The WHO study does not probe the commercial reasons for such widespread prevalence of smoking incidents in Hindi and Tamil films though it is evident that 'in-film advertising' (also termed 'product placement') is an effective strategy for financing costs of production and marketing. The ethics, however, of introducing irrelevant incidents of smoking into a creative medium like film, remains questionable. Also questionable is the deliberate introduction of often unnecessary scenes of alcohol consumption (where the opportunities for advertising particular brands are immense), drug use and offensive language.

Film Censorship: A Brief History

Film Censorship was set in motion in India when the Cinematograph Act of 1918 was made law from May 1920. It allowed the exhibition of films only after they had been certified as suitable for public exhibition. However, the exhibition of a film could be suspended and its certificate annulled in any Province on the authority of the District Magistrate or Commissioner of Police, pending the order of the Provincial Government, which could uncertify the film for the whole or part of the Province.

Censor Boards were accordingly set up in Bombay, Calcutta, Madras, Rangoon and Lahore. All members of the Boards were appointed by the Government. They consisted of the Commissioner of Police, the Collector of Customs, a member of the Indian Educational Services, and three prominent citizens representing the Hindu, Muslim and other communities.

Prior to the Act of 1918, total freedom did exist for the Indian film-maker and exhibitor, though some control was exercised under the Indian Penal Code and the Criminal Procedure Code. These were primarily concerned with obscenity, the wounding of religious sentiments, or inciting disaffection against the Government. Under the Act, the control was made more rigid and effective countrywide.

In the early days of censorship the Boards were "particularly sensitive to nudity, passionate or suggestive lovemaking, women in a state of drunkenness, anything that might show the white man in bad light, scenes of Western women in any contact with Oriental men and of course, any reference to political activity or ideology."[103]

Amendments to the Act of 1918 in later years made film censorship a function of the Provincial Governments. By far the largest number of films exhibited in India from the 1920s was American, and the British Government resented their influence.

In October 1927 an Indian Cinematograph Committee was appointed with an Indian, T. Rangachariar, as Chairman. It observed in its Report submitted two years later that censorship is certainly necessary in India, and is the only effective method of preventing the import, production and public exhibition of films which might demoralise morals, hurt religious susceptibilities or excite communal or racial animosities. But the coming of the talkies in India introduced new elements into censorship, and the Report was shelved.

During the war-years censorship was strictly enforced particularly with regard to political allusions. By Independence film making had become a losing proposition, and on June 30, 1949 an All India Cinema Protect Day was held to protest against the government's taxation policy. That crippling taxation policy is still the greatest restraint on film making in India. 60% of the gross collections go as entertainment tax to the coffers of State Governments.

The Cinematograph Act of 1952 continued the British tradition of severe censorship of films that made any references to the political situation or to communal groups. The guidelines of the Act are lifted almost entirely from the Hays Code, named after Will Hays, once Post-master General of U.S.A. While the Code has been scrapped abroad, the censors here still continue to swear by it.

In 1969, the Khosla Commission was appointed to report on the whole film industry. It recommended an autonomous Censor Board without any official government control the examination of a film as a whole and to allow kissing, nudity and violence,

---

[103] Aruna Vasudev: *Liberty and Licence in the Indian Cinema*, p. 22.

if they were integral to the theme. The Government reluctantly accepted the Report, and in 1974 a Bill was introduced in the Lok Sabha. However, the clamping of the emergency soon led to even stricter control by the Government. The guidelines by the government now forbade more than six minutes of violence in a film, though *Sholay* was cleared at the behest of the Centre. Indeed, the whims of the I & B Ministry decided which films should be given 'A' or 'U' Certificates. Political satires like *Kissa Kursi Ka* were banned.

The Janata regime, appointed a Working Group on National Films Policy. The Working Group's Report has criticised the rigid approach of the film censors against the exposure of corruption in the police and the Government's political leadership. Such an approach, says the Report, prevents creative film-makers from portraying social reality as it exists. Cinema, like literature, has to be given the freedom to make social and political comment, if it is to fulfil its function as a catalyst of social change. The Group has also opposed the Government's issuing of guidelines, and its acting as an appellate body. It suggests that the only aspect of censorship requiring the Government's guidelines is the sovereignty of the State, the security of the State, and friendly relations with foreign countries.

Rationale of Censorship: All citizens, says Article 19(1) and (2) of the Constitution, shall have the right to freedom of speech and expression, and then goes on to add, 'Nothing in this clause shall affect the operation of any existing law, or prevent the State from making any law, in so far as such law imposes reasonable restrictions on the exercise of the right conferred by the said clause in the interests of the sovereignty and integrity of India, the security of State, decency or morality, or in relation to contempt of court, defamation or incitement to an office'.

This is the key to the laws of censorship in the media in India. Reasonable restrictions on the fundamental right of freedom of speech and expression are sanctioned by the constitution. The State is therefore justified in imposing restrictions on the arts and the media. However, the restrictions imposed must be 'reasonable', and whether they are reasonable or not has to be decided by the courts.

K.A. Abbas challenged the censorship of films in general and pre-censorship in particular in the Supreme Court in November 1969. In its verdict delivered on September 24, 1970, the Supreme-Court said that 'censorship in India (and pre-censorship is no different in quality) has full justification in the field of exhibition of films. We need not generalize about other forms of speech and expression here for each such fundamental right has a different content and importance...The censorship imposed on the making and exhibition of films is in the interest of society. If the regulations venture into something which goes beyond this legitimate opening to restrictions, they can be questioned on the ground that a legitimate power is being abused. We hold, therefore, that censorship of films, including prior restraint, is justified under our constitution'.

The Central Board of Film Certification (CBFC)

The Central Board of Film Censors (since June 1, 1983 renamed the 'Central Board of Film Certification') is set up by the Central Government under the powers granted it by the Cinematograph Act (1952) and the Cinematograph (Censorship) Rules 1958. The Board is headed by a chairman, appointed by the Central Government and is assisted by not more than nine members. (This number has now been increased to 12-35 members; this has been done to facilitate the opening of more regional offices. Presently, there are offices at Bombay, Madras, Calcutta and Trivandrum, with Bombay as the headquarters.

Advisory Panels

Advisory Panels are constituted at each regional office by the Central Government which also decides, in consultation with the CBFC, the number of panel members for each office. The members are appointed by the Central Government in consultation with the CBFC. However, the Central Government may dispense with such consultation in the case of members whose number does not exceed one-third of the total number.

The members are appointed for a period of two years and may be re-appointed after the expiry of the term. The Central Government reserves the power to remove a member before the completion of the term. The member is entitled to a consultancy fee of Rs. 50/- for previewing a film or attending a meeting.

How Films are Censored

A film producer has, in the first place, to submit an application for a certificate to the CBFC. The fee charged is Rs. 100 per reel. The Examining Committee consists of a member from the Advisory Panel and an examining officer in the case of a short film, while in the case of a feature film four members from the Advisory Panel and an examining officer. The film to be examined must be complete in every sense, with the background music and all sound effects duly recorded on the film itself.

Under the Amendment Act, 1983, all previews of films for the purpose of certification and the reports and records related to it, will be treated as confidential. The names of members of the Examining Committee will not be disclosed to any official or non-official with the preview of a particular film or to any other person including the applicant or his representative. The applicant or his representative will not be allowed to be present inside the preview theatre.

This 'confidentiality clause' has been introduced to counter a judgement of the Madras High Court which stated that the CFBC must specify the guideline under which a film has been refused a certificate. Said the Court on February 7, 1983 in the case between Ramakrishna Cine Studio and the CBFC: 'The Central Board of Film Censors has to come out with specific reasons when it asks for cuts in a film and it must also furnish the particulars of guidelines under which cuts are sought to be effected to the film producer. If for any reason, the members of Committees (Examining or Revising) felt that any particular portion of film has to be cut, there could not be any 'confidentiality' about these opinions especially when the privilege was not claimed on the ground of public interest.'

The CBFC had directed the deletion of shots of President Reagan and Tamil Nadu Chief Minister M.G. Ramachandran, in a Telugu film starring N.T. Rama Rao, and produced by the Ramakrishna Cine Studio. The Court observed that by no stretch of the imagination could it be said to offend against public order, decency or morality under the Act, and the procedure followed by the Board was far from satisfactory.

Examining Committee

The recommendations of all the members of the Examining Committee are sent by the Examining Officer to the Chairman of the CBFC within three days of the preview. Within the next seven days, the producer is informed about the Certificate issued. Under the Cinematograph Act of 1952, films were certified 'U' (for unrestricted exhibition), and 'A' (for public exhibition restricted to adults only). But according to the new amendment, two more categories have been introduced. The first is 'UA' (for unrestricted public exhibition subject to parental guidance for children below the age of 12), and the second is 'S' (for public exhibition restricted to specialized audiences such as doctors, etc.)

The Board may, of course, ban a film or refuse to give it a certificate unless certain deletions in visuals and sounds are made. It may also offer to grant a 'U' instead of an 'A' provided suggested deletions are agreed to. In some cases where the Examining Committee is divided or where the producer makes a request for a reconsideration of the decision arrived at, a Revising Committee takes a second look at the film.

Revising Committee

The Revising Committee, under the new directives, consists of a chairman and not more than nine members selected from the Advisory Panel by the Chairman. No member of the Examining Committee can sit on the Revising Committee of the same film. It is stipulated that within three days of seeing the film, the recommendation of all the members have to be sent by the presiding officer to the chairman of the CBFC. Appeals against the CBFC's decisions are heard by the Film Certification Appellate Tribunal (FCAT) which was constituted in 1984. The Tribunal sits in New Delhi.

But the possession of a 'censor certificate' does not necessarily ensure the smooth exhibition of film throughout the country. Petitions can be filed in High Courts seeking a ban on a film. For instance, a private organisation had sought to ban Attenborough's *Gandhi* in a Jhansi Magistrate's court. In another case, the Allahabad High Court served notices on the writer, director and artistes of *Andha Kanon* directing them to show cause why action should not be taken against them for alleged contempt of court. And in Srinagar, the Chief Judicial Magistrate issued a bailable warrant against the producer of *Nikaah* on the charge that the film was produced with the intent to disrespect the laws of a minority community. In recent years, Shekar Kapoor's *Bandit Queen* and Mira Nair's *Kamasutra* have been subject to severe censorship. Besides, there are pressure groups that bring their opinions to bear on the kind of films that ought to be exhibited. They halt the screening of films by force, or take their complaints to the courts. Such has been the fate of *Parzania*, *So Bole Nihaal*, Deepa Mehta's *Fire* and *Water*, Ashutosh Gowarikar's *Jodha Akbar*, Kamal Hasan's *Dashavatharam*, and of several other films. In Gujarat, theatre managers did not dare screen the films of Shah Rukh Khan for fear of threats from Hindu fundamentalist groups. So, it is not enough for a film to get past the CBFC which takes its Guidelines from the Central Government. Excerpts from the Guidelines are given below.

Censorship Guidelines

The Cinematograph Act lays down that a film has to be certified keeping the interests of sovereignty, integrity and security of India, friendly relations with foreign states, public order, morality etc. in mind.

Under section 5B(2) the Central Government issues detailed guidelines.

A film is judged in its entirety from the point of view of its overall impact and is examined in the light of the period depicted in the film and the contemporary standards of the country and the people to whom the film relates, provided that the film does not deprave the morality of the audience. Guidelines are applied to the titles of the films also.

Objectives of film certification:

(a) the medium of film remains responsible and sensitive to the values and standards of society;
(b) artistic expression and creative freedom are not unduly curbed;
(c) certification is responsible to social changes;
(d) the medium of film provides clean and healthy entertainment; and
(e) as far as possible, the film is of aesthetic value and cinematically of a good standard.

Detailed Guidelines for certification:

(i) anti social activities such as violence are not glorified or justified;

(ii) the modus operandi of criminals, other visuals or words likely to incite the commission of any offence are not depicted;

(iii) scenes- showing involvement of children in violence as victims or perpetrators or as forced witnesses to violence, or showing children as being subjected to any form of child abuse;- showing abuse or ridicule of physically and mentally handicapped persons; and- showing cruelty to, or abuse of animals, are not presented needlessly

(iv) pointless or avoidable scenes of violence, cruelty and horror, scenes of violence primarily intended to provide entertainment and such scenes as may have the effect of de-sensitising or de-humanising people are not shown;

(v) scenes which have the effect of justifying or glorifying drinking are not shown;

(vi) scenes tending to encourage, justify or glamorise drug addiction are not shown; (vi-a) scenes tending to encourage, justify or glamorise consumption of tobacco or smoking are not shown;

(vii) human sensibilities are not offended by vulgarity, obscenity or depravity;

(viii) such dual meaning words as obviously cater to baser instincts are not allowed;

(ix) scenes degrading or denigrating women in any manner are not presented;

(x) scenes involving sexual violence against women like attempt to rape, rape or any form of molestation or scenes of a similar nature are avoided, and if any such incidence is germane to the theme, they shall be reduced to the minimum and no details are shown

(xi) scenes showing sexual perversions shall be avoided and if such matters are germane to the theme they shall be reduced to the minimum and no details are shown;

(xii) visuals or words contemptuous of racial, religious or other groups are not presented

(xiii) visuals or words which promote communal, obscurantist, anti-scientific and anti-national attitude are not presented;

(xiv) the sovereignty and integrity of India is not called in question;

> (xv) the security of the State is not jeopardized or endangered;
>
> (xvi) friendly relations with foreign States are not strained;
>
> (xvii) public order is not endangered;
>
> (xviii) visuals or words involving defamation of an individual or a body of individuals, or contempt of court are not presented;
>
> EXPLANATION:
>
> Scenes that tend to create scorn, disgrace or disregard of rules or undermine the dignity of court will come under the term 'Contempt of Court'; and
>
> (xix) national symbols and emblems are not shown except in accordance with the provisions of the Emblems and Names (Prevention of Improper Use) Act, 1950 (12 of 1950).

FOR FURTHER READING

A. FILM HISTORY

1. Erik Barnouw and S. Krishnaswamy: *Indian Film*, New Delhi: Oxford, 1980.
2. B.K. Karanjia: *A Many Splendoured Cinema,* Bombay: New Thacker's Fine Arts Press Pvt. Ltd, 1986.
3. B.D. Garga: *So Many Cinemas: The Motion Picture in India*, Bombay: Eminence Designs Pvt. Ltd, 1996.
4. Gulzar, Govind Nihalani and Saibal Chatterjee (Eds.): *Encyclopaedia of Hindi Cinema*, New Delhi: Encyclopaedia Britannica, Bombay: Popular Prakashan, 2003
5. Somnath Gupt: *The Parsi Theatre: Its Origins and Development*, Calcutta: Seagull, 2005.
6. Ashish Rajadhyaksha and Paul Willemen: *Encyclopaedia of Indian Cinema,* London: British Film Institute, 2000.
7. Brigitte Schulze: *Humanist and Emotional Beginnings of a*

Nationalist Indian Cinema in Bombay: With Kraceur in the Footsteps of Phalke, Berlin: Avinus, 2003.
8. Matthias Uhl and Keval J.Kumar: *Indischer Film: Eine Einfuehrung*, Bielefeld, 2004.
9. Yves Thoraval: *The Cinemas of India*, New Delhi: Macmillan, 2000.
10. Aruna Vasudev: *The New Indian Cinema*, New Delhi: Macmillan, 1996.
11. Aruna Vasudev: *Liberty and Licence in the Indian Cinema*, New Delhi: Vikas, 1978.
12. Aruna Vasudev and Philipe Lenglet (Eds): *Indian Cinema Super Bazaar*, New Delhi: Vikas, 1983, Rev. Ed. 1987.

B. FILM REPRESENTATIONS, POLITICAL ECONOMY AND THE NATION

13. Shakuntala Banaji: *Reading Bollywood: The Young Audience and Hindi Films*, New York: Palgrave Macmillan, 2006.
14. Derek Bose: *Brand Bollywood: A New Global Entertainment Order*, New Delhi: Sage Publications, 2006.
15. Derek Bose: *Bollywood Unplugged: Deconstructing Cinema in Black and White*, Bombay: English Edition Publishers & Distributors, 2004.
16. S. Chakravarty: *National Identity in Indian Popular Cinema (1947-1987)*, Bombay: Oxford University Press, 1996.
17. N. Manu Chakravarthy (Ed.): *Culturing Realism: Reflections on Girish Kasaravalli's Films,* Bangalore: Nudi Pustaka, 2007.
18. Shoma A. Chatterjee: *Subject: Cinema, Object: Women – A Study of the Portrayal of Women in Indian Cinema*, Calcutta: Parumita Publications, 1998.
19. Prem Chowdhry: *Colonial India and the Making of Empire Cinema: Image, Industry and Identity*, Manchester/New York, 2000.
20. Darius Cooper: *In Black and White: Hollywood and the Melodrama of Guru Dutt*, Calcutta: Seagull, 2005.
21. Chidananda Dasgupta: *Talking about Films*, Bombay: Orient Longman, 1977.
22. Chidananda Dasgupta: *The Painted Face*: India's Popular Cinema, New Delhi: Roli Books.

23. Chidananda Dasgupta: *Seeing is Believing: Selected Writings on Cinema*, New Delhi: Penguin/Viking, 2008.
24. Jigna Desai: *Beyond Bollywood: The Cultural Politics of South Asian Diasporic Film*, New York: Routledge, 2004.
25. Wimal Dissanayake and Malti Sahai: *Raj Kapoor's Films: Harmony of Discourse*, New Delhi: Vikas, 1988.
26. Rajinder Kumar Dudrah: *Bollywood: Sociology Goes to the Movies*, New Delhi: Sage Publications, 2006.
27. Rachel Dwyer and Divia Patel: *Cinema India: The Visual Culture of Hindi Film*, London: Reaction Books, 2002.
28. Rachel Dwyer: *Filming the Gods: Religion and Indian Cinema*, London/New York: Routledge, 2006.
29. K. Moti Gokulsing and Wimal Dissanalyake: *Indian Popular Cinema: A Narrative of Cultural Change*, Staffordshire: Trenthan Books, 1998.
30. Lalitha Gopalan: *Cinema of Interruptions: Action Genres in Contemporary Indian Cinema*, London: BFI Publishing, 2002.
31. Priya Jaikumar: *Cinema at the End of Empire: A Politics of Transition in Britain and India*, Kolkata: Seagull, 2007.
32. Lalit Mohan Joshi (Ed.): *Bollywood: Popular Indian Cinema*, London: Dakini Books.
33. Fareed Kazmi: *The Politics of India's Conventional Cinema*, New Delhi: Sage, 1999.
34. Connie Haham: *Enchantment of the Mind: Manmohan Desai's Film*, New Delhi: Roli Books, 2006.
35. Preben Kaarsholm (Ed.): *City Flicks: Indian Cinema and the Urban Experience*, Calcutta: Seagull, 2004.
36. Vinay Lal and Ashish Nandy: *Fingerprinting Popular Culture: The Mythic and the Iconic in Indian Cinema*, New York: Oxford University Press, 2006.
37. Ranjani Mazumdar: *Bombay Cinema: An Archive of the City*, Ranikhet: Permanent Black, 2007.
38. Ashish Nandy (Ed.): *The Secret Politics of our Desires: Innocence, Culpability and Indian Popular Cinema*, New Delhi: Oxford University Press, 1998.
39. M.A. Oomen and K.V. Joseph: *Economics of Film Industry in India*, Bombay: Academy Press, 1981.
40. Madhava M. Prasad: *The State and Culture: Hindi Cinema in the Passive Revolution*, Ph.D. Dissertation, University of Pittsburg, 1994.

41. Vijay Mishra: *Bollywood Cinema: Temples of Desire*, London: Routledge, 2001.
42. John Kenneth Muir: *Mercy in Her Eyes: The Films of Mira Nair*, Chennai: Westland Books, 2007.
43. Satyajit Ray: *Our Films, Their films*, Bombay: Orient Longman.
44. Gaston Roberge: *Chitrabani: A Book on Film Appreciation*, Calcutta: Chitrabani, 1974.
45. Gaston Roberge: *The Subject of Cinema*, Calcutta: Seagull Books, 1990.
46. Gaston Roberge: *Another Cinema for Another Society*, Calcutta: Seagull Books, 1985.
47. Manjunath Pendakur: *Popular Indian Cinema: Industry, Ideology and Consumerism*, Creskill, New Jersey: Hampton Press Inc. 2003.
48. Srividya Ramasubramaniam and Mary Beth Oliver: *Portrayals of Sexual Violence in Popular Hindi Films – 1997-1999*, Springer Netherlands, 2003.
49. *Sangeet Natak Akademi Journal*, No.100: Special issue on Hindi Film Music, April-June 1991.
50. *Symposium on Cinema in Developing Countries*, New Delhi: Publications Division, Government of India, 1980.
51. Jonathan Torgovnik: *Bollywood Dreams: An Exploration of the Motion Picture Industry and its Culture in India*, London, 2003.
52. P.G. Vaidyanathan: *Hours in the Dark*, Bombay: Oxford University Press, 1996.
53. Raminder Kaur and Ajay J Sinha (Eds.): *Bollyworld: Popular Indian Cinema Through a Transnational Lens*, New Delhi: Sage Publications, 2005.
54. Aruna Vasudev (Ed.): *Frames of Mind: Reflections on Indian Cinema*, New Delhi: Indian Council for Cultural Relations, 1995.
55. Valentina Vitali: *Hindi Action Cinema: Industries, Narratives, Bodies*, New Delhi: Oxford University Press, 2008.

C. REPORTS

1. *Report of the Indian Cinematograph Committee, 1927-28, Vols. 1-4*, New Delhi: Government of India, Central Publication Branch, 1928.
2. *Report of the Film Enquiry Committee*, New Delhi: Government of India, 1951.

3. *Report of the Enquiry Committee on Film Censorship*, New Delhi: Government of India, 1968.
4. *Report of the Working Group on National Film Policy*, New Delhi: Ministry of Information and Broadcasting, May 1980.

D. JOURNALS
1. *Cinema Vision India*, Bombay, Vols. 1-4.
2. *Cinema in India*, Bombay: National Film Development Corporation, 1987-1991.
3. *Deep Focus*, 2124, HAL II Stage, 16th 'B' Main, 1st 'A' Cross, Bangalore - 560 008.
4. *Cinemaya, Journal of Asian Cinema*, New Delhi.
5. *Journal of Arts and Ideas*: Special issue on 'Film Studies', No. 29, January 1996, (35 A/1 (II Floor), Shahpur Jat, New Delhi - 110049.)
6. *Journal of South Asian Cinema*, London.

E. WEB RESOURCES
1. www.nfaipune.nic.in (National Film Archive of India, Pune)
2. www.imdb.com (International Movie Data Base).
3. www.ibosnetwork.com (International Box Office Statistics)
4. www.screenindia.com (Web version of Screen, the weekly publication of the Indian Express Group)
5. www.filmfare.com (Web version of Filmfare)
6. www.boxofficeindia.com
7. www.indiafm.com
8. www.upperstall.com
9. www.cbfcindia.nt.nic.in (Official website of the Central Board for Film Certification/Censor Board).
10. http://miffindia.in (Mumbai International Film Festival)
11. www.idpaindia.org (Indian Documentary Producers Association)
12. www.filmsdivision.org
13. http://cat.sas.upenn.edu (Indian Cinema Database of Penn University).
14. www.sarai.net
15. www.studio-systems.com

REVIEW QUESTIONS

1. Trace the development of Indian Cinema from Dadasaheb Phalke to the early talkies. What were the main trends?
2. What are the characteristics of documentary films? What has been the achievement of the Films Division in the area of documentary films?
3. Why do you think the 'Regional Cinema' is catching up with the popularity of mainstream national cinema? Write on the achievements of the Marathi or Tamil cinema in recent years.
4. How has film censorship affected the content of mainstream commercial cinema?
5. How has Indian cinema benefited from the Government declaring it to be an 'industry'?
6. Has film censorship been effective in improving the quality of cinema in India?
7. How successful has the independent documentary movement been in playing the role of an opinion-making force?
8. Write short notes on:
   a) The Hindi Film Song
   b) 'Multiplex' Films
   c) Characteristics of the 'New Wave' or 'Alternative' Cinema
   d) Genres in Popular Indian Cinema
   e) Film Magazines
   f) Film Actors' Blogs

SUGGESTED PROJECTS

1. Watch two popular movies by the same director. What differences in theme and treatment do you notice? Has there been a development in the use of song-and-dance sequences, background music, dialogue, colour, etc.?
2. Watch two films in which your favourite star has an important role. Compare the two roles played. Which was played more convincingly? What are your reasons for preferring one role to the other?
3. Write out a script for a brief film on a well-known short story or fable. Divide the script into brief scenes/shots stating clearly whether they are set indoors or outdoors ('interior' or 'exterior').

4. The next time you watch a film, try to identify the different types of shots, the camera angles, and camera movements in a particular sequence (E.g. a song or dance or chase sequence). Also note how 'continuity' from shot to shot is achieved. Write a short account of the sequence.
5. Play the movie game, 'antakshari'. What does the game tell you of the role of songs in our films? Account for the popularity of the game show 'Antakshari' on television.
6. Write a critical review of a film you have seen recently.
7. Select two Sunday papers published in your city. Analyse the film review sections of the two papers. Compare their reviews of a film released during the past week. Compare their 'ratings' for the film.
8. Check out the official website of the Censor Board www.cbfcindia.nt.nic.in. How many films have been refused censor certificates during the previous year? Why?

RADIO BROADCASTING

Development of Radio as a Mass Medium

A combination of a number of discoveries of electro-magnetic waves, radio waves, the wireless telegraph and the triode amplifier valve) by technicians and scientists from different countries gave rise to the development of wireless telegraphy and later to radio broadcasting. 'It took ten years for wireless telegraphy, whose sole use was point-to-point telecommunication, from ship to ship and ship to shore, to become a broadcasting system that was one of the main media for mass culture. This shift from one type of technological and social usage to another took place in relation to two developments: First, the World War prompted the industrialization of wireless telegraphy; secondly, in the United States the radio created a communication environment in which amateurs could operate freely'.[1] 'Hams' (wireless telegraphy hobbyists) were used extensively during World War I.

Radio broadcasting needed the mass production of receivers and marketing for it to be commercially viable. This came about during World War I largely because of military requirements. After the War, radio found its commercial base and was given a social form 'through a combination of several traditions – those of telecommunications, mass industry and the press'.[2] The earliest radio transmissions in 1915 were by universities to disseminate news. The first radio stations were set up in Pittsburg, New York and Chicago in the 1920s to broadcast election news, sporting events and opera performances. By mid-1923 as many as 450 stations sprouted across the United States – all run by a pool of amateurs. (These stations were later connected by AT & T to form the National Broadcasting Company (NBC) in 1926. The following year, a number of

---

1   Flichy, 1995.
2   ibid.

independent stations clubbed together to form a second national network, the Columbia Broadcasting System (CBS)). The public service radio network, National Public Radio (NPR), was established much later.

In Britain and in Europe, however, radio broadcasting was felt to be much too important a mass medium to be left to private profit-oriented companies. Public service broadcasting supported by taxes or license fees rather than advertising-oriented commercial broadcasting found widespread favour. Thus it was that while the NBC and CBS were established as private commercial stations in the United States, the British Government took the initiative to set up the BBC in 1920 as an autonomous public service corporation. Other European countries established national public service networks, some directly under government control, others as autonomous establishments. Colonial powers like Britain and France opened broadcasting stations (BBC World Service and Radio France) in Asia and Africa to extend their governance over the local populations and to propagate their interests in politics and trade. The United States Government established the Voice of America.

Indian Broadcasting: The Early Years

Broadcasting was introduced in India by amateur radio clubs in Calcutta, Bombay, Madras and Lahore, though even before the clubs launched their ventures, several experimental broadcasts were conducted in Bombay and other cities. *The Times of India* records that a broadcast was transmitted from the roof of its building on August 20, 1921. However, the first licence granted for transmitting a broadcast was given only on February 23, 1922. The Radio Club of Calcutta was perhaps the first amateur radio club to start functioning (in November 1923), followed by the Madras Presidency Radio Club which was formed on May 16, 1924, and began broadcasting on July 31. Financial difficulties forced the clubs to come together in 1927 to form the Indian Broadcasting Company Ltd. IBC), a private company, 'fired by the financial success of European broadcasting'.[3]

Lionel Fielden, India's first Controller of broadcasting[4], tells the story of the early years of Indian Broadcasting in his autobiography[5].

"A group of Indian businessmen, fired by the financial success of European broadcasting, had floated a company in 1927, with a too meagre capital, built two weak little stations at Calcutta and Bombay. In the following three years they had gathered some 7,000 listeners and lost a great deal of money. They decided to go into liquidation. The Government of India, which then and later – with considerable wisdom – thought broadcasting a curse was thereupon bullied by the vested interests of radio dealers to buy up the transmitters. Having done so, it proceeded, quite naturally, to economise; file-writers in Delhi could hardly be expected to sanction public expenditure on music, drama and similar irrelevancies: it seemed obvious that all such frivolous waste should be avoided. The programmes accordingly deteriorated even from their former low standard and Indian broadcasting would have spiralled down to complete eclipse had not the BBC, at the critical moment, started an Empire programme on the short wave. Europeans in India rushed to buy sets; and since the Government had, by way of strangling broadcasting altogether, put an import duty of fifty percent on sets, even the 8000 extra sets purchased brought quite a deal of money under the broadcasting head. The dealers cried that broadcasting's profits must be used for broadcasting. The Government replied with the offer of a new station at Delhi and a man – me – from the BBC. But, however much English residents of India listened to the BBC – and to the radio dealers it did not matter, then, who listened to what as long as sets were sold – Indian broadcasting remained what it had always been..."[6]

---

3   Lionel Fielding: *The Natural Bent*, London: Methuen, 1960. See also the accounts of early radio broadcasting in Awasthy (1965), Mullick (1974), Duggal (1980), Masani (1985), Luthra (1986), and Chatterji (1987).
4   According to G.C. Awasthy's account though, P.G. Edmunds was the first Controller, and Lionel Fielden was the second Controller. Cf. Awasthy (1965), p. 7.
5   Lionel Fielden: *The Natural Bent*, London: Methuen, 1960.
6   op cit., p.159.

'All India Radio'

The government-run broadcasting set up was called the Indian State Broadcasting Service (ISBS), with Fielden its first Controller. Interestingly, ISBS was set up under the Department of Industries and Labour. Fielden brought to All India Radio – a name thought up by him – "a veneer of respectability, a little polish, some enterprise, a good deal of pride and prejudice, if not much sense and sensibility."[7]

How ISBS was turned into AIR in June 1936, is a fascinating tale told with relish by Fielden:

I had never liked the title ISBS which to me seemed not only unwieldy, but also tainted with officialdom. After a good deal of cogitation – which may seem ridiculous, now, but these apparently simple and obvious things do not always appear easily – I had concluded that All India Radio would give me not only protection from the clauses which I most feared in the 1935 Act, but would also have the suitable initials AIR. I worked out a monogram which placed these letters over the map of India. But, when I mooted this point I found that there was immense opposition in the Secretariat to any such change. They wanted ISBS and they thought it fine. I realized that I must employ a little unnatural tact. I cornered Lord Linlithglow after a Viceregal banquet and said plaintively that I was in a great difficulty and needed his advice. (He usually responded well to such an opening). I said I was sure that he agreed with me that ISBS was a clumsy little. After a slight pause, he nodded his long head wisely. Yes, it was rather a mouthful. I said that perhaps it was a pity to use the word broadcasting at all, since all Indians had to say 'broadcasting' – broad was for them an unpronounceable word. But I could not, I said, think of another title; could he help me? 'Indian State', I said, was a term which, as he well knew, hardly fitted into the 1935 Act. It should be something general. He rose beautifully to the bait. 'All India?' I expressed my astonishment and admiration. The very thing. But surely not 'broadcasting?' After some thought he suggested

---

7   R.K. Narayana Menon, *Mass Media in India 1979-80*, p.32.

'radio'? Splendid, I said – and what beautiful initials. The Viceroy concluded that he had invented it, and there was no more trouble. His pet name must be adopted. Thus, All India Radio was born.[8]

The War Years

The first daily news bulletin was introduced in 1936. But World War II necessitated the growth of a national network and an external service, and the installation of high power transmitters to expand coverage. Nazi propaganda was coming through loud and clear, and it needed to be countered. Thus was established the practice of all news bulletins being broadcast from one central newsroom. During the War Years as many as 27 bulletins were broadcast each day. Further, the External Services as also a Monitoring Service were set up as part of the Military Intelligence Wing. These were delinked when the war ended, and All India Radio was transferred to the Department of Information and Broadcasting in 1946, and it remained with that Department/Ministry until September 1997 when the Prasar Bharati (or Broadcasting Corporation of India), an autonomous statutory body, was constituted under the Prasar Bharati Act (1990).

Underground 'Congress Radio'

The leaders of the 'Quit India' movement had no access to either radio or the press. All India Radio was British imperialism's propaganda machine; the newspapers were heavily censored. The only alternative was the establishment of underground radio, using a dismantled transmitter. A group of young Congress freedom fighters (Usha Mehta, Vithaldas Khakar, Chandrakant Jhaveri) launched their shortlived Congress Radio on September 3, 1942 on 41.78 metres 'from somewhere in India' (though actually from Bombay). The broadcasts continued till November 11 of that year with a short

---

8   op.cit. p.193.

break from October 15 to 17 to raise the transmitter's power.[9] To escape detection the portable radio station was moved from place to place. However, the British police soon got wind of the underground broadcast centre. The police commissioner reported that the chief of the group was 'directly responsible to Ram Manohar Lohia for the success of the scheme, and that he also received the necessary funds from the latter.' The young radio enthusiasts were soon arrested and put on trial. In the radio case trial, Khakar was held to be the 'arch conspirator' and charged with spreading disaffection and hampering the war effort; he was awarded a five year prison term while the others were imprisoned for a year each.[10] Thus ended the nationalists' lone attempt to challenge the official All India Radio version of the freedom struggle.

All India Radio at Independence

On the eve of Independence AIR had yet to have a truly national network. With only six stations located at Delhi, Bombay, Calcutta, Madras, Lucknow and Tiruchirapalli, and four stations in the princely states of Mysore, Travancore, Hyderabad and Aurangabad, a mere 18 transmitters, and the number of receiver sets at just 250,000 for a population exceeding 325 million, drastic steps were called for. They came in the form of 'pilot' stations and low power transmitters installed near them, in the States and linguistic areas which knew no broadcasting so far. Within a couple of years, 25 stations had started functioning and the sales of sets picked up in the cities and towns, but the prices were far above the means of the rural classes. The introduction of the commercial channel 'Vividh Bharati' in October 1957 further increased the interest and popularity of radio as a mass communication medium. Ten years later, commercials became an integral part of Vividh Bharati. Yuvvani or the Voice of Youth went on the air on July 23, 1969 in New Delhi; other cities followed suit in the major Indian languages.

---

9   Madhu Limaye: 'The Voice of India', in *The Times of India*, September 9, 1992.
10 ibid.

THE MASS MEDIA - HISTORY, PRACTICES, VALUES

Table 20: Growth of AIR Network since Independence

Year	Number of Centres	Estimated Number of Radio Receivers (in Million)
1947	10	0.2
1951	21	0.7
1961	30	2.2
1971	65	12.8
1985	86	35.0
1986	90	50.0
1987	93	65.0
1988	94	80.0
1989	97	90.0
1990	105	100.0
1991	110	111.0
1995	177	115.0
2005	210	120.0
2007	219	132.0

In April 1976, Doordarshan was de-linked from All India Radio; this allowed radio in India to take off on its own instead of being looked upon as television's 'poor cousin'. FM services (first from Madras, and later from Jalandhar and other cities) were introduced; local stations (Nagercoil station, for instance); and hourly news bulletins were introduced by the mid-eighties. By the early nineties, phone-in programmes in Delhi, Pune and other cities were experimented with. A landmark achievement was the launch of the Sky Radio Channel on April 1, 1994, which enabled subscribers to receive 20 radio channels via satellite on their FM receivers. AIR's venture in 'radio paging' in 17 centres proved to be a disaster because of competition from private paging companies. But by the close of the millennium the mobile/cellphone revolution put paid to all such business ventures.

All India Radio in the late 1990s and Early Years of 2000

By 2008, All India Radio comprised a country-wide network of 219 Centres including 32 Vividh Bharati/Commercial Centres, 73 local radio stations and 114 regional stations. An estimated 115 million radio/transistor sets have access to AIR programmes; over 65 million of these sets in rural homes.

As one of the largest radio news organisations (employing over 12,000 persons) in the world, AIR puts out over 300 news bulletins every day on its national, regional and external services. Further, AIR's 'Home Service' programmes are beamed from 242 transmitters over 90% of the geographical area and 97% of the population, thus catering to most of the cultural and linguistic regions of the country. AIR's main sources of news, besides its 90 regular correspondents in India and seven abroad, and 246 part-time correspondents, include the two national news agencies, PTI and UNI, the Hindi news agencies, Univarta and Bhasha and ANI (Asia News International). AIR's Monitoring Units – which monitor most of the world's major broadcasting organisations' output – are also an invaluable source[11]. By early 2007, All India Radio was spending as much as Rs. 84 crore per annum on software alone.[12] Much of it was spent on royalty for music paid to the Phonographic Performance Ltd (PPL) and the Indian Performing Rights Society (IPRS), the representative associations of Indian music companies. The music companies of South India are represented by the South Indian Music Companies Association (SIMCA).

All India Radio Services

The National Service

The origin of the centrally-planned National Service (also called the primary service) goes back to World War II when news bulletins were broadcast from Delhi. The News Services

---

11 *INDIA -1998*, New Delhi: Research and Reference Division/Publications Division.
12 Working Group of Eleventh Five-Year Plan (2007-12) on Information and Broadcasting Sector, January 2007

Division plans and presents the news, newsreels, spotlight/ comment, and current affairs programmes. But the National Programmes of music, plays, features and talks are planned by the Director General and produced at regional centres. To boost the commercial revenue of AIR, commercials were allowed on the primary channel from April, 1982, and on over 55 selected stations from January 28, 1985.

The Regional Services

The Regional Services cater to major linguistic and cultural groups. Each State and Union territory serves the groups living in the areas covered by it. Except for news and national programmes of talks and music which are relayed from Delhi, the other programmes of each regional station directed at different groups such as farmers, workers, children, women, youth, are produced at the regional stations/centres. The National Service Programmes are broadcast over short-wave transmitters which makes it possible for regional centres to relay them.

In March 1995, AIR had 105 regional stations, with an average of four to five stations in each State. While Madhya Pradesh had as many as 11 stations, Uttar Pradesh had 10 stations, Andhra Pradesh, Rajasthan, Karnataka and Maharashtra had eight. The seven States of the North-East were well served with four stations in Arunachal Pradesh (Itanagar, Passighat, Tawang, and Tezu), three stations in Assam (Dibrugarh, Guwahat and Silchar), two each in Meghalaya (Shillong and Tura) and Mizoram (Aijawl and Lungleh), and one each in Nagaland (Kohima), Manipur (Imphal), and Tripura (Agartala).

The Local Service

An interesting development in recent years has been the setting up of local radio stations in different regions of the country. The Verghese Committee (1978) recommended a franchise system for promoting local radio for education and development. The need for local/community radio, using FM radio technology, was discussed and accepted during the Seventh

Plan period (1982-87). It was proposed that 73 districts out of a total of more than 500 launch local broadcast stations by 1992. Each local station was to have a reach of around 100 kilometres, and the thrust of the programmes was to be on indigenous folk formats and the participation of the local people.[13] The proposal appears to have been hijacked by the takeover of the FM channels by commercial broadcasters.

The first experiment in local/community radio with FM facilities was conducted in Nagercoil. The experiment was launched on October 30, 1984. In a paper presented at a workshop in Ahmedabad, the station director of the Nagercoil local radio station, observed, 'Local radio should identify with the interests of the local population, (and) the heart of the people should beat in every pulse of the programmes broadcast.'[14] Other experiments have been carried out in rural areas of Bangalore and Hyderabad.

Several NGOs use local radio to further their development activities. Chetana (Calcutta) and Ravi Bharati (Patna), for instance, record their programmes on adult education, in the field, using local talents[15]. The Communication Division of UNESCO actively supports such endeavours in India and other countries. Community radio has perhaps been most successful in South America where religious and social action groups use low-cost radio stations involving local communities in promoting development at the grassroots level.

The Vividh Bharati Service

The Vividh Bharati was started on 2nd October 1957, as a service of 'light entertainment' to compete with Radio Ceylon

---

13 For a detailed discussion cf. K.E. Eapen, 'India's Radio System: The Unmet Challenges of Local Broadcasting', Paper presented at IAMCR Conference, Sydney, August 18-22, 1996. See also K.E. Eapen (Ed.): *Role of Radio in Growth and Development*, Bangalore, 1987.
14 K. Anjaneyulu: 'Calling Down: Local Radio in India', Paper presented at DECU-ISRO Orientation Workshop on Local Radio, Ahmedabad, 1990. Cited in Eapen (1996): op cit.
15 Cf. Eapen (1996): op cit.

(now SLBC), which had begun directing a commercial service to India on powerful short-wave transmitters. Earlier, AIR had banned film songs on its programmes, for Dr. B.V. Keskar, a classical music enthusiast and the then Minister for Information and Broadcasting, held that film music was cheap and vulgar. Commercials were introduced on this service in 1967, and sponsored programmes in May 1970. Up to 1986, the revenue from commercials was almost Rs. 200 million per annum; in 1989 this revenue rose to Rs. 360 million. In the 1990s, the revenue was on average Rs. 370 million per annum[16]. By 2004-2005, AIR's revenues reached Rs. 1.58 billion.[17]

Initially, a daily five hour programme was put out and 60% of the time was devoted to film music. The rest of the time was given to devotional music, short plays, short stories and poetry recitals. At the end of 1990s, the service was on the air for 12 hours and 45 minutes every day, with an extra hour and a quarter on Sundays and holidays. Most of the programmes are produced in Bombay, except for a few local 'request' programmes, which are produced at regional stations. The proportion of film music on Vividh Bharati remains 60%, while classical and light classical music, folk and regional music constitute around 20% of transmission time. The channel also carries news bulletins and some "spoken-word" programmes.

The service can only be heard on medium-wave in and around cities, where the transmitters are located and can be picked up in remote areas of the countryside only on short-wave. The programmes are broadcast on two short-wave transmitters in Bombay and Madras, and on low-power medium-wave transmitters. AIR does not have a network of transmitters for Vividh Bharati, and therefore the 30-odd centres have to be regularly supplied with tape-recordings made many days in advance at Vividh Bharati headquarters.

The popularity of this channel (with an audience of over 250 million) has drawn away listeners from AIR and its many

---

16 All India Radio - 1995.
17 Vanita Kohli-Khandekar: *The Indian Business, New Delhi*: Response Books, 2006. p. 168.

regional centres. Masani observes that Vividh Bharati should have been planned as an independent service producing its own news, music, sports review and commentaries and other "spoken word" programmes to provide a real alternative to the listeners who did not care for the National or Regional Service.[18]

The Verghese Committee found that the programme-content of Vividh Bharati was 'interesting', but pointed out that it has ceased to be a "Variety Programme" and "has become an essentially repetitive film-disc programme"[19]. Accordingly, it recommended a review of Vividh Bharati, "so as to develop a genuine radio-originated light-entertainment programme inclusive of film music which could become a vehicle for much experimentation and innovation."[20]

External Service

Broadcasting today is regarded as 'part of the normal apparatus of diplomacy'. Short wave and long wave broadcasting have made it possible to beam programmes across frontiers to different parts of the world. Radio Moscow, Radio Beijing, the BBC, the VOA, Radio Deutsche Welle, Sri Lanka Broadcasting Corporation (SLBC), Radio Netherlands, Radio Vatican, South African Broadcasting Corporation (SABC), the Australian Broadcasting Corporation (ABC), and several other national broadcasting networks beam their programmes round the clock across frontiers. The television extensions of these broadcasters continue this cross-border tradition.

From 1939, when AIR inaugurated its External Services Division with a broadcast in Pushtu, India too joined in the game of diplomacy on the air. Today the Division broadcasts programmes to 155 countries in 25 languages, 17 of them foreign, the rest Indian. News bulletins are beamed round the

---

18 Mehra Masani : *Broadcasting and the People*, New Delhi: National book Trust, 1985, p.25.
19 *Akash Bharati (National Broadcasting Trust): Working Group on Autonomy for Broadcasting*, New Delhi: Publications Division, Ministry of Information and Broadcasting, 1978.
20 ibid.

clock to sensitive areas where we believe our point of view will be heeded, and where people of Indian origin have made their homes. The primary objective of the broadcasts is 'to project the Indian point of view on world affairs and acquaint overseas listeners with developments in India, along with information on various facets of Indian life, thought and culture.'[21]

A UNESCO report on international broadcasting takes a similar stand, stating that ideally the purposes of international broadcasts are (a) to present the best culture and ideas of the broadcasting country, (b) to present world news objectively, (c) to explain the broadcasting country's viewpoint on important world problems and to promote international understanding. The boom began in 1975 in Japan and a few years later in Europe and the United States.

With more than 80 countries around the world clamouring for the overseas listener's attention in 148 languages on 4,450 short-wave frequencies, the voice of India has slight chances of being heard. The only feedback AIR receives is by way of listeners' letters. The main target areas are Pakistan, Bangladesh, Afghanistan, the Arab States and Western Europe.

If the External Service and the general overseas service has not made any impact, the fault is not with the listener who does have an abiding interest in India, but with the quality of programmes put out as well as with the poor transmission. As the Verghese Committee's Report expressed it: 'AIR's External Service Broadcasts are only dimly heard in significant areas and we have the picture of an ill-planned service, a wasteful use of resources, a frustrated staff and dissatisfied listeners, whether overseas, Indians or foreigners at whom these broadcasts are directed'.[22]

School Broadcasts

Programmes for schools are broadcast from the metros and

---

21 *All India Radio - 1995 (Facts and Figures)*, New Delhi: Audience Research Unit, p. 14.
22 op.cit.

other centres. However, only around 20,000 out of more than 700,000 schools own radio sets, and not more than 40% of these schools switch on the sets more or less regularly. Few schools provide for the broadcasts on their time-tables.

The quality of the programmes is uneven, as few excellent teachers make excellent broadcasters. The responsibility of the broadcasts rests with AIR, not with educationists. AIR draws up programmes on the advice of Consultative Panels for School Broadcasts, comprising six members at each station. The Consultative Panels also have representatives of the State education department, principals of schools, and AIR. Teachers are not on the Panels, but work on the Subjects Committees which are meant to assist the Panels. The Panels are set up by AIR, and educationists are invited to serve on them for a fixed period.

Radio Formats and Genres

Radio programmes may be classified into two broad groups:
(1) Spoken word programmes, which include news bulletins, talks, discussions, interviews, educational programmes for schools and colleges, specific audience programmes directed at women, children, rural and urban listeners, drama, radio features and documentaries.
(2) Music programmes which include disc jockey programmes, 'countdown' shows, musical performances of all types and variety programmes (called 'magazine programmes').

It is obvious that a good number of programmes like drama, features and documentaries need both the spoken word and music. This is true in particular of programmes broadcast on Vividh Bharati and FM channels.

News Bulletins

News bulletins are put out by AIR almost every hour of the day in English and the various regional languages. The major bulletins are of 15 minutes' duration, while others are of only five minutes' duration. They present summaries of news stories in order of importance and interest-value. National and international happenings get pride of place, while regional and local news is read out if time permits. Human interest stories and sports news generally round off the major bulletins. AIR's news bulletins are much too formal in language, structure and presentation, suitable more for a lecture than a talk across the table which news reading really is.

Newsreels

Newsreels, generally of 15 minutes' duration, present 'spot' reports, comments, interviews, and extracts from speeches. A much more complex and expensive format than the news bulletin, it calls for skilled tape editing and well-written link narrations.

Documentaries/Radio Features

Documentaries or radio features are usually factual, informational in character and sometimes educational in intent. They bring together the techniques of talks and drama to tell the story of events, past or present or those likely to happen in the future. They may sketch the biography of a great leader, or merely offer an interpretation of the world around us, or teach us about peoples and cultures unfamiliar to us, or even inquire into social, political, economic or cultural problems. Indeed, any subject of interest is grist to the mill of a feature writer.

The use of a narrator interspersed with voices of real people or/and actors and of appropriate background effects and music bring a documentary/feature to throbbing life. In Fielden's words, 'a feature programme is a method of employing all the available methods and tricks of broadcasting to convey information or entertainment in a palatable form'.

Radio Plays

Radio drama is a story told through sound alone. The sound is of course that of dialogue and voices of people, background or mood effects, musical effects, atmospheric effects and the like.

Radio drama, like stage drama is based on conflict, uses characters and has a beginning, a middle and an end. Movement and progress, generally to a crisis or climax, must be suggested in radio drama through sounds. The voices of characters must be sufficiently distinguishable, one from the other, lest the listener gets confused. They must sound natural, speak true to character and above all, be interesting.

Radio listeners would be confused by the presence of more than three to four characters. In fact, the shorter the drama (the average duration is 30 to 60 minutes) the fewer should be the major characters. In the early years of Indian broadcasting, the radio play took on the characteristics of the theatre as it existed on the stage in a particular region. Radio plays were broadcast then for three hours at a time. In Bombay, Parsi, Gujarati and Urdu plays were frequently put on the air: in Madras, mythological plays proved very popular. It was Fielden who introduced the present norm of the 30-minute radio play on AIR.

Radio Talks

Radio talks are not public speeches; rather, they are chats with a friend who does not see you, but is nevertheless close and attentive to you. Radio talks should give the impression to a listener that the speaker is addressing him or her alone in an informal manner.

The words of a radio talk need to be kept simple and familiar, yet descriptive and powerful, and the sentences short and without dependent clauses and awkward inversions. Care should be taken to keep close to the rhythm of ordinary speech when writing the talk, and also when recording it. Radio talks have no definite structure. All that the listener expects from them is that they should be interesting and informative.

Music Programmes

Music programmes enjoy much greater popularity than talk shows, as is evident from the popularity of Vividh Bharati programmes. We enjoy music for its rhythms, melodies and harmonies and above all for the relaxation it provides. Like any talk show, a music programme must have unity and form. Disc jockey (DJ) programmes of 'pop' or 'disco', therefore should not be mixed up with classical or light classical music. Variety is the keynote to any music programme; the different items should be linked together with interesting comments, announcements and narration.

Movie trailers

Vividh Bharati's movie trailers are sponsored programmes usually of 15-30 minutes' duration. They are fast-paced, and packed with extracts of dialogue and songs from the film being advertised. The narrator links the elements with dramatic appeals and announcements. The names of stars, of the producer, director, playback singers and musicians figure prominently in the trailers.

Quizzes

Largely studio-based and inexpensive to produce, the quiz show is easily one of the most popular programmes for the family. It's the sense of participation and involvement in the quiz questions that makes the programme very enjoyable family fare.

Programme Composition of AIR

The major sources of AIR's programmes are in-house productions, outside productions, sponsored programmes, and programmes obtained under the Cultural Exchange and Programme Exchange Service, apart of course from those programmes available on commercial records, audio-cassettes, CDs, and DVDs. A small number of programmes are obtained from SAVE (the SAARC Audiovisual Exchange). However, for its news bulletins AIR is dependent on PTI and UNI for national and regional news, and to Reuters, Associated Press, AFP and other multinational news agencies for its foreign news coverage. The multinational news agencies route their copy via the national news agencies.

Music takes the lion's share of time (39.73%) on the Home Service excluding Vividh Bharati, with Spoken Word programmes claiming 37.78%, and News and Current Affairs the remaining 22.49% of the time.[23]

A detailed break-down of the music and spoken word programmes provides a clear view of AIR's programming policy. (See Tables 21 and 22 below):

Table 21: Music Progammes on All India Radio (1992)[24]

Music (Excluding Vividh Bharati)	Percentage with Reference to Total Music (231,050.35 Hours)
Classical Music	30.15
Folk Music	11.56
Light Music	21.65
Devotional Music	12.86
Film Music	19.73
Western Music	4.05
Total	100.00

AIR's mode of classifying spoken word programmes is rather eccentric, but it is clearly a pointer to its programme policy, and the pressures under which it functions. Women and Youth are given adequate time on spoken word programmes, while children, industrial workers and tribals appear to be lower in its priorities. Dr. B.V. Keskar's ghost continues to influence AIR's policy on music: Indian classical music dominates programming, followed by 'light music' (largely semi-classical), and 'film music'. The popular music of the masses such as folk music as well as the traditional music of India's numerous religious and tribal communities is surprisingly given the least attention.

---

23 *All India Radio - 1995*, p.39.
24 op.cit. p.39.

Table 22: Spoken Word Programmes on All India Radio (1992)[25]

Spoken Word Programmes (Excluding Vividh Bharati)	Percentage with Reference to Total Spoken Word (219,652.37 Hours)
Talks/Discussions etc.	26.58
Drama	6.97
Religious	0.49
Educational	
Women	3.67
Rural	13.59
Industrial	2.15
School/University	8.15
Children	2.46
Youth	10.33
Tribal	2.76
Armed Forces	3.17
Publicity	6.59
Others	13.09
Total	100.00

Broadcasting Policy

Until September 15, 1997, AIR was fully owned, controlled, and run by the Central Government. But this was not what the founding fathers intended. Jawaharlal Nehru believed that "we should approximate as far as possible to the British model, the BBC; that is to say it would be better if we had a semi-autonomous corporation under the Government, of course with the policy controlled by the Government, otherwise not being conducted as a Government department but as a semi-autonomous corporation".[26]

The Chanda Committee on Broadcasting and Information

---
25 op.cit. p.40.
26 Prime Minister Nehru's reply to a debate in the Constituent Assembly on March 15, 1948.

Media said in its Report in April 1966 that 'it is not possible in the Indian context for a creative medium like broadcasting to flourish under a regime of departmental rules and regulations' and therefore recommended an 'institutional change' so that AIR can be liberated; and separate corporations for Akashvani and Doordarshan.[27] In April 1970, four years later, the Indira Gandhi Government responded stating that 'the present is not an opportune time to consider the conversion of AIR into an autonomous corporation'. However, with effect from April 1, 1976, Television was separated from AIR and constituted into a new body, Doordarshan.

The Verghese Committee in February 1978 called for the establishment of a 'National Broadcasting Trust' called Akash Bharati as an "autonomous and independent public service". Accordingly, the Akash Bharati Bill, 1978 was introduced in the Lok Sabha by the Janata Government though it had some reservations about it. Later, the Trust came to be termed 'Prasar Bharati' by successive national governments.

Even after the formation of the Prasar Bharati, supposedly an autonomous body for public radio and television broadcasting, both radio (All India Radio or 'Akashvani') and television ('Doordarshan') continue to act as 'media units' of the Ministry of Information and Broadcasting. It is this same Ministry that remains the official policy-making body on the broadcasting system.

The Government's earlier monopoly of broadcasting rested on Article 246 of the Indian Constitution which states that Parliament has 'exclusive' powers to make laws with respect to any of the matters enumerated in List 1 of the seventh schedule. Item 31 in this list includes 'posts and telegraphs, telephones, wireless, broadcasts and other like forms of communication'. The Indian Telegraph Act of 1885 and the Indian Wireless Telegraphy Act of 1933 (which were drawn up during the British regime) continued to be in force, and to give the Government the legal right to a monopoly in broadcasting, besides the right to

---

27 Chanda Committee Report, New Delhi: Publications Division, 1966.

intercept and to censor mail. This exclusive monopoly of the use of the airwaves was struck down by the Supreme Court in 1995 when it declared that 'the airwaves are public property' and that the public is distinctive from the government. It directed the Central Government to constitute an autonomous broadcasting authority to license and regulate the use of the airwaves for broadcasting. In September 1997, the Prasar Bharati (or the Broadcasting Corporation of India) was established as an autonomous body to give effect to the Prasar Bharati Act (1990). The Broadcasting Bill (1997) was drawn up by the United Front government, and later revised by the Congress coalition government. Both these lapsed and so another attempt was made in 2005 to revive the defunct Broadcasting Bill. The Ministry of Information and Broadcasting wrote up yet another: the Draft Broadcasting Services Regulation Bill 2006 – the fourth such Bill in a decade. It was to be introduced in Parliament in late 2007 but, as in earlier attempts of Government to regulate broadcasting – the placement of the Bill was postponed to give time to the industry to evolve its own code for self-regulation. This has now turned into a ritual: 'a bill is introduced; opened for public comments; greeted with a torrent of adverse comments by the country's main media houses; the ministry concedes need for further consultation and organizes a few such events. Finally, the ministry, in acknowledgement of the strong sentiments of the media industry, accepts the need for further deliberations and defers the introduction of the bill in Parliament a little longer.'[28] (For a discussion of the Bill refer to the Section on Television).

Broadcasting Code

Current broadcasting policy is based on the AIR Code of 1970, which sets down that broadcasts on All India Radio will not permit:
(1) criticism of friendly countries;
(2) attack on religion or communities;

---

28 Sukumar Murlidharan: 'Broadcast Regulation: Narrow Consultations, Indifferent Results', *Economic and Political Weekly*, September 15, 2007, pp. 3690-92.

(3) anything obscene or defamatory;
(4) incitement to violence or anything against the maintenance of law and order;
(5) anything amounting to contempt of court;
(6) aspersions against the integrity of the President, Governors, and Judiciary;
(7) attack on a political party by name;
(8) hostile criticism of any State or the Centre; or
(9) anything showing disrespect to the Constitution or advocating change in the Constitution by violence; but advocating change in a constitutional way should not be debarred.

The Broadcasting Code also forbids 'direct publicity of an individual or of a commercial benefit to an organisation', and the use of 'trade names amounting to direct advertising'. The Code applies to criticism in the nature of a personal tirade, either of a friendly Government or of a political party or of the Central Government or any State Government. But it does not debar references to and/or dispassionate discussion of policies pursued by any of them.

The Code adds that 'if a Station Director finds that the above Code has not been respected in any particular or particulars by an intending broadcaster he will draw the latter's attention to the passage objected to. If the intending broadcaster refuses to accept the Station Director's suggestions and modify his/her script accordingly, the Station Director will be justified in rejecting his or her broadcast. Cases of unresolved differences of opinion between a Minister of a State Government and a Station Director about the interpretation of the Code with respect to a talk to be broadcast by the former will be referred to the Minister of Information and Broadcasting, Government of India, who will decide finally whether or not any change in the text was necessary in order to avoid violation of the Code'.

The Code and other restrictions on broadcasting are based on Clause 2 of Article 19 of the Indian Constitution. Other restrictions include the broadcasting of the news of the death of high dignitaries such as the President, the Vice-President, the Prime Minister and a few others only after it has been cleared by the Home Secretary. The AIR or Doordarshan correspondent has to get the news from him, inform the News Room, before it can be broadcast. This explains the excessive delay in the announcement of the news of Indira Gandhi's assassination, though the BBC had made it known worldwide four hours earlier. According to an agreement arrived at by all political parties in 1977, air time continues to be allocated for political broadcasting prior to national and state elections.

Frequency Modulation (FM) Broadcasts – (1997 – 2000)

FM radio broadcasts were introduced in Madras in 1977 and later at Jalandhar in 1992, but it was only in 1993 when time slots came to be leased to private companies that FM became synonymous with pop music and youth culture. On August 15, 1993 a Frequency Modulation (FM) Channel was launched in Bombay, with nine hours of radio time leased to private producers like Times FM, Radiostar and Radio Midday. Coincidentally, the music video channels, [V] and MTV were launched around the same time on Star TV. FM broadcasts ensured reception free from atmospheric noise and electric interference. The AIR stations of Delhi, Bombay, Panaji, Bangalore, Madras and Calcutta, sold FM slots to private producers.

All India Radio charged a fee of Rs. 3,000 per hour, but the private companies charged advertisers Rs. 250 - 300 for a ten-second commercial. The broadcasts in most of the cities were oriented to urban English-speaking youth, with western pop music dominating. Besides sponsored hit parades and count-downs, the FM programmes included chat shows, contests, and quizzes. Phone-ins, page-ins and write-ins were the strategies used to involve listeners. Advertising support for the leased slots was generous and as a result revenue began to soar. The new mass medium of urban India was ready to take off.

But there were several roadblocks on the way. The main roadblock to the further growth of private FM broadcasting until 2000 was the low percentage of FM radio sets[29], the reluctance of AIR authorities to let go of their control, and the attempts of the private broadcasters at that time (two of whom, The Times of India and Midday, are major newspaper publishers) to hold on to their monopoly. They resisted AIR's bid to raise the rates and lobbied against Indian companies with 25% foreign equity bidding for time on the FM channels.[30]

FM radio technology facilitates localisation of broadcasting, and the operation of a large number of stations. New York, for instance, has as many as 82 stations; London has 42, Manila 35 and Jakarta 29, while New Delhi has only five. Transmission bands for FM radio range between 80 and 108 Mhz, though the Indian government has kept 80-108 Mhz for its own services. Still, 13 frequencies are available for a whole lot of stations in different languages in multi-linguistic cities. AIR has extended FM broadcasting to many Indian cities.

FM Radio - *Auctioning the Airwaves*

The Supreme Court pronounced in 1995 that 'the airwaves are public property', and therefore could not be the monopoly of either government or business. The government interpreted the pronouncement as an imperative to privatize the airwaves. This rather strange interpretation led to the auctioning of the radio waves to the highest commercial bidders.

The monopoly of All India Radio ended in 1999 when the industry was opened up to private commercial FM Radio. In 2001, 108 FM radio licences for 40 cities (Phase I) were up for grabs. The largest winner for the ten-year license was the Entertainment Network India Ltd. (ENIL), the radio arm of the

---

29 According to NRS-1997, barely seven percent of the urban population claimed to listen to FM channels; according to *All India Radio - 1995 (p.92)*, there were only five million FM radio households out of a total of 11 million radio households in the country.

30 Cf. *Business Standard* (Bombay), March 2, 1998. See also *Screen* (Bombay), May 1, 1998, p.1,4.

Times of India Group. However, the exorbitant licence fees and other preconditions resulted in just 21 stations becoming operational. According to industry reports, in 2005 alone, private FM radio stations paid licence fees to the tune of Rs. 100 crore and, with total revenues of Rs. 150 crore, and losses of Rs. 70-80 crore, the resulting accumulated losses since April 2000 were approximately Rs. 250 crore.[31]

In early 2006, as many as 338 licenses for FM stations in 91 cities were auctioned off to the highest bidders – all private companies that were allowed to get up to 20% FDI. The Government mopped up Rs. 9 billion from the auction and was expected to receive around Rs. 390 million per annum as the minimum license fee. The second phase (December 2007) saw the auction of another 97 stations to 27 companies, this time for stations in smaller cities such as Bikaner, Trichy, Udaipur, Warangal, Agartala and Gangtok). This phase ushered in the Revenue Share Model to replace the Fixed License Model, that is from an ascending fee-based system (which escalated by 10% every year) to a revenue-share system (4%) with radio operators. The Government was expected to net Rs. 11 billion from the auction. (The third phase was scheduled for the end of 2008 with a promise of higher earnings).

Major media companies such as The Times of India, Living Media, Hindustan Times, Dainik Bhaskar, Jagran Prakashan, Midday, Zee TV, Star TV, Sun TV and Eenadu have gained immensely from the auction. There were also indications that news and current affairs programmes would be permitted on these stations. So would live ball-by-ball commentaries. In fact, this was a strong recommendation of both TRAI (Telecom Regulatory Authority of India) and the Working Group of the 11th Five Year Plan (2007-2012) on Information and Broadcasting. Public ownership of the airwaves was thereby given short shrift.

By the close of 2007, the FM radio industry was worth over Rs. 310 crores and was expected to grow to a thousand crore rupees by the end of the decade. BIG FM, Survan, Radio Mirchi,

---

31 'Radio Casting a Hypnotic Spell', *USP Age*, February 2007, pp.21ff.

Table 23: Newspaper Publishers in FM Radio Broadcasting

No.	Newspaper Publisher	FM Radio Stations
1.	Jagran Prakashan	Radio Mantra
2.	Midday Multimedia	Radio One
3.	Hindustan Times	Radio Fever
4.	ENIL/Times of India	Radio Mirchi
5.	India Today	Radio Today/Radio Meow
6.	Dainik Bhaskar	My FM
7.	Dinakaran	Suryan FM/'S' FM
8.	Malayala Manorama	Manorama Radio/Radio Mango
9.	Ananda Bazaar Patrika	Friends FM
10.	Pudhari Publications	Tomato FM
11.	Prabhat Khabbar	Radio Dhoom

Radio City and of course AIR's FM stations (Rainbow FM and FM Gold) were the main players, the scene was expected to explode with the auction of the Third Phase. Music, chat and utilities (traffic updates, public announcements) are the main drivers, since news and current affairs and live sports commentaries were yet to be allowed by the government; user-generated content was yet another aim of the broadcasters. However, several companies that have won licenses for radio stations appear to be reluctant to launch them in the small cities and towns primarily because of the uncertainty of revenues from advertising. Further, there has not been a remarkable uptake in the purchase of FM-enabled radio sets. In January 2007, the Working Group of Eleventh Five Year Plan found that out of the total number of 132 million radio sets, barely 78 million were FM receivers.[32] By the end of that year 281 FM stations had been operationalised, with as many of as 121 of these private stations; another 130 remained to be operationalised. The primary content of both AIR's FM and private FM stations is Hindi and regional film music. The composition of a typical radio hour is as under:

Music	67%
Advertising	14%
Jock Talk	9%
Channel Promotion	5%
Fillers/Snippets	4%
Others	1%

(Source: *Broadcast and CableSat*, July 8, 2008, pp.48-52.)

Radio continues to be primarily a family and home medium. But the early years of the 21st century have been witness to FM radio turning gradually into an outdoors (or Out-of-Home) medium. Around 30% of listening to radio is on mobiles, with most mobiles being FM-enabled sets. Nokia's handsets even had Radio City's logo marked on them. Another 15% tend to listen to FM radio outside the home – mostly in cars and autorickshas, but also in shopping malls, restaurants, and other open spaces where leisure and entertainment dominate.

The FM industry has got together to form the FICCI-Radio Forum. Initiated by FICCI, the Radio Forum would be required to face new challenges such as satellite radio, community radio, mobile radio, campus radio and internet radio, as well as attempts to regulate the industry through the new content code spelt out in the Broadcasting Bill (2007). The Forum would provide a platform for discussion with the government so that there would be mobility and flexibility in the government's radio policy. That policy does not allow private FM radio stations to carry news and current affairs programmes, or live cricket/sports commentaries. The FM radio industry had committed over half a billion dollars in licence fees and rollout costs in 18 months, according to the Forum's chairman. The Forum's core group has representatives from a host of companies including MBPL, Red

---

32 Working Group of Eleventh Five-Year Plan (2007-12) on Information and Broadcasting Sector, January 2007.

FM, BAG Films, Adlabs/ADAG, Radio Midday, India Today, Malayala Manorama, Win Radio and TAM Media.[33] The trade body of the industry is the Association of Radio Operators of India (AROI).

Radio Industry Revenues

The radio industry works in close collaboration with the Phonographic Performance Ltd., the body that represents the interests of music companies, and the Indian Performing Rights Society (IPRS) which charges royalty from radio stations. Most stations play music for about 18 hours every day; the cost of music works out to Rs. 1,320 per needle hour. Around 20 to 30% of the revenue (largely from advertising, sponsorship and product placements) goes to PPL for cost of music rights.[34] Other costs include: human resources, marketing and branding. A one-time entry/license fee for ten years amounting to Rs. 1,300 crores has been paid collectively by private FM stations.[35]

According to studies by Zenith Optimedia and FICCI-Price Waterhouse Coopers, the revenues of the radio industry in India has been steadily rising since the year 2000. The share of radio in overall advertising spend has been around three percent compared to the average of 8.7% worldwide (China: 4.4%; Thailand: 6.5%; Singapore: 9.4%)[36]. The bulk of the revenues have accrued to All India Radio. In 2005, for instance, All India Radio accounted for over 53% of the total revenues of Rs. 3.32 billion. The table below suggests that, whatever the strident complaints of private broadcasters, radio is indeed a profitable enterprise; the rush for FM radio auctions during the three phases of radio expansion (from 2000 to 2008) is clear testimony of this.

---

33 For a comprehensive list of FM stations in India cf. www.airwaves.net/india-fm-radio.htm
34 S. Bansal: 'Who's Listening to Radio' in *Business Standard*, July 14, 2007, p. II.
35 Ibid.
36 Source: Zenith Optimedia, October 2004.

Table 24: Radio Industry Revenues

YEAR	Amount in Rs. Billion
2000	1.76
2001	2.22
2002	2.57
2003	2.80
2004	2.92
2005	3.32
2006	3.68

Source: Zenith Optimedia, October 2006.

Table 25: Major Players in FM Radio After Phase II Rollout

No.	Company	No. of Stations	Of top 13 Towns
1.	Adlabs/BIG	44	7
2.	South Asia/Kaal Radio	45	10
3.	ENIL/Times of India	32	13
4.	Radio City	20	11
5.	Dainik Bhaskar	17	4
6.	BAG Films	10	0
7.	Zee/Century	8	0
8.	Thanthi/Today/Midday	7	1/3/7
9.	Hindustan Times/ Positive/ Rajasthan Patrika	4	40/1

Projected Growth of Indian Radio Industry

Of all the mass media, radio has the widest reach as well as the widest coverage. With over 132 million radio sets (of which 78 million are FM receivers), radio reaches almost the entire population of India; the geographical coverage too is nationwide (98.3%). The coverage of AIR's FM stations is about 31%, while that of the private FM stations a bare nine per cent.[37]

The FICCI-PriceWaterhouse-Coopers Report (2007)[38]

---

37 Data Source: Working Group Report of the 11th Five-Year Plan (2007-12) for the Ministry of Information and Broadcasting – 2007.
38 FICCI-PriceWaterhouse Coopers: *The Indian Entertainment and Media Industry*, 2007.

projects that the radio industry valued at three billion rupees in 2005, and growing at 32% per annum, is estimated to expand to Rs. 12 billion by 2010. The prospects for expansion have brightened up with the liberalization of the economy and of foreign investment in radio broadcasting. FDI up to 20% in an Indian radio company is now allowed. BBC Worldwide, Virgin Radio, and Astro have already tied up with Radio Midday, Radio Today and HT Media respectively. With licenses for as many as 338 FM radio stations in 91 cities of India, it appears that the steady growth of radio is here to stay. There are of course some restrictions: radio companies will not be permitted to run more than 15% of the total stations in the country. It is also quite likely that the ban on the transmission of news and current affairs programmes will be lifted by the Ministry of Information and Broadcasting. In mid-2008, the Times of India Group/Bennett, Coleman & Co. Ltd (BCCL), which owns 32 FM stations (under the label Radio Mirchi) around the country, acquired the London-based Virgin Radio network. This is perhaps a sign of the future growth of Indian FM radio.

Table 26: Growth in Number of FM Radio Stations

Year	No. of FM Radio Stations
2004	10
2005	10
2006	26
2007	281
2008	338 (Est.)

New Developments

Community and Campus Radio

The Ministry of Information and Broadcasting as also the Prasar Bharati have been unwilling to give up their monopoly on radio broadcasting. Brave attempts by individuals, social action groups and small communities have succeeded in putting 'community' radio on the map. Community radio relates to non-state and non-profit 'narrow-casting' where at least fifty per cent of the programmes are made by local communities. Take Raghav Mattoo of a small Bihari village, for instance. In early 2006, he ran a community radio station all on his own in a remote village in Bihar for several years – until the law caught up on him, and forced him to shut shop. He had had no training and spent just fifty rupees to put his community radio station together. The BBC called Raghav's 'Mansoorpur FM' the 'amazing do-it-yourself village FM radio station'.[39]

Community radio is characterised by community ownership and community participation. The production of programmes is a participatory community exercise, for the benefit of the whole community. Some of the community radio efforts over the years include Radio Ujjas in Bhuj (Gujarat), the Deccan Development Society's community radio initiative in Pastapur (Andhra Pradesh), Namma Dhawani in Budhikote, Karnataka, and Radio Alakal in Trivandrum. Also worthy of note are Kalanjiam (near Bangalore), Heval (Chamba) and Mandani Ki Awaaz (Bhanaj).

Some social activists came together in Bangalore in 1996 to hammer out a 'Bangalore Declaration' on Community Radio as an alternative to public service and commercial radio. These activists had noted that Nepal and Sri Lanka were far ahead in their support of Community Radio than India. Radio Lumbini, a community radio station in Nepal, broadcasts programmes in Bhojpuri and Avadhi; they could be picked up in neighbouring Bihar. Nepal has no separate policy on community radio but as many as half the 56 FM stations are run entirely as community radio stations.[40]

It was only as late as 2002 that government opened up FM radio to community groups and to university campuses, but only Campus Radio stations – as many as 17 of them – came up in quick succession in different parts of the country. These included university campuses such as Jamia Milia Islamia, IGNOU,

---

39 Sajan Venniyoor: 'Radio's Third Wave', Impact, January 13-21, 2007, pp32 and 34.
40 Ibid.

Annamalai and Pune Universities, and national media institute campuses such as FTII, SRFTI and IIMC. These are often called 'Community Radio' stations which they certainly are not. True Community Radio stations were still not encouraged, though the Working Group for the Eleventh Five Year Plan has made it clear that 'three to four thousand community radio stations can potentially come up'.[41] At the close of 2007, barely 26 community radio stations were on the air.

In November 2006 the Union Cabinet announced a new policy on Community Radio. The policy opened up FM radio licensing to civil society and voluntary organizations, registered societies, autonomous bodies, and public trusts registered under the Societies Act or similar acts. But individuals, political parties and their affiliates, and profit-making institutions were prohibited from applying. No license fee was required for community stations and advertising could not exceed five minutes per hour. The fear is that this kowtowing to advertiser interests could result in the commercialization of community radio. The lack of a continuous power supply in the rural areas would necessitate alternative energy sources such as solar and wind.

Social action groups and others are organizing themselves into a Community Radio Forum so as to be able to lobby with the government for concessions on taxes and duties for radio infrastructure and equipment, for inexpensive receiver-sets, but most importantly for lifting the current ban on news and current affairs. Only then could community radio become the voice of the voiceless millions in our land. A Community Radio Policy is proposed to be integrated into the draft Broadcasting Regulation Bill drawn up by the Ministry of Information and Broadcasting.

Digital Audio Broadcasting (DAB)

Several broadcasters, including All India Radio, have introduced DAB since the mid-1990s. DAB technology arose out

---

41 Working Group of Eleventh Five-Year Plan (2007-12) on Information and Broadcasting Sector, January 2007.

of a European project called Eureka-147 and broadcasting using this technology was launched by the BBC in 1995 in the London region. It transmits sound as computer code rather than as analogous waves; like compact disc (CD) technology it provides interference-free sound. Though primarily an audio medium, it can also carry multimedia services such as text, data files, graphics, pictures, and moving video. Thus, DAB listeners can listen to music accompanied by information and pictures on their computer screens. There are other uses too for the technology: it can be used for carrying tourist and travel information to computer terminals; to transmit traffic information to cars equipped with multi-media DAB receivers, and to send data to notebook computers and mobile phones. Music hardware multinationals like Philips, Sony, Panasonic, and Grundig announced the manufacture of DAB receivers in late 1997.[42]

Satellite Radio

With its headquarters in Washington D.C., WorldSpace (founded in 1990 by Noah A. Samara) is the only private satellite radio platform so far in India. WorldSpace's rivals at the global level include Sirius and XM, also based in the United States, though these do not as yet have a footprint in Asia. WorldSpace was free-to-air when it was launched in 2000 but since then has become a pay service, offering over 40 radio channels in several Indian languages and in a variety of genres, from Jazz, Classical, Old Hindi Film Music and Rock.[43] The Indian Government's Department of Science plans to set up its own multi-media satellite radio platform to provide satellite radio, video and data channels, according to a Consultation Paper on Satellite Radio (2005) issued by TRAI. However, satellite radio is not likely to take off in the country because it requires special radio receivers and as long as subscription costs remain unaffordable. With the free and easy availability of FM channels and numerous radio

---

42 'Better Radio, or TV's Poor Cousin?', *Business Standard/b.s. connect*, p.2.
43 Interview with Harshad Jain (Chief Marketing Officer, WorldSpace India): 'Satellite Radio: Expanding Its Reach', Broadcast and CableCast, May 2008, p. 48.

stations from around the world on the Internet, satellite radio is likely to remain just another technology for the dissemination of music, news and talk shows. In developed countries FM radio was introduced in the 1960s much before cable, the internet and satellite radio; in India private FM radio took off only after 2000 but the pace of growth has been rather tardy (barely six to eight per cent per annum, according to an ILT survey by MRUC (Media Research Users Council).[44]

Visual Radio

Visual Radio is a convergent technology that combines FM radio with the mobile phone. It's a radio built into a mobile device. Visual Radio shows you what's playing on the phone screen. Thus you can see information about the song you are listening to, or biography or picture of the artist, or you can download a ringtone of the song. While listening to a Visual Radio-enabled FM Channel you can switch interactive service on or off whenever you want to. You can of course switch off the data on the screen and just listen to the FM radio broadcast. Listeners pay only for the data service carried via General Packet Radio Service (GPRS). India is the third country in the world to offer such a service, commercially, though penetration is still limited only to those who have a particular series of the Nokia handsets. This value-added service provides rich textual and visual information, a gaming platform, and the potential of forming social networking communities. User-generated content (UGC), a vital aspect of social networking websites like www.orkut.com, www.myspace.com, www.secondlife.com and www.flickr.com, could also become part of the visual radio listening experience. As is the case with all other interactive media, advertisers are looking at these social networks as advertising vehicles to peddle their wares. Mobile Radio, on the other hand, provides access only to the FM Radio programmes; Visual Radio extends the Mobile Radio experience by adding

---

44 Quoted in S. Bansal: 'Who's Listening to Radio' in Business Standard, July 14, 2007, p. II.

text and visuals to accompany the music or the talk show. Radio Data Receivers (RDS) fitted in cars offer a similar facility: they allow text to be displayed on the radio's panel, like the name of the artiste or the title of the song.[45] The RDS can be used to show text advertisements. This new text-radio technology has been introduced by Clear Channel Communications and Infinity Broadcasting in the United States;[46] it is yet to be launched in India.

Radio on the Internet

Several public and commercial radio stations transmit their music and talk shows on the Internet. Most Indian FM channels have an active presence on the net; they have their own social network sites. Meow FM, for instance, has launched // meowfm.ning.com, and Radio City FM its social network www.planetradiocity.com. Radio NRI 'Bollywood and Beyond' is available via the Internet on AOL radio, Apple iTunes radio and RadioNRI.com all across North America. The majority of Indian radio stations on the Internet, however, have their source in the United States and United Kingdom. (See www.indianradio.com and www.live365.com for a complete list). Hindi film music dominates on these 'desi' radio sites as it does on FM stations and television music channels in India.

Ethics of Broadcasting

Radio and television were introduced in India to be the carriers of entertainment and education for the general public. Though introduced with 'public service' as the prime objective, both the electronic media have been widely used for government propaganda as well as for commercial interests. Non-broadcast media like video and cable are in the private sector and therefore know no control and no regulation. Attempts at regulating cable and satellite TV have not been very effective because of the large number of operators and sub-operators involved.

---

45 Vanita Kohli-Khandekar: *The Indian Media Business*, New Delhi: Response Books, 2006. p.176.
46 Ibid.

Where broadcast news is concerned, the ethics of broadcasting is very similar to those for the print media. These relate to questions of accuracy and fairness, of respect for privacy and the religious beliefs/practices of different communities, of the need for caution in reporting violence and communal disturbances, and in criticising judicial acts, of the right to reply, of respect for the confidentiality of sources, and of the need to eschew obscenity and vulgarity.

Take the coverage of Operation Bluestar by All India Radio and Doordarshan, for instance. Or, their announcement of the assassinations of Indira Gandhi and Rajiv Gandhi. What were the 'ethics' involved in their low-key coverage of the storming of the Golden Temple at Amritsar, and their rather late declaration of the news about the assassinations of the Gandhis? The professional journalist's view is that, irrespective of the consequences, news should be transmitted immediately after the event no matter what the event or who the persons involved. However, there is an alternative view that tragic news which affects an entire nation and which might lead to violence, may be withheld or delayed for a while till tempers cool down and the law and order situation is under control. This alternative view suggests that professional 'ethics' cannot take precedence as these professional journalistic ethics have been evolved in Western liberal democracies, and often have little relevance to the social and cultural needs of developing countries.

However, the misuse of the airwaves by government for blatant political party propaganda, or for criticism of opposition parties without representing their perspective, must be termed 'unethical'. Also 'unethical' is the false representation of rallies, strikes and 'bandhs' to suit the ruling party's interests. The deliberate non-coverage of events of public concern and also the banning of programmes expressing alternative views on controversial issues (e.g. Anand Patwardhan's 'Ram Ke Naam', Saeed Mirza's 'Kashmir' and the documentaries on the Bhagalpur blindings, police brutalities, the Bhopal disaster, the Gujarat massacre, etc.) is also considered 'unethical' since broadcasting is not the private property of any political party or commercial broadcaster, as the 1994 Supreme Court declaration that 'the airwaves are public property' has made amply clear. All India Radio's monopoly of news on radio is also questionable; so is the auctioning of the airwaves to private broadcasters for the rank commercialization of FM radio. Whatever happened to the 'public service' remit of radio broadcasting?

Listenership Surveys

The Audience Research Units of major All India Radio stations conduct 'listenership surveys' regularly to find out who its listeners are, which programs they listen to, and how popular its various programmes are. The marketing agencies that conduct National Readership Surveys also gather data about radio listeners. Two other agencies that conduct listenership surveys regularly are: Media Research Users' Council (MRUC) and Radio Audience Measurement (RAM), the latter a new division of the A C Nielsen and IMRB joint venture called TAM (Television Audience Measurement). The MRUC conducts the Indian Listenership Survey (ILT).

The ILT survey uses the Day-After-Recall (DAR) methodology; it is conducted in Mumbai, Delhi and Kolkata; in other cities a variety of research such as coincidental researches like the IMRB Car Tracks and IMRB Listenership Tracks, again based on the DAR methodology. The DAR methodology relies on recall of the previous day's listening to radio, the assumption by market researchers being that recall tells us everything about 'impact' and 'effectiveness'. What a naïve view of radio reception this is! Individual channels conduct their own research at different stages of production and transmission. Few attempts are made to fathom the complexity of the experience and after-effects of listening to radio. Here is what the CEO of Radio City told the trade magazine IMPACT: 'DAR essentially measures awareness of an FM station since it looks at the recall of a station the day after it is listened to. With radio, as a medium, it is very difficult to recall what one was listening to the previous day, thus the most salient brand gets recalled and saliency becomes a surrogate for listenership which is incorrect'.[47] Radio City itself uses a Brand Health Monitor which tracks various parameters including listenership. And the CEO of Red FM avers: Brand recall is being confused with actual listenership in DAR.[48]

Radio Audience Measurement (RAM) also tracks radio listenership but unlike ILT employs the 'diary method'. A panel of 480 individuals in each city (Bombay, Delhi, Bangalore and Calcutta) is selected from a broad panel of 3000 on the basis of household size, work status and other demographics. RAM ratings like those for TAM are available on a weekly basis. A comparative analysis of respondents' patterns of listening to radio and watching television will be made. The findings are available to subscribers every Thursday through software called 'radio advisor' that can be updated online for the latest results. To track listening habits of those on the move, a 'go' meter, an electronic radio tracking meter, is proposed to be introduced.[49]

Call-ins, SMSes and e-mails are other ways in which radio stations invite feedback from listeners. They serve as a reference check while scheduling songs on the stations. For instance, Radio City's Chennai station changed their programming to raise their English content to 70%, with the balance divided between Tamil and Hindi.[50] Radio One employs a research methodology that it terms Hit Music Testing (HMT). This involves constant testing of new music as well as consistent testing of old hits from all eras. This enables the station to generate indices by which it is able to generate a HIT Quotient (HQ) which tells it how much of a hit a song is, as well as a Fatigue Indicator (FI) that tells whether a song has gone out of favour with the listeners.[51] BIG FM says that it does Continuous Call-Out Research to test new

---

47 'Radio Talk: Radio delivers; it should get the $$$ to grow', IMPACT, 28 August 2006, pp.12-15.
48 Ibid.
49 Cf. PITCH, June 2007, pp.2-21.
50 'Radio Talk: Measured Music!', IMPACT, 11 December 2006, pp.16-17.
51 Ibid.

songs and play only the city's favourites.[52]

But the fundamental question that arises in all such attempts is: who really is a radio 'listener'? If Vividh Bharati or a private FM station is on the whole day long in a household, does it mean that every member of the household is a 'listener'? Indeed, for most Vividh Bharati listeners, the music provided is background music while they go about their household chores. This is equally true of the listener to FM broadcasts when on the move. His one or two hour daily drive to work becomes less tedious and boring when music or chatter on the FM channels is present in the background. Further, few members of a household listen very attentively to every programme, except perhaps to the news or announcements. So, most radio listeners, especially listeners to popular music programmes are in reality only 'secondary' and 'tertiary' listeners: not much attention is given to this musical wallpaper at home or in the office or while on the move. Both the survey methods – DAR (Day-After-Recall) and the Diary' are terribly flawed. Where listening to music on radio is one among several activities indulged in at the same time – and certainly not necessarily the most important activity – what can either method tell us about respondents' listening habits or preferences? The exercise of 'recalling' what one listened to on the previous day suggests that recall is equivalent to actual use; similarly, the daily recording of one's radio listening habits in a diary – a rather painstaking exercise – suggests that respondents can be relied upon to accurately jot down the radio channels and programmes they are tuned to the whole day long. Ultimately, the diary method too is dependent upon 'recall' which at its best is a very slippery and unreliable measure. The Audience Research Units (ARUs) of All India Radio and Doordarshan have been using the 'diary method' for years together and with much larger and more representative samples than that of the marketing agencies. The measurement of media audiences remains, in the final analysis, a very tricky business. It must go beyond counting heads and statistics if it is to be in any way meaningful.

---

52 Ibid.

FOR FURTHER READING

A. RADIO BROADCASTING
1. *All India Radio Handbook*, New Delhi, 2005.
2. Audience Research Unit, AIR: *All India Radio - 1995: Facts and Figures*, New Delhi, 1996.
3. G.C. Awasthy: *Broadcasting in India*, Bombay: Allied, 1965.
4. U.L. Baruah: *This is All India Radio*, New Delhi: Publications Division, 1984.
5. P.C. Chatterjee: *Broadcasting in India*, New Delhi: Sage, 1987; Second Rev. Ed. 1992.
6. K.S. Duggal: *What Ails Indian Broadcasting?*, New Delhi: Marwah Publications, 1980.
7. H.K. Luthra: *Indian Broadcasting*, New Delhi: Publications Division, 1987.
8. Mehra Masani: *Broadcasting and the People*, New Delhi: National Book Trust, 1976, 2nd Ed. 1985.
9. K.R. Mullick: *Tangled Tapes: The Inside Story of Indian Broadcasting*, New Delhi: Sterling Publications, 1974.
10. Vinod Pavarala and Kanchan K. Malik: *Other Voices: The Struggle for Community Radio in India*, New Delhi: Sage Publications, 2007.

B. REPORTS
1. *Radio and Television: Report of the (Chanda) Committee on Broadcasting and Information Media*, New Delhi: Ministry of Information and Broadcasting, 1966.
2. *Akash Bharati (National Broadcasting Trust): Report of the Working Group on Autonomy for Akashvani and Doordarshan*, Vols. I and II, New Delhi: Ministry of Information and Broadcasting, 1978.
3. *An Indian Personality for Television: Report of the Working Group on Software for Doordarshan*, Vols. I, II and III, New Delhi: Publications Division, Ministry of Information and Broadcasting, 1985.
4. Report of the Amit Mitra Committee on Radio Broadcast Policy, 2003, New Delhi: Ministry of Information and Broadcasting (Government of India).
5. Working Group Report of the 11th Five-Year Plan (2007-2012) on

Information and Broadcasting Sector, January 2007, New Delhi: Ministry of Information and Broadcasting (Government of India).
6. FICCI-PriceWaterhouse-Coopers Report: *The Indian Entertainment and Media Industry – Sustaining Growth, 2007.*

C. JOURNALS
1. Broadcast and CableSat (www.adi-media.com)
2. USP Age (Cf. Special issue on Radio Broadcasting, Vol. IV, No. 4. February 2007).
3. IMPACT
4. Brand Reporter
5. PITCH.

WEB RESOURCES

1. www.allindiaradio.org (All India Radio Services)
2. www.aiir.com (All India Internet Radio)
3. www.exchange4media.com (For current information on the FM radio business)
4. www.screenindia.com (For recent developments in radio broadcasting)
5. www.mib.gov.in (For Government documents on radio and television)
6. www.airwaves.net
7. www.mruc.net
8. www.adexindia.com
9. www.radioandmusic.com (For news on radio in India)

REVIEW QUESTIONS

1. What is the scope of radio in India? What are its special advantages as a mass medium of communication?
2. Trace the development of radio broadcasting in India since 1927.
3. How can you explain the popularity of Vividh Bharati?
4. What is the role of External Service broadcasts? What is the future of such broadcasts in the context of the globalisation of television?
5. The privatisation of FM broadcasting has proved to be

controversial. What are the restrictions imposed on private FM broadcasters?
6. Write short notes on:
   (a) Rural Broadcasting
   (b) The AIR Code
   (c) School Broadcasts
   (d) FM Channels
   (e) Community Radio
   (f) Campus Radio
   (g) Visual Radio
   (h) Radio on Mobile Telephones and on the Internet.

SUGGESTED PROJECTS

1. Organise a visit to the local radio station. Request a programme producer or assistant to show you around the station.
2. Listen to AIR's news bulletin at 9.00 p.m. and also to Doordarshan's news telecast at 10.00 p.m. on the same day. What differences do you find in the mode of presentation, the language employed, the order in which news stories are read? Which media do you think provided wider coverage?
3. Read the report of the main news item in today's papers. Rewrite the report for a radio news bulletin. (Remember to write the report for the 'ear', not for the eye!).
4. Do a radio feature on students' views on Direct-to-Home (DTH) broadcasting. Record the views of three or four students on a cassette. Intersperse these views with your own narrative on the cassette.
5. Write out a script for a radio play. Produce the play on a cassette with the help of your friends' voices.
6. Critically analyse an interview or a discussion you have heard recently on radio. How do you think it could have been made more interesting?
7. Write out a five-minute radio talk on a subject you are interested in. Record your talk on a cassette. Play it back to evaluate your performance.
8. Conduct a survey of the music genres that young people listen to on the FM radio stations of your city.

9. Play the role of an RJ (Radio Jockey). Introduce the top ten songs of the week to your FM audience. (How would you go about preparing yourself for the task?)
10. Conduct a study of the 'economics' of running an FM radio station. What are the costs involved? Where do the main revenues come from? How profitable is it to run an FM station?

TELEVISION

Early Experiments in Television

Experiments in television broadcasting were initiated during the 1920s in the United States and Europe. These experiments used a mechanical scanning disc that did not scan a picture rapidly enough. In 1923, however, came the invention of the iconoscope, the electric television tube. The inventions of the kinescope or picture tube, the electronic camera and TV home receivers arrived in rapid succession during the next few years and by the 1930s the National Broadcasting Corporation (NBC) had set up a TV station in New York, and BBC a TV station in London, offering regular telecast programmes. Germany and France too established television stations around the same time.

The World War put a brake on further developments in television, though in Nazi Germany television was widely used as an instrument of political propaganda.[1] Nazi party conventions were televised, but the top event in the first chapter of German television history was the 1936 Olympics in Berlin which was staged as a gigantic propaganda show for the Third Reich.[2] But by the late 1940s and early 1950s television had become a feature of life in most developed countries. In 1948, for instance, there were as many as 41 TV stations in the United States covering 23 cities through half a million receiving sets. Within a decade, the figure jumped to 533 stations and 55 million receivers. Canada, Japan and the European countries did not lag very far behind.

The age of satellite communication dawned in 1962 with the launch of Early Bird, the first communication satellite. The two big international satellite systems, Intelsat and Intersputnik began operating in 1965 and 1971 respectively and from then on the progress was phenomenal. Today, almost every country in the world has earth stations linked to satellites for transmission and reception. Communication satellites have literally transformed

---

1 Gerd Hellenberger: 'Television in West Germany', 1994, mimeo.
2 ibid.

the modern world into what Marshall McLuhan, the Canadian media sociologist, liked to call 'a global village' though political economists would rather term it a 'global market'.

In the decades that followed more sophisticated transmission techniques were invented employing optical fibre cable and computer technology. Japan succeeded in designing a computer-controlled network to carry two-way video information to and from households. The audio-visual cassette and the video tape recorder, closed circuit TV, and more recently cable television, pay-television, DTH (Direct-to-Home) television, HDTV (High Definition Television) and IPTV (Internet Protocol Television) have changed the course of the development of TV in new and unexpected ways. Digital compression technology, DTH, HDTV, and IPTV have enhanced the number of channels and media platforms which can be accessed, as also the quality of picture and sound transmission. Television programmes can now be 'streamed' to websites on the Internet and also to mobile telephones (Mobile TV) and other handheld devices. Flat-screen television sets with LCD and plasma screens of varying sizes have turned homes into mini-theatres and gaming arcades.

But this rapid growth has been rather lopsided. Some of the poor countries in Africa and Asia have still to possess their own domestic satellites or to provide an adequate number of production and transmission centres and receiving sets. The United Nations, UNESCO, UNDP and other world organizations have initiated several efforts to narrow this gap in technology hardware between the rich and poor countries, but, with newer technologies of information and leisure (such as the Internet and mobile telephony), this gap has widened even further.

The Story of Indian Television

For more than a decade, the Ministry of Information and Broadcasting managed to hold out against demands from educational institutions, industrialists, politicians and indeed the middle-classes in urban areas for the introduction of television. But then in 1959, Philips (India) made an offer to the

Government of a transmitter at a reduced cost. Earlier, Philips demonstrated its use at an exhibition in New Delhi. The Government gave in, with the aim of employing it on an experimental basis 'to train personnel, and partly to discover what TV could achieve in community development and formal education'.[3] A UNESCO grant of $20,000 for the purchase of community receivers and a United States offer of some equipment proved much too tempting to resist, and on September 15, 1959, the Delhi Television Centre went on air.[4]

The range of the transmitter was forty kilometres round and about Delhi. Soon programmes began to be beamed twice a week, each of 20 minutes' duration. The audience comprised members of 180 'teleclubs' which were provided sets free by UNESCO. The same organization concluded in a survey conducted two years later in 1961 that the 'teleclub' programmes had made 'some impact'.

Entertainment and information programmes were introduced from August 1965, in addition to social education programmes for which purpose alone TV had been introduced in the capital. The Federal Republic of Germany helped in setting up a TV production studio.

By 1970, the duration of the service was increased to three hours, and included, besides news, information and entertainment programmes, two weekly programmes running to 20 minutes each for 'teleclubs', and another weekly programme of the same duration called 'Krishi Darshan' for farmers in 80 villages. 'Krishi Darshan' programmes began in January 1967 with the help of the Department of Atomic Energy, the Indian Agricultural Research Institute, the Delhi Administration and the State Governments of Haryana and Uttar Pradesh. The programmes could easily be picked up in these States, as the range of the transmitter was extended to 60 kilometers.

The number of TV sets (all imported) in 1970 stood at around 22,000 excluding the community sets. By the mid-'seventies, however, Indian sets were in the market, and the number

---

[3] Bela Mody: 'The Commercialization of Indian Television', Paper presented at ICA Conference, New Orleans, 1988.
[4] ibid.

overshot the 100,000 mark in no time. By the early seventies the demand from the Indian cities, television manufacturers and the advertising industry as well as the Indira Gandhi Government's popularity contributed to the decision to expand the medium nationwide. By the end of the decade there were more than 200,000 sets in Delhi and the neighbouring states. The Bombay centre was opened in 1972, and in the following year, TV centres began to operate in Srinagar, Amritsar and Pune (only a relay centre). In 1975, Calcutta, Madras and Lucknow were put on the television map of the country. From January 1, 1976, 'commercials' came to be telecast at all the centres.

Another significant development during the same year was the separation of TV from All India Radio. Television now became an independent media unit in the Ministry of Information and Broadcasting, under the new banner – 'Doordarshan'. Thus cut off from its parent body, hopes were raised about improvement of the quality and duration of its service.

In 1977, terrestrial transmitters were put up at Jaipur, Hyderabad, Raipur, Gulbarga, Sambhalpur and Muzaffarpur, to extend television coverage to a population of more than 100 million. For the first time in the history of Indian broadcasting, political parties shared equal radio and TV time with the ruling party for their election campaigns.

Meanwhile, the success of the Satellite Instructional Television Experiment (SITE) brought India international prestige; the country appeared ready for satellite television. NASA, ITU-UNDP, Ford Aerospace were major foreign actors in this success; the minor actors were General Electric, Hughes Aircraft, the Massachusetts Institute of Technology, and representatives of Western nations at the ITU's World Administrative Radio Conference. The INSAT series of domestic communications satellites and microwave cable networks have provided the country the infrastructure for a national satellite hook-up. However, as the table below shows, access is still limited, and as the Joshi Committee Report (1983) found, the development of indigenous software continues to serve the urban elite in the main.

The Asian Games which were held in New Delhi in 1982 gave further impetus to the rapid expansion of the national television network. In the mid-1980s, a second channel was introduced first in New Delhi and Bombay, and later in the other metros; this second channel was to evolve into the popular Metro Entertainment Channel (or DD-2).

Table 27: Growth of Indian Television

Year	No. of Transmitters	No. of TV sets (in Million)	Total Population with Access to TV (in Million)
1976	8	0.5	2.9
1977	13	0.5	2.9
1978	15	0.7	4.1
1979	17	0.9	5.4
1980	18	1.2	6.9
1981	19	1.5	9.3
1982	19	2.1	12.6
1983	43	2.1	12.7
1984	46	3.6	21.8
1985	172	6.8	40.5
1986	179	11.0	52.5
1987	197	13.2	65.0*
1988	243	17.3	86.5*
1989	335	22.5	110.5*
1990	519	27.8	139.0*
1991	527	30.8	150.0*
1992	531	34.9	195.0
1993	542	40.3	218.8*
1994	564	45.7	241.8*
1995	672	52.3	246.0*
1996	743	54.0	270.0
1997	868	63.2	296.0
1998	897	69.1	326.0*
1999	984	75.5	356.0*
2000	1030	80.0	376.0*
2002	1244	81.6	380.0*
2003	1388	86.0	400.0*

* Estimates.
(Source: Doordarshan – 2003).

Table 28: Indian Households with TV Access (2004-07)

In Million	2004	2005	2006	2007 (Est.)	CAGR 2004-07
TV Households	102.0	109.0	112.0	115.0	4%
Pay TV Households	50.0	62.0	70.0	74.0	14%
Cable TV Households	50.0	61.0	68.0	70.0	12%
DTH Households	0.10	1.0	2.0	3.5	227%

(Source: FICCI-PriceWaterhouse-Coopers Report – 2008)

Enter: Film Directors and Film Stars

The entry of film directors and producers into the world of television was inevitable. Low-budget film directors like Basu Chatterjee, Ray, Benegal, Saeed Mirza, and Govind Nihalani went to television to express themselves. Chatterjee's crusading *Rajani* did leave a mark on the new medium; so did Mirza's politically and socially challenging *Nukkad*, and Nihalani's story of partition, *Tamas*, though Benegal failed to draw the viewers to his Sunday morning *Bharat Ek Khoj* (loosely based on Nehru's Discovery of India).

But it was the commercial box-office film-makers who succeeded in taking over television by storm. With their reverential and solemn versions of the religious epics, first the *Ramayana*, and later the *Uttar Ramayana* and the *Mahabharata*, television was returned to the mythologicals and the magic of early Indian cinema. In the early 'nineties the television viewer in north India was still in awe of the great religious epics, though ever so gently jolted into reality by hospital-based experiences (*Jeevan Rekha*, *Doctor Saheb*), political satires (*Kakaji Kahen*), and little gems from the South (*Malgudi Days*).

At the end of the century, that awe for religion and myth continued with every channel offering its own fare. Some perspicacious observers attributed this awe to the rise of religious fundamentalism in the country; others attributed it to the religious fervour inherent in Indian culture. In the early years of the 21st century, the 'K-Soaps' of Ekta Kapoor dominated the small screen; so did quiz, game shows and reality shows. Star's *Kaun Banega Crorepati* (a clone of 'Who Wants to be a Millionaire?) and Sony's search for an *Indian Idol* (a clone of 'American Idol') were runaway successes in 2004 and 2005. MTV grabbed the attention of the young with their Reality shows, *Roadies* and *Splitsvilla*. But they paled in comparison with the greatest success of them all – the 45 days of 59 T20 matches of the BCCI's DLF-Indian Premier League (IPL) in mid-2008. The exclusive global media and production rights (for a period of ten years) were won by Sony Entertainment Television (SET) and World Sport Group (Sony-World Sports Group) for US$ 1,026 billion. All the matches were telecast live at prime time on SET-Max. The IPL involved eight teams (a mix of Indian and international players) playing for and in eight zones (Mohali, Jaipur, Chennai, Mumbai, Kolkata, Bangalore, Delhi and Hyderabad). For television viewers and cricket-crazy fans in India and abroad it was in-stadium live entertainment par excellence. The final match on June 1 received a peak rating of 10.2 and an average rating of 7.7, according to aMap's people-meter readings. (For a discussion of the methodology of TV 'ratings', see Section III).

Table 29: Cricket on Television: The Biggest Money-Spinner

Channel	Rights	Value US$
ESPN-STAR	ICC Global Rights for 8 years	1.1 billion
SONY	Indian Premier League (IPL) for 10 years	1.026 billion
Zee 1	Indian Cricket League (ICL)	N.A.
Neo Sports	All domestic & international matches played in India	N.A.

(Source: *4Ps Business & Economy*, 15-28 February, 2008, p. 25)

Advertising Revenues

With the success of *Hum Log* and other soap operas like *Buniyaad* and *Khandaan*, Doordarshan's revenue from advertising soared, and the sponsorship of indigenous soaps, sitcoms and other serials provided a spurt to production, sometimes taken up by the advertising agencies themselves (such as Lintas' production of a popular detective serial, *Karamchand*). The religious epics, the *Mahabharat* and the *Ramayana*, which followed the soap opera format, with a harking back to the magic of the early Indian cinema, proved to be phenomenal successes on the small screen. Advertisers discovered a new advertising medium and they gave it all their support. By 1987, over 40 serials had been produced; on average two were being screened each evening at prime-time; foreign serials were gradually edged out, and so were several prime-time talk shows, film-based programmes, and quiz programmes. In 1987-88, Doordarshan's revenue shot up to Rs. 136.3 million, and further rose to Rs. 256 million at the end of 1990, and to a whopping Rs. 490 crores (Rs. 4900 million) in 1997-98. At the close of the 1990s, there were 58 million television sets in the country, with around 15 million connected to neighbourhood cable networks.[5] A decade later, this number rose to 210 million TV sets with over a third hooked up to cable and/or satellite networks; about six million sets were tuned to DTH services like DD-Direct, DISH-TV, Tata-Sky and Sun-Direct. Revenue streams for advertising included not just the traditional forms of advertising and sponsorship but increasingly also from subscription, pay-TV and Pay-Per-View, product-placements (in-programme advertisements), merchandising, and sales of electronic and DVD copies of successful programmes. For some channels like Zee, Sun and NDTV overseas subscriptions added considerably to their earnings. The Conditional Access System (CAS) which has been made obligatory in some cities allows TV viewers to watch cable and satellite TV via a set-top box and to pay only for the programmes/channels subscribed to. The system provides the broadcaster accurate information about the number of television sets tuned to their channels; there is no way the cable operator can now take the broadcaster or the Multi-System Operator

---

5   All data from *Doordarshan - 1997*, New Delhi: Audience Research Unit.

(MSO) (or even the entertainment tax collector) for a ride by 'under-reporting' the number of homes wired to cable and satellite TV.

Table 30: Doordarshan's Revenue from Advertising (1976-2006)

Year	Gross (In Rs.)
1976-77	77,18,000
1977-78	2,07,31,243
1978-79	4,97,26,582
1979-80	6,16,43,840
1980-81	8,07,50,300
1981-82	11,26,93,933
1982-83	15,88,74,060
1983-84	19,78,99,238
1984-85	31,43,45,326
1985-86	62,27,92,400
1986-87	21,93,00,000
1987-88	1,36,30,00,000
1988-89	1,61,26,00,000
1989-90	2,10,13,00,000
1990-91	2,56,00,00,000
1991-92	2,90,00,00,000
1992-93	3,60,23,00,000
1993-94	3,72,95,00,000
1994-95	3,98,00,00,000
1995-96	4,30,13,00,000
1996-97	5,72,73,00,000
1997-98	4,90,00,00,000
1998-99	3,99,32,00,000
1999-00	6,10,20,00,000
2000-01	6,37,50,00,000
2001-02	6,15,20,00,000
2002-03	5,53,82,00,000
2003-04	5,30,23,00,000
2004-05	6,65,27,00,000
2005-06	9,68,00,00,000

(Source: www.ddindia.gov.in/About +DD/Commercial+Service). Accessed on December 3, 2009.

Table 31: Leading Advertisers on Television

Top Ten Advertisers on Television (2008)		Top Ten Categories Advertised on Television (2008)	
Rank		Rank	
1	Hindustan Lever	1	Cellular Phone Service
2	Pepsico	2	Aerated Soft Drinks
3	Reckitt Benckiser India	3	Corporate/Brand Image
4	Coca-Cola India	4	Social Advertisements
5	ITC.	5	Toilet Soaps
6	Vodafone Essar	6	Shampoos
7	Smithkline Beecham	7	Toothpastes
8	Bharti Airtel	8	Cars/Jeeps
9	Colgate Palmolive India	9	Cellular Phones
10	L'Oreal India	10	DTH Service Providers

(Source: AdEx-India – 2008)

Distribution of Television Content

First, it was 'terrestrial television', limited to a transmitter's range, say of around 50 kilometers. So, Delhi and its neighbours in Haryana, Uttar Pradesh and Rajasthan were able to grab the first TV signals. And viewers in Bombay and its suburbs had to be content with fare provided by Delhi and the local Doordarshan studio. Then 'cable TV' made its appearance, first in Bombay's skyscrapers and later in cooperative housing societies in the suburbs – though mostly for watching Hindi films.

Satellite-based TV transmission proved to be successful during its dry run as part of SITE, but really took off nationwide only in the early 1990s with the arrival of STAR TV from Hong Kong. Satellite TV gave us access to both national and international channels and to programmes in different Indian languages. But satellite transmission needed to be married to terrestrial cable in order to make it affordable to around fifty per cent of TV households. Cable and satellite (C and S) television brought to an end the monopoly exercised by Doordarshan; as also to the monopoly of Hindi and English programming. Sun TV, Eenadu (ETV), Asianet and others set the pace for the rapid growth of television in South India; by the late 1990s these channels were garnering higher ratings and also higher advertising revenues than the Hindi and English channels.

The DTH (Direct-to-Home) delivery mode launched by Doordarshan in 2003 made it necessary to have a set-top box (STB) to receive signals direct from communication satellites; few could afford this additional investment even though most channels were free, and more significantly, it freed one from the clutches of cable operators. Later, the Zee TV and Star TV networks launched their own DTH service, Dish TV and Tata-Sky respectively. For the broadcasters it was a boon for it provided them with accurate data on the number of viewers; for the cable operators it was a threat to their business. What threatened their business further was the introduction of CAS. In January 2007, TRAI (Telecom Regulatory Authority of India) made CAS (Conditional Access System) obligatory for cable TV households in Delhi, Mumbai and Kolkata. (It was already obligatory in Chennai for some years, though without much success). CAS meant that households could pay only for the channels they chose to watch; here again the STB provided accurate data on viewership. TRAI imposed a flat subscription fee of Rs. 5 per month per channel for all channels and all cities. The price for MSOs and local cable operators (LCO) was fixed at Rs. 2.25 per month, and the revenue sharing between broadcaster, MSO and LCO fixed in a ratio of 45:30:25.[6]

HITS (Headend-In-The-Sky) is another delivery mode for television content. It delivers satellite channels to cable operators through a HITS rather than through an on-ground control room. So, a HITS operator encrypts all channels at a common facility and uplinks them to a satellite (HITS). The operator can download a whole bouquet from the satellite rather than downloading each channel, thus enabling him to go all-India and become digital as well as addressable. HDTV (High Definition TV) promised supreme picture quality for the small screen.

---

6 FICCI-PriceWaterhouse-Coopers Report: *The Indian Entertainment and Media Industry – Sustaining Growth*, 2008.

Mobile TV can also be provided by HITS; MTNL and BSNL have already introduced this facility for their subscribers; others like Bharati Airtel are bound to follow suit. Several TV channels like DD News and NDTV already 'stream' their news to the Internet besides offering their 'archives' for accessing programmes which one might have missed. By the end of the decade it is expected that Doordarshan will offer all its over 34 channels on a 'terrestrial digital' platform.

Distribution Technologies for Television Content

1. Terrestrial TV
2. Cable
3. Cable and Satellite
4. CAS (Conditional Access System
5. DTH (Direct-to-Home)
6. HITS (Headend in the Sky)
7. IPTV (Internet Protocol TV)
8. HDTV (High Definition TV)
9. The Internet
10. Mobile Telephones
11. Digital Terrestrial Television

Television Genres

Television News

A TV newscast cannot match the wide coverage and in-depth report of radio news. The time taken up by visual material does not allow for a probe, or even for adequate background information. Indeed, a TV newscast cannot present the most interesting and significant news since the cameras just cannot be present where such events take place (e.g., a coup, an invasion, a war, or a cabinet meeting).

A TV newscast is, however, the ideal medium for presenting ceremonial events like coronations, swearing-in-ceremonies, arrivals and departures of VIPs, signing of treaties, parades, inaugurations, and sports. Unfortunately, the hard-core news does not lie in these events – even if they are telecast 'live' – and constitute only a small percentage of the daily fare of news.

To begin with, the standard newscast in India employed the radio technique of reading out the news in a formal manner from a script (on cards or on an electronic 'teleprompter'), interrupted with an occasional still, a map, or a moving picture. Frequently, the news is tailored to the visuals available. With the acquisition of ENG (Electronic News Gathering) and the latest computerised graphics equipment, the number of visuals has increased. Indeed, the news bulletins of Doordarshan's channels, as also those of the many satellite channels, have in recent years taken on the format of 'magazine' programmes.

News Bulletins and Current Affairs

News bulletins, general news magazines, and panel discussions on public affairs are some of the popular news programmes on the over 40 news channels on Indian television. Major networks/bouquets like Doordarshan, Star, Zee, Sun, Eenadu, TV-18, Sahara, NDTV, TV Today and INX have at least one news channel as part of their bouquets. Business news channels too form part of networks like CNN, NDTV and Aaj Tak. Examples of these include CNBC, NDTV Profit, Awaz, and Zee Business. All these are either in Hindi or English, like most other programmes on the National Network. Visuals include slides, film clips, maps, diagrams, charts and other visual devices. As the news channels have few correspondent-cameramen posted overseas they depend largely on Reuters, Associated Press (AP) and Agence France Presse (AFP) for actuality footage of foreign news. The Asian Broadcasting Union helps out with its international news exchange system. Yet another important source is the Asia News International (ANI) wherein Reuters is the largest shareholder.

New Trends

Almost every major newspaper publisher in India owns at least one television and FM radio channel. So, the country's largest chain of newspapers, the Bennett Coleman & Co. Ltd./ Times of India Group, has *Times Now*, a television news channel in partnership with Reuters (the partnership came to an end in early 2008), and also a lifestyle channel called simply *Zoom*. The Times of India Group has also teamed up with the BBC to publish the latter's magazines. Living Media, the publisher of *India Today* (in English and four Indian languages) and a host of American/European magazines, such as *Cosmopolitan, Vogue,* and *Men's Health*, owns a bouquet of news channels: *Headlines Today, Aaj Tak,* and *Delhi Aaj Tak*. TV18, a television production house, has teamed up with CNN to launch *CNBC-TV 18* and *Awaaz*, two business news channels, and three general news channels: *CNN-IB, IBN-7* and IBN-Lokmat. Other major players in the news media include the Star network and the Zee network which run news, business news and entertainment channels. Eenadu, Sun, Sahara, Asianet and INX are the other Indian language networks that include news channels and sports channels in their bouquets. The public service Doordarshan network has a huge bouquet of over 34 channels, with DD News being their flagship news channel. BBC World and CNN-International too are major players in the Indian news media scene; other overseas players include Deutsche Welle-TV, ABC-Asia Pacific, CCTV and NHK.

Political parties have followed suit, launching their own channels to propagate their own ideologies. By the end of 2007, most major political parties in North and South India could boast of their own TV channels.[7] Thus, the Nationalist Hindu Party, the BJP, the Marxists of Kerala, the DMK and AIADMK of Tamilnadu, the Congress Party in Kerala, and even the Catholic Church have their own TV channels.

All the over 40 TV news channels, including the public service Doordarshan, are commercial in nature as their primary source of revenue is advertising. Only a few of them are pay/subscription channels.

---

7   For a critical analysis of the political-party-based TV channels in Tamilnadu, see Maya Ranganathan: 'Television in Tamilnadu Politics', *Economic and Political Weekly*, 2 December 2006, pp. 4947-4955.

It was probably the boom in the local retail market that prompted several TV channels to launch city-centric channels in Delhi, Mumbai, Chennai and Kolkata. It appears that the TV industry is going the newspaper way, with a similar revenue model. Local newspapers or local editions of national or regional newspapers have proved to be successful across the country in winning over advertisers and readers.[8] Aaj Tak and Sahara Samay-NCR started the trend in New Delhi; NDTV's MetroNation and INX News followed suit. Sahara Samay has six city-specific channels, one each in Uttar Pradesh, Madhya Pradesh, Chattisgarh, Bihar/Jharkand and Mumbai. NDTV and other networks have announced the launch of city-specific general entertainment channels in other Indian cities.

Advertising in the News

The news media in India are, as in other democracies, vigorously supported by the advertising and public relations industries. The print media receive the most generous support. As much as 48% of the total ad spend of Rs. 168 billion goes to the press. Television earns around 41% while radio, the internet and mobiles fetch less than five per cent each. Every news bulletin on every single news channel, including the public service Doordarshan, is heavily 'sponsored' by advertisers and is frequently interrupted for commercial breaks.

Besides, television news channels and news bulletins receive the biggest patronage where in-content ('soft advertising') is concerned. In 2006, for instance, the news bulletins obtained the highest secondage (56.2 million) or 18% share of total in-content advertising across all media genres, including feature films (16%), music shows (9%), soaps/drama (8%), and film songs (5%).[9]

The total ad spend across all media is a mere Rs. 16,000 crore (US$4000 million) with the press getting almost 50% of the

---

8   For a study of the 'localisatation' of Hindi newspapers cf. Sevanti Ninan: *Headlines from the Heartland*, New Delhi: Sage Publications, 2007.
9   *The Marketing White Book: 2007*, p.234.

advertising pie, and television another 43%. Commercial radio stations (which include All India Radio, Vividh Bharati, Rainbow FM and FM Gold) get barely three per cent. News and Current Affairs programmes are not allowed on private FM radio stations, according to the Government's broadcasting policy. Cross-media ownership and Foreign Direct Investment (FDI) too are restricted. For instance, telecom companies in the business of mobile telephony are not allowed to own more than 20% of a broadcasting company.

Table 32: *Growth of News Channels*

Year	No. of TV News Channels
2002	11
2003	18
2004	22
2005	34
2006	38
2007	+40
2008	+56

Source: TAM Media Express/Starcom

Table 33: *Major News Channels*

DD News	News 24
Zee News	Aaj Tak
Headlines Today	Star News
NDTV 24x7	NDTV-India
India – TV	Sun News
Eenadu (ETV News)	Manorama News
Times Now	Sahara Samay
CNN-IBN	CNBC-TV 18
IBN-Lokmat	Zee Business
IBN-7	CNBC-Awaz
India Live	NDTV Profit
Voice of India	News X

Crime-based Programmes on News Channels

Crime-based programmes, also called 'crime specials', have become an integral part of round-the-clock news channels. Each news channel has its own flagship crime show. The attempt is to 'reconstruct' and dramatize real-life crime stories. Crime stories often dominate the news channels in their primary news bulletins; crime shows extend these stories further, adding 'reconstructions', including eyewitness accounts, music and a breathless and dramatic narrative. The focus is on stories of rape, murder, theft, burglary and forgery. Some of the popular crime shows are 'Sansani' and 'Red Alert' on Star News, 'Crime Reporter' and 'Crime File' on Zee News, 'FIR', 'Crime and the City' and 'Dial 100' on NDTV-India, and 'Jurm' and 'Vardaat' on Aaj Tak. Besides crime-based stories, news channels have also turned to Reality TV shows and Lifestyle Shows to seduce the viewers away from the General Entertainment Channels (GECs). The foremost examples of Reality TV shows in recent years include the live dramatizations in 2004 of the plight of Guriya, the pregnant Muslim wife whose husband was thought to have been a deserter during the Kargill War in 1999; Prince, the little boy who was rescued from a well in Kurukshetra in 2006, and the many crime stories related to the capital's celebrities like Jessica Lal, Priyadarshini Mattoo and others. The late-night Lifestyle Shows that have apparently raised the TRPs of news channels like NDTV are 'Night Out' and 'Raat Baaki'. (For a fuller discussion of this genre, see Nalin Mehta: *India on Television*, pp. 185-192).

Spoofs on the News

Satirical take-offs on national and international news stories (E.g. Cyrus Broacha's *The Week that Wasn't* and Veer Das's *News on the Loose*, modeled respectively on NBC's *Jay Leno's Tonight Show* and CNN's *Not the Daily News* shows. Other spoofs on the news included: *Double Take* and *Sabse Politically Incorrect Kaun* (NDTV 24x7, NDTV-India), *Aisi Ki Taisi* (Aaj Tak), *Poll Khol* (Star News), and *Just Laugh Baaki Maaf* (India TV).

TV Documentaries or Features/Factual Television

Television documentaries, like cinema documentaries can

feature any subject of interest to a number of viewers, such as the state of pollution, poverty, famine, the cultural scene, or the plight of construction workers. The aims of documentaries are to enlighten, arouse, and motivate, or simply to entertain. The stress is on portraying real people and real situations, and on activity rather than on talk and commentary. In a documentary, it's the story that dictates film technique, not vice versa; film is exploited here as a tool to document reality, and not to display gimmicks of the cameraman or editor in shooting reality, even though the documentary is in essence a 'social construction' of reality.

The format of a TV documentary takes the form of a 'direct presentation' of the substance of a problem or an experience or a situation, by contrast with the 'discussion' in which a situation or problem may be illustrated, usually relatively briefly, but in which the main emphasis falls on relatively formal argument about it.[10] TV channels dedicated to the production and screening of documentaries include: Discover, Animal Planet, History, and Planet Earth.

Talk Shows

Talk Shows are of various types: interviews, discussions, and panel discussions with and without a live audience participating. Interviews are of various types: Personality interviews such as those in Karan Thapar's *The Devil's Advocate* and Shekhar Gupta's *Walk the Talk* where the attempt is to probe well-known personalities; 'In Conversation' and 'Vibrations' which focus on literary figures; Content Interviews, such as *We The People* and *The Big Fight* in which the message rather than personalities is of prime importance; and Group Interviews such as a Press Conference in which a group of press people hurl questions at the Prime Minister or a Cabinet or Chief Minister on sundry subjects of current interest.

---

10 Raymond Williams: *Television: Technology and Cultural Form*, p.79.

Children's Programmes

These are defined as programmes specially made for and offered to children, at certain special times.[11] Cartoons, puppet-shows, 'live' stories and plays, and educational items are some of the items that make up a children's show. Some children's programmes have been turned into quiz shows. Feature films in Hindi for children are screened occasionally. Television channels exclusively targeted at children and young people are: POGO, Hungamma, Disney, Nickleodeon, and Cartoon Network (CN).

'Talent Hunt' Shows

In the early days of Indian television, Doordarhan's National Programmes of Dance and Music brought India's foremost performers to the TV screen. The standard format of these programmes was an elaborate introduction in Hindi and English of the performer and his or her style, followed by a 'live' recital of various items. Each item was briefly explained in the two languages so that appreciation of the performance is enhanced. The programmes focussed on the classical and the folk forms. Light music programmes like *Aarohi, Sham-e-Ghazal* and *Bazm-e Quwali* also proved to be popular. They were compered by well-known figures and featured top-notch singers.

The arrival of multi-channel cable and satellite TV put paid to Doordarshan's monopoly, though some of the formats introduced by it were gladly adopted by the new channels. One of these was *Chhaya Geet* or *Chitra Geet*, the film based music programme which continues to be popular, though with far fewer slots devoted to it. It has a format all its own, with film clippings of old and new song-sequences put together in a haphazard manner. Similar programmes in Marathi, Gujarati, Tamil and other languages have also been extremely popular. However, the majority of such film-based programmes have been replaced by what in the industry are called 'talent-hunt shows' which are played out in lavish stage-sets and judged by well-known stars from the world of film music, fashion, arts and dance

---

11 ibid.

choreography. Talent hunt shows involve different types of quiz programmes, and a whole range of song, dance and acting competitions.

Most quiz-programmes and Game Shows are studio-oriented or involve the outdoors like *Amazing Race*. Advertisers provide their products as prizes for such shows. Examples of Quiz Shows are: *Wild Encounters*, and *Kudrath Namah*, while the popular Game Shows include *Family Fortunes*, *Antakshari* and *Close Encounters*. After the phenomenal success of *Kaun Banega Crorepati* compered by Amitabh Bachchan on the Star network, quiz-based game shows were introduced on several satellite channels, including Zee, Sony, Sun and Eenadu, but they remained pale imitations and, except for some of their initial episodes, did not find much of an audience. Later, talent hunt shows became the rage. These included: *Zee Cinestar Ki Khoj*, *Super Singer* (on Channel V), *Mr and Miss Bollywood* (Sahara), *Harsh Ki Khoj* (ESPN-STAR), *Chhota Veejay Hunt* (Nickleodeon), *Launch Pad* (Channel V), and *Captain Hunt* (Hungamma).

Such shows engage nationwide audiences since the mobile phone, SMS and the Internet have made it easy and cheap for viewers to take part in the choice of winners. Advertisers sponsor these shows and some corporate houses offer huge awards, prizes and gifts to the participants and winners. They are in fact a subset of Reality TV.

Some Talent Hunt Shows on Indian Channels

Zee Cinestar Ki Khoj	Chhota Veejay Hunt (Nick)
Indian Idol (Sony TV)	Launch Pad (Channel V)
Super Singer (Channel V)	Lakme Fashion (Zoom)
Mr & Miss Bollywood (Sahara)	Dus Ka Dum (Sony)
Harsha Ki Khoj (ESPN-Star)	Roadies (MTV)
Captain Hunt (Hungamma)	Splitsvilla (MTV)
Sa Re Ga Ma (Zee)	

Reality TV

The archetypal 'reality TV' programmes were *Big Brother,*

Survivor, Temptation Island, Fear Factor and *Real World*. Most of those that followed were largely clones of these formats. Other versions of the reality format include *Amazing Race, American Idol* ('Indian idol' in India), *Who Wants to be a Millionaire* ('Kaun Banega Crorepati?' in India), *Pop Stars, Dancing with the Stars, The Bachelor, The Apprentice,* and a host of contests in singing, dancing, dating and acting and stand-up comedy shows.

The format has its lineage in the Candid Microphone radio programmes (of the late 1940s) in which pranks were pulled on unsuspecting people. In 1953 Candid Camera shows debuted in the United States; in the mid-1960s the BBC reality TV series 'Seven Up!' was the rage.

Reality TV brings together three genres: the film documentary, the game show and the soap opera. A vital element in Reality TV is audience participation through voting via text messages from mobile telephones. Elimination of participants at every stage of the contest is voted upon by the audience and/or by a panel of judges. These formats radically change the relationship between media producers, participants and viewers, giving the impression that it is all 'democratic'; the reality is that the shows are deliberate constructions to engage the viewer, thus raising ratings and attracting advertisers. The focus, all the while, is on spectacles of extremity and cruelty, with aggressive competition underlining the whole show. The sub-categories of the Reality TV genre include: documentary style shows, game shows, self-improvement/makeover shows, dating shows, talk shows, hidden cameras and hoaxes.

The original formats of Reality TV were turned into intellectual property and sold to television stations around the world. So, unlike genres which are not copyright material, formats are, and permission for their use or adaptation has to be obtained. Thus the format of Big Brother, originally a Dutch programme, but owned by Endemol, was sold to Germany, Britain and even to India. The Indian version was called *Big Boss* with the participants/inmates of the 'house' being small time film stars and fashion models. Endemol, perhaps the world's largest owner of Reality TV formats, has also sold other formats like *The Apprentice*, to Indian television channels.

Indian Versions/Clones of Foreign Reality TV Shows

Who Wants to Be a Millionaire?	Kaun Banega Crorepati?
Fear Factor	Fear Factor India
Pop Idol /American Idol	Indian Idol
Dancing with the Stars/Strictly Dancing	Jhalak Didhlaja/Nach Baliye
Big Brother	Big Boss
Let's Make a Deal	Khulja Sim Sim
Night Fever	Kisme Kitna Hai Dum
The Power of Ten	Dus Ka Dum
Are you Smarter than a Fifth Grader?	Kya Aap Paanchvi Paas Se Tez Hain
Roadies	Roadies
Splitsville	Splitsvilla
Fear Factor	Khatron Ke Khiladi

In sum, Reality TV is a new type of narrative, a new type of storytelling that aims to imitate reality. It is format that presents unscripted dramatic situations and features 'ordinary' people rather than professional actors. Such shows 'fetishize the ordinary, elevate self-experience to the level of grand narrative and ultimate truth, exploit their subjects, and employ professionals who neglect the psychological hazards and ethical considerations of their involvement.'[12]

By mid-2008, however, audience fatigue with some reality shows had set in. The three seasons of *Kaun Banega Crorepati* (the first two with Amitabh Bachchan, the third with Shah Rukh Khan) were rated highly, but a similar strategy of using film stars like Shah Rukh Khan in *Kya Aap Paanchvi Paas se Tez Hain* and Salman Khan in *Dus Ka Dum* proved to be disasters, despite the huge budgets involved. The budget for the former was Rs. 150 crore – enough to start a news channel and to run it for a year.[13] The phenomenal success of the Indian Premier League's cricket

---

12 Sam Brenton and Reuben Cohen: *Shooting People: Adventures in Reality TV*, London: Verso Books, 2003.
13 Shantanu Guha Ray: 'Lights, Camera, Blackout', *Tehelka*, 5 July 2008, p.33.

matches with viewers and the moderate success of NDTV Imagine's *Ramayana* pointed to the need for Indian television to tell stories, not in terms of western soaps and reality shows but rather in terms of Indian cultural traditions and interests.

Religious Programmes

Religious/Spiritual programmes do comprise a popular genre in the Indian context. In recent years a number of religious channels have drawn millions of the faithful, each to his own religion. The Christian evangelical channels of the United States such as God TV, Miracle TV and TBN (Trinity Broadcasting Network) set the trend for other religious denominations. The major elements that make up religious TV programmes are discourses, readings from the scriptures, rituals and services, the singing of bhajans, and finally the request for donations. Some channels have introduced programmes on Ayurveda, Yoga, Vastu and Astrological Forecasts. Panjabi channels transmit the 'Gurbani' direct from the Golden Temple. The Indian religious channels are Sanskaar, Aastha, Zee Jagran, Jain TV, and the Christian channels (Jesus Calls, GOD, Miracle, TCTV (Tamil Christian TV), PowerVision and Velugu TV). The channels do not produce their own programmes; rather, they sell television time to religious leaders and sects that can afford to pay upfront for time-slots. So, for instance, Jain TV sells time-slots to Hindu, Christian, Muslim and Sikh groups. This business strategy of religious channels appears to be paying dividends.

Religious Channels	Religious TV Genres
1. Ashirwaad	1. Religious Discourses / Pravachans
2. Aastha	2. Bhajans / Hymns
3. God	3. Gurbani (Satsang)
4. Jagran (Zee Network)	4. Ayurved
5. Jesus Calls	5. Yoga
6. Sanskar	6. Astrological Forecasts
7. Power Vision	7. Vastu
8. TCTV	8. Religious/Mythological Movies
9. Velugu TV Network	9. Health and Nutrition Programs
10. QTV	10. Serials

Other TV Genres

Among the other formats of TV programmes are: reviews of films, recorded music and books, educational television (ETV) programmes, situation comedies ('Sitcoms'), soap operas, plays, talk shows, and stand-up comedy shows. The most interesting of these formats are the 'sitcom' and the 'soap opera'. Examples of 'sitcoms' include *Kakaji Kahen, The Flop Show, Zaban Sambhal Ke, Mr. Yogi, Dillagi,* and *Kya Baat Hai,* where humour, slapstick and satire come together in a loose narrative structure. A critical analysis of the introduction and development of the 'soap' genre on Indian television follows.

Soap Operas

Domestically-produced Indian-language television serials came into their own only in the mid 'eighties. For almost a decade since 1976 when the first commercials were allowed to be aired, Indian television was dominated by Hindi feature films and film-based programmes. But the only 'sitcoms', soap operas, detective or other TV genres telecast were from British, United States or German television. The British sitcoms shown during those early years of the national network were very regional in their humour and accent. Examples of these were *To the Manor Born, Some Mothers Do Love 'Em* and *Sorry*. However, British television also provided Indian viewers some of its foremost productions such as Bronowski's *Ascent of Man*, Kenneth Clark's *Civilization*, and nature documentaries by David Attenborough. American serials like *I Love Lucy* and *Startrek*, or German 'telematches' and detective series like *The Fox,* introduced Indian viewers to other kinds of foreign fare. Indian programmes that proved popular were quiz shows like *What's the Good Word?*, talk shows by Kamleshwar and Tabassum, and of course, sports programmes.

The Mexican 'Telenovela'

Indian television soap operas were directly inspired (not by American daytime soap opera) but by the success of Mexico's Televisa, a private commercial network, in producing popular melodramatic series such as 'Ven Conmigo' (Come with Me) which promoted family planning. The Mexican 'telenovela' (literally, a television novel) was in turn influenced by the Peruvian telenovela, 'Simplimente Maria' which told the story of a migrant girl who gets rich because of her skills in sewing with a Singer machine. The telenovela, as might be surmised, was sponsored by the Singer Company, the manufacturers of the machine. It is reported that the sales of the sewing machine in Latin American countries shot up dramatically.[14]

In 1983, David Poindexter, the President of the Centre for Population Communications International, New York, who had played a key role in popularizing the Mexican experience with development-oriented soap operas, arranged (at whose expense we don't know) for officials from India, Egypt, Nigeria, Kenya, and Brazil, to visit Mexico City and confer with Miguel Sabido, the producer. The Indian delegation was led by S.S. Gill, Secretary in the Ministry of Information and Broadcasting, who was later to be appointed the first Chief Executive Officer of the Prasar Bharati (Broadcasting Corporation of India).

Hum Log

On his return to Delhi, Gill got together a producer (Shobha Doctor, an ad person by profession), a director (P Kumar Vasudev), an executive producer (Satish Garg), and a script writer (Manohar Shyam Joshi) to produce India's first indigenous soap opera, *Hum Log*. 156 episodes of the serial were telecast twice a week from July 7, 1984 to December 17, 1985. The soap opera was sponsored by Maggi Noodles, a product of a Nestle subsidiary, Food Specialities Limited. The product was launched with the serial, and has today become a popular fast food in urban Indian households.

---

14 This account of the 'telenovela' and the circumstances that led to the making of Hum Log draws on two research articles: the first, 'Television Soap Operas for development in India' by Arvind Singhal and Everett Rogers, in *Gazette* (Amsterdam), Vol. 41, 1988, pp. 109-126; the second, 'Telenovelas in Latin America: A Success Story', by Everett Rogers and Livia Antala, in *Journal of Communication*, Vol. 35, No. 4, pp. 24-35.

'Hum Log' told the story of the ups and downs in the life of a North-Indian lower-middle class joint family with parallel stories which tackled the problems of smuggling, political corruption and underworld activities. Ashok Kumar, the highly respected film actor, wound up each episode with an authoritative exhortation on 'the message'. The family planning theme was first diluted and then almost dropped from the soap opera after the thirteenth episode. Several other revisions were introduced because of the feedback from viewers who made suggestions on the progress of the plot and the characterization.

Hum Log was proclaimed by the media and advertisers (the latter in particular) to be a phenomenal success. The Indian Market Research Bureau (IMRB), a unit of Hindustan Thompson Associates, a multinational ad agency, conducted a study which demonstrated that the soap opera registered its highest ratings in Delhi and Bombay, and the lowest in Calcutta and Madras. Moreover, it was much more popular among middle and lower income people than among the upper middle class who made up the large majority of TV owners. Doordarshan's Audience Research Unit also rated it a success. Singhal and Rogers of the Annenberg School of Communication, Los Angeles, surveyed 1,170 adults in 1987 and found that 90% of the respondents said they 'liked' the serial. But in Madras, only 48% of the respondents (much fewer than those from the North) reported that they had seen at least one episode.[15]

The success of *Hum Log,* but more significantly, the success of Maggi Noodles in the market place, led advertisers to promote indigenous soap operas on the box, and to spend more on television advertising. Prior to *Hum Log*, few advertisers had much faith in television as an advertising medium; by the time the first soap opera came to a close, advertisers were forced to queue up for 'commercial slots' frequently having to wait for ten months at a time. Doordarshan's revenue from advertising soared; the sponsorship of Indian serials provided a spurt to

---

15 Arvind Singhal and Everett Rogers: *India's Information Revolution*, New Delhi: Sage, 1988.

production, which was sometimes taken up by advertising agencies themselves. Indigenous serials came off the production studios in quick succession; soap operas like *Khandaan* and *Buniyaad*; sitcoms like *Yeh Jo Hai Zindagi*; televised adaptations of Indian and foreign short stories (by well-known film-makers like Satyajit Ray and Shyam Benegal); children's stories (e.g. *Ek, Do, Teen, Char*; *Vikram Aur Betaal*); and women-oriented stories (e.g. *Chehere*). By 1987, over 40 'serials' had been produced; on average two were being screened every evening. Foreign serials were edged out gradually; so were several primetime talk-shows, quiz programmes, and film-based programmes. Politically bolder news and current affairs programmes (such as *Newsline, Janavani,* and *Sach Ki Parchiyan*) were introduced, and then dropped without warning. Other popular Doordarshan serials were soaps such as *Humrahi, Aurat, Shanti, Itithas* and *Swabhiman*.

The proliferation of cable and satellite channels, beginning from the mid-1990s, brought about a steep increase in the number of soap operas on Indian television. The Star Network got off the mark with *Saans*, but it was together with Ekta Kapoor's TV production venture, Balaji Telefilms, that a new trend in the soap genre was introduced with what came to be called the 'K-series'. *Kyunki Saas Bhi Kabhi Bahu Thi*, the first in the series, has proved to be the longest running soap (it has run for 7.5 years and has had over a thousand episodes), followed by *Kahani Ghar Ghar Ki, Kahin To Hoga, Kasauti Zindagi Kay*, and a host of others. Balaji Telefilms churned out soaps for all the major networks. On Zee Network the K-soaps that ran were: *Koshish Ek Aasha, Koi Apna Sa, Kitty Party*, but there were non-K soaps too: *Tara, Banegi Apni Baat, Daraar, Hasratein, Aashirwaad, Parampara, Daraar* and *Dastaan*. Sony too had its share of day time and prime soaps; the K-soaps included *Kusum*, and non-K-soaps like *Ek Mahal Ho Sapna Ka, Heena*, and *Saaya*. But it was *Jassi Jaisi Koi Nahin* (a clone of the American soap *Ugly Betty*) that marked up the ratings week after week for Sony. Balaji Telefilms later teamed up with Star-Vijay and other South Indian networks to produce and dub the

K-soaps into languages other than Hindi. Meanwhile, several other TV production houses got into the business of soaps and reality shows.

Video and Cable TV (1980s and 1990s)

The early eighties saw the dramatic growth of the video industry in India. This followed close on the heels of Doordarshan opening up to advertising and sponsorship of soap-operas and other entertainment oriented programmes. Further, the switch-over to colour television, and the reduction of customs duties on imported television sets and VCRs/VCPs, paved the way for a video boom. By May 1985, there were about 5.5 million TV sets and at least half a million video-recorders/players in the country.

Indian advertising agencies were quick to transform video into a 'vehicle' for their business clients, despite the largely illegal and unorganised nature of the video industry. Indeed, the very fact that the industry was unregulated (like the advertising industry itself), made video attractive to advertisers. Rampant piracy forced many film producers to sell the video rights of their old and current films to Garwares, Bombino, Shemaroo, Super Cassettes, Esquire, Eagle and other companies.

The National Film Development Corporation (NFDC) too negotiated terms for video rights with Indian and foreign film producers. That the video rights would be misused to promote consumer products through advertising was not expected.

"Ad concessionaires" then stepped in to peddle audiovisual space on video. Video advertising was first restricted to export order cassettes, but the expanding home market was much too large to be overlooked by advertisers. The introduction of cable networks in the late 'eighties, first in Bombay's skyscrapers and later in 'colonies' and neighbourhoods of metropolitan areas, expanded the video market further. Consortia of leading video distributors were established. Perhaps the largest is Cable Video (India) Pvt. Ltd., which controls the home viewing and cable rights for over 3000 movies. The company is the sole ad concessionaire for these titles. Showtime Communication, a

Dalmia group company distributes the company's titles in Delhi. Others who have entered the cable industry include the State Video and Governments of Mizoram, Kerala and West Bengal, and Times Television.

The big spenders on video and cable include Nestle-India, Cadbury's, ITC, United Breweries and others. With over 50,000 cable operators across the length and breadth of the country, it is a free-for-all for advertisers, especially for those whose products cannot be advertised on Doordarshan. Such products are: alcoholic drinks, baby foods, pan masalas, cigarettes, underclothes, etc. Over rupees one crore was earned from advertisements on Cable in 1991, as against Rs. 253 crores (Rs. 2530 million) earned by Doordarshan. Advertisers are not deserting Doordarshan, but rather using cable as a supplementary medium. Cable offers the advantages of what is termed 'segmentation' of the market.

In all this frenzy to make easy and quick money from video and cable advertising, the greatest losers have been the film producers, Doordarshan, and video/cable viewers. Advertisements are seen to be a nuisance, especially when they are superimposed by 'crawlies'. The fast-forward button on the remote is of little use when almost every frame is thus appropriated by advertisers. But producers and viewers are fighting back. Organisations like INFACT and the Association of Video Rights Owners of India are putting pressure on Government to set up special 'anti-piracy cells' in each State to enforce the Copyright Act. A Copyright Enforcement Advisory Council has been established to consider effective ways of enforcing the Act. It has been suggested that a Copyright Council be established. It has also been suggested that the Indian Telegraph Act (1885), the Indian Wireless Telegraph Act (1933) and the Copyright Act (1957, Amended 1983) be revised to take into account recent developments in video, cable and satellite television.

Together with viewers, film producers planned to form Viewers' Associations to fight the blatant misuse of video and cable by advertisers. Their demand is for a Code for Advertising on TV, Video and Cable, so that viewers' rights are respected. They believe that the Code drawn up by the ASCI does not go far enough in dealing with Video and Cable. In November 1993, the Cable Operators Federation of India reached a consensus with the Ministry of Information and Broadcasting on the Cable Television Networks (Regulation) Bill. The Act, which was promulgated by an Ordinance in November 1994, made registration of cable companies with the Post Office obligatory. Further, all cable operators were obliged to transmit at least one Doordarshan channel, and to stop the relay of programmes and commercials of foreign satellite channels, which do not conform to prescribed codes and guidelines of the Indian Government.

Video, Cinema and Television (1980s)

Estimates of the number of video-cassette recorders (VCRs) and video-cassette players (VCPs) in India are hard to come by. Time was when flights to Singapore were known as 'VCR Flights'. In 1984, India Today put the estimate at close to three lakhs (300,000) with an average rate of growth at 20,000 every month. A study by the Indian Institute of Mass Communications, New Delhi, in 1985 put the figure at around five lakhs (or half a million). Video advertising agencies claimed that there were many more. In mid 1987, a survey by Mode Services for Prime Time put the number at 1.8 million; Contrast Advertising believed, however, that the number of VCR sets did not exceed one million. In early 1989, video companies claimed that the average figure for each film was 2.4 million viewers.

According to officials of the Film Federation of India, the video boom which followed the conclusion of the Asiad in 1982 in New Delhi, reached well over 400 towns in the country. The Study Team on Consumer Electronics reported in 1984 that 11 units in the organized sector and 60 units in the small scale sector have been granted licenses to manufacture 500 video-cassette recorders each per annum. However, despite the further liberalization of imports of electronic items, and the entry of several multinational manufacturers, recorders continue to be priced far above international prices. This gives a fillip to the illegal import and smuggling of sets. As regards video cameras, editing, duplicating and related technologies, the situation is very similar.

Video ownership is not the only means of access to video in India. Of the million or so viewers who watch video every day, the majority club together to rent video-players, or go to video-parlours, video restaurants, video clubs, or watch video while travelling on 'video buses'. It is estimated that a thousand video rental companies operate in each of the four metropolitan cities. In the other large cities, around a hundred to two hundred rental companies/shops operate. Besides, over 50,000 video parlours do brisk business. Of the number of video restaurants, video clubs and video buses it is impossible to calculate even the approximate number. (Cable and satellite TV has however brought about a dramatic decline in the video business).

The video has taken over the function of permanent and mobile cinema theatres. Paucity of exhibition outlets has always been a major constraint on the expansion of the industry. By the mid-'eighties, even remote areas in far-flung districts had access to video. In Madhya Pradesh, for instance, even tiny villages with a population less than 2,000 were equipped with videos. In the Chattisgarh region alone, 150 restaurants organize video shows regularly, with an admission fee of Rs. 5 per head. The Vindhya and Malwa regions too have easy access to video. Restaurant owners in Punjab, Orissa, Karnataka, Kerala and even remote north-eastern states have cashed in on the video craze. There has been a let-up in the video boom of the mid-'eighties because of the heavy hand of the law on video pirates. The whole video business even today is largely illegal as most tapes are transferred from film prints in a clandestine manner. Pirated cassettes reach India mainly from Dubai and Hong Kong. But Indian cinema producers and the NFDC (which has entered the video business in a big way) have banded together to have the Cinematograph Act amended to include films on videotape. The amendment has made it illegal to screen films on video or cable without certification from the Central Board of Film Certification. Further, video parlours and video restaurants in some states are required to pay entertainment taxes. And frequent raids conducted by the police on video parlours that screen 'blue' films or pirated versions, have deterred many an owner of video-parlours. Whereas earlier, cinema producers gave international video rights only to Esquire for distribution abroad, now they have begun to offer video rights for domestic distribution as well. To counteract the video 'menace', producers frequently resort to 'saturation releases' in theatres, and later sell the rights to video companies at moderate prices. For example, Gold Video flooded the market with 90,000 video copies of 'Shahenshah' at a mere Rs. 135 each.

Video for Social and Political Education (1980s)

Video is widely used in India at the time of regional and national elections to propagate the campaigns of political parties. For instance, during the 1984 national elections, Rajiv Gandhiji's speeches on videotapes were employed for electioneering: further over 500 copies of a 20-minute videotape of 'Maa' (on Indira Gandhi) were distributed. The opposition parties too exploited the new medium; over a hundred prints of a video film of the Tamilnadu Chief Minister, M.G. Ramachandran, undergoing treatment in a hospital in the United States, made the rounds in the South. The BJP, the Congress, and the Shiv Sena have used audio and video cassettes extensively for their political campaigns. 'Video-raths' (video vans) have now become a common sight at election time. In late 1993, the JAIN TV channel was launched to provide 'infotainment' – a mix of entertainment and politics.

Social service organizations like SEWA in Ahmedabad, and CENDIT in New Delhi are using the new medium for conscientizing marginalized groups. Besides, news and film magazines such as India Today, Hindustan Times and Stardust got into the video distribution business during the late eighties and early nineties. India Today's monthly Newstrack, Hindustan Times' Eyewitness and Stardust's Starbuzz, launched a new trend in 'video news magazines'.

Other film video magazines of the late 1980s were: 'Lahren',

'Chalte Chalte', 'Eknath', 'Movie Magic', 'Sitaron Ki Duniye', and 'Bush Film Trax'. Sportsweek introduced the sports video magazine, 'Sportstyle'. By late 1993, many of the video magazines had ceased production, owing to the explosion of cable and cross-border satellite channels on television. Some of the video news magazines like 'Newstrack' and 'Eyewitness' then managed to obtain slots on one of the many television channels. These attempts were the antecedents for the proliferation of around-the-clock news channels from 2002 onwards.

Cable Television

Until the arrival of cross-border satellite television, 'cable television' in India meant no more than the relay via cable of pirated video copies of popular Indian and American films, from a central control room. In Cable Television, programmes are 'piped' to viewers' sets from an ideally placed common antenna, instead of each viewer individually receiving signals from his/her private antenna. Such 'rediffusion' systems have now become fairly common in urban and rural India.

In North America, cable TV had its origins in the need for improved reception of television signals in hilly and remote terrain. Cable TV had the advantage of good reception from local transmitters and offers the possibility of relaying services from distant and foreign transmitters beyond the reach of domestic antennae. Further, cable TV facilitates access to multiple channels. In Canada and the United States, for instance, it is possible to hook up a television set to a dozen or more 'basic' and 'pay TV' channels. (Some of the channels available are: the Disney Channel, MTV (Music Television), news channels, shopping channels, movie channels, community and educational channels). The installation and rental charges are minimal.

In India, the hotel industry, public and private sector companies, housing colonies, high-rise buildings and co-operative housing societies pioneered the distribution of cable TV. Cable installations took off in the mid-eighties. Flats in skyscrapers, for instance, were wired up to central control rooms

Table 34: Growth in Cable TV Households

1984	100	1993	125,000
1985	450	1994	130,000
1986	80	1995	18,000,000*
1988	1200	1996	22,000,000*
1989	2000	1997	27,000,000*
1990	4000	1998	32,000,000*
1991	6000	1999	39,000,000*
1992	15,000	2000	40,000,000*
		2002	43,000,000*
		2003	48,000,000*
		2004	50,000,000*
		2005	55,000,000*
		2006	60,000,000*
		2007	70,000,000 *

* Cable TV Households

Sources: *INFA Yearbook, 2000-2001;* V.C. Khare: *'Cable TV Scenario in India'. Paper presented at International Broadcasting Cable and Satellite Conference, October, 1993; FICCI-PwC Report – 2008.*

from where video players transmitted programmes taped abroad, and Indian and foreign films on video tapes. Numerous housing colonies in Bombay's suburbs and in other cities are now 'cabled'. Cable owners have been restrained by the Bombay High Court from screening Indian films for which they have not received permission from the holders of copyright. Film producers have argued that 'home viewing' is distinct from 'the public viewing' which cable facilitates. Cable networks across the country have installed satellite dishes to pick up the television channels of STAR-TV and Doordarshan and to retransmit them via cable to around 20 million homes. At the close of the 1990s, there were over 200,000 cable networks in the country. Almost half of them were in 'building clusters', and a third in 'single-building systems. More than a third of the networks had from 250 to 750 subscriber homes, and 20% had from 1,000 to 1,500 subscriber-homes.[16] In the late 1980s, Multi-

---
16 The source of much of this data about cable TV in India is V.C. Khare's paper, 'Cable TV Scenario in India', presented at the International Broadcasting, Cable and Satellite Conference, New Delhi, October 1993.

Service Operators (MSOs) like SitiCable (of the ZEE TV Network), INCABLENET (of the Hinduja Group), Hathway and Sumangli Cable (of the Sun Network) forced the majority of cable operators to join one MSO or the other so as to keep up with the competition. In Bombay alone, INCABLENET had 600,000, and SitiCable 400,000 cable connections under their control out of a total of 1,200,000 connections. Small time cable operators controlled a mere 200,000 connections.[17] The arrival of satellite television like the Star Network in the early 1990s radically changed the structure of the whole cable business. Small cable operators could not afford the investments required to invest in infrastructure for the cable and satellite (C and S) business. Consolidation of small time operators under larger MSOs became the norm. So, by 2004, the number of cable operators was reduced to around 26,000 from the estimated 60,000 two years earlier. In Tamilnadu, the breakup of the Sun Network's monopoly in television and cable (owned by the Maran family) came about in 2007 with the launch of Kalaignar TV and the Royal Cable by Karunanidhi and family.

Satellite Television

However, direct-to-home (or DTH) technology which takes cross-border satellite programmes direct to viewers' homes without the intervention of cable operators, threatens to ruin the cable operators' business. DTH television is digital and interactive, and offers more than a hundred free and subscription channels. Rupert Murdoch's NewsCorp is leading the DTH revolution, having already established the BSkyB in Europe, the JSky B in Japan, and Tata-Sky on the Indian sub-continent.[18] In India, though, the DTH services of Doordarshan (DD-Direct)

---

17 Report in *The Times of India*, September 20, 1998, p. 1.
18 NewsCorp's other media interests include the Fox Network, Fox Sports, Kids Network, DirecTV, Twentieth Century Fox, the *New York Post* (in the United States), *The Times* and the *Sun* (in the United Kingdom), Sky (in Europe), TGRT TV channel (Turkey), *The Australian* and *The Telegraph* (in Australia) and the Internet portal www.indya.com, the interactive social network www.myspace.com and the video-sharing website www.indyarocks.com.

and Zee TV (DISH-TV) preceded the launch of Tata-Sky. Reliance's Big TV, Sun-TV, Bharti Airtel and Videocon and other major players in the media business have also applied for DTH licenses.

The satellite TV revolution in urban India was ushered in by five-star hotels in Bombay and Delhi which brought the 'live' coverage of the Gulf War to the small screen via the CNN (Cable News Network) of Atlanta, Georgia. STAR-TV (with four channels) was launched in 1991 when there were around 11,500 cable networks in the entire country. In Delhi alone, there were at the time around 45,000 households linked to cable TV. (STAR-TV added a fifth channel – the BBC World Service, on October 14, 1991). The number of cable networks increased steadily as it became clear that only a dish antenna would be necessary to transmit STAR-TV channels to basic cable-linked households. Around 78% of the cable households could access the STAR-TV network.

An ARU (Audience Research Unit) study conducted in 1992 covered ten cities and towns: Delhi, Bombay, Madras, Calcutta, Hyderabad, Bangalore, Lucknow, Nagpur, Jaipur and Cuttack. These cities and towns represented different sizes of population, different levels of cable penetration, and different levels of knowledge of English and Hindi. The study estimated that none of the satellite TV programmes had more than eight per cent viewing and very few programmes reached even five per cent. The programmes with higher than five per cent viewing were feature films, serials, cartoon shows and news. The study concluded: It appears that most of the satellite TV viewing is chance viewing. The programmes are yet to build up a loyal audience. The reasons are obvious: the programmes are in English and even for a majority of English knowing people the accent in the dramatic programmes is not easy to comprehend.

The study added that 'the VCR programmes of the local operator had good viewing which went up to 24% at times. These were mostly feature films, some new and other popular hits of yester years. Generally, the local VCR peaked in the afternoons and after 10.00 p.m. when feature films in the local languages were put on the cable network'. An IIMC survey of 300 respondents in Delhi conducted in January 1992 arrived at a similar conclusion.

The major effect of the mushroom growth of cable and satellite television has been on the advertising revenue earned by Doordarshan and the print media. Advertisers of sanitary napkins, pan masalas, alcoholic drinks, jewellery and other products which are banned on Doordarshan have begun capitalising on Star-TV's five channels. Other advertisers too are taking advantage of the lower rates of Star-TV and Zee TV, especially in the area of premium brands of soaps, consumer items and consumer durables. Doordarshan launched a metro channel and four other channels which are available via satellite in any part of the country, in a bid to win back the top advertisers. Doordarshan's efforts are bearing fruit since advertisers and advertising agencies are provided opportunities to produce programmes on the Metro and the national networks.

The effects of satellite television on other mass media such as the cinema, radio, recorded music and even the press have been equally remarkable. Though the production of films continues at the same rate as in earlier years (around a thousand per year), several cinema theatres have been forced to close down, especially in Mumbai and other cities of Western India. The 'privatisation' of FM radio in the metros is clearly a fallout of the widespread access to satellite and cable television, and an attempt to combat the popularity of the MTV channel on STAR-TV. The recorded music industry too has been forced to change its strategies to keep pace with the interests of the 'MTV-generation'.

The press has not escaped the onslaught either. With round the clock news on BBC World, CNN (Cable News Network), Star News, and Zee India News, Indian newspapers find that their reports cannot match the immediacy of satellite networks which present, as the claim goes, 'news as it happens'. In an effort to compete, Indian newspapers and magazines have introduced visuals and colour as well as interesting layouts to keep the attention of their readers. Besides, both newspapers and magazines now present news stories in the form of 'snippets' and 'briefs', and features that are investigative and analytical in nature. Several publications, such as *Bombay* (of the Living Media Group) and *The Illustrated Weekly of India* (of the Times of India Group) have fallen by the wayside.

Satellite television has had some influence undoubtedly on the socio-cultural environment of the urban and rural groups that afford access to the cable and satellite channels. The soap operas, sitcoms, talk shows and game shows of the American, British and Australian networks often deal with subjects that are of little relevance to Indian society; yet they are eminently watchable. Zee TV's shows are pale imitations of the American genres. The openness with which topics related to sex and violence are discussed or enacted, is passe in affluent societies; it is not so in most Eastern cultures. Constant exposure to 'images' and ideas from dominant and powerful cultures give rise to media and cultural imperialism. During the 'seventies and 'eighties, the non-aligned countries brought up this issue in UNESCO and other fora, and pleaded for a New World Information and Communication Order (NWICO), wherein the flow of information between the countries of the North and of the South would be 'fair, equal and balanced', and not predominantly from North to South. The United States and Britain saw this struggle as a 'communist plot', and walked out of UNESCO.

The reporting of the BBC, CNN and ABC News on culturally and politically sensitive issues over the satellite channels has been far from commendable. Apparently, they have little concern for the possible repercussions of their frequently provocative visuals and reports. Some national governments have pointed out that this is tantamount to 'interfering in the internal affairs' of Asian nations under the guise of providing world news.

Ownership, Control and Regulation of Television

Like All India Radio, Doordarshan was until November 1997

a 'unit' of the Ministry of Information and Broadcasting. The Government of India, of course, always claimed that Doordarshan enjoyed 'functional autonomy' in its programming and administration, but no matter what the claims, the Ministry has remained the real decision-making body. A fair amount of freedom was permitted in the selection and production of entertainment programmes. But news and current affairs programmes were closely monitored by the Ministry. That remained the practice since Independence no matter which political party was in power in Delhi.

The question of the ownership and control of India broadcasting was first raised during a discussion in the Constituent Assembly. Pandit Nehru, however, dismissed the issue with these words: "My own view of the set-up for broadcasting is that we should approximate as far as possible to the British model, the BBC; that is to say, it would be better if we had a semi-autonomous corporation under the Government, of course with the policy controlled by the Government, otherwise being conducted as a Government department but as a semi-autonomous corporation. Now, I do not think that is immediately feasible." Though that was the first Prime Minister's personal view, it remained the official position until 1964 when the Chanda Committee was established to look into the whole issue afresh.

The Chanda Committee

The Chanda Committee recommended that a Broadcasting Corporation should be established by an act of Parliament in which its objectives should be clearly laid down. It emphasised that 'the scope of Government's authority should be clearly defined and be free of ambiguity. The right to require the Corporation to broadcast certain programmes as also the right to veto broadcasts in certain subjects may be reserved to Government. It must be understood that such powers must be sparingly used and only when the national interest so demands. These reservations would automatically define the accountability of the Minister of Parliament. We also consider that the Act itself should lay down the authority and powers of the Governors to prevent possible encroachment'.

Accordingly, it recommended a Board of Governors (no more than seven) to be headed by a Chairman. 'The Chairman should be a public figure with a national reputation for integrity, ability and independence, and the members should be drawn from diverse fields of national life and enjoying a reputation in his particular field'. The Committee left selection to the Government itself, and the term of office of Governors was restricted to six years with two members retiring every other year in rotation. It argued that conditions for creativity could only be fostered by decentralisation of authority down to the regional and local levels.

The Verghese Committee

The Verghese Committee recommended the setting up of a National Broadcast Trust (or Akash Bharati) under which a highly decentralised structure would operate. It did not see the need for autonomous corporations or even a federation of State Government Corporations. Neither did it support the idea of two separate corporations for radio and television. However, besides asserting that the Trust should be an independent, impartial and autonomous organisation, the Committee wanted 'the autonomy of the corporation and its independence from government control to be entrenched in the Constitution'.

The Committee recommended that the Trust be supervised by a Board of Trustees (or Nyasi Mandal) consisting of 12 members who would be appointed by the president on the recommendation of the Prime Minister from out of a list of names forwarded by a nominating panel comprising the Chief Justice of India, the Lok Pal and the Chairman of the UPSC. The Chairman and three members would be full-time members while the other eight members would be part-time. It would be the responsibility of the Board of Trustees to appoint the Controller-General Broadcasting, the Directors and other senior personnel.

The Controller-General would head the Central Executive Board and will be ex-officio Secretary to the Board of Trustees. The Central Executive Board, in co-ordination with Zonal Executive Councils, would be responsible for implementing the policies and directives of the Board of Trustees. Programming would necessarily be decentralised and producers down to the local levels would enjoy 'a significant measure of autonomy'.

The Joshi Working Group on Software for Doordarshan

Though the Joshi Working Group was not asked to go into the question of broadcasting autonomy, it did stick its neck out in stating bluntly that 'functional freedom' did not exist at all in Doordarshan, despite government claims. However, it noted that the crucial issue is not 'autonomy versus government control' but 'urgent reforms in structure and management styles for support to creativity'. It, therefore recommended the creation of an institutional arrangement which provided co-ordination and interaction among political, administrative and communication spheres for policy guidelines and evaluation of software. Further, it recommended the establishment of a National Doordarshan Council to tender advice to the Minister on the broad social objectives and the modes of TV programming. The Joshi Working Group however, did not favour the freeing of broadcasting from the control of the I and B Ministry. It had no objection to Doordarshan receiving directives from the Minister or his deputy.

The Prasar Bharati Bill (1989)

The Prasar Bharati Bill (1989) is based largely on the Verghese Report (1978) and the Prasar Bharati Bill (1979) that was introduced by the Janata regime in Parliament in May 1979. There are some basic differences too. While the Prasar Bharati Bill favours the creation of a Broadcasting Corporation through an Act of Parliament, the Verghese Report clearly wanted broadcasting autonomy to be a part of the Indian Constitution. This would be necessary to ensure that no future government would tamper with the freedom and independence of the corporation. Further, a Trust in the service of the public was what the Verghese Report envisaged; the present Bill proposes a 'Corporation' which does not have statutory dignity and power. The objectives that the present Bill sets out for the corporation are taken almost verbatim from the Verghese Committee's objectives for the National broadcast Trust. Yet it does not go as far as the Verghese Report which wanted the Ministry of Information and Broadcasting to shed its responsibility for broadcasting altogether. The bill manages to sneak in a representative of the Ministry as a part-time Governor. This is not the 'full autonomy' the Verghese Committee had in mind.

The Verghese Committee warned against 'copying blindly' the structure and organisation of western broadcasting institutions. The structure envisaged by the new Bill is patterned closely on that of the British Broadcasting Corporation; even the nomenclature is similar. Moreover, the Verghese Report underscored the need for a decentralised structure with powers delegated at regional and local levels; the present Bill says little about devolution of the powers of the Central Governing and Executive Boards. The Bill does not also go into the question of 'franchise stations' for educational institutions or of independent radio and television producing agencies. On the matter of the selection of the Chairman of the Board of Governors too, the Bill departs from the Verghese recommendations. Instead of the nominating panel consisting of the Chief Justice of India, the Lok Pal and the Chairman of the UPSC, the present Bill would rather include the Rajya Sabha Chairman, the Press Council Chairman and a nominee of the President. Similarly, it deviates radically on the composition of the Broadcasting Council/ Complaints Council. Indeed, the current Bill is far closer in content, form and spirit to the Prasar Bharati Bill (1979) than to the Verghese Report's recommendations.

B.G. Verghese, Umashankar Joshi and other Committee members reacted strongly to the 1979 Bill. Both felt that the then Government had been 'distrustful' of the people and that the extent of autonomy provided in the Bill had been considerably diluted; there was no provision, they remarked, for any decentralisation of the functioning of the proposed broadcasting corporation. These objections can be raised against the 1989 Bill too. The Bill became an Act in 1990 with the approval by all political parties in the Lok Sabha and Rajya Sabha.

Prasar Bharati Act (1990)

The first step the ruling Congress government took in response to the 'invasion' by cross-border satellite television was to set up the Varadan Committe (1991) to re-examine the Prasar Bharati Act (1990). The Varadan Committee suggested that Doordarshan should devote 'at least 20% of total broadcasting time on each channel to socially relevant programmes'. Further, 'no more than ten per cent in terms of time of the programmes broadcast should be imported'. It also recommended that 'while dealing with any matter of controversy, the programmes shall present all points of view in a fair and impartial manner'.

The United Front Government went a step further. It sought to draw up a comprehensive National Media Policy that would take into account questions such as decentralisation of television, regulations, cross-media ownership, participation by foreign media houses, role of advertising, and uplinking from Indian territory. The Ram Vilas Paswan Committee was set up for this purpose in 1995. It submitted a 104-page working paper with 46 recommendations on public and private electronic media, newspapers, news agencies, and film. The Committee had hammered out a consensus on National Media Policy. Some of the recommendations were incorporated in the Broadcasting Bill introduced in parliament in May 1997. The Nitish Sengupta Committee (1996) was constituted in 1996 to have another look at the Prasar Bharati Act and to suggest amendments. It submitted its report in August of the same year.

The Broadcasting Bill (1997)

In mid-May 1997, the Broadcasting Bill was introduced in Parliament. A Joint Parliamentary Committee headed by Mr.

Sharad Pawar of the Congress (I) was constituted to have a second look at some of the controversial clauses such as cross-media ownership, licencing procedures, extent of foreign equity to be permitted, and uplinking services for private satellite channels.

The Bill made it mandatory for all channels whether Indian or foreign to transmit their programmes from Indian territory. Licences for satellite channels would be granted only to Indian companies, and they would be allowed up to 49% foreign equity. No foreign equity for terrestrial channels would be allowed.

The Bill banned cross-media ownership (newspaper publishing houses can have no more than 20% equity in television or cable companies), and foreign ownership. Besides, no advertising agencies, religious bodies, political parties or publicly funded bodies would be granted a licence to own a TV company. Direct-to-home (DTH) services would be licensed only to two companies after a bidding process.

The Cable Television Networks (Regulation) Act would stand repealed once the Bill came into effect.

The Broadcasting Bill was introduced in direct response to the Supreme Court of India's direction to the Central Government in February 1995 'to take immediate steps to establish an independent autonomous public authority representative of all sections and interests in the society to control and regulate the use of the airwaves'. The Supreme Court was opposed to the privatisation of broadcasting, observing that 'private broadcasting, even if allowed, should not be left to market forces, in the interests of ensuring that a wide variety of voices enjoy access to it. The Court saw 'a potential danger flowing from the concentration of the rights to broadcast/telecast in the hands of (either) a central agency or of a few private broadcasters'.

(Draft) Broadcast Regulation Bill (2007)

The Draft Broadcast Regulation Bill (2007) recognizes that 'the airwaves are public property' and therefore 'it is necessary to regulate the use of the airwaves in the national and public interest'. The Bill proposes the establishment of an independent authority, the Broadcasting Regulatory Authority (BRAI) for the purpose of regulating and facilitating the development of broadcasting services. The mandatory registration for cable operators under the Cable Television Networks (Regulations) Act, 1995, will continue. All television channels, whether Indian or foreign, would also be required to register and to comply with the Programme Code and Advertising Code laid down in the 1995 Act. However, registration/license of channels could be suspended or revoked by the Central government where the content was (i) prejudicial to friendly relations with a foreign country, (ii) threatened public order, communal harmony or the security of the state.

The Bill spells out the Public Service Obligations of Broadcasters in Chapter 2 (11):
(a) Share of content produced in India shall not be less than 15% of the total content of a channel broadcast every week;
(b) Share of public service/social messaging through advertisements shall not be less than 10% of the total content of a channel broadcast every week;
(c) Share of public service/socially relevant programme content shall not be less than 10% of the total content of a channel broadcast every week.

The Bill also makes it mandatory for broadcast channels to transmit at least two Doordarshan channels and one regional channel of a state in the prime band (2:7), the Lok Sabha and Rajya Sabha channels (2:7), as well as to share certain sports broadcast signals with the public service broadcaster, Doordarshan (2:6).

In order to prevent monopolies and to ensure diversity of news and views the Bill limits paid up equity of the broadcasting service provider to 20%, and an overall ceiling of 15% for the whole country.

Perhaps the most controversial of the clauses in the Bill is 3:23 which sets out the Powers and Functions of Authorized

Officers: (i) to inspect, search and seize equipment, (ii) to prosecute on a written complaint by the Licensing Authority, and (iii) to ensure that terms and conditions of the Licensing Authority are not violated. 'Authorized Officers' are: (i) a district magistrate, or (ii) a sub-divisional magistrate, or (iii) a commissioner of police.

The Content Code

The draft Content Code hammered out by the Information and Broadcasting Ministry together with broadcasters and advertisers, recommends that all programmes be slotted into three categories: universal (U), under parental guidance (U/A) and adult (A). Where a programme has one scene or portion that could be considered adult content, then the entire programme has to be slotted as such. Adult content will be permitted only from 11.00 pm to 4.00 am, while U/A programmes may be on air only after 8.00 pm.

For content regulation each broadcast service provider (BSP) will have to categorise content on basis of theme, subject matter, treatment, language and audiovisual presentation. It is up to the BSP to ensure that all programmes are broadcast according to the scheduling rules. The Content Code provides a list of eight themes/subjects:
1. Crime and Violence
2. Sex, Obscenity and Nudity
3. Horror and Occult
4. Drugs, Smoking, Tobacco, Solvents and Alcohol
5. Libel, Slander and Defamation
6. Religion and Community
7. Harm and Offence
8. Advertisements and General Restrictions.

The Code spells out the parameters of 'self-censorship' – a practice which broadcasters are keen on adopting. The three-tiered system includes a content auditor at the level of the channel, a peer or industry review of the violation, and the third level of the Broadcasting Regulatory Authority of India (BRAI).

So, each channel or network will be expected to appoint a 'content auditor' who will be the points person for complaints and feedback from the public. The content auditor will be responsible for categorizing the content though the chief editor of the channel will be responsible for any programme that does not meet the norms of the Code. It is the auditor who will be expected to report to the ministry violations. The second tier is a consumer complaints committee that will include industry representatives, consumers and members of civil society groups. The committee will have the power to stop telecast of a programme, edit objectionable portions, and direct the broadcaster to carry a disclaimer, warning or apology. At the final tier, the complaint can be referred to BRAI which has the authority to take the programme off the air or even to ban the channel or charge penalties.

These proposed regulations which are spelt out in the Broadcasting Bill (2007) have been resisted by the television broadcasters and the entire industry. The Bill was to be introduced in Parliament at the end of 2007. However, the News Broadcasters Association and other bodies quickly got together to draw up their own Code of Ethics and Broadcasting Standards which they said would function on the principle of self-regulation.

Response: The News Broadcasters Association's Code of Ethics

The News Broadcasters Association (NBA), a collective of 12 Indian broadcasters which run 25 channels, drew up a Code of Ethics and Broadcasting Standards in 2008 to counter the regulations of the Draft Broadcasting Bill which put the onus of regulating news programmes and news channels on the Ministry of Information and Broadcasting. The NBA collective includes TV Today Network Ltd., NDTV Ltd., Times Global Broadcasting Co. Ltd., TV 18 Group and Sun TV Network.

In a kind of Preamble, the Code states that 'electronic journalists should accept and understand that they operate as trustees of the public and should therefore make it their mission to seek the truth and to report it fairly with integrity and independence. Professional journalists should stand fully accountable for their actions.' Journalists are urged to maintain impartiality and objectivity in reporting, and to ensure neutrality. On crime reporting, journalists are asked to ensure that crime and violence are not glorified, and that the victims of crime are protected.

The Code stresses that 'sting and undercover operations should be a last resort and no sex and sleaze, or use of narcotics or psychotropic substances' will be allowed to be used. Channels must not intrude on private lives or personal affairs unless in the public interest. With regard to sex, nudity and pornography the Code makes it clear that 'channels will not show explicit images of sexual activity or sexual perversions or acts of sexual violence like rape/molestation, or show pornography or the use of sexually suggestive language'. Television channels should not glorify superstition and occultism.

Since the NBA excludes the majority of broadcasters, its writ will not run outside the collective. Self-regulation will have little impact if there is no effective machinery to monitor or to reprimand broadcasters that do not adhere to the Code. The Code was made public in late April 2008; two months later most channels were merrily flouting all the norms laid down in their sensational reporting of the Arushi and Hemraj murder case in Noida. The Ministry of Information and Broadcasting had to step in to pull the offending channels like *India Live*. In February 2008, the Ministry issued Guidelines for State and District-level Monitoring Committees for private television channels to keep an eye on channels infringing the Programme and Advertising Codes spelt out in the Cable Television Network (Regulation) Act of 1995. (See below for excerpts from the Act). The Committees would also deal with complaints from the public on programme content. This task of monitoring would be taken over by the proposed Broadcasting Regulatory Authority of India once it is established under the Broadcasting Bill/Act.

Television for National Development

Public television in India, according to various Prasar Bharati and Doordarshan publications, has the following social objectives:

1. To act as a catalyst for social change
2. To promote national integration
3. To stimulate a scientific temper in the minds of the people
4. To disseminate the message of family planning as a means of population control and family welfare
5. To provide essential information and knowledge in order to stimulate greater agricultural production
6. To promote and help preserve environmental and ecological balance
7. To highlight the need for social welfare measures including welfare of women, children and the less privileged
8. To promote interest in games and sports
9. To create values of appraisal of art and our cultural heritage.[19]

This, however, is official stated policy; a close examination of the programming and scheduling suggests very different priorities. See Table 35 below which shows a breakdown of the composition of programme genres. Social information and development programmes are way down the list comprising barely 2.4% of total broadcasting time; in contrast entertainment serials make up 30.4% and news and current affairs programmes 31%. It is clear where the public broadcaster's priorities lie.

---

19 *Doordarshan - 1997*, New Delhi: Audience Research Unit, Directorate-General, Doordarshan.

Table 35: Programme Composition by Format and Content – Doordarshan Channels (2003)

	National Network %
News and Current Affairs	31.9
General/Social Information	2.4
Serials/Plays/Skits	30.4
Culture	4.7
School & University Education	8.5
Film/Film-based Entertainment	8.7
Sports	10.5
Miscellaneous	2.9

(Source: *Doordarshan – 2003*, p. 20)

Educational Television (ETV)

As the above table indicates, school and university educational programmes make up just 8.5% of total broadcasting time on Doordarshan's many channels. Private commercial broadcasters fare no better. The distinct advantage of using television for formal and non-formal education is that large numbers across the length and breadth of the land can be reached simultaneously. Experts in various fields of education can offer their services to the whole nation. The main disadvantage, of course, is the enormous expenditure involved not only in production and transmission, but for reception of programmes. Although television access is widespread, receiver-sets are still beyond the reach of the majority of the urban and rural poor who are in need of further education.

Visual demonstrations of rare and complex material markedly improve understanding of many aspects of the physical sciences, of medicine, of geography and of the elements of drama and history.

England, Japan and the United States have a fairly well developed educational TV service. The British Open University makes wide use of TV-time over BBC to beam its various faculty programmes. The United States' Public Television's School Programmes serve teachers and students in the classroom and at home. Besides, the National University Consortium consisting of seven U.S. Colleges offers college credit courses on public television. An integral part of the courses of the Open University and the N.U.C. is the tutorial system under which students work with qualified tutors living in the same cities or towns.

Delhi TV took the decision in 1961 (when it covered only the twin cities and was still at an experimental stage) to broadcast curriculum-based lessons on selected subjects, particularly on science. The aim was to improve standards in the teaching of science at the secondary level. At the time, few Delhi schools had laboratory facilities, and further, there were few qualified science teachers. These disadvantages were sought to be overcome by the visual medium of TV.

Teachers and students responded with enthusiasm to the new teaching aid. The experiment was made possible by financial assistance from the Ford foundation. It was evaluated in 1969 by a UNESCO expert, Paul Neurath, and he concluded that ETV had amply proved its usefulness as 'an aid to the teaching of science subjects'. Though Delhi TV covers a much larger area now, and many more receivers have been installed in schools there has been no significant development in the educational programmes put out. Indeed, there has been a decline in interest. According to an NCERT (National Council of Educational Research and Training) survey on the utilisation of educational TV in schools under the Delhi administration, only 38% of the 500 schools provided with receivers in the secondary classes for which lessons are telecast every week, switched on to the programmes. Some of the reasons: poor maintenance of receivers, shoddy viewing conditions in the classrooms, indifference among teachers and students.

Doordarshan Centres in Mumbai, Chennai, Kolkata, Srinagar and other cities transmit educational programmes in English and

Science for primary and secondary classes. The unfortunate part of these 'lessons' is that they provide little knowledge of general interest, adhering strictly to the school curriculum and the classroom format. The camera moves outdoors only for short periods. The English language lessons are well-planned, but presented by teachers and students using a variety of accents and pronunciation.

With the extension of satellite and micro-wave facilities to almost the entire country and the installation of many more studios and transmitting centres, Doordarshan will inevitably increase its educational telecast across the length and breadth of the land. But what needs to be done before this take-off stage is close co-ordination between the centre and the states on ETV. It must be noted that the broadcast media are under Central Government control, while education is a State Government subject under the Constitution. The way out could be the setting up of an autonomous board of educationists, social scientists and media experts at the state levels. This has been recently initiated by granting 'autonomy' to the SIETs (State Institutes of Educational Technology).

A further development has been the launch of an educational channel called 'Gyan Darshan' by Doordarshan. The Indira Gandhi National Open University (IGNOU) is the main broadcaster on this channel, but the EMRCs and AVRCs have also now come on board to provide 'enrichment' educational programmes. However, since Gyan Darshan is a satellite channel it cannot be accessed by those who do not subscribe to the cable and satellite networks. Few cable operators are willing to carry this channel on their networks thus limiting its access to a largely urban elite.

Television and Higher Education

The Verghese Committee set up by the Janata regime in 1978 strongly recommended granting broadcast franchises to educational institutions. This would empower national institutions of higher learning to use low-power radio or television transmission solely for the propagation of quality education to large masses of students and others.

The UGC Higher Education Project launched in August 1984, serves this purpose. Known as Countrywide Classroom, and coordinated by the Consortium for Educational Communication (CEC), New Delhi, its ETV programmes are beamed across the country every weekday morning and afternoon. 1700 colleges have been provided with free colour TV sets (few colleges have bought sets from their own funds), the number of community sets stands at 60,000. However, a good number of programmes telecast continue to be of foreign origin (mainly from Britain, United States, West Germany and Russia), though indigenous programmes, produced at seven EMRCs (Educational Media Research Centres) and eight AVRCs (Audio Visual Research Centres) set up in different parts of the country, are increasing their contribution steadily. According to a 1993 ADMAR study, the UGC programmes have a viewership of over 19 million. Of these, 12 million watch the programmes at least once a week, and around seven million are regular viewers, watching two-to-five transmissions per week, though only 45% of the regular viewers are students. The launch of a round-the-clock educational channel called Gyandarshan by Doordarshan has given a fillip to educational programming in English, Hindi and the regional languages. A private educational television channel called 'Topper' was launched in 2007 with the objective of coaching students for various school and college examinations.

Major Television Networks

1. Doordarshan Network (+30 channels and DD-Direct)
2. NDTV Networks plc. (NDTV-India, NDTV-24/7, NDTV Profit, NDTV MetroNation, NDTV Imagine, NDTV Imagine Showbiz, NDTV Good Times, NDTV Lumiere)
3. ZEE Telefilms: (Zee News, Zee Business, Zee Sports, Zee Movies, Zee Music, Zee Next, Zee-Chavees Taas, Zee Gujarati, etc.)
4. STAR TV Network: (17 channels: Star Plus, Star One, Star

World, Star Utsav, Star Sports-ESPN, Star Gold, Star Movies, Channel V, Star News, Star Ananda, Star-Vijay TV, Star-Majha, etc.)
5. Sun TV Network (+24 channels: Sun TV, Sun News, Surya, Kiran, Gemini, Udaya, Ushe, etc.)
6. Raj TV: (Raj, Raj Digital Plus)
7. Jaya TV
8. UTV Entertainment Television (Bindass, Bindass Movies, World Movies, UTV Movies, UTVi)
9. Sony Entertainment TV(SET) (now Multi Screen Media): (SET, SET-Max, SET-Pix)
10. Eenadu (ETV): (ETV News, ETV Marathi, ETV Gujarati, ETV Urdu, etc.)
11. TV Today Network: (Aaj Tak, Headlines Today, Aaj Tak Tez, Delhi Aaj Tak)
12. SaharaOne Media (Sahara Samay, Sahara Delhi)
13. INX Media (News X, 9X, 9x Music)
14. Global Broadcast News (GBN): CNN-IBN, CNBC, IBN-7, IBN-Lokmat)
15. Asianet
16. Amrita TV
17. Television-18 (CNBC-TV 18, CNBC-Awaz, Colours)
18. Viacom (MTV, VH-1, Nickleodeon, Colours (with TV-18),
19. Times Global Broadcasting Ltd./BCCL (Times Now, Zoom)
20. Manorama (Manorama News)
21. Broadcast Worldwide (Tara News, Tara Muzik, Tara Talkies, etc.)
22. Bangla Entertainment (Channel Eight)
23. Disney (Hungamma, etc.)
24. BAG Films & Media Ltd. (E-24, News 24, Bliss 24, Life 24)

Table 36: Newspaper Publishers Owning Television Networks

Newspaper Publishers	Television Networks
The Times of India/BCCL	Reuters-Times Now/Zoom
Dinakaran	Sun TV Network
Eenadu	Eenadu TVNetwork (ETV)
India Today/Living Media	Aaj Tak/Headlines Today
Jagran Prakashan	IBN - Channel 7
Sahara	Sahara
Ananda Bazaar Patrika	Star News, Star-Majha, Star Ananda
Malayala Manorama	Manorama TV

Television and Corporate Social Responsibility

Television, cable and satellite TV producers have not drawn up any Code of Ethics for regulating practices in the profession. While television producers (and also 'independent producers' making programmes for Doordarshan) are required to follow the 'AIR Code' and other guidelines issued by the Central Government, cable and satellite TV producers follow a policy of crass commercialism. Any programme which attracts advertisers and brings in some viewers is telecast-worthy. There appears to be a certain indifference to questions of ethics and morality among professional media persons. Television programmes are not subject to any kind of censorship, though feature films, short films and video films which may be screened on television channels, need a censorship certificate from the CBFC. Television advertising films too are not subject to pre-censorship. However, the guidelines listed in Sections 6 and 7 of the Cable Television Networks Regulations Act (1995) are binding on television programmes and commercials (see below for excerpts from the Programme Code and Advertising Code). It is under this Act that the Information and Broadcasting Ministry banned FTV, AXN and Janmat channels for short periods in 2007.

Even as STAR - TV imposes largely western-type entertainment and news programmes on Asian audiences, Doordarshan imposes a North-Indian Delhi-centric culture on the whole country. It is very likely that the Metro channels and the five additional national channels will continue this 'unethical' practice. The pluralism of cultures in India will not be presented because of advertisers' influence on programming, and Doordarshan's unwillingness to take on a 'public service' role. The staple fare on Doordarshan, cable, and satellite channels is mainstream commercial cinema. Even films and soap operas meant for adults are telecast at times when children cannot be kept from watching. Explicit scenes of sex and violence are the main ingredients of such films. How 'ethical' is such telecasting?

Further, how 'ethical' is the presentation of violence in news programmes? The violence of war, the violence of the police against citizens, and the violence of famines, droughts and floods? The violence of poverty? The BBC wallows in the portrayal of emaciated bodies in the Sudan and Somalia.

Individual privacy is rarely respected when it comes to portraying death on television. Frequently, the cameras zoom in on the wan face of the dead person, or the agonised face of a widow, or a close relative. What is the earthly 'news value' of such representations?

The BBC World Service relishes showing us 'library pictures' of trishul-swinging sadhus in Ayodhya over and over again on a day when the whole nation is tense with communal frenzy. Do broadcasters owe it to their profession to 'give the news as it happens' without being concerned about the consequences to the community? Further, to portray all post-Ayodhya riots in India only in communal terms (despite the obvious economic and political grounds for such flare-ups) is to betray the persistent colonial mentality of the BBC. (The BBC, it must be noted, is extremely cautious and spare in its use of provocative visuals when it presents news of IRA-bombings and Ulster rioting).

The satellite channels are beyond the regulation of any Government. Protests of Governments of Asian countries often go unheeded. Advertisements for liquor and tobacco are banned on Indian and most other Asian television networks. But the satellite channels have begun showing 'surrogate' advertisements of different brands of liquors, and of pan masalas. There is little concern for the 'ethics' of advertising, or for that matter, with the 'ethics' of broadcasting. The TV viewer has to take it or leave it: advertisements interfere every few minutes with his right to information and his right to healthy entertainment, but he does not protest and so continues to be exploited. The introduction of the TiVo digital video recorder (DVR) to assist viewers to delete or skip the commercials has been vehemently resisted by the industry.

Guidelines for the Indian Television Industry

The Ministry of Information and Broadcasting, TRAI (Telecommunications Regulatory Authority of India) and other Government bodies issue regulations and guidelines to the television industry on issues such as norms for satellite transmission, subscription fees for cable, satellite and DTH operators, and even on programme content and advertising. Excerpts from some of these regulations/guidelines are given below:

The Cable Television Networks (Regulation) Act, 1995/The Cable Television Networks Rules (1994)

6. Programme Code. –

(1) No programme should be carried in the cable service which:-
   (a) Offends against good taste or decency;
   (b) Contains criticism of friendly countries;
   (c) Contains attack on religions or communities or visuals or words contemptuous of religious groups or which promote communal attitudes;
   (d) Contains anything obscene, defamatory, deliberate, false and suggestive innuendos and half truths;
   (e) Is likely to encourage or incite violence or contains anything against maintenance of law and order or which promote anti-national attitudes;
   (f) Contains anything amounting to contempt of court;
   (g) Contains aspersions against the integrity of the President and Judiciary;

(h) Contains anything affecting the integrity of the Nation;
(i) Criticises, maligns or slanders any individual in person or certain groups, segments of social, public and moral life of the country;
(j) Encourages superstition or blind belief;
(k) Denigrates women through the depiction in any manner of the figure of a woman, her form or body or any part thereof in such a way as to have the effect of being indecent, or derogatory to women, or is likely to deprave, corrupt or injure the public morality or morals;
(l) Denigrates children;
(m) Contains visuals or words which reflect a slandering, ironical and snobbish attitude in the portrayal of certain ethnic, linguistic and regional groups
(n) Contravenes the provisions of the Cinematograph Act, 1952.
(o) Is not suitable for unrestricted public exhibition.

Explanation – For the purpose of this clause, the expression "unrestricted public exhibition" shall have the same meaning as assigned to it in the Cinematograph Act, 1952 (37 of 1952);

(2) The cable operator should strive to carry programmes in his cable service which project women in a positive, leadership role of sobriety, moral and character building qualities.

(3) No cable operator shall carry or include in his cable service any programme in respect of which copyright subsists under the Copyright Act, 1972 (14 of 1972) unless he has been granted a licence by owners of copyright under the Act in rest of such programme.

(4) Care should be taken to ensure that programmes meant for children do not contain any bad language or explicit scenes of violence.

(5) Programmes unsuitable for children must not be carried in the cable service at times when the largest numbers of children are viewing.

7. **Advertising Code.** –
(1) Advertising carried in the cable service shall be so designed as to conform to the laws of the country and should not offend morality, decency and religious susceptibilities of the subscribers.
(2) No advertisement shall be permitted which-
  (i) derides any race, caste, colour, creed and nationality
  (ii) is against any provision of the Constitution of India.
  (iii) tends to incite people to crime, cause disorder or violence, or breach of law or glorifies violence or obscenity in any way ;
  (iv) presents criminality as desirable;
  (v) exploits the national emblem, or any part of the Constitution or the person or personality of a national leader or a State dignitary;
  (vi) in its depiction of women violates the constitutional guarantees to all citizens. In particular, no advertisement shall be permitted which projects a derogatory image of women. Women must not be portrayed in a manner that emphasises passive, submissive qualities and encourages them to play a subordinate, secondary role in the family and society. The cable operator shall ensure that the portrayal of the female form, in the programmes carried in his cable service, is tasteful and aesthetic, and is within the well established norms of good taste and decency;
  (vii) exploits social evils like dowry, child marriage.
  (viii) promotes directly or indirectly production, sale or consumption of-
    (A) cigarettes, tobacco products, wine, alcohol, liquor or other intoxicants;
    (B) infant milk substitutes, feeding bottle or infant food.
(3) No advertisement shall be permitted, the objects whereof, are wholly or mainly of a religious or political nature; advertisements must not be directed towards any religious

or political end.

(3A) No advertisement shall contain references which hurt religious sentiments.

(4) The goods or services advertised shall not suffer from any defect or deficiency as mentioned in Consumer Protection Act, 1986.

(5) No advertisement shall contain references which are likely to lead the public to infer that the product advertised or any of its ingredients has some special or miraculous or super-natural property or quality, which is difficult of being proved.

(6) The picture and the audible matter of the advertisement shall not be excessively 'loud';

(7) No advertisement which endangers the safety of children or creates in them any interest in unhealthy practices or shows them begging or in an undignified or indecent manner shall not be carried in the cable service.

(8) Indecent, vulgar, suggestive, repulsive or offensive themes or treatment shall be avoided in all advertisements.

(9) No advertisement which violates the standards of practice for advertising agencies as approved by the Advertising Agencies Association of India, Bombay, from time to time shall be carried in the cable service.

(10) All advertisement should be clearly distinguishable from the programme and should not in any manner interfere with the programme viz., use of lower part of screen to carry captions, static or moving alongside the programme.

Guidelines for Advertising on AIR and Doordarshan

a. Advertisement on cigarettes, bidis or tobacco products, pan masala, alcoholic drinks and other intoxicants, gold and silver jewellery, precious stones are not allowed for broadcast.

b. The spots on aerated water (soft drinks) should contain statutory declaration that it contains no fruit juice/fruit pulp and is artificially flavoured and does not contain BVO.

c. Medicinal products should be accompanied by 5 copies of the script (in Hindi or English), 5 copies of the list of ingredients (with percentage) and a sample to get the approval of the Drugs Controller before broadcast.
d. Medicinal spots are always accepted as fixed spots.
e. Ads should not contain any exaggerated, superlative or misleading claim.
f. All those engaged in advertising are strongly recommended to familiarize themselves with the legislation affecting advertising in this country, particularly the following Acts and the Rules framed under them as amended from time to time:
   i. Drugs and Cosmetics Act, 1940
   ii. Drugs Control Act, 1950.
   iii. Drugs and Magic Remedies (Objectionable advertisements) Act, 1954.
   iv. Copyright Act. 1957.
   v. Trade and Merchandise Marks Act, 1958
   vi. Provision of Food Adulteration Act, 1954.
   vii. Pharmacy Act, 1948.
   viii. Prize Competition Act, 1955.
   viii. Emblems and Names (Prevention of Improper Use) Act, 1950
   ix. Consumer Production Act, 1990.
   x. Indecent Representation of Women (Prohibition) Act, 1986.
   xi. Code of Ethics for advertising in India issued by the Advertising Council of India.
   xii. Code of Standards in relation to the advertising of medicines and treatments.
   xiii. Standards of Practice for Advertising Agencies.
   xiv. Code for Commercial Broadcasting, copy of which may be had from the Central States Unit.
g. Advertising shall be so designed as to conform to the Laws of the Country and should not offend against morality, decency, and religious susceptibilities of the people.

h. NO ADVERTISEMENT SHALL BE PERMITTED WHICH
   i. derides any race, caste, colour, creed and nationality;
   ii. is against any of the directive principles, or any other provision of the Constitution of India:
   iii. tends to incite people to crime, cause disorder or violence, or breach of law of glorifies violence or obscenity in any way:
   iv. presents criminality as desirable;
   v. adversely affects friendly relation with Foreign States;
   vi. exploits the national emblem, or any part of the Constitution or the person or personality of a national leader or state dignitary.

Code for Commercial Advertising on Doordarshan

This Code was presented to Parliament in mid 1987. It incorporates the Indecent Representation of Women Act and the Consumer Act, both of which were passed by parliament in 1986. It suggests 33 Do's and Don'ts for advertisers. Here are some of them.

Advertisements should conform to laws and should not offend against morality, decency and the religious susceptibilities of people.

The success of advertising depends on public confidence and no practice should be permitted which tends to impair this.

The Director General shall be the sole judge of the Code.

The following advertisements should not be permitted:
1. Ads which deride any race, caste, colour, creed and nationality, or are against the Directive Principles or the Constitution.
2. Ads which tend to incite people to crime or cause order or adversely affect friendly relations with foreign states.
3. Ads which exploit national emblem, any part of the constitution, or the person/personality or national leaders or state dignitaries.

4. No advertisement shall be presented as news:
5. Ads which have any relation to religion, political or industrial dispute.
6. Ads which promote chit funds, money lenders, jewelry fortune letters, foreign goods, and private saving schemes.
7. Guaranteed goods will have to be made available to Director-General of Doordarshan for inspection if necessary.
8. No disparaging or derogatory remarks of other products or comparison with them should be made.
9. Ads which portray women as passive or submissive.
10. Ads which are likely to startle viewers such as gunfire, sirens, bombardments, screams, and raucous laughter.

FOR FURTHER READING

A. BROADCASTING HISTORY, CULTURE AND IDEOLOGY

1. Audience Research Unit, *Doordarshan* - (Annual Surveys), New Delhi: Ministry of Information and Broadcasting.
2. Melissa Butcher: *Transnational Television, Cultural Identity and Change: When STAR Came to India*, New Delhi: Sage Publications, 2003.
3. P.C. Chatterjee: *Broadcasting in India*, New Delhi: Sage, 1987.
4. N.L. Chowla: *Listening and Viewing*, New Delhi, 1991.
5. David French and Michael Richards (Eds.): *Contemporary Television: Asian Perspectives*, New Delhi: Sage, 1996.
6. David French and Michael Richards (Eds.): *Television in Contemporary Asia*, New Delhi: Sage, 2000.
7. K. Moti Gokulsing: *Soft-Soaping India: The World of Indian Television Soap Operas*, London: Trentham Books, 2004.
8. Nilanjana Gupta: *Switching Channels: Ideologies of Television in India*. New Delhi: Oxford University Press, 1998.
9. Vanita Kohli-Khandekar: *The Indian Media Business*, New Delhi: Response Books, 2006. Second Ed.
10. Prabha Krishnan and Anita Dighe: *Affirmation and Denial: Construction of Femininity on Indian Television*, New Delhi: Sage Publications, 1990.
11. H.R. Luthra: *Indian Broadcasting*, New Delhi: Publications Division, 1986.

12. Purnima Mankekar: *Screening Television, Viewing Cultures: An Ethnography of Television, Womanhood and Nation in Post-Colonial India*, Durham N.C.: Duke University, 1999.
13. Nalin Mehta: *India on Television: How Satellite News Channels Have Changed the Way We Think and Act*, New Delhi: HarperCollins, 2008.
14. Srinivas Melkote, Peter Shields and Binod C. Agrawal (Eds.): *International Satellite Broadcasting in South Asia*, New York: University Press of America, 1998.
15. Mridula Menon: *Indian television and Video Programmes:* Trends *and Policies*, New Delhi: Kanishka Publishers, 2007.
16. A. Mitra: Television *and Popular Cultures: A Study of Mahabharat*, New Delhi: Sage Publications, 1993.
17. Anjali Monteiro: 'Official Television and Unofficial Fabrications of the Self: The Spectator as Subject' in Ashish Nandy(Ed.): *The Secret Politics of Our Desires*, New Delhi: Oxford University Press, 1998.
18. Sevanti Ninan: *The Magic Window*, New Delhi: Penguin 1996.
19. Mehra Masani: *Broadcasting and the People*, New Delhi, National Board Trust, 1985.
20. Latika Padgaonkar: *The Killing Fields,* New Delhi: UNESCO, 2000.
21. David Page and William Crowley: *Satellites over South Asia*, New Delhi: Sage, 2001.
22. Arvind Rajagopal: *Politics after Television – Hindu Nationalism and the Reshaping of the Public in India*, Cambridge University Press/Foundation Books, 4764/2a Ansari Road, Daryaganj, New Delhi. 2000.
23. Amrita Shah: *Hype, Hypocrisy and Television in Urban India*, New Delhi: Vikas Publications, 1997.
24. Arvind Singhal and Everett Rogers: *India's Communication Revolution: From Bullock Cart to* Cyber Mart, New Delhi: Sage, 2001.
25. Waheeda Sultana: *Women and Media – Women in Soap Operas.*
26. Namita Unnikrishnan and Shailaja Bajpai: *Impact of Television Advertising on Children*, Sage Publications, New Delhi, 1995.
27. U. Zacharias: 'The Smile of Mona Lisa: Postcolonial Desires, Nationalist Families and the Birth of Consumer Television in India', *Critical Studies in Mass Communication*, Vol. 20. No. 4, pp. 388-406.

B. REPORTS

1. *AKASH BHARATI - National Broadcast Trust,* Vols. 1 & II, (New Delhi: Publications Division, Ministry of Information and Broadcasting, 1978).
2. *An Indian Personality for Television: Report of the Working Group on Software for Doordarshan.* Vol. I & II New Delhi: Publications Division, 1985.

WEB RESOURCES

1. www.indiantelevision.com (For news and trends on Indian television)
2. www.ddindia.com (Doordarshan)
3. www.ddindia.net (Doordarshan on the Internet)
4. www.ddnews.com (Doordarshan's News Channel)
5. www.mib.nic.in(For all official documents published by Ministry of Information and Broadcasting)
6. www.thehoot.org (For critical articles on Indian TV)
7. www.screenindia.com (News and updates on a weekly basis from Screen)
8. www.cableandsatellite.com (Cable and Satellite Magazine)
9. www.adi-media.com (Broadcast and CableSat Magazine)
10. www.balajitelefilms.com
11. www.cable-quest.in

REVIEW QUESTIONS

1. What factors came together to promote the development of television in India?
2. How has television affected the performance of other mass media in India?
3. What influences have radio and television had on other media, and on Indian life?
4. How has cross-border satellite TV revolutionised the media scenario in India?
5. What has been the role of advertising and 'product placements' in TV programming?

THE MASS MEDIA - HISTORY, PRACTICES, VALUES

6. What is TV 'scheduling'?
7. Write short notes on:
   (a) Cable and Satellite Television
   (b) Television Genres and Formats
   (c) Reality TV
   (d) Soap Operas
   (e) CAS and DTH
   (f) The Broadcasting Bill
   (g) Sports Channels
   (h) Religious Channels
   (i) 'Sting' Operations on News Channels.

SUGGESTED PROJECTS

1. Critically analyse the format and content of two popular TV programmes. What 'genre/s' do they belong to?
2. Visit a TV Station to find out how it is organised, and how it produces programmes.
3. Write a script for a short television play. Note the differences between a radio script and a television script.
4. Interview a television personality or a programme producer about his/her work.
5. What are the differences between news on radio and news on TV? Do a content analysis of a radio news bulletin and a television news bulletin beamed on the same evening.
6. Watch a TV news bulletin. Note down the various news items in the order in which they are reported. What do you think is the basis of this order? Are there any 'news values' at work here? Do you agree with the way news is 'ordered'?
7. Make a list of the 'game shows' on Indian TV. Find out which original formats they are 'clones' of.
8. Analyse the TV schedule given in your daily newspaper. Make a list of the television 'genres' mentioned in the schedule. Discuss the historical origins of these 'genres'.
9. Look up the website www.tamindia.com. Find out the TV ratings for the previous week's programmes. What are the methods used for 'rating' programmes?

10. Go to the site www.indiantelevision.com. What does it say about the 'current trends' in Indian television? Describe these 'trends' in your own words.

RECORDED MUSIC INDUSTRY

The Indian recorded music industry had its beginnings in 1907 when the Gramophone Company of India (Gramco, or better known as HMV) opened an office in Calcutta, though gramophones were being imported since 1898. The gramophone came to Tamilnadu in the early twenties, and it was something of a revolution since it was the first time that music became accessible to all, irrespective of caste or class.[1] The first recording of an Indian song took place in 1902 in Bombay. During the first decade of the arrival of the gramophone in India, the records released were confined to classical music, though eventually folk songs, patriotic songs and devotional hymns (bhavgeet) also came to be recorded and sold in large numbers.

But it was only when the talkies became popular around 1931 that the record industry really took off. Gramco's sales were initially of English songs but in a few years Indian artistes, especially the mehfil and quwali singers too had their songs recorded and issued on discs. The standard disc at the time was seven inches in diameter, and had a speed of 78rpm. This restricted the length of a song to three and a half minutes. Later, 12 inch discs were introduced to provide for an extra minute of playing time.

The EMI (Electrical and Musical Instruments Ltd.) was established on April 20, 1931, through a merger of Columbia Company and Gramophone Company; the German Odeon and the French Pathe soon joined the group. Thus in the early thirties EMI was the largest music company in India and the world, though the individual units continued to use their individual labels: HMV, Twin, Zonophone and Columbia.

Music Industry after Independence

Gramco ruled the roost until first Polydor and then the Indian Record Company (INRECO) entered the Indian music market, in 1969 and 1973 respectively. In 1982, CBS/Tata launched its own

---

1   Theodore Bhaskaran: *The Message Bearers*, Madras.

venture at the height of the disco fever in Bombay. (The company was later taken over by R.V. Pandit). In the seventies, the Indian music industry's combined turnover stood at Rs. 30 million. During the next decade it rose dramatically to Rs. 200 million, and in the mid-nineties to a whopping Rs. 7,500 million. By the turn of the century, the industry was worth around Rs. 10,000 million.

According to one estimate, the global music industry is now worth over $30 billion, out of which India's share is barely $250 million. However, while worldwide almost 95% of the music sold is in the form of compact discs (CDs), in India compact discs comprise a mere six per cent of all music sold; audio-cassettes, which are much cheaper, continue to dominate the Indian market of a hundred million consumers.[2] CD players have to be imported at inflated prices and are thus far beyond the reach of these consumers.

Almost every major international player in the global music business has a presence now in India. These include EMI-Virgin Records, Sony Music Entertainment, Warner Bros, Polygram, Gramco (formerly HMV), BMG-Crescendo, CBS Records, and others. EMI, a London-based company, has a joint venture with the RPG's Gramaphone Company of India, and Warner Bros has tied up with Delhi-based Music Today, a unit of Living Media, the publishers of India Today. Indian companies include T-Series, Bombino Music, Magnasound, Oriental Records, Plus Music, Super Records, Venus, Tips, Time, Zee Music, Padmini Music, Superhits, Concord, Pan Music and several others. Tape recorder production is mostly in the hands of around 600 units in the small scale sector. Over a million cassette-recorders/players are sold each year. On average, 25 million music cassettes are sold every month, with over 10 million, according to the Indian Music Industry Association (IMI) (affiliated to the International Federation of Phonographic Industry (IFPI) being pirated versions. The Indian music industry was estimated in 1995 to be worth Rs. 899 crores, growing at 15-20% per annum

---

2 Report of the MTV-Times Forum seminar in Bombay, *Screen*, July 15, 1998.

on average.³ In 2003 the FICCI-KPMG Report estimated that the revenues of the Indian music industry, including both the organized and unorganized sectors, amounted to Rs. 6.2 billion, a decline of 23% from the previous year; the decline was attributed to: lackluster performance of the film industry; high cost of acquisition rights and increased piracy levels.⁴ IMI representatives believe that pirated music sales comprise around 40% of the Indian music market.⁵ But the 2008 FICCI-PriceWaterhouse Coopers Report⁶ suggests that the industry is steadily growing but has yet to make a mark at the international level. It valued the Indian recorded music industry to be around Rs. 1500 crores (US$300 million) and was expected to double in five years.⁷ The overseas market was estimated to be about ten per cent of the total market, with some labels selling over 400,000 units in around 20 countries.⁸ Further, the mobile music industry was worth as much as the mainstream recorded music industry. The Report estimated the size of the mobile music industry (ring tones, caller ringback tones) to be about Rs. 720 crores.⁹

Major Indian Music Labels

1. Saregama India Ltd.
2. Sony-BMG
3. Super Cassette
4. Yash Raj Music
5. T-Series
6. Tips
7. Music Today
8. Times Music
9. BIG Music
10. Universal Music
11. Eros International
12. EMI
13. Virgin
14. Warner Music

---

3   Cf. Aarti Dua and Vikram Bhat: 'Developing an Eye for Music', *Business Standard*, January 1, 1997.
4   FICCI-KPMG Report on The Indian Entertainment Sector, 2003, p.57.
5   ibid.
6   FICCI-PriceWaterhouse-Coopers Report: Indian Entertainment and Media Industry – Sustaining Growth-2008.
7   Ibid.
8   Ibid.
9   Ibid.

The 'Remix' Phenomenon

'Remix albums' turned into a rage in the eighties and nineties because of the growing interest among young music listeners in the cities in disco rhythms and superior sound quality. At the same time, their interest in old film songs remained intact. The new 'remixed' music was produced by re-recording old numbers with a new beat (popularly known as 'jhankar' beat). This generally involved first re-recording the rhythm track and then superimposing a vocal track on it. Where the music company had the rights to the song, the original vocal track would be used; else, the vocal track too would be re-recorded. Almost all music majors in India are involved in the business of 're-mixes', with T-Series, Tips and Venus the leaders in the field. Examples of successful remix albums are HMV's 'Mere Sapnon Ki Rani', Polygram's Rahul and I (an Asha Bhosale remix album). Over two hundred remix albums were released in 1997 and 1998.[10] The practice of recording 'remixes' or 'cover versions' has become even more rampant with further developments in digital technologies for recording and also for storage and playback such as MP3, iPods, Zunes and iPhones. Thanks to the ubiquitous presence of the Internet and mobile telephones, the music industry has several revenue streams beyond radio, television and physical sales of audio-cassettes and CDs. Indeed, the declining sales of the latter can be attributed to the growth of the Internet and the ease with which millions can freely download music and share music files with netizens around the world. In order to fight such practices, music companies now offer their recordings on the Internet and mobile telephones for a nominal fee but even this is resented. The industry is as a result plagued by plagiarism and rampant piracy.

Music Genres

Film songs and film music continue to dominate the Indian music industry, though it is not just Hindi Bollywood that reigns supreme; Tamil, Telugu, Malayalam, and Kannada reign in the

---

10 Jaya Wagle: 'Re-mixes Move Up the Charts', *Screen*, July 25, 1997, p.33.

South, and Panjabi and Bhojpuri in the North. This holds true for other genres too: devotional music, for instance, is produced in different Indian languages and for the many religious groups that comprise the diverse populations of our land. Classical and semi-classical of both Hindustani and Carnatic traditions too are produced in terms of the many instrumental and vocal practices extant in different regions of India. Folk music traditions have a minor share of the market but they are in one way or other present in most genres.

Genre	Market Share
Film Music	65 – 70%
Indi-Pop	10 – 15%
Devotional Music	10%
Classical Music	5%
International Music	5%
Other Genres (Regional etc.)	5%

(Source: Vanita Kohli-Khandekar: *The Indian Media Business*, p. 144.)

'Indi-pop' Challenges Film Music

Two events in Asian broadcasting provided a fillip to Indian interest in international music in the eighties and nineties. The first was the initiative taken by Doordarshan in 1982 to telecast the pre-Grammy and the Grammy Awards; the second was the launch exactly a decade later of two satellite music channels: MTV and [V]. Later, the Zee TV and other major television networks launched their own music channels. Music videos (called 'promos' sometimes), which are provided free to the satellite music TV channels, have now become the major marketing instrument; other marketing strategies include road shows, live concerts and sponsored events. More than 75% of the cost of launching a pop album (average cost is estimated at two million rupees) is spent on marketing.[11] Channel V and MTV air the music videos for free, but other satellite channels have different rates for telecasting the videos.[12]

11 Dua and Bhat, *op. cit.*
12 Dua and Bhat, *op cit.*

Until the mid-nineties, popular music in India was synonymous with film music, and the recorded music industry was totally oriented to such music, with some attention given to classical, semi-classical, religious and folk music, and ghazals and quwalis. Indi-pop (or Indian pop) made its appearance in 1994 with Alisha Chinai breaking into the scene with her album entitled 'Made in India'. Its title song was launched as a music video on Star TV's [V] music channel. Perhaps for the first time in non-film popular music, the sales soared to 2.2 million copies. Later in the same year another unknown singer, the Panjabi pop singer Daler Mehndi stormed his way to the top of the charts with his Bhangra-based 'Bolo Ta Ra Ra', recording sales of 1.5 million copies. Here too the satellite music channel played a major role in promoting the singer. The following year saw the Colonial Cousins sell 400,000 copies and Lucky Ali (with his album entitled 'Sunoh') sell over half a million copies. Nusrat Fateh Ali Khan and Javed Akhtar's 'Sangam' also sold half a million copies each during the same year. 'Indi-pop' had arrived. Other singers who made their mark in this non-film genre included Baba Sehgal, Shweta Shetty, Remo Fernandes, and A.R. Rehman. In recent years, a variety of singers has topped the charts; these include Abhijeet Sawant, Himesh Reshammiya, Rabbi Shergill, Sukhvinder Singh, Sonu Nigam, Shaan, Sunidhi Chauhan and Adnan Sami. In south Indian music industry, singers like Ilayaraj, A.R. Rahman, S.P. Subramaniam continue to rule the roost. Singers from all over the country have now come together to establish the Singers Association of India (SAI) to represent their interests with music companies and also with PPL and IMI.

Music on Radio and Television

FM radio stations, satellite radio (like WorldSpace) and television channels are major avenues for the growth of the music industry. Much of the programming on FM radio channels, like AIR's Vividh Bharati, is dedicated to music, primarily to film music. This is equally true of round-the-clock music channels on television. But besides the dedicated music channels, television programming on all general entertainment channels (GEC) in the various Indian languages includes several music-based genres. 'Talent hunt' programmes focused on singing, dancing and acting are based largely on Indian film music. The most successful perhaps has been 'Indian Idol' on the Sony channel (using the American Idol format) which involves the selection of the most talented singer in the country. The first Indian Idol winner was Abhijeet Sawant who turned into a singing star overnight. His album has sold over 900,000 copies. Channel V organised a talent hunt programme called 'Popstars' which involved the nationwide search for a five member all-girl band of singers. Called Viva, the winning band of girls released two albums and then went their separate ways. A similar vein a music project called 'the Underground' was conducted by Saregama India in the pubs, and clubs of Mumbai, Delhi and Kolkata in 1980 to select 30 music performers (bands, artistes and DJs). Saregama produced three tracks on CDs called the Underground Delhi, The Underground Mumbai and The Underground Kolkata and the new original artistes received advances against royalties. Further, young film makers were invited to produce 30 music videos which were uploaded on www.myspace.com and viewers had to select the winning videos. The whole project was marketed by My Space, a leading daily and on mobiles.[13] This trend in the search for new and original singers and in marketing their talent suggests the music industry is desperate to move away from the age-old dominance of film music.

Main Music Channels on Indian Television
1. MTV
2. Channel V
3. VH – 1
4. Zee Music
5. BFU Music
6. Sun Music
7. Gemini Music
8. SS (Southern Spice)
9. 9X M
10. Enter Ten
11. Music India
12. ETC

---

13 Report in *Screen*, Mumbai, 3 July 2008. p. 26.

According to Rhythm House (Bombay) figures, over three per cent out of the 21,000 titles sold in India is in the Indi-pop category, that is, as many as 600 titles. In terms of turnover, however, it is 11% of all sales. This is expected to soar to 30% by the end of the century.[14] Music majors are delighted with this development since they find that Indi-pop is a cheaper alternative to exorbitant payments for purchase of film music rights. Some companies such as Gramco and Polygram have moved into film production with the focus on song numbers so that even where the film fails, music sales could make up for the losses at the box-office. Polygram's film *Khamoshi* and Gramco Film's *Sapnay*, for instance, made Rs. 15 million each from sales of recorded songs.[15] The advent of the music company in film production, it is widely believed, has boosted the quality of Hindi music.

Hindi film music continues to be the most popular category of the music scene, with a little more than 50% of the market dedicated exclusively to this genre. Audiocassettes of the music of the two blockbuster films, *Dilwale Dulhaniya Le Jayenge* and *Hum Apke Hain Kaun* have sold over 10 million copies. Indi-pop has cornered 35% of the market while international (western) music has around 15%.[16]

The other categories such as regional language film music, classical and semi-classical music, devotional music and folk music have also gained in popularity during recent years. Two of India's largest publishing houses, Living Media (publishers of *India Today*) and Bennett-Coleman & Co. Ltd. (BCCL) (publishers of the *Times of India*) have entered the music business with their Music Today and Times Music labels respectively. They have set the current trend for diversification and cross-media ownership in the country's entertainment industry.

The Indian music industry is worth over Rs. 1,150 crores. The phenomenal rise of the mobile telephone industry, the Internet,

---

14 ibid.
15 Report in *The Economic Times*, May 24, 1997.
16 Report of the MTV-Times Forum seminar in Bombay, *Screen*, July 15, 1998. p.

music channels on television and FM radio stations during the first decade of the new millennium provided the music industry additional revenue streams. Ring-tones and music downloads helped the cash registers of the music labels to buzz again. Ringtone downloads alone gave the industry an additional revenue of Rs. 400 crores. The increase in the number of music channels and music-based television shows and contests gave further hope to the ailing music industry.[17] Liberalisation of the media industries led to some music companies tying up with multinational labels and also to the tapping of resources through the issue of IPOs. International music companies such as I K Multimedia, Native Instruments, and Cakewalk have got together to form the International Music Software Trade Association (IMSTA) to create awareness of software piracy. SudeepAudio.com from India has joined as a member from India. Further, FICCI (Federation of Indian Chamber of Commerce and Industry) has joined IMI (Indian Music Industry) in a national initiative against piracy.[18] With a force of over 80 retired police officers and direct contacts with sub-inspectors and other officers, raids are conducted regularly on pirates and counterfeiters.

FOR FURTHER READING

1. Aziz Ashraf: *Light of the Universe: Essays on Hindustani Film Music*, New Delhi: Three Essays Collective, 2003.
2. Ganesh Anantharaman: *Bollywood Melodies: A History of the Hindi Film Song*, New Delhi: Penguin, 2008.
3. Bhaskar Chandavarkar: 'Tradition of Music in Indian Cinema', *Cinema in India*, April 1987, pp.8-11.
4. Bhaskar Chandavarkar: 'Now It's the Bombay Film Song', *Cinema in India*, July-September 1987, pp.18-23.

---

17 Abhilasha Ojha: 'What's Wrong with India's Music Industry?' www.rediff.com. 5 September 2005.
18 Cf. Vijay Lazarus's Powerpoint presentation entitled 'FICCI National Initiative Against Piracy', www.ficci.com/media-room/. 26 April 2007.

5. Bhaskar Chandavarkar: 'The Power of the Popular Film Song', *Cinema in India*, April-June 1990, pp.20-24.
6. G.N. Joshi: 'A Concise History of the Phonograph Industry in India', *Popular Music*, Vol. 7, No. 2 (May 1987), pp. 147-156.
7. Ann E. Kaplan: *Rocking Around the Clock: Music Television, Postmodernism, and Consumer Culture*, New York: Methuen, 1987.
8. Peter Manuel: *Cassette Culture: Popular Music and Technology in North India*, New Delhi: Oxford University Press, 1993.
9. Ashok Ranade: *On Music and Musicians of Hindoostan*, New Delhi: Promila Publications, 1984.
10. Ashok Ranade: *Hindi Film Song: Music Beyond Boundaries*, New Delhi/Chicago: Promila Publishers/Bibliophile South Asia, 2006.

WEB RESOURCES

1. www.ficci.com/media-room/
2. www.televisionpoint.com
3. www.musicandradio.com

SUGGESTED PROJECTS

1. Draw up a list of your ten favourite singers or musicians. Which 'music labels' publish/distribute their work?
2. Listen to a recording of your favourite music video. What are the elements in the video that make it appealing to you and your friends?
3. Find out which international/multinational music labels have a presence in the Indian music industry. What are the music genres that they specialize in publishing in India?
4. Make a list of the websites on the Internet that provide you free access to the different Indian music genres.
5. Listen to the songs in your favourite album. Then write a music review for a Sunday newspaper.
6. Find out which newspapers and magazines publish a regular column on popular music releases.

BOOK PUBLISHING

The Beginnings

The beginnings of the book publishing industry in India can be traced to the establishment of the first printing presses in Goa in 1566, and in Tranqabar (near Madras) and Serampore (near Calcutta) two hundred years later in the 18th century. Between 1801 and 1832, the Serampore Mission Press alone published 212,000 volumes in fifty languages. The volumes were not restricted to religious books in English and the Indian languages; indeed, a substantial number was devoted to secular and educational materials.[1] It was only after the colonial government's decision in 1835 that all higher education would be through the medium of English that book publishing came to be dominated by English because of the need for textbooks in that language.[2] In 1881, a survey of books published in Bombay Presidency indicates that 931 books in European and Indian languages were published. Of these, only 117 were in European languages; the other books were in Marathi, Gujarati, Kannada, Sindhi and Hindi, with a few in Sanskrit, Persian and Arabic and two each in Zend and Magadhi.[3] Thus, only 12% of the books published in the Bombay Presidency were in English as against 40% today.[4]

The Indian branches of major British publishers were the first to capitalise on the demand for textbooks in English for high schools and colleges. Many British publishers like Macmillan, Kegan Paul and John Murray established a 'colonial' library – a list of books to be shipped only to India.[5] By the thirties, Indian publishers too had entered the business of textbook publishing,

---

1 Samuel Israel: 'Indian Publishing' in Jane R. Caleb (Ed.): *Christian Publishing: The Indian Experience*, New Delhi: ISPCK, 1984, pp.23-29. See also Samuel Israel: *A Career in Book Publishing*, New Delhi: National Book Trust, 1996.
2 Samuel Israel: 'Indian Publishing', p.24.
3 ibid.
4 ibid.
5 Sridhar Balan: 'Turned on by Indian Books', *The Times of India*, 13 May 2005, p.12.

and despite shortages of paper during the war years considerable progress was made in the field. The publication of fiction and non-fiction as well as scholarly books also progressed moderately. Pre-independence publishing of books of general interest was largely influenced by the national struggle for freedom. Even much of the fiction written in those times reflected these national concerns. Thus general publishing in India during the years between the wars was often politically and socially oriented. Much of such material was published in the Indian languages, but a majority of the longer works were in English.[6]

The years of World War II witnessed a growth in political and social consciousness, and this gave rise to political publishing; this trend continued in the years preceding independence and the decade that followed the attainment of independence. The rapid expansion of education across the newly formed linguistic states in the country, and with this the establishment of the libraries in schools, colleges, universities and other institutions of learning, led to the further expansion of the book publishing industry. Immediately after independence, several Indian publishers moved into textbook publishing for schools (where British publishers still dominated), but the 'nationalisation' of this sector brought an end to such ventures. University textbooks continued to remain in the private sector, but here too the United States and British publishers dominated with their cheap reprints of standard texts in medicine, engineering, the natural and social sciences and literature. A Subsidy Scheme assisted some Indian publishers of university textbooks.

Publishing after Independence

During the fifties and sixties the publishing industry grew steadily, but suffered a severe setback in the early seventies when the official prices of paper shot up and there was an acute scarcity of supplies. The Government stepped in with a control and concessional regime of paper production and supply. In

---

6 Samuel Israel, op cit

1967, the National Book Development Board (later the National Book Development Council) was established to promote the development of the book trade and industry. Besides setting up bodies like the National Book Trust and the Raja Ram Mohan Roy Educational Resource Centres, the Central Government launched a number of schemes for the publication of low-cost editions of foreign reprints, and a massive programme of bringing out university level books in Indian languages. In this programme, the Centre finances and coordinates the work of State institutions and universities engaged in the work of translation, compilation, writing and publishing of university level books in Indian languages.[7]

The Indian book publishing industry today is a 'cottage industry'[8] comprising the public and private sectors. In the public sector, book enterprises range from those of the various ministries of the Central and State Governments to semi-official and state-funded bodies such as the National Book Trust, the Children's Book Trust, the Sahitya Akademi and the Indian Standard Institution. Over 450 agencies in the public sector publish on a regular basis. The leading publishing house in the public sector is the Publications Division, a unit of Ministry of Information and Broadcasting. The unit was established in 1941 as a branch of the Bureau of Public Information and publishes 21 journals and around a hundred book titles each year in English, Hindi and other Indian languages.

The private sector is organised around small and medium-sized firms. It is estimated that there are around 10,000 small publishers, 2,000 medium-sized publishing firms, and 300 large publishing houses. No more than around 25 of the large publishers are equipped with adequate distribution facilities, sources of capital and professional expertise. The small and medium-sized publishers release books sporadically. A good number of authors publish their own books.

India is one of the top ten publishers in the world, and the

---

7 D. Raghavan: *An Introduction to Book Publishing*, New Delhi: Institute of Book Publishing, 1988. p.16.
8 ibid. p.20.

third largest publisher of books in English (around 11,400 titles per annum) next only to Great Britain (95,000 titles) and the United States (51,800 titles).[9] On average, around 22,000 new titles are brought out each year, with over half the titles being in English. The share of titles in Hindi is around 15%, Tamil around 9%, Marathi 7.5%, and Bengali 6.5%. However, India's share in the world's book market is barely three per cent. This works out to about 20 books per million of India's population in comparison with 420 books per million of the population of Europe.

According to Balan, a publishing professional, there are about 16,000 publishers in the country producing an estimated 70,000 titles every year. The annual turnover of the industry is estimated at Rs. 700 crore. A good 40% of the titles are in English, making India the largest producer of books in the English language after the UK and the US.[10] However, as Table 37 shows, the Indian book publishing industry has a long way to go to catch up with the per capita book title output of the developed countries.

Table 37: Per Capita Book Title Output (International)

Year	Country	Per Capita Output Per 100,000 People
2000	United States	43.2
2000	United Kingdom	212.2
2000	Germany	100.0
2000	France	87.0
2005	China	9.9
2004	India	6.3

(Data Source: The Book Publishing Opportunity in India-2007)[11]

---

9   Source of number of titles published: UNESCO Statistical Yearbook 1996 and Human Development Report 1997. Quoted in Ulla Carlsson and Cecilia von Feilitzen (Eds.): *Children and Media Violence*, UNESCO/Nordicom, 1998, pp.281-283.
10 Sridhar Balan, op. cit
11 'The Book Publishing Opportunity in India: A Macro-view', www.prayatna.typepad/publishing/2007/09/the-book-publis.html. Accessed on 20 April 2008.

Table 38: Output of the Indian Book Publishing Industry

Year	No. of Titles	Year	No. of Titles
1950-51	1,289	1978-79	18,584
1954-55	18,559	1979-80	16,466
1959-60	10,741	1980-81	17,158
1964-65	13,095	1983-84	14,202
1973-74	17,600	1986-87	16,970
1975-76	22,000	2003-04	70,000
2004-05	75,000*	2005-06	80,000*

* Estimates (Compiled from UNESCO Statistical Yearbooks; Altbach et al; Israel (1996); Balan (2005)

Paperbacks and Textbooks

The paperback movement was ushered into India by Jaico Publishing House in the 1940s, just a few years after the launch of Pocket Books in the United States, Penguin Books in Britain and Albatross Series in Germany.[12] Hind Pocket Books too went into paperback book publishing two decades later. Some of its titles in English, Hindi, Urdu and Panjabi have had print-runs of over 100,000 copies. Their nationwide distribution channels have ensured phenomenal sales. Hind Pocket Books' series on self-improvement, India's poet-saints, Indian language fiction and translations of popular writers in regional languages have earned it the gratitude of book lovers. Its book club, Gharelu Library Yojana, which has a membership of more than a hundred thousand ensures regular sales of its titles. Star Publications (Private) Ltd. too has made a name for itself in the world of paperbacks. Taking their cue from HPB and Star, other major publishers have set up their paperback units. Orient Longman's paperback unit is Sangam, Arnold-Heinemann's is Mayfair, Oxford University Press' is Three Coins, Vikas's is Bell Books, Vision's is Orient Paperbacks, and Sage India's is Response.

---

12 Cf. 'How It All Began: A Swift History of American Mass Market Paperbacks', *Publishers Weekly*, May 26, 1989.

Thus it is that renowned Indian and foreign writers have come within the reach of the literate masses.

In the area of children's literature, India Book House, the National Book Trust and the Children's Book Trust, Chandamama and Living Media are the leaders. However, the number of titles for children barely exceeds 500, excluding titles in comics. With a child population exceeding 45% of the total, such an output is woefully inadequate. Children's Book Trust is perhaps the only non-government organisation dedicated solely to publishing books for children in Hindi and English.

The craze for comics mushroomed in the early 1980s after the success of the Amar Chitra Katha series of India Book House. Launched by Anant Pai and India Book House, the series sold around a hundred thousand copies each fortnight. The focus was on biographies of eminent men and women and Indian myth and folklore. New titles were issued every year, some of them translated into several Indian and foreign languages. According to one estimate over 86 million copies of around 436 titles were sold abroad. Indrajal Comics of the Times of India Group proved very successful in the Indian and export market. Other titles in the series included *Phantom, Bahadur and Garth*. In 2005, riding on the wave of the mobile telephone boom, comics found a new media platform: 'momics' or comics for mobiles.[13] India Book House now plans to re-market the whole Amar Chitra Katha series as animation films for the big screen, 'momics' for the multimedia mobile and as 'video games' for the PC and consoles.[14]

However, the most lucrative sector of Indian book publishing continues to be the textbook sector. The nationalisation of the text book industry (especially for schools) hit the private sector hard, even as it gave rise to a racket in cheap guides and texts brought out by small publishers. The National Book Trust, the National Council for Educational Research (NCERT), the University Grants Commission (UGC), the Indian Council for

---

13 See Bindu Nair: 'Comics Make Way for Momics', *Impact*, May 23-29, 2005.
14 Ibid.

Social Science Research (ICSSR) and other autonomous bodies succeeded in marketing a good number of subsidised textbooks in English and the regional languages. Around 200 million copies of school and college textbooks are sold each year in the entire country. Besides, a fairly large library market in the states and relatively low publishing costs make book publishing an attractive investment opportunity for the informal business sector.

The Multinational Presence

Multinational book publishers tend to be dominant in all the sectors of Indian book publishing: fiction, non-fiction, school and college textbooks, dictionaries and encyclopaedias. Indian book publishing in English, for instance, is dominated by Orient Longman, Oxford University Press, McGraw-Hill and Thomson/ Pearson Learning for academic literature and by Rupa (which has a tie up with Harper Collins) and Penguin (which has a joint venture with Ananda Bazar Patrika) for general fiction and non-fiction titles. Oxford University Press (India) is a full-fledged subsidiary of Oxford University Press, with offices in the four metros and showrooms in six cities. It exports over a quarter of its Indian titles. Few books in English have print runs exceeding 3500 copies. The best selling authors in the Indian fiction category include Shoba De, Vikram Seth and Amitav Ghosh. British publishers account for over 55% of total imports from India; British book exports to India amounted to £6.4 million in 1991 and £17.2 million in 1995.[15]

The major book distribution outlets are India Book House, IBD and Westland Distribution. India Book House distributes the publications of Penguin India, and also children's books, mass market books as also cookery, management and coffee-table books. Penguin India has given its travel books to IBD for distribution, and also has its own regional network in four major cities. IBD has exclusive distributorship rights for most foreign

---

15 Devina Dutt: 'The Hardsell Begins', in *Business India*, January 27, 1997, p.118-120.

travel publications. IBH is the exclusive distributor for *Fortune International*, *The Economist* and the *Asian Wall Street Journal*, and also owns the chain of Crossword book stores, and promotes Book Clubs, while IBD runs the Fountainhead retail leisure stores in Bangalore and Madras.[16] Among other multinational publishers active in India are Harper-Collins, Random House, Hachette, Scholastic, Picador and Westland.

Westland Distribution is a collaboration between the Landmark retail chain and East-West Books (Madras), covering 250 booksellers in the region. East-West Books represents 40 United States and British publishers including Academic Press, Routledge and Faber and Faber. It also distributes the publications of Rupa and Rupa Harper-Collins. Perhaps the biggest publisher in the world is Bertelsmann which recently acquired Random House, the largest publisher in the United States. On the international scene, 'the old model in book publishing was signing big authors; the new model is marketing'.[17] Over 60% of books are now sold in chains and supermarkets, through book clubs, and over the Internet. The Bertelsmann Book Club has more than 25 million members in 19 countries, while Amazon.com, the world's largest cyber bookstore, sells over a million titles every year. Most of the major Indian publishers are now on the Internet, offering their entire catalogues and also e-shopping facilities directly to customers around the world. Publishing houses like the *Indian Express*, *The Times of India*, *Oulook*, Jaico Books and Hind Pocket Books have launched their own book clubs.

New Trends in the New Millennium

The central government's import policies, the domination of the industry by English language publishing, the strong multinational presence, piracy and above all the exorbitant price of paper, are the major areas of concern for the Indian book publishing industry. Import policies are meant to give an impetus

---

16 ibid.
17 Report in *The Economist/Economic Times*, April 5, 1998.

to indigenous publishing, and to help Indian publishers to compete with the multinational houses. Imported books form an important financial base for the Indian book industry, since there is a demand for the novels of major fiction writers such as John Grisham, James Hadley Chase, Harold Robbins and Irving Wallace, and for scholarly academic textbooks in medicine, engineering, and computers. So, piracy of imported fiction is rather worrisome to Indian publishers; so is the practice of the flooding of the Indian book market by 'remainders' from the United States and Britain, which are sold at throw-away prices to Indian importers. 'Remainders' is a tag pinned on books that have outlasted their utility in the west, and so have little sale value. In Mumbai, for instance, the book industry is worth around Rs. 2,000 million annually, out of which Rs. 600 million turnover comes from sales of imported books, and the 'remainder' business accounts for Rs. 200 million. Some of the established distributors who deal in imported books also deal in 'remainders'. Another common practice in Mumbai for private distributors of American books like Rajesh and Co. buy 'job lots' and dispose them off to pavement dwellers. Reprinting of popular Western titles, especially of textbooks and novels, is yet another common practice. Publishing houses like Prentice Hall, Tata-McGraw Hill (now McGraw-Hill), and Thomson/Wadsworth (now Pearson Education India) have churned out low-priced Indian editions of Western titles. Rupa and Jaico have been the leaders in the field, but Penguin too entered the reprint business in the eighties. Among the publishing houses active in the non-technical field have been IBH, Orient Paperbacks, Vision Books, Harper-Willis and L.B. Publishers. For technical books Wiley-Eastern, Affiliated East-West Press, Sterling Publishers, Allied Publishers and Oxford-India have been the leaders.[18]

At the dawn of the second millennium, however, things began to look up for the Indian book publishing industry. Liberalisation

---

18 M.A. Deviah: 'Reprint Boom in Book Industry', *The Indian Express*, January 26, 1992.

had opened up the trade in books to the global market. The government allowed 74% foreign direct investment in the publishing business and 100% in trading companies engaged in the export of books. Publishers of non-news magazines and journals were permitted 100% FDI. And several multinational publishers began outsourcing their editing, designing, printing and distribution jobs to Indian publishers. Indian reprints of foreign publications became a widespread practice owing to the growing market of English readers. This resulted in popular novels and even textbooks in medicine, engineering, management and mass communication being made available to Indian readers – at more affordable prices. It also made a small dent in the business of book piracy.

National book fairs have now become a regular feature of the book retail landscape; several Indian book publishers are frequent participants at international book fairs at Frankfurt and London. In 2007, for instance, 173 publishers participated in the Frankfurt Book Fair where an Indian pavilion was installed; over 300 Indian publishers visited the Fair. Training programmes in book publishing have yet to become a part of the university curriculum; Indira Gandhi National Open University (IGNOU) has pioneered a Diploma Course in Book Publishing, via its Distance Learning programme.

Book exports climbed from Rs.33 crore in 1991 to Rs. 360 crore in 2003.[19] And during the same period the export of print jobs grew from Rs. 12.3 crore to Rs. 94.2 crore. Indian and multinational publishers are now integrated into the global market and outsourcing pre-press and printing work to India has become widespread. The retailing of books too has been revolutionised with the growing nationwide chains of bookstores (Crossword, Landmark, Higginbothams, Wheeler), with some of them teaming up with supermarkets, shopping malls, music stores, restaurants and coffee shops to give books a greater visibility in the urban landscape. India Today has begun to publish a monthly list of 'Top Ten Bestsellers' compiled for it by

---

19 Sridhar Balan, op. cit

the market research agency, ORG-MARG. However, the source of the data gathered is only from 15 retail outlets in six cities of India. The Sunday papers too regularly publish their own lists of 'bestsellers' in fiction and non-fiction; the Book Review page has returned to most newspapers and news magazines.

The dramatic rise in general literacy, urbanization and the retail trade has given a fillip to book publishing not only in English but also Hindi, Tamil, Malayalam, Bengali and other Indian languages. Tamil publishing is one such success story, with New Horizon Media perhaps exemplifying the trend for the future of Indian publishing. Taking a cue from Indian media conglomerates, it raised funds from venture capital or private equity investors – perhaps the first venture capital investment in the Indian book publishing industry. New Horizon published a mere 50 titles in 2004 but now publishes around 500 titles across three languages and seven imprints, with each title selling an average of 2,500 copies.[20] Its Tamil stock market primer, *Alla Alla Panam*, for instance, has sold 25,000 copies every year since 2004.[21] It publishes biographies, travelogues, corporate histories and translations of well-known English books. It has an unorthodox approach to book distribution and retailing. It distributes its titles not just to regular bookshops but also to medical stores, supermarkets, temple shops, saree shops and even restaurants. It uses mobile vans to take the books around to 20 small towns of Tamilnadu and organizes regular 'road shows' to promote book reading.[22] Indian language book publishing is set to challenge the monopoly of English; newspaper publishers like *Dainik Jagran, Dainik Bhaskar, Malayala Manorama, Deenathanthi* and many others have shown how this could be done.

According to the Federation of Publishers and Bookstores Association of India (FPBAI), by 2010 India is slated to become a publishing hub and the publishing outsourcing industry alone

---

20 Samanth Suramanian: 'Making a Mark: How a Tamil Publisher Sells Books Like Toothpaste', MINT, 2 June 2008, p. 1.
21 Ibid.
22 Ibid.

is worth US$ 1.1 billion and the whole industry is valued at Rs. 7,000 crore.[23] However, the loss to piracy is estimated to be about 25%; the Association of Publishers in India (API) in its annual report (2005) estimates the loss to be Rs. 2500 crore.[24] The Washington-based IIPA (International Publishers Association) estimates the loss to the book trade because of piracy, including illegal photo-copying, to be as high as 39%.[25] It thus appears that the book publishing trade has to re-think its five-century old 'business model' in the age of the new media and the Internet, just as the cinema, music, radio, television, video and other media industries have been forced to do. It needs to lobby for a nationwide library movement and to chalk out a vision for a future where digital libraries, e-books, audio-books, m-books, etc. are likely to be vital modes of access to information and knowledge.

FOR FURTHER READING

1. Philip Altbach: *Publishing in India: An Analysis*, New Delhi: Oxford University Press, 1975.
2. Philip Altbach: A. Arboleda and S. Gopinathan (Eds.): *Publishing in the Third World: Knowledge and Development*, London: Mansell, 1985.
3. K.S. Duggal: *Book Publishing in India*, New Delhi: Marwah, 1980.
4. Federation of Indian Publishers: *Sixty Years of Book Publishing in India*, New Delhi, 2007.
5. Rob Francis: *India Publishing Market Profile*, London: Publishers Association, 2008.
6. Samuel Israel: *A Career in Book Publishing*, New Delhi: National Book Trust, 1996.
7. D.N. Malhotra and Narendra Kumar (Eds.): *Fifty Years of Book Publishing in India Since Independence*, New Delhi: Federation of Indian Publishers, 1998.

---

23 Report in The Times of India, 18 March 2006.
24 Ibid.
25 Ibid.

8. D.N. Malhotra: *Dare to Publish*, New Delhi: Clarion Boos, 2005.
9. D.N. Malhotra: 60 Years of Book *Publishing in India*, New Delhi: Federation of Indian Publishers 2007.
10. D. Raghavan: *An Introduction to Book Publishing*, New Delhi: Institute of Book Publishing, 1988.
11. Tejeshwar Singh: 'Publishing in India: Crisis and Opportunity', in Altbach, Arboleda and Gopinathan (1975).

JOURNALS

1. *The Publisher's Post* – a weekly newsletter on book publishing and selling in India. (cf. www.dogearsetc.com/thepost/)

WEB RESOURCES

1. www.fipindia.org (Official site of the Federation of Indian Publishers)
2. books.google.com (Provides partial /full access to digitised books and libraries)
3. www.amazon.com (World's largest retailer of books)
4. www.firstandsecond.com
5. www.sageindia.com
6. www.jaicopub.com
7. www.iipa.com

REVIEW QUESTIONS

1. Give a brief account of the development of the Indian book publishing industry after Independence.
2. What are the constraints under which the Indian book publishing industry functions?
3. What is the role of the multinationals in the Indian book publishing industry?
4. What are the major areas of concern for Indian book publishing houses?
5. How have developments in DTP and printing technology affected the book publishing business?

FOLK MEDIA

The folk or traditional arts of India have from ancient times been used for moral, religious, and socio-political purposes. Rarely have they been resorted to for pure entertainment alone, though they are often packed with spontaneity, boisterousness and humour. Indeed, they have been, down the ages, schools of learning, courts of justice, and discussion for a representative of the public sphere. In contrast to the modern mass media, the traditional media are personal, familiar, and more credible forms, with the majority of literate and illiterate identifying with their formats, genres, and contents. However, these forms need to be used with understanding and sensitivity. Vulgarization could set in if they are left to the mercy of urban elites. A deliberate distortion of the forms could easily alienate the masses. Meddling with folk forms which are alien to the idea of communication on contemporary topics shows scant respect for them. It must also be noted that folk forms are religion, community, caste, culture, and language/dialect-specific and bear values and associations often unique to them; these need to be taken into account in any attempts at adaptation or 'modernization'.

Advantages of the Folk Media

The folk media are close to the hearts and minds of the people; so their appeal is at a personal and intimate level. Further, their familiar format and content, as also the local and colloquial dialects used, make for clarity in communication. Cross-cultural communication hurdles are not encountered here. The numerous groups and different forms available for specific homogeneous groups and for specific purposes can be exploited to cater to people of different regions, on home ground as it were. Rapport is immediate and direct; the barriers to communication almost non-existent.

Folk media are available to all and sundry, and enjoyed by persons of different age groups – all at a very low cost. The greatest advantage of the folk media over the electronic media is their flexibility in accommodating new themes. For instance, comments on current events can be introduced into the traditional form of the *tamasha* or the *jatra*, or even the *keertan*. These are hardly ever interpreted as interpolations, as they are not 'pure' forms. Indian folk forms have a generous mix of dialogue, dance, song, clowning, moralising and prayer. True, they cater to small audiences at a time, but these audiences are so completely caught up in the folk forms, that the impact on them is at a much deeper level. Folk media, unlike the electronic media, involve and often invite, audience participation. The *Keertana*, *Alha* and various street theatre genres are good examples of this. The folk art forms satisfy our innate need for self-expression, for moral instruction combined with entertainment, and for the dramatic and the lyrical. The folk media preserve and disseminate in a lively manner, the traditions and cultures of our forefathers.

From a country-wide perspective the folk and traditional media are still the only 'mass' media, in the sense that they have their roots in the tradition and experience of a large majority of the population, and also that they have a reach much more extensive than any of the modern technological media. It must be noted, however, that the numerous religious, caste and linguistic groups across the 25 States of the country have their own distinctive folk and traditional media, though there has been liberal intermingling and interaction among them. With the advance of the communication technologies in the country, there has also been some interaction between the traditional and the technological media: the traditional have introduced 'film-style' songs and other elements of the cinema into their folk forms; and the technological media like cinema and television have integrated folk themes and formats into their techniques. The beginnings of cinema and television suggest that there is often a continuity between the folk and the audiovisual media. The first Indian film, *Raja Harishchandra*, was a mythological; the earliest soaps (albeit religious in character) were the *Mahabharat* and the *Ramayana*.

Public and private organizations use the folk and traditional media on a large scale in their efforts in community and national development. The largest public body thus involved is the Song and Drama Division, a 'unit' of the Ministry of Information and Broadcasting. Ministry publications describe the 'unit' as its 'live media wing' which utilizes the traditional folk and contemporary state forms like puppets, plays, dance-dramas, ballads, and harikathas 'for purposes of social communication, projecting the development activities in the country especially in the rural areas'.[1] The Division functions at three levels; at its headquarters in New Delhi, at eight regional Centres in various parts of the country, and at nine sub-Centres at district headquarters. The Division has over 40 departmental troupes, several sound and light units, and 'registered parties' which are made up of eminent performers in the folk arts.[2]

The majority of private organizations utilizing the folk and traditional media are 'social action groups' (SAGs) owing allegiance to various political, social and religious bodies. Marxist and Christian groups are perhaps the most active groups here. It is difficult to estimate the number of such groups or the nature of their use of the folk media. What is also difficult to investigate is the manner in which they are funded. Several foreign funding agencies are actively involved in the social work of these SAGs, with the connivance of the Central Government which desperately needs foreign exchange. Other private organizations such as theatre groups in West Bengal, Maharashtra, Tamilnadu and Kerala, employ traditional media like street theatre, dance-dramas, community festivals, religious epics, and proscenium style plays to disseminate social messages or just to keep these media alive. The politics and economics of the folk media industries is a field largely neglected by scholars. The main areas of contention relate to the funding of social action groups by foreign agencies, Central Government control over funds, and the varied approaches to the use of the folk and

---

1 Ministry of Information and Broadcasting: *Annual Report 1997-98*, New Delhi.
2 ibid.

traditional media for the purpose of empowering the marginalised.

Electronic Media and Folk Media

Under the impact of the more sophisticated, more glamorous and more 'powerful' electronic media, the folk art forms cannot but be transformed, even vulgarized. Even while bold attempts to preserve the original forms continue to make some headway, principally by the National School of Drama, and directors like E. Alkazi, Girish Karnad, Karanth, Habib Tanvir, Badal Sircar, and those of IPTA (Indian People's Theatre Association), the change is evident. The vulgarization of the rural forms has already started with the introduction of film-style *geet* and dance in the *jatra, tamasha* and *nautanki*. At the same time it is heartening to see how skillfully the new media are exploiting the traditional or folk forms to convey contemporary messages on radio and television, particularly in programmes for farmers and workers.

It is this integrated approach that will strengthen the efficacy of both technology-based and folk media. A happy combination of the modern and the traditional would make for a practical approach, though it must be seen to it that the folk forms are not crushed in the unequal competition with the new media. It is, however, unlikely that the electronic media will completely replace the traditional media; rather, what is more likely is that they will appropriate the folk media for their own political and business purposes.

Folk Theatre Forms

The folk theatre is impolite, rude, vulgar. It shocks prudes. The secular forms – tamasha, bhavai, nautanki, and Naqal – dominating the northern and western parts of India are replete with sexual jokes. It is considered improper for women to watch these plays.[3] In contrast with the more sober and sophisticated classical theatre, folk theatre is 'unselfconscious, spontaneous,

---

3 Balwant Gargi: *Folk Theater of India*, Bombay: Rupa & Co., 1991, p.3.

boisterously naive'.[4] Further, the folk has mass appeal, and a universality which the classical lacks. The classical Indian drama grew out of pageants, rituals, mimes, and ancient folk forms. But the Indian folk theatre forms as enacted in urban and rural India today are barely four to six hundred years old.

Tamasha

The tamasha is an extremely lively and robust form of folk theatre of Maharashtra, going back to over 400 years. The most celebrated patron of this folk form was Bajirao II, the last of the Peshwas, who introduced professional women singers into it for the first time. Another important development was the introduction of the jester, nicknamed Songadya who acted also as the 'master of ceremonies'. His witty remarks, often bordering on the lewd, and replete with double entrendes expose the hero to ridicule in the presence of the heroine.

In the main, tamasha (which means 'fun') is pure commercial entertainment, with the star performer being the female artiste who has to sing the favourite songs of the patrons as they shout out "Daulat Ziada" (May the wealth of the donor increase!). The form had originally no religious or social message to convey, except in the more refined type of tamasha called dholki-barris (folk drama troupes) which dealt with philosophical and moral questions. It takes its name from the dholki, a cylindrical two-sided drum, and its leading player is the shahir, the people's poet. A chorus of six to eight male singers-cum-performers, and two or more female dancer-singers make up the rest of the troupe.

It is this type (though often regarded as banavat, artificial) that has been extensively used by Marathi dramatists like Anna Bhau Sathe, P.L. Deshpande, Vasant Sabnis, Vasant Bapat and V.D. Madulkar to comment on contemporary life. Also known as *loknatya,* the dramatic form has been well exploited to sway public opinion on social and political affairs.

The more vigorous and bawdy form of tamasha is called

---

4   ibid.

sangeet-barris (song troupes) and is believed to be the genuine or real (assal) form. It has a cast of three to six women dancer-singers (one of whom is the star artiste), a tabla player, and a harmonium and tuntun player.

A tamasha performance whether in the banavat or assal mode, starts with a prayer called gan to Ganesh. It is followed by Gaulan, a milkmaid scene in which robust and lusty songs, dances and sketches about Krishna and his many gopis are enacted.

Vag (story) is the next element – the most important in the performance. The vag is told in the form of dialogue, song and dance and is based on stories derived from myth and folk-lore. It is in this section that satirical (and often salacious) comments are made on contemporary social and political problems. During the freedom struggle against the British, the vag was successfully used for political propaganda. Today, government-sponsored tamasha troupes exploit this section to educate the masses on family planning.

The 'vag' section begins with a chorus changed at a high pitch to introduce the audience to the plot. As the story unfolds in stages, song and dance sequences like the lavani and the powada are woven into its structure. The lavani (transplantation) was originally a harvest song but in tamasha, it depicts love, separation, reunion, changing and fickle love and sometimes social conditions through song and dance sequences performed by professional dancing girls.

Powada or Pawala

The Powada of Maharashtra is a folk ballad form which shot into prominence during the 16th century. It is dramatic in nature, and is dominated by tales about the events of history. It is sung to the accompaniment of musical instruments like daph, tuntune, and Majira, generally by a group with a leading voice. While singing, the leader indulges in dramatic gestures, describing the heroic deeds, which lend effect to the whole performance.[5] The

---

5 S. Parmar: Traditional Folk Media in India, New Delhi: Geka Books, 1975, p.75.

tempo is heightened by a refrain or chorus which rounds off each stanza.

The tamasha needs no elaborate stage props or costumes, and place and time are suggested through gestures, movement and dialogue. Generally the women artistes wear the nine-yard Maharashtrian sari of loud colours, and the males wear kurta-pyjama, a dark jacket and a pheta as headgear. The popularity of the tamasha is not restricted to Maharashtra. The response in Delhi to *Ek Tamasha Achhha Khasa*, scripted in Hindi, demonstrates the potential of the form, as also to its immense popularity. Bertolt Brecht's *Three Penny Opera* has been enacted as a tamasha entitled *Teen Paisacha Tamasha*.

Dangi tamasha: An interesting variation is the tamasha performed by the Dangi tribals of Gujarat. The roles of the women are played by men, who dance with the same gay abandon as the dancing girls. The Dangi tamasha narrates stories of kings and historical figures, and is interspersed with songs and dances. As in the Maharashtrian tamasha, so in the Dangi tamasha, there is a farceur whose antics are as amusing. Besides, it features a question-and-answer session in verse.

Keertana

The Keertana (or Harikatha or Harikeertan as it is sometimes called) is a kind of concentrated drama, a monodrama in which one gifted actor enters swiftly a whole series of characters and moods. The ancient sage Narad is believed to have invented and practised the form with great success. It is believed to have spread from Maharashtra to Karnataka and Tamilnadu about 150 years ago. Mainly associated with the bhakti movement in religion and literature, it has been used by saints like Kabir and Tukaram to preach the Hindu faith, and also to bring about social reform and political change. It is such a potent weapon in social education that Lokmanya Tilak is reported to have said that if he were not a journalist, he would have been a Keertankar.

Three types of the Harikatha or Harikeertan are popular in

Maharashtra: the traditional or Naradiya Harikatha, the Warkari Harikatha, and the Nationalist Harikatha. The Nationalist Harikatha is exploited by the Central and State Governments to educate the masses on family planning, development activities, democratic values and national integration – with the help of kathakars or keertankars. All India Radio and Doordarshan too use the Keertana form for broadcasts beamed at industrial workers and rural audiences.

The Warkari Harikatha is current in Maharashtra in two styles. In the more popular style, it takes the form of devotional worship among Warkaris of the Dnyaneshwar-Tukaram sect. The Keertankar selects episodes or verses from the writings of the two saints and chants them. He then explains their spiritual significance with the help of several stories from the Hindu epics and scriptures. The 'sermon' is interspersed with the singing of bhajans by all present.

The second style is a one-man show, more sophisticated and elaborate, but also more interesting. The keertankar begins the keertana with a theme song from a religious book, and explains and comments on it. He then goes on to narrate an interesting episode from the life of Sri Krishna or any other god, and brings out its moral and spiritual meaning. The theme song is then sung again.

In the second half of the Keertana, the sermon is continued on the same episode, but with rhetorical questions and satirical comments on contemporary subjects thrown in. In the Keertankar's hands, the Keertana is not only a means of worship but of popular education and entertainment as well.

Keertana (Gujarat): Gujarat's temple tradition of Keertan Sangeet, like that of Harikeertan in Maharashtra, has been a popular medium of mass education entertainment for centuries. It came into vogue in the wake of the Vaishnava paramapara. The themes of Keertan Sangeet form a wide variety and are usually based on significant episodes from the epics. The trained singers embellish their narration with suitable songs set to Hindustani ragas and also resort to some sort of abhinaya in the course of their performances.[6]

Yakshagana

Yakshagana is 'the song of the Yaksha', the most popular folk drama of Karnataka first performed in the 16th century. Its themes are from the Bhagavata but with a lot of local flavour. As with other Indian folk drama genres, Yakshagana is full of song and repartee. The narrator here is known as the Bhagavata who sings verses and exchanges witty remarks with the players, and handles the cymbals and songs. Besides, there is the jester, Hanumanayaka, as also kings, villains and demons – all elaborately (and frightfully!) made up.

The late Shivaram Karanth was largely responsible for injecting new life into this dying drama form by setting up his own troupes for performances all over the country. Girish Karnad's play *Hayavadan* employs the Yakshagana folk form.

Dashavatar

The Dashavatar is a religious folk theatre form of South Konkan. It is a Konkani variation of the Yakshagana of Karnataka, perhaps first launched by a priest called Gore about 400 years ago.

The Dashavatar is a re-enactment of the ten incarnations of Vishnu, and the story of the Lord and his devotees. It is generally performed within the precincts of a temple, for it is regarded as an act of worship. Male artistes alone are allowed to play various roles, even those of women. Men of 12 different castes including the Shudra take part in the worship of the local gods.

The hallmark of this folk form is improvisation, to cater to the preferences of the villagers of different areas. Indeed, 'the presentation becomes a free for all. Gods, priests, social and community leaders are ridiculed with the alacrity and wit of a

---

6 For a more detailed discussion of the role of folk theatre traditions in development, cf. Tevia Abrams: 'Folk Theatre in Maharashtrian Social Development Programmes', in *Educational Theatre Journal*, Vol. 27 (1975), pp. 395-407.

wild brat. Even Ganapati, without whose presence as an idol in the petaro (a large rectangular basket) and a character for the invocation ceremony no Dashavatar performance can take place, is not spared. You greedy fellow, declares the priest, demanding sweets when sugar is scarce and expensive. The God Vishnu also comes in for ridicule, his countless progeny and the limit set by the red triangle campaign. The rakshasas also lose the battle comically'.[7]

Nautanki

The Nautanki is a North Indian folk drama form performed on an open and bare stage. It gets its name perhaps from the charming Rani Nautanki of Multan whose young lover disguised himself as a woman to gain entry into her chambers. Like other Indian folk drama forms, the nautanki has a simple dramatic structure comprising small units linked by a Ranga or Sutradhar, the narrator. The themes are derived from the ancient epics and from folklore like the tale of Laila and Majnu, or the heroic deeds of Amar Singh Rathod and Sultana Daku.

Music is of prime importance in this folk drama, for it provides the pace and tempo required. The main musical instruments used are the makkara (kettle drum) and the dholak. As in opera, the dialogues are sung to popular folk melodies and now, even to popular film tunes. The Nautanki forms most popular these days are Bahertabil Chaubola, Doha, Lawani, Thumri, Dara, Sher, Ghazal and Quawwali. These dramatic forms can easily be adapted to make social and political comments on contemporary events and leaders.

Ramlila and Raslila

The Ramlila celebrates the story of the Ramayana, while the Raslila focuses on the exploits of Lord Krishna and his love for Radha. The Ramlila is enacted all over north India in September and October during the Dashahara festival; the Raslila, a dance-drama, is performed on various occasions in Vrindaban, Gujarat,

---

7 Sheela Barse, in *Sunday Standard*, March 1, 1981.

Maharashtra, Manipur and Kerala.

The Ramlila is made up of a cycle of plays based on the life of Rama. Varanasi and Ramnagar are the focal areas for the celebrations and the pageants. The plays usually begin with the birth of Rama and the cycle continues for thirty days, ending with his coronation. The cast is exclusively male, with boys under 14 playing the roles of Rama, Lakshmana, Bharata, Shatrughna, and Sita. In the Raslila too, the roles of Krishna, Radha and the gopis are played by young boys. Religious fervour characterise both these folk theatre traditions.

Jatra

The origin of jatra (journey), the folk theatre of Bengal and Orissa, is obscure, though it is very likely that the form got its name because of the nomadic habit of its performers. To begin with, Jatra compositions focussed on episodes from the lives of Krishna and Radha, and proved to be successful in propagating the Bhakti cult, and later the Shakta cult. In the 18th century, however, erotic elements were injected into the form which were soon snuffed out by Motilal Ray, and Mukunda Das, who used it with great effect to spread the nationalist spirit. Utpal Dutt has used the jatra in his plays as an instrument for political education.

Whatever the themes taken up, the basic structure and style of the jatra has remained unchanged. Singing interludes by the chorus (juri), loud and high pitched acting and rhetorical flourishes characterise the form even today.

Bhavai

The Bhavai is the foremost folk theatre form in Gujarat. A stylised medieval dramatic form, the Bhavai has a Ranglo and a Naik, besides other characters. The Ranglo is the stock-character who is the jester or clown of the play, while the Naik is the Sutradhar or manager with whom he carries on a bantering dialogue.

Like the court-jester, the Ranglo (or Vidushaka) enjoys the privilege of poking fun at local leaders, of making satirical comments on current affairs, of exposing social and political evils, and of extemporizing on subjects of concern to his audience. He has the freedom to connect the past with the present and relate the drama to the contemporary scene. He also acts as a liaison between the audience and the players.

A Bhavai performance starts with a devotional song in honour of Amba, the presiding deity. Ganesh, her son then appears on the stage in symbolic form, hiding his face behind a brass plate. He will show himself in his true form only at the end of the performance.

The initial formalities over, the wail of the Bhungalo (trumpet) announces the first of the series of veshas (playlets) to be staged. Each vesha is a complete short play in itself, with a loose structure that allows for a lot of improvisation. Besides dialogue, mime, fantasy, acrobatics, magic tricks, dance and song are the other elements that allow free play to the genius of the participants.

The ragas of the music in a Bhavai are largely classical. Popular musical forms like bhajans, dohas, garbas and ghazals make the Bhavai an extremely lively folk theatre experience. In addition, the delicate footwork of the garba (folk dance of Gujarat) and the more classical dance-forms in colourful costumes make it a feast for the eye. Ketan Mehta's film *Bhavni Bhavai* has superbly translated this folk drama tradition into cinematic language.

Therukoothu

In Tamilnadu, the traditional media include puppetry, Puravi Attam (Horse Dance), Nizhal Attam (Shadow Dance), Theru Koothu (Street Drama), Kazhai Koothu, Kalatchem and Villupattu. The Theru Koothu is the best known of these. The therukoothu is Tamilnadu's street theatre, bringing together dance and the classical literary forms – prose (iyal), music (isai) and drama (natakam). It is believed to have evolved from villupattu (ballad) and nondi-natakam (a morality play).

In the manner of other Indian folk traditions, religion and downright buffoonery mix freely in the Tamil street theatre in its treatment of themes like Valli's marriage to Karthikeya, Arjun's penance and Harischandra's meeting with the god of death, Yama. Again, as is common in our folk plays, the Therukoothu has stock characters like Koothadi (clown) and the God Ganesh. In recent times the form has been turned into a musical play, the sangeetha natakam, both on stage and screen.

Puppetry

Puppetry has fascinated children and adults of all climes for centuries. In India, four styles of puppetry have proved popular in different parts of the country.

Sutradharika: Puppets are manipulated with long strings in Rajasthan, Orissa, Karnataka, Tamilnadu and Andhra Pradesh. The costumes used generally belong to those seen in the folk theatre of a particular State. For instance, Orissa puppets, known as Sakhi Kundhei are dressed Gombeyatta in the Yakshagana mode. In Tamilnadu, the puppets are operated by strings and rods, and are called Bommalattums. The strings of each puppet are attached to an iron ring on the head of the puppeteer, which leaves him free to operate the puppets with his hands.

Rod Puppets: Rod puppets, known in West Bengal as putul nauch, are also dressed in the Jatra manner. Rod puppets are large in size, and are fixed to heavy bamboo sticks which are tied to the puppeteer's waist.

Shadow Puppets: Shadow Puppets (Chhaya Putli) are the favourite form in Andhra Pradesh (locally known as Thohu Bommalutta), Karnataka, (Togalu Combe Atta), Kerala (Tholpava Koothu), and Orissa (Ravan Chhaya). Shadow puppets are flat figures made from tanned hide and painted with vegetable dyes. They are illuminated from behind so that their shadows fall on a transparent cotton screen. The stories projected by shadow puppets are generally taken from the Hindu epics, the Ramayana and the Mahabharata.

Hand Puppets: Glove or hand puppet shows are most popular in Orissa, Kerala and Tamilnadu. The free use of the puppeteer's hand lends a rare strength and vitality to the movements of a puppet's head and arms, and the wrist lends flexibility and power to a puppet's body. Hand-puppets are fashioned on Kathakali characters in Kerala, and are played in almost the same manner. The musical accompaniment is provided by musicians and a chorus of singers. In Orissa, the gloved puppeteer squats on the ground with a drum under his knee. He sings, and beats the drum with one hand and with the other brings the puppets to life.

Puppetry versus Films: The Union Bank of India and the Life Insurance Corporation have used the medium of puppetry in Uttar Pradesh, to arouse the interest of the rural folk in bank savings, and insurance policies. A pilot study by the Indian Institute of Mass Communication on the comparative effectiveness of puppetry and a documentary film in two villages near Delhi showed that the cheaper traditional medium could be as effective as film. Women in particular responded more favourably to the puppet shows than to the films.

That finding has led to the Films Division and the Children's Film Society going in for 'puppet films'. Doordarshan too capitalises on the puppet figure in programmes for children.

Street Theatre

There has been an explosion of 'street theatre' activity in India in the eighties and nineties. One study estimates the existence of about 7,000 'street theatre' groups in different parts of the country, with the largest number in West Bengal, Andhra, Tamilnadu and Kerala. The main groups involved in this type of popular theatre activity are 'social action groups' (SAGs), health and agricultural extension workers, student activists, political parties, religious reformers and women's organizations.

The formal origins of Indian street theatre can be traced to the radical political theatre in the 'forties in Calcutta. It emerged not from folk or traditional theatre form but rather from the tradition of Indian adaptations of Western proscenium theatre, popular at the time in urban centres. To begin with, it was Marxist-inspired. It was as it were driven to the 'streets' because theatres would not stage such political plays which were characterized by vivid portrayal of real events, popular language and minimal props. It was the Bengal Famine that perhaps first triggered such activity. In 1944, Bijon Bhattacharya, a founder of Indian People's Theatre Association (IPTA) staged perhaps the first street play. It was called 'Nibanna', and told of the exploitation of peasants by Bengali landowners. IPTA popularized the street-corner play in the early 'fifties during the Bandimukti Andolan. Other politically motivated groups also took to the form in the 'seventies and the 'eighties to mobilize the marginalized groups. The slaying of the IPTA activist, Safdar Hashmi, during a street performance in Delhi in early 1989, led to the form being given wide coverage in the national press.

The most influential proponent of Indian street theatre has been Badal Sircar who has argued for a 'theatre of commitment'. He has been, in turn, considerably influenced by Grotowski's 'poor theatre' and Schechner. Sircar's work stands out for its emphasis on 'body language', on dialogue directed straight at the audience and on the involvement of the audience. It is to be noted that street plays are culture-specific and employ local folk theatre forms, local songs and dances, and the local dialect. For instance, 'Sahiar', a women's group in Baroda, uses Gujarati folk forms like *bhavai* and *garba*, and the Jan Natya Mandali (of Andhra Pradesh) uses local forms like 'oger ratha'.

Women's groups in Delhi, Bombay, and in rural Andhra, Kerala and Maharashtra have used street theatre to raise social consciousness on issues like suttee, dowry, sex discrimination in education and employment, exploitative advertising, and discriminatory laws of inheritance and divorce. In Kerala, the KSSP has employed street theatre to popularize science and literacy.

FOR FURTHER READING

1. Appavoo, J. Theophilus: *Folklore for Change*, Madurai: Tamilnadu Theological Seminary, 1986.
2. *Communication Research Trends*, London: 'Popular Theatre', 1988 (Nos. 1 & 2).
3. Gargi, Balwant: *Folk Theater of India*, Bombay: Rupa and Co., 1991.
4. Julia Hollander: *Indian Folk Theatres*, London: Routledge, 2007.
5. Malik, Madhu: *Traditional Forms of Communication and the Mass Media in India*, Paris: UNESCO, 1983.
6. Mukhopadhyay Dungadas: *Lesser Known Forms of Performing Arts in India* New Delhi: Sterling, 1978.
7. Parmar, S.: *Traditional Folk Media in India*, New Delhi: Geka Books, 1975.
8. Parmar, S.: *Folk Music and Mass Media*, New Delhi: Communication Publications, 95/2 Tatarpur, Tagore Garden, 1977.
9. Ranganath, H.K.: *Not a Thing of the Past: Functional and Cultural Status of Traditional Media in India*, Paris: UNESCO, n.d.
10. Manorma Sharma: *Musical Heritage of India*, New Delhi: APH Publications, 2007.

WEB RESOURCES

1. www.culturopedia.com
2. www.yakshagana.com
3. www.chandrakantha.com

REVIEW QUESTIONS

1. Why are folk media important in Indian communication? What are their advantages compared to the electronic media?
2. Name the major folk theatre forms popular in your district/State. Discuss any two of them.
3. Lokmanya Tilak is believed to have said, "If I were not an editor, I would be a Keertanakar". Why do you think he was so attracted to the Keertana tradition?
4. Write on the different types of puppetry popular in India.

5. Write short notes on:
   (a) Lavani and Powada
   (b) Warkari Harikatha
   (c) The role of the Sutradhara in folk theatre.
   (d) Use of the folk media for literacy campaigns.
   (e) 'Antakshari' as an urban folk form.

SUGGESTED PROJECTS

1. Select a simple folk form of your village/region and use it to talk (or sing) about a contemporary problem.
2. Listen to a radio programme, or watch a television programme that makes use of folk media for mass education. Do you think it has been successfully used?
3. Compare two programmes on radio or television that adapt folk media to talk about a current social problem.
4. Organise a debate on the proposition:
   "The folk media should be allowed to die a natural death with the coming of the mass media and new media."
5. Put together a scrap-book on the folk theatre traditions of your State.
6. Draw up a list of Internet websites that deal with the Indian folk media.
7. Select a popular folk media of your own city/village/state. Make a Powerpoint presentation on the selected folk medium.
8. Make a list of popular films that use the folk media in the stories they tell. Is the use convincing?

ADVERTISING AND PUBLIC RELATIONS

Advertising and Public Relations are not 'mass media' in the way that the press, the cinema, radio, TV and the folk media are. They are not so much mediating technologies for reaching the masses as commercial uses of the mass media to get across persuasive messages to large numbers of customers with the primary purpose of selling products, services and ideas. Advertising and Public Relations are thus 'applied' mass media. Advertising and public relations have indeed been the engines of growth for the mass media since much of the financial support for the development of the technological media has come from business and industry. Both business and industry need large-scale advertising and public relations to make their wares known in the marketplace. This has resulted in a certain 'interdependence' of the media and business. Further, since other social institutions too (such as politics, education, religion, and art and culture) need to speak to the public and to publicise their activities, they are required to make use of the media as well. As a consequence, advertising and public relations have become so closely intermeshed with the mass media that the distinction between the media as public fora and as tools of publicity for business and other social institutions has become gradually blurred. Advertising and public relations thus hold the key to understanding both the form and substance of modern mass communication. Indeed, the history of mass communication has been largely shaped by the needs of advertising and public relations on the part of business, government and other social, political and cultural institutions.

Both advertising and public relations are forms of publicity, but with a difference. Advertising is paid for, and is direct and explicit; media users for the most part recognise advertisements for what they are, and know who has paid for them, as well as who the sponsors are. Advertising rates for the various media are in the public domain and so the 'adspend' can be calculated. The source of the advertisement is also known; so is the name of the agency that created or produced it. Public Relations, however, is subtle and often unrecognised by the general public. It is not paid for directly, and the sponsor is rarely mentioned. That is largely true for 'press or media relations', 'advertorials' and lifestyle/celebrity (or 'Page Three') journalism; however, in PR activities such as community services, exhibitions, cultural and sports events, health camps and so on, the sponsor's name is widely publicised.

An advertisement is thus a public announcement with the avowed purpose not so much to inform as to persuade the public to buy a product, a service or an idea. According to the Drugs and Magical Remedies (Objectionable Advertisements) Act of 1954, an advertisement includes 'any notice, circular, label, wrapper, or other document and any announcement made orally or by means of producing or transmitting light, sound or smoke'. Public Relations, on the other hand, is 'the deliberate, planned and sustained effort to establish and maintain understanding between an organisation and its public'. This is how the Institute of Public Relations, London, has defined Public Relations; it is a definition accepted by the Public Relations Society of India (PRSI), a trade association established in 1958.

History and Development of Advertising

The origin of advertising as a public announcement is traceable to the town crier and the village drummer. These used their lung-power to shout out their own or others' messages. The messages could relate to government proclamations or even to sales of goods on 'market days'. Then there were signs on shops or drinking houses to indicate the name of the shop owner or of the shop. The highly urbanized cities of Mohenjodaro and Harappa must have employed some form of advertising to sell the many types of art and craft items that these ancient civilizations were famous for.

Excavations in Pompeii and other ancient cities have also thrown up evidence of some form of advertising in the pre-modern period. Says one advertisement in Latin found in

Pompeii: 'A copper pot has been taken from this shop. Whoever brings it back will receive 65 cesterces. If anyone shall hand over the thief, he will receive an additional reward'. Such a public announcement has a striking resemblance to modern 'classified' advertisements. Further, the excavations suggest that notices of theatre performances, games, entertainments, and other public events were painted on the walls of the busy centres of the city. This was also the practice among the ancient Romans: they used 'albums' (places in walls made smooth and white for writing or carving), stone tablets and even playing cards for making announcements of public interest. Public notices were placed in the 'Acta Diurna', a wall-newspaper which provided daily news of Senate politics.

Modern Advertising

Modern advertising was made possible by the invention of printing, and the subsequent attempts to print notices, posters and bills in large numbers. However, it was the industrial revolution in Europe, combined with large scale urbanization and mass production of goods, and the growth of the publishing business that brought about the expansion of competitive advertising. The eighteenth and nineteenth centuries in Europe and the United States were witness to massive migrations of people from rural to urban areas, there to work in factories and live in crowded unhygienic conditions. The industrial revolution proved to be a success on the back of the working-classes, and the availability of large markets in the 'colonies' from where cheap raw materials could be bought.

Mass production resulted in the need to market the products as they rolled out of factories. Advertising was hit upon as a powerful tool to stimulate public demand for standardized factory products. It was welcomed by the growing printing and publishing trade as it subsidized their costs of production; this went a long way in keeping the price of newspapers low. By 1861 there were as many as 5,000 newspapers and magazines in the United States, with several of them publishing more advertisements than news or articles. 'Space sellers' entered the business world to act as middlemen or brokers between the manufacturers and the press.

The first modern 'advertising agency' started operating around 1875, when N.W. Ayer and Son of Philadelphia offered to produce advertisements and also to contract for space in the press. The growth of advertising as a service industry and as a profession was rapid. In 1917, the American Association of Advertising Agencies and the Association of British Advertising Agencies were founded. By the 'twenties, ad agencies were offering such 'facilities' as campaign planning, budgeting and even market research. Besides, they began to extend their business beyond the press to outdoor advertising and direct mail.

The industrial revolution, the growth of the press and of advertising had its impact on the Indian industry and economy. This impact was felt most in the metropolitan cities of Calcutta, Bombay, Delhi and Madras.

History of Indian Advertising

The history of Indian advertising parallels the history and development of the Indian press. The first newspaper started by James Hicky on January 29, 1780, was called the 'Bengal Gazette' or the 'Calcutta General Advertiser'. Its very first issue carried a few advertisements, which were mostly informative. To 'advertise' meant merely to 'inform' until the end of the eighteenth century, and the early newspapers and periodicals announced births, deaths, arrivals of ships (and of women as well) from England, sales of household furniture, etc. Some journals like the 'Bengal Journal' (first published in 1785) even offered to print Government advertisements free. The front page of several such journals carried only advertisements. But before long, persuasive copy began to replace mere information. This is evident from the appearance of punch lines such as 'superior to anything of the kind hitherto imported' and 'warranted of the first quality'. The rhetoric of advertising now included words like 'elegant', 'most elegant and superb' and 'handsome'.

Discounts and special services also began to be offered by the beginning of the nineteenth century. By the dawn of the nineteenth century the pattern of advertising revealed a definite change in the direction of hard selling. New products and services established themselves on the market through the advertisement columns of newspapers and periodicals. Even daily newspapers, which began to appear about this time, announced themselves through advertisements in existing periodicals. The power of advertising (as also of the press) increased rapidly with the growth in trade and commerce.

By 1830 around three dozen English dailies and periodicals were being published on a regular basis in India. By mid-century, however, the number rose to a hundred, with ten from North India, 17 from Bombay and the rest from the south. With the increasing impact of the industrial revolution on India, the number of advertisements from British business houses rose sharply.

'Agents' flourished at the time as space contractors, obtaining advertisements for newspapers and periodicals on a commission basis. Frequently, the 'agents' also helped out even with the copy, layout and printing. Leading newspapers like *The Statesman* and *The Times of India,* which had their own advertising departments, offered their facilities to 'agents'. This was advantageous to both the advertiser and the publisher; for the advertiser, it saved the bother of preparing a suitable layout for his advertisements; for the publisher, it assured a certain uniformity of standard in the advertisements appearing in its columns. This practice was perhaps responsible for turning advertising into a distinct profession. These 'agents' were forerunners of the 'advertising agencies' of a later period. However, true to their original function, agencies continued to be 'space sellers'.

Advertising in the early 20th century

Two events were responsible for the growth of Indian advertising agencies in the early twentieth century. The first was the Swadeshi Movement (1907–1911) which gave an impetus to indigenous industries; the second was the installation in 1907 of the first rotary linotype machine by the *Statesman* of Calcutta.

In a few years' time, other papers too installed the new machine which made it possible to produce a cheap newspaper with a large national circulation. The first Indian ad agency, the Indian Advertising Agency, was launched around this time, and is still going strong. The Calcutta Advertising Agency started operations in 1909, and B. Dattaram's in 1915. The main function of these agencies was to secure advertisements from manufacturers, retailers and other business firms and to get them published in the press.

However, the Indian advertising agencies found it difficult to compete with the British agencies. The major British agencies of the 1920's and 1930's were: Alliance Advertising Associates, Publicity Society of India (which specialized in outdoor publicity in Calcutta), L.A. Stronach and Co., Bombay, D.J. Keymer (now Ogilvy and Mather), and J. Walter Thompson (now Hindustan Thompson Associates). They catered to the needs of the affluent British and Indian elites living in the metropolitan cities. Mass consumer items like tea and cigarettes were rarely advertised by them. The idiom and rhetoric of their advertising copy was alien to the Indian experience.

But during the war, press advertising was exploited to raise funds for the war effort. Thus it was that the language of the people came to be employed on a wider scale than hitherto. This experience taught Indian professionals in advertising how to motivate large sections of the Indian population.

Ad agencies established during this period included Alliance Advertising Association Ltd. at Bombay, started by the British India Corporation of Kanpur to sell its manufactured goods. Mr. L.A. Stronach, the manager of Alliance, bought up the Bombay branch of the agency and started in 1922 his own agency, L A Stronach and Co., with a branch in London. It provided production and media services to advertisers (unlike the space-selling agencies) and so even manufacturers of competing products or brands had to use his services. Stronach's captured several British accounts including major tyre and automobile manufacturing companies.

The Inter-War Years

During the inter-war years a few Indian agencies too sprang up, the most notable being the Modern Publicity Co. in Madras, the Calcutta Publicity (1924), Central Publicity Service (1925) in Bombay and Calcutta, and the Oriental Advertising Agency in Tiruchirapalli (1925). Among British agencies launched were D.J. Keymers which opened an office at Calcutta in 1928, and a while later a branch in Bombay. J. Walter Thompson opened an office at Bombay in 1928 and later at Calcutta. Outdoor advertising took off about this time, since it came to be realized that the press reached only a tiny percentage of the population. In 1926 Mr. I.S. Taylor set up the Publicity Society of India to exploit advertising possibilities on trams, kiosks and other outdoor media. The Vasudeva Publicity Service was started in Delhi to carry out outdoor publicity campaigns in Uttar Pradesh, Punjab and Delhi. In 1931, the first full-fledged Indian ad agency, the National Advertising Service, was established. Among the other Indian agencies to be launched during this period were: New India Publicity Co. (1930), Paradise Advertising Agency of Calcutta (1928), Mr. V. Sista's Sales and Publicity Service (1934), Alpha Advertising Service (1937), Lintas and Press Syndicate (1938), and P.S. Mani and Co. (1939). In February 1939, the Indian and Eastern Newspapers Society (IENS) was established as a central organisation of the newspaper-owners of India, Burma and Ceylon. The Society looked after the interests of newspaper publishing houses; an indirect effect of the formation of the IENS was the standardization of ad agency practices. The Society prescribed the minimum qualifications of ability, experience, and resources required for accreditation to IENS, and to be eligible for a uniform rate of commission. Strict enforcement of the accreditation rules went a long way in eliminating some unhealthy practices of ad agencies. The IENS sought to foster better publisher-agency relationship.

The establishment of the Advertising Agencies Association of India (AAAI) in 1945, and the Audit Bureau of Circulation (ABC) in 1948 helped to bring some order to the competitive field. The AAAI (3A's of I) came to be recognized as a representative body of the profession, with the authority to represent its interests and problems. A Joint Standing Committee, comprising representatives of AAAI and the IENS (now INS, the Indian Newspaper Society) was formed later. The ABC gave some credibility to the claims of newspapers regarding their circulation. Earlier, such claims had no standing, even when supported by auditors' certificates.

Post-Independence Advertising

Following World War II and Indian Independence, the British-owned agencies were sold to Indian business. Several agencies, however, retained an 'affiliate' status with the main branches of the agencies in London. They continue to enjoy this status even today, though American multinational agencies have replaced affiliation with British agencies.

At Independence, the advertising business was well on its way to growth and expansion. Partition did not touch the business at all. The introduction of multi-colour printing, improved printing machines (like offset and web offset), and the development of commercial art gave the ad business a further fillip. Besides selling space, advertising agencies began to offer many more services, such as art work, organisation of fairs and exhibitions, market research, and public relations consultancies.

The Indian Society of Advertisers (ISA) was formed in 1951, and in May 1958, the Society of Advertising Practitioners, was established. The Audit Bureau of Circulation had been set up in 1948, and the Advertising Agencies of India, in 1952. The Commercial Artists' Guild came into existence in the late 1950s, and advertising clubs were formed in Calcutta and Bombay to promote higher standards. The phenomenal growth in the media, especially television and cable in the 1990s gave a boost to Indian advertising. Market research and readership surveys have led to the further professionalization of the business. Readership surveys were first conducted by individual publishing houses like the *Hindu* and the *Times of India,* or individual publications like the *Readers' Digest.* Since the 1980s, market research agencies such as ORG, MARG, IMRB, MODE, TAM and A.C. Nielsen have been conducting National Readership Surveys (NRS), Indian Readership Surveys (IRS) and regular Television Rating Points (TRP) measurements to provide advertisers with statistical data and even 'models' on which to base their media plans. A variety of computer software assist media planners to work out their advertising schedules.

At the end of the first decade of the new millennium Indian advertising was a two billion rupee industry with around 1,200 agencies and 10,000 professionals and growing at 15-20% per annum. The Public Relations industry too was worth as much and with as many professionals, but surging ahead at 30-35% per annum, according to reports in trade journals and the annual FICCI-PriceWaterhouse Coopers' surveys. Media training and management institutes across the country are churning out advertising and PR professionals by the hundreds to meet the needs of a booming economy. How these developments impact upon the mass media and their role as the nation's 'public sphere' and the Fourth Estate is a matter of grave concern. Already, the lines between news and advertising/public relations and also between news and entertainment have become blurred, and journalism has turned into 'churnalism' thanks to the proliferation of print, broadcast and digital news media.

Evolution of the Public Relations Industry

During World War I, the United States set up a Committee on Public Information with the task of propagating the aims and ideas of the American Government. The Soviet Union and the Communist International also established similar organs for Public Relations. Other national governments too set up

Information Offices for public relations activities. The British Government in India set up the Central Bureau of Public Information in 1923. (The same Bureau was re-named the Public Information Bureau (PIB) after independence).

But it was during the Depression in the United States during the 1930s that there was a spurt in corporate PR, mainly to counteract the dramatic rise in public suspicion and distrust of business, industry and the Government. The experience of the Depression had taught the corporate world that selling products for profit, and advertising in the various media, was not enough. They needed the goodwill and trust of the communities they served. They therefore sought to raise the image of American business so as to win the understanding and acceptance of the public. The range of strategies they employed to achieve this came to be termed 'Public Relations'.

Perhaps the earliest venture in Public Relations by Indian industry was the publicity conducted in London in 1920 by the Great Indian Peninsular Railway to promote travel in India. The House of Tatas started their Public Relations Department as early as 1945. The British government, of course, had employed PR strategies using print, film and radio media, especially during the years of World War II, to win Indian support for its policies; so had Anglo-Indian business and industry to build up its public image as serving the interests of India.

The Need for Public Relations

During the pre-industrial period, business and social relations were simple, straightforward and on a person to person basis. That was possible because business and society were much less complex in structure and character than they are today, and competitiveness was minimal. Following the Industrial Revolution in Europe and the United States, business and society underwent a total transformation. Business organisations mushroomed, competing one with another for attention and profit, and urban society became pluralistic, comprising as it did men and women from different classes and groups, of varying educational, religious and social backgrounds. In such a complex capitalist society, advertising and public relations were necessary to fight the competition. The mass media came to serve this function for business and administration. Governments too found it necessary to use the mass media to publicise and justify their policies and plans to the people.

Public Relations emerged as the strongest weapon to do so. Of equal importance was bringing to the attention of the public the contributions of business to society and to the community. They sought thereby to raise the 'image' of business and government so as to win the understanding and acceptance of the public. Public relations activities would be guided by truth and honesty in providing full information to the public. Complaints from consumers would be invited and welcomed, and a general attempt would be made to serve and to build the community, rather than exploit it for purely commercial purposes. The need for Public Relations today is therefore inherent in the very nature of modern business and government. Business cannot rest satisfied with production, distribution and the making of profits. It must involve itself with community activities (what is now termed 'Corporate Social Responsibility' (CSR)), and inform the public on a regular basis what its achievements and failures are. The various 'publics' it has direct relations with (distributors, retailers, customers, opinion leaders, government) must understand the nature of business, and why it is important to the community. Public Relations thus provides a channel through which business can talk to the various 'publics', and the 'publics' in their turn can talk back to business. This is the ideal; on the ground, however, public relations continues to be a one-way channel. This is clearly evident in the small number of business or government organisations that take the trouble to reply to the letters of complaint from customers. The Consumer Protection Act of 1986 as well as the recent Right to Information Act of 2006 will now force them to take greater heed. But the function of Public Relations is not merely to combat criticism or complaints, but rather to create goodwill, trust and understanding, and in building up a favourable climate in which an organisation can function.

The PR industry in India has now been 'invaded' by multinational players, forcing the major home-grown agencies to tie up or even sell out to them. Public Relations used to be one of the activities of advertising agencies until the 1990s; today it is a highly specialized management and marketing function dedicated to building the reputation and public image of commercial, political and cultural organizations. 'Reputation Management', 'Image Management' and 'Crisis Management' have come to be the primary functions of PR in the new millennium. Specialities within Public Relations profession include Healthcare PR, Food Service PR, Technology PR, Public Affairs PR, Labour Relations, etc.

Major PR Agencies in India
- Genesis Burson-Marsteller
- Perfect Relations
- Adfactors PR Pvt. Ltd.
- Corporate Voice/Weber Shandwick
- 20:20 Media
- Good Relations
- Ogilvy PR Worldwide
- Synergy Public Relations
- Pressman Advertising and Marketing Ltd.
- Vaishnavi Communications
- Sampark Public Relations.
- Shabbdanjali Communication Services
- Hanmer and Partners

The Business of Advertising and Public Relations

Both the advertising and public relations industries are multi-million rupee businesses. While advertising expenditures and revenues can be estimated from the rates for each medium and each vehicle (though it is widely known that most rates are negotiated rather than fixed), the expenditures on public relations are difficult to estimate. Most organisations club their expenditures on advertising and PR together, as advertising is often a tool of PR, and vice versa. The annual surveys of the advertising industry conducted for instance by the PITCH magazine and Madison Media, provide separate breakdowns for advertising and marketing spends, but do not provide any clue as to PR spend. In business management parlance, however, advertising and PR are both vital elements of the 'marketing mix'. Could it be then that expenditure on PR is included under the 'marketing' head? While the primary role of advertising is to sell a product, service or idea (or at least to stimulate a demand for it), Public Relations aims at creating a climate for such a sale, a climate of trust and goodwill. Thus PR includes several areas such as Employee Relations (Internal PR), Government Relations, Shareholder Relations, Community Relations, Customer Relations (External PR). The tools of PR include house journals, brochures and booklets, press handouts, press conferences, press visits, websites, blogs, online social networks, exhibitions, welfare activities, sponsorships of community events, etc. Indeed, any gesture on the part of an organisation which provides a positive image (or perception) of it to the public and contributes to the evolution of a climate of trust, goodwill and understanding is an instance of Public Relations. The traditional mass media (the press, radio, television and cinema) and the 'new' digital media (the internet, mobile telephony, digital radio and television, multimedia) are the information and communication technologies at the service of both advertising and PR, the very engines of media growth and prosperity.

The largest multinational group of advertising agencies active in India is WPP which includes four Indian agencies: JWT (formerly HTA), Ogilvy and Mather, Contract and the media buying agency, Mindshare. This one group alone accounts for sixty per cent of the total Indian advertising business; the top advertising agencies listed below account for as much as 80%, according to the 5th Pitch-Madison Survey (2008). India's top ten advertising agencies are all part of international advertising networks; most of them are subsidiaries. The total annual adspend over the last six years has been as follows:

Table 39: Total Annual Adspend (2003-2008)

Year	Adspend (in crores)
2003	Rs.9,328
2004	Rs.10,354
2005	Rs.11,195
2006	Rs.14,505
2007	Rs.17,690
2008	Rs.21,582 (Est.)

Table 40: India's Major Advertisers

1.	Hindustan Uni-Lever	9.	Hero Honda
2.	Procter & Gamble India	10.	Videocon International
3.	Reckitt & Benckiser	11.	Colgate
4.	Nokia	12.	Nestle India Ltd.
5.	Dabur India Ltd.	13.	Bajaj Auto Ltd.
6.	Paras Pharmaceuticals	14.	Godfrey Phillips India Ltd.
7.	Bharti Airtel	15.	Amity University
8.	Pepsico	16.	Coca Cola

According to the 5th Pitch-Madison Survey (2008), the major products and services advertised in the print media were: mobile phone services, toilet soaps, shampoos, two-wheelers, toothpastes, cars, internet services and soft drinks. Print media received the biggest slice of the advertising cake (47.9%), followed by television (40.2%), outdoor/OOH (7.2%), radio (2.7%), Internet (1.4%) and cinema (0.6%).

Table 41: India's Top Advertising Agencies

A. Multinational Agencies
- WPP
- Lowe
- Rediffusion
- EuroRSCG
- Dentsu
- Leo Burnett

B. Joint Ventures
- Percept-Hakuhodo
- Publicis-Ambience
- BBDO-R K Swamy
- FCB-Ulka

C. Home-Grown Agencies
- Mudra Communications
- Madison
- MAA
- Pressman Advertising and Marketing
- Concept

(Source: 5th Pitch-Madison Survey, 2008)

Types of Advertising

Advertising can be categorised in various ways. The most common mode of classifying various forms of advertising is in terms of product or service. In the press, ads are generally classified into 'classified' and 'display' types; in cinema, cable and television, ads are classified into 'stills' and 'live'. Where the focus of attention is the medium, the classification is in terms of 'print', 'electronic', 'cinema', 'outdoor'(or Out-Of-Home), 'Online' and 'mobile/cellphone' advertising.

Product, Service and Institutional Advertising

Advertisements can be classified according to different categories such as ad theme (or 'advertising platform'), media, product. Broadly speaking, there are three types of advertising, where the content or theme is concerned.

The first is *product advertising*. This is the most common type of advertising. The items advertised are consumer products, consumer durables. The dominant focus is the product itself rather than the name of the company or manufacturer. The advertising tells a story about the product, evokes an image or images of it, turns it into something unique. A certain aura is created about the product as though it were a dream product, for instance, satisfying special needs and wants. The whole approach is playful, relaxed, dream-like. Most often, hardly anything is told about the product. Such ads are low in information but high on style. Ads of soft drinks, energy drinks, fast foods, textiles, belong to this type. So do consumer durables such as refrigerators, TV and video sets, musical systems, furniture items. Consumer product advertising is the type readers, listeners and viewers are exposed to most of the time. It is the type that tends to promote attitudes and lifestyles which praise acquisition and consumption at the expense of higher values. Consumer ads play on emotions, change real human situations into stereotypes, exploit anxieties and employ techniques of direct and indirect persuasion. Thus, consumer ads do not sell soap but glamour and charm; they do not sell soft drinks or chocolates but a happy and carefree lifestyle. Indeed, consumer advertisements more than other types, conjure up a fantasy world where it neither rains nor blows, where the women exude charm, the men are macho, and children little cherubs all eager for the goodies of life. Thus they are extremely low on information but high on wit, rhetoric and style.

Classified Advertising

At the other extreme is *classified advertising* which provides valuable information in a dry matter of fact manner. Useful information about the employment market ('situations vacant' and 'situations wanted'), about births, deaths, engagements and marriages, about change of names, about accommodation and housing (accommodation available and accommodation wanted), about the availability of various services such as tuitions, and about various items on sale. Matrimonial advertisements are frequently downright casteist, racist and sexist, but they fill the weekend papers. Service advertising focuses on 'services' such as professional training, coaching classes, consultancies, advertising, public relations, market research, education, public speaking, institutes, management training, travel agencies, hotels, tourism, and others. The approach here is usually more direct, and information oriented.

Public Service Advertising

Then there is *public service* or *social service* advertising. The newest term for it is 'development' advertising. This type of advertising focuses on social issues like family planning, national integration, pollution, care for the aged and the disabled, cautious driving, campaigns against alcohol, drugs and smoking. Their primary purpose is public education through hard-hitting didactic messages. They do not sell products or services but 'ideas' and 'messages'.

Industrial Advertising

This type differs from others in that machinery and large outlays are involved. The descriptions in such ads are therefore precise and technical; the appeal is down-to-earth and rational. The presentations are mostly factual since the target audience is technical personnel of industrial companies.

Corporate or Institutional Advertising

The aim here is to build a good public image for a corporate. This type focuses on a company's activities in research, development and quality control, on its sponsorship of educational, cultural and sports programmes, and on its consumer service and social service programmes. The advertising technique employed for the purpose is information oriented, rather than rhetorical. The large display of the 'achievements' of State Governments, the telephone and telecommunications authorities, the Indian railways serve a similar purpose. Institutional Advertising has as its objective the creation of a good public image of the company rather than of the product. The company, for instance, is presented as serving the public through sponsorships of cultural, sports and social events, as supporting charities and social service causes. Generally, such advertising does a public relations job for the company.

Institutional advertising may be of the 'patronage institutional advertising' type. The primary objective is to sell; persuade readers to patronise a particular retailer or store. A second type of institutional advertising is 'public relations institutional advertising'. For instance, during an industrial strike, a company informs the public about what it has done for the workers. Finally, there is what may be termed 'public service institutional advertising', where the company tries to create the image of how public-spirited it is by talking about its contribution to the development of the community.

Financial, Hospitality and Political Advertising

Since the 1980s the advertising of issues of corporate shares and bonds came as a boon to the print and electronic media. With many IPOs subscribed, the market turned competitive. The business press has begun to flourish as a result. Yet another little known advertising type is that of Legal Tenders and Legal Notices, and other public notices. Display advertising for appointments in the country and overseas, especially in West Asian countries, has also proved popular. Advertising for Hotels and Tourists (targeted at the domestic and foreign tourist), particularly by State Governments, Tourism Boards, Airlines, Travel Agencies, Passport and Visa Assistance, has seen a big boost. During election time, political advertising/marketing takes pride of place in the press though most advertising agencies are reluctant to enter this domain.

Outdoor or Out-Of-Home (OOH) Advertising

This has largely been an unorganized advertising industry up until the end of the 20th century. But the emergence of national and local OOH agencies have brought about a semblance of order in a chaotic business. The following are some of the top OOH agencies:
- Madison Outdoor Media Services (MOMS)
- Times OOH (The Times of India Group)
- Jagran Engage (Dainik Jagran Group)
- Ads World
- Prime Site
- Graphic Ads
- Kinetic
- Skyline Outdoor Media
- MPG's (Media Planning Group) Active

Outdoor sites belong for the most part to local municipalities and each city draws up its own rules and regulations for OOH advertisers. Further, there is a multiplicity of civic authorities, with each vying to profit from the sale of public spaces. Despite strictures from the Supreme and High Courts, advertising agencies and civic bodies collude to deface the urban landscape. Express ways, national highways and even winding roads up to the many hill resorts that dot the Indian sub-continent are not spared.

OOH advertising includes a vast range of publicity media, from wall-paintings, posters, buses, trains, bus-shelters, train stations, airports, billboards and hoardings (illuminated and non-illuminated) to electronic 'signages' such as liquid electronic displays (LED). Shopping malls, supermarkets, multiplexes, interactive kiosks, and game arcades are other new media that offer opportunities for advertising. In 2008, the OOH business was worth over two billion rupees.

Online Advertising

During the last decade or so the new digital media have given rise to new forms of advertising; the Internet which was once free of all advertising has now emerged as the advertising medium par excellence for reaching consumers worldwide. The global reach of the Internet, the competitive rates and above all the accuracy of its measurement of 'hits', 'page-views' and 'click-throughs' make it an attractive advertising vehicle. Banners, pop-ups, buttons, displays, and now 'searches', 'blogs' and social networking sites are widespread types, though it is 'search engine' advertising that has proved to be the most profitable. Every major search engine or search portal offers to match topics of search with targeted advertising. Online advertising includes interactive marketing, social networking, email-marketing, blogging, podcasting and displays. Google's AdWords and AdSense have been the pioneers in this form of 'contextual' online advertising, particularly after it acquired eQuantive, an advertising company for six billion dollars in 2007. Rediff.com and indiatimes.com display ads through Google's AdSense. Google has teamed up with Yahoo to extend its advertising reach. It is estimated that Google earns two million dollars an hour from search-engine advertising.[1] How does Google rank advertisements on its search site and how much do advertisers pay? It appears that the ranking of ads is based on a combination of bid price (the amount advertisers are willing to bid for a certain keyword) and click-through-rate (the frequency with which users click on an ad) and that advertisers pay Google only when a surfer clicks on their ads.[2] Google India (www.google.co.in) offers search and translation facilities in English, Hindi, Tamil, Telugu, Bengali and Marathi. The India chapter of You Tube (in.youtube.com) offers video-sharing (and advertising) opportunities to Indians worldwide; NDTV has used it extensively for its shows and IIT, Chennai, has uploaded over 1600 lectures to the site.

---

[1] Migiel Helft: 'The Hands that Keep the Google Money Machine Running', *DNA Money*, 4 June 2008, p. 22.
[2] Ibid.

The online media competes with offline media for advertising revenue, and in several areas such as books, music, electronics, films, travel, recruitment and matrimonials, online media have an edge. Even blogs, emails and podcasts are replete with advertising messages. In 2007-08 Internet advertising was worth Rs. 225 crore in India compared to Rs. 60,000 crore in the United States. But this is no surprise, for barely 5.3% of India's population has access to the Net compared to 71% in the United States.

Zedo, an ad serving network based in San Francisco, has developed a 'behavioural targeting' software that keeps track of websites visited and serves relevant 'contextual' ads as the surfer is talking on a social networking site. Ten per cent of Zedo's ad volumes are served in India.[3] And Fox Interactive Media has developed a 'hypertargeting' technology that places Internet users in 'buckets' based on their search interests. Microsoft and NewsCorp's My Space exploit this technology to 'serve' ads to online surfers.

Viral advertising too has taken off through social networking websites such as Orkut, MySpace, Second Life, yaari.com, craigslist.com and others. This is an advertising message that is passed on from one virtual contact to another or from one group to another by email or blogs or social networks. It is akin to the buzz that is created through word-of-mouth publicity. Then there is 'user-generated' publicity that is promoted by commercial organizations such as the Sunsilk haircare brand (Cf. www.sunsilkgangofgirls.com). The 'gang' has now turned into a virtual community of over 20,000 'gangs' and over 200,000 registered members aged between 16 and 24, though most members are from the big cities. It is indeed a commercial 'virtual space' where young women talk about beauty, careers, fashion, fitness and relationships.

Mobile Advertising

The mobile/cellphone 'revolution' in India has provided yet

---

3 Ibid.

another opportunity to advertisers and PR professionals. It has in fact proved to be a windfall. For the over 300 million cellphone users, however, voice and text messages from marketing agencies around the clock have turned out to be a veritable nuisance. The Do-not-call (DNC) register has had little effect on tele-marketers despite the threat of penalties by TRAI. Instead of the 'opt-out' facility provided to mobile phone subscribers, an 'opt-in' facility needs to be offered so that only those subscribers who want to receive marketing messages are targeted by advertisers. But it appears that advertisers persist in imposing themselves on media users come what may. It is no wonder that the rate of 'ad avoidance' in all the mass media has been rising over the last decade. The 'right to commercial information' which advertisers declare at every fora to be a 'fundamental' right does not necessarily extend to making a nuisance of oneself. The new technology that assists marketers in their attempts to reach mobile subscribers is termed 'Blue-casting'; it beams advertisements (in the form of video-clips, ringtones, sound-bites, MP3 tracks, games, and wall-papers directly to Bluetooth-enabled mobile phones. Geo-targeting and tracking of subscribers wherever they are has now transformed mobile phones into yet another 'media vehicle' for advertisers. Mobile advertising in India has 7-8% of the market, while display ads have 60-65% and search engine ads 30-35%.[4] 'Embedded' advertising in cinema and television, 'insert' media in credit-card, phone and electricity bills, and 'direct mail' via email are other forms of advertising that promise to woo customers in the future.

Nature and Role of Advertising and Public Relations

Private business organisations usually engage 'accredited' or recognised advertising, PR agencies and media agencies to conduct their public campaigns for them. Some large companies such as Larsen and Toubro, and Voltas have their own

---

4 K.K. Sruthijith: 'Battle Intensifies for Ad Revenues in India's Online Space', MINT, 9 June 2008, p.06.

advertising and PR Departments; others like Reliance, Kirloskar and Hindustan Lever's have started their own ad agencies (which also accept work from other companies). The specialised PR agency is a recent development in India; right from the evolution of advertising, most ad agencies also helped out with PR work. Ad agencies plan, produce and distribute advertisements on behalf of advertisers (termed 'clients' or 'accounts) in accordance with a 'brief'. Advertising, PR and media agencies are commercial organisations in their own right, providing 'services' to manufacturing, business, government and other institutions. They function as intermediaries between advertisers and the media, buying 'time' in the electronic media and 'space' in the print media. They earn their profits from commissions provided by advertisers and the various media organisations. However, recent developments in Indian advertising (such as the rise of global media agencies) have threatened the continuation of the commission system.

Advertising/Account Planning

Since the costs of advertising are so high, it is considered extremely important to plan the advertising of a product, a service or an institution. A full page advertisement in *The Times of India* or *The Indian Express* could cost over three lakh rupees; a 10 second ad before a prime time saas-bahu soap opera on television costs over one or two lakh rupees. The rates depend on a number of factors such as readership and circulation in the case of print media, and GRPS in the case of television. On the Internet, advertising rates depend on position (home page, for instance), the type (banner, button, links, etc), the hits or page views, and so on. This is, of course, besides the costs of production. Careful planning at every stage of the process (account planning, campaign planning, media planning) is essential if the advertiser's budget is to be spent purposefully.

Advertising planning involves making certain what the specific objectives are, who is the target audience (TA), what is the nature of the message to be conveyed (the Unique Selling Proposition, for example), the positioning of the product or service, and the budget to cover production and media costs. It also involves pre-testing to find out how a sample of the target audience 'reads' the advertisement. Sometimes, an ad can turn people off by its language or illustration; certain negative images of rival products or brands can turn the target audience hostile to the product. Images that exploit the female body to sell products are under attack by consumer groups.

Media planning is the selection of appropriate media or a combination of media for 'placement' of advertisements. Thus ads targeted at women are 'placed' in women's magazines or women's pages of weekend newspapers, though it needs to be remembered that women read other magazines too, and that men read women's magazines. (Does this explain why the 'sexiest' ads are to be found in women's magazines?) For women executives, there is the *Executive Women's Digest*, and for upper-class men, monthly magazines like *Debonair*, *Gentlemen* and *Maxim*. Curiously, products and diets for slimming appear in health and nutrition magazines.

Media Buying and Selling

Most of the world's largest multinational media buying and media selling agencies are active in India, either on their own or in collaboration with Indian agencies. There are few restrictions on foreign investments in the advertising and PR business. Media Planning service/consultancy is now provided by these Media Agencies to advertisers, unlike earlier practices in advertising where Media Planning was an integral part and function of Advertising Agencies.

Global Media Networks
1. Group M (Mindshare, Maxus, MEC, Motivator, Mediacom)
2. Omnicom Madison
3. Publicis Groupe Media
4. Interpublic Media Council
5. Havas
6. Aegis

Indian Media Agencies
1. OMD
2. Starcom MediaVest
3. Mindshare
4. Mediaedge: cio (MEC)
5. Universal McCann
6. Mediacom
7. Zenith Optimedia

Table 42: Media Share in AdSpend (2007)

Media	AdSpend (Rs. Crore)	AdSpend (Percentage)
1. Print	8470	47.9
2. Television	7110	40.2
3. Outdoor/OOH	1275	7.2
4. Radio	480	2.7
5. Internet	250	1.4
6. Cinema	104.5	0.6
TOTAL	17,690	100.0

(Source: 5th Pitch-Madison Media Survey – 2008)

Testing Advertising Effectiveness

Advertising effectiveness relates to the extent to which an advertisement has been successful in winning over the maximum number of customers to purchase the product or service. While there may be other incidental effects of advertising (the company's image may improve; goodwill for the company may be created; the product may be bought just once to compare it with others; dissatisfaction with rival products may grow), the ultimate test of effectiveness is its impact on potential and current customers. Effectiveness, of course, is related to the goals of an ad campaign.

Several psychological tests have been devised to pre-test and post-test advertising copy and advertising campaigns. These evaluate readability and comprehension, changes in attitudes and perceptions, and credibility or believability. The 'Consumer Jury' is a technique that is frequently employed in the initial stages of a campaign. A small group of potential customers is brought together to discuss and evaluate the copy and the visual. Coupon-Return Analysis is another technique for measuring response and effectiveness. Sometimes, mechanical devices such as the eye movement camera, the 'galvanometer' and the 'electroencephalograph' are used to measure physical responses to an advertisement. Then there are Projective Techniques, borrowed from clinical psychology, which attempt to unearth the real views of respondents through 'word-association', 'sentence completion', 'cartoon-strip completion', 'mapping' and other tests.

Principles of Advertising

Advertisers and ad agencies believe that customers have needs and desires which can be fulfilled through the purchase and use of products and services. Following Abraham Maslow's 'hierarchy of needs', they assume that the basic human needs are: physiological, safety, love, esteem and self-actualisation. Advertising works largely through appeal to emotions of envy, fear, anxiety about one's appearance and the lack of status. In consumer product advertising, in particular, customers are cajoled into 'joining the crowd', 'having fun', 'improving one's status and appearance', and 'keeping up with the Joneses'.

It is widely assumed that advertising works if the AIDCA formula is followed. The formula sums up the principles of advertising. The name of the formula is derived from the initial letters of the words: Attention, Interest, Desire, Conviction and Action.

The formula suggests that the attention and interest of consumers must be gained first before the process of stimulating desire, imparting conviction and urging action in advertisements can bring about a change in buying behaviour. The fact, however, is that buying behaviour (or consumer psychology) is a very complex matter, and that advertisements comprise only one of the many elements that might result in a decision to make a purchase. We are not usually carried away by advertisements unless the products themselves are of some value or use to us. After all, we do not have a lot of money to throw around.

Advertisements grab Attention by their size, colour, visualization, layout, positioning or by a striking headline or slogan or appeal. They create Interest by holding out to consumers the hope or the promise of achieving something or being someone. Further, they stimulate Desire for the product by various strategies such as making you feel 'exclusive' or 'modern' or 'with-it', or perhaps by offering discounts or other incentives (say a free 'pager' for buying a fridge or a TV). Finally, advertisements impart Conviction (say by showing film stars using the brand) and urge Action ('For quick pain relief take Anacin'; 'Always use Johnson's body cream for your baby').

Public Relations in Industry

Public Relations is a communication technique frequently used in dealing with employees, trade unions, trade associations (internal 'publics') and also with the government, the press and other media, rival industries and organisations, and the general public (external 'publics'). The most widespread methods of communication with 'internal publics' include house journals, bulletins, letters, emails, SMS, blogs, and meetings; some of the methods for talking to 'external publics' are: press releases, press conferences, direct mail, company websites, social networks, exhibitions, sponsorship, event marketing, viral marketing, etc.

Public Relations Departments organise and maintain an efficient system of internal and external communications. They perform a council function for management and workers as well as for the public. Thus a vital function of the PR Department is to ensure a streamlined communication system, a system that keeps channels of communication open all the time to people within an organisation as well to the various external 'publics'.

The 'House Journal'

The 'house' or company journal is a regular or occasional publication which is distributed free to all employees, and sent out to dealers, shareholders and other well-wishers of the company. The journal enters the homes of most workers and thus helps information about the company to reach the public. The overall function of a house journal is to act as a bond between far-flung members of a corporate family. It counteracts any tendency to dehumanize and impersonalize the company's efforts in the pursuit of profits and wealth. Further, it helps engender participation in the organisation's activities. It promotes discussions on such questions as safety, productivity, and welfare. Ideally, the house journal should also involve the community, and should take up issues like environmental protection, national integration, discrimination, poverty and unemployment. In reality, however, the house journal is employed to act as the 'voice' of the management. It is a continuation of the top-down communication that takes place in the organisation.

Most house journals give prominence to messages from the company's chairman, to glossy pictures of workers' kids, and to articles by executives. The achievements of the company and of the employees on the sports field, in competitions and in community activities are also highlighted. In the ultimate analysis, the house journal is an excellent tool of publicising the company's achievements. The house journal is edited and brought out by the Public Relations Department of a company. More than a thousand house journals and company newsletters are published in India, with a print order of over a million copies. Several titles are now on the Internet, but also distributed as hard copies. Indeed, much of corporate communication now takes place on the Internet via emails, chats, IMs, blogs and social networks.

Table 43 : Titles of House Journals of Some Public and Private Sector Companies

	Company	House Journal
1.	Thermax Ltd.	Fireside
2.	Air India	Magic Carpet
3.	Reserve Bank of India	Without Reserve
4.	Hindustan Lever Ltd.	Hamara
5.	Bank of India	The Teller
6.	Telco Ltd.	Telco Parivar
7.	Indian Hotels Co. Ltd.	Apna Taj
8.	Pfizer Ltd.	The Crucible
9.	Mahanagar Telephone Nagar Ltd.	Antarang
10.	Indian Iron and Steel Co. Ltd.	Yours Faithfully

Media Relations

Perhaps the most efficient and cost effective technique for building up the corporate 'image' of an organisation is Press or Media Relations. The media provide an organisation a means of talking and listening to the public. With the pervasive presence of the media, customers tend to use the media to make their complaints about products and companies. And organisations, in their turn, use the media to make their point of view known to the community.

However, the media comprise only one of a whole gamut of techniques for creating goodwill and for winning over public opinion. This technique involves keeping the media regularly informed about the achievements and developments of an organisation. Some strategies that have been evolved over the years for keeping in touch with the media are: Media Contacts, Press Releases, Press Conferences and Press Visits. Most companies today have their own websites and conduct their PR work over the Internet. Some have launched social networking spaces where their dealers, distributors and customers can interact with one another as members of 'electronic communities'.

Public opinion is an elusive entity, but people's opinions and images of organisations are formed more by personal experiences and exchanges with primary and secondary groups than by the media. This is not to suggest that the media have no role to play; they are significant mediators, but have to contend with other equally 'significant others' such as parents, siblings, peers and personal experiences.

Going Beyond Media Relations

Public Relations used to be largely associated with Media Relations. Since the emergence of the 'new' digital and interactive media Public Relations has developed into a much more comprehensive professional practice taking within its ambit activities such as Corporate Communications, Event Management, Crisis Management, Investor Relations, Financial

PR, Brand PR, and Internal Communications PR. Media Relations continues to be a vital activity in Public Relations which in turn is considered as only a part of Integrated Marketing Communication (IMC).

Advertising and Corporate Social Responsibility

Do advertising people have a responsibility only to their clients – to sell their products or services or ideas, using any strategy in the bag as long as it wins customers and influences people? What about the responsibility to the social, cultural and moral values of the community in which they function? Ad people are, after all, citizens of a community, and it is as citizens that they have a duty to build rather than destroy the values of that community – unless, of course, those values degrade human dignity (e.g. the caste system, dowry, bonded labour). In the effort to promote commercial prosperity, advertisers cannot afford to turn their backs on the social and cultural environment in the community. For, it is within the context of their own social and cultural environment that people most easily understand and accept the messages of advertising. An exotic environment may grab attention, and even perhaps hold the interest for a while, but will rarely persuade and convince as effectively.

The Indian Institute of Mass Communication, New Delhi carried out in 1982, a wide-ranging study on *Advertising and Social Responsibility*. It involved an analysis of over 3,500 ads in 35 English and 27 Hindi magazines. As part of the study, the Institute also did a survey of consumers' reactions to advertising in Delhi. The majority (62%) of the consumers interviewed felt that advertising was important and relevant in present day society, but wanted ads to be "checked for the validity of claims made, and censored to avoid socially irresponsible advertising". They felt that 'a number of ads exaggerated product qualities; the products were often not as good as their advertisements claimed', and that a fair amount of ads used women to attract attention, though often the portrayal of women was not necessarily desirable, or even relevant.

The IIMC analysis revealed that 'one out of every five ads featured a female model', whereas a male model appeared in only one out of every seven ads. In more than 10% of the ads featuring female models, their presence was unnecessary. They were there merely as attention-getters or as 'props'. Ads for cigarettes and textiles were found to be particularly guilty of this approach. Further, 'more than nine out of every ten cigarette ads portrayed a sophisticated, luxurious and snobbish atmosphere.' Ads for fabrics, ready-made garments, cosmetics, jewellery, leather goods and toiletries were also found to portray a highly westernised, showy and snobbish life-style. This was mostly true of the ads appearing in English magazines.

Kamala Bhasin and Bina Agrawal's investigation of the commercial jingles heard on the Vividh Bharati service of All India Radio provide further evidence of socially irresponsible advertising. The jingles promoting 'Jolly' TV sets and 'Cool Foam' Mattresses, to name only two, clearly promote the dowry system. Other jingles convey an image of Indian women as housewives solely preoccupied with cosmetics, clothes and similar adornments, and as stupid, gullible and superstitious.

TV advertisements present a very similar picture. The commercials on TV depict a woman essentially as a consumer. Cosmetics and clothes promise the development of a woman's potentiality to entice the right man; they portray a smart but very capable housewife who is clever at using things in the kitchen, which are appreciated and approved even by the mother-in-law. She is also presented as a very devoted and loving wife and mother. The mass of working class women and their problems are nowhere in the picture.

So outraged are the members of several women's organisations at this degrading image of women purveyed in the mass media that they have formed a Committee on the Portrayal of Women in the Media. Other social organisations have raised their voices against obscene film-posters which are not subject to censorship like the films they advertise. Often, the scenes depicted in the posters are not to be seen in the films, or have been deleted at the instance of the Censor Board.

Advertisements appearing on public service television and radio have to be approved by Doordarshan and AIR authorities. However, advertisements on private television channels (and they comprise the majority), in newspapers and magazines, and on outdoor sites are not regulated by any guidelines. It's a free-for-all in this very competitive market, with advertisers sometimes taking recourse to unethical practices to fight the competition. Liquor manufacturers and advertising agencies have drawn up a code of self-regulation for advertising of hard drinks on cable and satellite television channels. But 'surrogate advertising' of well-known liquor brands continues with the impression being given that soda, playing cards, cassettes, glass crockery and other items are being advertised. (Doordarshan and All India Radio are prohibited from carrying liquor advertisements on any of their channels). The Code of Ethics drawn up by the Advertising Standards Council of India (ASCI) has had some impact.

Ethics in Advertising and Public Relations

Advertising and PR organisations are well aware that consumer groups and the public are often critical of the 'manipulative' and 'deceptive' methods resorted to by some advertisers and PR professionals. The trade associations that represent these professionals have drawn up Codes of Ethics with the hope of regulating and disciplining practices in Advertising and Public Relations. The Advertising Standards Council of India (ASCI), a voluntary body (of over 250 members who together represent almost 70 per cent of the industry) which brings together advertisers, ad agencies and the media, has drawn up a detailed and elaborate Code (see below). It has also established a Consumer Complaints Council (CCC) to examine complaints received from the public or from advertising agencies. The ASCI has also, in collaboration with the Society of Indian Automobile Manufacturers (SIAM), drafted Guidelines on Advertisements for Automotive Vehicles. The Guidelines

state that advertisements should not:
a) Portray violation of traffic rules
b) Show speed maneuverability in a manner which encourages unsafe or reckless driving, which could harm the driver, passengers and/or the general public
c) Show stunts or actions which require professional driving skills, in normal traffic conditions, which in any case should carry a readable cautionary message drawing viewer attention to the depiction of stunts.

Further, SEBI has drawn up a Code for the issue of IPOs and other types of financial advertising. These Codes are enforced through a process of self-regulations; most advertisements found to be 'offensive' or infringing established ethical practices in the industry are immediately withdrawn.

The Public Relations Society of India (PRSI) has not yet formulated a Code of Ethics for its members; it has declared, however, that its members are committed to the International Code of Ethics, drawn up by the International Public Relations Association (IPRA) in Athens in 1965, and later modified at the annual meeting of the IPRA Council held in Teheran on April 17, 1968. A second trade association is the Public Relations Consultants Association of India (PRCAI) established by seven PR firms; this body has its own Code of Conduct which is similar to the Athens Code. Both Codes are spelt out below. (India's National Public Relations Day is April 21.)

CODE OF THE ADVERTISING STANDARDS COUNCIL OF INDIA (ASCI)

CHAPTER I

To Ensure the Truthfulness and Honesty of representations and claims made by Advertisements and to safeguard against misleading Advertisements.

(1) Advertisements must be truthful. All descriptions, claims and comparisons which related to matters of objectively ascertainable fact, should be capable of substantiation. Advertisers and advertising agencies are required to produce such substantiation as and when called upon to do so by the Advertising Standards Council of India.

(2) Where advertising claims are expressly stated to be based on or supported by independent research or assessment, the source and date of this should be indicated in the advertisement.

(3) Advertisements should not contain any reference to any person, firm or institution without due permission; nor should a picture of any generally identifiable person be used in advertising without due permission.

(4) Advertisements shall not distort facts nor mislead the consumer by means of implications or omissions. Advertisements shall not contain statements or visual presentations which directly or by implication or by omission or by ambiguity or by exaggeration are likely to mislead the consumer about the product advertised or the advertiser or about any other product or advertiser.

(5) Advertisements shall not be so framed as to abuse the trust of consumers or exploit their lack of experience or

knowledge. No advertisement shall be permitted to contain any claim so exaggerated as to lead to grave or widespread disappointment in the minds of consumers. For example:

(a) Products shall not be described as 'free' where there is any direct cost to the consumer other than the actual cost of any delivery, freight or postage. Where such costs are payable by the consumer, a clear statement that this is the case shall be made in the advertisement.

(b) Where a claim is made that if one product is purchased another product will be provided 'free', the advertiser is required to show as and when called upon by The Advertising Standards Council of India that the price paid by the consumer for the product which is offered for purchase with the advertised incentive.

(c) Claims which use expressions such as "Up to five years guarantee" or "Prices from as low as Y" are not acceptable if there is a likelihood of the consumer being misled either as to the extent of the availability or as to the applicability of the benefits offered.

(d) Special care and restraint has to be exercised in advertisements addressed to those suffering from weakness, any real or perceived inadequacy of any physical attributes such as height or bust development, obesity, illness, impotence, infertility, baldness and the like to ensure that claims or representations, directly or by implication, do not exceed what is considered prudent by generally accepted standards or medical practice and the actual efficacy of the product.

(e) Advertisements inviting the public to invest money shall not contain statements which may mislead the consumer in respect of the security offered, rates of return or terms of amortisation; where any of the foregoing elements are contingent upon the continuance of or change in existing conditions, or any other assumptions, such conditions or assumptions must be clearly indicated in the advertisements.

(f) Advertisements inviting the public to take part in lotteries or price competitions permitted under the law or which hold out the prospects of gifts shall state clearly all material conditions so as to enable the consumers to obtain a true and fair view of their prospects in such activity. Further, such advertisers shall make adequate provision for the judging of such competitions, announcement of the results and the fair distribution of prizes or gifts according to the advertised terms and conditions within a reasonable period of time. With regard to the announcement of results, it is clarified that the advertiser's responsibility under this section of the Code is discharged adequately if the advertiser publicizes the main results in the media used to announce the competition as far as is practicable, and advises the individual winners by post.

(6) Obvious untruths or exaggerations intended to amuse or to catch the eye of the consumer are permissible. Provided that, they are clearly to be seen as humorous or hyperbolic and not likely to be understood as making literal or misleading claims for the advertised product.

CHAPTER II

To ensure that Advertisements are not offensive to generally accepted standards of Public Decency.

Advertisements should contain nothing indecent, vulgar or repulsive which is likely, in the light of generally prevailing standards of decency and property, to cause grave or widespread offence.

CHAPTER III

To Safeguard against the indiscriminate use of Advertising in situations or for the promotion of products which are regarded as Hazardous to society or to Individuals to a degree or of a type which is Unacceptable to Society at Large.

(1) No advertisement shall be permitted which:
   (a) Tends to incite people to crime or to promote disorder and violence or intolerance.
   (b) Derides any race, caste, colour, creed or nationality.
   (c) Presents criminality as desirable or directly or indirectly encourages people – particularly children to emulate it or conveys the modus operandi of any time.
   (d) Adversely affects friendly relations with a foreign state.

(2) Advertisements addressed to children shall not contain anything, whether in illustration or otherwise, which might result in their physical, mental or moral harm or which exploits their vulnerability. For example, no advertisement
   (a) Shall encourage children to enter strange places or to converse with strangers in an effort to collect coupons, wrappers, labels or the like.
   (b) Should depict children leaning dangerously outside windows, overbridges or climbing dangerous cliffs and the like.
   (c) Should show children climbing or reaching dangerously to reach products or for any other purpose.
   (d) Should show children using or playing with matches or any inflammable or explosive substance; or playing with or using sharp knives, guns or mechanical or electrical appliances, the careless use of which could lead to their suffering cuts, burns, shocks or other injury.

(3) Advertisements shall not, without justifiable reason, show or refer to dangerous practices or manifest a disregard for safety or encourage negligence.

(4) Advertisements should contain nothing which is in breach of the law, or omit anything which the law requires.

(5) Advertisements shall not propagate products, the use of which is banned under the law.

CHAPTER IV

To ensure that advertisements observe Fairness in Competition such that the Consumers need to be informed on choices in the market-place and the canons of generally accepted competitive behaviour in Business are both served.

(1) Advertisements containing comparisons with other manufacturers or suppliers or with other products, including those where a competitor is named are permissible in the interests of vigorous competition and public enlightenment, provided:
 (a) It is clear that aspects of the advertiser's product are being compared with what aspects of the competitor's product.
 (b) The subject matter of comparison is not chosen in such a way as to confer an artificial advantage upon the advertiser or so as to suggest that a better bargain is offered than is truly the case.
 (c) The comparisons are factual, accurate and capable of substantiation.
 (d) There is no likelihood of the consumer being misled as a result of the comparison, whether about the product advertiser or that with which it is compared.
 (e) The advertisement does not unfairly denigrate, attack or discredit other products, advertisers of advertisements directly or by implication.

(2) Advertisements shall not make unjustifiable use of the name or initials of any other firm, company or institution, nor take unfair advantage of the goodwill attached to the trade mark

or symbol of another firm or its product or the goodwill acquired by its advertising campaign.

(3) Advertisements shall not be so similar to other advertisements in general layout, copy, slogans, visual presentations, music or sound effects as to be likely to mislead or confuse consumers.

PRSI'S CODE OF ETHICS

International Code of Ethics for Public Relations which was adopted by the Public Relations Society of India at its 1st National Conference at New Delhi on 21-4-1968.

Considering that all Member countries of the United Nations Organisation have agreed to abide by its Charter which reaffirm "its faith in fundamental human rights, in the dignity and worth of the human person" and that have regard to the very nature of their profession, Public Relations practitioners in these countries should undertake to ascertain and observe the principles set out in this Charter,

Considering that apart from "rights", human beings have not only physical or material needs but also intellectual, moral and social needs, and that their rights are of real benefit to them only insofar as these needs are essentially met,

Considering that, in the course of their professional duties and depending on how these duties are performed, Public Relations practitioners can substantially help to meet these intellectual, moral and social needs,

And lastly,

Considering that the use of techniques enabling them to come simultaneously into contact with millions of people gives Public Relations practitioners a power that has to be restrained by the observance of strict moral code.

On all these grounds, the Public Relations Society of India hereby declares that it accepts, as its moral charter the principle of the following Code of Ethics, and that if, in the light of evidence submitted to the Society, a member of this Society should be found to have infringed this Code in the course of his professional duties, he will be deemed to be guilty of serious misconduct calling for an appropriate penalty.

Accordingly, each Member of this Society, Shall Endeavour

1. To contribute to the achievement of the moral and cultural conditions enabling human beings to reach their full stature and enjoy the indefeasible rights to which they are entitled under the "Universal Declaration of Human Rights";
2. To establish communication patterns and channels which, by fostering the free flow of essential information, will make each member of the group feel that he is being kept informed, and also give him an awareness of his own personal involvement and responsibility and of his solidarity with other members;
3. To conduct himself always and in all circumstances in such a manner as to deserve and secure the confidence of those with whom he comes into contact;
4. To bear in mind that, because of the relationship between his profession and the public, his conduct – even in private – will have an impact on the way in which the profession as a whole is appraised;

Shall Undertake

5. To observe, in the course of his professional duties, the moral principles and rules of the "Universal Declaration of Human Rights";
6. To pay due regard to, and uphold, human dignity, and to recognise the right of each individual to judge for himself;
7. To establish the moral, psychological and intellectual conditions for dialogue in its true sense, and to recognise the right of the parties involved to state their case and express their views;
8. To act, in all circumstances in such a manner as to take account of the respective interest of the parties involved: both the interests of the organisation which he serves and the interests of the public concerned;

9. To carry out his undertakings and commitments which shall always be so worded as to avoid any misunderstanding, and to show loyalty and integrity in all circumstances so as to keep the confidence of his clients or employers, past or present, and of all the publics that are affected by his actions;

Shall Refrain From

10. Subordinating the truth to other requirements;
11. Circulating information which is not based on established and ascertainable facts;
12. Taking part in any venture or undertaking which is unethical or dishonest or capable of impairing human dignity and integrity;
13. Using any "manipulative" methods or techniques designed to create subconscious motivations which the individual cannot control of his own free will and so cannot be held accountable for the action taken on them.

PRCAI'S CODE OF ETHICS

All the members of PRCAI agree to the following:

- To maintain the highest standards of professional endeavour, integrity, confidentiality including financial propriety and personal conduct.
- Deal honestly and fairly in business with employers, employees, clients, fellow professionals and other professions and the public.
- To value the customs, practices and codes of clients employers, colleagues, fellow professionals, other professionals all over India.
- To take all reasonable care for best employment practice giving no space for complaint of unfair discrimination on any grounds
- To be in the legal and regulatory frame works affecting the practise of public relations all over India.

- Encourage professional training and development among members of the profession.
- To respect and abide by this code and related notes of guidance issued by PRCAI and encourage others to do the same.

Principles Of Good Practice

Integrity
- Honest and responsible regard for the public interest.
- Checking the reliability and accuracy of information before dissemination.
- Never mislead the clients, employers, employees, colleagues and fellow professionals about the nature of representation or what can be competently delivered and achieved.

Competence
- Being aware of the limitations of professional competence: without limiting realistic scope for development, being willing to accept or delegate only that work, for which practising is done by skilled and experienced professionals.
- Where appropriate, collaborating on projects to ensure the necessary skill base.
- Transparency and conflicts of interest, (circumstances which may give rise to them) in writing to clients, potential clients and employers as soon as they arise
- Ensuring that services provided are costed and accounted for in a manner, which confirms to accepted business practice and ethics.

Confidentiality
- Safeguard to the confidences of present and former clients and employers
- Being careful to avoid using confidential and 'insider' information to the disadvantage or prejudice of clients and employers, or to self-advantage of any kind.
- Not disclosing confidential information unless specific

permission has been granted or the Public interest is at stake or if required by law.

Maintaining Professional Standards
- PRCAI members are encouraged to spread awareness and pride in the public relations profession where practicable such as:
- Identifying and closing professional skills gaps through Professional development programme
- Offering work experience to students interested in pursuing a career in Public Relations.
- Participating in the work for the institute through the committee structure, special interest and vocational groups training and networking events.
- Encouraging employees and colleagues to join and support the PRCAI
- Sharing Information on good practice with members and equally referring perceived examples of poor practice to the association.

FOR FURTHER READING

A. PROFESSIONAL ADVERTISING AND PUBLIC RELATIONS
1. Sushil Bahl: *Making PR Work*, New Delhi: Wheeler Publishing, 1994.
2. K.R. Balan: *What the Management Defines... Public Relations Defines*, New Delhi: Sterling Publishers Pvt. Ltd., 2003.
3. Rama Bijapurkar: *We Are Like That Only: Understanding the Logic of Consumer India*, New Delhi: Penguin, 2008.
4. Anil Basu: *Public Relations: Problems and Prospects*, New Delhi: Space Age Publications.
5. Samar Basu: *The Public Relations Practitioner*, Calcutta: Shibamaya Prakashani, 1993.
6. G.C. Banik: *Effective Public Relations in Public and Private Sectors*, Mumbai: Jaico Publishing House, 2002.

7. Rita Bhamani: *The Corporate Peacock: New Plumes for Public Relations*, Mumbai: Rupa and Co.
8. Arun Chaudhari: *Indian Advertising (1780-1950)*, New Delhi: Tata-McGraw-Hill Publishing Co. Ltd, 2007.
9. S.A. Chunawala, Keval J. Kumar, K.C. Sethia et al: *Advertising Theory and Practice*, Mumbai: Himalaya Publishing House, 2007.
10. L.A. Eerayayil and J. Vadakuncherry: *Public Relations at the Cutting Edge*, Trivandrum: Police Training College.
11. Joseph Fernandez: *Corporate Communications: A 21st Century Primer*, New Delhi: Response Books, 2004.
12. Subir Ghosh: *Public Relations Today in the Indian Context*, Calcutta: Rupa and Co., 1995.
13. Ajit S. Gopal: *Public Relations for a Better World*, New Delhi: Har-Anand, 1995.
13. Vanita Kohli-Khandekar: *The Indian Media Business*, New Delhi: Response Books, 2005.
14. A.G. Krishamurthy: *Desi Dream Merchants*, New Delhi: Tata-McGraw-Hill, 2005.
15. Subroto Sengupta: *Brand Positioning*, New Delhi: Tata-McGraw-Hill, 1990.
16. C. Sardana (Ed.): *Applied Public Relations in the Indian Context*, New Delhi: Har-Anand Publications, 1999.
17. Sanjay Tiwari: *The (Un)Common Sense of Advertising: Getting the Basics Right*, New Delhi: Response Books/Sage Publications, 2003.
18. June Valladares: *The Craft of Copywriting*, New Delhi: Response Books, 2003.
19. Anupama Vohra: *Advertising on Television*, New Delhi: Wadhwa & Co., 2005.

B. CRITICAL ANALYSIS OF ADVERTISING AND PUBLIC RELATIONS

20. Katherine Toland Frith (Ed.): *Advertising in Asia: Communication, Culture and Consumption*, Ames: Iowa State University Press, 1996.
21. Keval J. Kumar: *Advertising: A Critical View*, Pune: Nirali Prakashan, 1992.
22. J. M. Kaul: *Public Relations in India*, Calcutta: Natyaprakash.

23. W.S. Kline Leiss and Sut Jhally: *Social Communication in Advertising*, New York: Methuen, 1986.
24. National Council of Applied Economic Research (NCAER): *Socio-Economic Effects of Advertising in India*, New Delhi, 1993.
25. Ram Sehgal: *Mixed Feelings: My Advertising Years*, New Delhi: Tata-McGraw-Hill, 2006.
26. Krishnamurthy Sriramesh (Eds.): *Public Relations in Asia: An Anthology*, Singapore: Thomson Learning, 2004.
27. K. Sriramesh and D. Vercio (Eds.): *The Global Public Relations Handbook: Theory, Research and Practice*, Marwah N J: Lawrence Erlbaum Associates, 2003.
28. Namita Unnikrishnan and Shailaja Bajpai: *The Impact of Television Advertising on Children*, New Delhi: Sage Publications, 1996.

C. JOURNALS

1. PITCH
2. IMPACT
3. USP Age (cf. Special issue on 'The Future of Public Relations', June 2008)
4. Brand Reporter
5. 4Ps
6. Public Relations Voice
7. The Marketing White Book (Annual from Business World)
8. Journal of Creative Communication (MICA/Sage Publication).
9. Campaign India
10. Outdoor Advertising

WEB RESOURCES

1. www.adage.com (Advertising Age)
2. www.exchange4media.com (News site on Indian advertising and marketing)
3. www.agencyfaqs.com
4. www.indiaprwire.com
5. www.prcai.org (Public Relations Consultants Association of India)
6. www.gfpr.org (Global Forum for Public Relations, Hyderabad)

7. www.magindia.com (Discussions on Indian Advertising)
8. www.icirrus.com
9. www.tamindia.com (Television Audience Measurement)
10. www.adexindia.com (Advertising Trends in India)
11. www.lovemarks.com (Insights from CEO, Saatchi & Saatchi)
12. www.allaboutoutdoor.com
13. www.esomar.org
14. www.prwatch.org
15. www.corporatewatch.org
16. www.ascionline.com (Advertising Standards Council of India)
17. www.auditbureau.org (Audit Bureau of Circulation)

REVIEW QUESTIONS

1. Distinguish between the following:
   (a) Advertising and Public Relations
   (b) Product advertising and Institutional/Corporate advertising
   (c) Classified and Display Advertising
   (d) Media Planning and Account Planning
   (e) Internal PR and External PR
2. Why is it important to plan an advertising campaign? What are the important points to keep in mind while planning a campaign?
3. What is the AIDCA formula? Does it work?
4. What is 'media planning'? What kind of background information does a media planner need?
5. What are 'Projective Techniques' in advertising research? What are the limitations of such techniques?
6. How has the Internet changed practices in PR and Advertising?
7. Why has it become 'crucial' for PR Departments and Agencies to monitor and even to participate in blogs, chat-rooms and social networks? How ethical is this practice?

SUGGESTED PROJECTS

1. Select your favourite daily newspaper. Mark all the different types of advertisements you come across on the various pages. Categorise them into different types. Now find out which type is predominant. Why do you think this is so? Why are there no advertisements on the Editorial page?

2. Go to the business page of a daily newspaper. Mark all the ads, then read through the news reports and mark the ones you feel are the result of Public Relations. How does the content of the ads differ from that in the news reports?
3. Plan the publication of a House Journal. How would you collect articles and photographs? What types of news items and articles would you highlight? Which items would you upload to the company's website?
4. You are the PRO of a private company. Organise a Press Conference to announce the launch of a new product.
5. Write out a Press Release on the occasion of the visit of a distinguished industrialist to your company.
6. Sketch a rough plan for a House Journal for your company on the occasion of its golden jubilee.
7. Plan a website for doing Public Relations for your company.
8. Conduct a Case Study of the Public Relations strategies employed by a manufacturing/service/IT company in your city.
9. Conduct a 'Communication Audit' for a selected firm. Recommend strategies for improving internal and external communications of the firm.
10. Track the 'image' of an IT company in two major newspapers of your city. Conduct a content analysis of news stories and features about the company over a period of three months.

SECTION III
PSYCHOLOGY AND SOCIOLOGY OF MEDIA AUDIENCES

Communication and the Social Sciences

Communication is an inter-disciplinary area of study taking within its compass the disciplines of political science, economics, literature, statistics, philosophy, psychology, sociology, linguistics and anthropology. The origins of the subject are traceable to Germany and the United States in the early twentieth century. It was a time when European sociologists like Max Weber, Emile Durkheim, Georges Simmel and later the Chicago School of Sociologists, began to raise questions related to the role of the press in society. In later years, with the rise of the Third Reich, both Germans and Americans were worried about Nazi propaganda, and were searching for the most effective strategies to propagate and to counter it. Then there were American advertisers making vigorous attempts to maximize profits through manipulation of customer behaviour. The growth of the press, cinema and radio was dramatic during the pre-World War II years. It was therefore natural that some of the basic questions raised by political scientists, sociologists and psychologists at the time related to questions of perceptions, attitudes, beliefs and behaviour in the new context of media pervasiveness.

By the 1960s, however, it came to be accepted in the disciplines involved that 'attitudes' were infinitely complex phenomena, and were not subject to easy manipulation, though development communication researchers such as Daniel Lerner, Lucian Pye, Wilbur Schramm and Everett Rogers persisted in imposing their 'modernization' model of development using the mass media. Meanwhile, the mass media grew from strength to strength and with breakthroughs in electronics and telecommunications came to regulate the whole of society. It made inroads into the home, and revolutionised social life. So all-pervasive did the media become that sociologists were obliged to accept it as a 'social system' and as an 'industry' in its own right. They went to the extent of saying that the mass media had created a 'mass' society and a 'mass' culture. 'Critical' schools focussed attention on the media product, the media professionals and on business/political groups that owned and controlled the media. The political and economic contexts in which media functioned was of crucial interest to them. They called into question the commercialization and politicization of the mass media – which they termed 'cultural' or 'consciousness' industries. The Frankfurt School of Social Research pioneered these attacks on the mass media in the 1940s. Later, two schools of 'critical' scholars that campaigned for this new approach to media studies in the 1970s and 1980s were: (1) The 'Cultural Studies' School (led by Raymond Williams, Richard Hoggarth and Stuart Hall), and (2) The 'Political Economy' School (led by Peter Golding and Graham Murdock of the Centre for Mass Communication Research, Leicester University, and Nicholas Garnham of the Polytechnic of Central London.)

As the philosopher Kellner points out, 'radicals have conceptualized television as part of 'an ideological state apparatus' (Althusser), as 'a mind manager' (Herbert Schiller), as 'the cultural arm of the industrial social order' (George Gerbner), as 'an instrument that maintains hegemony and legitimates the status quo' (Tuchman), as a 'looking glass' that provides a distorted and ideological view of social life (Rapping), as an instrument that 'invents reality' according to the needs and imperatives of corporate capitalism' (Parenti), and as a propaganda machine that 'manufactures consent' to the existing political socio-political order (Herman and Noam Chomsky).[1] So, while the classic 'critical' theory of the Frankfurt School (Herbert Marcuse, Walter Benjamin) was predominantly negative in its view of television, and media as an instrument of

---

1   Douglas Kellner: *Television and the Crisis of Democracy*, Boulder: Westview Press, 1990. p.6.

domination, Kellner says he follows Walter Benjamin, Bertolt Brecht and Enzensberger who conceptualise television as 'a potential instrument of progressive social change'.² But even this approach attributes too much power to the effects of the media. Considerable revisions in the approach of scholars to media studies took place in the late 1980s, with the end of the Cold War and the emergence of 'the active viewer' in reception research.³ Further revisions came about when the novelty of television wore off and the 'new' convergent media, especially the Internet and mobile telephony, introduced interactivity, asynchronicity, mobility, flexibility and user-friendliness into mass communication.

Media Audiences

The definition of a 'media audience' depends on one's perspective of the role of communication in society. If for instance, we look upon communication as a commodity or as merchandise, and media as tools for selling that commodity, a 'media audience' for us would be no better than a potential market for products and services. On the other hand, if we consider communication to be a social good, a public resource and a public service, a 'media audience' would be a participative and dialogic community, and the media as serving the educational, informational and cultural needs of the community. Further, if communication to us is a tool for persuasion and propaganda to promote certain political, religious or moral views, then a 'media audience' is 'the masses' that need to be indoctrinated.

A 'media audience' is unlike say an audience for a political meeting, a theatrical performance, a street performance, a mela or a lecture. Sociologists like to define an audience as a 'conventionalized crowd' assembled together. A media audience, however, is more than a conventionalized crowd, but rather a

---
2   Ibid.
3   Cf. Janice Radway: *Reading the Romance*, Ien Ang: *Watching Dallas*, David Morley : *Family Television*. (See below for further references to work on 'reception' and the 'active viewer'.

collectivity, an aggregate of persons who are readers, listeners, and viewers of different media or their various components. However, this 'collectivity', is not collected together at one place or even at one time. Though in most cases, members of the audience are attending components of one medium or another at the same time, time-shift recording (audio and video) has made it possible to listen to radio or to watch television and films at one's own convenience. Later, digitization and media convergence made it possible to experience the same on a variety of reception platforms. Hence what makes a media audience a conventional group is the fact that they are attending to the same components. That audience has come together (not in time and space) but in the common act of reading, listening or viewing. Time, distance, geography and discrete media technologies and reception platforms have become immaterial.

The composition of the group is predictable in some ways; unpredictable in others. So is the reception of the audience. The quality and nature of the response too is largely unknown. While it is true that a particular component or a medium has 'caused' the audience, the audience too has in a way 'caused' the medium; the audience has influenced the form and substance of the medium, its genres and its components. Indeed, the various genres and components/programmes are part of, and have often been taken from the socio-cultural experience of the audience. Audiences therefore, 'read' the messages of the media in terms of that experience; they 'negotiate' its various meanings, accepting or rejecting or 're-reading' the open and the latent (explicit and implicit) layers of meaning. Audiences generally do not interact with media messages as a 'mass' (as Raymond Williams observed the 'mass' exists only in the minds of the elite) but rather as a family, a cultural group, a social class, a caste or tribal group. The media, therefore, are not out there unrelated to their audiences, but an integral part of the social history and cultural values of the audience.

The Audience as 'Market'

Mass media audiences are the subject of much research in India. Most of the research, however, is what is aptly termed 'market research'. The primary objective of market research is to provide advertisers and advertising agencies with quantitative data about the access and exposure of selected ('segmented') audiences to the various mass media or to their various components. Such collection of data rarely goes beyond 'head-counting' though tall claims are generally made about 'qualitative' methodologies also being employed. Armed with such 'reliable' data (believed to be 'scientifically' collected), advertisers can 'slot' their advertising spots in newspapers or magazines with the highest readership among audiences that have a good purchasing power (often termed 'target audience') or on the radio or TV programmes which have the highest 'rating' or even on websites, search engines, blogs and social networks that have the highest number of 'page-views', 'hits' or 'click-throughs'. Among professional advertisers and marketing managers such an exercise is known as 'media planning' but more ambitiously, 'media research'.

So, if I want to sell a new soft drink or a new brand of soap to upper middle class housewives, I would be advised by the 'media planner' to place my advertisement in a single medium or in a combination of media (the 'multi-media' campaign) most regularly read or watched by my target audience. That potential market for my product is the 'media audience' for the market researcher. It is a deliberately selected segment of the whole audience, selected for its market value, not for its potential as an audience as such. From the perspective of the 'market researcher' and 'media planner', therefore, an audience is a 'construct', carved out of a larger group with the sole purpose of persuading (and manipulating) that segment of the audience to buy a product or service. To the market researcher and the advertiser, then, a media audience is a group of potential customers for products and services advertised in the media.

Advertisers and market researchers are not the only

professional group that studies media audiences. Psychologists, sociologists, anthropologists and other social scientists too look at audiences from their own diverse perspectives. Of course, they could assist market researchers in their efforts, and many do so. In fact this is how media audience research began, in the first place, in the United States. Academics were funded by business and government to look at the 'effects' of the mass media; changes in perceptions, attitudes, opinions and beliefs were scrutinized to study the role of the media in bringing about changes in consumer behaviour. Later, this selling out to business and government came to be termed 'administrative research' as against the more serious 'critical' research of social science. Thus, research for the purpose of exploiting the media for persuasion and propaganda was 'administrative'; research which questioned and challenged the status quo, which looked at the media as a social system, an institution and an industry, was 'critical'. Administrative research focussed on media audiences as 'consumers', as passive receivers; critical research turned the searchlight on the media themselves, studying their hidden meanings and their production processes; this approach considered audiences as subjects and as citizens. In recent years, communication researchers have begun looking at families, women, children and other groups in terms of their interactions with TV and with other members of the group. The methods used for such research have been largely qualitative, such as ethnographic observation, participant-observation, and in-depth group discussions[4]. Similar research methods are employed to study the activity of Internet surfers and mobile telephone users.

The Psychology of Audiences

Group Influences
A group is a collection of people who share some common

---

4   Cf. James Lull: *World Families Watch Television*, Newbury Park: Sage, 1989; David Morley: *Family Television*, London: Comedia, 1986; Roger Silverstone: *Television and Everyday Life*, London:Routledge, 1994; Michael Charlton and Ben Bachmair: *Media Communication in Everyday Life*, Munich: K.G. Saur, 1990.

characteristics, and who interact with one another. A social group is 'any number of persons who share a consciousness of membership and of interaction'. Thus we belong to social groups like the family, the community, the caste, the trade union, the professional associations, political parties, student bodies, graduates, teachers and the like. No man is an island; he is a member not of one group alone, but of many groups, and many move from one group to another through one's long life and career. No matter how strong-willed an individual one is, the pressure of groups shapes to a large extent one's attitudes, beliefs, values and opinions. Groups are a vital social reality from which there is little escape. They, much more than the mass media or the new media, are the agents of change as well as of resistance to change. Group-leaders (or opinion leaders) play an important role in the behaviour of the group. It is only the rare individual who defies the group and sets off on his or her own no matter what the consequences. But then he or she goes on to become a member of some other group or groups.

Types of Groups

The group that is most intimate and close is known as the primary group. Such for instance are the family, the peer group, the gang or the clique. The three conditions that give rise to primary groups are: (a) a close physical proximity, (b) the small size of the group, which makes for face-to-face association and co-operation, and (c) the lasting nature of the bond or a relationship like that between a husband, wife and children.

The secondary or peer group, on the other hand, is characterized by a less close relationship between members. Although secondary groups sometimes provide pleasant human relationships, sociability is ordinarily not their goal. So, while primary groups are relationship-oriented, secondary groups are goal-oriented and much less cohesive. Examples of secondary groups are: the college, the school, the various organizations and unions, the army, film and other entertainment societies, and clubs and political parties. Then there are castes, tribes, religious and linguistic communities, and regional groups. These groups, like the primary groups, exercise a strong influence on our thought and behaviour even determining the prejudices with which we watch mass media programmes.

The influence of a group on the attitude of an individual is generally treated in terms of the concept of 'reference group'. A more specific concept than secondary group, it is a group that an individual takes as a frame of reference for self-evaluation and attitude formation. Such a group has the function of setting and enforcing standards of conduct and belief. It also serves as a standard against which people compare themselves and others.

But our 'reference group' differs from situation to situation. For instance, when we watch a cricket test match our reference group is the nation we belong to, not usually the religious group we are members of. So also, for the middle-classes the reference group would be the upper class whose riches and lifestyles they aspire to. Consequently, reference groups are not necessarily the groups of which we are members, but rather the groups we long or wish to be members of. It is these groups that provide us the 'frame of reference' in terms of which we respond to communication. This is not to discount the role of primary and secondary groups in our understanding of and response to communication. The term 'interpretive communities'[5] perhaps comes closest to describing the groups that shape and influence our reaction to the messages of the various media.

As more and more of us become part of 'virtual communities' on the Internet we begin to relate to new social formations and groups which cut across all regional, national and cultural borders. Cyberspace is borderless, timeless and even spaceless but 'real' nevertheless despite being totally virtual. For, the 'news groups', 'social networks' and 'virtual communities' we become part of are inhabited by real people, no matter how faceless they might be. Some virtual groups (social networks for instance) are anonymous (the members take on different

---

5 James Lull: 'The Social Uses of Television', *Herman Communication Research*, 1980 (6), pp. 197-209. See also Thomas R. Lindlof: 'Media Audiences as Interpretive Communities', in *Communication Year Book 11*, ed. J.A. Anderson, Newbury Park, CA: Sage, 1988, pp. 81-102.

'avatars'), others (such as 'newsgroups') where members are named and know each other. The membership of such groups is not fixed: new members join in; old members fall away. Virtual groups exercise little or no influence on their members though it is possible that people who live alone and have few friends are more likely to be influenced than most others. Relationships in the virtual world can of course sometimes blossom into relationships in the real world.

The 'Mass' Audience

The large number of members who are supposed to make up 'the mass' come from all walks of life. They are, therefore, a heterogeneous group or groups with little interaction among themselves. If they are organised at all, the organisations are loose and flexible. Further, the members comprising 'the mass' are anonymous not only to each other, but to the communicator himself. They are united only by the medium and the message. It is in other words, a 'mass media audience' – yet another indefinite concept in the infant discipline of mass communication.

A 'mass audience' is larger than an audience for a lecture, or for a musical or theatrical performance. But what about a 'mass meeting' or a 'mass rally' addressed by a political leader in Mumbai or Delhi? The term 'mass', therefore, lacks precision in meaning and becomes intelligible only when used in a specific context and related to certain kinds of behaviour, institution or structure. It is in fact an elastic epithet devoid of any precise scientific content and more likely to reveal the point of view of the person using it, than to clarify the phenomenon in question.

A 'mass' audience is, consequently, a very large (another imprecise word!) audience that is the creation of the modern electronic and digital mass media. It is the result of a new technology that is directed at mass production and wide dissemination of communication. The exact size of audience or readership which gives rise to mass communication cannot be specified, but it must be 'large' relative to audiences for other means of communication such as a lecture or play, and large in relation to the number of communicators. This holds true also for audiences that surf, interact, play and shop on the Internet.

Nature of a 'Mass' Audience

Indeed, this audience is a collectivity unknown prior to the age of electronics. It is as McQuail writes, 'an aggregate of individuals united by a common focus of interest, engaging in an identical form of behaviour and open to activation towards common ends; yet the individuals involved are unknown to each other, have only a restricted amount of interaction, do not orient their actions to each other and are only loosely organised or lacking in organisation. The composition of the audience is continually shifting; it has no leadership or feelings of identity'.[6]

In India, television is largely a family activity; few families own more than one television set. Further, barely fifty per cent of television households have access to cable and satellite channels; only a tiny minority of households have access to DTH networks. While the large majority of India's television viewers watch Hindi channels (and most general entertainment channels are in that language) there is a significant number, particularly in South India, that opt to watch channels/networks that air programmes in their own regional languages. Audiences are thus segmented in terms of their languages as much by their interests and tastes.

A 'national mass audience' comes into existence only when a popular film is screened or when India is playing in a cricket test match. The 'live coverage' of an India Premier League (IPL) or a World Cup series brings about such a 'mass audience'. But by and large what we do have are 'local audiences' united by common languages, cultures and interests. These local groups function as social-cultural groups within the amorphous larger groups and at least indirectly influence the interactions with the mass media.

The 'local audiences' in India have a dynamic of their own. The pulls and pressures of the family, the caste, religion,

---

[6] Denis McQuail: Towards a Sociology of Mass Communication, Collier-Macmillan, 1969, p.10. See also: Denis McQuail: Audience Analysis, London: Sage, 1997.

community, language, and profession are much stronger than any power of the mass media to institute a new way of thinking or a new way of life, except perhaps at a superficial level.

The expectation of great persuasive power, says McQuail[7], from the new media has been largely misplaced. The fault lies partly in a failure to appreciate that the selection of communication content by whatever means disseminated, and its significance to the audience, will both be governed by existing mechanisms of social control, and partly in a tendency to regard the audience member as isolated and abstracted from his social environment. From the first of these stems a false assumption of discontinuity and novelty of content, and from the second a misleading conception of the vulnerability of the individual to mass persuasion.

The Public and Public Opinion

A public is a dispersed group of people interested in and divided about an issue, engaged in discussion of the issue, with a view-to-registering a collective opinion which is expected to affect the course of action of some group or individual. Or, as Kuppuswamy defines, a spontaneous collection of people in response to a certain kind of situation.[8]

What unites the members of a public is an issue or controversy, not their togetherness, either physical or intellectual. Indeed, the members may hold different views on an issue, belong to as many publics as they like, and be involved only slightly in an issue. Further, a 'public' has no fixed size, and no fixed place where its members gather. The 'spontaneous collection' is largely intellectual and takes place now through the mass media. Divided though its members be, the movement of the public is in the direction of a collective decision but always through discussion in various forums. It is goal-oriented, wanting to take society along with its collective view, or what is properly

---

7 ibid. p.49.
8 B. Kuppuswamy: *Communication and Social Development in India.*

called 'public opinion'.

A public, however, is not one composite group, but a number of interest groups, often working at odds with one another. The large majority of the groups are indifferent, disinterested and detached unless the issue at stake radically affects their way of life. Shopkeepers, for example, will generally remain uninvolved in the affairs of state, but when any legislation on hoarding of essential commodities or on octroi is passed, they will assert their strength through a 'bandh' call. Students are up in arms when college or examination fees are raised. The small interest groups, therefore, aim at promoting their own causes by mobilizing the public in their favour. The better organised they are, the greater is the pressure they bring to bear on the public, and on 'public opinion'.

Public Opinion

'There are few political fantasies as enduring as that labelled public opinion,'[9] but journalists, pollsters, politicians and marketing people pursue them relentlessly. In general, however, 'public opinion' is a belief or view prevalent among a large number of interest groups (or at least their leaders) that comprise a public. It is not necessarily representative of all the people, nor is it a unanimous opinion. It is not as the ancient Romans would say *vox populi*, the voice of the people. The extent to which it is representative differs from issue to issue. It will depend on a number of factors, such as the cultural levels of the various groups and the methods habitually adopted by their members for resolving intra-group and inter-group disputes, the facilities available to them for forming and articulating a balanced judgement on the question at issue, the degree to which the interests affected are mutually compatible and the depths of emotion at which they are felt as vital by the groups concerned; and above all, the measure of confidence that the people have in the administration's responsiveness to public opinion expressed

---

9 D. Nimmo and J. Coombs: *Mediated Political Realities*, New York: Longman, 1983, p.173.

in a variety of ways.[10]

Nature of Public Opinion

Since public opinion is always shifting, inconsistent and often contradictory, Shah concludes that 'generally, public opinion is likely to be a bundle of disparate, often conflicting, opinions rather than a unanimous or near unanimous judgement offered by the body of citizens for the guidance of the government. Only on rare occasions will it appear as the voice of the people, either because the issue is of transparent simplicity and cuts across sectional interests, or because it touches certain deep-seated emotions of a large majority of the people affected by it.' For instance, public opinion in India favoured the government's support of the liberation struggle of Bangladesh, but opposed the clamping of the 'emergency'. But it is divided over whether India should go in for nuclear power plants and for defence ballistic missiles like 'Agni' and 'Prithvi', and even whether the Pokhran-II tests were necessary.

The 'Two-step flow' of Information

The mass media play an important role in the formation of public opinion on various issues. However, the messages conveyed by the media are invariably mediated by the opinion leaders of groups. As Katz and Lazarsfeld put it, 'ideas seem to flow from radio and print to opinion leaders and from them to the less active sections of the population'. Village level workers or the Panchayat leaders are, for instance, opinion leaders in rural areas, and heads of committees and associations, the opinion leaders in the urban areas. It is they who interpret the messages of the media for their groups. But opinion leaders are usually leaders in one content area, and not in another. For example, in the matter of adopting new agricultural techniques the village level worker (VLW) may be the leader, while in political affairs, the Panchayat head may be the opinion leader.

---

10 A.B. Shah: 'Public Opinion in Indian Democracy', in *Society, Economy and Polity in India*, Bombay, 1984. p. 393.

It needs to be noted, however, that the 'two-step flow' of information does not ensure that the required information reaches the people most in need. Opinion leaders are very

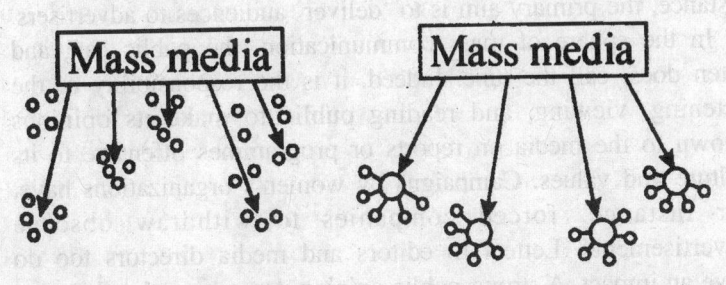

Fig. 4: Two-Step Flow[11]

○ - Isolated individuals constituting a mass
○ - Opinion leader
⊙ - individuals in social contact with an opinion leader

selective in the kind of information they pass down to peasants and workers. Indeed, mass media use is a group activity involving family, friends and the local community – not an isolated, individual activity.

Mass Media and Public Opinion

Our selection and 'reading' of components/items of the various media is influenced by the social and cultural groups we belong to. The way we see and hear and interpret programmes too depends upon the same sections. In other words, the culture, language, religion, caste and other groups we are members of provide us the frame of reference for interacting with the mass media. Thus public opinion is formed only indirectly by the mass media, and by information from other sources like rumours, street propaganda and of course, our own interests. By themselves alone the mass media have little power in forming public opinion. Besides, it needs to be noted that the mass media

---

[11] Denis McQuail and Sven Windahl : *Communication Models for the Study of Mass Communication*, London: Longman, 1993.

are not always engaged in attempts to mould public opinion, but more often that not, in trying to meet public needs and/or to sell consumer goods and services. For commercial broadcasters, for instance, the primary aim is to 'deliver' audiences to advertisers.

In the sphere of mass communication, the public can, and often does, call the tune. Indeed, it is the responsibility of the listening, viewing, and reading public to make its opinions known to the media on reports or programmes offensive to its culture and values. Campaigns by women's organizations have, for instance, forced companies to withdraw obscene advertisements. Letters to editors and media directors too do have an impact. A strong public opinion does shape the character of the mass media for better or for worse. It is the responsibility of the public to see that the pressures brought to bear on the media are for the better. An indifferent, undiscriminating public will get what it deserves − reporting and programming of indifferent quality. Peggy Charren's movement Action for Children's Television (ACT) paid off after years of public mobilisation: every American television channel is now required to allocate at least ten per cent of the total broadcast time to children's programmes. The movement in India for 'community radio' spearheaded by some NGOs has similarly paid dividends with the mushrooming of independent community radio stations.

Agenda Setting

The hypothesis of this socialisation and learning theory is that 'the mass media by paying attention to some issues and overlooking others will affect public opinion: people will tend to know about those things dealt with by the mass media and adopt *the order of priority* set by media'. The term 'agenda setting' itself was coined by Malcolm McCoombs and Donald Shaw in 1976. They went on to argue that 'audiences not only learn about public issues and other matters through the media; they also learn how much importance to attach to an issue or topic from the emphasis the mass media place upon it'. For example, in reflecting what candidates are saying during an election campaign, the mass media set the agenda of the campaign. This ability to affect cognitive change among individuals is one of the most important aspects of mass communication.' These are claims for the media which are difficult to verify. It is true that the media prioritise the news in terms of headlines and placement of stories. But it is equally true that people pay greater attention to stories of personal interest to them and their groups. Indeed, it would be nearer the truth to say that the media more often than not 'reflect' rather than 'set' the agenda. Individuals, groups, institutions, political parties and governments – all have their own agenda, and they lobby hard to set the media's agenda through press conferences, press releases, press visits, sponsorships, advertisements, gifts and other means. The major sources of news for the media are influential elites of society, and they (together with the media proprietors' interests) usually set the agenda for what the media highlight and underplay. It must be conceded, however, that there are sections of the media which play a marvellous 'watchdog' role; truth to sell, there are other sections that play the 'lapdog' role with no concern at all for their audience's information needs.

Issues	Differential media attention	Consequent public perception of issues
X_1	▭▭▭▭▭▭▭▭▭▭	X_1
X_2	▭▭▭▭▭▭	X_2
X_3	▭▭▭▭	X_3
X_4	▭▭▭▭▭▭▭▭▭▭▭	X_4
X_5	▭▭	X_5
X_6	▭▭▭▭▭▭▭▭▭▭▭▭	X_6

Fig. 5 : McCoomb and Shaw's Agenda-Setting Model[12]

---

12 Ibid.

The Spiral of Silence Model

The supposed agenda-setting role of the media is related to what Elisabeth Noelle-Neumann, a German media sociologist, calls the 'spiral of silence'. From her analysis of the election scene in Germany, she assumes that individuals just hate to be isolated from their fellow-beings and so tend to follow dominant opinions rather than express their own points of view openly.

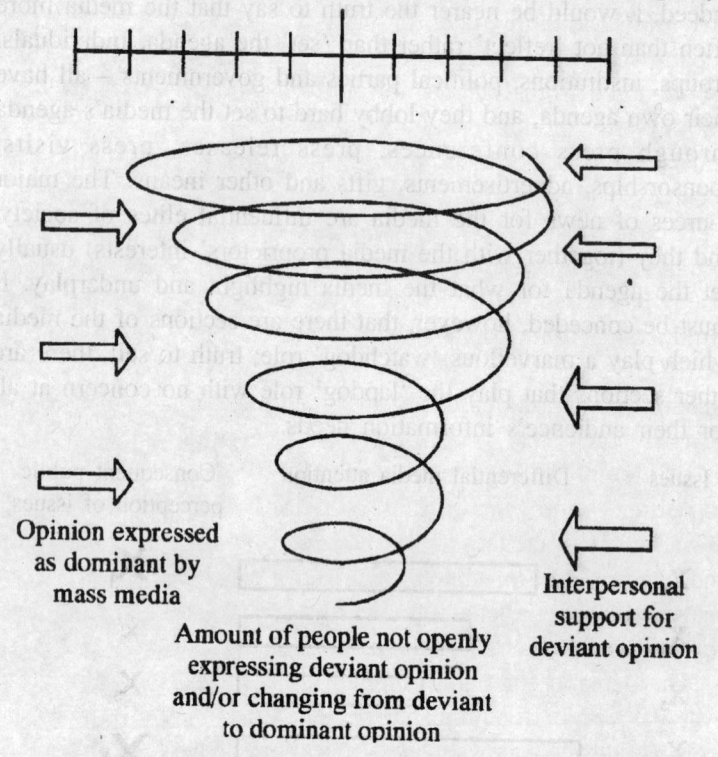

Opinion expressed as dominant by mass media

Amount of people not openly expressing deviant opinion and/or changing from deviant to dominant opinion

Interpersonal support for deviant opinion

Fig. 6 : Elisabeth Noelle-Neumann's Spiral of Silence Model[13]

Public Opinion Surveys

Among the most respected public opinion research organisations in the U.S.A. is the institute founded by George Gallup –

---
13 Ibid.

the Gallup Organisation. The Louis Harris Poll organisation comes a close second, leaving the hundreds of other survey organizations analysing public opinion way behind. In India, ORG-MARG, IMRB, MRAS, MODE and others are the survey organisations, regularly carrying out public opinion polls. The results are reported widely in the media, and possibly exert some influence in shaping public opinion in the cities, and in providing valuable data to the government and its various departments. An Opinion Poll selects a random sample, say a few hundred from each region, up to a total of around 2000 or 3000. With modern probability methods of sampling and statistics, it is believed that it is possible to calculate the accuracy of the sample. Yet, the margin of error ranges from 3-4 per cent. Since 1952, Gallup polls have erred by 1.2 percentage points in their predictions for national elections in United States. The polls carried out by IMRB, a research unit of the ad agency, Hindustan Thompson Associates (now JWT), or by ORG-MARG, on public attitudes to various issues, and in particular election predictions based on the Gallup system are claimed to be fairly accurate.

Errors in polling occur generally because of inadequate sampling, poor phrasing of questions and the drawing of unwarranted inferences from meagre data. Errors in tabulation and analysis are not uncommon. Moreover, the variables in the analysis of human behaviour are so many that it is impossible in any survey to take all of them into account.

The demand for public opinion polls in India has increased over the years. Big publishers like to find out how the public feels about their newspapers, magazines and books. PR and advertising professionals like to know if they succeed in their efforts to build up a favourable image for companies and their products, through consumer surveys. Governments and political parties are interested in researching public attitudes to social and economic issues, or to the popularity of a leader. Indeed, Opinion Polls themselves are now considered big news stories. Several newspapers and television channels conduct daily SMS polls on all kinds of political and social issues, asking respondents to answer 'Yes' or 'No'. This makes a mockery of public opinion since it is ridiculous to reduce every issue, no matter how complex it is, to a Yes/No response. It's more ridiculous (and manipulative and deceptive) for newspapers and television channels to display results of these polls without indicating anywhere how many in all (the sample) responded, and how representative the sample was. The only beneficiaries of these daily polls are telecom service providers and the media, the public be damned!

Opinion Polls and Elections

The Election Commission has at times banned the publication of the results of opinion polls and exit polls for about a fortnight during which the national elections are held. This is primarily because of the possibility of opinion polls influencing voters.

Even when the results of opinion polls are made public in the print or electronic media, the Election Commission has spelt out some guidelines. These include the need for the media to state very clearly who are the sponsor/s of the poll, the size of the sample, how it was constituted, and its geographical spread. Further, the 'margin of error' should be made clear. The Press Council too has recommended similar guidelines for the publication of opinion poll results.

A section of the news media has criticised these guidelines arguing that they infringe the constitutional right to freedom of speech and expression. However, it is this same section of the Indian news media that sponsors many opinion polls and publishes their results prominently without ever revealing the sample size and the margin of error. The results (and predictions too) are often laid out attractively in charts and graphs showing only percentages: a clear case of fraud and deception.

Assessing Opinion Polls

Consequently, in any analysis of public opinion polls the following questions need to be asked to assess their real worth:

(1) Who sponsored the survey? What were the motives for the sponsorship?
(2) How exactly were the questions worded? Could a different phrasing or ordering of the questions give another set of findings?
(3) What percentage of the population was sampled? What was the basis of the sampling?
(4) What was the size of the sample? How many responded to the survey?
(5) What is the margin of error allowed for?
(6) Are any of the findings based only on part of the total sample? Do all the 'generalisations' about the population follow from the data gathered and processed?
(7) How was the interview conducted – by phone, mail, face to face at home, or in the office?
(8) What was the timing of the interview in relation to other social, economic and political events?

Media and Politics

There exists an intimate relationship between the political process and the mass media. The functions of mass communication in the sphere of politics are of grave importance to India, since more than anything else, the mass media are fully exploited by our leaders for political propaganda, but the truth is that even the largely private-owned press is charged with political news, biased frequently in favour of one party or another.

In the first place, mass communications should provide the citizen the means to understand the substance of policies. Secondly, they should perform an 'amplifying function', by giving wide publicity to the actions and views of important individuals. Thirdly, they should provide the common fund of information necessary for the formation of public opinion and the conduct of the political process. Further, the mass media should attempt to provide standards by which political actions can be judged, the common frame of reference which must unite rulers and ruled in a democratic political structure. The media, therefore, could help, considerably in public participation in national and regional policies. However, the reality is that the coverage of politics by the mass media is often fragmented and superficial. The sensational and the transient are given predominance over the kind of information relevant to political education about political leaders and parties which are of great significance to the political outcome.

Moreover, except perhaps in the cities, the media do not exercise much influence in national or state elections. For one thing, the spread of the mass media is mostly restricted to the urban areas; for another, local leaders wield an influence that overshadows any media impact. The limited impact of the mass media was evident in the result of the 1977, 1980 and 1985 elections. Both the public and the private media played up the benefits of emergency rule; yet the ruling Congress Party was routed at the polls. Similarly, the Janata regime spared no effort in publicising the 'excesses of the emergency'; yet, the emergency regime was returned to power with a resounding victory in 1980.

During the 1989 Tamilnadu assembly elections the broadcast media went all out to project the Indira Congress; yet the DMK won hands down. In recent elections too, the print and broadcast media have not had much of an influence on the way the Indian voter selected parliamentary and assembly candidates. Recent parliamentary and assembly elections too have demonstrated time and again that it takes much more than the mass media to win over the Indian voter.

It appears, therefore, that the mass media are powerless against more mighty factors such as caste, community and religion. Interpersonal communication is given much greater credence than group media or mass media. One major reason for this is perhaps the lack of credibility of the mass media as they are, for the most part, urban and elite-oriented and have little relevance to the rural masses. It is clear then that people are, by and large, active interpreters of the mass media: they frequently reject or even oppose political messages in the media. The innate intelligence of voters is often under-estimated; ask the pollsters and psephologists how often they have had to eat humble pie!

Persuasion and Propaganda

Persuasion is the art of winning friends and influencing people. It's an art that does not employ force or deliberate manipulation of people's minds. Its success depends rather on attention to and comprehension of the persuader's message, and acceptance of it voluntarily, as well as on the content of the message, the manner of presentation, and other crucial situation/cultural factors. Of equal importance are predispositional factors such as responsiveness to emotional appeals, to logical arguments and to prestigeful sources.

However, the resistance to persuasive communication is no less strong. It's not as easy as media people imagine to 'brainwash' or persuade or manipulate people's minds. Mass communication generally fails to produce any marked changes in social attitudes or actions. The slight effects brought about by the mass media reinforce prevailing beliefs and values of an audience. The mass media are in fact status quoist and conservative. They are usually not a major force for social change.

Audience Expectations: The degree of acceptance of messages that comes over the mass media is related to the initial expectations of an audience. In an instructional situation, for example, acceptance is high because the audience expects to be helped by the communicator. But in a persuasive situation, interfering expectations operate to decrease acceptance. These include (1) expectations of being manipulated, (2) expectations of being wrong in assessing the message, and (3) expectations of social disapproval from one's community or group which does not share the communicator's views.

Further, some people are more easily persuaded than others. Educated people are, for instance, likely to be persuaded more effectively when the presentation refutes the arguments of the other side, while projecting one's own, and uneducated and uninformed people are taken in by a one-sided presentation. Changes in attitudes generally come about after a lapse of time than immediately.

Propaganda

Propaganda is the deliberate manipulation by means of symbols such as words, gestures, flags, images, monuments, music and the like, of people's thoughts or actions with respect to their beliefs, values and behaviours. Propaganda, therefore, is not casual or instructional communication. It is opposed to any free exchange of ideas, for the propagandist never doubts his own beliefs and value system, and the necessity of propagating them to others. His is a closed mind, for unlike the educator or the persuader he presents only one side – his side – of an issue, for no other side exists for him. He does not trust the listener to make up his own mind; the propagandist decides what kind of mind others should have.

Vladimir Lenin made a distinction between 'propaganda' and 'agitation'. Propaganda, he held, was the reasoned use of arguments from philosophy, history and science to influence the educated and reasonable few. Agitation, on the other hand, was the use of emotional slogans, Aesopian parables, and half-truths to influence the uneducated, the semi-educated, and the unreasonable. However, people's response to propaganda or 'agitation' is not as simple as is often made out to be. In most cases, they respond favourably if they share the ideology of the propagandist, but are rather hostile if they get the impression that they are being taken for a ride. So it is clearly possible that some groups and individuals would resist messages that come to them over the media, especially those like advertising they do not trust. It is also possible that some groups remain neutral or indifferent in the face of propaganda, or are even turned off by shame-faced attempts to brainwash them. It is, therefore, often impossible to say how precisely audiences will react to attempts of propagandists and campaigners to manipulate them. The

'India Shining' campaign by the BJP Government prior to the 2004 national election was for instance completely rejected by the electorate.

Audience Measurement: The 'Ratings' Game

Attempts to measure audiences for radio, television and other media are no more than mechanical head-counting exercises. The use of measuring devices such as the people meter, the diary or DAR (Day-After-Recall) fails to provide us accurate accounts of the 'experience of watching and listening'. For several years now, both All India Radio and Doordarshan have had Audience Research Units (ARUs) at the major production centres. Each production centre has a research cell headed by an audience research officer and assisted by a staff of six to seven research personnel. Doordarshan has Audience Research Units in 19 Kendras; the research is coordinated by the Director, Audience Research, at New Delhi. The research methods employed by AIR and Doordarshan include listenership and viewership surveys (largely quantitative), summative and evaluation studies, feed forward studies, and market surveys. The arrival, however, of private cable and satellite TV networks in the early 1990s challenged the monopoly of Doordarshan. Market research agencies such as IMRB, MRAS-Burke and ORG-MARG were quick to enter the 'ratings' game, though they had launched initiatives to conduct ratings-related research already in the early 1980s.

Audience Surveys

The three most common methods employed for conducting television audiences surveys are: the recall method, the consumer panel (or diary method), and 'people meters' (earlier known as 'tammeters'). The 'people-meter method' comprises three technologies: a meter-display unit (MDU), a remote control (or keypad) and a Central Data Storage Unit (CDSU). The MDU records the times when the television set is 'on' and how many members of the family have pressed the number on the remote control button that has been assigned to each of them. Guests too can press the number/s assigned for them. However, the meters are not cameras: they do not make a video recording of what is going on in front of the screen or whether the person who pressed his assigned button on the remote control is physically present in the room when the set is on. The meters can be connected directly to telephone lines, and these in turn to central computer data storage units. Laptop computers too could be used by the rating agencies to download the record from the meters. Generally, this mechanical recording is combined with panel surveys and interviews to obtain a clearer picture of audience response.

People meters were first used in 1988, but market research agencies in India began subscribing to the meter data only in 1995 when cable and satellite viewing had taken off, especially in the metros.

The Indian Market Research Bureau (IMRB) and ORG-MARG pioneered the use of 'people meters'; the IMRB system was called TAM (Television Audience Measurement) and the ORG-MARG system IMTAM. To begin with, a small sample of around 1500 households had their television sets wired to the set-top meters. TAM and INTAM merged in 2002 to form TAM Media Research which is a 50:50 joint venture of AC Nielsen and IMRB/Kantar. This company conducts the research and presents its 'ratings' every week for both C & S (cable and satellite) and non-C and S television households across the country. (IMRB/Kantar is the marketing division of J. Walter Thompson, India's largest advertising agency). The TAM sample is 7000 television households selected randomly from 148 towns which have a population larger than 100,000 (Class I cities). Thus the whole of Bihar, Jharkand, Orissa and the North-East has no meter-households and the whole of rural India finds no place whatsoever in the survey. TAM tracks minute-by-minute data not only on programmes but also on advertisements 'watched' for up to 15 seconds, for over 300 channels. Since 2008, TAM has established an Elite Panel to track viewership of

SEC-A and SEC-B viewers in the major cities.

Since early 2007, a second 'rating agency called aMap (Audience Measurement and Analytics Ltd.)) has begun offering 'overnight ratings' to broadcasters and other clients, using a similar people meter technology but grabbing viewership data from the meters every night through GSM cellphone calls. Employing a Virtual Private Network (VPN) technology, aMap (based in Ahmedabad) is able to provide overnight 'ratings' and viewing demographics online to its subscribers. aMap currently has people meters installed in a sample of a thousand households but plans to increase the sample up to 20,000 in the next few years. It has now developed a software called 'Dashboard' to enable broadcasters, advertisers, corporates and advertising agencies to tract second-by-second viewers' response to programmes and advertisements. It assists production houses like Balaji, Endemol and Miditech to revise the plot of their shows overnight.

Doordarshan Audience Research Television (DART) uses the consumer panel method. A panel of 4700 respondents in 33 cities are requested to keep a diary of their viewing over a certain period. DART 'ratings' are primarily for DD's national, regional and metro channels. The method has its weaknesses in terms of reliability and validity. Since the panel member has to keep a record of his viewing habits, there is every likelihood that he will watch more programmes than he would normally like to; the desire to please the marketing agency can be very strong. This is equally true of the personal interview as a method of evaluating viewer reactions.

Television 'ratings' are calculated in terms of 'Television Rating Points' (or TRPs), where one TRP is equivalent to one per cent of the total TV viewing population. Most broadcasters and market research agencies prefer to use the currency of GRPs (Gross Rating Points); these are calculated by summing up the TRPs for an entire week. All that the 'ratings' tell us, however, are a mechanical record of the activity on the people-meter and the keypad. This is a totally one-dimensional approach to the rich family experience that television is. Further, the 'ratings' give us no idea whatsoever of the attention or the interest paid to programmes and advertisements nor do they give us any inkling of whether they were liked or not, or even whether television was watched at all. Broadcasters, advertisers, media agencies and others pay thousands to subscribe to the rating agencies but most are dissatisfied with what they see week after week. Attempts are afoot to evolve 'alternatives'.

The members of three professions bodies – Indian Broadcasting Foundation (IBF), the Indian Society of Advertisers (ISA) and the Advertising Agencies Association of India (AAAI) – have now come together to establish the Broadcast Audience Research Council (BARC), an independent non-profit research-oriented company to work on an alternative to TAM and aMap ratings and also to conduct broadcasting research. TRAI and the Ministry of Information and Broadcasting have supported this initiative and have officially recognized the BARC as a self-regulatory body for the Indian broadcasting industry. However, in a July 2008 draft paper on 'Measurement of Television Audiences' (see www.trai.gov.in) TRAI has recommended that there should be two representatives of the Ministry on the BARC's Board of Directors and one representative on the Technical Committee. It has also recommended that there should be no cross-holding between the rating agencies and broadcasters, advertisers and advertising agencies in order to make the rating system transparent, neutral and credible. The three recommendations have not gone done well with the professional bodies.

Readership Surveys

National Readership Surveys (NRS) are conducted regularly by the Operations Research Group (ORG) and/or the Indian Market Research Bureau (IMRB), the research unit of the multinational ad agency, Hindustan Thompson Associates (now J. Walter Thompson), on behalf of a syndicated body comprising advertisers, advertising agencies, the national press and also All

India Radio and Doordarshan. The NRS investigates the readership of over 480 titles: dailies, weeklies, bi-weeklies and monthlies – in over 475 towns of 57 regions across the length and breadth of the country. The towns selected, however, are publication centres of dailies. By a process of 'cluster sampling', over 55,000 households in these towns are surveyed, the number of households in each town proportionate to its population. All men and women above the age of 12 are questioned for about an hour on the basis of a structured questionnaire.

The NRS is claimed to be the most thorough readership survey in the country. It provides exhaustive data (available to its clients on CDs and as soft copies on the Internet) on readership, radio listenership, cinema and TV viewership, internet usage and SMS and internet usage on mobile telephones. Other data made available is a 'readership profile' – the socioeconomic characteristics of the readers as well as the degree of duplication among publications and between media.

The first NRS was carried out in 1970 by the Operations Research Group (ORG) under the sponsorship of the Indian Society of Advertisers and the Advertising Agencies Association of India. It covered a sample size of 55,622 households in 254 towns and 704 villages. NRS-II was carried out in 1977 by ORG and IMRB together, while NRS-III was conducted by IMRB and MARG. Rural India did not form part of the survey in both NRS-II and NRS-III. The third was carried out in 1985 in 463 towns and covered 322 publications besides television, radio and cinema. The sample was over 54,000 adults. The survey found that the press reaches almost half the urban adult population; the reach is higher among men (60%) than among women (30%). NRS III also noted that the English press had an 'up-market profile', and the regional language press a 'mass market profile'. Besides, it revealed that the country is 'gradually moving from a single media environment to a multi-media environment'.

NRS-IV was conducted by IMRB in 1990 but ORG carried out a parallel survey a year earlier. NRS-IV covered both urban and rural areas and both print and electronic media, including video and Cable viewership. The classification of households was on the basis of social class rather than on income.

NRS-V was carried out in 1995, and NRS-VI in 1997.

Since 1997 the NRS has been carried out for the National Readership Studies Council (NRSC) by a consortium of market research agencies comprising IMRB, MODE and AC-Nielsen. The NRS-2006 survey, for instance, had a sample size of 284,373 households and examined the readership of 535 publications (230 daily newspapers and 305 magazines). The comprehensive survey revealed that these publications reached 222 million individuals, 45% of them in urban areas and 19% in rural areas. Further, daily newspapers reached 25% of the households surveyed and magazines only eight per cent. NRS-2006 also surveyed the viewership of television, cable and satellite, trends in radio listenership, the use of the Internet, and ownership and usage of cellular phones. It found that radio reached barely 27% of the population and cinema around 39 million film-goers. Satellite television reached as many as 230 million viewers. Where readership of newspapers and magazines was concerned, the survey showed that 40% of the urban population were regular readers, with Kerala registering the highest percentage, followed by Tamilnadu and Gujarat, though the most read language was Hindi (18%). Barely 12% of urban Indians read English newspapers. Surprisingly, 20% of the literate urban population said they did not read at all.

Indian Readership Survey (IRS)

Since the mid-1990s, the NRS has had a serious competitor: Indian Readership Survey (IRS). The IRS was launched in 1995 with the objective of 'setting an industry standard for readership and other media measurement, and to provide insights on media and product consumption as consumer behaviour patterns'. IRS is a random sample survey with a sample of 240,000 respondents in urban and rural India.

Like the NRS, however, the IRS uses the 'masthead method' wherein the title and logo of newspapers are shown to respondents and they are asked: Have you seen? Have you read this paper yesterday (in the case of a daily), last week (for a weekly magazine) or previous fortnight (for a fortnightly). The Recent Reading Technique (the RR Method) is also used by both NRS and IRS.

The IRS has an annual sample size of 209,076, covering 12-year old individuals living in urban and rural markets. A remarkable feature of the IRS is that it is a continuous survey conducted over 10 months, year after year. It also studies TV viewership and channel penetration.[14] The IRS is now conducted in two Rounds every year. The fieldwork for the survey is conducted by Hansa Research on behalf of the Media Research Users' Council (MRUC). The MRUC recently drew up a Code of Conduct after Hansa Research reported that some publications were trying to influence survey results.

Limitations of Readership Surveys

Several questions can be raised against this total market-biased research of both NRS and IRS. If questions on 'readership' are limited to asking, 'which papers have you seen?' (the Masthead Method), not what you have actually 'read', one must challenge the very claim of the survey being on readership. One is therefore led to conclude that the readership surveys are nothing more than a 'consumer' or 'market' survey the ultimate purpose of which is after all to 'rate' newspapers so that advertising is attracted to them. The results of the surveys are widely used by newspapers to make the claim that they are 'the best', 'Number One'. The no-holds-barred media wars since the late 1980s can be traced to this new-fangled craze for American style surveys and public opinion polls. The commitment to serve the public has, as a result, given way to a commitment to advertising and to business interests. Both the NRS and the IRS do not go beyond the head-counting exercise which is of course of some interest to advertising and marketing agencies because it is the only estimate we have of 'readership'. Media Planners

---

14 Cf. *Advertising and Marketing*, May 15, 1998, for details.

are totally dependent on this exercise to chalk out their advertising strategies though they remain confused by the many contradictions in the two national readership surveys; it's impossible to say which is more credible. A 'single currency' for the print media is a demand that is currently making the rounds among members of the Indian Newspaper Society (INS), the NRSC and the MRUC. It is likely that NRSC and MRUC will soon merge and that INS would take up that responsibility of conducting a credible national readership survey. However, the question of who is a newspaper 'reader' and what the 'reading experience' brings to our lives and to that of our families will

FOR FURTHER READING

1. Ien Ang: *Desperately Seeking the Audience*, London: Routledge, 1991.
2. Sonia Bathla: *Women, Democracy and the Media, Cultural and Political Representations in the Indian Press*, New Delhi: Sage Publications, 1998.
3. T.R. Lindlof (Ed.): *Natural Audiences*, Norwood, NJ: Ablex, 1987.
4. Denis McQuail: *Towards a Sociology of Mass Communication*, London: Collier-Macmillan, 1969.
5. Denis McQuail: *Mass Communication Theory : An Introduction*, London: Sage, 1986, Rev. 2008.
6. Denis McQuail: *Audience Analysis,* London: Sage, 1997.
7. Andal Narayanan: *The Impact of TV on Viewers*, Bombay: Somaiya, 1987.
8. Maya Ranganathan: 'Television in Tamilnadu Politics', *Economic and Political Weekly*.
9. *Cable Television: Glitter or Gloom,* New Delhi: Indian Institute of Mass Communication, 1992.
10. Rachel Dwyer and Christopher Pinney (Ed.): *Pleasure and the Nation: The History, Politics and Consumption of Public Culture*, Oxford: Oxford University Press, 2001.

WEB RESOURCES

1. www.tamindia.com
2. www.comminit.com
3. //mruc.net
4. www.rnib.nic.in
5. www.audiencemap.com

REVIEW QUESTIONS

1. How is Communication an 'interdisciplinary area of study'?
2. What is a 'media audience'? Distinguish between the 'functionalist' and 'critical' approaches to the study of media audiences?
3. How do advertisers and marketing people look at 'media audiences'?
4. What possible influences do the mass media have on Public Opinion?
5. What are the ways of ascertaining Public Opinion? How reliable are they?
6. Who are Opinion Leaders? What role do they play in our interaction with the mass media? Discuss the 'two-step' flow model of communication.
7. What are the characteristics of a 'mass audience'?
8. What is the influence of primary and secondary groups on our response to the mass media?
9. Write critical notes on:
   (a) Opinion Polls and Exit Polls
   (b) Persuasion and Propaganda
   (c) National Readership Surveys
   (d) TRPs
   (e) Media and Politics

SUGGESTED PROJECTS

1. Conduct an opinion survey on the attitudes of students in your class/college or of people residing in your building/co-operative

society to advertising in the mass media. Draw up a suitable questionnaire for the purpose.
2. Make a list of the groups in your class/college. What are the grounds on which such groups are formed? What is the attitude of these groups to one another?
3. Make a list of opinion leaders whose views probably influence you as you listen to or watch (a) a sports programme on radio on TV; (b) an entertainment programme on radio or T.V., and (c) as you read the political news in your newspaper

SECTION IV

USES AND EFFECTS OF THE MASS MEDIA

The Meaning of 'Effects'

'Media effects' means different things to different people. A psychologist, for example, has 'psychological' effects in mind when talking about media effects; the sociologist, the 'social' effects, the anthropologist, the 'cultural' effects, the political scientist the 'political' effects, the economist the 'economic' effects, the preacher, the 'moral' effects, the advertiser, the 'market' effects... and so on. Parents too are concerned about the amount of time their children spend with television, music, films, mobile phones and the Internet and the effects this might have on their children's behaviour and attitudes. Then there are school teachers who worry about their students' exposure to misinformation in the mass media and on the Internet, and the police who scapegoat the media for social violence and delinquency. So, any attempt to understand 'effects' must necessarily take into account the perspective from which the 'effects' are being investigated.

Further, 'effects' are of various types and various gradations too. They may be short-term, medium-term or long-term; they may be deep or profound, or transient or superficial as in the case of fashions, mannerisms, and life-styles. Then there are influences of a passing nature or of a more permanent nature.

Can influences be termed as 'effects'? How are 'influences', 'effects' distinct from 'impacts', or are they mere synonyms for the same social phenomena? Few media sociologists have subjected the inadequacy of everyday language to fathom the complexity of media effects to any kind of critical scrutiny.

But what precisely are 'the media'? Are they the technologies (printing presses, the telegraph, telephones, radio and TV sets, audio and video recorders, video and movie cameras, satellites, computers, etc.) or the 'genres', the 'programmes' (the software) or the contents of individual media? Or, are they the cultural and entertainment industries which are today one of the fastest growing businesses owned and run by large media conglomerates? Or, are they the many media organisations involved in the production, storage, distribution and exhibition of media materials? The sheer imprecision in all talk about 'the media' and 'effects' seems to be characteristic of the social sciences. But then, it must be conceded, the social sciences are not 'exact' sciences like the physical and natural sciences. For, while the social sciences study human beings and their behaviour in different situations, the natural sciences study minerals, plants, and animals where consistency and predictability are the order of the day.

Moreover, social scientists and media professionals rarely consider the infinite variety of 'uses' the different media and the different programmes are put to, in different contexts. In most cases, the use of the term 'effects' is misleading because it suggests that the media "do something" to people, as though people are inorganic creatures, who do not bring their own personalities to play in the communication process. It also implies that the media are actors, and that the people are acted upon. So while the media are active, audiences are unresponsive if not passive. These assumptions about media and audiences have their origin in Aristotelian linear models of communication where persuasion is seen as the primary goal of all communication.

The truth is that we have little precise knowledge or proven data about media effects since they invariably take place in combination with a whole lot of social, economic and cultural variables. Do effects relate to change, however slight, in attitude and behaviour (both elusive terms and comprehensive in meaning)? Perhaps. The extent of change (if any) depends on the variations in the desires and inclinations of individual members of an audience, and in the way they as individuals and as members of different social and cultural groups respond to various types of stimuli from the mass media. It has to be noted, moreover, that people can be influenced without paying attention and without changing at all, that there is often no relationship between what a person learned, knew or recalled on the one hand and what he did or how he felt on the other! It follows therefore that one can learn things without believing them, believe things without doing them, and do things without learning or believing them!

Interaction, Not Effects

The 'interaction' (a much more comprehensive and accurate term than 'effects') between media and human beings is an extremely complex phenomenon. It becomes even more complex when we realize that there are a great variety of media offering numerous programme genres, and also the fact that there are a whole variety of people and groups listening, viewing, and reading in a countless number of socio-cultural environments. Perhaps, the only safe conclusion on 'effects' (or 'interactions') of the media is the one arrived at by Bernard Berelson several years ago: "Some kinds of communication on some kinds of issues, brought to the attention of some kinds of people under some kinds of conditions have some kinds of effects."

Theories of Media Effects

Several theories related to the effects or changes brought about by the media on individuals and society have been propounded by both 'functionalist' and 'critical' schools of communication. The 'functionalist' theorists begin with the assumption that the media have a role and a function in society: to stabilise, reinforce and maintain the consensus in society. They do not see the question of power and conflict as a major driving force in society; they assume that the competition among the various groups in society allows for free and fair play, and all groups have an equal chance to dominate and to control. The 'critical' theorists, on the other hand, place the struggle for power among social classes/groups at the centre of society; the mass media are invariably employed by the dominant class to propagate its ideology. Further, while the 'functionalists' research media effects using empirical quantitative methods, the 'critical' theorists are so not much concerned with effects as the cultural and political context in which media experiences take place, the ownership and economics of the media, and the various ways in which audiences 'read' the media.

Effects Theories

These theories range from one extreme position of all-powerful wide-ranging effects of the media, to the opposing extreme position where the media have no effects at all. At the one extreme are writers and researchers like Marie Winn who take the media, especially television, to be a 'plug-in drug'[1]; at the other extreme is Joseph Klapper who concluded from his longitudinal research that media succeed only in 'reinforcing' old attitudes, habits, and beliefs[2]. In between, are the 'negotiation' or interaction theorists who suggest that effects, like meanings of media texts, are ultimately 'negotiated' by audiences. (This is sometimes termed the 'mediation perspective')[3]. Most media theories deal directly with the 'effects' of the content of programmes on opinions, attitudes, perceptions, beliefs and social behaviour. The theories have their basis largely in research on television and film, though some in speculation or personal experience. The largest number of studies has been on the effects of violence in television programmes on the behaviour of children and adolescents; others on the effects of propaganda on personal opinion and on voting behaviour. Since early effects research was based on the 'persuasion' model of communication (the Lasswell model and the Shanon-Weaver model, for instance) and carried out by social psychologists, the results often pointed to strong effects, for that is what they were looking for in the first place. The

---

1 Marie Winn: *Children Without Childhood*, Hammondsworth:Penguin, 1981.
2 Joseph Klapper: *The Effects of Mass Communicatin*, New York: Free Press, 1960.
3 Cf. Jesus Martin Barbero: *Mediation*

social contexts in which the media were experienced (say the family, the home, the theatre, the school or the peer group) were rarely taken into account. The stimulus-response experiments to measure effects were frequently carried out in laboratories using mechanical pre-test and post-test methods of research. Thus the results they obtained turned out to be along expected lines.

Reinforcement: Limited Effects Theory

Joseph Klapper and others, for example, believed that media reinforce existing values and attitudes. Only then, after all, can programmes of the media be popular with a majority of social groups which have an interest in the perpetuation of their own traditions and statuses. Lazarsfeld and Merton held that the mass media 'cannot be relied upon to work for changes, even minor changes, in the social structure'[4].

Catharsis and Narcosis

Some mass communication theorists (Lazarsfeld, Merton, and Winn for instance) argue that media have a 'narcotizing dysfunction' that distracts audiences from real problems and in fact prevents their doing anything about them. In other words, the mass media have a drug-like addictive effect, lulling audiences into passivity and a sense of elation. Exposure to a flood of information, say Lazarsfeld and Merton, may serve to narcotize rather than energize the average reader or listener. As an increasing amount of time is devoted to reading and listening, a decreasing share is available for organized action. The interested and informed citizen can congratulate himself on his lofty state of interest and information and fail to see that he has abstained from decision and action.... He comes to mistake *knowing* about problems of the day for *doing something* about them.

First proposed in 1948, the theory appears dated particularly after the galvanizing impact the mass media had in bringing the Vietnam War to an end, and in throwing Nixon out as a result of

---

4 Cf. R K Merton: *Social Theory and Social Structure*, Glencoe, IL: Free Press, 1957.

the reporting on Watergate. Of course, several other social factors too played a vital role. In India, the press publicity given to excesses of the emergency, particularly through underground literature, did contribute to bringing about an end to the Emergency regime.

Closely related to the 'narcosis' theory, is the 'Catharsis' theory of media effects. Seymour Feshbach, the main exponent of the theory, argued that the media have a 'cathartic' effect on people that somehow purges them of many anti-social and unfulfilled desires, frustrations and feelings of hostility. In one of his laboratory studies, Feshbach subjected college students to savage insults and criticism at the hands of experimenters; the 'experimental group' was then shown an aggressive film of a brutal boxing-match, while the 'control group' was shown a dull film. When they were later questioned about their opinions of the experimenters, those students who had seen the film on boxing felt less hostile to their experimenters than those students who were shown the 'control' film.

However, in an almost identical laboratory experiment by Leonard Berkowitz, the experimenters were introduced to the students as either a boxer or a rhetoric student. The students were then exposed to either a violent boxing film or a neutral non-violent film. Later, they had the chance to give electrical shocks (under the pretext of a separate experiment) to the 'boxer' or the rhetoric student. It was found that those students who had seen the boxing film gave the largest number of shocks to the 'boxer'. Berkowitz concluded that the boxing film was responsible for the aggressive response of the students.

Other experiments have revealed that children in particular are likely to imitate violence in films if the violent actions in the film are rewarded.

Laboratory experiments are by their nature artificial for they cannot re-create the different conditions, environments, and states of mind in which violent films are seen. The reactions to violence in films can be very varied as is well demonstrated in Philip Schlesinger's work on 'Women Viewing Violence' and

'Men Viewing Violence' at the Stirling Media Research Institute.

The 'narcosis' and 'catharsis' theories represent extreme views. So does Ernest Van den Hag's view that 'mass communications, taken together are demeaning, debasing and depersonalizing instruments of manipulation at worst; middle-class hedonism at best'. Yet another extreme theory is that of Frederic Wertham which says that the content of the media is 'corruptive in general and specifically teaches materialism, brutality, antisocial behaviour and callousness towards other humans'.

Incidental Effects

In contrast, Aldous Huxley took the stand that media indeed do teach people things, but most of them are of no consequence; they also have effects, but mostly in unimportant and trivial facets of our lives although we may think that they are important. These trivial facets are fashions, mannerisms, mating habits, and food habits. As Schramm, Lyle and Parker found in their study of children and television, 'television could be an especially effective agent of incidental learning while the child is still young. This is because at that time it seems so real'[5].

Uses and Gratifications

By the 1950s and sixties, communication researchers began to fine tune their methods and their theories. Elihu Katz, Denis McQuail and Michael Gurevitch introduced what they termed the 'uses and gratifications' theory of media effects[6]. They turned their attention to how audiences used the media to live out their fantasy lives and to seek out other gratifications, or even to inform and educate themselves about the world and its people. Thus media 'effects' were related to the needs and activities of audiences. The theory was largely concerned with the selection, reception and nature of response of audiences to

---

5   W. Schramm, J. Lyle and E. Parker: *Television in the Lives of our Children*, Stanford, CA: Stanford University Press, 1961.
6   Elihu Katz, Jay G Blumler and Michael Gurevitch: 'Utilization of Mass Communication by the Individual' in J G Blumler and E.Katz (Eds.): *The Uses of Mass Communication*, pp.19-32, Beverly Hills, CA and London: Sage Publications.

the media, the assumption being that individual members in an audience made conscious and motivated selection of channels and programmes. It was also assumed that audiences made supplementary and compensatory uses of the mass media.

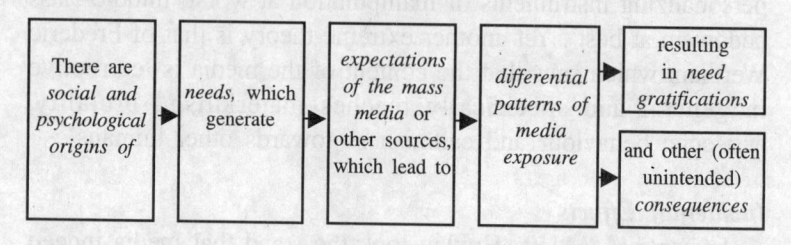

There are social and psychological origins of	→	*needs,* which generate	→	*expectations of the mass media* or other sources, which lead to	→	*differential patterns of media exposure*	→	resulting in *need gratifications*
					→	and other (often unintended) *consequences*

Fig. 7 : Uses and Gratifications Model of Mass Communication[7]

Cultivation or Cultural Indicators Theory

George Gerbner's dissatisfaction with effects research led him to evolve a sophisticated theory grounded on his longitudinal research on American television. He and his team undertook a content analysis of television programmes, looking at portrayals of gender, violence, the family, portrayal of minorities, and then matched these with actual situations, behaviours and attitudes in American society.[8] Take the portrayal of crime, for instance. Gerbner concluded that there was a 'cultivation' or enculturation effect on audiences highly exposed to television. Audiences 'adopted' the perceptions and values which were consistently portrayed in different programme genres. Gerbner and his team attempted to move beyond the analysis of effects on individual behaviour and to analyse communication systems at a social structural level. Television was seen as the arm of the industrial and military establishment, an agent of social control.

---

7   Denis McQuail and Sven Windahl: *Models for the Study of Mass Communication,* London: Sage Publications.
8   George Gerbner: 'Cultural Indicators - The Third Voice', in G. Gerbner, L Gross and W Melody (Eds): *Communications Technology and Social Policy,* pp.553-73, New York: Wiley.

Technological Effects – McLuhanesque Perspective

"The medium is the message", wrote Marshall McLuhan, setting the controversy over media effects on its head. No matter what the contents of programmes, he argued, people will watch television; it commands their attention as no other medium has. He warned like a doomsday prophet that "the electronic media are transforming every aspect of man's life and re-structuring civilization, not so much by the content of their messages, as by the nature itself of television, movies, computers and other media." Mass communications, therefore, are neither good nor bad, but rather mystical devices that possess powers to change the way mankind lives and thinks. For instance, Indian cities are already witnessing some changes in eating, sleeping and socialising habits as a result of the introduction of television.

Reflex Effects

A rather different kind of effect on which no theory has yet been built is the impact of media among and within themselves. Mass communicators are known to review each other's work, and reporters carefully go through rival papers, and switch on to news programmes on the air. It is no surprise, therefore, that 'copycatting' in content and form has become a common phenomenon. Let a topic be introduced in one paper, and the others take it up with a vengeance. So when a 'health' programme proves popular on TV, every newspaper introduces a 'health' column.

Then there are the effects of new media upon the old, and vice versa. The formats of Doordarshan's newscasts and features have in fact been copied from All India Radio and magazines are all profusely illustrated because of the impact of television. Again, short stories first published in the papers or magazines, are turned into radio, TV and cinema scripts. All these inter-media and intra-media effects may be called 'reflex effects' or 'bandwagon effects'.

Impact of Cable and Satellite: Perceptions of Viewers

In January 1992, the Indian Institute of Mass Communication

conducted a survey in New Delhi of the 'perceptions' of viewers on the socio-cultural impact of cable and satellite television. The following were some of the conclusions of the survey. (However, 'perceptions' of viewers do not amount to any kind of 'impact' or effect):

(i) While 84 per cent of the respondents found the MTV programmes entertaining 60 per cent felt that they would have a socio-cultural effect on the younger generation. The reactions included the view that the younger generation will adopt the western life-style, that MTV will hamper their studies and they will be more inclined to migrate to the West. However, some respondents felt that the younger generation will become smarter and more aware because of this exposure.

(ii) With regard to BBC, while 58 per cent of the respondents felt that it has "wide, in-depth and balanced coverage", surprisingly 42 per cent felt that "stories about India sometimes reflect bias and distortion of facts".

(iii) About 80 per cent of the respondents felt that foreign serials were entertaining. An equal percentage opined that "STAR serials are more imaginative and creative" (than Doordarshan). Yet, 35 per cent felt that foreign serials are 'not relevant to our culture, history, region and society'; and 42 per cent said that the foreign serials "are always glorifying Western society and their culture, which will adversely affect our children and youth".

(iv) With regard to films shown on the "VCR Channel" of cable systems, the audience was almost exactly divided between those who felt that "the number of films shown ...... is too many" and those who stated that "their number was just right". As many as 70 per cent felt that the moral and ethical values of our society will be affected by the onslaught of films. While there was concern about the depiction of sex and violence, some felt that there is already so much exposure to this (through other sources) that cable TV will not make much difference.

(v) A substantial proportion of respondents (between 45 and 62%) were worried about the negative effects of cable TV on children. A majority (57%) feel that "children will be adversely affected". The sports activities of children will be curtailed, felt 62 per cent, while 51 per cent felt that reading and other creative activities will be adversely affected. (See Section III for details of other research efforts).

Effects of Media on Education

Right from pre-Independence days, attempts have been made by both government and private groups to use the media for educational purposes. Dadasaheb Phalke, the pioneer of Indian cinema, made educational documentaries such as 'The growth of a Pea plant' and 'How to Make a Film' besides fictional films. Radio experiments in the use of radio for promoting literacy and education were conducted as early as the 1930s. Television was introduced into India by the Nehru Government with the primary aim of exploiting the medium for distance education. B.G. Verghese's Chattera experiment attempted to use the daily newspaper to educate urban Delhites about rural people and their problems.

The most ambitious attempt to exploit the mass media for education was of course, SITE (Satellite Instructional Television Experiment). It sought to educate rural people in six States of India about the need for family planning, improved agriculture, hygiene, nutrition and health care. Classroom-type instructions were also provided to school children.

Today, Doordarshan devotes at least ten per cent of its telecast time to educational or enrichment programmes for farmers, school children, youth and other groups. It has taken to promoting literacy on a nationwide scale. UGC's 'Countrywide classroom' and IGNOU's transmissions are ambitious post-SITE attempts to use television for higher education. 'Gyan-darshan', an exclusively educational channel, was launched by Doordarshan in 2004. A second educational channel called 'Topper' went on air in 2008 to help students prepare for their school examinations.

Do media educate? How effective are the mass media in educating the people of our country? What are the 'effects' of media on 'education'? These are all loaded and difficult questions to which there can be no straight cut-and-dry answers. Literate and educated people benefit much more from educational media than the less literate and educated, unless the education-oriented programmes are specifically geared to the needs, interests and levels of specific groups. This is an essential condition of any educational programme on any medium to have some kind of 'effect'. Even before groups and regions can benefit from education through the print or the electronic media, they will need to become 'media literate'. Media literacy precedes or is simultaneous with the skill to learn from the media.

The folk media are perhaps much more effective in promoting the message of literacy than any of the mass media. In Kerala, Maharashtra, Andhra Pradesh and other states, folk forms of the local regions have been utilised both by voluntary social action groups and by government-supported literacy campaigns. For example, in Maharashtra, literacy campaigns have used folk musical forms such as lavani, powada, gondhal, jagar and others. During the campaign, cultural teams went out to the different villages on Kalajathas. 'The main thrust of the messages conveyed through song, dance and discussions was literacy. However, it was reported that other issues such as mother and child care, family planning, watershed management, the problem of alcoholism and dowry, small savings and agricultural development were also conveyed'. In some campaigns, the message of literacy was spread by relating the folk forms to local festivals: akshar kandlis and akshar rangoli at the time of Diwali and Akshar Ganpathi at the time of the popular festivals of Maharashtra. In the campaign at Sindhdurg, haldikumkum celebrations were widely used to mobilise women and to bring them together to discuss issues related to their everyday lives. However, in all these campaigns, there were few attempts to place literacy in the context of political, social and economic structures in the rural and urban areas.⁹

It appears then that the media by themselves (whether modern or folk) do not promote literacy. Nor is commitment enough. The social structures obtaining at the grassroots need to be taken into account, as well as the infrastructure in the form of schools, teachers, volunteers, post-literacy facilities, and the caste and communal divides. A factor often overlooked is the time available to agricultural and industrial workers to respond in any meaningful way to literacy drives in the media.

The Mass Media and the Indian Family

The proliferation of TV, cable and satellite channels in India is of great concern to parents and teachers. With so much time given to watching the small screen, parents are worried that little or no time will remain for conversation in the family, for family get-togethers and for family visits. However, parents must acknowledge that they too spend a lot of time with television, and that frequently they exercise no control on what their children watch and when. Further, parents frequently use television as a baby-sister or as an excuse for staying at home.

Two early studies of television and the Indian family, Andal Narayanan's *Impact of Television on Viewers*,[10] and Neena Behl's close look at what happens to one Indian village when television is introduced in it,[11] suggest that television plays a vital role in influencing family relationships. But when the novelty of the medium wears off and it becomes part of the furniture ('the box in the corner') it appears that the effects on the family are not as

---

9 For further details, see D. Saldanha: 'Cultural Communication in Literacy', *Economic and Political Weekly*, May 15, 1993. pp. 981-989.
10 Andal Narayanan: *Effects of Television on the Indian Family*, Bombay: Somaiya Publications, 1985.
11 Neena Behl: 'Equalizing Status: Television and Tradition in an Indian Village', in James Lull (Ed.): *World Families Watch Television*, Newbury Park: Sage Publications, 1988, pp.136-157. See also J.S. Yadava and Usha V. Reddi's 'In the Midst of Diverstiy: Television in Urban Indian Homes', in the same book.

worrying as they were first thought to be. True, multi-channel television often creates friction among siblings, or between parents and children, or even between parents themselves. But then TV also helps to bring a family closer especially when all members enjoy a popular programme together. It provides topics for conversation, for expressing opinions and for family discussions. A lot depends upon what the members of the family do with television. Since few Indian families can afford more than one TV set, gathering around the TV set is similar to the earlier practice of gathering round a fireplace. The family, like any other social institution, is a power structure. The exercise of power in the home, in earlier times, was through the breadwinner, generally the man of the house. The remote control device now puts power in the hands that hold it. Ethnographic and focus group studies of the place of television in the lives of families clearly point to the remote control in most families being held by male rather than female members. However, in many Indian homes where the female is dominant, the remote control is invariably in the hands of the mother. In some families though, the remote control is in the hands of the children.[12]

Five recent studies on the controversial role that Doordarshan played in the mid-1980s in promoting the Hindu nationalist agenda through serials based on the epics, Mahabharata and Ramayana, and thus changing the face of Indian politics, are worthy of attention here. The first is Mitra's 1993 study of genres on Indian television; a content-analysis of Mahabharat on Doordarshan.[13] The other three use ethnographic methods to analyse audience reception of Indian television serials. Gillespie looks at the TV viewing experience of British Panjabi families of Southall, particularly as they watch Doordarshan's Mahabharat and compare it with Peter Brooks' version on British television.[14] Mankekar takes a close look at 25 families of Delhi

---

12 Cf. Keval J Kumar: 'Television in the Lives of Indian Families: An Ethnographic Study', Paper presented at the International Television Studies Conference, London, 1988.
13 A. Mitra: *Television and Popular Culture*, New Delhi: Sage Publications, 1993.

in an attempt to fathom how they make sense of television post-Mandal riots,[15] while Raghavan sits down with 20 upper middle class and middle class families in Ahmedabad to figure out their pleasure of watching the longest running Hindi soap opera, *Kyunki Saas Bhi Kabhi Bahu Thi*.[16] And Rajagopal, employs discourse analysis and other methods to understand the role of television in the rise of the Hindutva movement in India and North America.[17]

Children and the Mass Media

Without communication an individual could never become a human being; without mass communication an individual could never become part of modern society. Socialisation is a life-long active process, beginning on the day of one's birth. The child learns to socialise from the parents and the social groups he or she belongs to. As children grow up they come into contact with other social groups, but their basic loyalties are to their own primary and secondary groups which provide them their sets of attitudes, beliefs, and norms of behaviour. Children come under three kinds of social control: (1) tradition orientation – social control based on tradition; (2) inner orientation – social control achieved through standards, guidelines or values existing in each individual; and (3) external or other orientation – social control achieved by conformity to standards existing in other persons and groups.

The child of today comes into contact with groups other than those in school; for instance, through the mass media, which give

---

14 Marie Gillespie: *Television, Ethnicity and Cultural Change,* London: Routledge, 1995.
15 Purnima Mankekar: *Screening Culture, Viewing Politics: An Ethnography of Television, Womanhood, and Nation in Post-colonial India,* Durham N C: Duke University Press, 1999.
16 Priya Raghavan: *Family, Politics and Popular Television: An Ethnographic Study of Viewing Indian Serial Melodrama,* Unpub. Ph.D. dissertation submitted to Victoria University, March 2008.
17 Arvind Rajagopal: *Politics After Television: Religious Nationalism and the Reshaping of the Indian Public in India,* New York: Cambridge University Press, 2001.

him/her access to remote groups and their cultures. Besides, the mass media provide models of behaviour, and norms of living. The child begins to imitate them, particularly in cases where he or she is least integrated into the family or the peer group. Such children rely heavily on media advice and models; while others do not since their activities outside the home provide them greater stimuli and other role models.

But the socialisation effects of mass media cannot match the power of the home, the neighbourhood and the school where interpersonal relationships exist.[18] In contrast, socialisation through the mass media is depersonalised and hence effective mainly in the peripheral areas of life. One would expect a national outlook to follow from a wide exposure to national news and social advertisements in the mass media. But communalism continues to hold out against all attempts at national integration through the media – so deep-rooted are our attitudes and beliefs. So also social evils like the dowry system, child marriages, caste conflicts, foeticide and the like persist. The mass media are not a panacea for social or economic underdevelopment as some governments are prone to believe. Even interactive media like the Internet, computer games and mobile telephony may have little influence in bringing an end to these evils.

In any study of media influence on children, or on the influence of children's interests and needs on the media, the age-group is an important variable. Other equally important variables are social class, religious and cultural background, linguistic background and community. It has been found from research by Jean Piaget and others that the pre-operational child (aged 5 years and below), responds differently from the child belonging to the concrete operations stage (6 to 11 years) or to the formal operations stage (11 to 12 years). To illustrate, young children aged five and below see a series of separate and fragmentary

---

18 Cf. Robin McRon: 'Changing Perspectives in the Study of Mass Media and Socialisation', in James D. Halloran (Ed.): Mass Media and Socialisation, pp.13-44, Leicester: IAMCR, 1975, for a detailed discussion.

incidents rather than the story of a film. They do not invariably recognise the identities of the principal character throughout the film, and they tend to believe implicitly what they see on TV to be real. And, interestingly, they sometimes read incidents into the plot from their own imaginations, or add incidents and events that they think should have occurred.[19]

The 6 to 11 year old child, however, understands the story of a film, but still understands only the concrete physical behaviour of film performers. Only at the age of 10 or 11, does he usually understand the feelings and motivations and put himself in the shoes of a character.

The 11 to 12 year old comprehends films as efficiently as adults, and comes to realize the make-believe fantasy world of films. He also gradually begins to understand the emotional relationships in films, and to appreciate some and dislike other aspects of films. Besides, he can imagine hypothetically the sorts of relationships which may exist between film characters even if the relationships are not presented on the screen.[20] Recent ethnographic and semiotic studies of children's interaction with television suggest that children make for a 'lively audience' and are highly discriminating and critical viewers.[21]

Children and Indian Television

Children below the age of 16 comprise about 40 per cent of the population of India. Yet barely five per cent of total telecast time on GEC channels (General Entertainment Channels) is directly aimed at children; this is equally true of other mass media too: radio, fiction and documentary cinema, and the press. On television, programmes for children devote the largest chunk

---

19 Grant Noble: *Children in Front of the Small Screen*, London; Constable, 1975.
20 Cf. Kevin Durkin: *Television ,Sex Roles and Children*, Milton Keynes: Oxrod University Press, 1985, for a good discussion of how children understand the language of advertising. For an Indian study cf. Namita Unnikrishnan and Shailaja Bajpai: *Impact of Television Advertising on Children*, New Delhi: Sage Publications, 1995.
21 Cf. Patricia Palmer: *The Lively Audience*, Sydney: Macmillan, 1988; Bob Hodge and David Tripp: *Children and Television: A Semiotic Approach*, Oxford: Polity Press, 1986.

of time to animation films, muppet shows, game shows, reality shows and talent-hunt series. American animation series like 'Spiderman', 'He-man', 'Mickey and Donald', and a host of others feature regularly on Indian television channels. The advertisements that usually accompany them relate to toys and dolls. Interestingly, terrorist-related toys like 'G I Joe', 'Barbie' dolls, sold by India toy manufacturers like Funskool, an MRF-controlled company based in Goa, and Leo Toys of Blowplast company, are advertised regularly on children's programmes. Funskool is a collaborator of a subsidiary of Hasbro, the world's largest toy manufacturer, and the makers of 'G I Joe'; Leo Toys collaborates with Mattel, the second largest toy manufacturer in the United States. Mattel produces toys like hotwheels, scrabble, pictionary and Superman. It has also produced the TV series on 'He-man' to promote the sale of their toys. It has set up a Barbie Friends Club, 'an interactive club where children could emulate the role model'. The members of the club – over 12,000 of them between the ages of 6 and 12 years at a subscription fee of Rs. 95 each – write letters to Barbie and she writes back to them. It is claimed that Barbie receives over a hundred letters every day.[22]

Should Indian television channels allow themselves to become commercial medium for the peddling of transnational manufacturers and their toys? All children's channels look upon kids as 'consumers' who enjoy immense 'pester power'.

In the mid-1980s when there wasn't a single channel for children, the Joshi Committee warned against this 'cultural invasion', but Doordarshan and later the private channels have paid no heed to the warning. The Joshi Committee Report also observed that 'reviews of children's reaction to film and television in India have indicated that animation is not always successful with Indian child audiences. Unfamiliarity with the technique sometimes makes it difficult for Indian children to identify the characters and objects.' For Indian children to

---

22 Anita Sharan: 'Coming Closer to the Consumer', *Brand Equity/The Economic Times*, July 14, 1993.

comprehend them it is necessary to keep the drawings in animation films simple and realistic, and the message needs to be conveyed in a direct manner. It therefore urged that research-based software be produced so that programmes are appropriate in terms of the child's level of development as well as his or her life situation.

The Joshi Committee Report (1984) learned from its extensive analysis of television software that 'most of our children's programmes seem to have been designed for the upper-class child. This is somewhat paradoxical: the ultimate objective is to use television for education purposes, and it is the urban child who least needs additional educational inputs. Instead, television programmes should be directed primarily towards disadvantaged children in rural and urban areas'[23]. The irony is that 'disadvantaged children' do not possess or have access to television receivers.

The Joshi Report also noted that children's programmes are among the most substandard of all programmes produced. Indeed, children's programmes are considered child's play; producers who are under-utilized at other work are allocated the children's programme section. Further, the time slotted for telecasting children's programmes is generally at the beginning of the evening's transmission, when most children should be playing outdoors.

Except for SITE studies of children's response to educational programmes, and a few other studies, we have little significant research on children's use of, or interaction with, the mass media.[24] The comic strips that daily newspapers, Sunday newspapers, and magazines publish regularly for young readers are mostly 'syndicated' comics from the United States. Columns for children frequently include quizzes, contests, comic strips and stories. Children's magazines like *Chandamama* (in different

---

23 *An Indian Personality for Television: Report of the Working Group on Software for Television*, Vols. I, II and III.
24 Cf. Keval J. Kumar: 'Impact of Mass Media on Young People', Paper read at a National Seminar, Shillong, June 1995, for the findings of a survey conducted in Bombay.

languages), Champak and JAM are few and far between.

While there is a National Film Foundation for Children and Young People, and children's film festivals are organized sporadically, very little attention is in fact paid to the production of films for children on a regular basis. The Films Division, on the other hand, is the foremost producer of short animation films, either directly educational in nature, or telling popular stories from the Panchatantra or the wealth of Indian folktale tradition.

Children's Programmes on Doordarshan

A 1995 study by Anura Goonasekera[25] reveals the attention given by Doordarshan to programmes for children. The table below gives the data for one week in January 1995. The predominance of animation programmes (19.3%) stands out among Doordarshan's fare for children. It is also remarkable that foreign programmes clearly dominate this category (63.89%). This is equally true of children's channels (Hungamma, Disney, POGO, Cartoon Network, Nickleodeon, etc.) that have been launched during the last few years by private TV networks. One does not see many original indigenous programmes on children or youth channels except perhaps for some game shows and reality shows.

Representations of Women in the Mass Media

The Joshi Committee Report observed in 1984 that Doordarshan is 'dominated by feature films and film-based programmes that exploit the female form to titillate and/or, through their socially insensitive approach, simply trivialize and debase the image of womanhood'. It therefore urged not only a reduction of the number of future films and film-based programmes on television but, more positively, "the incorporation of the 'women's dimension' in all programmes" and "the need for a

---

25 Anura Goonasekera: 'Children's Voice in the Media: A Study of Children's Television Programmes in Asia' in Ulla Carlsson and Cecilia von Feilitzen (Eds.): *Children and Media Violence*, UNESCO, 1998, pp.201-213.

Table 44 : Telecast of Children's Programmes on Doordarshan (1995)

Programme Type	Duration in Minutes per week		Total Broadcast Time per year in		As Percentage of all Children's Programmes
	Local	Foreign	Minutes	(Hours)	
Animation	85	150	12220	(203.66)	19.83
Puppets	-	-	-	-	-
Story Telling	-	90	4680	(78.00)	7.59
Serial/Drama	60	60	6240	(104.00)	10.12
Pre-School Magazine	20	-	1040	(17.33)	1.69
Magazine Information	70	-	3640	(60.66)	5.91
Information/ News	-	-	-	-	-
Magazine Entertainment	110	-	5720	(95.33)	9.28
Quiz/Games	60	-	3120	(52.00)	5.06
Pop Music	-	-	-	-	-
Religious	-	-	-	-	-
Cultural/ Traditional	30	-	1560	(26.00)	2.53
Other Programme Types	450	-	23400	(390.00)	37.97
TOTAL	885	300	61620	(1026.98)	100.00

separate focus on and for women."

Other recommendations of the Joshi Committee Report included the following:
(1) The improvement of women's condition, status and image be defined as a major objective of Doordarshan.
(2) The formulation of clear guidelines regarding the positive portrayal of women on television, and a system of monitoring the implementation of these guidelines.
(3) The redefinition of the image and the promotion of the male 'ideal' as one who is carrying and willing to share in household, childcare and contraceptive responsibilities.

(4) The need for orientation courses for all Doordarshan policy makers, programming and production staff so that they are sensitised to social issues with particular reference to women's issues and their implications in society.
(5) The careful scrutiny (by a special committee) of all advertisements shown on television, to ensure that they do not portray women in derogatory and stereotyped ways.
(6) The need for a weekly programme on viewers' views, in which the audience, critics, commentators, women's organizations are called upon to analyse and evaluate the week's programmes.
(7) The involvement of Mahila Mandalas in the installation of community television sets, and in community viewing arrangements in rural areas.

Women's organizations across the country (such as AWAG in Ahmedabad, Vimochana in Bangalore, and the Committees on Portrayal of Women in the Media, in New Delhi and Bombay), periodicals like *Manushi* and *Stree*, and Departments of Women's Studies in universities, have been active in carrying out research on representations of women in the various mass media. Several serious studies, involving both quantitative and qualitative methodologies, have been conducted; the majority of them are available, however, only in mimeo.

Women on Doordarshan

Doordarshan's portrayal of women in its various programmes has been subjected to close critical analysis by a number of researchers. Two major studies are: *Affirmation and Denial: Construction of Femininity on Indian Television* by Prabha Krishnan and Anita Dighe (1990)[26], and *Vision Unveiled* by Nandini Prasad (1994)[27]. The first study was conducted by Krishnan, Dighe and Rao in 1986. Programmes over a period of

---

26 Prabha Krishnan and Anita Dighe : *Affirmation and Denial: The Construction of Femininity on Indian Television*, New Delhi: Sage Publications, 1990.
27 Nandini Prasad : *Vision Unveiled: Women on Television*, New Delhi: Friedrich Ebert Stiftung, 1994.

15 days (a sample of 30 news programmes, 30 special interest group programmes, 55 general enrichment programmes, 33 art and entertainment programmes, 27 fiction-oriented and cinema programmes, 186 commercials and two audience-contact programmes – a total sample of 363 items) were scrutinized for women-related references. The largely quantitative analysis indicated certain definite trends:

In the first place, news related to women did not exceed 2.5 minutes out of the total 20 minutes. Women were news makers in less than ten per cent of the 30 news programmes telecast, mostly in the foreign news items that related to Margaret Thatcher and Corazon Aquino. Further, women invariably figured in the political news as wives, mothers, daughters of well-known men. They also appeared frequently as members of audiences and as victims of some calamity or accident. A significant number of women appeared as shoppers. In development-oriented news items, women featured as workers in tea plantations, sericulture poultry farming, etc., and as beneficiaries of welfare schemes. In women's programmes the focus was on the woman at home. The 'experts' in these programmes were men; in farmers' programmes all the experts were men; women, however, compered most children's programmes.

Where commercials were concerned, the lifestyles promoted were largely elitist; the models in the commercials were overwhelmingly light-skinned. In voice-overs, male voices were presented as 'authoritative'; female voices as informative and 'seductive'. Women featured in all categories of commercials, but they were dominant in ads for foods, grooming and household items.

Nandini Prasad's Study

Prasad's content analysis of Doordarshan programmes was carried out in 1992, using a large sample of two and a half months of national news bulletins. The sample extended from October 1 to December 15, 1992, with every second day's bulletin comprising the sample, i.e. a total of 38 news bulletins. Prasad found that a mere 20 news items during the entire period related to women. Of the 20 news items, 5 related to social issues, 3 to mobilising public opinion on women's issues, and 11 to other women-related issues. Prasad's examination of the portrayal of women in Doordarshan's advertisements reveals that out of a total sample of 210 ads, 63 showed women in 'traditional' roles, 35 in a 'non-traditional' role, and 117 in a 'neutral manner'.

Descriptive analyses of the portrayal of women in popular television serials include those by Leela Rao[28], Jyoti Punwani[29] and others.

Women in Radio Programmes

Less than two per cent of broadcasting time on radio is devoted to programmes on or for women, yet over 25 per cent of radio advertising is directed at women, in the form of advertisements on cosmetics, food products, beverages and fabrics. The songs selected for broadcast on All India Radio and Vividh Bharati are 'by and large on religious themes or depicting themes of coy young women waiting to be married'[30]. The plays convey the message of the ideal woman who is a housewife and mother. If she is employed, then surely she must be neglecting her home and children. Stereotypes of women are reinforced in songs, plays and commercial jingles.

An exhaustive study of the portrayal of women in Hindi and Gujarati films was conducted in 1976 by Ila Pathak and her colleagues at AWAG[31]. Their analysis of 12 Hindi and six Gujarati films showed that the films emphasised young, beautiful

---

28 Leela Rao: 'Portrayal of Women on Indian Television: Stri, Shakti and Sita: The Search for Identity', Paper presented at the International Television Studies Conference, London, 1988.
29 Jyoti Punwani: 'Portrayal of Women on Television' in Rehana Ghadially (Ed.): *Women in Indian Society: A Reader*, New Delhi:Sage Publications.
30 Neera Desai and Maitrey Krishnaraj (Eds.): *A Decade of Women's Studies in India*, Bombay: Allied, 1988.
31 Quoted in John Lent: 'Women and Mass Communication: The Asian Literature', *Gazette*, 1985, Vol. 35, pp.123-142.

and sexually attractive women; portrayed women in terms of their relationship to men; depicted women in traditional female occupations; and as overwhelmingly emotional, dependent, superstitious, and irrational beings. Besides, they stressed marriage as a goal for women, and offered a double standard of morality.

Dasgupta and Hegde did a quantitative analysis of 30 Hindi films available on video in a mid-Western city in the United States, with the objective of investigating how they dealt with 'mistreatment' of women[32]. The analysis led them to conclude that mistreatment was not a central concern of any film; that mistreatments (such as physical battering, assault, rape, homicide) occurred regularly when women step out of their traditional roles; and that mistreatment served the common function of returning straying women to their stereotypical and socially approved behaviour patterns. The recurrence of mistreatments on the Hindi screen was, therefore, an established mechanism to monitor and perpetuate the patriarchal order. Another study by Vijaya Mulay revealed that women continue to be portrayed in traditional ways, and that in a few films, women beatings were popularized as a form of taming and romancing[33]. Madhu Kishwar, editor of *Manushi*, found that Films Division documentaries on family planning contained a strong sexist bias: they underscored the importance of sons over daughters, the responsibility of family planning as a woman's duty, and the general passive nature of women[34].

Women and Print Media

Studies of the print media have focused on the reporting of rape cases in the press ('as merely spicy news stories'), the presentation of women in women's sections of newspapers, general interest magazines and women's magazines. Ammu Joseph and Kalpana Sharma critiqued the news media's

---
32 Shanti Dasgupta and Radha S Hegde: 'The Eternal Receptacle: A Study of Mistreatment of Women in Hindi Films' in Ghadially, op. cit.
33 Quoted in Lent, op. cit.
34 Quoted in Lent, op. cit.

presentation of women's issues in their study, *Whose News?*[35]

Ila Pathak's study of women's sections in the Gujarati dailies of Ahmedabad, for instance, found that there were hardly any articles devoted to a serious discussion of women's problems at home or in society[36]. Dasgupta's look at the Sunday editions of four English dailies found that articles on women were middle-class and urban-biased, and were restricted to a limited range of themes which did not take into account the political and economic realities of Indian women[37].

An analysis of fiction in three women's magazines and two general interest magazines concluded that they contained 'images and norms which should discourage female employment, particularly in higher-status occupations'.[38]

Women's magazines have come in for a lot of criticism. Often, they are no more than a mixed bag of recipes, tips on beauty aids, romantic stories, features on women's issues, and discussions on gender problems, and of course women-oriented advertisements. Butalia found that, the advertisements, even in women's magazines, were sexist[39]. Aminu Amin's 1982 study of 'Commercial Ads and the Great Health Robbery of Women and Children' showed how advertisers and manufacturers play on the susceptibility and vulnerability of women consumers and cheat them into buying food products, cosmetics, sanitary napkins, soaps and detergents that are positively harmful to the health of their families. The study also revealed that 'men in advertisements are fully clothed, appear confident and dignified' while the women are presented as glamorous but in traditional roles. Further, 'wares for men were sold for durability and economy; those for women for beauty and glamour'.[40] Kalia's analysis of the language used in Indian school textbooks also

---

35 Ammu Joseph and Kalpana Sharma: *Whose News?,* New Delhi: Sage Publications.
36 Quoted in Lent, op. cit.
37 Quoted in Lent, op. cit.
38 Quoted in Lent, op. cit.
39 Quoted in Lent, op. cit.
40 Aminu Amin: 'Commercial Ads and the Great Health Robbery', Mimeo.

concluded that it was clearly 'sexist'.[41] Another analysis of the textbook series called *Let's Learn English* concluded that women were few in number when it came to central characters, and they were shown as either mothers or teachers.[42]

Two anthologies, *Practising Journalism* and *21st Century Journalism in India*, edited by Nalini Rajan,[43] touch on the current status of women in the print media. In the first anthology, V. Geetha[44] analyses the 'female victim story' as a genre in the Tamil popular press; in the second, Ammu Joseph[45] revisits 'the gender factor', this time with reference to the tsunami news story. She attempts to answer two crucial questions: Can there possibly be a gender angle to the tsunami story? Is it at all reasonable to call for a gender perspective while covering the post-tsunami situation?

Women in the Media Professions

Besides the question of 'representations', the focus of research has been the job opportunities for women, especially at decision-making levels, in the production, administration and technical departments of the various media. The most widely discussed is S.R. Joshi's study for UNESCO entitled *Invisible Barriers: Women at Senior Levels*.[46] It analyses the status of women's employment at senior levels in Doordarshan. It found that women headed three out of 18 stations; that at the Delhi station 40 per cent of producers are women. Another important finding was that 'although overall employment figures were not available, 28 per cent of the producers at two other stations are

---

41 N.N. Kalia: 'Women and Sexism: Language of Indian School Textbooks' in Ghadially, op. cit.
42 Quoted in Lent, op. cit.
43 Nalini Rajan (Ed.): *Practising Journalism: Values, Constraints, Implications*, New Delhi: Sage Publications, 2005; Nalini Rajan (Ed.): *21st Century Journalism in India*, New Delhi: Sage Publications, 2007.
44 V. Geetha: 'Gender, Identity and the Tamil Popular Press' in Rajan, op.cit. pp.115-124
45 Ammu Joseph: 'The Gender Factor' in Rajan, op.cit. pp.29-44.
46 S.R. Joshi: Invisible Barriers: *Women at Senior Levels of Decision-Making in Doordarshan*, Paris:UNESCO, 1985.

women, with responsibility for determining the content of programmes'. Besides, one-third of the women at these levels are unmarried, compared to only one-tenth of the men. The women have fewer children, and are better educated though mostly in the arts, compared to the men, half of whom had gone for courses in science, engineering and commerce. According to the study, a large proportion of the women thought that there would be a change in programme content with an increase in the proportion of female employees, programme quality would improve and a more balanced perspective would emerge.

But there are more women in senior positions in the government-owned radio and television than in the press which continues to be male-dominated. A 1987 study[47] by the Women and Media Group, Bombay, discovered that women journalists are mainly on the staff of women's magazines; the women journalists in the daily newspapers and the news magazines also confine themselves to women-related issues and 'soft' news stories. Gita Aravamudan's study[48] of the status of women journalists in Kerala, the state with the highest literacy in the land, found that most are employed by women's magazines, or hold desk jobs; dailies such as *Malayala Manorama* and *Kerala Koumadi* however, did not employ women as a matter of policy. Robin Jeffrey analysed the place of women in the Indian language press as well as how they are reported in *Malayala Manorama* and other papers.[49] Rami Chhabra tells the story of how women journalists in India struggled to break the glass ceiling.[50]

Need for Audience Studies

A largely neglected area in women-and-the-media studies has

---

47 S.Sharma et al: 'Women and the Media in South Asia', *Media Asia*, 14 (4), 1987.
48 Quoted in S. Sharma et al, op. cit
49 Robin Jeffrey: *India's Newspaper Revolution*, New Delhi: Oxford University Press, 2000. pp.170-177.
50 Rami Chhabra: 'Women and the Media – Staking the Turf – To What End Today' in AshaRani Mathur (Ed.): *The Indian Media: Illusion, Delusion and Reality*, New Delhi: Rupa and Co., 2006. pp.67-76.

been audience research. Most of the audience research available has been conducted by market researchers where women are taken to be 'consumers'. The kind of research questions that need to be looked at are: How do women from different social classes 'read' the stereotypes in the various mass media and their genres? Do they, for instance, swallow the stereotypical representations hook, line and sinker, or reject or even 're-read' them? Again, how are programmes for women on radio and television produced? Who takes the vital decisions on programme content? Does the very fact that women are producers necessarily add a women's dimension to the programme? Women film directors like Aparna Sen and Sai Paranjpe have sensitized us to women's issues, but so have Satyajit Ray, Kumar Shahani, Mani Kaul, Basu Chatterjee, and Shyam Benegal. Further, women-centred serials on Doordarshan (*Rajani; It's A Woman's World*, *Kashmakesh*, *Chehre*, *Poornima*, *Rathachakra*, *Rathen Au Bhai Hain*, *Swayamsiddha*, *Basanti*, *Shanti*, and several others) and also on Star Plus (the K-serials), Zee TV and Sony TV have attempted, some with greater success than others, to probe the woman/gender question through interesting narratives. Ekta Kapoor, the prolific producer of Indian soap operas, continues to perpetuate rabidly conservative images of middle class women and the Hindu joint-family.

Further, several women have entered print and electronic journalism, but one wonders whether this alone has made any difference to professional values and news values – which have been evolved and moulded by patriarchy, politics and the market. The core of professional journalism is still 'hard news'; 'soft news' which women reporters and feature-writers are generally asked to cover, is considered less important.

Media and Consumerism

To most advertisers, people are not customers or even people but mere 'consumers'. Advertisers seek to entice target consumers to consume as much as possible, as frequently as possible, and with as much relish and envy or vanity as possible. It is not without significance that we are urged to buy and to consume wherever we are and whenever we switch on the radio, TV, cable or satellite TV, or read newspapers and magazines. Day in and day out we are bombarded with print and electronic messages promising us fun, frolic and happiness if we 'consume'. It does not matter whether we have the purchasing power to try out 'impulse products' like ice-creams, chocolates, candies, or soft drinks, but if we do not consume like the rest of the world we are likely to be left behind in the rat-race.

It is not only advertising that directly promotes consumption beyond one's means, but also 'sponsored' programmes and columns and supplements. The subtle messages of soap-operas, quiz and game shows (where expensive prizes are gifted by business and industrial houses), elite-oriented news and current affairs programmes, sports programmes, fashion shows, children's magazines and programmes, cartoon shows, 'advertorials' and almost every programme – all tell one persuasive story: consume or be damned. Advertisers like to believe that the consumer enjoys the freedom of choice. He is, after all, not compelled to buy. He must learn to live within his means. What is more, the consumer is not a moron; she is your wife!

The question that needs to be raised is: Do the mass media which thrive on advertising lead to excessive consumption in society, or is it the other way around: Does an affluent and economically developed society or community persuade the mass media to turn consumerist? It is true that both manufacturing and service industries in developed economies spend more on advertising and media relations than those in developing economies. However, it is equally true that the world's biggest markets for consumer product as well as for consumer durable are in the less developed countries. Further, during the past decade or so, growth in advertising expenditure in Asian countries has been steadily rising, while it has been reduced in the United States and other western countries.

In sum, consumerism is a fall-out of an industrial society, especially a society that swears by the economic laws of the free market and a liberal democracy. The assumption of such a society is that an 'invisible hand' controls the forces that compete freely with one another, and that justice and equity is promoted by such competition. The reality is that in a so-called open and free market the law of the jungle prevails, and only the most aggressive survive. Public welfare and concern fall by the wayside. The Indian experience of 'privatization' and 'liberalization' during the decades that followed suggests that some 'regulation' is imperative if the public weal is to be maintained.

Violence in the Media and Violence in Society

Over three thousand studies have been conducted during the past forty years in the United States alone that suggest that there is a 'correlation' between social aggression and the viewing of violence on the big and small screens. According to the American Psychological Association, by the time an average American child is ten or eleven years old, he/she would have seen 8,000 murders and 10,000 acts of violence on television.

Few studies on the subject have been conducted in India, and Indian children are not yet exposed to the excessive violence that American children are, at least on television. However, with the arrival of satellite television which is dominated by American films and television programmes, the Indian child is no doubt likely to be exposed to more and more violent fare. Of course, popular Indian films too have a surfeit of violence, much of it stylised, but some of it vivid and realistic, often bordering on the pornographic. There have been cases of children and adults imitating on-screen violence and the modus operandi of gangsters, robbers and murderers. Such cases get prominent coverage in the press and other media. But all this does not lead one to the conclusion that cinema or television violence is the primary or even the secondary cause of violence in our society. At the most, screen violence may be one of the many contributory factors. More influential factors are poverty, frustration, unemployment, revenge, family clashes, urban decay, loss of self-esteem, a sense of failure – in other words, a combination of sociological, psychological, economic and cultural factors. In any case, the 'correlations' that the American studies have found between screen violence and individual acts of violence do not mean that screen violence has 'caused' the violent behaviour. Statistical correlations, however significant, may point to an 'association' but hardly ever to a cause-and-effect relationship. What is of greater concern is the effect of 'desensitization' which could result from repeated exposure to scenes of violence in programmes, news and cartoons. Exposure to violence constantly and on a daily basis can desensitize us to violence in real life: violence against women and children, for instance, will shock or move us much less than we ought to as human beings. Further, we might be convinced that violence is a part of society, and that it is normal, even glamorous to be aggressive and 'macho' in one's behaviour. It might lead us to believe that some groups (for instance, tribals, dalits and leftists) are 'naturally' violent, and such stereotypes might endure.

Violence in the News

Violence in the news and in comic strips is rarely talked about. While the portrayal of violence in the press and broadcast media is condoned because it is 'factual' and deals with real-life incidents, the caricatures of violent fights and clashes between heroes and villains are condoned because they are presented in a light and humorous manner. There have been few Indian or even Asian studies on the influence of such violent portrayals on society or on how these portrayals often reflect violence in society.

A 1995 study sponsored by AMIC, Singapore, of television violence in six Asian countries concluded that where American-origin fare dominated, as in the Philippines and Thailand, the violent scenes were more numerous than in indigenous programmes, though this was not the case in Japanese television.

The violence on the Indian television screen was found to be mostly in the popular Hindi and regional language films. A recent study, again by AMIC, on the coverage of the American invasion of Iraq in the newspapers of five Asian countries including India, suggests that there were different perspectives to the war.[51]

The Indian Institute of Mass Communication, New Delhi, undertook a study of television violence in 1996, using the Gerbner model of 'cultivation analysis'.

But violence is not related to crime alone. It must take into account state violence, like that of the police and the armed forces, or the violence of the law which does not bring the guilty to book, or which delays justice, or worse, punishes the innocent. Such violence too is sometimes the subject of cinema and television. The portrayal of such violence could help raise consciousness and thus lead to social reform (E.g. the film *Ardh Satya*, and the television serial, *Tamas*).

Violence in the mass media is frequently associated with sex. Indeed, rape or forced sex is the most violent crime that is often depicted graphically on the big and small screen. In recent years, a rape sequence has almost become obligatory in the popular film. Rape sequences are sometimes followed by scenes of blood and gore, since scores have to be settled and the rape avenged. Further, villains need to frequent night clubs where titillating cabarets are put on for their entertainment.[52] The censors come down heavily on a few films, but the majority of popular films are 'passed' as okay for the entire family. Foreign television soap-operas, sitcoms, detective serials, music videos, reality shows, and even game shows and sports relays (especially those from the United States, Australia, Hong Kong and Britain) have dollops of sex and violence, often verging on soft-core

---

51 See Crispin Maslow: Crispin Maslow et al: 'Framing Analysis of a Conflict: How Newspapers in Five Asian Countries Covered the Iraq War', *Asian Journal of Communication*, Vol 16, No. 1 (2006). pp.19-39.
52 For a recent study, see Srividya Ramasubramaniam and Mary Beth Oliver: *Portrayals of Sexual Violence in Popular Hindi Films – 1997-99*, Springer Netherlands, 2003.

pornography. Doordarshan and the numerous private cable and satellite TV channels, have begun screening such programmes and making 'clones' of them for the Indian viewer. Crime stories and crime-based programmes are regular fare on the over 50 television news channels; they are often presented as voyeuristic entertainment at a breathless pace, without the slightest concern for the sensitivity of the victim or that of the viewer.

FOR FURTHER READING

1. Binod C. Agarwal and Mira Aghi: *Children and Television in India*, New Delhi: UNICEF, 1986.
2. Kamla Bhasin and Bina Agrawal: *Women and Media Analysis: Alternatives and Action*, New Delhi: Kali for Women, 1984.
3. Ulla Carlsson and Cecilia Feleitzen (Eds.): *Children and Media Violence*, Paris: UNESCO, 1998.
4. Ulla Carlsson and Cecilia Feleitzen (Eds.): *Children and Media: Image, Education, Participation*, Paris: UNESCO, 1999.
5. Kirsten Drotner and Sonia Livingstone (Eds.): *The International Handbook of Children, Media and Culture*, London: Sage Publications, 2008.
6. Ammu Joseph and Kalpana Sharma: *Whose News?: The Mass Media and Women's Issues*, New Delhi: Sage.
7. Prabha Krishnan, Anita Dighe and Purnima Rao: *Affirmation and Denial: Sex Role Patterns in Doordarshan*, New Delhi: Sage, 1988.
8. Crispin Maslow et al: 'Framing Analysis of a Conflict: How Newspapers in Five Asian Countries Covered the Iraq War', *Asian Journal of Communication*, Vol 16, No. 1 (2006), pp.19-39.
9. Andal Narayanan: *The Impact of TV on Viewers*, Bombay: Somaiya, 1987.
10. Nandini Prasad: *Vision Unveiled*, New Delhi: Friedrich Ebert Stiftung, 1994.
11. Michael Traber (Ed.): *Globalisation, Mass Media and Indian Cultural Values*, New Delhi: ISPCK, 2003.
12. Namita Unnikrishanan and Shailaja Bajpai: *Effects of Television Advertising on Children*, New Delhi: Sage, 1995.

13. Leela Rao (Ed.): *Women and the Mass Media*, Bangalore: Media Centre, 1992.
14. Joseph Velacherry: *Social Impact of Mass Media in Kerala*, New Delhi: ISPCK, 1993.

JOURNALS

1. Asian Journal of Mass Communication
2. Media Asia
3. Communicator
4. Vidura
5. ICCTR Journal

WEB RESOURCES

1. www.aocmedialiteracy.com (United Nation's Alliance of Civilizations' Initiative on Media Literacy)
2. www.museum.tv (Archive for Television Programmes)
3. www.dissent.com
4. www.counterpunch.com
5. www.medialens.org
6. www.fair.com
7. www.thehoot.org

REVIEW QUESTIONS

1. What are the problems involved in talking about media effects?
2. Describe and comment on the well-known theories of 'media effects'.
3. How do children react to television violence, say in WWF? Enumerate the different types of TV violence.
4. What role do the media play in Indian Politics? Do you think they influence voting patterns in any significant manner?
5. What are the factors that need to be taken into account in any study of the impact of advertising on our buying behaviour?
6. Write short notes on:
   (i) Women and the Mass Media
   (ii) Socialisation Effects of the Media
   (iii) The Mass Media and Politics

(iv) Media as promoters of consumerism
(v) Influence of the media on family interaction patterns
(vi) Sex and Violence in the Media.

SUGGESTED PROJECTS

1. Examine the results of a recent election at the national or regional/local level. Did the media influence the result in any way? What are the other forces that affected the results.
2. Conduct a brief survey of the 'attitudes' of students to the examination or caste-system. Draw up a brief questionnaire. What factors do you find influence these attitudes? Suggest how these attitudes can be changed.
3. Examine the violent scenes in two films seen in the cinema or on TV. Which of the scenes are realistic and which stylised/ritualised? Comment on the violence in television news bulletins.
4. Critically analyse any two ads which you believe have had a particularly strong impact on you.

SECTION V

MEDIA, CULTURE AND DEVELOPMENT

'Development Communication' or DevCom has now become a widely established sub-discipline in Communication Studies in India. Most university departments of Communication/Journalism as well as private media institutes (the latter far exceeded the former by 2008) teach courses in this sub-discipline though indigenous research efforts remain few and far between. Much of the research continues to be carried out and published by Indian scholars overseas. But even these efforts do not often go beyond the functionalist research questions that relate to 'diffusion', 'effects', 'uses and gratifications' and 'cultural indicators'. Research that attempts to grapple with the tough social-structural and critical questions continues to remain on the margins.

The attempt in this chapter is to trace the historical evolution of the field, the emergence of the 'dominant paradigm', its apparent 'passing away', the several responses to it in the way of 'alternative' approaches based on 'participation', 'empowerment' and 'self-reliance' and of course the 'revival' of the dominant paradigm each time a new communication technology emerges. (Currently, it is the mobile telephone that has become the centre-piece of development strategies; a decade earlier it was the internet). The focus on the role of the mass media in national development has given way to questions about the centrality of the new digital and mobile media (the information and communication technologies or ICTs) in the process of economic, social and cultural development. Often overlooked in such discussions are the institutional and social structures that pervade every level of Indian society and the scant resources at the command of the marginalized and the oppressed. ICTs are perceived to be the panacea for 'under-development' as though bridging the 'digital divide' and/or the 'mobile divide' is the key to resolving the 'development divide' in urban and rural India.

The Cultural Context of 'Development'

'Development' is perhaps one of the most fiercely debated concepts in contemporary social science. The concept is often equated with 'modernisation', 'industrialisation', 'social change', 'progress', and 'growth', and like these other terms is invariably seen as something desirable and positive for society in general, and for the community in particular. Also, 'development' as a socio-economic phenomena is seen as necessary, even inevitable; as good and salutary. Rarely is development discussed as possibly hazardous and destructive of the environment, or in terms of social values and cultures. Indeed, rarely is development framed in the context of history, culture and values, or looked at in relative terms. Development is in the main seen as absolute, inevitable, and universal; it is promoted as a laudable goal no matter what the society, the culture, the people and their resources and traditions.

The concept of 'development' has evolved since World War II from a narrow economistic term into a comprehensive and dynamic one, taking within its ambit almost every aspect of human existence. For, in its fundamental meaning, all 'development' is human development; the focus of development is the human being, the quality of his/her life, and the environment in which that quality of life is sustained. The early concept of development overlooked the human and the environmental factors. Having been inspired by the Western industrialisation process, the concept was initially restricted to 'an almost exclusive concern with a narrowly conceived economic dimension and to reliance on a traditional Western market-oriented model of industrialisation and growth.' The stress was on modernisation imposed from above, at the expense of tradition and culture.

New dimensions were added to the original concept in the 1950s. The social dimension, through such aspects as health and education, was then given prominence. But the talk of such notions as 'functional literacy' and 'human resources' revealed that the concept of development was still dominated by economic growth theories. Rural development and communications were yet to be given any serious thought.

From the 1970s, however, the development concept was refined and broadened through the addition of first, the ecological dimensions: population, food, employment, human sentiments, and later, science and technology, including technology transfer. In keeping with the trend today towards more holistic paradigms, there is a growing recognition of still another crucial dimension: the cultural dimension, or seen from another angle, the communications and information dimension.

Development, therefore, is a whole; it is an integral value-loaded, cultural process; it takes in the natural environment, social relations, education, production, consumption and welfare. The approach to development depends upon the local cultural or national situations, as much as on local knowledge and experiences, and not on any outside model. In other words, development springs from the heart of each society, relying on its history and traditions, as also its own strengths and resources as far as possible.

Until the 1960s, economic theories of development explained 'underdevelopment' as a consequence of industrial and technical backwardness, while sociological theories put the blame on the superstition and fatalism of the illiterate masses. Thus, the quickest solution to 'underdevelopment' was believed to be the borrowing of 'modernization' strategies of Western societies which were deemed to be 'developed. These strategies, however, needed the necessary know-how as well as the capital which the industrialized countries alone could provide at the time. So multinational corporations (MNCs) were allowed to enter the poorer countries to provide this capital and know-how. International aid agencies and financing institutions like the World Bank, the International Monetary Fund (IMF) and USAID, too rushed in to assist the poorer countries; so did specialists and advisers in 'development'. Two such advisers who had a great influence on Indian approaches to development were Wilbur Schramm and Everett Rogers, the first a UNESCO adviser on development communication to the Government of India, and one who helped establish the Indian Institute of Mass

Communication; the second, also an adviser to the Indian government, but who promoted innovation and diffusion research in Indian agriculture and information technology.

Development Communication

'Development Communication' (or simply 'Devcom') emerged as a field of mass communication studies during the post-World War II years when the countries of Asia, Africa and South America were asserting their right to independence, self-reliance and non-alignment. These very same countries were in a hurry to find solutions to the most urgent needs of their people: the eradication of poverty, illiteracy and unemployment. Colonial rule had established massive bureaucracies, skeleton transport and communication infrastructures, few educational and professional institutes, and fewer industries and public services. Centralized economic planning, large-scale industrialisation and the development of the mass media appeared at the time to be the most effective strategies for 'catching up' with the industrialized nations. This indeed was the advice proffered by Western financial institutions, United Nations experts, and foreign advisers to national governments.

'Modernization' Models of Development Communication

Perhaps the most influential work in the emergence and growth of Development Communication as a field of mass communication studies was Daniel Lerner's *The Passing of Traditional Society*, sub-titled 'Modernizing the Middle-East'.[1] But this study was not the work of an individual but rather part of a large research project of the Bureau of Applied Social Research (BASR), at the Columbia University in New York City. Its earlier avatar was the Office of Radio Research at Princeton University. Paul Lazarsfeld, an Austrian researcher who was to have a seminal influence on early media research, was brought

---

1 Daniel Lerner : *The Passing of Traditional Society: Modernizing the Middle-East*, New York: Free Press, 1958.

in by the CBS to head the Bureau. In the earlier stages of the Office and the Bureau's existence, much of the funding came from the Rockfeller Foundation.[2]

Lerner's project was funded by the Voice of America (VOA) which was keen on finding out the extent of listenership to this overseas service which was promoted and funded directly by the United States government. The Cold War against the Soviet Union and Communism was a major driving force for the establishment of the VOA (and later Radio Free Europe, Radio Liberty, Radio Marti and Radio Free Asia), and for supporting such research projects.

Lerner was an Intelligence Officer of the United States army during the War, and was now involved in social research projects. He looked upon the mass media, especially radio, as the means for bringing about the development of newly-independent nations. They were the 'mobility multipliers', forces which would motivate people to turn their backs on tradition and embrace 'modernization', which a close reading of his novelistic account of his experiences in the Middle East reveals, he equated with 'Westernization'. He regarded his model of 'modernization' to be universally relevant and applicable. The media were for Lerner, powerful tools for changing people's perceptions, attitudes and aspirations. Exposure to the media would stimulate 'empathy' – the capacity to distance oneself imaginatively from one's immediate circumstances and to take an interest in matters that do not bear directly to everyday life. 'With the development of empathy, the self becomes more expansive, desirous, open-ended; rather than seeing oneself as located at a fixed point in an unchanging order of things, one sees one's life as a moving point along a trajectory of things imagined. Like the grocer of Balgat, the empathetic self can imagine a world beyond the immediate locale, a world of risks and opportunities in which a new life can be forged through the continuous assimilation of actual and

---

2   See the interview with Frank Stanton, then CBS President, in Peter Ludes (Ed.): *Visualising the Public Sphere*, Muenchen: Wilhelm Fink Verlag, 1994. pp. 54-55.

vicarious experience.'[3] At least that was what he argued for in his romantic paean to the 'modern' in the fascinating tale of his encounters in the Middle East.

Diffusion of Innovations

Everett Rogers, the pioneer of 'diffusion' studies of media technologies, was an Iowa farm-boy trained in modern agriculture. He found his home community less than impressed with his stock of innovations in agriculture; outside his country he had a marked influence in the field of agricultural extension, through his textbook on *The Diffusion of Innovations*, which over the years has been expanded and updated into the second and third editions.[4]

Rogers developed his concepts and theories of the diffusion of innovations from a synthesis of diffusion research studies in the United States, and in later editions, of diffusion studies in the developing world as well. Rogers defined an 'innovation' as 'an idea perceived as new by the individual'. 'It really matters little, as far as human behaviour is concerned', he added, 'whether or not an idea is 'objectively' new as measured by the amount of time elapsed since its first use or discovery. It is the newness of the idea to the individual that determines his reaction to it.' In later editions, however, an 'innovation' is no more just an 'idea'; it is also a 'practice or object perceived as new by an individual.' Indeed, by the third edition, Rogers begins to use 'technology' as a synonym for 'innovation', and to urge the adoption of a 'convergence model' that stresses the intricacy of 'interpersonal

---

[3] See John B Thompson: *The Media and Modernity: A Social Theory of the Media*, Stanford University Press, 1995. p. 188-192, for a recent (unusually favourable) re-evaluation of Lerner's empirical research on the role of media exposure in 'modernisation'. Thompson acknowledges that Lerner's work is now dated and also that it is 'ethno-centric' but goes on to pay tribute to him for his emphasis on 'the fact that the media play a crucial role in the cultural transformation associated with the rise of modern societies'.

[4] Everett M. Rogers: *Diffusion of Innovations*, Glencoe, Illinois: Free Press, 1962; Everett K. Rogers and F. Shoemaker: *Communication of Innovations*, New York: Free Press, 1973; 3rd Ed. 1982.

communication networks' that are in operation during the process of diffusion.

In the mid-1970s, Rogers proclaimed the 'passing of the dominant paradigm'[5] – the modernization model – though apparently excluding his own 'diffusion of innovation' model, the basic principles of which were derived from the United States' experience of agricultural extension. He propagated his model of modernization in developing countries urging that it had cross-cultural applications. Rogers' work was in fact an extension of Lerner's; he adopted Lerner's notions of 'empathy', 'cosmopoliteness', and 'attitude change'; his unit of analysis was the individual, and his main concern was with the 'social mind', and the change of culture, attitudes and ideas.

Mass Media as 'Magic Multipliers'

Wilbur Schramm extended the arguments of Lerner and Rogers in favour of 'modernization' through the mass media – which he termed 'the magic multipliers'.[6] His work was part of the efforts of the United Nations and UNESCO for 'a programme of concrete action to build up press, radio broadcasting, film and television facilities in countries in the process of economic and social development. The survey on which the book was based was carried out by UNESCO during a series of meetings in Bangkok, Santiago and Paris.

To Schramm, as to mainstream social scientists of the time, the mass media were 'agents of social change', 'almost miraculous' in their power to bring about that change. Schramm argued that the mass media could help accomplish the transitions to new customs and practices (the 'innovations' of Rogers) and, in some cases, to different social relationships. Behind such changes in behaviour must necessarily lie substantial changes in attitudes, beliefs, skills and 'social norms'. The process, he

---

5 Everett M. Rogers: 'Communication and Deveopment: The Passing of the Dominant Paradigm', pp. 121-47, in Everett M. Rogers (Ed).): *Communication and Development: Critical Perspectives*, Sage, 1982.
6 Wilbur Schramm: *Mass Media and National Development*, Stanford: Stanford University Press, 1964.

elaborated was simple: first, the awareness of a need which is not satisfied by present customs and behaviour; second, the need to invent or borrow behaviour that comes close to meeting the need. Hence a nation that wants to accelerate the process of development will try to make its people more widely and quickly aware of needs and of the opportunities for meeting them, will facilitate the decision process, and will help the people put the new practices smoothly and swiftly into effect. Schramm went further than Rogers in taking account of cultural linkages, in acknowledging 'resistance to change' and in urging 'an understanding participation'. However, his model of communication was still manipulative of behaviour towards the desired end of innovation adoption; it still cited as empirical evidence a strong correlation between high media exposure and development. Schramm argued forcefully that the mass media had the potential to widen horizons, to focus attention, to raise aspirations and to create a climate for development. They also had the potential to confer status, to enforce social norms, to help form tastes, and could affect attitudes lightly held. He was optimistic about the potential of the mass media (and also the educational media such as programmed instruction, language laboratories, electronic digital computers) in all types of education and training. Unlike Rogers, he conceded though that 'the mass media can help only indirectly to change strongly held attitudes and valued practices'.

He therefore recommended that 'a developing country should review its restrictions on the importing of informational materials, should not hesitate to make use of new technical developments in communication, in cases where these new developments fit its needs and capabilities'. The challenge, he concluded, was to put the resources and the power of modern communication skillfully and fully behind economic and social development. He described as fortuitous, 'almost miraculous' that modern mass communications should be available to multiply informational resources. So carried away was Schramm by his messianic role that he observed in a final flourish: 'it is hardly possible to imagine national economic and social development without some modern information multiplier; and indeed, without mass communication probably the great freedom movements and national stirrings of the last few decades would never have come about at all'. Such was the faith of the purveyors of 'modernization' models.

The assumption in 'modernization' theories of Development was that societies evolved from one stage to another, from 'traditional' to 'transitional' to 'modern', and thence to 'postmodern' or 'post-industrial' societies. Largely influenced by Social Darwinism, early social theorists like Max Weber, Karl Marx, Emile Durkheim and others took society to be an organism that evolved and grew in a linear and orderly logical manner rather than in a random chaotic manner. Societies grew and flourished on the Darwinian principle of 'the survival of the fittest'. Rostow, for instance, argued that every society followed a five-step model of transition from a traditional to a modern industrial society: the traditional society, preconditions for take-off, take-off, drive to maturity and the age of mass consumption.[7]

Dependency/Structuralist Models

By the mid-1970s, however, evaluation reports of 'extension' programmes in the non-aligned world indicated that the consequences of 'modernization' had been disastrous. While there had been some successes in agricultural, health, nutrition and educational extension programmes, the main beneficiaries were the better-off sections of society. There was little evidence of the hoped for 'trickle down' effect; the diffusion of innovations that was believed to have brought about the Green Revolution, for instance, benefited the richer landowners and farmers, and the expansion of the mass media network was used for political propaganda or for the entertainment of the urban middle-class rather than for development purposes. Indeed, the knowledge-gaps between the haves and the have-nots had

---

7 W.W. Rostow: *The Stages of Economic Growth: A Non-Communist Manifesto, 1960.* Quoted in Srinivas Melkote: *Communication for Development in the Third World: Theory and Practice*, New Delhi: Sage, 1991.

widened since access to the mass media was still restricted to the elites. Where serious attempts to use mass media for development were made, bureaucracies and their collusion with the better-off and higher-caste groups rendered most projects ineffective. Rural social structures were such that all attempts to reach the poorest of the poor were scotched.

At the international level, the main beneficiaries were the big powers and their industries, the multinational companies and the financing banks and institutions. The harmful effects of 'modernisation' policies were incalculable. Several countries in Africa and South America were turned into one-crop cultures (the single crop was usually a 'cash crop' needed in industrialized countries) and into importers of food grains. Further, large scale industrialization and urbanization (the 'hallmarks of modernisation') had led to massive migration from rural areas to the cities, and greater technological dependence on the more advanced countries. This dependence was also increased in the information and cultural industries (both in hardware and software) since the principle of 'free flow' prevailed.

'Dependency' models came to the fore in the early 1970s as a reaction to 'modernization' models. These new theories were the product of the application of Marxist theories of imperialism, though both Marxists and non-Marxists were instrumental in articulating them. There were in fact various influences at work, such as 'liberation theology', Freirian thinking on the pedagogy of the oppressed through 'conscientization', Schumacher's advocacy of 'appropriate technologies', popular grassroots movements (e.g. formation of 'base Christian communities' in several Latin American countries, and the Sarvodaya Movement in Sri Lanka), and alternative communication strategies (e.g. radio schools in Latin America, and people's theatre in India).

The original version of 'dependency and underdevelopment' theory was outlined by Paul Baran[8] and Andre Gunder Frank.[9]

---

8   Paul Baran: *The Political Economy of Growth*, New York: Monthly Review Press, 1967.
9   Andre Gunder Frank: *Capitalism and Underdevelopment in Latin America*, New York: Monthly Review Press, 1967.

The primary concern was finding out the causes of backwardness of the non-aligned countries within the dynamics of the world capitalist system. They assumed that 'underdevelopment' was due, not to some 'original state of affairs' but the result of the same historical process by which the now developed capitalist countries became economically advanced and industrialized. Thus, Baran argued that underdevelopment was the obverse side of development; the capitalist countries had become 'developed' by exploiting the colonies for centuries. Such economic exploitation had left the colonies with a narrowly-specialized, export-oriented primary production structure managed by an elite which shared the cultural lifestyle and tastes of the dominant classes in capitalist states. This elite continues to perpetuate the rule of the ex-colonies; hence a kind of neo-imperialism still prevails.

Andre Gunder Frank elaborated the theory by postulating three 'laws' of motion of the process of development and underdevelopment, and coining the twin concept 'metropolis-satellite', to characterize the nature of imperialist economic relations. The ties of dominance and dependency, he explained, run in chain-like fashion throughout the global capitalist system, with 'metropolitan' (or 'centre') states appropriating the surplus from the 'satellites' (or 'periphery').

The Economic Commission for Latin America (ECLA) under the leadership of Raoul Prebisch propounded 'dependency theory' along similar lines. It saw a 'structural' link between development and underdevelopment. ECLA's economists emphasised self-reliant development through industrialization import-substitution though under the aegis of foreign investment. However, the consequence of following this strategy led to greater rather than less dependence on advanced countries – for finance, marketing, capital goods, technology design, etc. Indeed, it led to even further underdevelopment, what with the presence of foreign industrial subsidiaries, and the growing balance-of-debts situation, the dumping of obsolete equipment and technologies. Thus 'dependency theories' lost their radical appeal to the peasants and workers.

A structuralist who merits attention here is Emile McAnany, who focuses attention both on the external and internal structures in society and communications in order to explain 'underdevelopment'.[10] He argues that social, economic and political structures enter into the formation of the problems of the poor. He believes that communication has a modest role to play in development, but the necessary condition of this role will be some changes in the environment other than the addition of information. (Manuel Castells' recent work on the potential of mobile telephony for global development endorses such a cautious approach: 'Wireless communication is no panacea for development. But development projects, from all corners of the planet, are embracing the potential of new technology and are using it for their own purposes according to what they are able to achieve.')[11]

'Alternative' Approaches to Development

The 1980s and '90s saw a number of critical scholars proposing approaches to development communications that were alternative to both the 'modernization' and 'dependency' approaches. These were in the main non-Marxist approaches; they rejected the economism and universal relevance of earlier models. The focus of these 'alternative' approaches has been on the social and cultural identities of nations as well as on the external factors that inhibit all-round development. Some of the communication scholars associated with these 'culturalist' approaches include Goran Hedebro[12], Jan Servaes[13], Majid Teharanian[14] and Hamid Mowlana.[15]

---

10 Emile McAnany (Ed.): *Communication in the Rural Third World*, New York: Praeger, 1980.
11 Manuel Castells et al: *Mobile Communication and Society: A Global Perspective*, Cambridge. Mass.: The MIT Press, 2007. p. 243.
12 Goran Hedebro: *Communication and Social Change in Developing Nations: A Critical View*, Ames: Iowa State University Press, 1982.
13 Jan Servaes: 'Towards an Alternative Concept of Communicatio and Development', Media Development, 4: 2-5.
14 Majid Teharanian : 'Paradigms Lost' in *Media Development*, 1985 (4).
15 Hamid Mowlana and L.J. Wilson: *Communication Technology and Development*, Paris: UNESCO, 1988.

Jan Servaes has developed his 'multiplicity model' in a series of publications during the last two decades.[16] Shirley White, Tom Jacobson, Sadanand Nair and Joseph Ascroft[17] have elaborated on their 'participatory' and 'empowerment' models of Development Communication, in two edited volumes. Srinivas Melkote and Steeves have introduced a strong value-orientation into their 'liberation theology' perspective of the discipline[18]. (For a recent summing up and critique of these various alternative approaches to devcom, see Robert White's 2004 paper)[19]. 'Empowerment is central to the process of development', White concludes his review, 'but empowerment needs to be located within a broader framework, which sees the goal of development as the cultural and political acceptance of universal human rights'. Social movements and non-government social action groups do certainly have a crucial role to play in grassroots initiatives provided of course the focus is on the empowerment of dalits and other oppressed groups rather than on the organizations themselves.

Other contemporary scholars have underlined the need for 'self-reliance' in any attempt at national development. Non-aligned nations in particular have made demands in international fora like the United Nations for the establishment of a new international economic order (NIEO) and a 'new world information and communication order' (NWICO) so that the domination of the world economy by the big powers is reduced. Self-reliance models attempt to link the NIEO with the need for national development strategies based on autonomous development. No longer is development envisaged to be an

---

16 Jan Servaes : *Communication for Development: One World, Multiple Cultures*, Gresskill NJ: Hampton Press. 1999.
17 See Thomas Jacobson and Jan Servaes (Ed.): *Theoretical Approaches to Participatory Communication*, Gresskill NJ: Hampton Press. 1999; Shirley White, K.S. Nair and Joseph Ascroft (Eds.): *Participatory Communication: Working for Change and Development*, New Delhi: Sage. 1994.
18 Srinivas Melkote and Leslie H. Steeves: *Communication for Development in the Third World: Theory and Practice for Empowerment*, New Delhi: Sage. 2001.
19 Robert A. White: 'Is 'Empowerment' the Answer? Current Theory and Research in Development Communication' , Gazette, Vol. 66, No. 1, pp. 7-24.

externalization movement whose motor of development of trade and technological transfers from outside but as a process of mobilization of local resources with a view to satisfying local needs. The Arusha Programme for collective self-reliance and the Framework for Negotiations drawn up in February 1979 by the Group of Seventy-seven, gives expression to this strategy. The success of the Non-Aligned Movement, China's Great Leap Forward, and the writings of Mahatma Gandhi, Mao Tse Dong and Paulo Freire have provided the inspiration for self-reliant development.

Rajni Kothari, Director of the Centre for the Study of Developing Societies, New Delhi, has been a well-known advocate of the 'self-reliant' and 'humane' development model.[20] However, he stresses the need for looking at self-reliance in 'the context of the rise of new movements and new actors on the scene'. The new movements are the ecological, the feminist, the movements for peace and for self-determination and democratization. The human rights movement too is gathering strength among bonded labour, the landless, miners, fisherfolk, ethnic minorities and women. But these movements are pitted against governments that are increasingly becoming militarized through arms deals, and against elites that indulge in rampant consumerism. Further, there is a 'transnationalization' of the world's economy; indeed a revival of old paradigms of development through a free market economy, monetarism, export-oriented growth, free trade zones, the adoption of new technologies, and the depoliticization of development. The role of communication in such a situation, urges Kothari, is to be 'part and parcel of the struggle for human liberation, freedom and justice, strengthening the struggles of communities, cultures, and of the marginalized, and to make their voices heard. Communication should be a process that contains the forces of backlash and the forces of transformation and survival. The human rights dimension needs to be built into the new development paradigm; human survival, and a just,

---

20 Rajni Kothari: 'Communication for Alternative Development' in *Development Dialogue*, 1984 (1-2).

demilitarized and humane society should be the main aims of this development paradigm. Kothari sees human survival as a dynamic force projecting a positive alternative to the theory of progress and the goal of affluence, one that finds dignity in genuine equity and in diverse cultures working out their own strategies in local movements for democracy and autonomy. Global problems, local solutions, he argues, is no mere slogan; it is the very condition of human survival.[21]

Revival of 'Modernization' Models

The dominant paradigm of modernisation never really 'passed'. Though several communication and development scholars turned their back on it, national governments, the power blocs and the transnationals continued to practise and propagate the old paradigms. 'Catching up' with the advanced industrialized countries continues to remain the ambition of national governments. What is more, the new technologies offer governments greater means of control and surveillance over their large populations.

As the 1980s drew to a close, there was a vigorous revival of 'modernization' both in theory and practice, particularly in the aftermath of rapid developments in telecommunications and the new technologies. Rural development was once again the focus of attention but not through the mass media as much as through 'telecommunications'. The term 'telecommunications' entered the field of development communication in the early 1980s and came to include not only the broadcast media but also the telephone and related technologies such as teleconferencing, audio conferencing, and satellite communications. Several rural telecommunications projects were launched – in Alaska, India, Indonesia and the South Pacific – mainly with the assistance of international donor agencies. The evidence from these projects seemed to indicate that there were linkages between telephony and rural development, that telephony was a cause rather than a

---

21 For a critical study of Indian social movements, see Rajendra Singh: *Social Movements : Old and New: A Post-Modernist Critique*, New Delhi: Sage.

consequence of development.²²

The organizations promoting this 'revival' were the International Telecommunication Union (ITU), the OECD, the World Bank, USAID, IBD (the Inter-American Development Bank), and IPDC. The Maitland Commission Report²³ became the bible of this telecommunication approach to development. Some of the assumptions of this approach were: telecommunication use benefits the society and the economy, improves cost-benefits of rural social service delivery, improves cost-benefits for rural economic activities, permits more equitable distribution of economic benefits, and facilitates social change and improved quality of life.

Other 'new' technologies too, such as video, computers, the internet and even mobile telephony, are currently being propagated as tools for quickening the pace of development. Manuel Castells, for instance, believes that 'the Internet is the fabric of our lives... a fundamental instrument for development in the Third World'.²⁴ He states that 'the new model of development requires leap-frogging over the planetary digital divide. It calls for an Internet-based economy, powered by learning and knowledge-generation capacity, able to operate within the global networks of value, and supported by legitimate, efficient political institutions. It is in the shared interest of humankind that such a model emerges while there is still time.'²⁵

Castells' three volumes on the *Economy, Society and Culture: The Information Age*²⁶ take us through the many multicultural dimensions of his concept of the 'Network Society', and the suggestion clearly is that 'networking' is a complex, open,

---

22 Heather E. Hudson: *When Telephones Reach the Village: The Role of Telecommuniction in Rural Development*, Norwood NJ: Ablex, 1984.
23 Maitland Commission: *The Missing Link: Report of the Independent Commission for Worldwide Telecommunications Development*, Geneva: ITU, 1984.
24 Manuel Castells: *The Internet Galaxy*, Oxford University Press, 2001. p.5.
25 Ibid. p. 271.
26 Manuel Castells: *The Information Age: Economy, Society and Culture*, Volume 1: *The Rise of the Network Society*, Oxford: Blackwell Publishers. Volume 2: *The Power of Identity*, Volume 3: *End of Millennium*, Oxford: Blackwell Publishers, 1996-2000.

dynamic, flexible, elaborate and comprehensive social, cultural, political and economic process. While information technology is at the centre of his vision of the Network Society, it has to be acknowledged that there are several segments of society (besides those termed 'the Fourth World') which are outside it, and yet an integral part of it. Besides, his understanding of Information Technology is all-inclusive: the old and the new media, print and broadcast media, telecommunications, the internet, intranets, the works. He does not consider the inevitable development of societies from one stage to another until they reach the level of 'network societies'. Indeed, he makes it clear that he does not subscribe to this point of view and that 'there is no predetermined direction in which societies evolve ... full of surprises.'[27]

Further, he is emphatic that diffusing the Internet 'without altering the context of its appropriation will not reverse the current situation, in which fifty per cent of humankind barely survives with less than a dollar a day; hence the need for a broader development strategy'.[28] In a similar vein, Castells et al warn governments against over-optimism about the mobile phone as a tool for 'leapfrogging' in the context of development.[29] They argue that 'one of the most important identifiers of the potential developmental impact of mobile telephony could be its contribution to moving developing countries as close as possible to a universal telecommunications service, which has been shown to be the critical-mass level at which telecommunications began to exhibit significant impacts on economic growth in advanced countries'.[30] Yet, 'to be effective, mobile communication technology needs to exist in concert with developments in other areas of economic and social

---

27 Manuel Castells: The *Rise of the Network Society*, Oxford: Blackwell Publishers, 1997.
28 Manuel Castells: *The Internet Galaxy*, Oxford University Press, 2001.
29 Manuel Castells et al: *Mobile Communication and Society: A Global Perspective*, Cambridge, Mass.: The MIT Press, 2007. p. 216. Cf. Chapter 8: 'Wireless Communications and Global Development: New Issues, New Strategies'.
30 Ibid.

infrastructure (for example, better trunk roads and postal systems)'.[31]

ICT, the Internet and Mobile Telephony for Development

The Technology Mission and the Telecommunications Commission launched in India in the late 1980s were dedicated to development through technology. Urgency has been attached to the modernization of communication infrastructure. In 1981, a Committee on Telecommunication was set up by the Indian Government. The Committee recommended that digital technology for both switching and transmission be used in future telecommunication networks. In 1984 the Centre for Development of Telematics (C-DOT) was established to develop indigenous digital switching equipment. The phenomenal expansion of telephony, the liberalization of government policy in the area of electronics and computers, and the opening up of the Indian economy to foreign capital, has been the result of the new thrust towards technological solutions. In 1998, the BJP-led coalition at the Centre, established a National Task Force on Information Technology and Software; later, the States followed suit with their own Information Technology committees, to liberalise the sector, and thereby promote private enterprise and foreign investments. Both the Centre and the States went all out to woo telecom and IT multinationals such as AT & T, Microsoft, IBM, Oracle and others to set up shop in India. That trend persists, with the majority of Fortune 500 companies now having a significant presence in the metros and state capitals of the country.

Several public and private sector organizations have sought to tap the potential of information and communication technologies (ICTs) for national development. Rogers and Singhal[32] present a heartening account of the success of what they call 'cyber-marts' in rural India. More than 5,000 'e-chaupals' have been set up by

---

31 Ibid.
32 Everett Rogers and Arvind Singhal: *From Bullock-Carts to Cyber-Marts: India's Communication Revolution*, New Delhi: Sage. 2001.

ICT which have been instrumental in disseminating timely information to 3.5 million farmers in 35,000 villages about prices (in local, national and international markets) and also in curtailing the role of the middle-man in the distribution of products.

Three recent edited compilations describe some of these attempts from different parts of the country.[33] Sreekumar's study,[34] however, takes issue with these enthusiastic accounts of the role of ICTs in rural development. In his critical analysis of three typical projects to bridge the digital divide, two private and one state/district government, he sheds light on the grassroots problems involved. The three projects in using 'cyber-kiosks' to provide economic opportunities to women, dalits and other marginalized groups as well as to enhance their participation in the democratic process and in e-governance, were: (i) Village Knowledge Centres, established and promoted by the M.S. Swaminathan Research Institute (Pondicherry), (ii) TARA Kendras, by a group called Development Alternatives, with cyber-kiosks in Bhatinda (Panjab) and Bundelkand (Uttar Pradesh); and (iii) Gyandoot Soochanalyas (Information Centres), set up by the district administration in Dhar (Madhya Pradesh). All these three projects have won international acclaim and several awards for their development enterprises. However, Sreekumar found from his close observation and interviews at the three centres that discrimination in terms of caste and gender regarding access and use persisted and that higher castes and men grabbed most of the resources and the economic opportunities. Thus, the power-structures at the grassroots rural level continued to determine access to the cyber-kiosks in rural areas.

---

33 See S. Bhatnagar and R. Sechware (Eds.): *Information and Communication Technologies in Development: Cases from India*, New Delhi: Sage, 2000; I. Pringle and S. Subramanian (Eds.): *Projects and Experiences in ICT Innovation for Poverty Reduction*, New Delhi: UNESCO. 2004; G. Parayil (Ed.): *Political Economy and Information Capitalism in India: Digital Divide, Development Divide and Equity*, Basingstoke: Palgrave Macmillan. 2006.

34 T.T. Sreekumar: 'Cyber Kiosks and Dilemmas of Social Inclusion in Rural india', *Media, Culture and Society*, Vol. 29, No. 6, 2007. pp.869-889.

Need for National and International Regulations

Telecommunications, computing, video, interactive video, mobile telephony and other new technologies are not necessarily 'appropriate' to all non-aligned countries. In fact, the use of these capital technologies could only lead to further dependence on transnational corporations and the power-blocs that support them. Free enterprise and export-oriented economies in southeast and east Asia, for instance, have succeeded in 'catching up' with the industrialized powers, though at tremendous human and environmental cost. Development economists hold them up as 'models' to other non-aligned countries, but socio-economic and geopolitical conditions vary so much from country to country that all talk of 'models' of communication or development support communication seems irrelevant. In the ultimate analysis, the search for grand universal paradigms of development communication is futile; each country or community must find its own path in terms of its values and culture, its resources and ideals, but respecting human rights, basic-needs, social justice, and the world's fragile ecology and its ever-depleting energy and other natural resources. International regulations on arms trade, the dumping of poisonous wastes, the activities of transnational corporations who are often a law unto themselves, the use of space for commercial and military purposes, the trade imbalances between and among nations, outsourcing of manufacturing and services, global migration and human trafficking, are imperative for the survival of nations and of mankind itself.

Media, Development and Social Change: The Indian Context

From the early stages of the introduction of the mass media in India various attempts were made to exploit their potential for developmental purposes. The 'nationalist' press (termed the 'native' press by the dominant Anglo-Indian press) sought to bring about social and religious reforms in Indian society. Raja Ram Mohan Roy set the pace for such a development-oriented press.

As early as 1933, rural radio listening communities were formed in Bhiwandi (near Bombay) and rural programmes were broadcast regularly in Marathi, Gujarati and Kannada. Allahabad and Dehra Dun beamed their first rural broadcasts in 1936, and by 1939 there were over a hundred community radio sets for rural listening in the North West Frontier Province alone.

Broadcasting as Public Service

The Indian Broadcasting Company had been set up only on July 15, 1927 (earlier there were radio clubs at Bombay, Madras and Calcutta), with the assurance by its Chairman, Sir Ibrahim Rahimtoola, that the earnest desire of the Board of Directors would be to work broadcasting in a spirit of public service; no matter what the problems of distance, and of different languages and cultures might be. But in three years' time the company faced liquidation, and so the Government took it over most unwillingly on April 1, 1930, renaming it the Indian State Broadcasting Service (ISBS) and later AIR. More than public service, however, the Government was concerned with the prevention of grave menace to the peace and tranquility of India; and accordingly the Governor-General was given 'unrestricted powers' to deal with such a menace under the Indian Wireless Telegraphy Act (1935). The Act continues to be in operation to this day.

Mahatma Gandhi, The Communicator

The Government take-over transformed Indian broadcasting into a political instrument, highly centralized and controlled. Rural development programmes were broadcast in the local languages, and community sets installed in rural areas, but the main thrust of broadcasting was political. The World War and the need to counteract enemy propaganda and to hold in check the rising nationalist aspirations under the leadership of Mahatma Gandhi necessitated further expansion of broadcasting, and of stricter control. At Independence there were nine AIR stations and a few independent native stations, but providing no access to the leaders of the freedom struggle. Mahatma Gandhi spoke just once over radio, and that was three months prior to his assassination. Yet he was able to mobilize the masses (even in the remotest areas) who themselves had little access to the mass media.

Gandhiji did make good use of the nationalist press and his own journals – *Young India*, *Navijivan*, *Indian Opinion* and *Harijan* – but these were restricted in influence to the urban literates of the country. But he knew that the secret of reaching out to the hearts of the millions in the rural areas was the age-old oral tradition, and the padyatra (pilgrimage on foot). There was no substitute for direct, non-mediated communication through meetings and discussions, through song and prayer, and through the folk media.[35]

Role of TV in Promoting Literacy and Social Change

Two experiments in rural television were conducted in the mid-1970s with the prime objective of bringing about social change and development. Both were launched in 1975; the more ambitious programme was SITE – the Satellite Instructional Television Experiment; the second was the more modest Kheda Communication project.

SITE (Satellite Instructional Television Experiment)

In 1967 a UNESCO expert mission conducted, with the co-operation of the Indian Government, a study on the use of a satellite for national development. It recommended that since conditions were favourable such a start should be made. Accordingly, in 1969, the Department of Atomic Energy entered into an agreement with the National Aeronautic and Space Administration (NASA) of the United States for the loan of a

---

[35] For a more detailed discussion of Gandhi as a mass communicator, see Keval J. Kumar: 'Mahatma Gandhi as a Mass Communicator' in Gnana Robinson (Ed.): *Communicating the Gospel Today*, Madurai: Tamilnadu Theological Seminary, 1986, pp. 171-197. See also Keval J Kumar: 'Gandhi's Ideological Clothing' in *Media Development* (London), Vol. 31, No.4, 1984, pp. 19-21.

satellite free of cost for one full year starting from August 1975. It was the first experiment ever to relay educational television programmes direct (not from relay stations) from a satellite to receivers (with front-end converters) in 2400 villages (some without electricity) scattered over six selected regions in Orissa, Madhya Pradesh, Bihar, Rajasthan, Andhra Pradesh and Karnataka. Besides, conventional receivers in 2500 villages and towns got the programmes through earth transmitters which picked up the satellite signals through Receive-only Stations.

SITE *Programmes*

The four-hour telecast beamed every day from earth stations at Delhi and Ahmedabad concentrated on programmes on education, agriculture, health and family planning. These were planned and produced by AIR at Production Centres set up in Delhi, Hyderabad and Cuttack, with the help of committees which included Central and State Government representatives and experts from universities, teacher training colleges, and social workers. Besides, the ISRO (Indian Space Research Organisation) set up its own Audio-Visual Instruction Division to plan and produce programmes according to schedule.

However, as the satellite had only one video channel and two audio channels it could transmit just one picture at a time with synchronised sound in two different languages. So it was possible to beam programmes to only two linguistic regions at a time.

School Telecasts: Of the 4-hour daily telecast, an hour and a half was aimed at pre-primary and primary school children aged 5 to 12. During this duration, programmes were telecast for 22 minutes each day in Telegu, Kannada, Oriya and Hindi – and were watched on community receivers installed in schools, so that TV was regarded as part of the education system. (Adults watched social education programmes later on the same sets).

The goals of these school broadcasts were two-fold:
(1) To make school more interesting, and so reduce the drop-out rate.
(2) To improve children's basic concepts and skills, promote

aesthetic sensitivity, instill habits of healthy living, bringing awareness of modernisation of life and society.

However, the social evaluation report on SITE in two volumes by ISRO, published in September 1977, observes on page 5 of the Foreword:

'The observed fact that the school enrolment of the drop-out rate was not affected by the introduction of TV in schools proves that these factors depend primarily on social and economic parameters and not on the attractiveness or otherwise of the school curriculum; the children do not have an independent choice in the matter. So unless circumstances are changed so that parents do not have to make use of child labour for economic reasons, TV in schools is not going to affect enrolment or the drop-out rate'[36].

Agriculture: The Ministry of Agriculture set out the following objectives for SITE:
(1) Dissemination of information and demonstration of dry land farming etc., advice on poultry and animal husbandry, recommendation of practices for crops and their management, and so forth.
(2) Broadcast of information regarding organisations in districts which are responsible for supply of agriculture inputs such as seeds, fertilisers, implements, and for services in marketing, credit and so forth.
(3) Giving advice and demonstration on pests and their control.
(4) Broadcast of weather forecasts and market trends.
(5) Narration of success stories of farmers, preferably within the region, and other relevant news.

SITE had an ambitious goal in promoting new agricultural practices like dry-land farming and use of fertilisers, pest control, market trends and weather forecasts. It broadcast programmes on agriculture for 30 minutes each day for each linguistic group, plus 30-minute entertainment programmes in Hindi.

---

36 SITE: Social Evaluation Report, Vols. I and II, Ahmedabad: ISRO, September 1977, p. 5.

The ISRO Report states that there was 'some gain though it is not statistically significant'. The Foreword points out that 'some case histories of these innovations indicate that the farmers adopted only those practices which did not demand additional expense on infrastructure. They were also secretive about their intentions till the time that they achieved success'.

Health: Though one year is too short a period for adopting innovations in health practices, the Report says that SITE gave rise to 'modest gains'. On the practice of seeking medical aid for the delivery of babies, the change brought about was 'minimal', the reason being that 'adoption of this practice depended on the availability of health personnel in the village and also on the ability of the people to afford services'. On nutrition, the social scientists were unable to collect data.

Family Planning: Much was expected from SITE in the area of family planning. The Report, however, concludes that though the adaptation of vasectomy was between two to four per cent higher in the SITE villages, this figure was unreliable, because of over-reporting by males during the emergency. Hence the figure is 'statistically not significant' and the survey admits that a year's time was too brief to change an important social practice. Thus, 'in the practical aspects of nation building on which programmes were telecast during SITE, viz., agricultural and animal husbandry, health and nutrition, family planning and in telecasts for schools we find that the gains were rather meagre'.

SITE was a valuable learning experience for both hardware and software people of the media. The hardware people realized that keeping sets in working order for a year was no mean task, even though most of the SITE villages were not very far from cities and towns. During the first month, for instance, only 70% of the sets were in working order, and this figure declined to 33% in some cases in subsequent months. There was a dramatic decline too in the number of people viewing the programmes, particularly among women and children. This was despite the fact that over 50% had never been exposed to other mass media, and over a third of them were first generation consumers of the media. Part of the blame could be put on the low participation of the village level, block level and higher functionaries of development departments in the programmes. The village level workers and the health staff only occasionally viewed the telecasts, and none of them either participated or guided discussion after the telecasts as was expected of them.

SITE Evaluation Studies

It was not surprising therefore, that most viewers considered television a source of recreation rather than of education and development. As the SITE Evaluation Studies by the Planning Commission as well as by the Space Application Centre, Ahmedabad, testify, there were no appreciable gains in the adoption of agricultural practices, or of family planning methods. Children learnt hardly anything from the content of the science education programmes, and women precious little from the programmes on health and nutrition. The SAC study reveals that the programmes were incomprehensible to many viewers, and that inappropriate use of telecast language was the single most important factor that affected comprehension of the programmes especially in the Hindi states. The Planning Commission's evaluation, on the other hand, makes it out that 'TV played an important role for gain in knowledge in the field of animal husbandry (72%), agriculture (60%) and health (45%) on the ground that 89% could *recall* the main message of the programmes. It also discovered that 75% of the respondents felt the developmental programmes were on the whole useful, and by and large conformed to the local customs, beliefs and practices.'

Soon after the conclusion of SITE in 1986, six terrestrial transmitters started beaming programmes to 40% of the SITE villages. The SITE Continuity Centres – Jaipur, Raipur, Gulbarga, Hyderabad, Sambalpur and Muzaffarpur – were designed to provide developmental support in liaison with the respective State Governments. The scheme envisaged that, as beneficiaries, the State departments should shoulder a major responsibility in the distribution system. But the State Governments were not equipped to take over the responsibility of installation and maintenance of the sets; so the sets were transferred to Doordarshan. The Panchayat Raj departments of Andhra Pradesh and Orissa have taken up the scheme, now termed the SITE continuity project.

Kheda Communications Project

The Kheda Communications Project, on the other hand, has made remarkable progress under the charge of the Space Applications Centre, Ahmedabad. Launched at the same time as SITE, it has over the past 14 years chalked out a part all its own in the use of television for development. (Attempts to wind up the popular project were made in 1986-87, but the local villages resisted the move by 'hugging' on to the transmitter).

Kheda is a small district in central Gujarat surrounded by two predominantly tribal districts and the industrial districts of Ahmedabad and Baroda. 607 Community TV sets have been installed here in 443 villages and are owned by the community, but maintained by the State Government. The sets are kept in the buildings of the Milk Producers' Co-operative Society or the Panchayat Ghar.

The programmes (for over an hour every day) are produced by Doordarshan and the Space Application Centre. What is distinct about these programmes is that they result from constant interaction with the people. They have their origin in the lives of the local people and are in simple Charotari, a dialect of Gujarati. They are not telecast till pre-testing in the field is done, and feedback obtained. There have been numerous occasions when the programmes have been drastically revised or even dropped altogether.

Take for instance, one of the early serials *Chatur Mota* on the subjects of dowry and widow remarriage. It proved to be an extremely popular serial. The intention was to highlight the dominance and authoritarianism of the conservative Chatur as head of the family, and to show the growing challenge to him of younger and more enlightened people. However, "the presentation was so realistic, and so habituated were most people to this kind of dominance by traditional ideas that the programmes lulled rather than provoked; the form and presentation drowned the content, and instead of instigating a revolt against the Chatur Motas of the world, only succeeded in further establishing their right to dominate and dictate." It also came to be realized that the problems of dowry and widow remarriage were basically middle-class problems, not of the poor of Kheda.

The SAC software team scrapped the serial at once, and produced instead a different serial on untouchability, minimum wages, and the need to co-operate to fight exploitation. It proved to be equally popular, as it featured the poorer classes and portrayed their problems. Social researchers stationed in the villages also found that the majority of viewers were from the poorer classes, and women and children were more regular viewers than men. Indeed, in the early months of the Project, over 50% of the audience was made up of children. Accordingly, a series for children was launched.

In the weekend series for women, the most successful were *Dadi ma Ni Vaton* (Wise Women's Talks), *Hun Ne Mara Ae* (I and My Husband), and *Jagi Ni Jus To* (When I Wake Up and See). The goal of the series was to generate self-confidence, provide a sense of equality and create a realization of social worth and economic importance. The attempt was to wean the rural poor from superstition, wasteful expenditure, evils of child marriage, and to provide new skills. In the majority of the programmes, the format used was group discussion, and where real problems had to be highlighted, dramatization in a studio setting was the preferred format.

Kheda: Evaluation Studies

Four evaluation studies of Kheda carried out over a decade indicate that more women than men gained knowledge from TV viewing though their number was small, particularly in the areas of health, nutrition and family planning. This could be because

TV in a community viewing situation provides direct access to information which in most cases is not available to them. After all, women have very little exposure to other mass media and little urban contact too.

The Kheda team's commitment, however, was not merely to be disseminators of knowledge and awareness. They found it necessary and desirable to forge links with 'user' departments particularly the Agriculture, Health and Animal Husbandry departments at the State levels, as well as with the district and village level extension services of these departments and agencies like Amul and others.

So when they produced a series on cottage industries suitable for landless labourers and their families, and involving little or no cost, they worked in collaboration with a training institute, mailed instruction manuals to all interested, arranged for training, for bank loans, and finally even for marketing the products. In their efforts to take an integrated view of development, the Kheda scientists learnt a lot about the bureaucracy and the problems involved in getting people to adopt obviously beneficial trades.[37]

Kheda Credo

The focus of the Kheda Communications Project was, however, not so much on the diffusion of technical innovations, as on (1) exposing the oppression and bondages in the present social and economic system in such a way as to heighten understanding; (2) mobilising the community and the individual himself to break away from these bondages and (3) promoting self-reliance among the individuals and the community.

Development, therefore, to the Kheda team, implied a break from the status quo, from inertia; it implied movement, change. And change required a certain attitude, motivation, and of course, appropriate physical and social infrastructure. It implied, moreover, social change, education, awareness, and of course,

---

37 See also S.R. Joshi: 'Community Television: A Tool for Community Action?', *Gazette*, 38:43-57.

economic development – which could not take place in isolation.

The Kheda team believed that communication could play a major role in accelerating development, and their attempt in Kheda is to use TV – and also to supplement it by other means – for development in the broadest meaning of the term.[38]

The Power of TV?

How powerful then is television as an instrument of change and development? S.R. Joshi, a social researcher in the Kheda team, had this to say at a 1983 Seminar in Baroda: TV is described as a powerful medium. This statement has to be taken with a pinch of salt. The effectiveness of TV depends on a host of factors like infrastructure support, practicability of recommendations, follow-up on the programmes, etc. The choice of the medium, he added, should be determined not by the glamour but by assessing the needs of the situation, people, and experiences of the educator. TV therefore should not be selected only because it is there or because of fancy. The Kheda experiment has been wound up, but an attempt to replicate it is currently under way in the villages of Jhabua district in Madhya Pradesh.

Radio Rural Forums

Very similar in concept to Kheda, were the Radio Rural Forums or 'Charcha Mandals'. Started in Pune in 1959 in collaboration with UNESCO, they were based on the Canadian farm forum project. By 1965 the number of Mandals (of 15-20 members) rose from 900 to 12,000 in various parts of the country, but they reached only the more advanced sections of the rural population, leaving others untouched as the Report of the Study Team on Five Year Plan Publicity (1965) indicated. Membership of the Mandals, says the Report, shows a fairly high preference for the more advanced sections of the village community, with the small farmers, landless cultivators, artisans,

---

38 Cf. SEMINAR, No. 232 for a detailed account of the Kheda Communication Project.

craftsmen and women having only a token inactive membership. More than 70,000 community radio sets were installed all over the country in the early 1970s, but the Vidyalankar Committee found that 50% of them were not in working order on any given day. The 'transistor' revolution in the more prosperous villages gradually put paid to the experiments in community listening.

During the mid-1990s fresh attempts were made to revive community or local radio, both by All India Radio and social action groups. This new thrust towards local radio for development is best summed up in the 'Bangalore Declaration on Radio' proclaimed in September 1996 at a Consultation of more than sixty persons representing All Indian Radio, universities, NGOs involved in development activities, journalists and members of the broadcasting establishment.[39] The organisation that was the driving force of the Declaration was a voluntary social action group VOICES – a unit of Madhyam Communications of Bangalore. The group has now launched the country's first Community Radio in Chitradurga. The radio programmes are broadcast in the dialect of the local people and the focus of news and entertainment programmes is health and family welfare, women's empowerment, micro-credit, watershed management, rural development and non-formal education.[40]

Rural Broadcasts

Since 1966 All India Radio has been putting out Farm and Home Broadcasts to keep farmers informed on the use of fertilisers, pesticides, seeds and new implements. There are 59 such units in the country, but they are inadequately staffed, due to lack of personnel qualified in agriculture. The Rural-Urban programmes, and the Intensive Nutrition programmes introduced some years ago cater in the main to rural elites. All AIR stations beam programmes for rural audiences, but these add up to a measly 7% of the total transmission time. Moreover, hardly any of the minority castes and tribals figure in the programmes. A

---

39 Bangalore Declaration on Radio, September 1976, Bangalore: VOICES.
40 Report in *The Times of India*, Bangalore, July 9, 1998.

1979 survey showed, for instance, that Punjab Harijans felt that radio was unfair to them, and that there was no broadcast of exclusive interest to them. They complained that they were often excluded from the community radio centres.[41] (Cf. Section on 'Radio' for a discussion of the role of Community Radio in development).

Media and Family Planning

Family planning has been adopted as a national policy since the early 1950s. During the 1960s, Extension Officers in family planning were posted at select AIR centres. They worked in close co-ordination with government and voluntary agencies. Radio, films and the press carried the message of family planning to the masses in feverish campaigns that reached their climax during the Emergency. Diffusion studies carried out by the National Institute of Community Development, Hyderabad, demonstrate that 'extensive awareness' among people of the principles and practice of family planning was brought about, but that the gap between awareness and acceptance was very wide. A UNESCO study conducted in 1969 points to the same conclusion, and recommends the use of the oral–and traditional– media for propagating the message. Writes G.N.S. Raghavan, "If the practitioners of traditional media internalise the message of family planning and incorporate it into some of the locally popular tunes, for group singing, or singing accompanied by dance, there will be achieved an interaction and reinforcement of the message, in a pleasant and persuasive form, which can be rivalled by no other means of communications."

And, Dr. Bhaskara Rao of the Centre for Media Studies, New Delhi, found from his survey of the usage of the condom in rural and urban areas that only 6% of potential users of the condom in rural areas used the device, whereas 20% used it in urban areas. He also found that interpersonal communication between

---

41 For the story of the long struggle for community radio in India, see Vinod Pavarala and Kanchan K. Kumar: *Other Voices: The Struggle for Community Radio in India*, New Delhi: Sage, 2007.

health workers and others was more effective in propagating the family planning message rather than any mass media. Indeed, the most effective canvasser for family planning has been a person sterilized himself who passes on the message by word of mouth. The interpersonal relationship of the opinion leaders with the local people is also of great importance, as also the availability of the devices, the purchasing power of the local people, and the social and religious sanctions of the community.

Traditional Media and Development

What are the clear advantages of using traditional media, of even integrating them into the mass media? In India, such media have played a role in the communication and promotion of new ideas and the adjustment to a new or evolving social or political situation. We know that interpersonal exchanges cannot be dispensed with in the effort to change attitudes and behaviour. The folk media allow for such interactions, for they are essentially participatory, flexible, and familiar. Since they are not usually pure art forms, developmental messages can be introduced through them. A note of caution is necessary here: only those folk forms that lend themselves easily (without shocking the audience) to the propagation of developmental messages must be employed. Care must be taken also to see that the forms are not vulgarised (as they often are in the mass media). It is evident that the local people identify most with their own folk forms and the characters in them (the performers, if they are well known, are liked by the audience, and respected for their talent and skills). What is more, the forms – drama, song and dance, religious discourses – can be adapted to suit local conditions, local dialects and local concerns and interests.

Song and Drama Division

The Central Government has realized the potential of the folk media in bringing about development. It has set up a Song and Drama Division under the Ministry of Information and

Broadcasting. The Regional Offices of this body work in collaboration with the Field Units and are also helped out by Block Development Officers, Village Level Workers, extension officers and other local leaders. Over 43 departmental troupes and 500 private troupes sponsored by the Song & Drama Division put up nearly 20,000 performances each year. The programmes include folk plays, poetry recitation, (Kavi Sammelan, Mushaira, Kavi Darbar), folk recitals like Qawalis, Pall, Villupatu, Ra, Kakigan, puppet shows, religious discourses (Harikatha, Bhagwat Katha, Daskathia), folk songs and folk dances. However, the troupes comprise largely urban-bred artistes whose chaste literary language is unfamiliar to the dialect-speaking rural folk and fail to reach the poor in remote areas, who have little exposure to any of the media. This should surprise no one, for only in a few villages are all castes permitted to share the same source of water. The Dalits are the most deprived – of water and the media. There is a total of 82 million Dalits, and of these over 80% live in rural areas, often isolated from higher caste groups. More than 50% of them are landless labourers, and a mere 15% literate. 68% of Dalit children don't go to any school. No media take care of their needs for development.

The Press and Development

The press occasionally divulges the inhuman treatment meted out to them in Bhelchi and other places, their poverty and their patient suffering. Development journalism has brought them into the press, but on the whole its role is that of a silent spectator, sometimes pleading on their behalf, but by and large ineffectively. Out of 20,000 publications, the rural press accounts for less than 500 publications, and most of them are government handouts, or brought out by agricultural institutes, for the rural elite. Take Hamara Desh, for example, published in 12 languages, or Sewagram, a rural paper published for the last 30 years in Uttar Pradesh, where over 6,000 Krishi-Charcha

Mandals meet twice a week to discuss the week's news. The main aim of Sewagram is to promote better farming.

B.G. Verghese's experiment in Chhatera village was an isolated attempt to highlight development-related issues in a daily newspaper of New Delhi, the *Hindustan Times*.[42] In early 1969, the *Hindustan Times* started a regular fortnightly column entitled 'Our Village Chhatera'. The village is 25 miles northeast of Delhi, off the Grand Trunk Road, with a population of 1,500, comprising mainly landowning jats and Brahmin landless labourers. The inaugural column appeared on February 23, 1969, as the cover-story in the Sunday magazine section of the Hindustan Times. It carried a photograph of a group of children grazing sheep, with one Harijan girl carrying a lamb on her shoulder. This romantic scene contrasted with the actual squalor and poverty reported in the column. Soon, the village was turned into a news event when it was reported that one villager died owing to the collapse of an old swing bridge; officials, extension workers, social workers, and private companies visited the village. A new bridge was built, a bus service was started, the branch of a national bank opened, loans provided by the bank for the purchase of buffaloes, tractors, and fertilizers, and for the digging of wells and tubewells. The Department of Atomic Energy installed community television sets in 80 villages besides Chhatera to test a biweekly farmers' programme, Krishi Darshan. The community sets brought together different communities, and broke down the traditional segregation of men and women. The Usha Sewing Company donated sewing machines to the village mahila mandals, and other companies introduced pesticides and fertilizers to the village.

In 1972, this experiment in developmental journalism was extended to Chhatera's two neighbouring villages, Majra and Barota. Majra's Harijan weaving community was urged to form a cooperative and to improve their product designs; they were assisted in exporting their products. In Barota, the *Hindustan*

---

42 George Verghese: *Project Chhatera - An Experiment in Development Journalism*, Singapore: AMIC, 1976.

Times worked with the Yuvak Kalyan Sabha to assist the village in starting a nursery school, a first aid class, a reading room and a mobile library. Besides, a newspaper and magazine agency was established. The overseas edition of the *Hindustan Times Weekly* carried the column on the rural experiments in developmental journalism.

In 1993, the *Indian Express* devoted one page every week to developmental issues, but this practice was wound up abruptly after a year. *The Times of India* and *The Hindu* too have carried a series of heart-rending reports sent in by P. Sainath from some of the poorest villages of India.[43] Mukul Sharma of the *Navbharat Times*, New Delhi, has contributed a series of articles on the role of the environment on human lives.[44]

Voluntary Agencies/Social Action Groups

Those who have taken up development as a mission have been largely voluntary agencies, and co-operatives. The story of Dr. Kurien and his several 'Anands' in the country are too well-known to bear recapitulation[45]. His extensive use of a feature film like Shyam Benegal's *Manthan*, and short films to spread the spirit of 'cooperatives' is worthy of note. However, his primary medium has been meetings and discussions with the local people. This was also the main communication strategy in the Chipko (Hug the Tree) Movement of the 1970s which waged a grassroots struggle in the Tehri Gerhwal district of Uttaranchal for the preservation of forests and the fragile natural

---

43 See P. Sainath's *Everbody Loves a Good Drought* for an analysis of the potential of Development Journalism.
44 Mukul Sharma: *Landscapes and Lives: Environmental Dispatches on Rural India*, Oxford University Press, New Delhi, 2001. See also Darryl D'Monte: 'The Greening of India's Scribes' in Nalini Rajan (Ed.): *Practising Journalism: Values, Constraints, Implications*, Sage, New Delhi, 2005, pp. 89-102.
45 For a recent experiment in women's empowerment in the Cooperative Development (CD) program of the National Dairy Development Board (NDDB), see Michael J. Papa, Arvind Singhal, Dattaray V. Ghanekar and Wendy H. Papa: Organising for Social Change Through Cooperative Action: The (Dis)Empowering Dimensions of Women's Communication, *Communication Theory*, Vol. 10, No. 1, February 2000, pp. 90-123.

environment of the Himalayan region.[46]

Less well-known is the late Manibhai Desai, founder of the Bharatiya Agro-Industries Foundation (BAIF), at Uruli Kanchan, near Pune. Desai persuaded the local people to take to cattle development through artificial insemination, and promoted reforestation. Like Dr. Kurien, he had no need of the mass media in his efforts to bring about change and development; he won the hearts of the people by involving them in his projects. "I do believe", said Desai, "that the ultimate beneficiary is vitally important for the success of a programme, even though this may mean a longer implementation period. Also, the programmes designed must be related to the local resources available in the local areas".

Drs. Mabel and Rajnikant Arole have since 1970 built up the strength of the community and mobilised resources among 100,000 agricultural workers scattered around the village of Jamkhed in Ahmednagar District. Through a network of trained villagers, mostly illiterate, the people (mainly Harijans and tribals) are linked to the Health Centre, which has diagnostic facilities and arrangements for emergency cases and in-patient beds. Says Rajnikant Arole, "Health is only a tool for the development of the people. It has to become a people's programme. Through health care the village communities have to build up a leadership and have to come together to fight against their exploitation." The process has indeed already begun.

The Jamkhed idea, like the Anand idea, has snowballed. Health Centres at Behrampur (Orissa) and elsewhere have begun springing up. Then there are young groups such as SEWA (Self-Employment Women's Association), Ahmedabad, the Rural Community Development Association (RCDA), Gram Vikas, the KSSP (Kerala), the Sarvodaya Units, MOTT (Mobile Orientation Training Team) and a host of other Social Action Groups (SAGs) around the country involved in rural and urban

---

[46] For a recent account see, Hemant Shah: 'Communication and Marginal Sites: the Chipko Movement and the Dominant Paradigm of Development Communication', *Asian Journal of Communication* (Singapore), Vol. 18, No. 1, March 2008. pp. 32-46.

developmental programmes – all of which closely involve the local people themselves. Several NGOs and Social Action Groups now work in partnership with Central and State governments in the various areas of rural development.

FOR FURTHER READING

1. Graham Chapman, Keval Kumar, Caroline Fraser and Ivor Gaber: *Environmentalism and the Mass Media: The North-South Divide*, London/New York: Routledge, 1997.
2. O.P. Dhama and O.P. Bhatnagar: *Education and Communication for Development*, New Delhi: Oxford/IBH, 1980.
3. Walter Fernandes (Ed.): *People's Participation in Development*, New Delhi: Indian Social Institute, 1984.
4. Paul Hartmann, B.R. Patel and Anita Dighe (Eds): *Mass Media and Village Life in India*, New Delhi: Sage, 1989.
5. Neville Jayaweera (Ed.): *Rethinking Development Communication*, London: Sage, 1988.
6. Kirk Johnson: *Television and Social Change in Rural India*, New Delhi: Sage Publications, 2000.
7. P.C. Joshi: *Communications and Nation-Building – Perspectives and Policy*, New Delhi: Publications Division, 1985.
8. B. Kuppuswamy: *Communication and Social Development in India*, Bombay Sterling, 1976.
9. Srinivas R. Melkote: *Communication and Development in the Third World: Theory and Practice,* New Delhi: Sage, 1991. Second Edition, 2000.
10. Bela Mody: *Designing Messages for Development Communication: An Audience Participation-Based Approach*, New Delhi: Sage Publications, 1986.
11. Uma Narula and W.B. Pearce: *Communication as Development: A Perspective on India*, Southern Illinois University Press, 1986.
12. Peter Gonsalves: *Clothing for Liberation: A Communication Analysis of Gandhi's Swadeshi Revolution*, New Delhi: Sage, 2009.
13. G.N.S. Raghavan: *Development and Communication in India: Elitist Growth and Mass Deprivation*, New Delhi: Gyan, 2005.
14. Niranjan Rajadhyaksha: *The Rise of India: Its Transformation*

from Poverty to Prosperity, Singapore: John Wiley, 2007.
15. National Council of Applied Economic Research (NCAER): *India – Human Development Report*, 2000.
16. Vinod Pavarala and Kanchan K. Malik: *Other Voices: The Struggle for Community Radio in India*, New Delhi: Sage, 2007.
17. Ronald E. Ostman (Ed.): *Communication and Indian Agriculture*, New Delhi: Sage Publications, 1989.
18. *Rural Development and Communication Policies*, New Delhi: Indian Institute of Mass Communication, 1980.
19. S.C. Sharma: *Media, Communications and Development*, Jaipur: Rawat, 1987.
20. Rajendra Singh: *Social Movements: Old and New: A Post-Modern Critique,* New Delhi: Sage, 2000.
21. Arbind Sinha: *Mass Media and Rural Development*, New Delhi, Concept 1985.
22. Krishan Sondhi: *Problems of Communications in Developing Countries*, New Delhi: Vision 1980.
23. H.K. Ranganath: *Using Folk Entertainment to Promote National Development*, Paris: UNESCO, 1980.
24. I.P. Tiwari: *Communication Technology and Development*, New Delhi: Concept 1985.
25. Pradip N. Thomas (2002): 'Beyond the Pale: Poverty in an Era of Cutting Edge Communications: A View from India', *Media Development*, 2/2002, pp. 50-58.
26. Shirley White, K. Sadanand Nair and Joseph Ascroft (Eds.): *Participatory Communication: Working for Change and Development*, New Delhi: Sage, 1995.

WEB RESOURCES

1. www.onthecommons.org
2. www.comminit.com
3. www.infochangeindia.org
4. www.oneworld.org
5. www.thehoot.org

REVIEW QUESTIONS

1. What, according to your experience, is the role of mass

communication in the development of a country?
2. How can the mass media contribute to social change?
3. Name some of the 'models' of development communication? Which model do you think describes best the Indian experience?
4. What are the reasons for the revival of 'modernization' models every time a new communication technology (video, computing, the internet, mobile telephony) emerges?
5. How far can television be effective in serving the ends of national development? Discuss SITE and Kheda.
6. The media are full of reports about a 'shining', 'rising' and 'incredible' India. How do you as a media student respond to this 'marketing' of the nation?
7. Write critical notes on:
   (i) Mass media and Family Planning.
   (ii) Barriers to the use of mass media for national development.
   (iii) Role of Documentary TV Channels (e.g. Discovery, History, Animal Planet) in Promoting Education and Literacy.
   (iv) Cyber Kiosks and e-Choupals in rural India.
   (v) 'Outsourcing' in IT/ITES as a Development Strategy.

SUGGESTED PROJECTS

1. Write a report on the social changes brought about in your village/society/colony after the introduction of cable and satellite television. If there have been no changes, explain why.
2. Draw up a list of communication devices you use on a daily basis. What do you predominantly use them for: entertainment, information or education? What have you learned from this exercise about Development Communication?
2. Make a list of the practical information you come across in the various media. Which media provide the most practical information? Why do you think it is so?
3. Conduct a survey of the 'cyber-cafes' in your neighbourhood. How have they contributed to the development of the neighbourhood?
4. Organise a debate or a group discussion on the advantages and disadvantages of using television/telecommunications/information technologies/mobile telephony for rural development.

SECTION VI

INFORMATION TECHNOLOGY, TELECOMMUNICATIONS AND THE INTERNET

From Stand-Alone Technologies to 'Convergence'

The concluding decades of the 20th century were witness to revolutionary developments in the mass media, telecommunications and information technologies. The old mass media technologies were stand-alone isolated technologies: radio, television, cinema, the press and book publishing were looked upon and used as distinct and discrete technologies. Telecommunications (primarily the telegraph and the telephone) developed on their own, and were never considered as 'mass media'. This was also the case with developments in computers and other information technologies, which too were not taken to be 'mass media'. A computer was just a computer, a telephone just a telephone and a television set just a box in the corner for watching broadcast programmes. This separate and stand-alone identity was reinforced in government administration, where the mass media, telecommunications and computer technologies were under the charge of three different ministries: Information and Broadcasting, Department of Telecommunications (DoT), and the Ministry of Communications and Information Technology. This was further reinforced in the Indian university system where departments of communication and journalism remained isolated from developments in telecommunications and computer science, which of course had their own separate departments. Such was the case with cinema as well: film studies was in university departments (Jadavpur University for instance) while professional training in film production was the responsibility of film institutes like the Film and Television Institute of India (FTII), Pune, or the Film Institute in Guindy, Chennai.

Besides, ownership of such technologies too was generally

restricted to one or two of the media. In Europe and the developing countries, radio and television were government-owned and government-run, though the press and book publishing remained the monopoly of the private sector. Film-making was in both the public and private sectors: the feature film industry was in private hands, while newsreels, documentaries, short films and animation films were the responsibility of the public sector.

Few attempts were made to combine the different print and electronic media; cinema films were shown on the small screen with the help of a 'telecine chain' (an electronic device which can transfer film material to standard TV format), but one could not read the newspapers on computer screens or listen to the radio on television. The 'two-in-one' combined the radio and the audio-recording and playback technologies. The video-recorder was an add-on to television, and to begin with was used primarily for 'time-shifting'. This was the beginning of the asynchronous and interactive elements in the 'new media'. No longer were listeners and viewers tied down to the exposure of radio and TV programmes at the same time as others; this greater control of the electronic media was gradually leading to the 'de-massification' of the media. Audio and cassette recorders, the walkman, and later the personal computer, the internet, MP3, VCD and DVD players, iPods and mobile phones, were further examples of greater audience control over content, as well as over the time and place of media exposure. The earlier concept of a 'mass audience' was giving way gradually to a newer concept which took into account factors like flexibility, asynchronicity, and interactivity. (Fragmentation of the 'mass audience' came about first with multi-channel cable/satellite television and the proliferation of local FM radio stations, and later with dramatic developments in digital and mobile technologies).

Further, in telecommunications, the telephone and the telegraph remained isolated from the mass media, except as 'carriers' of information. Audio and video cassette recording and playback technologies extended radio and television, giving them the facility of 'delayed' or flexible exposure. Simultaneity of listening and viewing gave way to media access at one's own convenience.

Communication satellites, cable, fibre optics, wireless technologies, networked computers and the internet changed the very nature of mass media and telecommunications. When the computer appeared on the scene in the 1970s and 1980s, it was a stand-alone desktop technology; interactive, but discrete. Computers could not 'talk' to each other; compatibility was a critical stumbling block. Apple-Macs, Apricots, Tangerines, Amstrads and IBMs were often incompatible, and could not read or understand one another. Magnetic tapes and later floppy disks had to be used to transfer or copy data or graphics from one computer to another.

The 'modem' (an abbreviation of 'MOdulation' and 'DEModulation) revolutionised the entire stand-alone approach. It is an electronic device which changes analogue to digital signals and vice versa. It brought together the media, the computer and telecommunication technologies so that computers in different parts of the world could start 'talking' to each other using the international telephone networks and the supporting satellite and cable hardware. Electronic mail (or e-mail) and the Internet with its World Wide Web were developed in quick succession. Convergence of the various mass media, computers and telecommunication technologies now became possible, reaching its acme in the multi-media systems so common today for the transfer and exchange of information, data, graphics and sound. One could now watch films and video on the computer screen, or surf the Internet on the television screen. One could also use the computer for sending and receiving fax messages, electronic mail, for surfing the Internet, and even using the NetPhone for phoning and tele- and video-conferences. Digitisation was the key here, aided by miniaturisation, satellite communication, digital compression, optical fibre and comparatively low-costs and user-friendliness. The mobile telephone with its many value-additions (SMS, MMS, email, chat, internet search and surfing, camera, video camera, personal organizer, music player, ring tones, wallpapers, alarm clock, stopwatch, calculator, games, etc.) came to exemplify the very embodiment of the emerging 'age of convergence'. By mid-2008, there was a larger number of mobile phones (over two hundred million and increasing at the rate of 6.5 million every month) in the country than fixed-line phones or computer terminals, radio sets, television sets and internet connections. The mobile phone had been transformed into the mass communication (yet quintessentially inter-personal) medium par excellence.

History of Information Technology in India

India did not lag behind in the introduction of the new information technologies though, to begin with, the progress was tardy, and largely restricted to the elites in urban areas, and to teachers and researchers in national science and research institutes. The first computers to be installed in India were imported in the 1960s and 70s. Most were second- and third-generation IBM mainframes using transistors. The major importers were government departments and large corporations. By 1978, India had 800 mainframes maintained by the public sector company, Computer Maintenance Corporation (CMC), after the withdrawal of IBM. The decade also saw the emergence of a few Indian producers: ECIL, ICIM, Bull-PSI, and others. Developments in microcomputing, the convergence of computer controls with telecommunications, communication satellites, fibre optics and digital switches, as well as liberalisation in import policies, led to the rapid growth of the computer industry in India, though all the while it remained 'an assembly-oriented industry'.[1] The mushrooming of computer training institutes and university degree courses in computer science provided the much-needed personnel needed for creating

---

1 *Report on Computers and Peripherals*, Vols. I and II, New Delhi: Bureau of Industrial Costs and Prices, 1989, p.1.

the software and maintaining the hardware in the growing industry.

New Computer Policy - 1984

The Rajiv Gandhi government initiated the 'information revolution', opening up the Indian market to foreign investors; gradual privatisation and deregulation of first telecommunications and later other industries, reducing import and excise duties on electronic goods, computer hardware and software, and providing other incentives for the development of the information industries. The man Rajiv Gandhi chose to lead the revolution in telecommunications was Sam Pitroda, a non-resident Indian technocrat who had made good in the United States, and who passionately believed that India could leapfrog into the age of information, if only it embraced the new information technologies.

He was appointed Chairman of the Telecommunication Commission, and later telecommunication adviser to the Prime Minister. He established the Centre for the Development of Telematics (C-DOT) which would design and fabricate digital automatic switching equipment for rural (RAX) and urban (MAX) telephony. Pitroda lived up to his reputation of getting things done, but in the process he trod on many bureaucrats' toes. One section of the media wowed him; the other lambasted him for the hype he created about the potential of telecommunications for the nation's development. Pitroda shared Rajiv Gandhi's vision of a modern India competing with advanced industrialised nations in the new age of information, the post-industrial age. However, while urban India was swamped by multinational brands of consumer goods, the latest hardware and software, value-added services like cellular telephony, paging, and a plethora of cable and satellite channels, the rural areas and the urban poor were untouched by such happenings. Liberalisation and re-structuring of the economy in the early 1990s both under the Congress and the United Front regimes, so as to promote foreign investment and private business, re-enforced this urban approach. Leftist economists dubbed this approach an instance of 'selling out to the multinationals'. Pitroda returned to India to head the education mission when the Congress Party-led coalition came to power in 2004.

The Private Phone STD/ISD Booth Phenomenon

Perhaps the most striking development in Indian telecommunications in the three decades preceding the new millennium was the phenomenal growth of what are popularly known as 'STD booths' in cities and small towns across the land (though by the late 1990s this turned out to be a pale shadow of the mind-boggling explosion of the cellular mobile phone). This was the beginning of the privatisation of the basic phone service. Licences were freely given by the Department of Telecommunications to small-time shopkeepers and operators: unemployed graduates, the handicapped, and women. All that was required was a hole in the wall for a telephone connection. In mid-1998, Maharashtra alone had over 20,000 STD/PCOs, around 15,000 local PCOs, and 30,000 village public telephones. The unexpected proliferation of mobile cellular telephony dealt a severe blow to the ever greater expansion of the public telephone system (of which the STD booth revolution was an integral part). By 2005, however, the phenomenal uptake of mobile telephones led to the gradual decline of visitors to STD booths in the metros and large cities. The liberalization of the Government's telecommuni-cations policy was voted a resounding success.

National Telecommunications Policy (1994)

In May 1994, the Government of India announced a new telecommunication policy which threw open the basic telephone service to the private sector. Value-added services (such as electronic mail, paging, cellular telephony, video conferencing, audio and video text services, data services and VSATs) had already been liberalised two years earlier, in July 1992. Foreign companies were permitted up to 49% equity, with two operators (one private company competing with the public sector unit) for each circle in the basic telephone service, and two private operators competing with each other in the value-added services. The primary objective of the New Telecommunication Policy was to provide telephone connections to all villages in India, and to offer telephones on demand by May 1997. While the value-added sector has had many bidders (including several multinational companies) and has taken off in the large cities, the objectives for the basic telephone service were far from fulfillment by mid-June 1998, as few private investors were willing to risk their venture capital in the poorer telecom circles (Bihar, Orissa and the North-East, for example). Even those companies that won bids for licences were reluctant to launch the basic service; half of the 20 circles in the country did not have any bidders among the private operators. The widespread complaint was that the license fees were exorbitant (Rs.210 million to be paid over three years), and the tariffs unreasonable. The real fear was that the telecommunication market was not large enough to make for profitable ventures.

In August 1996, India had a tele-density (number of telephones per 100 persons) of 1.27 in comparison with 1.7 in Indonesia, 2.0 in the Philippines, and 3.4 in China.[2] The growth rate had been impressive: from 5.07 million lines in 1991 to 13.48 million lines in 1997. But rural India continues to be ill-served: barely fifty per cent of the 600,000 villages have the basic telephone service. By mid-2007, the tele-density had shot up to 14, with over one hundred and fifty million telephone connections, more than a hundred million of them wireless mobile phones, serviced by 22 companies running 42 networks in 28 'circles' around the country.

VSAT systems comprise small earth stations that communicate with one another via a central earth station (the 'hub'). A signal from one VSAT is uplinked to a satellite, downlinked to

---

2 Business India Survey, March 24, 1997, pp.123-143.

the hub and then relayed to another VSAT via the satellite. These systems are used by different branches of a bank or any other customers, or by agents or distributors. The main VSAT operators in India are Hughes-Escorts Communications Ltd. (HECL), a leading user of this technology is the National Stock Exchange. The VSNL (Videsh Sanchar Nigam Limited) is a partner with other national and international companies for plastic and automatic international roaming voice telecommunications such as Iridium and ICO-Global.

Regulating Telecommunications

Structure of the Telecom Industry

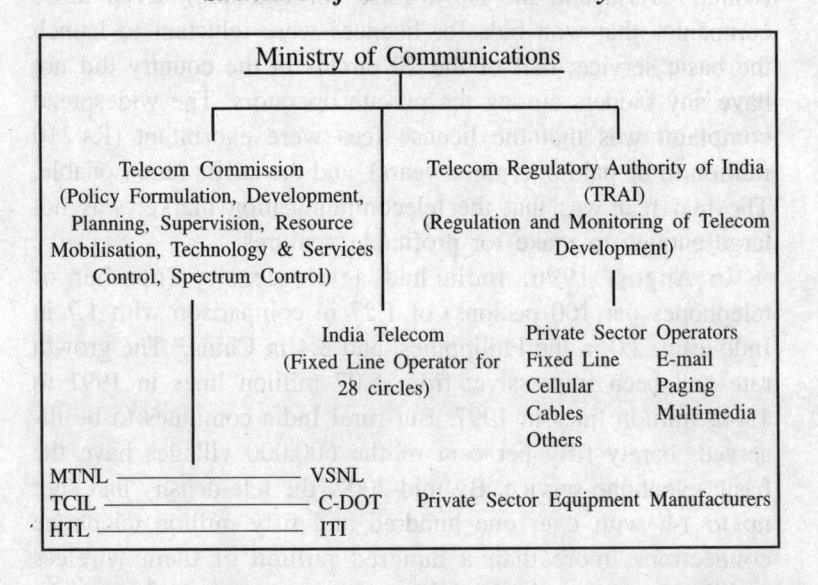

```
                    Ministry of Communications
                              |
         ┌────────────────────┴────────────────────┐
   Telecom Commission                  Telecom Regulatory Authority of India
(Policy Formulation, Development,                  (TRAI)
 Planning, Supervision, Resource      (Regulation and Monitoring of Telecom
 Mobilisation, Technology & Services              Development)
   Control, Spectrum Control)
                              |
              India Telecom            Private Sector Operators
          (Fixed Line Operator for     Fixed Line    E-mail
                28 circles)            Cellular      Paging
                                       Cables        Multimedia
                                       Others
   MTNL ─────────────── VSNL
   TCIL ─────────────── C-DOT     Private Sector Equipment Manufacturers
   HTL  ─────────────── ITI
```

The Telecom Regulatory Authority of India (TRAI) was constituted in February 1997, as an overall regulatory body to monitor the nation's telecom services and to sort out disputes among operators and between the Department of Telecommunications (DoT) and private operators. The Indian Paging Services Association (IPSA) and the Cellular Phone Operators Association of India (COAI) represent the interests of the paging and cellular phone companies. The rapid proliferation of cellular telephony in the new millennium rang the death knell of the pager in India. The consumers have interests too but they have not been so well-served. For instance, the quality of service offered by the operators cries out for improvement, and despite the DNC (Do Not Call) register, the telemarketers continue to harass the unwary mobile user.

Information Technologies: Developments in India

Prior to liberalisation of the computer industries, the Indian government's policy was on 'self-reliance through import substitution'. The setting up of the Electronics Corporation of India (ECIL) and the Computer Maintenance Corporation (CMC) under the public sector was part of this policy, as much as the side-lining of the multinational IBM. Liberalisation by the Rajiv Gandhi government in the mid-1980s and by the Narsimha Rao government in the early 1990s gave a fillip to joint ventures with multinational companies. Import duties for hardware and software were slashed and incentives offered for private investment in the industry. Over forty multinational companies such as Texas Instruments, Motorola, Honeywell, IBM, Digital, Hewlett-Packard and Microsoft have set up operations in Bangalore, Hyderabad, Gandhinagar, Pune, and other cities, primarily for exporting software. Indian software exports are tied to the Unites States market which accounts for up to 58% of export destinations, with Europe at 20%.[3] Computer software is thus one of the largest foreign exchange earners for India. India's share of the global software business is 16.7% for customised software, but only .05% of the product and package market.

A second area of impressive growth has been in the education and training sector. Indian software education is also an export item: the National Institute of Information Technology

---

3   John Sinclair and Linda Hamphill: *The Social Determinants of Demand for Convergent Communication Services in the Asian Region: The Case of India*, Melbourne: Victoria University of Technology, 1997, p.11.

(NIIT), its leading institution, is an exporter of educational software and provides courses through offices in Southeast Asian capitals[4]. National institutes offering advanced training in computers number 1,675, training over 55,000 professionals every year. Around a hundred doctorates in computer science and over 2,000 M.Techs, and 14,060 B.Techs besides 2,250 M.Scs and 2600 B.Scs, and 16,200 diploma graduates are trained every year.[5]

The Indian information technology industry is growing at the annual rate of more than 35%, with software and services alone worth over US$ 50 billion, according to NASSCOM estimates. 'Bodyshopping', a common practice in the United States and other countries, involves employing Indian software professionals overseas at low wages. More common is the practice now of contracting companies in India to service foreign clients; most of this exported software is in the form of customized work for corporate clients in the United States.[6] Business process outsourcing (BPO) and information technology enabled services (ITES) have witnessed a boom during the last two decades. Technology Parks are being established in collaboration with Singapore, South Korea and other nations in Bangalore, Hyderabad, Bhubaneshwar, Trivandrum, Gurgaon, Pune and other cities to promote the software and applications industry. Indian IT companies have a 38% share in the global IT market; in Karnataka alone over a million are employed in IT and allied industries. The city of Bangalore has more than 1,600 IT companies of which 622 are MNCs, and more than 300,000 IT workers. It was expected that by 2020 India would have over 47 million skilled IT professionals; yet, according to N.R. Narayanmurthy, only 25% of the students in India have the necessary skills. If outsourcing were to move to China, South

---

4 John Sinclair and Linda Hamphill: op cit., p.12.
5 S. Chandrasekhar: 'Manning the Internet Forece', in *Economic Times*, June 17, 1996, p.12.
6 John Sinclair and Linda Hamphill: op cit., p.12.

Korea and Europe over 74 million jobs in India would be affected.[7]

Table 45 : Top Ten Indian Exporters of Computer Software

1. Tata Consultancy Services
2. Wipro Corporation
3. HCL Technologies
4. Tata Unisys
5. Infosys Technologies
6. Satyam Computer Services
7. NIIT Ltd.
8. DSQ Software
9. Visualsoft Technologies
10. Hughes Software

The Information Revolution

How did the Information Revolution differ from the Industrial Revolution of the 19th century? The Industrial Revolution ushered in the factory system at the hub of which was the division of labour and a capitalist mode of production. Mass production of goods and their mass distribution in the markets of the world were the driving forces. Both depended on massive labour recruitment. This was the origin of the need for the mass media which would promote the mass-produced goods to potential customers in cities and villages. The manufacturing industries were labour-intensive, while the new service industries were capital intensive. What gave a fillip to these developments were new modes of energy like steam, gas and electricity, and faster modes of transport like the railways, the automobile and the aircraft.

The concept of 'information society' gained widespread currency in the 1970s and 1980s to explain the social, economic and technological changes that were taking place during those decades in advanced industrialised societies. The social changes

---

[7] N R Narayanmurthy, in the D V Narasimha lecture on 'Indian Software Industry: Opportunities and Challenges', Bangalore, 3 January 2005.

included the entry of entertainment media and computers in the home, and the growth of telecommuting, that is working from home. The divisions between home and the factory or office were breaking down. The main work telecommuters did was gathering, processing and storing information with the help of personal computers.

Where the economy was concerned, more workers were involved with information-related industries (travel, tourism, hospitality, banking, insurance) than the production of commodities for a mass consumer market. This was because such production had been moved to developing countries where low-paid labour was easily available. Later, this was known by the euphemism, 'outsourcing'. Industrialised economies were therefore gradually turning into 'information economies'; they were non- polluting, were capital-intensive, and were oriented to 'service' rather than 'production'.

But it was the technological changes that made the new kind of social changes and economic changes possible. The innovations in information and communication technologies brought about by the integration of telecommunications, mass media and computing, promised greater flexibility, greater efficiency and lower costs.

In sum, these societies were on the way to becoming information-centred societies. Their primary resource was information of all kinds rather than production of consumer goods. Some sociologists believed that an 'information revolution' was taking place, a complete break from the 'industrial revolution' of the eighteenth and nineteenth centuries.

The Japanese writer, Yoneji Masuda, pioneered the use of the term 'information society' to describe a society which would eventually 'move to the point at which the production of information values became the formative force for the development of society'.[8] Daniel Bell, the American sociologist,

---

8 Quoted in William J. Martin: *The Global Information Society*, London: Aslib/Gower, 1995, p.2.

and author of 'The Coming of Post-Industrial Society', preferred the term 'post-industrial society' to describe the same socio-economic process, and Alvin Toffler and John Naisbett, authors of 'Future Shock' and 'Megatrends' respectively, popularised the concept of 'information society'. However, the information that has been transformed into a resource and a commodity is technology-mediated, most of it in digital form. Since different countries are at different stages of the adoption of information technologies, we have several 'information societies' rather than only one type. Indeed, every society is in a sense an information society, for information and communication is what holds it together, despite its many diversities and rivalries. An alternative view suggests that the information society is a continuation of the industrial society rather than a revolutionary break from it, as consumer-oriented free-market capitalism is still at its heart. Others like William Martin[9] would rather label it a 'broadband society' since it is telecommunications (rather than computers and the media) which has become the true catalyst for change. Vincent Mosco of Canada has opted for the more vivid term, the 'pay-per society'.[10] But by the closing years of the last century, Manuel Castell's prolific and influential writings on the 'network society' (more recently 'the mobile network society'), especially his trilogy on the Information Age had established the term 'network society' as the most widely accepted label for the technology-oriented contemporary world.[11] For Castells 'the network society is a social structure based on networks operated by information and communication technologies based in microelectronics and digital computer networks that generate, process, and distribute information on

---

9 op.cit.
10 Vincent Mosco: *The Pay Per Society: Computers and Communication in the Information Age*, New Jersey: Ablex, 1989.
11 Manuel Castells: *The Information Age: Economy, Society and Culture*, Volume 1: *The Rise of the Network Society*, Oxford: Blackwell Publishers. Volume 2: *The Power of Identity*, Volume 3: *End of Millenium*, Oxford: Blackwell Publishers, 1996; *The Internet Galaxy* (1995); *Mobile Communication and Society: A Global Perspective*, Cambridge, Mass: The MIT Press, 2007.

the basis of the knowledge accumulated in the nodes of the networks... it is a formal structure... a system of interconnected nodes.'[12] This ICT-based and ICT-centred society, it is evident, excludes the majority of the world's population.

The 'Information Superhighway'

This image or metaphor for a wired universe interlinked by networks of computers was popularised by Al Gore, the Vice-President of the United States, in the early 1990s. The information highway is an electronic network that connects libraries, corporations, government departments and individuals.

The information superhighway can be defined as 'an information and communication technology network which delivers all kinds of electronic services – audio, video, text, and data – to households and business'.[13] It is usually assumed that the network will allow for two-way communication which can deliver 'narrow-band' services like telephone calls as well as 'broad-band' capabilities such as video-on-demand, teleshopping, games, and other 'interactive TV' multi-media applications. Services on the superhighway can be one-to-one (telephones, electronic mail, fax, etc.); one-to-many (broadcasting, interactive TV, videoconferencing, etc.); or many-to-many (bulletin-boards and forums on the Internet).[14]

The examplar of the 'Information Superhighway' is the Internet which had its roots in the need during the mid-1960s for linking military computer researchers in the United States.[15] The United States Defense Department established a computer

---

12 Manuel Castells: 'The Network Society: From Knowledge to Policy' in Manuel Castells and Gustavo Cardoso (Eds.): *The Network Society: From Knowledge to Policy,* Washington DC: Centre for Transatlantic Relations, 2006. p.7.
13 William H. Dutton et al: 'The Politics of Information and Communication Policy: The Information Superhighway' in William H. Dutton (Ed.): *Information and Communication Technologies: Visions and Realities,* Oxford: Oxford University Press, 1996, p.391.
14 ibid.
15 Peter Golding: 'Worldwide Wedge: Division and Contradiction in the Global Information Infrastructure' in *Monthly Review,* Vol. 48, July-August 1996, pp.70-85.

network that permitted military contractors and universities involved in military research to exchange information. This was the origin of Arpanet, the network of the Pentagon's Advanced Research Project Agency (ARPA).[16] In 1975, Arpanet which had grown from four to about one hundred nodes was handed over to the Defense Communication Agency. Meanwhile, in the 1980s, the National Science Foundation developed its own academic networks (NSFNET), providing researchers access to super-computers at Cornell, Illinois, Pittsburg and San Diego. It comprised high capacity telephone lines, microwave relay systems, lasers, fiber optics and satellites. The NSF network became a backbone connecting several other networks of educational agencies, government agencies and research organisations. The cost of the backbone was borne by NSF, with members funding the cost of their local networks including cost of outsiders who entered the system.

By 1990, NSFNET had replaced Arpanet. This later developed into the INTERNET, a network of networks. Up to this time, access to the networks was 'universal' and free in academic and research institutions. In 1992, NERN or the National Education and Research Network, or 'enhanced Internet' permitted the exchange of more and lengthier material, even full-motion video. Doctors could send x-rays and cat-scans to faraway colleagues in other countries, students could access the Library of Congress, and have whole books transmitted to them, and farmers and weather pundits could receive maps from satellite phones. NSFNET was shut down in 1995, opening the way for the private operation of the Internet.[17]

Commercialisation of the networks began when the Internet was opened up to private service providers like Prodigy, Delphi, Genie, America Online (AOL), and Compuserve. The World Wide Web was developed at the European Centre for Particle Research in 1989, but took off only in 1993 when software

---

16 For a different perspective on the origins and history of the Internet, see Manuel. Castells: *The Internet Galaxy*, pp.9-35.
17 Manuel Castells: *The Internet Galaxy*, Oxford University Press, 2001. p.12.

developed at the University of Illinois, and subsequently elsewhere, created 'browsers' and graphical interfaces making the search and interrogation of 'pages' on the WWW possible. Hundreds of 'sites' were placed on the Web, but the number of commercial (.com) sites soon outnumbered the education (.edu), government (.gov) and organisation (.org) domain names.[18] Newspapers, magazines, radio, television and cable channels from around the world set up their own websites, offering news services, headline news, accompanied with colourful graphics. The services were offered free to begin with, but gradually most of the services were restricted to 'subscribers' or to 'registered users'.

The Internet in India

The Department of Science and Technology (India) established the ERNET in India, serving to link the institutes of science and technology across the nation. Later, the universities and other teaching and research institutes too were linked together. Other networks the government of India established included NICNET (for administration and planning), Indonet (for access to specialized information through satellite communication), and Railnet (for the Indian Railways' ticketing, scheduling and planning activities).[19]

By mid-1998, most major Indian newspapers, magazines, publishing houses, political parties, commercial firms, banks, etc. had their own sites; so did most State governments, All India Radio, Doordarshan, police departments, municipalities and non-government organisations.

However, one could not wade through the cornucopia of information on offer without encountering 'banner' advertisements and pop-ups on almost every home page. The information offered was replete with propaganda and hype. Surfing the Net often turned into an irritating experience,

---

18 ibid.
19 Sandhya Rao and N. Chinna Natesan: 'Internet: Threat or Opportunity for India?', *Media Asia*, Vol. 23, No. 2, pp. 96-99.

especially with the frequent breaks in power supply and the Internet Service Providers (ISPs) tendency to let the sites 'hang' intermittently. The accessing of e-mail too turned into a nightmare: one could not read one's mail without having to leap over 'junk mail' (also termed 'spam' or unsolicited mail).

The Symantec Internet Security Threat Report estimates that as much as 76% of e-mails originating from India are spam, compared to the world average of 56%.[20] The Report adds there is no dearth of viruses, phishing scams and malicious software codes (termed 'bots') in India, and that at least 40 command and control servers control bot-infected computers. On any given day, says the Report, there are around 277 active bot-infected computers in the Indian internet scenario.[21]

Entertainment rather than information is the primary motivation for accessing the Net; games, pornography and sex chat lines and cross-national prostitution have proved extremely popular in the United States and elsewhere. The lack of control over the Net has led to the development of 'blocking' software (such as NetNanny and SurfWatch) to protect children and young people from obscenity and pornography on the Net.

Advertising and commercial interests have taken over the Internet, and e-commerce is on the upswing. Perhaps one of the greatest success-stories has been the 'virtual' bookstore, Amazon.com. It has no physical bookstore any where in the world, but has more titles for sale than any other, with offers of up to 40% discount on its titles. Orders are placed online and payment too can be made online using one's credit card (at one's own risk of course). The marketing of other products too, especially computer software programmes, browsers, computer games, music albums and films has caught on. Once security of payment is assured through introduction of encryption technology, the Web is bound to be transformed into the largest cross-national shopping mall in the world. Indeed, if one were

---

20 '76% e-mails from India are Spam', Report in *Hindustan Times*, Mumbai, 2 June 2007, p. 1.
21 Ibid.

to go by the amazing commercial success of amazon.com, google.com, ebay.com, the numerous travel, matrimonial, games and jobs portals on the Worldwide Web, the Internet has already been turned into the latest medium for advertising, marketing and public relations. Free e-mail facilities offered by Hotmail, Yahoo, Google, Rediffmail, Indiatimes, and a host of others around the world are not free at all: ads clutter their home pages, unsolicited direct mail and regular pop-ups have to be tolerated. This is true also of the search engines that these portals and others like Wikipedia provide; customised online advertising distracts you on every single page. Moreover, many of the search engines like Google flout privacy laws when they retain the histories of search of each individual for two years, often using them to build databases which are sold to marketers, and most worryingly for targeting web searchers in terms of their interests revealed in such histories. The EU has challenged these practices of Google. Google Earth has also got into trouble over its invasion of privacy when it reveals the interiors of homes and roadside shops. The Government of India has protested to Google against the unwitting disclosure of its defence establishments around the country.

The Internet, Civil Society and Social Movements

However, the numerous positive benefits of the Internet must not be overlooked. It has helped to network non-Government organisations in India and across the world, social action groups fighting for peace, human rights, gender equality, the environment, AIDS awareness and numerous other global concerns in different continents. News blogs such as www.indymedia.org, www.onthecommons.com, www.indiauncut.com, have created 'alternative' forms of journalism that provide different perspectives on the world news. Bloggers in Iraq, Iran,[22] China and Myanmar have been offering 'inside' accounts

---

22 Cf. Nasrin Alavi: *We are Iran: The Persian Blogs*, Brooklyn N.Y.: Softskull Press, 2005.

of happenings on the ground in these countries.

The Internet has indeed become a force to reckon with: for lobbying with authorities on various issues at local, national and international levels. Civil society and the public sphere have gained immensely from the national and global reach of the internet[23]. For instance, action groups were instrumental in bringing the world's attention to the attempted genocide in Bosnia-Herzogovina, the struggle of peasant movements in South America, the anti-WTO protests in 1999 in Seattle and other cities, and more recently (in late 2007 and March 2008) to the worldwide protests against the US invasion of Iraq and the Myanmarese and Chinese governments crackdown on Buddhist and Tibetan monks demonstrating for democracy and human rights.[24] The internet, especially blogs, played a crucial role in 'disaster management' during the tsunami in Asia, disseminating information around the world about the tragedy and putting out appeals for donations and assistance. It has been a tremendous boon for researchers who wish to conduct surveys and interviews in different parts of the world.

Family and Social Networks

Communities like the overseas Chinese, non-resident Indians, and groups with common interests have come together to form 'electronic communities'. Electronic mail assists families, relations and friends scattered across the country and the globe to keep in touch ('sociability'), and to organize their daily lives, a phenomenon Castells terms 'microcoordination'... 'Communication technologies materially allow the post-patriarchal family to survive as a network of bonded individuals, in need of both autonomy and support at the same time. As people rebuild and extend their lives along their networks, they bring with them into these networks, and into their networking devices, their

---

23 Report in Hindustan Times, Mumbai, 2 June 2007. p. 1.
24 For a more detailed analysis of the role of the Internet in Social Movements, see Castells: The Internet Galaxy, Chapter 5. See also www.comminit.com/en/drum_beat_222.html.

values, perceptions, and fears.'[25] Thus it appears that the internet is just 'an extension of life as it is, in all its dimensions, and with all its modalities.'[26]

Social network sites like www.orkut.com, www.myspace.com, www.youtube.com, www.secondlife.com, www.hi5.com, www.bigadda.com, www.yaari.com, www.ishare.com, (some of which are also blogs and video-sharing sites) and numerous other similar sites (including the 'social bookmarking' sites like www.reddit.com, www.digg.com, www.del.ic.ious.com and www.facebook.com) on the Web help create new virtual communities where discussion and exchange of ideas through words, images and sounds take place across national and regional borders. Some of them are closely monitored for 'hate speech', obscenity, issues of privacy and human rights, the protection of intellectual property rights and the misuse in general of public space; most, unfortunately, are not. Viacom (owner of MTV, Paramount and Nickleodeon), for instance, initiated a one billion dollar lawsuit against Google and its YouTube subsidiary, for infringement of copyright; Universal Music has similarly charged MySpace. Yet another 'cyber-crime' is 'cybersquatting' wherein a trademarked domain name is registered – or one very similar to it – for the purpose of profiting from selling it or blackmailing the owner of the domain name. The exploitation of the worldwide web for marketing ideas, products and companies is rampant. The foremost example in the Indian context is www.sunsilkgangofgirls.com. The 'Dove' brand and others too are following suit.

Yet, despite the global reputation of India being far ahead of most developing nations in information technology, the uptake of digital media like the Internet has been unimpressive compared with the growth of the traditional mass media. At the close of 2007, no more than 42 million Indians had regular

---

25 Manuel Castells et al: *Mobile Communication and Society*, p. 126.
26 Manuel Castells: *The Internet Galaxy*, p.118.

access to the Internet, for instance. Access to the Internet is fairly widespread in the cities, though mainly via cyber-cafes, schools, colleges and offices; the cost of access at home is still unaffordable for most Indians. Home access to the net is limited to a small minority of the upper middle class in Tier 1 and Tier 2 cities. The situation in rural areas is far worse. Except for around five thousand e-choupals (Internet kiosks/dhabas) and a few other community computer centres, rural India is poorly served. The largest segment of Internet users is in the 18-35 age group; this comprises half of all users. But only 66% of these are 'active users', that is those who use the net at least once a month. Most are 'ever' users', those who access the net once in a way.[27]

Globalisation

Like the 'information superhighway', 'globalisation' is yet another hype term in Information Technology. Globalisation, it is assumed, flows automatically from the wide pervasiveness of information technologies, the internet and the information superhighway, across the length and breadth of the globe. It assumes also that proliferation of the various information and communication technologies is worldwide, that users of information technologies make up the majority of the world's population with no obstacles to access whatsoever, and that it is public service widely and freely available to one and all. While over two billion people across the world access the Internet it is often forgotten that these belong to elite educated groups in the richer countries. By no means is access universal; nor is it affordable to the vast majority of the world's population. There is indeed a yawning gap between the information-rich and the information-poor, and this gap is growing, since the costs of access are nowhere getting any easier or cheaper. The 'digital divide' is a grim reality both in the developed and the

---

27 *The Marketing White Book:* 2007. pp.251-253.

developing economies of the world. According to a recent survey (2007) by the Internet and Online Association, India had around 25 million Internet users; barely 30% of them were online for more than 20 hours a week.

According to one estimate, in 1996, 64% of all hosts in the world were in the United States; 17% were in Western Europe; four percent in Asia; Eastern Europe, Africa and Central and South America accounted for around one percent each.[28] Another estimate suggests that out of the 13 million hosts in the world in the same year, around eight million were in the United States; the UK and Germany had around 600,000 each; South Africa had just over 80,000 and India had around 2,000. At the end of 1996, a search suggested that barely three out of the over 1,400 Internet-based electronic newspapers were from the continent of Africa[29]. What is more, most Internet sites and databases are located in the United States; so Internet Service Providers (ISPs) such as VSNL in India and ISPs in other countries have to lease links to American backbones. United States 'carriers' charge $20,000 for 2mbps circuit monthly rental, as against only $3,000 to ISPs in the United States itself.[30] Thus, a 'google' or 'yahoo' or msn.com search yields information and data that is largely based on sources in the United States; this holds true also for searches on news.google.com, youtube.com, gettyimages.com and the many other search engines for videos, images, music, television shows, etc. So, while the circulation of information is indeed global, the sources of information and the way such sources are prioritized are certainly not. This is best illustrated when you search for news about India on news.google.com. US news agencies, newspapers, radio news (Voice of America) and television news (CNN, ABC, CBS, NBC and Fox) get top ranking.

---

28 Quoted in Colin Sparks: 'Newspapers, the Internet and Democracy', in *Javnost/The Public*, Vol. III (1996), 3, p. 53.
29 ibid.
30 Report in Business Standard, February 26, 1998.

While computing, the internet and wireless mobile telephony form the backbone of globalisation, the term encompasses more than technology: family, democracy, the economy and culture too play a vital role in shaping the uses and values of technology.

E-Commerce, E-Banking and E-Governance

Electronic Commerce involves the production, advertising, sale and distribution of products via telecommunication networks. It includes intranets and extranets. E-commerce via the Internet has already made inroads into traditional business and trade at both local and global levels. Shopping via the Internet ('e-shopping') especially for computer hardware, software, books, music cassettes and compact discs is becoming commonplace among Internet users. By the turn of the century, it is estimated that e-commerce was worth over $300 billion. The United States is pushing for e-commerce to be a free trade zone and devoid of any tax regimes whatsoever.

E-Banking has become fairly widespread in India. The majority of nationalized and private sector banks have computerized their services, offering facilities like internet banking, electronic transfers, and digital payments. Several multinational banks have outsourced their customer services to call centers in India and other developing countries. However, foolproof security is still a great concern, especially after it was discovered that some employees of Mphasis BPO used personal information such as bank account numbers, PIN numbers, credit card and passport details to siphon off Rs. 1.83 crore to benami accounts.[31] The British tabloid *The Sun* carried a frontpage report entitled 'Your life for sale' which claimed that call centre workers in India are 'flogging' details of Britons' bank accounts[32]; British banks, however, have rubbished the report.

E-Governance has been taken up by the Central and State

---

31 Cf. 'BPO firms jittery after British paper exposes call centre fraud' in The Indian Express, June 24, 2005, p. 1.
32 Ibid.

governments with some seriousness. Land and other records as well as the multiplicity of forms that need to be filled up for applications, permissions, taxes, etc. can now be downloaded from web sites of the various departments of the civil administration. Bus, retail and air bookings as well as hotel rooms can now be made on the net; so can reservations for seats in cinema theatres, stage shows, etc. All kinds of bills and taxes can be paid through secure sites on the net. Undoubtedly, this has made for greater transparency and higher efficiency.

National Task Force on Information Technology

The Vajpayee government set up the Prime Minister's Task Force on Information Technology in mid-1998 under the chairmanship of Prof. M.G.K. Menon, to formulate a comprehensive IT policy. Its Action Plan report made 108 recommendations on ways of speeding up the nation's development in the various information technologies. It recommended the privatisation of internet services (then under the monopoly of the public sector Videsh Sanchar Nigam Ltd. (VSNL)), the waiver of licence fees for private Internet Service Providers (ISPs) allowing even cable operators and ISD/STD-booth operators to use their infrastructure to enhance internet access, and zero duty on all IT products by 2002 A.D. It further recommended that software and IT be treated as a priority sector by banks for five years, and that students, teachers and schools be offered computers at reduced prices. The Task Force wanted every ISD/STD booth in the country to be turned into an 'information kiosk' providing access to the internet and related services like e-mail. Internet access nodes are to be installed in all districts. The Action Plan envisaged pumping $7 billion so as to step up India's software exports to $50 billion by year 2008. Besides, it proposed the setting up of a corpus fund of Rs. 1,000 crore (Rs. 10,000 million) by the Government to be distributed to software companies through public sector banks. The Congress-led coalition has continued this policy of providing generous support to the IT industry. Several of the

Special Export Zones (SEZs) have been allotted to companies in IT and ITES sectors.

Mobile Telephony

Since the early years of the second millennium the fastest growing media sector has been mobile telephony. It has left the other flourishing media sectors such as television and the internet far behind. It's been called a 'magical device'[33], a 'miraculous technology'[34]. It's believed to be the fastest growing communication technology in the continent of Africa[35], followed closely by two of the world's most populous countries, India and China. Indeed, the mobile or cellular phone is slowly but steadily being transformed into the media and communication technology par excellence of the future. It is light-weight, portable, user-friendly, and by middle class standards, fairly inexpensive; it's a very personal device: a faithful companion that nearly always stays with you. It combines the characteristics of the traditional and the new media; it feeds off the traditional media such as recorded music, photography, cinema, radio, television, and the press, and uses the new media to extend its storage, processing and distribution capacities. 'The boundary between the cellular phone as a medium of interpersonal communication and as a mass medium for the distribution of SMS, Web pages, videos and games is dissolving.[36] Mobile telephony is gradually merging with mobile computing. In fact, mobile telephony has the potential of empowering individuals and groups; it is interpersonal, immediate and extremely convenient; it has the potential to contribute to the new public sphere. This is the primary attraction of the mobile phone as a medium for development. However, the mobile telephone continues to remain an elite medium of communication: the

---

33 The Economist (2005): 'Man's best Friend: Not a dog, but a mobile phone', in A Survey of Consumer Power, April 2, pp.8-10.
34 ibid
35 Ibid.
36 Jan Van Dyke: 'Digital Media' in John Downing et al (Eds.): *The Sage Handbook of Media Studies*, London: Sage Publications, 2005.

majority of the urban and rural poor in India and China have little or no access to the mobile phone technology; the infrastructure for mobile telephony does not exist in rural India and China, where the majority of the population lives. Globally too, it is an elite medium as barely 25% of the world's populations owns and uses the device, even though 80% lives within range of a mobile network.[37]

Table 46 : Growth of Telephone Subscriber Base (1997-2008)

Year	Fixed Line Phones (Million)	Mobile Phones (Milliion)
1997	14.54	0.34
1998	17.8	0.88
1999	21.59	1.2
2000	26.51	1.88
2001	32.44	3.58
2002	37.94	6.43
2003	40.62	12.69
2004	42.58	33.6
2005	46.91	52.21
2006	46.78	93.04
2007	40.38	162.52
2008	37.18	250.93

(Source: Telecommunications Regulatory Authority of India – March 2008)

By the close of 2008, the 300 million mark had been crossed with growth in the fixed phone market unable to keep pace with the steady rise in mobile phone subscriptions. As the above table suggests, the gradual decline of fixed-line subscribers was unstoppable despite lower tariffs. The majority of wireless subscribers (up to 90% in some of the 28 telecom 'circles') had opted for the pre-paid schemes. Prices of low-end phones fell remarkably; so did those of high-end (camera phones, games- and FM-radio enabled phones, 3G) cell phones. The Indian

---

[37] The Economist. *op.cit.*

telecom market was ripe for the launch of the Blueberry and Apple's 'i-phone'. And 4G phones were on the way with faster data speeds and WiMax, LTE (Long Term Evolution) and UMB (Ultra Mobile Broadband) networks promised.

Some telecom service providers have begun offering 'news alerts' as a value addition service (VAS) on mobile phones. These are in the form of SMS messages. School exam results, cricket scores, results of contests, emergency messages, scotching rumours by authorities are other kinds of 'news alerts' which are offered by mobile operators. Other newspapers, news channels and telecom operators offer 'news alerts' via email. BBC, CNN, IBN and NDTV were the first to offer these services free. Further, the majority of daily newspapers and news channels pose questions for audiences to respond to via email or SMS. Polls are conducted on a daily basis by the news media on questions and issues of the day. However, while the results of the polls are widely discussed by anchors and experts, the total sample of respondents and their representative nature is rarely revealed.

In India, the major investments in telecom have come from domestic rather than foreign sources. Foreign equity up to 49% is permitted in private telecom ventures, but few transnational companies have availed of this, except for AT & T, British Telecom and some others. It is in the mobile handset sector that foreign companies have ruled the roost. The market shares of major handset makers (both GSM and CDMA) are as follows:

Telecom Co.	Market Share
Nokia	31.2%
Motorola	19.2%
Samsung	10.9%
LG Electronics	7.2%
Siemens	6.9%
Others	24.6%

(Source: Cellular Operators Association of India, quoted in a Report in *Business & Economy*, 2005, p.22)

Though telecom services, especially in the fixed line sector, began as a monopoly, the liberalisation of Indian telecom in the early 1990s has given rise to a host of private operators all across the country offering both fixed and mobile services, and competing fiercely among themselves and with the state operators such as BSNL and MTNL. VSNL held the monopoly until recently for the international telecom market, but this too has been whittled down after it was acquired by Tata's. The major players in the mobile phone arena are: Bharti Telecom (Airtel), Aircel Ltd (Aircel, Essar), Idea Cellular Ltd, Hutchison Max Telecom Ltd (Orange), Fascel Ltd (Hutch), Hutchison India Ltd (Oasis Cellular), BPL Mobile, Escotel Mobile, Spice Communications Ltd (Spice), Reliance India Ltd (Reliance India Mobile), RPG Telecom, Koshika Telecom Ltd (Ushafone) and others, indeed, there exist at least half a dozen private companies competing with each other and with public sector companies such as BSNL (CellOne) and MTNL (Dolphin) in the major cities. Private operators now account for 43% of India's telecom services revenues (Voice and Data, July 2005). In late 2007, Vodafone, Europe's largest mobile telephone operator took over Hutch and became India's largest operator too.

Major Mobile Phone Service Providers

1. Vodafone
2. Bharti Airtel
3. Spice Communications
4. BPL Mobile
5. Idea Cellular Ltd.
6. Reliance Communications/RComm
7. Tata Indicom
8. Tata Teleservices
9. Tata Teleservices Maharashtra Ltd.
10. BSNL (Public Sector)
11. MTNL (Public Sector)
12. VSNL

Serving the Urban and Rural Poor

The New Telecommunication Policy was to provide telephone connections to all 600,000 villages in India. 'Universal service' became the avowed public policy. Over the last decade, hardly any of the 22 private telecom companies has made any contribution to taking either the basic or the mobile service to rural India. Their argument remains that the license fees were too high and that the tariffs were unreasonable. It is only the public sector companies such as BSNL that has fanned out into the villages. More than a third of the villages are yet to be connected. Rural China too has been ill-served by its four telecom companies.

Some mobile service providers have teamed up with NGOs to take information technology and the telephone to rural communities. BT, AT & T, Bharti Group and Escotel, for instance, have tied up with NGOs working with the urban and rural underprivileged. Perhaps the best known of these is the Grameen Phone Sewa (Village Phone Service) started by Escotel to connect 3000 villages where there are no means of communication; each village has been given one cellphone at half the cost and also a free connection.[38]

Social and Cultural Implications

Telecommunications and information technologies were developed in advanced industrialised societies to serve their needs and interests. These societies needed capital-intensive labour-saving technologies to make up for high labour costs and low populations. The 'new' technologies brought about speed, efficiency and a non-polluting environment. As the technologies became cheaper with greater volumes of users, business and administration needed fewer and ever fewer workers. Thus several workers were rendered redundant or were provided part-time jobs. The worst sufferers were women who worked as

---

38 Thomas, Thomas K: 'Communicating Where It Matters', *Business Standard*, 4 February 2001. p. 9.

typists, stenographers, telephone operators, packers, etc. The low-paid jobs were the first to go.

Two Bombay economists, Sudha Deshpande and L.K. Deshpande, suggest that since the 1980s, when economic liberalisation was introduced in India, female employment has increased. The female work participation rate – the ratio of women workers to their population – had increased to 9.74% in 1991 from 8.3% in 1981. In urban areas, there were 178 women workers for every thousand male workers in 1991 compared to 139 in 1981.[39] However, the increase in female employment was most likely in the low-paying traditional manufacturing industries rather than in high paid technology-oriented services.

Computer technologies changed the very nature and meaning of work and employment. Work took on a new orientation, related more to the storage, processing, retrieval and distribution of information than to traditional modes of labour and industry. Information was thus turned into a commodity which had a market price instead of being a public resource and a public good available to all in the community. Further, computer technologies tend to turn work and service into something impersonal, mechanical, routine, though less laborious; certainly more efficient, neater, faster but one that lacked the personal touch.

The vulnerability of the new information technologies to attacks by hackers, crackers, and viruses as well as to breakdowns without prior warning is extremely worrying. Computers can go on the blink at airports, railway stations, supermarkets, water and power stations and even in hospitals leading to chaotic situations. September 11, 2001 and other acts of terrorism in India and worldwide demonstrated how fragile the internet and telecommunication backbone is in a crisis situation. This is especially so in countries like India where breakdowns in power supply are frequent and unexpected. It is widely assumed that corruption is reduced with the introduction

---

39 Neeraj Kaushal: Report in the Times of India, 1992.

of computers in administration, but the securities scam in Bombay demonstrates that computers can play a role in promoting corruption too. Counterfeiting, cloning of credit cards, access to ATMs, e-banking, flooding of email boxes, pop-ups, spamming, the constant need to update anti-virus softwares and to block banner, pop-up and in-your-face advertising .... the list of social and cultural concerns is endless. Stalking, human and sex trafficking, pornography, entrapment of children by pedophiles, bullying and harassment by class-mates and colleagues have been facilitated by the internet and mobile telephony. Driving on the information super-highway is indeed fraught with several risks. And what is most distressing is that the entire responsibility for protecting the vulnerable sections of society rests with the users themselves.

The Gaming Industry

Information Technology has changed the very nature of entertainment and leisure activities. Computer and video games ('Cyber gaming') have become a vital part of the entertainment industry. A major spin-off of the new digital and mobile technologies is the mushrooming of the gaming industry which has now (at the global level) surpassed the cinema, television and music industries as a revenue earner. By 2008 there were over 80 million gamers worldwide and the revenue from gaming exceeded a billion dollars. Sony's Playstations, Microsoft's Xbox and Nintendo Gamecube (as also handheld devices such as the Nintendo DS and Sony PSP) have turned gaming into a new cultural industry. Sony, Microsoft and Nintendo are the global players in this competitive game console market. Other global corporations active in developing and publishing games online and other media platforms include Vivendi Universal; independent publishers include Electronic Arts, Activision, Ubisoft and Take-Two. Indian IT and ITES companies are reaping a harvest from the 'game design and development' industry, a huge chunk of which is 'outsourced' by these major global corporations.

But gaming itself is still a nascent industry in India though game arcades are gradually being integrated into the 'multimedia experience' of amusement parks, shopping malls and cinema multiplexes which are under construction in metros and the large cities and towns. Moreover, almost every major portal on the net offers free and subscription-based downloads of different genres of computer games (E.g sports games, driving games, puzzle games). And so do most mobile phone service providers, as a value-added service. Several game-based web portals have proved popular with young gamers. They promote the formation of 'virtual gaming communities' and online worlds where players live what could be termed a 'second life' – 'socializing, trading, building, battling and 'levelling up' the player-character, most commonly as part of organized 'guilds' or clans of players.'[40]

The city of Pune (with a population of three million) has over 10,000 'gamers'; popular games include 'War Craft', 'Counter Strike', 'Need for Speed', 'Sim City' and 'Ragnarok'.[41] Children and young people are the major 'gamers', and parents and teachers are concerned that some of the games promote aggression and hatred.[42] Other non-metro cities where the gaming bug has caught on include Bangalore, Hyderabad and Ahmedabad. Some innovative teachers have developed games for learning and enhancing language and communication skills. Reliance, Zee, Sify and other media companies are active in the gaming business. Sify Gamedrome, a gaming chain with over 230 gamedromes in 66 cities is among the largest gaming ventures; Reliance's Zapak Digital Entertainment has more than 500 gaming cafes all over the country. It is teaming up with Chinese and others to license games for Indian players. Animax/

---

40 Rune Klevjer: 'The Cultural Value of Games: Computer Games and Cultural Policy in Europe' in Peter Ludes (Ed.): *Convergence and Fragmentation: Media Technology and the Information Society,* Bristol: Intellect, 2008. pp.71-90.
41 Report in The Times of India, Pune, 7 May 2005, p. 2.
42 See Simon Egenfeldt-Nielsen and Jonas Heide Smith: 'Playing with Fire: How Do Computer Games Influence the Player', Sweden: NORDICOM, 2005, for an interesting analysis in the European context.

Sony too is another major player; it held a 51-day national gaming tournament called AGGC-2007 and featured games like Counter-Strike, FIFA, Defense of the Ancients, and Gunz Online. Gaming is indeed evolving from a nascent stage to a lifestyle hobby.

Online, PC, mobile and arcade games, while borrowing from the story-telling and entertainment strategies of the cinema (especially animation, fantasy and science fiction genres), offer a more interactive and 'immersive' experience than the uni-directional mass media. They provide amusement and pleasure that involve the gamer intimately; there's a feeling that one is in total control, with the drama and excitement providing an exhilarating multimedia and multimodal experience. These are the pleasures that make computer games 'addictive'. Indeed, contemporary trends in advertising, television and cinema suggest that the new techniques developed in the virtual reality of games have been carried over into these visual media. The growing sophistication in animation, 3-D graphics, lighting, texture and sound, first used in the games industry has transformed the music video and other television and film genres. The online journal www.gamestudies.org provides interesting insights into this new media industry from the perspective of designers, gamers and social researchers.

The gaming industry has given a fillip to the animation industry in India. Animation has grown into a 1.5 billion industry with outsourcing work proving to be a major revenue spinner. Most Indian animation companies are located in Bangalore, Trivandrum, Hyderabad and Pune. Disney Studios has initiated a joint venture with Rajshri Productions to make animation films like 'Roadside Romeo'. Other Hollywood studios too have co-production deals with Indian animation companies. Mythologicals appear to make the most successful animation features, several episodes from the Mahabharat and Ramayana, with Hunaman being a favourite. Toonz has produced 'Hanuman', 'the Return of Hanuman' and 'Shiva', and other animation studios have made a splash with 'Ganesh' and 'Ghatothkach'.

Online Gambling Industry

From gaming to gambling on the Internet is a move that is inevitable. Though gambling on the Net is outlawed in the United States, it is not so in Europe and other parts of the world. In India, regulation of Internet gambling is still not in place. The Information Technology Act (2000) does not address the issue at all; this is perhaps because the Public Gambling Act (1867) deals with the issue and it applies to online as much as to other forms or platforms for gambling. The Asian Cyber Law Institute has pointed out that 'online gambling is a serious issue that has not been addressed under any Indian law. The Internet makes it very easy for any person to gamble using a web site which may be hosted anywhere in the world. The anonymity offered by the Internet allows operators of fraudulent web sites to dupe unsuspecting surfers of their money and escape prosecution. It therefore recommends that 'appropriate amendments may be made in the Gambling Prevention Act to address online gambling'.[43] Offline betting on cricket and other games is rampant in the country; it appears that there is no way that online gambling can be curbed or regulated since it is supported by a global ring of operators who know they are above the law. Regulation of online gambling can be effective only at the international level. The Internet has indeed been turned into the world's largest casino and its most profitable enterprise. Websites that auction products and services, such as www.ebay.com, gaming sites (www.zapak.com, www.games2win) and numerous e-shopping sites that peddle a whole range of consumer products and services have also proved that 'monetization' of the web is possible.

InfoWars, Hate Speech

The Internet has also been transformed into a global 'public

---

43 www.cyberlaws.org. Accessed on 15 April 2008.

agora' or an open forum for democratic discussion but also for the dissemination of 'hate speech' and 'infowars' and 'swarming'. Other issues of concern are the impact of the Internet and IT on education (e-learning), the authority of the nation-state, the culture of digital spaces (e.g. digital cities, outsourcing, software parks, silicon valleys) and human relationships. Information technologies make it quite easy for governments, revenue and police departments to keep a close watch on citizens, and to invade their privacy. At the same time, they can also afford challenges to hackers to break into the computers of government and private organisations, as the breaks into the computers at the Pentagon, the Bhabha Atomic Research Centre, Bombay, and other research and defence establishments around the world has revealed. 'Infowars' have become as vital as deadly weaponry to win the hearts and minds of people. Military victories have become meaningless without the support of the masses. Hence the attempts of the US to deface the English language version of Al-Jazeera on the Internet (english.aljazeera.net) and to prohibit its global television network in the country. However, the Voice of America (VOA), Radio Marti and Radio Free Asia and the external service broadcasting channels of several countries continue to wage 'infowars' round the clock across the globe. The 'infowars' have now been extended to cinema, television, the internet, blogs, social networks and even to video, computer and mobile games.

FOR FURTHER READING

1. Arjun Appadurai: *Modernity at Large: Cultural Dimensions of Globalization*, New Delhi: Oxford University Press, 1996.
2. Manuel Castells: *The Information Age: Economy, Society and Culture*, Volume 1: *The Rise of the Network Society*, Oxford: Blackwell Publishers. Volume 2: *The Power of Identity*, Volume 3: *End of Millennium*, Oxford: Blackwell Publishers, 1996.

3. Manuel Castells: *The Internet Galaxy*, Oxford: Oxford University Press, 2001.
4. Manuel Castells and Gustavo Cardoso: *The Network Society: from Knowledge to Policy*, Washington DC: Centre for Transatlantic Relations, 2006.
5. Manuel Castells et al: *Mobile Communication and Society: A Global Perspective*, Cambridge, Mass.: The MIT Press, 2007.
6. Carl J. Dahlman and Anuja Utz: *India and the Knowledge Economy: Leveraging Strengths and Opportunities*, 2005.
7. Ashok V. Desai: *India's Telecommunication Industry: History, Analysis, Diagnosis*, New Delhi: Sage Publications, 2005.
8. Anthony P. D'Costa and E. Sridharan: *India in the Global Software Industry: Innovation, Firm Strategies and Development*, London: Palgrave Macmillan, 2004.
9. Peter Ronald DeSouza (Ed.): *Contemporary India: Transitions*, New Delhi: Sage Publications, 2005.
10. Government of India, Ministry of Industry (1989): *Report on Computers and Peripherals*, Volumes I and II, New Delhi: Bureau of Industrial Costs and Prices.
11. Indian Academy of Social Sciences: *Social Perspectives of Microprocesors and Information Technology*, Allahabad: Vindhya Prakashan, 1988.
12. Joseph M. Grieco: *Between Dependency and Autonomy - India's Experience with the International Computer Industry*, Berkeley and Los Angeles: University of California Press, 1984.
13. Richard Heeks: *India's Software Industry*, New Delhi: Sage, 1996.
14. Peter Ludes (Ed.): *Convergence and Fragmentation: Media Technology and the Information Society*, Bristol: Intellect, 2008.
15. Robin Mansell: *The New Telecommunications: A Political Economy of Network Evolution*, London: Sage, 1993.
16. William J. Martin: *The Global Information Society*, London: Aslib/Gower, 1995.
17. Vincent Mosco: *The Pay-Per Society: Computers and Communication in the Information Age*, New Jersey: Ablex, 1989.
18. Srinivas Melkote and Sandhya Rao (Eds.) (2002): *Critical Issues in Communication: Looking Inward for Answers*, New Delhi: Sage Publications.
19. Ali Mohammadi (Ed.): *Global Communication and International Relations*, London: Routledge.

20. Tejeswani Niranjana, P Sudhir and Vivek Dhareshwar (Eds.): *Interrogating Modernity – Culture and Colonialism in India*, Calcutta: Seagull Publications, 1993.
21. T.K. Oommen: *Alien Concepts and South Asian Reality*, New Delhi: Sage Publications, 2003.
22. Sam Pitroda: *Exploding Freedom*, New Delhi: Allied Publications, 1992.
23. A.N. Rai: *Digital Communication in India*, New Delhi: Authorspress, 2000
24. Arvind Rajagopal: *Politics after Television – Hindu Nationalism and the Reshaping of the Public in India*, Cambridge: Cambridge University Press, 2001.
25. Arvind Singhal and Everett K Rogers: *India's Information Revolution*, New Delhi, 1989.
26. Arvind Singhal and Everett K Rogers: *India's Communication Revolution: From Bullock-Carts to Cyber Marts*, New Delhi: Sage Publications, 2001.
27. C.R. Subramanian: *India and the Computer: A Study of Planned Development*, New Delhi: Oxford University Press, 1992.
28. Pradip N. Thomas: 'Copyright and the Emerging Knowledge Economy in India', *Economic and Political Weekly*, June 16, 2001.
29. Thomas, Pradip and Jan Servaes (Eds.): *Intellectual Property Rights*, New Delhi: Sage, 2005.
30. Daya Kishan Thussu: *International Communication: Continuity and Change*, London: Arnold, 2000.
31. Daya Kishan Thussu (Ed.): *Electronic Empires: Global Media and Local Resistance*, London: Arnold, 1998.
32. Janet Wasko and Vincent Mosco (Eds.): *Democratic Communications in the Information Age*, Toronto: Garamond Press, 1992.

WEB RESOURCES

1. www.trai.gov.in (Telecommunications Regulatory Authority of India)
2. www.siliconindia.com
3. www.siliconvalley.com
4. www.iamai.in (Internet and Mobile Association of India)
5. www.contentsutra.com

6. www.bangalorenet.com
7. www.nasscom.com
8. www.icann.com (Official site of Internet Consortium that governs the Net)
9. www.isoc.org (Official site of the Internet Society that oversees the development of the Internet worldwide)

REVIEW QUESTIONS

1. How has the integration of telecommunications, electronics and computers changed the nature of Information Technology?
2. Comment on the Indian government's policy on telecommunications since 1994.
3. What are some of the cultural and social implications of recent developments in the New Information Technologies?
4. What are the origins of the Internet? How has the Internet changed the nature of communication and of business?
5. How has the proliferation of mobile phone among young people influenced familial and social relations? Has this resulted in a 'youth culture'?
6. Write short notes:
    (a) TRAI
    (b) E-Mail
    (c) SMS
    (d) Social Networking Sites
    (e) Electronic Communities
    (f) Privatisation of Fixed-Line and Mobile Telephone Services
    (g) Games and music on mobile phones

SECTION VII

MASS MEDIA, INTELLECTUAL PROPERTY RIGHTS (IPR) AND THE 'PUBLIC DOMAIN'

As the Indian economy races to transform itself into an 'Information Society' and an emerging economic power, it will necessarily have to take into account the implications of being an active member of the World Trade Organisation (WTO) and the global cultural regime that this organisation has introduced in the form of the Trade Related Aspects on Intellectual Property Rights Agreement (TRIPS). Mass media, information and culture, it is assumed under the TRIPS regime, are private property that can be traded across the world for profit without any concern for universal access, human rights, free speech, affordability, public service, fair play and balance. Other assumptions are that 'culture can be legitimately appropriated for private commercial purposes, that cultural works are original, that without protection there would be no cultural production and that without royalties there would be no other sources of revenues.'[1] The consequence is that the public domain, that is 'the commons' has been distributed to the highest bidding entrepreneurs and these are then sold back to the richest sections of the community, while the indigent majority are left out in the cold. Such a commodification of culture and the public sphere gives rise to a socio-cultural situation where the knowledge gap widens and so does the rich-poor divide. This dominant approach is led by the late capitalistic belief that economic growth and success can only be measured by the commodification of not just capital and labour but also information, culture and the mass media.

'All information today, digital or non-digital, is becoming converted into property available for a fee. Intellectual Property Rights (IPR) have become the means for sustaining and

---

1 Cees Hamelink: 'Intellectual Property Rights' in Pradip N. Thomas and Zaharom Nain (Eds.): *Who Own the Media?*, Penang: Southbound, 2004, pp.43-47.

extending the market for knowledge as property. Consequently, there has been a shrinking of ideas in the public domain. The enforcement of copyright has become big business in India as Hollywood, software manufacturers and the music industry enforce their writ on the Indian cultural industries.'[2] The commercial significance of IPR became evident from the late 1970s when international trade in intellectual trade took off. An international survey conducted by Skilbeck in the late 1980s found that such trade contributed on average as much as 2.7% to GDP.[3]

Hamelink[4] estimates that 'copyright industries were surpassing in economic importance such sectors as automobile manufacturing. In the USA, for instance, the copyright industries are the second largest contributor to GDP and still growing yearly. In 1990 they were estimated to contribute 5.8% to GDP'.

The Indian economy appears to be going the way of industrialised societies in emphasising rapid growth in the Information Technology and services sector as against its traditional strengths in the agricultural and manufacturing sectors. According to data released recently by the Indian government, the share (as proportions of (GDP) of agriculture is down 0.9 percentage points to 25.3 and that of manufacturing 0.4 percentage points to 14.7; however, the service sector now constitutes nearly 60 percent of GDP.[5]

This chapter analyses the implications of the IPR regime, particularly Article 14.3 of the TRIPS Agreement, for Indian broadcasting. It traces the historical development of this Agreement in the context of the failure of the major powers to accept the recommendations of the MacBride Report (1981) on the New World Information and Communication Order

---

2 Pradip N. Thomas: 'Taking Stock of IT Developments and the Political Economy of communications in India' in Michael Traber (Ed.): *Communication in Theological Education: New Directions,* New Delhi: ISPCK, 2005.
3 Quoted in Cees Hamelink: The Politics of World Communication, London: Sage Publications, 1998. p. 127.
4 Ibid.
5 Quoted in Editorial in *The Times of India*: 'Beyond Numbers', 3 February 2006, p. 12.

(NWICO). The paper raises critical questions on the relationship between writers and broadcasting rights. And between broadcasters and those who make home recordings and others who rent out or sell copies on videos, CDs, DVDs as well as over the Internet, the mobile telephone and the iPod. But the major question that will be raised in this discussion relates to the rights of the general public to universal access, and the responsibility of national broadcasters to serve and to protect the public domain and the public sphere. The primary question that arises then is: How do communities and nations protect their cultural knowledge and cultural rights against the onslaught of global forces such as the WTO, of which TRIPS is an integral strategy?

IPR: An Historical Perspective

'Intellectual Property' relates to the ownership of 'intangible' property such as ideas, various forms of literary and artistic expression, broadcasting and the mass media, folklore, and the new media; indeed any mode of expression, whether technical or non-technical, which has a commercial value. These laws encompass four separate and distinct types of intangible property: (i) Patents, (ii) Copyright, (iii) Trade marks and Trade names, and (iv) others such as industrial designs, trade secrets and other confidential information. All these are collectively referred to as 'intellectual property'. Of these, Copyright directly applies to the mass media and to cultural rights.

The IPR regime has sought to equate the literary and artistic with private property by terming it 'intangible property'. Thus, intellectual property is seen as an asset that can be sold, bought, exchanged, licensed, reproduced, or donated like any other form of private property. Further, as with private property, the owner of intangible property has the right to prevent its unauthorised use or sale. All member states of the WTO (formerly GATTS – the General Agreement on Trade and Tariffs) are obliged to legislate at a national level to comply with the various agreements. The WTO was established at the Uruguay Round in

April 1994; TRIPS – the Trade-Related Agreement on Intellectual Property Rights – is a major instrument to protect intellectual property worldwide. The apex body for arbitration and mediation is the World Intellectual Property Organisation (WIPO). This organisation promotes and administers the Paris Convention on Industrial Property, the Patents Cooperation Treaty, the Berne and Rome Conventions on Copyright and Related Rights, and the Madrid Agreement on Trade Marks. But the body that has wielded its power to bully both developed and developed countries into servile submission to the dictates of private corporations and the United Sates government has been the International Intellectual Property Alliance (IIPA). This alliance was forged in the early 1980s by US-based multinational corporations such as Pfizer, IBM, Monsanto and others to offset the 'free-riding' and 'copy culture' then prevalent in developing countries.[6]

The IIPA was also forged in response to the MacBride Declaration (1981) hammered out by UNESCO to bring about a New World Information and Communication Order (NWICO). The main demand of the Declaration was for 'a free and balanced flow of information' to replace the existing one-way free flow of information from the developed to the developing world. The United States, Britain and Singapore walked out of UNESCO in protest.[7]

The Uruguay Round of GATT in 1986 was the response of the United States, Britain and some other developed countries to MacBride. It witnessed the arm-twisting of the IIPA and the United States Government in the formation of WTO and the decision to start negotiations on TRIPS and counterfeit goods. By 1995 an IPR text was ready for adoption at Marrakesh,

---

6 Vishwas H. Devaiah: 'TRIPS: A Tale of the Shrinking Ocean Called 'Public Domain' (An El Nino in the Information Age)', Inforchange News and Features, May 2004. www.infochangeindia.org/IPRIb.jp.

7 Cf. Dwayne Winseck: 'The WTO, Emerging Policy Regimes and the Political Economy of Transnational Communications' in Marc Raboy (Ed.O: *Global Media Policy in the New Millennium*, Luton: the University of Luton Press, 2002. pp. 19-37.

Morocco, and by January 1 of the following year, TRIPS came into effect for all member states of WTO. Brazil and India were the last to fall in line.

Membership of the WTO now meant that the common standards laid down in TRIPS were binding on all member states. Indeed, TRIPS was the first multilateral agreement which obliged all member countries of the WTO to provide protection to seven types of IPRs: copyright and related rights, patents, trademarks, geographical indications, industrial designs, layout designs and trade secrets. TRIPS thus married trade laws with intellectual property rights.[8] The lack of a strong opposition from either the developed or the developing world led to the setting up of higher standards of protection.[9]

India's Copyright Act

India's Copyright Act of 1957 was amended in 1994 and later in 1999[10] to comply with the demands of TRIPS which incorporated all the principles and practices laid down in the Rome and Rome Conventions of 1961 and 1971 respectively, as well as the subsequent Paris Convention in 1971. Moreover, institutes to administer the demands of the Act were established in the form of the Copyright Office, the Registrar and Deputy Registrars of Copyrights, and the Copyright Board (Sections 9-11). India promulgated the International Copyright Order (1991) which was subsequently superseded by the International Copyright Order (1999) in pursuance of the Berne Convention where the member countries agreed to extend protection of copyright to areas beyond the territorial limits of nations.

Further, the amendments made in the Copyright Act in 1999 in Chapter VIII ('Rights of Broadcasting Organisations and of Performers') extended the provisions to certain other countries provided there were reciprocal provisions in those countries. At the same time, the provisions provided for the empowerment of

---

8 Devaiah op. cit.
9 Ibid.
10 *Copyright Act (1957) as amended in 1994 and 1999*, Law Publishers, Allahabad, 2006.

the Central Government to restrict the rights of foreign broadcasting organisations and performers if they failed to give adequate protection to rights of broadcasting organisations or performers. The Government of India has also established the Copyright Enforcement Advisory Council to enforce IPR all across the country. The penalty for infringement of copyright has been made more stringent with increase in fines and duration of imprisonment.

The Meaning of 'Copyright'

Copyright is generally defined as an 'exclusive right granted to the owner of an original work (e.g. lyrics, movies, computer programs, paintings, designs, logos) for a limited period of time. Copyright inheres not in ideas but rather in the unique expression of ideas. Copyright offers a legal protection granted to an artist or creative writer to reproduce, prepare derivative works, distribute, perform and display the work publicly. Interestingly, the Copyright Act (1957) does not attempt to define 'Copyright' but rather describes its various types and spells out at great length what constitutes or does not constitute 'infringement' of copyright.

There are three types of works in which copyright subsists, according to both TRIPS and the Copyright Act of India, in almost identical terms:

1. Original, literary, dramatic, musical and artistic works. Literary works includes tables, compilations, and computer programs; dramatic works includes plays, staged plays, scripts, recitations, and choreography; and artistic works include painting, sculpture, drawing, comic strips, and photographs.
2. Cinematograph films
3. Sound recordings, such as on tapes, records, disks, perforated rolls, etc.

Adaptations and Derivative Works

Adaptations and derivative works are also protected. For

instance, translations, remixes, dramatisations, musical arrangements which can be re-cast, transformed, or adapted. A derivative work consists of, for instance, editorial revisions, annotations, elaborations or other modifications which as a whole represent an original work of authorship.

The Copyright Act (1957) (1.3) offers an elaborate explanation of what 'adaptation' means:
- in relation to a dramatic work, the conversion of the work into a non-dramatic work;
- in relation to a literary work or an artistic work the conversion of the work into a dramatic work by way of performance in public or otherwise;
- in relation to a literary or dramatic work, any abridgement of the work or any version of the work in which the story or action is conveyed wholly or mainly by means of pictures in a form suitable for reproduction in a book, or in a newspaper, magazine or similar periodical;
- in relation to a musical work, any arrangement or transcription of the work; and
- in relation to any work, any use of such work involving its re-arrangement or alteration.

Indian Broadcasting

This section applies directly to practices in Indian broadcasting. Several made-for television films, dramas, soap operas, and documentaries are direct or loose adaptations of dramatic and artistic works. Satyajit Ray's television film, *Sadgati*, for instance, tells a Premchand short story of the same title; so is *Malgudi Days* an adaptation of R.K. Narayan's novels. The television serial *The Sword of Tipu Sultan* is based on an historical novel; some soap operas are straight adaptations of Mexican telenovellas, and Govind Nihalani's *Tamas* was based on a novel of the same title. Dubbed, sub-titled and 'remakes' of films and TV serials and game shows in different Indian languages have become the norm in the entertainment industries.

Further, 'clones' or adaptations of successful American and European films and TV shows are quite widespread. The most widely acclaimed of these has been Star TV's 'Kaun Banega Crorepati?' Intellectual property rights are granted to each new adaptation and to each separate delivery platform (cable, satellite, videos, CDs, DVDs). Thus, 'ringtones' on mobiles based on songs or tunes from films, radio and TV are copyright protected.

A recent study of television viewership in South India using a sample of over 47,000 respondents suggests that local language programmes are extremely popular and that Hindi serials evince very little interest.[11] The study also found that producers of local language serials often stretched and distorted original short stories, novels and scripts so as to increase the number of episodes, say from 52 (as originally agreed upon with writers) to 130 and even 260 episodes.

Rights of Broadcasters

Copyright is granted to both the first and subsequent authors of adaptations or derived works. However, in film and television the adaptation while being protected by copyright is granted to the producer rather than the author. The two main rights that copyright includes are: economic rights and moral rights. Economic rights relate to rights of reproduction, broadcasting, public performance, etc. Moral rights, on the other hand, include an author's rights to object to any distortion or other modifications of his work that might be prejudicial to his/her honour or reputation.[12]

'Related Rights' refers to a category of rights granted to performers, phonogram producers and broadcasters. In the United States, United Kingdom and India, these rights are incorporated under the general rubric of copyright. But in France and Germany they are termed 'neighbouring rights'; the

---

11 K. Kunhikrishnan: 'Literary Work and TV Rights', *The Hindu Business Line*, 4 May 2003.
12 Ibid.

argument is that these works do not meet the same requirement of personal intellectual creativity as literary and artistic works. For instance, the production of a CD or broadcast program is taken to be an activity of technical and organisational character rather than the expression of personal intellectual creativity. But such works need to be protected, so goes the argument, because of their economic value and also because they are easy to imitate.

Following the 1961 Rome International Convention for the Protection of Performers, Producers of Phonograms and Broadcasting Organisations, Article 14 of TRIPS entitled 'Protection of Performers, Producers of Phonograms (Sound Recordings) and Broadcasting Organisations' spells out what is protected:

In respect of a fixation of their performance on a phonogram, performers shall have the possibility of preventing the following acts when undertaken without their authorizations: (i) the fixation of their unfixed performance and the reproduction of such fixation; (ii) the broadcasting by wireless means and the communication to the public of their live performance.

Producers of phonograms shall enjoy the right to authorize or prohibit the direct or indirect reproduction of their phonograms.

Broadcasting organisations shall have the right to prohibit the fixation, the reproduction of fixations, and the re-broadcasting by wireless means of broadcasts, as well as the communication to the public of television broadcasts of the same.

Provisions of Article 11 in respect of computer programs shall apply mutatis mutandis to producers of phonograms and any other right holders in phonograms.

The terms of protection are 50 years to performers and producers of programs and 20 years to broadcasters. (TRIPS Art. 14).

In almost the same vein, The Copyright Act (1957) (Chapter VIII) grants every broadcasting organisation a special right to be known as 'broadcast reproduction right' in respect of its broadcasts. The broadcast reproduction right shall subsist until twenty five years from the beginning of the calendar year next following the year in which the broadcast is made.

The following acts are listed as infringing the broadcast reproduction right without the licence of the owner of the right (S.37):

(a) re-broadcasting of broadcast, or
(b) causing the broadcast to be heard or seen by the public on payment of charges, or
(c) making any sound recording or visual recording of the broadcast, or
(d) making any reproduction of such sound recording or visual recording, or
(e) selling or hiring to the public or offering for such sale or hire any such sound recording or visual recording.

Satellite and Cable Broadcasting

Developments in the new technologies such as cable and satellite television have made the protection of 'intellectual property' more complicated. In the existing copyright conventions (the Berne Convention, the Universal Copyright Convention and the Rome Convention) there were no references to the distribution of signals through cable networks or by broadcast satellites since these techniques developed and were deployed after the enactment of the treaties[13]. The questions these developments raised related to whether cable and satellite transmission of signals constituted 'broadcasting' and whether the distribution and reproduction of such signals amounted to infringement of copyright. The Brussels Convention (1974) on 'Relating to the Distribution of Programme-Carrying signals Transmitted by Satellite' took up the issue and urged member states to 'take adequate measures to prevent the distribution on or from its territory of any programme-carrying signal by any distributor for whom the signal emitted to or passing through the satellite is not intended'.[14] The Convention provides protection

---

13 Hamelink (1998).op. cit. p. 109.
14 Ibid.

to the signals but not to the messages they carry. A later meeting in March 1985 confirmed that direct broadcasting of works by means of a satellite should be defined as broadcasting in the sense of the copyright conventions and should be thus protected.

Doctrine of Fair Use

'Fair Use' is a vital principle in copyright law. While an original work in art, literature, music, etc. comes within the ambit of copyright law, the public has to be allowed to freely use segments or parts of copyright materials for purposes of commentary and criticism. The Copyright Act (1957) (VIII.39) allows for this 'private use' with reference to broadcasting. The following acts are therefore not seen as infringing broadcast reproduction right:
- the making of any sound recording or visual recording for the private use of the person making such recording, or solely for purpose of bona fide teaching or research; or
- the use, consistent with fair dealing, of excerpts of a performance or of a broadcast in the reporting of current events or for bona fide review, teaching or research; or
- such other acts, with any necessary adaptations and modifications which do not constitute infringement of copyright under Sec. 52.

Sec. 52 spells out rather elaborately 'certain acts' which do not amount to infringement of copyright. The emphasis again is on 'a fair dealing' with literary, dramatic or artistic works, and 'private use' such as for research, criticism or review, the bona fide use by educational institutions, such as in a collection mainly composed of non-copyright matter, or the performance of a literary, dramatic or musical work by the staff and students of the institution, or of a cinematographic film or a sound recording if the audience is limited to such staff and students, the parents and guardians of the students and persons directly connected with the activities of the institution, or the communication to such an audience of a cinematograph film or sound recording

(52.i).

Home Taping, Rentals, Piracy

The key to understanding recent developments in IPR is by coming to grips with the forces released by 'digitisation' and the subsequent 'convergence' of the old and the new technologies. No more are leisure technologies stand-alone and discrete; digitisation has facilitated bundling of technologies and softwares. Indeed, all information today, whether biological or non-biological, has become digitised, for the digital code has brought about the convergence of the old and the new media, and also of information technology with genetics. And, since digital information in varied formats such as voice, still and moving image and text can be readily stored, processed, retrieved and transferred almost instantly, it can be traded across borders without let or hindrance.

An area of concern for authors, film makers, music composers, playwrights and other creative artists is the 'broadcasting' of their work on a host of delivery platforms: radio, television, the Internet, and more recently over the mobile phone. Further, advances in audio and video recording technologies have facilitated the diffusion of broadcast material through videos, CDs and DVDs which may be sold or rented out. Home recording of radio and television broadcasts for personal use is considered 'fair use' of copyright material, and so is the renting out of recorded videos, CDs and DVDs. However, public screenings of TV programmes, especially to a paying audience, is an infringement of copyright; so is the playing of music and songs from films, radio and TV programmes in concerts, cafes, night clubs, and other public places. And reproduction of copyright material – even for personal use – without permission or a license amounts to 'piracy'.

Conclusions

Canada and the European Community and its Member States has so far succeeded in excluding 'cultural industries' from free trade agreements with the US (O'Connor: 2002). Their argument is they need to protect 'national cultures' and 'cultural diversity which they define as 'artistic and cultural expression, popular culture, traditional knowledge, linguistic diversity' (ibid.). The exemptions taken by the EC on MFN (Most Favoured Nation) treatment are mainly to promote the audiovisual sector. Hence the current status for European cultural industries within WTO Trade negotiations is exemption from WTO Rules on MFN and National Treatment for free trade in services. France and Canada have proposed the introduction of a new international instrument for trade in cultural goods and services that is monitored by cultural rather than trade officials and observers.

This, of course has not cut much ice with the WTO Secretariat. Perhaps India and other developing countries should team up with the EU and Canada to re-negotiate TRIPS to protect its own cultural diversity and to cry halt to the appropriation of culture by private commercial interests such as the multinational corporations. It is time to turn the clock back and return the mass media and culture to the public domain. This could perhaps be effected, as Larry Lessig proposes, by adding to 'copyright' a 'copyduty' – the legal duty of copyright holders to assure public access'.[15]

FOR FURTHER READING

1. Larry Lessig: 'Life, Liberty, Copyright', *The Atlantic Monthly Unbound*, 10 September 1988.
2. Lawrence Liang, A. Mazamdar and Suresh M. (2004): 'Copyright/ Copyleft: Myths about Copyright', *Infochange News and Features*, May 2004.
3. Noel Anne O'Sullivan: 'International Policy of Trade in Audio-Visual Services: the Rights of Citizens to Information in a Global Political and Economic Community', Paper presented at IAMCR Conference, July 2002.

---

15 Larry Lessig: 'Life, Liberty, Copyright; *The Atlantic Monthly Unbound*, 10 September 1988.

4. Pradip N. Thomas: 'Copyright and Emerging Knowledge Economy in India', *Economic and Political Weekly*, Vol. 36, No. 24, June 16, 2001. pp. 2147-2156.
5. Anurika Vaish (Ed.): *IPR and Broadcasting Rights*, New Delhi: Shree Publishers and Distributors, 2008.

WEB RESOURCES

1. http://www.iprlawindia.org
2. http://www.infochangeindia.org
3. http://onthecommons.org
4. http://www.wipo.int

REVIEW QUESTIONS

1. What do you understand by 'Intellectual Property Rights' in the context of broadcasting? Whose 'rights' do they refer to?
2. What is the 'public domain' perspective of IPR? Why is it crucial to protect the 'public domain'?
3. What measures has the Indian Government introduced to enforce Copyright in the print and electronic media?
4. 'Copyright is granted to both the first and subsequent authors of adaptations or derived works'. Give examples of 'adaptations or derived works' from Indian television.
5. What has been the role of WTO and TRIPS in enforcing IPR worldwide?
6. How does the IPR regime threaten local cultures?

SUGGESTED PROJECTS

1. Find out who owns the copyright for a reality show like 'Indian Idol'. What adaptations has the show made to the original reality show?
2. Who holds the copyright for a feature film made in India? For how many years is this copyright valid?

3. List the various revenue-streams for a Bollywood film. Who holds the copyright for each of the streams?
4. In the music industry who holds the copyright for the music and the lyrics?
5. In daily newspapers who holds the copyright to reports, features, columns and editorials? For how many years? Look up the Copyright Act.